9th Workshop on Representation Learning for NLP (RepL4NLP-2024)

Bangkok, Thailand
15 August 2024

ISBN: 979-8-3313-0174-3

Printed from e-media with permission by:

Curran Associates, Inc.
57 Morehouse Lane
Red Hook, NY 12571

Some format issues inherent in the e-media version may also appear in this print version.

Printed with permission by Curran Associates, Inc. (2025)

Association for Computational Linguistics
209 N. Eighth Street
Stroudsburg, Pennsylvania 18360

Phone: 1-570-476-8006
Fax: 1-570-476-0860

acl@aclweb.org

Additional copies of this publication are available from:

Curran Associates, Inc.
57 Morehouse Lane
Red Hook, NY 12571 USA
Phone: 845-758-0400
Fax: 845-758-2633
Email: curran@proceedings.com
Web: www.proceedings.com

ACL 2024

The 9th Workshop on Representation Learning for NLP (RepL4NLP-2024)

Proceedings of the Workshop

August 15, 2024

Association for Computational Linguistics (ACL)
317 Sidney Baker St. S
Suite 400 - 134
Kerrville, TX 78028
USA
Tel: +1-855-225-1962
acl@aclweb.org

Introduction

The 9th Workshop on Representation Learning for NLP, organized by SIGREP, aims to continue the success of the first eight workshops in the series. The RepL4NLP workshop was introduced as a synthesis of several years of independent *CL workshops focusing on vector space models of meaning, compositionality, and the application of deep neural networks and spectral methods to NLP. With the widespread adoption of neural network architectures (and especially Transformer models), representation learning has become a central concept in NLP research. RepL4NLP provides a forum for discussing recent advances on these topics, ranging from the development of new representations for various tasks and applications to the analysis of existing representations, e.g., with respect to generalization and robustness.

In most NLP applications, the goal is to understand, interpret, and generate human language text, extract linguistic information from raw text or to transform linguistic observations into an alternative form, e.g., from speech to text or from one language to another. Traditional statistical models relied heavily on discrete categories that are parameterized individually (e.g., each word or n-gram in a language model gets its own parameter); Representation learning—whether using spectral methods, probabilistic models, or deep neural networks—offers an alternative: by learning continuous, multidimensional representations of discrete objects (e.g., words, tags, labels, phrases, sentences), models can find representations that enable them to solve tasks more effectively. As learning representations has now been adopted as the de-facto approach to building models in NLP, their widespread use raises important questions towards further understanding them.

Organizing Committee

Workshop Organizers

Chen Zhao, New York University Shanghai
Marius Mosbach, Mila - McGill University
Pepa Atanasova, University of Copenhagen
Seraphina Goldfarb-Tarrent, Cohere
Peter Hase, University of North Carolina at Chapel Hill
Arian Hosseini, Mila - University of Montreal
Maha Elbayad, Meta AI
Sandro Pezzelle, University of Amsterdam
Maximilian Mozes, Cohere

Program Committee

Reviewers

Taichi Aida, Tokyo Metropolitan University
Gábor Berend, University of Szeged
Ondřej Bojar, Charles University Prague
Bridger Bridger, Holistic Intelligence for Global Good
Necva Bölücü, CSIRO
Muthu Kumar Chandrasekaran, Accenture
Anni Chen
Danlu Chen
Lin Chen, Facebook
Yue Chen, Microsoft and Indiana University
Catherine Chen, University of California Berkeley
Minhao Cheng, Pennsylvania State University
Heeyoul Choi, Handong Global University
Manuel Rafael Ciosici, USC/ISI
Wenliang Dai, NVIDIA
Christopher Davis, University of Cambridge
Vladimir Eidelman, FiscalNote, Inc.
Maha Elbayad, FAIR
Sergey Feldman, Allen Institute for Artificial Intelligence and Data Cowboys
Matthias Gallé, Cohere
Félix Gaschi, University of Lorraine
Shahriar Golchin, University of Arizona
Ashim Gupta
Gustavo Hernandez Abrego, Google
Julia Hockenmaier, University of Illinois, Urbana Champaign, University of Illinois, Urbana Champaign and University of Illinois, Urbana Champaign
Valentin Hofmann, Allen Institute for Artificial Intelligence
Dae Yon Hwang, Amazon AGI
Katharina Hämmerl, CIS, LMU Munich
Etsuko Ishii, The Hong Kong University of Science and Technology
Hamish Ivison, University of Washington
Fran Jelenić
Josip Jukić, Faculty of Electrical Engineering and Computing, University of Zagreb
Hirotaka Kameko, Kyoto University
Jaeyoung Kim, Seoul National University
Hyunjong Kim
Shankar Kumar
Matthieu Labeau, Télécom ParisTech
Seungil Chad Lee
Fei-Tzin Lee, Columbia University
Yitong Li, Huawei Technologies Co., Ltd.
Tao Li, Google DeepMind
Kai Liu, Clemson University
Zhu Liu
Chen Cecilia Liu
Holy Lovenia, AI Singapore

Yiwei Lyu
Kimberly Mai, University College London, University of London
Danil Malaev, MTS
Sheikh Mannan
Sneha Mehta
Antonio Valerio Miceli Barone, Università di Palermo, Università di Palermo, Università di Pisa and University of Edinburgh
Ashutosh Modi, IIT Kanpur
Vishvak Murahari, Princeton University
Alberto Muñoz-Ortiz
Inderjeet Jayakumar Nair, University of Michigan - Ann Arbor
Nikita Nangia
Vivi Nastase, University of Geneva
Abhijnan Nath
Chau Nguyen, University of Western Australia
Stephen Obadinma, Queen's University
Tsuyoshi Okita, Kyushu Institute of Technology
Ankur Padia, Philips Research North America
Jungsoo Park, NAVER
ChaeHun Park
Vipul Raheja, Columbia University, Grammarly and International Institute of Information Technology Hyderabad
Surangika Ranathunga, Massey University
Narutatsu Ri
Frank Rudzicz, Dalhousie University
Kaushik Ram Sadagopan, Meta
Hassan Sajjad, Dalhousie University
Avneesh Saluja, Netflix
Lingfeng Shen, ByteDance Inc.
Keisuke Shirai, Kyoto University
Shashwat Singh, International Institute of Information Technology Hyderabad
Karolina Stanczak, Mila - Quebec Artificial Intelligence Institute and McGill University, McGill University
Sho Takase, LINE Corporation
Shuai Tang, Amazon Web Services
Olga Tsymboi, Sber AI Lab and Moscow Institute of Physics and Technology
Sowmya Vajjala, National Research Council Canada
Eva Maria Vecchi
Qingyun Wang, University of Illinois, Urbana Champaign
Fanyu Wang, Monash University
Hai Wang, Samsung
Rodrigo Wilkens, UCL
Chenghao Xiao
Zhenping Xie, Jiangnan University
Zhikun Xu, Arizona State University
Tiezheng YU, The Hong Kong University of Science and Technology
Takateru Yamakoshi, The University of Tokyo
Sohee Yang, University College London, University of London, Department of Computer Science, University College London, University of London, DeepMind and Google
Majid Yazdani, Leeroo
Hee Suk Yoon, Korea Advanced Institute of Science & Technology

Eunseop Yoon, KAIST
Hong Yu, Apple
Kai Zhang
Wenbo Zhao, Amazon
Wenxuan Zhou, Zoom
Dong Zhou, Guangdong University of Foreign Studies
Vilém Zouhar, Department of Computer Science, ETHZ - ETH Zurich

Invited Speakers

Mor Geva, Tel Aviv University
Dieuwke Hupkes, Meta
Hassan Sajjad, Dalhousie University
Edoardo Ponti, University of Edinburgh

Table of Contents

Learning Contextualized Box Embeddings with Prototypical Networks

Kohei Oda **Kiyoaki Shirai** **Natthawut Kertkeidkachorn**
Japan Advanced Institute of Science and Technology
{s2420017,kshirai,natt}@jaist.ac.jp

Abstract

This paper proposes ProtoBox, a novel method to learn contextualized box embeddings. Unlike an ordinary word embedding, which represents a word as a single vector, a box embedding represents the meaning of a word as a box in a high-dimensional space: that is suitable for representing semantic relations between words. In addition, our method aims to obtain a "contextualized" box embedding, which is an abstract representation of a word in a specific context. ProtoBox is based on Prototypical Networks, which is a robust method for classification problems, especially focusing on learning the hypernym–hyponym relation between senses. ProtoBox is evaluated on three tasks: Word Sense Disambiguation (WSD), New Sense Classification (NSC), and Hypernym Identification (HI). Experimental results show that ProtoBox outperforms baselines for the HI task and is comparable for the WSD and NSC tasks.[1]

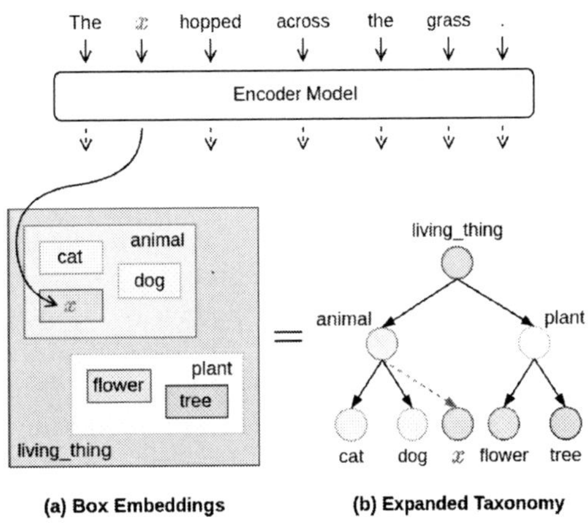

Figure 1: Example of contextualized box embedding and its application to New Sense Classification and Hypernym Identification.

1 Introduction

Word embedding is an abstract representation of a word, usually as a vector in a high dimensional space. Nowadays, word embeddings are widely used in models based on deep learning. Word embedding can represent the meaning not only of a word itself (Mikolov et al., 2013) but also of a word in a context. For example, BERT (Devlin et al., 2019) is often used to obtain vector representations of words in a given sentence. In this paper, we call such word embeddings "contextualized word embeddings." In addition, box embedding (Dasgupta et al., 2020) is a kind of word embedding, which represents a word not with a point but with an area in vector space. While an ordinary word embedding is primary used to measure the similarity between two words, box embeddings can be used to capture other semantic relations between words such as that between a hypernym and a hyponym. However, past studies of box embeddings did not well consider the context of the word, that is, the box embedding was not contextualized.

Contextualized word embeddings can be regarded as "sense embeddings," since a word may have two or more senses and convey one of those possible senses in a specific context. Word Sense Disambiguation (WSD) (Navigli, 2009) is a task that aims to identify the meaning of a word in a context. Most previous work on WSD has focused only on the senses in a predefined inventory and has ignored new (not predefined) senses. However, senses of words change day by day and new senses are constantly created (Yu and Xu, 2023). It is preferable that a WSD system can handle a new sense by classifying a word even if it is being used in a new sense, and, if possible, explaining the meaning of the new sense.

In this paper, we propose ProtoBox, a method to produce a contextualized box embedding of a word in a given context. In general, box embeddings can represent hypernym–hyponym relations between

[1]Our code is available at: `https://github.com/iehok/ProtoBox`.

Proceedings of the 9th Workshop on Representation Learning for NLP (RepL4NLP-2024), pages 1–12
August 15, 2024 ©2024 Association for Computational Linguistics

words, as illustrated in Figure 1 (a). If a box of word w_a subsumes the box of another word w_b, w_a can be regarded as a hypernym of w_b. Such relations between words can be represented as taxonomy (Figure 1 (b)). Our ProtoBox can produce contextualized box embeddings. For example, a box embedding of x in the sentence "The x hopped across the grass." can be obtained as shown in Figure 1 (a). Contextualized box embeddings enables us to judge that x has a new sense when the box embedding of x does not overlap any other box embeddings of fine-grained senses such as "cat" and "dog". In addition, "animal" can be identified as a hypernym of x, since the box embedding of x is subsumed by that of "animal". Identification of a hypernym can provide a rough explanation of a new sense, i.e., x is a kind of an animal. Furthermore, ProtoBox can expand the existing taxonomy by adding a new node x to the structure as shown in Figure 1 (b).

We evaluate ProtoBox with three tasks: WSD, New Sense Classification (NSC), and Hypernym Identification (HI). Three datasets of different domains, one is large and two are small, are used to thoroughly evaluate our proposed method. Experimental results show that ProtoBox is better than or comparable to the baselines for WSD and NSC, and always outperforms the baselines for HI.

The contributions of this paper are summarized as follows:

- We propose ProtoBox, a new method to learn contextualized box embeddings based on Prototypical Networks (Snell et al., 2017).
- We propose a method to construct an mini-batch to learn hypernym–hyponym relations between senses in the contextualized box embeddings.
- We empirically evaluate the effectiveness of ProtoBox for three down-streaming tasks: WSD, NSC, and HI.

2 Related Work

2.1 WSD

Many recent WSD methods use glosses (sense definitions) and lexical relations (e.g., hypernym–hyponym relations) to improve their performance (Huang et al., 2019; Kumar et al., 2019; Bevilacqua et al., 2020; Bevilacqua and Navigli, 2020; Blevins and Zettlemoyer, 2020; Scarlini et al., 2020; Barba et al., 2021). However, the accuracy of WSD for infrequent senses tended to be lower than that for the whole of the test data (Maru et al., 2022).

To address this problem, Chen et al. (2021) proposed MetricWSD, a method to learn contextualized embeddings using Prototypical Networks (Snell et al., 2017). Prototypical Networks is a meta learning method that works better on imbalanced data. MetricWSD achieved a state-of-the-art WSD performance without additional lexical information such as glosses or lexical relations.

Generationary (Bevilacqua et al., 2020) is another approach for WSD. First, a definition of a sense for a given word is generated by BART (Lewis et al., 2020). Then, the similarity score between the generated definition and each definition of the target word in WordNet (Miller, 1995) is calculated by Sentence-BERT (Reimers and Gurevych, 2019) and the most similar sense chosen to be the predicted sense. Generationary aims not only to improve the performance at WSD but also explain a new sense. This paper also tries to explain the meaning of a new sense using trained contextualized box embeddings. Instead of generating a definition of a new sense, a hypernym of a new sense is identified as a coarse meaning of it.

2.2 Taxonomy Expansion

Taxonomy Expansion is the task to infer a hypernym of a new concept (Bordea et al., 2016). It has been actively studied. Recent methods improved the performance by using graph neural networks (Shen et al., 2020) and learning the shortest path between a target concept and the root concept (Yu et al., 2020). Some methods (Aly et al., 2019; Ma et al., 2021) used Hyperbolic space (Nickel and Kiela, 2017) learn hypernym–hyponym relations. This paper also presents a method of Taxonomy Expansion, but a hypernym of a new concept is guessed by contextualized box embeddings.

2.3 Contextualized Box Embeddings

There have been a few studies that have applied contextualized box embeddings to some tasks. The Entity Typing task is a multi-label classification problem to predict appropriate types such as "event" and "person", for a target in a context (Choi et al., 2018). Onoe et al. (2021) represented target entities by contextualized box embeddings, and also represented types of entity by dedicated box embeddings. The model was trained so that the contextualized box embedding of the target entity was enclosed by the box embeddings of its type of entity.

Jiang et al. (2023) proposed a method for Taxonomy Expansion by learning the box embeddings of concepts. The box embeddings of entities in the existing taxonomy were derived from their definition sentences. The model, which converts a sentence to a contextualized box embedding was trained by hypernym–hyponym pairs in the taxonomy so that the box embedding of a hypernym enclosed that of a hyponym. Although the above studies presented methods to learn contextualized box embeddings, we adapt another approach. Specifically, our framework follows that of Prototypical Networks, which can work well for imbalanced training data. We expect that our method can learn appropriate box embeddings for infrequent senses.

3 Proposed Method

This section describes the details of ProtoBox, our proposed method to train contextualized box embeddings. We first explain box embeddings, as background, in subsection 3.1, then explain ProtoBox in the succeeding subsections.

3.1 Box Embeddings

Single vectors represent items as points, while box embeddings represent items as boxes. Box embeddings can naturally represent asymmetric relations like hypernym–hyponym relations by the overlap of two boxes. In this work, a box embedding $\mathbf{b}$ is constructed from two vectors $\mathbf{c}$, the center of the box, and $\mathbf{o}$, an offset from $\mathbf{c}$. $\mathbf{c}$ is the center of a box and $\mathbf{o}$ is the offset from $\mathbf{c}$. Note that the dimensions of $\mathbf{c}$ and $\mathbf{o}$ are equal. The area of the ith dimension of the box embedding is defined as the range $[c_i - o_i, c_i + o_i]$.

Given two boxes $\mathbf{b}_i$ and $\mathbf{b}_j$, the probability that $\mathbf{b}_i$ encloses $\mathbf{b}_j$ can be defined as

$$P(\mathbf{b}_j|\mathbf{b}_i) = \frac{\mathrm{Vol}(\mathbf{b}_i \cap \mathbf{b}_j)}{\mathrm{Vol}(\mathbf{b}_i)}, \quad (1)$$

where $\mathbf{b}_i \cap \mathbf{b}_j$ is the are of the overlap of $\mathbf{b}_i$ and $\mathbf{b}_j$, and $\mathrm{Vol}(\mathbf{b})$ is the function that calculates the volume of $\mathbf{b}$.

The hard definition of the probability in Equation (1) often leads a serious problem for training box embeddings. When two boxes have no overlap, $P(\mathbf{b}_j|\mathbf{b}_i)$ is zero, causing the training to halt due to the vanishing of the gradient. Therefore, in general, a soft definition is often used. Following previous work (Onoe et al., 2021; Jiang et al., 2023), we use Gumbel Box (Dasgupta et al., 2020), one of the box embeddings that calculates the above probability with a soft definition. Specifically, the probability that $\mathbf{b}_i$ encloses $\mathbf{b}_j$ is calculated with the Gumbel distribution.

3.2 MetricWSD

Since ProtoBox is an extension of MetricWSD (Chen et al., 2021), we first briefly introduce the latter. The left side of Figure 2 shows an overview of MetricWSD. It is a model for WSD, based on Prototypical Networks. The training data is a collection of sentences including a target word (e.g., 'dog') labeled with its gold sense (e.g., dog.1). It is divided into two sets: a support set and a query set. Each sentence in the support set is converted to a contextualized word embedding (or sense embedding) by a model f_θ. In MetricWSD, BERT (Devlin et al., 2019) is used as f_θ. The prototype vector of each sense (e.g., dog.1, dog.2) is defined as the average of the contextualized word embeddings of that sense. Next, the sentences in the query set are converted to contextualized word embeddings by the same model f_θ, and then the loss is calculated by the distances between the query vector and the prototype vectors. Finally, the parameters of the model, θ, are updated so that the loss becomes minimized. At the inference, a test sentence is converted to an embedding by f_θ, and then the similarities between it and the prototype sense vectors are calculated, and the most similar sense is chosen.

3.3 Learning Contextualized Box Embeddings

The right side in Figure 2 shows an overview of ProtoBox. In our method, MetricWSD is modified in three ways. First, instead of a single vector, a sentence is converted to a box embedding by the model. Following previous work (Onoe et al., 2021), we add a Fully Connected Layer (FCL) after BERT. For a sentence x where the zth word is the target word, its contextualized box embedding is obtained as follows:

$$\mathbf{b} = f_\theta(x, z) = \mathrm{FCL}(\mathrm{BERT}(x)[z]). \quad (2)$$

The input of FCL is $\mathrm{BERT}(x)[z]$, the contextualized word embedding of the zth word when x is entered to BERT. The output of FCL forms the box embedding $\mathbf{b}$, which is equally divided into two vectors $\mathbf{c}$ and $\mathbf{o}$ by $\mathbf{b} = [\mathbf{c}, \mathbf{o}]$.

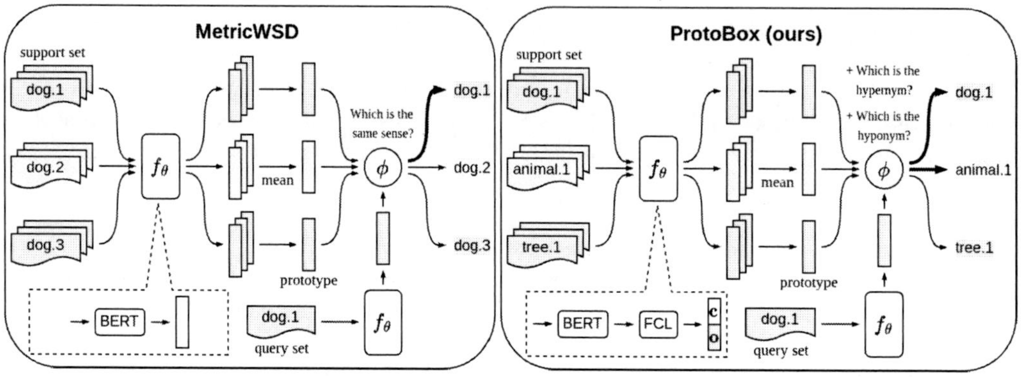

Figure 2: Overview of MetricWSD and ProtoBox (ours).

Second, the episodes are constructed differently. In Prototypical Networks, a mini-batch used to train a model is called an "episode." On the one hand, an episode is a set of instances with different senses of the same target word in MetricWSD. On the other hand, an episode is a set of instances with different senses of multiple target words (e.g. dog.1, animal.1, and tree.1) in ProtoBox. The details of the construction of an episode will be explained in subsection 3.4.

Third, the loss is calculated between a query representation (contextualized box embedding) $\mathbf{b}^q$ and each prototype representation (sense box embedding) $\mathbf{b}^p$. Given a query set $\mathcal{E}_Q = \{x_1, x_2, ..., x_{N_Q}\}$, box embedding of each sample x_i is computed by

$$\mathbf{b}_i^q = f_\theta(x_i, z). \tag{3}$$

Let us suppose $\mathcal{C} = \{s_1, s_2, ..., s_{N_C}\}$ is the set of the senses (of different words) in the entire support set and $\mathcal{E}_{P_j} = \{x_{j1}, x_{j2}, ..., x_{jN_P}\}$ is the support set of the jth sense s_j. The prototype representation of s_j, $\mathbf{b}_j^p$, is defined as the mean of the box embeddings of the samples in the support set:

$$\mathbf{b}_j^p = \frac{1}{N_P}\sum_{i=1}^{N_P} f_\theta(x_{ji}, z). \tag{4}$$

In the above two equations, z stands for the position of the target word in the sentence.

Following Onoe et al. (2021), we use the binary cross-entropy loss between the prototype sense s_j in the support set and the sample x_i in the query set:

$$\begin{aligned} l(\mathbf{b}_j^p, \mathbf{b}_i^q) = &- \delta\cdot\log P(\mathbf{b}_j^p|\mathbf{b}_i^q) \\ &- (1-\delta)\cdot\log(1 - P(\mathbf{b}_j^p|\mathbf{b}_i^q)). \end{aligned} \tag{5}$$

Here, δ is 1 if the prototype sense s_j is equal to the sense of x_i or s_j is a hypernym of x_i, otherwise 0. Finally, the total loss $\mathcal{L}$ is defined as follows:

$$\mathcal{L} = \frac{1}{N_Q N_C}\sum_{i=1}^{N_Q}\sum_{j=1}^{N_C}\frac{1}{2}(l(\mathbf{b}_j^p, \mathbf{b}_i^q) + l(\mathbf{b}_i^q, \mathbf{b}_j^p)).$$

Intuitively, the model f_θ is trained so that contextualized box embeddings of the same sense overlap each other and a contextualized box embedding of a hypernym encloses that of a hyponym.

3.4 Episode Construction

The training data of ProtoBox is a collection of "sense instances." A sense instance is an example sentence including a certain sense of a target word. To train the model, the training data is divided into episodes. Note that each episode is a pair of support and query sets, $(\mathcal{E}_S, \mathcal{E}_Q)$. The following sets are made: (1) $\mathcal{W}$, a set of small number of randomly chosen target words, (2) $\mathcal{P}_S$, a set of senses of the target words in $\mathcal{W}$, and (3) $\mathcal{P}_\mathcal{H}$, a set of direct hypernym senses of the senses in $\mathcal{P}_S$. Then, several senses in $\mathcal{P}_S$ and $\mathcal{P}_\mathcal{H}$ are chosen as the prototype senses, thus the support set is formed by sense instances of those prototype senses. The query set is made up of the sense instances of the senses in $\mathcal{P}_S$ that are mutually exclusive with the support set. We limit the number of the target words in each episode to N_W, the maximum number of the prototype senses to N_C, the maximum number of sentences for each prototype sense to N_P (the maximum number of sentences in the entire support set is $N_C \times N_P$), and the maximum number of the sentences in the query set to N_Q.

Algorithm 1 shows how the episodes are constructed. First, N_W words are randomly chosen

Algorithm 1 Construction of Episodes

1: $\mathcal{D}^{\text{train}}$: the training data
2: $\mathcal{V}$: all words in the training data
3: $\mathcal{E} \leftarrow \emptyset$
4: **while** $\mathcal{V} \neq \emptyset$ **do**
5: $\quad \mathcal{W} \leftarrow \text{RANDOM}(\mathcal{V}, N_W)$
6: $\quad \mathcal{V} \leftarrow \mathcal{V} \setminus \mathcal{W}$
7: $\quad \mathcal{P}_S \leftarrow \bigcup_{w \in \mathcal{W}} \text{SENSEOFWORD}(w)$
8: $\quad \mathcal{P}_\mathcal{H} \leftarrow \bigcup_{s \in \mathcal{S}} \text{DIRECTHYPERNYMS}(s)$
9: $\quad$ **if** $|\mathcal{P}_S| + |\mathcal{P}_\mathcal{H}| > N_C$ **then**
10: $\quad\quad$ /* ensure $|\mathcal{P}_S| + |\mathcal{P}_\mathcal{H}| = N_C$ */
11: $\quad\quad \mathcal{P}_\mathcal{H} \leftarrow \text{RANDOM}(\mathcal{P}_\mathcal{H}, N_C - |\mathcal{P}_S|)$
12: $\quad \mathcal{E}_S \leftarrow \emptyset; \mathcal{E}_Q \leftarrow \emptyset$
13: $\quad$ /* $\mathcal{D}_s^{\text{train}}$: sense instances of s in $\mathcal{D}^{\text{train}}$ */
14: $\quad$ **for** $s \in \mathcal{P}_S$ **do**
15: $\quad\quad \tilde{\mathcal{E}}_S \leftarrow \text{RANDOM}(\mathcal{D}_s^{\text{train}}, N_P)$
16: $\quad\quad \mathcal{E}_S \leftarrow \mathcal{E}_S \cup \tilde{\mathcal{E}}_S$
17: $\quad\quad \mathcal{E}_Q \leftarrow \mathcal{E}_Q \cup (\mathcal{D}_s^{\text{train}} \setminus \tilde{\mathcal{E}}_S)$
18: $\quad$ **for** $s \in \mathcal{P}_\mathcal{H}$ **do**
19: $\quad\quad \mathcal{E}_S \leftarrow \mathcal{E}_S \cup \text{RANDOM}(\mathcal{D}_s^{\text{train}}, N_P)$
20: $\quad \mathcal{E}_Q \leftarrow \text{RANDOM}(\mathcal{E}_Q, N_Q)$
21: $\quad \mathcal{E} \leftarrow \mathcal{E} \cup \{(\mathcal{E}_S, \mathcal{E}_Q)\}$
22: **return** $\mathcal{E}$

(line 5). Second, all senses of the randomly chosen target words are kept as $\mathcal{P}_S$ (line 7), and all direct hypernym of those senses are kept as $\mathcal{P}_\mathcal{H}$ (line 8). The senses in $\mathcal{P}_S$ and $\mathcal{P}_\mathcal{H}$ are used as the prototype senses. More precisely, all the senses in $\mathcal{P}_S$ are kept as prototype senses, while the rest are randomly chosen from $\mathcal{P}_\mathcal{H}$ so that the total number of prototype senses becomes N_C (lines 9–11). Then, the randomly chosen N_P instances for each prototype sense are kept as the support set $\mathcal{E}_S$ (lines 15–16, 19), while the N_Q instances of the senses in $\mathcal{P}_S$, which were not selected in the support set, are chosen as the query set $\mathcal{E}_Q$ (lines 17, 20). Note that the function $\text{RANDOM}(S, n)$ randomly chooses n samples at most from the set S; all samples are chosen when $|S| < n$. The above procedure is repeated until all words in the training data have been used to make episodes.

Since instances of hypernym senses as well as all the senses of a target word are included in the support set, ProtoBox can consider not only the sense discrimination, as does MetricWSD, but also the hypernym–hyponym relations in the training of the model that produces contextualized box embeddings.

4 Applications of ProtoBox

This section describes how ProtoBox is applied to three tasks: Word Sense Disambiguation, New Sense Classification, and Hypernym Identification.

4.1 Word Sense Disambiguation

Task Definition The goal of Word Sense Disambiguation (WSD) is to select the most appropriate sense of the target word w in a given context x from a predefined inventory $\mathcal{S}_w$ of senses.

Method First, we get the contextualized box embedding $\mathbf{b}^q$ of w in x. Second, we create the sense embedding $\mathbf{b}_i^p$ for each sense s_i in $\mathcal{S}_w$ from the training data. Finally, we calculate the similarity score between $\mathbf{b}_i^p$ and $\mathbf{b}^q$ using Equation (6), which measures by how much two box embeddings overlap, then the most similar sense is chosen to be the predicted sense.

$$\text{sim}(\mathbf{b}_i^p, \mathbf{b}^q) = 2 \times \frac{P(\mathbf{b}_i^p|\mathbf{b}^q)P(\mathbf{b}^q|\mathbf{b}_i^p)}{P(\mathbf{b}_i^p|\mathbf{b}^q) + P(\mathbf{b}^q|\mathbf{b}_i^p)} \quad (6)$$

4.2 New Sense Classification

Task Definition The goal of New Sense Classification (NSC) is to classify the target word w in a given context x, whether it has a new sense or not. In this study, new senses are defined as senses that do not appear in the training data.

Method First, we get $\mathbf{b}^q$ and $\mathbf{b}_i^p$ in the same way that WSD does. For all senses s_i in $\mathcal{S}_w$, if $\text{sim}(\mathbf{b}_i^p, \mathbf{b}^q)$ is smaller than a threshold α_{s_i}, w in x is predicted to be a new sense, otherwise not.

Then α_{s_i} is determined for each sense using the training and development data. Let $\mathcal{D}_{s_i}^{\text{dev}}$ be a set of sense instances of s_i in the development data. The threshold is set to be

$$\alpha_{s_i} = \frac{1}{|\mathcal{D}_{s_i}^{\text{dev}}|} \sum_{j=1}^{|\mathcal{D}_{s_i}^{\text{dev}}|} \text{sim}(\mathbf{b}_i^p, \mathbf{b}_j^q), \quad (7)$$

where $\mathbf{b}_i^p$ is the box embedding of the prototype sense s_i and $\mathbf{b}_j^q$ is the box embedding of the jth instance in $\mathcal{D}_{s_i}^{\text{dev}}$. That is, α_{s_i} is determined as the average similarity between the sense instance of s_i in the development data and the prototype sense s_i in the training data. When there is no sense instance of s_i in the development data, the threshold is set to the average of α_{s_i} for all senses.

4.3 Hypernym Identification

Task Definition Hypernym Identification (HI) is the task of predicting a hypernym of a new sense. Specifically, for a given new sense of a target word w in a context x, we choose and rank the top ten senses that are most likely to be a hypernym of it.

Method First, we get the contextualized box embedding $\mathbf{b}^q$ of w in x and the box embeddings of the prototype senses $\mathbf{b}_i^p$ as in the WSD task. Then, the set $\mathcal{H}$ of candidates of hypernym senses is created:

$$\mathcal{H} = \{s_i \mid P(\mathbf{b}_i^p|\mathbf{b}^q) > \beta\}, \quad (8)$$

where β is a pre-defined threshold. Next, we choose the sense where the difference of the volume of $\mathbf{b}_i^p$ and $\mathbf{b}^q$ is the smallest as the best hypernym sense u.

$$u = \arg\min_{s_i \in \mathcal{H}} |\mathrm{Vol}(\mathbf{b}_i^p) - \mathrm{Vol}(\mathbf{b}^q)| \quad (9)$$

The motivation to consider the difference of the volumes is that when the volume of the box embedding is large, the sense may be an abstract concept and not likely to be a direct hypernym of an input new sense. Finally, all other senses are ranked by their similarity with u (using Equation (6)) and the top nine senses are chosen to make the final ranked list of the hypernyms.

5 Experiments

5.1 Dataset

Following the WSD framework proposed by Raganato et al. (2017), we use SemCor 3.0 (Miller et al., 1994) as the training data, SemEval-2007 (Pradhan et al., 2007) as the development data, and Senseval-2 (Edmonds and Cotton, 2001), Senseval-3 (Snyder and Palmer, 2004), SemEval-2013 (Navigli et al., 2013), SemEval-2015 (Moro and Navigli, 2015) as the test data. All datasets are corpora annotated with sense labels defined by WordNet (Miller, 1995).

In this work, the only the senses of nouns in the datasets are used. In WordNet, senses of nouns connected by hypernym–hyponym relations form a Directed Acyclic Graph of which the root is the synset "entity.n.01". We create three datasets: $\mathcal{D}_{\text{living\_thing}}$, $\mathcal{D}_{\text{artifact}}$, and $\mathcal{D}_{\text{entity}}$. These datasets consist of instances of hyponyms of "living_thing.n.01", "artifact.n.01", and "entity.n.01" in WordNet, respectively. Here, $\mathcal{D}_{\text{entity}}$ is a large dataset that includes all nouns, while $\mathcal{D}_{\text{living\_thing}}$ and $\mathcal{D}_{\text{artifact}}$ are smaller ones including a restricted number of nouns.

Training data The statistics of the training data $\mathcal{D}^{\text{train}}$ are presented in Table 1. The sizes of $\mathcal{D}^{\text{train}}_{\text{living\_thing}}$ and $\mathcal{D}^{\text{train}}_{\text{artifact}}$ are almost the same, while $\mathcal{D}^{\text{train}}_{\text{entity}}$ is much larger than they are.

	$\mathcal{D}^{\text{train}}_{\text{living\_thing}}$	$\mathcal{D}^{\text{train}}_{\text{artifact}}$	$\mathcal{D}^{\text{train}}_{\text{entity}}$
#senses	1,713	1,939	12,760
#words	1,809	1,994	11,029
#instances	15,838	8,708	84,962

Table 1: The statistics of the training data.

Development and test data The development and the test data for the WSD task are constructed from instances including a target word that has multiple senses and its gold sense appears in the training data. Statistics are shown in Table 2. It is found that a considerable number of test instances have infrequent senses.

	$\mathcal{D}_{\text{living\_thing}}$		$\mathcal{D}_{\text{artifact}}$		$\mathcal{D}_{\text{entity}}$	
	ALL	≤ 10	ALL	≤ 10	ALL	≤ 10
dev	13	5	9	5	125	54
test	190	66	78	40	2,514	992

Table 2: The number of instances in development and test data for WSD task. "ALL" means all instances. "$\leq$ 10" means instances of a sense that appears in the training data less than or equal to 10 times.

The development and the test data for the NSC task are constructed from instances including a target word that appear in the training data. The instances are labeled as "new sense" if its gold sense does not appear in the training data, otherwise as "not new sense". The statistics are shown in Table 3.

	$\mathcal{D}_{\text{living\_thing}}$		$\mathcal{D}_{\text{artifact}}$		$\mathcal{D}_{\text{entity}}$	
	new	not	new	not	new	not
dev	0	23	0	18	7	144
test	20	500	12	221	295	3,379

Table 3: The number of instances in development and test data for NSC task. "new" and "not" mean new sense and not new sense, respectively.

The development and the test data for the HI task are constructed from instances whose gold senses do not appear in the training data. The statistics are shown in Table 4. The gold hypernym is determined by WordNet.

	$\mathcal{D}_{\text{living\_thing}}$	$\mathcal{D}_{\text{artifact}}$	$\mathcal{D}_{\text{entity}}$
dev	2	2	11
test	107	32	658

Table 4: The number of instances in development and test data for HI task.

5.2 Settings

Baselines We prepare two baselines: vanilla BERT (BERT-NN) and MetricWSD (Chen et al., 2021). These models output a contextualized embedding (single vector) $\mathbf{r}$ for a given sense instance. In BERT-NN, the embedding of a prototype sense are obtained by the average of the vectors of sense instances derived from the pre-trained BERT. The similarity between two vectors $\mathbf{r}_i$ and $\mathbf{r}_j$ is defined as the dot product $\text{sim}(\mathbf{r}_i, \mathbf{r}_j) = \mathbf{r}_i \cdot \mathbf{r}_j$.

The baselines perform WSD and NSC in the same way as our method, except that the similarity between two instances is measured by two single vectors. In HI, the baseline chooses the ten most similar senses to make up a ranked list of hypernym senses.

Parameters For all models in BERT-NN, MetricWSD, and ProtoBox, we use bert-base-uncased as the BERT model. We set the number of dimensions of the output layer of FCL to 256 (i.e. the size of $\mathbf{c}$ and $\mathbf{o}$ is 128), N_W is 32, N_C is 128, N_P is 5, and N_Q is 64. As for the hyperparameters for the fine-tuning of BERT, the learning rate is set to 1e-5. The number of epochs is optimized, that is, it is varied from 1 to 200 and the best value is chosen using the development data.

5.3 Results and Analysis

Word Sense Disambiguation Table 5 shows the accuracy on the WSD task. As can be seen from the column "ALL", our ProtoBox outperformed the two baselines for $\mathcal{D}_{\text{living\_thing}}$, but was comparable for $\mathcal{D}_{\text{artifact}}$ and $\mathcal{D}_{\text{entity}}$. We guess that the poor performance on $\mathcal{D}_{\text{entity}}$ was caused by the scale, that is, our method failed to obtain appropriate contextualized box embeddings when it was applied to many sense instances. The reason why ProtoBox was worse than MetricWSD on $\mathcal{D}_{\text{artifact}}$ may not be a scale issue, but the semantic domain of the target noun, since the sizes of $\mathcal{D}_{\text{living\_thing}}$ and $\mathcal{D}_{\text{artifact}}$ were almost the same.

A similar tendency for the disambiguation of infrequent senses can be seen in the column "≤ 10". Surprisingly, BERT-NN achieved the best accuracy on $\mathcal{D}_{\text{entity}}$, although the pretrained BERT model was just applied without fine-tuning. MetricWSD and ProtoBox still suffered from the data sparseness when they were applied to the large dataset.

New Sense Classification The results on the New Sense Classification task are shown in Table 6. Comparing the F1-score, ProtoBox was comparable to MetricWSD on $\mathcal{D}_{\text{living\_thing}}$ and $\mathcal{D}_{\text{entity}}$, and significantly worse on $\mathcal{D}_{\text{artifact}}$. The poor performance for NSC for the senses of artifacts was coincident with the results of the WSD task, where ProtoBox was worse than MetricWSD on $\mathcal{D}_{\text{artifact}}$. The F1-score of BERT-NN on $\mathcal{D}_{\text{living\_thing}}$ was notable as it was better than that of MetricWSD and ProtoBox. ProtoBox is designed to learn hypernym–hyponym relations between senses, but such knowledge may not be indispensable for New Sense Classification. This might be the reason why ProtoBox could not outperform MetricWSD.

Hypernym Identification Following previous work on Taxonomy Expansion (Shen et al., 2020; Yu et al., 2020; Jiang et al., 2023), we evaluate the baselines and ProtoBox in term of three metrics: accuracy (ACC), Mean Reciprocal Rank (MRR), Wu-Palmer similarity (W&P) (Wu and Palmer, 1994). Accuracy measures the agreement ratio between the gold hypernym and the highest ranked hypernym, while Wu–Palmer similarity measures how closely these two hypernyms are located in WordNet. The parameter β described in subsection 4.3 is set to 0.5, 0.7, or 0.9.[2]

The results on the HI task are shown in Table 7. ProtoBox outperformed the baselines in all three evaluation metrics on the three datasets. In particular, the difference between ProtoBox and the baselines was significant on $\mathcal{D}_{\text{living\_thing}}$. The many gold hypernyms in the test data of $\mathcal{D}_{\text{living\_thing}}$ were "person.n.01", which were correctly predicted by ProtoBox. On the other hand, on $\mathcal{D}_{\text{artifact}}$ and $\mathcal{D}_{\text{entity}}$, the differences in terms of ACC and MRR between ProtoBox and the baselines were small. However, a significant difference of W&P was confirmed, indicating that ProtoBox could predict hypernyms closer to the correct ones. Finally, the performance of ProtoBox was sensitive to the parameter β, especially in terms of ACC and MRR. Investigating how to optimize β would be the important future work.

[2] β was not optimized due to the insufficiency of the development data.

Model	$\mathcal{D}_{\text{living\_thing}}$ ALL	$\mathcal{D}_{\text{living\_thing}}$ ≤ 10	$\mathcal{D}_{\text{artifact}}$ ALL	$\mathcal{D}_{\text{artifact}}$ ≤ 10	$\mathcal{D}_{\text{entity}}$ ALL	$\mathcal{D}_{\text{entity}}$ ≤ 10
BERT-NN	.816	.727	.744	.775	.579	**.602**
MetricWSD	.821	.773	**.872**	**.925**	**.711**	.588
ProtoBox (ours)	**.884**	**.788**	.859	.875	.707	.584

Table 5: Accuracy of WSD task. "ALL" indicates the results for all senses, and "$\leq$ 10" for infrequent senses.

Model	$\mathcal{D}_{\text{living\_thing}}$ A	P	R	F	$\mathcal{D}_{\text{artifact}}$ A	P	R	F	$\mathcal{D}_{\text{entity}}$ A	P	R	F
BERT-NN	**.744**	**.099**	**.700**	**.174**	**.682**	.069	.417	.119	**.656**	.119	.515	.194
MetricWSD	.712	.055	.400	.096	.674	**.119**	**.833**	**.208**	.633	**.138**	**.678**	**.229**
ProtoBox (ours)	.704	.053	.400	.094	.618	.086	.667	.152	.628	.132	.651	.219

Table 6: Results of New Sense Classification task. A, P, R, and F mean accuracy, precision, recall, and F1 score, respectively.

Model	β	$\mathcal{D}_{\text{living\_thing}}$ ACC	MRR	W&P	$\mathcal{D}_{\text{artifact}}$ ACC	MRR	W&P	$\mathcal{D}_{\text{entity}}$ ACC	MRR	W&P
BERT-NN	–	.150	.259	.754	.094	.150	.567	.068	.113	.460
MetricWSD	–	.103	.219	.767	.062	.170	.505	.073	.124	.494
ProtoBox (ours)	0.5	.439	.502	.855	.125	**.179**	.628	.061	.084	.539
	0.7	.533	.570	.876	**.156**	.175	**.644**	.081	.113	.558
	0.9	**.579**	**.604**	**.877**	.062	.076	.621	**.100**	**.126**	**.565**

Table 7: Results of Hypernym Identification task.

5.4 Optimization of Number of Dimensions

We analyzed how the performance of WSD was influenced by the number of the dimensions of the box embeddings **c** and **o**. In this experiment, the number of dimensions of the box embeddings was set to $\{32, 64, 128, 192, 256\}$. Table 8 shows the accuracy of WSD on the development data of $\mathcal{D}_{\text{entity}}$. It was found that the best performance for both "ALL" and "$\leq$ 10" was obtained when the number of dimensions was set to 128. Therefore, as described in subsection 5.2, the number of dimensions was set to 256 (128 + 128). For NSC and HI tasks, we did not optimize this since the development data was small, but set it to be the same number as for the WSD task.

Dimension	ALL	≤ 10
32	.744	.593
64	.784	.630
128	**.792**	**.685**
192	.752	.630
256	.736	.574

Table 8: Accuracy of WSD task on the development data for different number of dimensions of **c** and **o**.

6 Conclusion

This paper proposed ProtoBox, an expansion of MetricWSD to learn contextualized box embeddings. The representations of words in a context were changed from single vectors in MetricWSD to box embeddings in our ProtoBox, since box embeddings are suitable to represent semantic relations between senses such as the hypernym–hyponym relation. Additionally, we proposed a method to construct episodes to train the model to produce the contextualized box embeddings. We evaluated ProtoBox on three tasks: Word Sense Disambiguation (WSD), New Sense Classification (NSC), and Hypernym Identification (HI). ProtoBox outperformed the baselines in terms of all evaluation metrics in the HI task. This was reasonable, since ProtoBox was designed to take the hypernym–hyponym relation into account when training the contextualized box embeddings. In addition, ProtoBox achieved a performance comparable with the baselines for the other sense related tasks, WSD and NSC.

In the future, the scalability of ProtoBox should be improved. As reported in subsection 5.3, the performance of ProtoBox was degraded when the number of sense instances was large. A more efficient and precise method to learn contextualized box embeddings should be investigated. In addition, the definition of the prototype representation (the box embedding of a sense) can be reconsidered. Currently, the prototype representation is an average of box embeddings of the elements in the support set. However, it can be a box that includes all the elements in the support set. It is worth to explore better ways to obtain the prototype representation.

Limitations

In the experiments, ProtoBox was only applied to nouns. Additional experiments are required to investigate how ProtoBox can work well for other parts of speech, such as verbs.

The parameter β in the HI task was not optimized due to the insufficiency of the development data. It is worth investigating how to find an appropriate threshold in the future.

We did not compare ProtoBox with other methods of contextualized box embeddings such as Onoe et al. (2021) and Jiang et al. (2023) in the experiments, since the target tasks were not completely the same as the three tasks in this paper. However, empirical comparison is necessary to clarify the contribution of our method.

Ethics Statement

Since ProtoBox was developed using the established datasets for WSD that have been widely used in the community and contain no private information, there is no concern for data and privacy.

References

Rami Aly, Shantanu Acharya, Alexander Ossa, Arne Köhn, Chris Biemann, and Alexander Panchenko. 2019. Every child should have parents: A taxonomy refinement algorithm based on hyperbolic term embeddings. In *Proceedings of the 57th Annual Meeting of the Association for Computational Linguistics*, pages 4811–4817, Florence, Italy. Association for Computational Linguistics.

Edoardo Barba, Tommaso Pasini, and Roberto Navigli. 2021. ESC: Redesigning WSD with extractive sense comprehension. In *Proceedings of the 2021 Conference of the North American Chapter of the Association for Computational Linguistics: Human Language Technologies*, pages 4661–4672, Online. Association for Computational Linguistics.

Michele Bevilacqua, Marco Maru, and Roberto Navigli. 2020. Generationary or "how we went beyond word sense inventories and learned to gloss". In *Proceedings of the 2020 Conference on Empirical Methods in Natural Language Processing (EMNLP)*, pages 7207–7221, Online. Association for Computational Linguistics.

Michele Bevilacqua and Roberto Navigli. 2020. Breaking through the 80% glass ceiling: Raising the state of the art in word sense disambiguation by incorporating knowledge graph information. In *Proceedings of the 58th Annual Meeting of the Association for Computational Linguistics*, pages 2854–2864, Online. Association for Computational Linguistics.

Terra Blevins and Luke Zettlemoyer. 2020. Moving down the long tail of word sense disambiguation with gloss informed bi-encoders. In *Proceedings of the 58th Annual Meeting of the Association for Computational Linguistics*, pages 1006–1017, Online. Association for Computational Linguistics.

Georgeta Bordea, Els Lefever, and Paul Buitelaar. 2016. SemEval-2016 task 13: Taxonomy extraction evaluation (TExEval-2). In *Proceedings of the 10th International Workshop on Semantic Evaluation (SemEval-2016)*, pages 1081–1091, San Diego, California. Association for Computational Linguistics.

Howard Chen, Mengzhou Xia, and Danqi Chen. 2021. Non-parametric few-shot learning for word sense disambiguation. In *Proceedings of the 2021 Conference of the North American Chapter of the Association for Computational Linguistics: Human Language Technologies*, pages 1774–1781, Online. Association for Computational Linguistics.

Eunsol Choi, Omer Levy, Yejin Choi, and Luke Zettlemoyer. 2018. Ultra-fine entity typing. In *Proceedings of the 56th Annual Meeting of the Association for Computational Linguistics (Volume 1: Long Papers)*, pages 87–96, Melbourne, Australia. Association for Computational Linguistics.

Shib Dasgupta, Michael Boratko, Dongxu Zhang, Luke Vilnis, Xiang Li, and Andrew McCallum. 2020. Improving local identifiability in probabilistic box embeddings. *Advances in Neural Information Processing Systems*, 33.

Jacob Devlin, Ming-Wei Chang, Kenton Lee, and Kristina Toutanova. 2019. BERT: Pre-training of deep bidirectional transformers for language understanding. In *Proceedings of the 2019 Conference of the North American Chapter of the Association for Computational Linguistics: Human Language Technologies, Volume 1 (Long and Short Papers)*, pages 4171–4186, Minneapolis, Minnesota. Association for Computational Linguistics.

Philip Edmonds and Scott Cotton. 2001. SENSEVAL-2: Overview. In *Proceedings of SENSEVAL-2 Second International Workshop on Evaluating Word Sense Disambiguation Systems*, pages 1–5, Toulouse, France. Association for Computational Linguistics.

Luyao Huang, Chi Sun, Xipeng Qiu, and Xuanjing Huang. 2019. GlossBERT: BERT for word sense disambiguation with gloss knowledge. In *Proceedings of the 2019 Conference on Empirical Methods in Natural Language Processing and the 9th International Joint Conference on Natural Language Processing (EMNLP-IJCNLP)*, pages 3509–3514, Hong Kong, China. Association for Computational Linguistics.

Song Jiang, Qiyue Yao, Qifan Wang, and Yizhou Sun. 2023. A single vector is not enough: Taxonomy expansion via box embeddings. In *Proceedings of the ACM Web Conference 2023*, pages 2467–2476.

Sawan Kumar, Sharmistha Jat, Karan Saxena, and Partha Talukdar. 2019. Zero-shot word sense disambiguation using sense definition embeddings. In *Proceedings of the 57th Annual Meeting of the Association for Computational Linguistics*, pages 5670–5681, Florence, Italy. Association for Computational Linguistics.

Mike Lewis, Yinhan Liu, Naman Goyal, Marjan Ghazvininejad, Abdelrahman Mohamed, Omer Levy, Veselin Stoyanov, and Luke Zettlemoyer. 2020. BART: Denoising sequence-to-sequence pre-training for natural language generation, translation, and comprehension. In *Proceedings of the 58th Annual Meeting of the Association for Computational Linguistics*, pages 7871–7880, Online. Association for Computational Linguistics.

Mingyu Derek Ma, Muhao Chen, Te-Lin Wu, and Nanyun Peng. 2021. HyperExpan: Taxonomy expansion with hyperbolic representation learning. In *Findings of the Association for Computational Linguistics: EMNLP 2021*, pages 4182–4194, Punta Cana, Dominican Republic. Association for Computational Linguistics.

Marco Maru, Simone Conia, Michele Bevilacqua, and Roberto Navigli. 2022. Nibbling at the hard core of Word Sense Disambiguation. In *Proceedings of the 60th Annual Meeting of the Association for Computational Linguistics (Volume 1: Long Papers)*, pages 4724–4737, Dublin, Ireland. Association for Computational Linguistics.

Tomas Mikolov, Ilya Sutskever, Kai Chen, Greg S Corrado, and Jeff Dean. 2013. Distributed representations of words and phrases and their compositionality. *Advances in Neural Information Processing Systems*, 26.

George A. Miller. 1995. Wordnet: A lexical database for english. *Commun. ACM*, 38(11):39–41.

George A. Miller, Martin Chodorow, Shari Landes, Claudia Leacock, and Robert G. Thomas. 1994. Using a semantic concordance for sense identification. In *Human Language Technology: Proceedings of a Workshop held at Plainsboro, New Jersey, March 8-11, 1994*.

Andrea Moro and Roberto Navigli. 2015. SemEval-2015 task 13: Multilingual all-words sense disambiguation and entity linking. In *Proceedings of the 9th International Workshop on Semantic Evaluation (SemEval 2015)*, pages 288–297, Denver, Colorado. Association for Computational Linguistics.

Roberto Navigli. 2009. Word sense disambiguation: A survey. *ACM Comput. Surv.*, 41(2).

Roberto Navigli, David Jurgens, and Daniele Vannella. 2013. SemEval-2013 task 12: Multilingual word sense disambiguation. In *Second Joint Conference on Lexical and Computational Semantics (*SEM), Volume 2: Proceedings of the Seventh International Workshop on Semantic Evaluation (SemEval 2013)*, pages 222–231, Atlanta, Georgia, USA. Association for Computational Linguistics.

Maximillian Nickel and Douwe Kiela. 2017. Poincaré embeddings for learning hierarchical representations. *Advances in Neural Information Processing Systems*, 30.

Yasumasa Onoe, Michael Boratko, Andrew McCallum, and Greg Durrett. 2021. Modeling fine-grained entity types with box embeddings. In *Proceedings of the 59th Annual Meeting of the Association for Computational Linguistics and the 11th International Joint Conference on Natural Language Processing (Volume 1: Long Papers)*, pages 2051–2064, Online. Association for Computational Linguistics.

Sameer Pradhan, Edward Loper, Dmitriy Dligach, and Martha Palmer. 2007. SemEval-2007 task-17: English lexical sample, SRL and all words. In *Proceedings of the Fourth International Workshop on Semantic Evaluations (SemEval-2007)*, pages 87–92, Prague, Czech Republic. Association for Computational Linguistics.

Alessandro Raganato, Jose Camacho-Collados, and Roberto Navigli. 2017. Word sense disambiguation: A unified evaluation framework and empirical comparison. In *Proceedings of the 15th Conference of the European Chapter of the Association for Computational Linguistics: Volume 1, Long Papers*, pages 99–110, Valencia, Spain. Association for Computational Linguistics.

Nils Reimers and Iryna Gurevych. 2019. Sentence-BERT: Sentence embeddings using Siamese BERT-networks. In *Proceedings of the 2019 Conference on Empirical Methods in Natural Language Processing and the 9th International Joint Conference on Natural Language Processing (EMNLP-IJCNLP)*, pages 3982–3992, Hong Kong, China. Association for Computational Linguistics.

Bianca Scarlini, Tommaso Pasini, and Roberto Navigli. 2020. With more contexts comes better performance: Contextualized sense embeddings for all-round word sense disambiguation. In *Proceedings of the 2020 Conference on Empirical Methods in Natural Language Processing (EMNLP)*, pages 3528–3539, Online. Association for Computational Linguistics.

Jiaming Shen, Zhihong Shen, Chenyan Xiong, Chi Wang, Kuansan Wang, and Jiawei Han. 2020. TaxoExpan: Self-supervised taxonomy expansion with position-enhanced graph neural network. In *Proceedings of The Web Conference 2020*, pages 486–497.

Jake Snell, Kevin Swersky, and Richard Zemel. 2017. Prototypical networks for few-shot learning. *Advances in Neural Information Processing Systems*, 30.

Benjamin Snyder and Martha Palmer. 2004. The English all-words task. In *Proceedings of SENSEVAL-3, the Third International Workshop on the Evaluation of Systems for the Semantic Analysis of Text*, pages 41–43, Barcelona, Spain. Association for Computational Linguistics.

Zhibiao Wu and Martha Palmer. 1994. Verb semantics and lexical selection. In *32nd Annual Meeting of the Association for Computational Linguistics*, pages 133–138, Las Cruces, New Mexico, USA. Association for Computational Linguistics.

Lei Yu and Yang Xu. 2023. Word sense extension. In *Proceedings of the 61st Annual Meeting of the Association for Computational Linguistics (Volume 1: Long Papers)*, pages 3281–3294, Toronto, Canada. Association for Computational Linguistics.

Yue Yu, Yinghao Li, Jiaming Shen, Hao Feng, Jimeng Sun, and Chao Zhang. 2020. STEAM: Self-supervised taxonomy expansion with mini-paths. In *Proceedings of the 26th ACM SIGKDD International Conference on Knowledge Discovery & Data Mining*, pages 1026–1035.

A Visualization of Box Embeddings

To verify whether ProtoBox could learn appropriate relations between senses, we visualize box embeddings of several prototype senses. Figure 3 represents box embeddings of animal.n.01 and dog.n.01 trained by ProtoBox from $\mathcal{D}^{\text{train}}_{\text{living\_thing}}$. The horizontal axis represents the dimensions of the boxes, while the vertical axis represents the intervals of each dimension $[c_i - o_i, c_i + o_i]$. It is found that the box of animal.n.01 almost encloses that of dog.n.01, indicating that animal.n.01 is a hypernym of dog.n.01. This is also supported by the fact that P(animal.n.01 | dog.n.01) = 0.999. Therefore, the model learned the hypernym–hyponym relation between animal.n.01 and dog.n.01. Next, let us consider cat.n.01 and dog.n.01, for which there is no hypernym–hyponym relation in WordNet. Looking at Figure 4 and the two probabilities P(cat.n.01 | dog.n.01) = 0.146 and P(dog.n.01 | cat.n.01) = 0.089, the two boxes seem to not overlap very much. Even though cat.n.01 and dog.n.01 are conceptually similar, ProtoBox can learn that there is no hypernym–hyponym relation between them.

Figure 5 shows box embeddings of building.n.01 and house.n.01 trained by ProtoBox from $\mathcal{D}^{\text{train}}_{\text{artifact}}$, and Figure 6 shows box embeddings of hotel.n.01 and house.n.01. The box embeddings of those senses are also adequate. That is, the box of building.n.01 almost encloses that of house.n.01, and the boxes of hotel.n.01 and house.n.01 do not overlap very much.

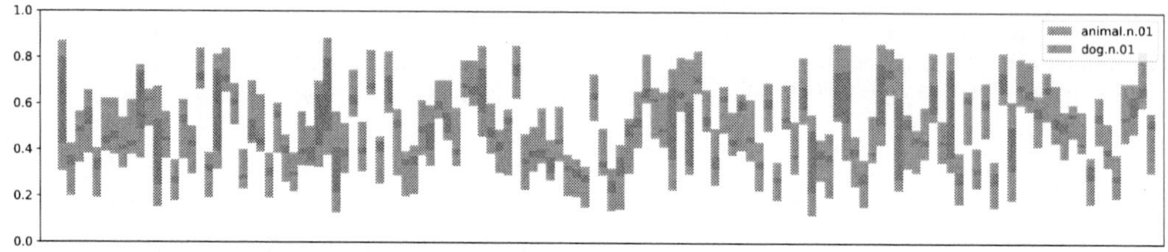

Figure 3: Box embeddings of animal.n.01 and dog.n.01 trained from $\mathcal{D}^{\text{train}}_{\text{living\_thing}}$. $P(\text{animal.n.01} \mid \text{dog.n.01}) = 0.999$, $P(\text{dog.n.01} \mid \text{animal.n.01}) = 3.12\text{e-}9$.

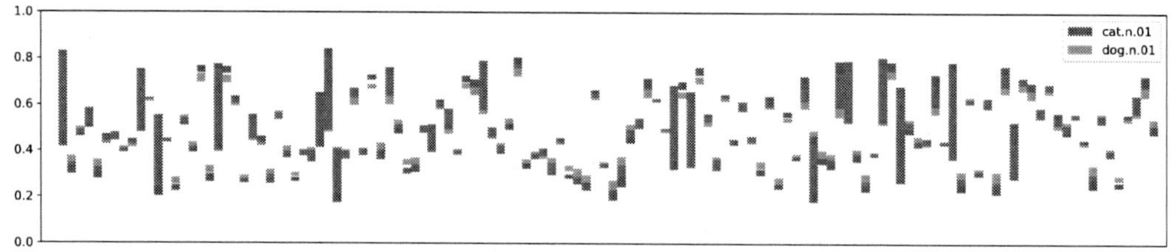

Figure 4: Box embeddings of cat.n.01 and dog.n.01 trained from $\mathcal{D}^{\text{train}}_{\text{living\_thing}}$. $P(\text{cat.n.01} \mid \text{dog.n.01}) = 0.146$, $P(\text{dog.n.01} \mid \text{cat.n.01}) = 0.089$.

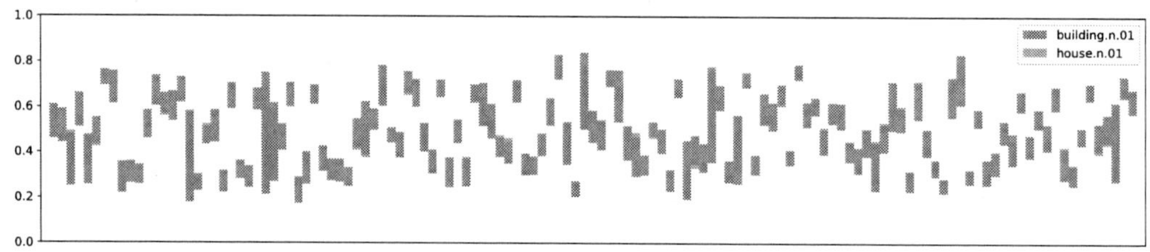

Figure 5: Box embeddings of building.n.01 and house.n.01 trained from $\mathcal{D}^{\text{train}}_{\text{artifact}}$. $P(\text{building.n.01} \mid \text{house.n.01}) = 0.766$, $P(\text{house.n.01} \mid \text{building.n.01}) = 2.97\text{e-}4$.

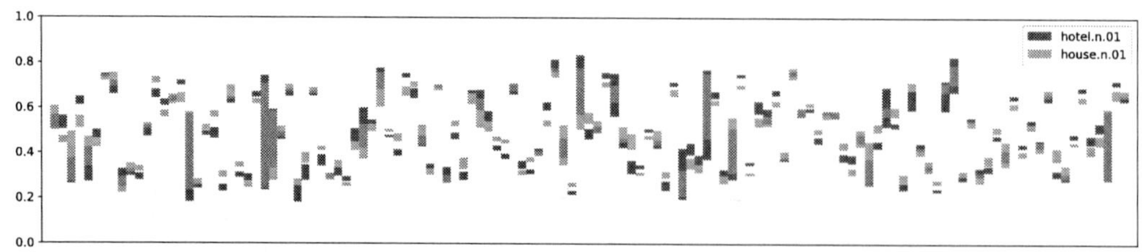

Figure 6: Box embeddings of hotel.n.01 and house.n.01 trained from $\mathcal{D}^{\text{train}}_{\text{artifact}}$. $P(\text{hotel.n.01} \mid \text{house.n.01}) = 0.011$, $P(\text{house.n.01} \mid \text{hotel.n.01}) = 0.013$.

DomainInv: Domain Invariant Fine Tuning and Adversarial Label Correction For Unsupervised QA Domain Adaptation

Anant Khandelwal
Applied Scientist, Microsoft India
anantk@microsoft.com

Abstract

Existing Question Answering (QA) systems are limited in their ability to answer questions from unseen domains or any out-of-domain distributions, making them less reliable for deployment in real scenarios. Importantly, all existing QA domain adaptation methods are either based on generating synthetic data or pseudo-labeling the target domain data. Domain adaptation methods relying on synthetic data and pseudo-labeling suffer from either the need for extensive computational resources or an additional overhead of carefully selecting the confidence threshold to distinguish noisy examples from the training dataset. In this paper, we propose unsupervised domain adaptation for an unlabeled target domain by transferring the target representation close to the source domain without using supervision from the target domain. To achieve this, we introduce the idea of domain-invariant fine-tuning along with adversarial label correction (DomainInv) to identify target instances that are distant from the source domain. This involves learning the domain invariant feature encoder to minimize the distance between such target instances and source instances class-wisely. This eliminates the possibility of learning features of the target domain that are still close to the source support but are ambiguous. The evaluation of our QA domain adaptation method, namely DomainInv, on multiple target QA datasets reveals a performance improvement over the strongest baseline.

1 Introduction

Over the past few years, machine learning models have been widely deployed in production. However, making them work satisfactorily in production requires a substantial amount of high-quality annotated data, which is expensive and time-consuming. Therefore, it is of utmost importance to build generalizable models that can perform well on unseen datasets. However, due to the mechanism of *domain shift* or *bias* in the training dataset (Ben-David et al., 2010, 2006), it is challenging to directly transfer knowledge from the model trained on the source domain to the unlabeled target domain. In this paper, we studied this phenomenon specifically for the case of extractive Question Answering (QA) systems.

Extractive QA systems perform the task of identifying the most relevant answer for a given question within a context or paragraph. The answer is represented as a sub-span of the context, with start and end positions predicted by the QA model. The training data for QA essentially consists of triplets specifying the question, answer, and context. The input to the model is a question and context presented as running text separated by a separator. The model is trained to predict the most relevant start and end positions in the context (Seo et al., 2016; Chen et al., 2017; Devlin et al., 2019; Kratzwald et al., 2019).

These QA systems also face performance degradation at test time, as questions and contexts can vary widely in complexity. The same question may be phrased in the simplest or most complex ways, and the answer may involve reasoning or follow a complex extraction pattern that is challenging to generalize with a limited annotated training dataset. Recent works (Fisch et al., 2019a; Miller et al., 2020; Zeng et al.) have explored this issue, proposing solutions such as using labeled target domain data or incorporating feedback during training (Daumé III, 2007; Kratzwald et al., 2020; Kamath et al., 2020). Others (Yue et al., 2022c, 2021) have employed synthetic or pseudo-labeled data to train these systems and enhance their generalization to out-of-domain distributions. However, it is important to note that pseudo-labeled data is prone to noise, and obtaining accurately labeled data requires considerable human labeling effort.

In this paper, we focus on unsupervised domain adaptation (UDA), which does not require labeled target domain data. There are numerous

Proceedings of the 9th Workshop on Representation Learning for NLP (RepL4NLP-2024), pages 13–25
August 15, 2024

works towards achieving domain-invariant representations, categorized into 1) optimizing the discrepancy between domain representations (Yue et al., 2022c, 2021), and 2) adversarial learning (Lee et al., 2019b; Cao et al., 2020). However, in general there exists different distance metrics for minimizing domain discrepancy, for example (Gretton et al., 2006) leverage maximum mean discrepancy (MMD) as the distance measure between source and target domain distributions. Similar to MMD, CMD (central moment discrepancy) (Zellinger et al., 2017), Wasserstein distance (WD) (Shen et al., 2018), sliced Wasserstein distance (SWD) (Kolouri et al., 2019), multi-kernel MMD (Long et al., 2015), joint MMD (Long et al., 2017) are other alternative measures.

Inspired by generative adversarial networks (GAN) (Goodfellow et al., 2014), adaptation methods based on adversarial learning have also shown promising results (Ganin et al., 2017; Xie et al., 2018; Pei et al., 2018; Saito et al., 2018; Lee et al., 2019a). Adversarial learning methods propose the idea of using the domain discriminator to distinguish whether the incoming sample is from the source or target domain, while the feature generator tries to fool the discriminator by generating domain-invariant features. During the process of creating domain-invariant representations, the generator positions the target representation near the source domain decision boundaries. However, these representations are misaligned with respect to the source classes, leading to a degradation in performance (Lee et al., 2019a).

Some works rely on high-confidence pseudo-labels (Yue et al., 2022c; Deng et al., 2019) for the target domain. However, this method of generating synthetic data for the target domain imposes an additional computational overhead. Moreover, target pseudo-labeling can have adverse effects on adaptation if it generates too many incorrect labels above the confidence threshold. Some works propose minimizing the distance between tokens from the target instances and those of the source support contrastively (Yue et al., 2022c). However, in practical scenarios, the target domain can be completely asymmetrical, necessitating the alignment of the pre-trained source model with the target domain before optimizing for domain-invariant representations. In this paper, we propose an adaptation framework called **DomainInv** (illustrated in Figure 1), which can perform domain adaptation without training an answer classifier with noisy pseudo-labeled data. This eliminates the need to filter out that noise before training on the target domain, as opposed to the existing SOTA method in (Yue et al., 2022c). Our approach involves learning domain-invariant features through domain-invariant fine-tuning along with adversarial label correction. This is done to identify target instances that are far apart from the source domain and optimize them to lie near the source support, class wisely. **Main Contributions of this paper are as follows**:

- We propose the unsupervised domain adaptation framework called DomainInv for extractive QA. The framework can address the *domain shift* phenomenon without the need for explicit training of an answer classifier with pseudo-labeled data. The noise in pseudo-labeled data, which is challenging to filter out, deteriorates the performance of the answer classifier and, consequently, hinders its ability to generalize well to the target domain.

- We propose the idea of 1) Domain Invariant Fine Tuning and 2) Adversarial Label Correction together, aiming to minimize the distance between the source and target domain representations class-wise (start and end) in an iterative manner.

- We evaluated our framework on multiple QA datasets as target domains without accessing their answers during training. DomainInv outperforms the strongest baseline for QA domain adaptation, which adapts the model by explicitly training on pseudo-labeled target domain.

2 Related Work

In the past few years, there has been an increasing interest in learning generalized representations through various learning paradigms, namely, unsupervised, multi-tasking, and transfer learning (Peters et al., 2018; McCann et al., 2018; Chronopoulou et al., 2019; Phang et al., 2018; Wang et al., 2018; Xu et al., 2019). Specifically, recent studies have explored the generalization capability of reading comprehension systems (Golub et al., 2017; Fisch et al., 2019b; Talmor and Berant, 2019; Yue et al., 2021, 2022c,b). Our interest in this paper lies solely in unsupervised approaches for domain adaptation, where target domain data is unlabelled. The approaches used for unsupervised

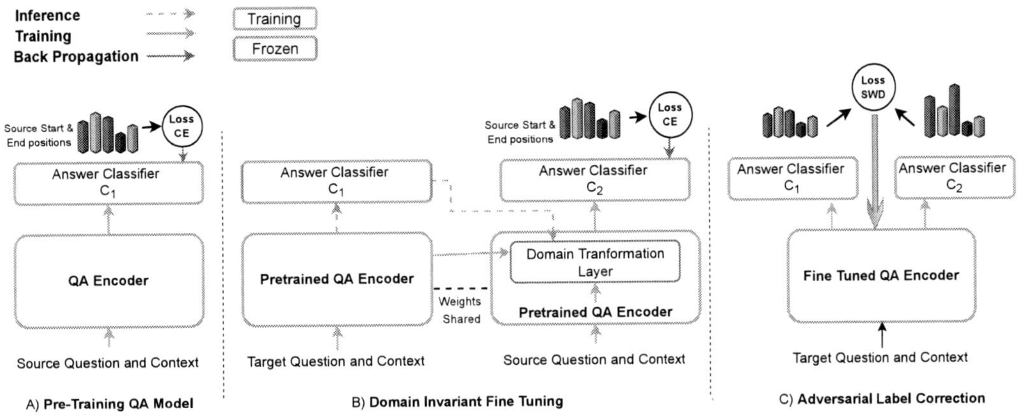

Figure 1: DomainInv: A Robust Framework for QA Domain Adaptation. It proposed to utilize domain invariant fine-tuning followed by adversarial label correction to overcome the limitations associated with domain invariant fine-tuning, demonstrating the noise free domain adaptation.

domain adaptation are broadly categorized into the following main themes: 1) Contrastive Learning, 2) Self-Supervision, and 3) Adversarial Learning.

Contrastive Learning: Contrastive learning methods (He et al., 2020; Caron et al., 2020; Chen et al., 2020; Yue et al., 2022c, 2021) aim to learn a feature encoder that generates similar features for the same input (obtained from different augmentations) and different features for any other input and its augmentations. Specifically for QA, (Sun et al., 2018; Du et al., 2017) have generated synthetic QA samples through Question Generation (QG). Leveraging these samples improves performance in out-of-domain distribution (Yue et al., 2021; Golub et al., 2017; Tang et al., 2017; Lee et al., 2020; Tang et al., 2018; Shakeri et al., 2020; Yue et al., 2022a; Zeng et al., 2022). Additionally, contrastive learning has been applied to minimize the discrepancy between the source and target domains using Maximum Mean Discrepancy (MMD) (Gretton et al., 2006). They learned to minimize the distance for averaged token features (Yue et al., 2022c) among answer and non-answer tokens in source and target domains and maximize the distance between them.

Self-Supervision: There are many works in computer vision that have explored the use of self-supervision for unsupervised domain adaptation, all aligned with the common objective of minimizing the discrepancy (distance) between domains (Kang et al., 2019; Wang et al., 2021; Thota and Leontidis, 2021). Although the objective is similar to that of contrastive learning, models learned through contrastive learning have been shown to perform better (Shen et al., 2022). Apart from the MMD (Gretton et al., 2006) criterion used in (Yue et al., 2022c), other metrics like central moment discrepancy (CMD) used in (Zellinger et al., 2017) directly match order-wise differences of central moments. Wasserstein distance, employed to measure the distance between two probability distributions, has been explored in (Shen et al., 2018; Kolouri et al., 2019). The method in (Yu et al., 2020) learns sentence representations for text matching between asymmetrical domains. In our approach, we consider the use of sliced Wasserstein distance (Kolouri et al., 2019). Instead of minimizing the distance between representations for domains, this distance is applied to minimize the distribution learned for the start and end tokens in QA domain adaptation.

Adversarial Learning: The objective of adversarial learning is also based on the idea of minimizing domain discrepancy. The main concept of domain adversarial learning is to learn domain-invariant representations through an adversarial loss between the feature generator and discriminator, similar to GANs (Goodfellow et al., 2014). Some works that use domain adversarial learning include (Ganin et al., 2017; Tzeng et al., 2017; Bousmalis et al., 2017; Yang et al., 2020; Long et al., 2018; Pei et al., 2018). Additionally, there are methods (Yue et al., 2022c) that explored the use of target data along with pseudo-labels to train the target classifier. In contrast to this, we have explored the use of adversarial loss to identify and correct mistakes in labels during target-aware source fine-tuning, aiming to learn domain-invariant representations for the target domain.

3 Setup

Problem setup for unsupervised domain adaptation(UDA) consider the labeled source domain $\mathcal{D}_s$ and unlabelled target domain $\mathcal{D}_t$. The goal is to maximize the performance on target domain by only training with labeled source domain data and unlabelled target domain data as in (Cao et al., 2020; Shakeri et al., 2020; Yue et al., 2021, 2022b,c).

Data: Specifically, for the case of QA domain adaptation we describe the labeled source domain $\mathcal{D}_s$ data as samples consisting of triplets, $\{c_s^{(i)}, q_s^{(i)}, a_s^{(i)}\} \in \mathbf{X}_s$, consisting of context $c_s^{(i)}$, question $q_s^{(i)}$ and answer $a_s^{(i)}$, where each triplet is obtained from the training data $\mathbf{X}_s$. Similarly, the unlabelled target domain $\mathcal{D}_t$ data consists of samples with pair $\{c_t^{(i)}, q_t^{(i)}\} \in \mathbf{X}_t$ consisting of only context $c_t^{(i)}$ and question $q_t^{(i)}$, obtained from unlabelled training data $\mathbf{X}_t$. Here, in our case of QA domain adaptation the answer is the start and end position in the context since we are working with extractive QA systems.

Model: We approach the problem of QA domain adaptation as training the model function f which predicts an answer $a_t^{(i)}$ given the context $c_t^{(i)}$ and question $q_t^{(i)}$ from $\mathbf{X}_t$, denoted as $a_t^{(i)} = f(c_t^{(i)}, q_t^{(i)})$. This requires to optimize the function f for maximum performance on target domain $\mathcal{D}_t$, given $\mathcal{D}_s$. Mathematically, this is denoted as:

$$\min_f \mathcal{L}(f, \mathbf{X}_t; \mathbf{X}_s) \tag{1}$$

where $\mathcal{L}$ is the loss function. We adopt the two fold training scheme to maximize performance on target domain namely, Domain Invariant Fine Tuning and Adversarial Label Correction which will be discussed in the following sections.

4 DomainInv Framework

4.1 Overview

The proposed DomainInv framework consists of two main components: 1) **Domain Invariant Fine Tuning** and 2) **Adversarial Label Correction** for domain adaptation, as shown in Figure 1. We start with a pre-trained QA model f, fine-tuned on the source domain $\mathcal{D}_s$ as in (Cao et al., 2020), with an additional batch norm layer. The answer classifier $\mathcal{C}_1$ predicts the start and end indices in the context. During domain invariant fine-tuning, we incorporate the use of the target domain $\mathcal{D}_t$ to augment the style of pseudo-answer and non-answer tokens to the source domain. This results in another answer classifier $\mathcal{C}_2$, which possesses target domain style information while still being trained on the source domain. With the answer classifier $\mathcal{C}_2$, there are instances in the target domain $\mathcal{D}_t$ for which the answer differs from the one obtained using $\mathcal{C}_1$. We identify these instances as those which are far apart from the source domain, and the QA model is least confident about them. During adversarial correction, we minimize the distribution between these two classifiers and update the BERT encoder to generate features for the target domain closer to the source domain. This ensures that the classifier $\mathcal{C}_2$ predicts the answer as if it were operating on the source domain, aligning the features for the target domain with those of the source domain.

4.2 Domain Invariant Fine Tuning

In this section, we will explain in detail the process we have followed for domain invariant fine-tuning. Let the trained QA model on source domain is denoted as f, it is a BERT model with $\mathbf{L}$ layers of transformers (Vaswani et al., 2017). Specifically, let $\mathcal{C}_1$ be an answer classifier, and θ_g be the encoder parameters for this source-domain QA model.

During domain invariant fine-tuning (shown in Figure 2), we propose to feed the style information of the target domain $\mathcal{D}_t$ to the source domain QA model at each layer $l \in \mathbf{L}$, as illustrated in Figure 2. We keep the weights shared between the two encoders to allow the target domain information to be updated in the BERT encoder with the supervision of the source domain. Let $\phi(x, x')$ be the learnable domain shift vector between the source instance x and the target domain instance x', and $\mathcal{M}(x, \phi(x, x'))$ be a learnable domain transformation layer, which is introduced at the top of each transformer layer $l \in \mathbf{L}$ of model f. Cumulatively, it transforms the parameters of the source domain classifier $\mathcal{C}_1$ to the target-aware classifier $\mathcal{C}_2$ and updates encoder parameters θ_g with the style of the target domain.

Domain Transformation Layer: The domain transformation layer $\mathcal{M}$ is expected to fuse the domain shift vector with the hidden states (which were fine-tuned for the source domain) at each layer of the transformer. The domain shift vector ϕ should solely capture the information that is different from the source domain. This categorizes the vector containing any extra information in the target domain compared to the source domain, ir-

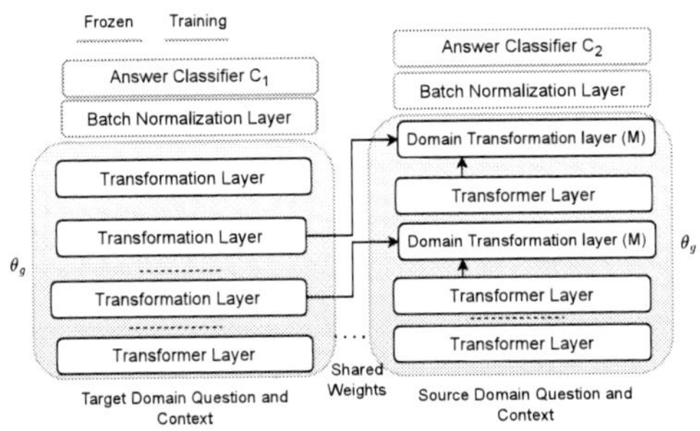

Figure 2: Domain Invariant Fine Tuning with Domain Transformation Layer

respective of its position in the context. This can be achieved by taking the difference between the average pooled vector of hidden states at each layer obtained for the source and target domains. Let $\mathbf{H}_s^{(l)}$ and $\mathbf{H}_t^{(l)}$ be the hidden states obtained at layer l for the source domain and target domain, respectively. Then, the domain shift vector at layer l between two instances is given as:

$$\phi^{(l)}(H_t^{(l)}, H_s^{(l)}) = avg(WH_t^{(l)}) - avg(WH_s^{(l)}) \tag{2}$$

where, $W \in \mathbf{R}^{k \times d}$ are the linear transform parameters shared across layers. Then, the domain transformation layer $\mathcal{M}$ is given as:

$$\mathcal{M}(H_s^{(l)}, \phi^{(l)}(H_t^{(l)}, H_s^{(l)})) = H_s^{(l)} + W^T \phi^{(l)}(H_t^{(l)}, H_s^{(l)}) \tag{3}$$

The expression $W^T\phi^{(l)}(H_t^{(l)}, H_s^{(l)}) \in \mathbf{R}^d$ is added to all hidden states at layer l corresponding to the source domain. This design of the domain shift vector follows the identity property, i.e., $\phi(x, x) = 0$. This allows us to plug in the domain transformation layer only at the time of training, while at the time of inference for the target domain, it is, $\phi^{(l)}(H_t^{(l)}, H_t^{(l)})) = 0$. However, it is required to carefully choose the value of k, which is a hyperparameter, because it assumes the domain shift information lies in the k-dimensional subspace where the difference between two domains can be minimized to make them appear similar.

QA Domain Transformation: Specifically, for the case of QA domain adaptation, we can't apply the domain shift across all the tokens uniformly, as there are underlying differences between the context, question, and answer tokens. Hence, it would be wise to calculate ϕ_A, ϕ_C, and ϕ_Q for Answer, Context, and Questions, respectively. Since we only have context and questions in the target domain, the answer is the pseudo-answer obtained from the classifier $\mathcal{C}_1$, where the weights of $\mathcal{C}_1$ are frozen, and the BERT encoder parameters θ_g are shared during fine-tuning. These will be updated jointly along with classifier $\mathcal{C}_2$ (initialized with the fine-tuned classifier $\mathcal{C}_1$), as shown in Figure 2. At the end of domain transformation fine-tuning, we obtain another target-aware classifier $\mathcal{C}_2$ and updated encoder parameters θ_g which are the fine-tuned parameters on the target-aware source domain with supervised cross-entropy loss $\mathcal{L}_{ce}$. Note that here pseudo labels on target domain is not directly involved in training answer classifier $\mathcal{C}_2$.

$$\min_f \mathcal{L}_{ce}(f, \mathbf{X}_s || \mathbf{X}_t) \tag{4}$$

where f consists of parameters θ_g and parameters in classifier $\mathcal{C}_2$ and $\mathcal{M}$. During training, we randomly select samples from the target domain, ensuring the batch size matches that of the source domain, and an additional constraint to include parallel instances with the same question types (denoted as $\mathbf{X}_s || \mathbf{X}_t$). We employ the dependency parser, semantic role labeling, and named entity recognition (NER) to detect the question types, as done in (Keklik, 2018).

4.3 Adversarial Label Correction

We have introduced adversarial label correction based on the fact that during domain invariant fine-tuning, we relied on the pseudo-labels obtained from classifier $\mathcal{C}_1$. However, these labels are noisy and prone to error accumulation, potentially leading to erroneous alignment of the source and target domain. The domain shift information in the k-dimensional subspace may be captured incorrectly, resulting in similar performance degradation as observed in the approaches (Yue et al., 2022c, 2021) where pseudo-labels are used to train the answer classifier. However, these methods (Yue et al., 2022c, 2021) overlook the fact that domain adaptation can result in target features lie far apart from the source domain for similar semantics that are ambiguous and hence error-prone. To mitigate this, we propose the idea of reducing the inconsistency between domains by generating target features near the support of source classes. In our case, this refers to the starting and ending indices for the answer classifier for different question types.

In Equation 4, fine-tuning occurs with the target-aware source domain, resulting in the answer classifier $\mathcal{C}_2$. This learns the distribution of start and end classes given the style of the target domain $\mathcal{D}_t$, but these can be error-prone, mainly due to two reasons: 1) The target pseudo labels obtained from $\mathcal{C}_1$ are erroneous, and 2) The target domain information makes the classifier $\mathcal{C}_2$ difficult to learn the correct distribution of start and end classes on the source domain. Collectively, this happens when the target instances are far apart from the source domain and require explicit optimization for such cases. Hence, we make use of the adversarial loss to first identify the samples of the target domain that are far apart from the support of the source domain. We then update the parameters of answer classifiers $\mathcal{C}_1$ and $\mathcal{C}_2$ with θ_g (obtained after domain invariant fine-tuning) frozen to maximize the discrepancy due to such instances. Specifically, we update $\mathcal{C}_1$ first keeping $\mathcal{C}_2$ fixed and then $\mathcal{C}_2$ with updated $\mathcal{C}_1$. Subsequently, we minimize the parameters of θ_g to generate target domain features near the source domain for start and end classes. Mathematically, this has been written as the minmax game of learning domain invariant representations:

$$\min_{\theta_g} \max_{\mathcal{C}_1,\mathcal{C}_2} \mathcal{L}_{lc}(X_t) \tag{5}$$

where $\mathcal{L}_{lc}$ is the label correction loss optimized for the target domain for maximum performance. The discrepancy maximizing term has been mathematically formulated as the Sliced Wasserstein Distance(SWD) between the representation as in (Kolouri et al., 2019) learnt for start and end classes by classifier $\mathcal{C}_1$ and $\mathcal{C}_2$ respectively. Let $\mathcal{G}$ denote the BERT encoder with parameters θ_g, the loss is written as:

$$\min_{\mathcal{C}_1,\mathcal{C}_2} \mathcal{L}_{ce}(f, \mathbf{X}_s||\mathbf{X}_t) - \sum_{k\in\{s,e\}} \mathcal{L}_{swd}(\mathcal{C}_1^k(G(X_t)), \mathcal{C}_2^k(G(X_t))) \tag{6}$$

where $\mathcal{C}_1^k(.)$, $\mathcal{C}_2^k(.)$ for all $k \in \{s, e\}$ denotes the probability distribution obtained from classifier $\mathcal{C}_1$ and $\mathcal{C}_2$ for starting and ending indices s and e. This loss updates both classifiers on target aware source domain only for those instances where parallel target domain instances are inconsistent. Since both $\mathcal{C}_1$ and $\mathcal{C}_2$ trained to predict the start and end indices for the source domain, one with source domain features only and another on source augmented with target domain features. Hence, the classifier $\mathcal{C}_2$ can predict the different start and end indices for those instances where $\mathcal{C}_1$ is incorrect for target domain. Hence we update the classifier $\mathcal{C}_1$ first and then update $\mathcal{C}_2$ using updated $\mathcal{C}_1$. Adjusted answer classifiers results in updated domain discrepancy for the non-confident target predictions and hence we need to update the parameters θ_g so as to generate the target domain features near to source support class wisely. This has been achieved by minimizing the loss function:

$$\min_{\mathcal{G}} \sum_{k\in\{s,e\}} \mathcal{L}_{swd}(\mathcal{C}_1^k(G(X_t)), \mathcal{C}_2^k(G(X_t))) \tag{7}$$

Finally, at the end we use the Encoder $\mathcal{G}$ and answer classifier $\mathcal{C}_1$ as the domain adapted QA model. End-to-end training of DomainInv Framework is shown in Algorithm 1 (in Appendix B).

5 Experiments

Datasets: We consider the source domain $\mathcal{D}_s$ as **SQuAD v1.1** (Rajpurkar et al., 2016) following (Yue et al., 2022c, 2021; Shakeri et al., 2020; Cao et al., 2020; Lee et al., 2020). **SQuAD v1.1** is a well known annotated QA dataset where paragraphs (context) are from Wikipedia articles. Target Domains $\mathcal{D}_t$ are considered from MRQA Split 1 (Fisch et al., 2019b), namely, **NaturalQuestions** (Kwiatkowski et al., 2019), **HotpotQA** (Yang et al., 2018), **SearchQA** (Dunn et al., 2017), **TriviaQA** (Joshi et al., 2017), **NewsQA** (Trischler et al., 2016). The dataset details we have considered for target domain is given in Appendix A.

Baselines: We trained our DomainInv Framework on top of the fine-tuned QA model on source domain, adopted from BERT with an additional batch normalization layer, as in (Cao et al., 2020). This fine-tuned BERT model, trained on the source domain, acts as the naive baseline. However, to further assess the robustness of our framework in QA domain adaptation, we adopted the following state-of-the-art (SOTA) baselines: 1) **QADA** (Yue et al., 2022c): QA Domain Adaptation (QADA) leverages hidden space augmentation for enriching the training dataset and used attention-based contrastive learning for domain adaptation. 2) **CAQA** (Yue et al., 2021): Contrastive Domain Adaption for Question Answering (CAQA) combines question generation and contrastive domain adaptation to learn domain-invariant features, so that it can capture both domains and thus transfer knowledge to the target distribution 3) **DAT** (Tzeng et al., 2017; Lee et al., 2019b): Domain Adversarial Training (DAT) follows the known adversarial training and uses the [CLS] token in BERT as a discriminator to learn the generalized features from both source and target domains after training with labeled source domain 4) **CAQA*** (Yue et al., 2021, 2022c): Instead

Model	HotpotQA EM / F1	NaturalQ. EM / F1	NewsQA EM / F1	SearchQA EM / F1	TriviaQA EM / F1
(1) **Zero Shot Target Performance**					
BERT	43.34/60.42	39.06/53.7	39.17/56.14	16.19/25.03	49.70/59.09
(2) **QA Domain Adaptation Target Performance**					
DAT (Lee et al., 2019b)	44.25/61.10	44.94/58.91	38.73/54.24	22.31/31.64	49.94/59.82
CASe (Cao et al., 2020)	47.16/63.88	46.53/60.19	43.43/59.67	26.07/35.16	54.74/63.61
CAQA (Yue et al., 2021)	46.37/61.57	48.55/62.60	40.55/55.90	36.05/42.94	55.17/63.23
CAQA* (Yue et al., 2021, 2022c)	48.52/64.76	47.37/60.52	44.26/60.83	32.05/41.07	54.30/62.98
QADA (Yue et al., 2022c)	50.80/65.75	52.13/65.00	45.64/61.84	40.47/48.76	56.92/65.86
DomainInv(Ours)	**52.92/66.71**	**54.97/68.80**	**45.96/61.88**	**40.92/49.88**	**57.78/66.64**
(3) **Supervised Training Target Performance**					
BERT (10K Samples)	49.57/66.65	54.81/67.98	45.92/61.85	60.21/66.96	53.87/60.42
BERT (All Samples)	57.96/74.76	67.08/79.02	52.14/67.46	71.54/77.77	64.51/70.27

Table 1: QA Adaptation Performance on Target Domains

of question generation in CAQA, this baseline uses the same process of generating pseudo labels and self-supervised adaptation as in QADA. 5) **CASe** (Cao et al., 2020): Conditional Adversarial Self-Training (CASe) is an unsupervised domain adaptation method that iteratively performs self-training on high-confidence pseudo-labels and incorporates conditional adversarial learning.

Training, Evaluation and Implementation: Following (Cao et al., 2020; Yue et al., 2022c), we trained the naive baseline of the BERT model with an additional batch norm layer after the encoder (in PyTorch by Hugging Face, using the base-uncased pretrained model with 12 layers and 768-dim hidden state). Specifically, we used a learning rate of $3 \cdot 10^{-5}$ and trained for 2 epochs with a batch size of 12, optimized using the AdamW optimizer with 10% linear warm-up on the source domain $\mathcal{D}_s$. Following (Lee et al., 2020; Shakeri et al., 2020; Yue et al., 2021), we evaluated exact matches (EM) and F1 score on the dev sets. The rest of the baselines are implemented according to the methods described in their corresponding papers.

For the DomainInv Framework, we ran the domain invariant fine-tuning followed by adversarial label correction and repeated this for 10 epochs with the AdamW optimizer, learning rate of 10^{-5}, with 10% linear warm-up. During fine-tuning, we generated the labels for the target domain using the classifier $\mathcal{C}_1$, which is frozen during fine-tuning, and sampled parallel samples of the target domain with question types of source domain samples in a given batch size of 12. During fine-tuning, there is only one hyperparameter named k for the domain transformation layer, which has been searched for the best value in [64, 128, 256, 512, 768]. Eventually, the best value of 256 works for us in almost all cases and is the one with the maximum performance on the source domain $\mathcal{D}_s$ during fine-tuning. After domain invariant fine-tuning, the obtained classifiers $\mathcal{C}_1$, $\mathcal{C}_2$, and encoder $\mathcal{G}$ are trained with adversarial label correction. We stopped the training in between if there is no decrease in the loss described in equation 7 for the continuous 3 epochs in a row.

5.1 Experimental Results

Table 1 presents the results for QA domain adaptation performance on various target domains, as described in Section 5. We grouped our results and analysis into three main categories, namely: 1) **Zero short Target Performance**: This reports the results on the target domain with the BERT fine-tuned model without any domain adaptation on the target domain, serving as a *lower bound* for domain adaptation approaches. 2) **QA Domain Adaptation Target Performance**: This reports the results due to various domain adaptation methods, including DomainInv.. 3) **Supervised Training Target Performance**: This reports the results following the supervised training of BERT on the target domain using randomly selected 10K samples, along with all source domain samples, to establish the *upper bound* performance for QA domain adaptation approaches. QA domain adaptation performance (shown in Table 1) using the DomainInv

Model	HotpotQA EM / F1	NaturalQ. EM / F1	NewsQA EM / F1	SearchQA EM / F1	TriviaQA EM / F1
DomainInv(Ours)	**52.92/66.71**	**54.97/68.80**	**45.96/61.88**	**40.92/49.88**	**57.78/66.64**
w/o Adversarial Label Correction	51.60/64.07	53.91/65.21	45.88/61.86	39.81/46.98	56.98/65.32

Table 2: Ablation Study: QA Adaptation Performance on Target Domains by different components of DomainInv

Framework outperforms all the domain adaptation baselines across all target domains and is well beyond the naive baseline. In fact, almost all the domain adaptation baselines outperform the naive baseline by a significant margin on all target domains. However, BERT performs poorly (compared to domain adaptation baselines) on some target domains, namely, Natural Questions and SearchQA, due to two main reasons: 1) BERT does not understand the style of Natural Questions; even if the Wikipedia article is the same, the real user questions style is different from the one asked in SQuAD v1.1. 2) BERT does not understand the long form of contexts, which is usual in SearchQA, and it learns to focus on the nearby tokens similar to those in SQuAD v1.1.

However, the actual or more effective answer is also present in the long context. Compared to the worst QA adaptation baseline, DomainInv outperforms BERT on these two domains on average by 2.64% in EM and the other domains by 1.2% in EM. This is the main reason we adopted the domain style-based transformation layer and the corresponding fine-tuning, which can make BERT understand different contexts and questions. The DomainInv Framework outperforms all baselines; on average, it outperforms the best baseline by 2.59% and 2.17% in EM and F1, respectively. Moreover, our framework outperforms supervised training with 10K target data, additionally on Natural Questions and NewsQA, as compared to QADA (best baseline), which outperforms the supervised baseline of 10K target data only on HotpotQA and TriviaQA. We reported all the results after averaging the inference results from 10 rounds.

5.2 Ablation Studies

In Table 1, we compared the DomainInv framework against the strongest baseline named QADA. However, this comparison does not detail the importance of each component of DomainInv, namely, domain invariant fine-tuning and adversarial label correction. The absence of these components can cause a maximum drop of 5.17% compared to the best baseline QADA, highlighting the advantage of using DomainInv over other domain adaptation approaches. However, the contribution of each component towards performance gain is still unknown. Hence, we studied the performance (mentioned in Table 2) of DomainInv after removing the adversarial label correction component only, since removing the domain-invariant fine tuning as well results in the source-domain trained BERT model, for which the zero-shot performance is already mentioned in Table 1. The performance drop in Table 2 clearly depicts the advantage of adversarial label correction. For target domains, namely HotpotQA, Natural Questions, and NewsQA, the performance of DomainInv w/o adversarial label correction in terms of EM is still higher than that of QADA. However, in SearchQA, it goes below the performance of QADA. This indicates the important insight into the functioning of adversarial label correction. For long contexts like in SearchQA, where matching the answer exactly requires significant correction, and in Natural Questions, where the question style has changed but the context is still the same (i.e., Wikipedia articles), requiring only minor correction in labels. This proves the effectiveness of the label correction component in the DomainInv framework.

6 Conclusion

In this paper, we proposed a novel QA domain adaptation framework called DomainInv. It is an unsupervised algorithm that does not require the use of labeled target domain data, nor does it depend on synthetic data or pseudo-labeled target domain. DomainInv comprises two key components: 1) Domain Invariant Fine Tuning, which fine-tunes the QA model using the target style on the source domain, and 2) Adversarial Label Correction, which identifies target distributions that are far apart from the source domain and optimizes the feature generator to bring them closer to the source support class wisely. Evaluation of DomainInv showed that it outperforms all baselines, achieving superior performance and establishing a new benchmark.

Limitations

In this section, we highlights certain limitations of DomainInv that were not covered in the paper. In the domain invariant fine-tuning, we introduced a new layer called the domain adaptation layer, which computes the difference between the average pooled representations of the source and target domains. However, this design assumes equal importance for all tokens in both domains at each layer, overlooking the influence of the self-attention mechanism on token distribution. To rectify this, future work should explore incorporating attention-weighted representations before calculating the difference. Additionally, in the adversarial label correction, we proposed adjusting the feature encoder solely based on the target domain, neglecting the potential benefits of jointly aligning both source and target domains. Further research could explore these aspects for improvement.

References

Shai Ben-David, John Blitzer, Koby Crammer, Alex Kulesza, Fernando Pereira, and Jennifer Vaughan. 2010. A theory of learning from different domains. *Machine Learning*, 79:151–175.

Shai Ben-David, John Blitzer, Koby Crammer, and Fernando Pereira. 2006. Analysis of representations for domain adaptation. In *Advances in Neural Information Processing Systems*, volume 19. MIT Press.

K. Bousmalis, N. Silberman, D. Dohan, D. Erhan, and D. Krishnan. 2017. Unsupervised pixel-level domain adaptation with generative adversarial networks. In *2017 IEEE Conference on Computer Vision and Pattern Recognition (CVPR)*, pages 95–104, Los Alamitos, CA, USA. IEEE Computer Society.

Yu Cao, Meng Fang, Baosheng Yu, and Joey Tianyi Zhou. 2020. Unsupervised domain adaptation on reading comprehension. In *Proceedings of the AAAI Conference on Artificial Intelligence*, volume 34, pages 7480–7487.

Mathilde Caron, Ishan Misra, Julien Mairal, Priya Goyal, Piotr Bojanowski, and Armand Joulin. 2020. Unsupervised learning of visual features by contrasting cluster assignments. In *Proceedings of the 34th International Conference on Neural Information Processing Systems*, NIPS'20, Red Hook, NY, USA. Curran Associates Inc.

Danqi Chen, Adam Fisch, Jason Weston, and Antoine Bordes. 2017. Reading Wikipedia to answer open-domain questions. In *Proceedings of the 55th Annual Meeting of the Association for Computational Linguistics (Volume 1: Long Papers)*, pages 1870–1879, Vancouver, Canada. Association for Computational Linguistics.

Ting Chen, Simon Kornblith, Mohammad Norouzi, and Geoffrey Hinton. 2020. A simple framework for contrastive learning of visual representations. In *Proceedings of the 37th International Conference on Machine Learning*, ICML'20. JMLR.org.

Alexandra Chronopoulou, Christos Baziotis, and Alexandros Potamianos. 2019. An embarrassingly simple approach for transfer learning from pretrained language models. In *Proceedings of the 2019 Conference of the North American Chapter of the Association for Computational Linguistics: Human Language Technologies, Volume 1 (Long and Short Papers)*, pages 2089–2095, Minneapolis, Minnesota. Association for Computational Linguistics.

Hal Daumé III. 2007. Frustratingly easy domain adaptation. In *Proceedings of the 45th Annual Meeting of the Association of Computational Linguistics*, pages 256–263, Prague, Czech Republic. Association for Computational Linguistics.

Zhijie Deng, Yucen Luo, and Jun Zhu. 2019. Cluster alignment with a teacher for unsupervised domain adaptation. In *2019 IEEE/CVF International Conference on Computer Vision (ICCV)*, pages 9943–9952.

Jacob Devlin, Ming-Wei Chang, Kenton Lee, and Kristina Toutanova. 2019. BERT: Pre-training of deep bidirectional transformers for language understanding. In *Proceedings of the 2019 Conference of the North American Chapter of the Association for Computational Linguistics: Human Language Technologies, Volume 1 (Long and Short Papers)*, pages 4171–4186, Minneapolis, Minnesota. Association for Computational Linguistics.

Xinya Du, Junru Shao, and Claire Cardie. 2017. Learning to ask: Neural question generation for reading comprehension. In *Proceedings of the 55th Annual Meeting of the Association for Computational Linguistics (Volume 1: Long Papers)*, pages 1342–1352, Vancouver, Canada. Association for Computational Linguistics.

Matthew Dunn, Levent Sagun, Mike Higgins, V. Ugur Güney, Volkan Cirik, and Kyunghyun Cho. 2017. Searchqa: A new q&a dataset augmented with context from a search engine. *CoRR*, abs/1704.05179.

Adam Fisch, Alon Talmor, Robin Jia, Minjoon Seo, Eunsol Choi, and Danqi Chen. 2019a. MRQA 2019 shared task: Evaluating generalization in reading comprehension. In *Proceedings of the 2nd Workshop on Machine Reading for Question Answering*, pages 1–13, Hong Kong, China. Association for Computational Linguistics.

Adam Fisch, Alon Talmor, Robin Jia, Minjoon Seo, Eunsol Choi, and Danqi Chen. 2019b. Mrqa 2019 shared task: Evaluating generalization in reading comprehension. In *EMNLP 2019 MRQA Workshop*, page 1.

Yaroslav Ganin, Evgeniya Ustinova, Hana Ajakan, Pascal Germain, Hugo Larochelle, François Laviolette, Mario Marchand, and Victor Lempitsky. 2017. *Domain-Adversarial Training of Neural Networks*, pages 189–209. Springer International Publishing, Cham.

David Golub, Po-Sen Huang, Xiaodong He, and Li Deng. 2017. Two-stage synthesis networks for transfer learning in machine comprehension. In *Proceedings of the 2017 Conference on Empirical Methods in Natural Language Processing*, pages 835–844, Copenhagen, Denmark. Association for Computational Linguistics.

Ian Goodfellow, Jean Pouget-Abadie, Mehdi Mirza, Bing Xu, David Warde-Farley, Sherjil Ozair, Aaron Courville, and Yoshua Bengio. 2014. Generative adversarial nets. In *Advances in Neural Information Processing Systems*, volume 27. Curran Associates, Inc.

Arthur Gretton, Karsten Borgwardt, Malte Rasch, Bernhard Schölkopf, and Alex Smola. 2006. A kernel method for the two-sample-problem. In *Advances in Neural Information Processing Systems*, volume 19. MIT Press.

Kaiming He, Haoqi Fan, Yuxin Wu, Saining Xie, and Ross Girshick. 2020. Momentum contrast for unsupervised visual representation learning. In *2020 IEEE/CVF Conference on Computer Vision and Pattern Recognition (CVPR)*, pages 9726–9735.

Mandar Joshi, Eunsol Choi, Daniel Weld, and Luke Zettlemoyer. 2017. TriviaQA: A large scale distantly supervised challenge dataset for reading comprehension. In *Proceedings of the 55th Annual Meeting of the Association for Computational Linguistics (Volume 1: Long Papers)*, pages 1601–1611, Vancouver, Canada. Association for Computational Linguistics.

Amita Kamath, Robin Jia, and Percy Liang. 2020. Selective question answering under domain shift. In *Proceedings of the 58th Annual Meeting of the Association for Computational Linguistics*, pages 5684–5696, Online. Association for Computational Linguistics.

G. Kang, L. Jiang, Y. Yang, and A. G. Hauptmann. 2019. Contrastive adaptation network for unsupervised domain adaptation. In *2019 IEEE/CVF Conference on Computer Vision and Pattern Recognition (CVPR)*, pages 4888–4897, Los Alamitos, CA, USA. IEEE Computer Society.

Onur Keklik. 2018. *Automatic question generation using natural language processing techniques*. Ph.D. thesis, Izmir Institute of Technology (Turkey).

Soheil Kolouri, Kimia Nadjahi, Umut Simsekli, Roland Badeau, and Gustavo Rohde. 2019. Generalized sliced wasserstein distances. *Advances in neural information processing systems*, 32.

Bernhard Kratzwald, Anna Eigenmann, and Stefan Feuerriegel. 2019. RankQA: Neural question answering with answer re-ranking. In *Proceedings of the 57th Annual Meeting of the Association for Computational Linguistics*, pages 6076–6085, Florence, Italy. Association for Computational Linguistics.

Bernhard Kratzwald, Stefan Feuerriegel, and Huan Sun. 2020. Learning a Cost-Effective Annotation Policy for Question Answering. In *Proceedings of the 2020 Conference on Empirical Methods in Natural Language Processing (EMNLP)*, pages 3051–3062, Online. Association for Computational Linguistics.

Tom Kwiatkowski, Jennimaria Palomaki, Olivia Redfield, Michael Collins, Ankur Parikh, Chris Alberti, Danielle Epstein, Illia Polosukhin, Jacob Devlin, Kenton Lee, Kristina Toutanova, Llion Jones, Matthew Kelcey, Ming-Wei Chang, Andrew M. Dai, Jakob Uszkoreit, Quoc Le, and Slav Petrov. 2019. Natural Questions: A Benchmark for Question Answering Research. *Transactions of the Association for Computational Linguistics*, 7:453–466.

Chen-Yu Lee, Tanmay Batra, Mohammad Haris Baig, and Daniel Ulbricht. 2019a. Sliced wasserstein discrepancy for unsupervised domain adaptation.

Dong Bok Lee, Seanie Lee, Woo Tae Jeong, Donghwan Kim, and Sung Ju Hwang. 2020. Generating diverse and consistent QA pairs from contexts with information-maximizing hierarchical conditional VAEs. In *Proceedings of the 58th Annual Meeting of the Association for Computational Linguistics*, pages 208–224, Online. Association for Computational Linguistics.

Seanie Lee, Donggyu Kim, and Jangwon Park. 2019b. Domain-agnostic question-answering with adversarial training. In *Proceedings of the 2nd Workshop on Machine Reading for Question Answering*, pages 196–202, Hong Kong, China. Association for Computational Linguistics.

Mingsheng Long, Yue Cao, Jianmin Wang, and Michael I. Jordan. 2015. Learning transferable features with deep adaptation networks. In *Proceedings of the 32nd International Conference on International Conference on Machine Learning - Volume 37*, ICML'15, page 97–105. JMLR.org.

Mingsheng Long, ZHANGJIE CAO, Jianmin Wang, and Michael I Jordan. 2018. Conditional adversarial domain adaptation. In *Advances in Neural Information Processing Systems*, volume 31. Curran Associates, Inc.

Mingsheng Long, Han Zhu, Jianmin Wang, and Michael I. Jordan. 2017. Deep transfer learning with joint adaptation networks. In *Proceedings of the 34th International Conference on Machine Learning - Volume 70*, ICML'17, page 2208–2217. JMLR.org.

Bryan McCann, Nitish Shirish Keskar, Caiming Xiong, and Richard Socher. 2018. The natural language decathlon: Multitask learning as question answering. *CoRR*, abs/1806.08730.

John Miller, Karl Krauth, Benjamin Recht, and Ludwig Schmidt. 2020. The effect of natural distribution shift on question answering models. In *Proceedings of the 37th International Conference on Machine Learning*, ICML'20. JMLR.org.

Zhongyi Pei, Zhangjie Cao, Mingsheng Long, and Jianmin Wang. 2018. Multi-adversarial domain adaptation. In *Proceedings of the Thirty-Second AAAI Conference on Artificial Intelligence and Thirtieth Innovative Applications of Artificial Intelligence Conference and Eighth AAAI Symposium on Educational Advances in Artificial Intelligence*, AAAI'18/IAAI'18/EAAI'18. AAAI Press.

Matthew E. Peters, Mark Neumann, Mohit Iyyer, Matt Gardner, Christopher Clark, Kenton Lee, and Luke Zettlemoyer. 2018. Deep contextualized word representations. In *Proceedings of the 2018 Conference of the North American Chapter of the Association for Computational Linguistics: Human Language Technologies, Volume 1 (Long Papers)*, pages 2227–2237, New Orleans, Louisiana. Association for Computational Linguistics.

Jason Phang, Thibault Févry, and Samuel R. Bowman. 2018. Sentence encoders on stilts: Supplementary training on intermediate labeled-data tasks. *CoRR*, abs/1811.01088.

Pranav Rajpurkar, Jian Zhang, Konstantin Lopyrev, and Percy Liang. 2016. SQuAD: 100,000+ questions for machine comprehension of text. In *Proceedings of the 2016 Conference on Empirical Methods in Natural Language Processing*, pages 2383–2392, Austin, Texas. Association for Computational Linguistics.

K. Saito, K. Watanabe, Y. Ushiku, and T. Harada. 2018. Maximum classifier discrepancy for unsupervised domain adaptation. In *2018 IEEE/CVF Conference on Computer Vision and Pattern Recognition (CVPR)*, pages 3723–3732, Los Alamitos, CA, USA. IEEE Computer Society.

Min Joon Seo, Aniruddha Kembhavi, Ali Farhadi, and Hannaneh Hajishirzi. 2016. Bidirectional attention flow for machine comprehension. *CoRR*, abs/1611.01603.

Siamak Shakeri, Cicero Nogueira dos Santos, Henghui Zhu, Patrick Ng, Feng Nan, Zhiguo Wang, Ramesh Nallapati, and Bing Xiang. 2020. End-to-end synthetic data generation for domain adaptation of question answering systems. In *Proceedings of the 2020 Conference on Empirical Methods in Natural Language Processing (EMNLP)*, pages 5445–5460, Online. Association for Computational Linguistics.

Jian Shen, Yanru Qu, Weinan Zhang, and Yong Yu. 2018. Wasserstein distance guided representation learning for domain adaptation. In *Proceedings of the Thirty-Second AAAI Conference on Artificial Intelligence and Thirtieth Innovative Applications of Artificial Intelligence Conference and Eighth AAAI Symposium on Educational Advances in Artificial Intelligence*, AAAI'18/IAAI'18/EAAI'18. AAAI Press.

Kendrick Shen, Robbie M Jones, Ananya Kumar, Sang Michael Xie, Jeff Z. Haochen, Tengyu Ma, and Percy Liang. 2022. Connect, not collapse: Explaining contrastive learning for unsupervised domain adaptation. In *Proceedings of the 39th International Conference on Machine Learning*, volume 162 of *Proceedings of Machine Learning Research*, pages 19847–19878. PMLR.

Xingwu Sun, Jing Liu, Yajuan Lyu, Wei He, Yanjun Ma, and Shi Wang. 2018. Answer-focused and position-aware neural question generation. In *Proceedings of the 2018 Conference on Empirical Methods in Natural Language Processing*, pages 3930–3939, Brussels, Belgium. Association for Computational Linguistics.

Alon Talmor and Jonathan Berant. 2019. Multiqa: An empirical investigation of generalization and transfer in reading comprehension. In *Proceedings of the 57th Annual Meeting of the Association for Computational Linguistics*, pages 4911–4921.

Duyu Tang, Nan Duan, Tao Qin, and Ming Zhou. 2017. Question answering and question generation as dual tasks. *CoRR*, abs/1706.02027.

Duyu Tang, Nan Duan, Zhao Yan, Zhirui Zhang, Yibo Sun, Shujie Liu, Yuanhua Lv, and Ming Zhou. 2018. Learning to collaborate for question answering and asking. In *Proceedings of the 2018 Conference of the North American Chapter of the Association for Computational Linguistics: Human Language Technologies, Volume 1 (Long Papers)*, pages 1564–1574, New Orleans, Louisiana. Association for Computational Linguistics.

Mamatha Thota and Georgios Leontidis. 2021. Contrastive domain adaptation. *CoRR*, abs/2103.15566.

Adam Trischler, Tong Wang, Xingdi Yuan, Justin Harris, Alessandro Sordoni, Philip Bachman, and Kaheer Suleman. 2016. Newsqa: A machine comprehension dataset.

E. Tzeng, J. Hoffman, K. Saenko, and T. Darrell. 2017. Adversarial discriminative domain adaptation. In *2017 IEEE Conference on Computer Vision and Pattern Recognition (CVPR)*, pages 2962–2971, Los Alamitos, CA, USA. IEEE Computer Society.

Ashish Vaswani, Noam Shazeer, Niki Parmar, Jakob Uszkoreit, Llion Jones, Aidan N Gomez, Łukasz Kaiser, and Illia Polosukhin. 2017. Attention is all you need. *Advances in neural information processing systems*, 30.

Alex Wang, Amanpreet Singh, Julian Michael, Felix Hill, Omer Levy, and Samuel Bowman. 2018. GLUE: A multi-task benchmark and analysis platform for natural language understanding. In *Proceedings of the 2018 EMNLP Workshop BlackboxNLP: Analyzing and Interpreting Neural Networks for NLP*, pages 353–355, Brussels, Belgium. Association for Computational Linguistics.

Rui Wang, Zuxuan Wu, Zejia Weng, Jingjing Chen, Guo-Jun Qi, and Yu-Gang Jiang. 2021. Cross-domain contrastive learning for unsupervised domain adaptation. *CoRR*, abs/2106.05528.

Shaoan Xie, Zibin Zheng, Liang Chen, and Chuan Chen. 2018. Learning semantic representations for unsupervised domain adaptation. In *Proceedings of the 35th International Conference on Machine Learning*, volume 80 of *Proceedings of Machine Learning Research*, pages 5423–5432. PMLR.

Yichong Xu, Xiaodong Liu, Yelong Shen, Jingjing Liu, and Jianfeng Gao. 2019. Multi-task learning with sample re-weighting for machine reading comprehension. In *Proceedings of the 2019 Conference of the North American Chapter of the Association for Computational Linguistics: Human Language Technologies, Volume 1 (Long and Short Papers)*, pages 2644–2655, Minneapolis, Minnesota. Association for Computational Linguistics.

Guanglei Yang, Haifeng Xia, Mingli Ding, and Zhengming Ding. 2020. Bi-directional generation for unsupervised domain adaptation. *CoRR*, abs/2002.04869.

Zhilin Yang, Peng Qi, Saizheng Zhang, Yoshua Bengio, William Cohen, Ruslan Salakhutdinov, and Christopher D. Manning. 2018. HotpotQA: A dataset for diverse, explainable multi-hop question answering. In *Proceedings of the 2018 Conference on Empirical Methods in Natural Language Processing*, pages 2369–2380, Brussels, Belgium. Association for Computational Linguistics.

Weijie Yu, Chen Xu, Jun Xu, Liang Pang, Xiaopeng Gao, Xiaozhao Wang, and Ji-Rong Wen. 2020. Wasserstein distance regularized sequence representation for text matching in asymmetrical domains. In *Proceedings of the 2020 Conference on Empirical Methods in Natural Language Processing (EMNLP)*, pages 2985–2994, Online. Association for Computational Linguistics.

Xiang Yue, Ziyu Yao, and Huan Sun. 2022a. Synthetic question value estimation for domain adaptation of question answering. In *Proceedings of the 60th Annual Meeting of the Association for Computational Linguistics (Volume 1: Long Papers)*, pages 1340–1351, Dublin, Ireland. Association for Computational Linguistics.

Zhenrui Yue, Bernhard Kratzwald, and Stefan Feuerriegel. 2021. Contrastive domain adaptation for question answering using limited text corpora. In *Proceedings of the 2021 Conference on Empirical Methods in Natural Language Processing*, pages 9575–9593, Online and Punta Cana, Dominican Republic. Association for Computational Linguistics.

Zhenrui Yue, Huimin Zeng, Ziyi Kou, Lanyu Shang, and Dong Wang. 2022b. Domain adaptation for question answering via question classification. In *Proceedings of the 29th International Conference on Computational Linguistics*, pages 1776–1790, Gyeongju, Republic of Korea. International Committee on Computational Linguistics.

Zhenrui Yue, Huimin Zeng, Bernhard Kratzwald, Stefan Feuerriegel, and Dong Wang. 2022c. Qa domain adaptation using hidden space augmentation and self-supervised contrastive adaptation. *arXiv preprint arXiv:2210.10861*.

Werner Zellinger, Thomas Grubinger, Edwin Lughofer, Thomas Natschläger, and Susanne Saminger-Platz. 2017. Central moment discrepancy (CMD) for domain-invariant representation learning. In *5th International Conference on Learning Representations, ICLR 2017, Toulon, France, April 24-26, 2017, Conference Track Proceedings*. OpenReview.net.

Huimin Zeng, Zhenrui Yue, Ziyi Kou, Lanyu Shang, Yang Zhang, and Dong Wang. 2022. Unsupervised domain adaptation for covid-19 information service with contrastive adversarial domain mixup.

Huimin Zeng, Zhenrui Yue, Yang Zhang, Ziyi Kou, Lanyu Shang, and Dong Wang. On attacking out-domain uncertainty estimation in deep neural networks.

A Benchmark Datasets

The dataset details we have considered for target domain is given as follows:

- **NaturalQuestions**: A real world QA dataset with questions that are actual user questions, and contexts as Wikipedia articles, which may or may not contain the answers (Kwiatkowski et al., 2019)
- **HotpotQA**: A reasoning based QA dataset with multi hop questions and supporting facts (Yang et al., 2018)
- **SearchQA**: QA dataset where context built by crawling through Google Search. However, this is based on existing QA pairs for which the context is extended. More details in (Dunn et al., 2017)
- **TriviaQA**: A reasoning based QA dataset containing evidences for questions asked (Joshi et al., 2017)
- **NewsQA**: QA dataset with news as contexts and questions with answers not from simple matching and entailment. (Trischler et al., 2016)

B Algorithm

We presented the end-to-end DomainInv algorithm as follows:

Algorithm 1 `DomainInv` Training for UDA

Require: Labeled Source $\{\mathcal{X}_s, \mathcal{Y}_s\}$; unlabelled Target $\{\mathcal{X}_t\}$, hyperparameter k, fine tuned QA model with encoder $\mathcal{G}$ and Classifier $\mathcal{C}_1$ and classifier $\mathcal{C}_2$ initialized with $\mathcal{C}_1$.
Step 1: Update $\mathcal{G}$, $\mathcal{C}_2$ on Source Domain (with target style augmentation) using Domain Invariant Fine-Tuning as in Equation 4

while $\mathcal{G}, \mathcal{C}_1, \mathcal{C}_2$ still converging **do**
  Step 2: Update $\mathcal{C}_1$, $\mathcal{C}_2$ on target aware source set to maximize the sliced Wasserstein distance (SWD) on target instances as in Equation 6
  Step 3: Update $\mathcal{G}$ to minimize the SWD as calculated earlier according to Equation 7
end while

Relevance-aware Diverse Query Generation for Out-of-domain Text Ranking

Jia-Huei Ju[1*] **Huck Chao-Han Yang**[2] **Szu-Wei Fu**[2]
Ming-Feng Tsai[3] **Chuan-Ju Wang**[4]
[1]University of Amsterdam [2]NVIDIA Research
[3]National Chengchi University [4]Academia Sinica
j.ju@uva.nl, {hucky, szuweif}@nvidia.com,
mftsai@nccu.edu.tw, cjwang@citi.sinica.edu.tw

Abstract

Domain adaptation presents significant challenges for out-of-domain text ranking, especially when supervised data is limited. In this paper, we present ReadQG[1] (Relevance-Aware Diverse Query Generation), a method to generate informative synthetic queries to facilitate the adaptation process of text ranking models. Unlike previous approaches focusing solely on relevant query generation, our ReadQG generates diverse queries with continuous relevance scores. Specifically, we propose leveraging soft-prompt tuning and diverse generation objectives to control query generation according to the given relevance. Our experiments show that integrating negative queries into the learning process enhances the effectiveness of text ranking models in out-of-domain information retrieval (IR) benchmarks. Furthermore, we measure the quality of query generation, highlighting the underlying beneficial characteristics of negative queries. Our empirical results and analysis also shed light on potential directions for more advanced data augmentation in IR. The data and code have been released.

1 Introduction

Many domain-specific tasks lack supervised data, posing challenges for many neuarl approaches. Recently, Thakur et al. (2021) introduce an out-of-domain (OOD) information retrieval (IR) benchmark across diverse scenarios and domains. Their findings indicate that many neural text ranking models demonstrate limited effectiveness in such contexts. These tasks primarily struggle with adaptation (Gururangan et al., 2020), highlighting the issues of insufficient task- and domain-specific labeled data.

To address this, one line of research propose utilizing synthetic training data for adapting text ranking models (Ma et al., 2021; Bonifacio et al., 2022; Wang et al., 2022). These approachees employ generative models to first learn document-to-query mapping from rich-resource datasets such as MSMARCO (Bajaj et al., 2018). Subsequently, a document and its generated query can be treated as a relevant pair for fine-tuning text ranking models. Recently, these methods have been further refined with instruction-tuned large langugage models (LLMs) (Brown et al., 2020a; Chung et al., 2022). Such LLM-driven query generation can produce more informative query through in-context (Jeronymo et al., 2023) or few-shot learning (Dai et al., 2023).

Document
(Title) animals environment general health health general weight philosophy ethics. *(Text)* Being vegetarian helps the environment ... Modern farming is ...

Relevance-aware Queries
1.0 why do you think meat is bad for a planet earth
0.9 what is the philosophy of vegetarian
...
0.7 what is a vegetarian diet?
0.6 what is deforestation in asian countries
....
0.1 what is an asian diet
0.0 what is the difference between food and a burger

Figure 1: An example of generatie negative query from document inputs by ReadQG.

Compared to these works, in this study, we introduce **Re**levance-**a**ware **D**iverse **Q**uery **G**eneration (ReadQG), aiming to generate more informaive synthetic queries with lightweight generative models. Specifically, we generate both positive and (hard) negative queries from the same document, as illustrated in Figure 1. Our hypothesis is that a set of diverse relevance-aware queries can enhance relevancy representation of texts in unseen domains. To achieve this, we develop the instruction prompt and relevance prompt embeddings. The instruction prompt directs LLMs to generate query, while rel-

[*]Work partially done as an research assistnat at Academia Sinica.

[1]https://github.com/DylanJoo/readqg

Proceedings of the 9th Workshop on Representation Learning for NLP (RepL4NLP-2024), pages 26–36
August 15, 2024 ©2024 Association for Computational Linguistics

evance prompt captures and conrols the *relevance dynamic* between docuemnt and multiple queries. Moreover, we develop two strategies to diversify our generated queries: self-contrastive loss and sequence calibration loss (Zhao et al., 2023). These strategies prevent ReadQG from degeneration (i.e., falling back to naive relevant query generation).

Finally, to exploit positive and negative queries genereted by ReadQG, we integrate the query-based objectives into the training process of text ranking models. Our experiments demonstrates that models fine-tuned on our synthetic data outperform the original model in terms of passage re-ranking efftiveness on the BEIR benchmark. In addition, we define and propose two metrics to measure the quality of generated queries. We observe that the query exhibiting both diversity and relevancy provide useful signals for passage re-ranking models to learn, emphasizing the importance of hard negative query.

To sum up, we propose a domain adaptation pipeline with ReadQG, tailored for out-of-domain text ranking. Our empirical results show that hard negative queries could provide useful signals. Further, the domain adaptation pipeline is built with lightweight generators and text ranking models, achieving improved effectiveness but more efficient in terms of inference time and computational costs. More details can be found in our results (Section 6.1) and our analysis (Section 6.2).

2 Backgrounds

Data augmentation in IR. Numerous IR studies have pioneered in the area of data augmentation for domain adaptation. For instance, QGen (Ma et al., 2021) used synthetic query with documents to facilitate the adaptation of bi-encoder as domain-adaptive dense retrieval. This can also be combined with negative mining techniques (Xiong et al., 2020), leading to enhanced effectiveness (Wang et al., 2022). Recent data augmentation techniques in IR have further been improved by the advancements in instruction-tuned large language models (LLMs) (Brown et al., 2020b; Chung et al., 2022). InPars (Bonifacio et al., 2022) showed that specific in-context prompting can enhance the quality of generated queries. Moreover, Promptagator (Dai et al., 2023) introduces few-shot in-context learning to bridge the gap between in-domain and out-of-domain data. Typically, all these methods center aorund augmenting synthetic queries derived from unseen document and utilizing them as additional training data.

Query Generation. Since the documents in out-of-domain corpus are usually available, we in this work focus on the query generation instead of document generation (Gao et al., 2022). Particularly, Nogueira et al. (2019) first explored the role of query generation in IR. Oguz et al. (2022) also showcased that increasing the number of synthetic queries enhances domain adaptation capability, while Lin et al. (2023) further validated diverse queries can bridge the gap between zero-shot and supervised setups. Question generation can also plays a cruicial role in improving robustness of question answering (QA) systems (Bartolo et al., 2021; Lee et al., 2020) and has broader impacts in various NLP applications such as summarization (Lyu et al., 2021) or building retrieval-intensive QA datasets (Min et al., 2020).

Diverse and controllable text generation. We further extend the concept of query generation to controllable text generation in NLP area. Similar to our goal, Cho et al. (2019) propose capturing the one-to-many relationship between texts, such as dcument-to-summaries. However, due to the discrete nature of text generation, controlling sequence diversity is challenging and often required specialized learning settings (Bowman et al., 2016) or model adjustments (See et al., 2017). Text decoding strategies also significantly influence the results (Holtzman et al., 2020). Many ongoing research focus on designing constraints and objectives, such as unlikelihood (Welleck et al., 2020) or additional constrative-like learning signals (Liu et al., 2022; Zhao et al., 2023). We hypothesize recent LLMs could transform the notion of continuous relevance and present them with divese queries, thereby improve the domain adaptation of out-of-domain text ranking.

3 Methodologies

In this work, we utilize synthesized out-of-domain training queries to tackle the domain-mismatch issues. We will first provide an overview of our domain adaptation pipeline in Section 3.1; it is also illustrated in Figure 2. Following this are the details of the two main stages in ths pipeline, including out-of-domain data augmentation and domain-adaptive fine-tuning.

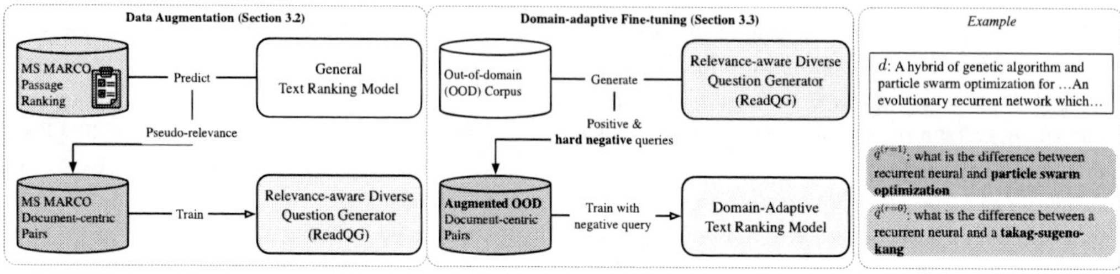

Figure 2: The domain adaptation pipeline for out-of-domain text ranking. The first block is for data augmentation (ReadQG, Section 3.2), and the second block is domain adpative fine-tuning (Section 3.3) with our augmented dataset. The last block is an example pairs we used for training text ranking models.

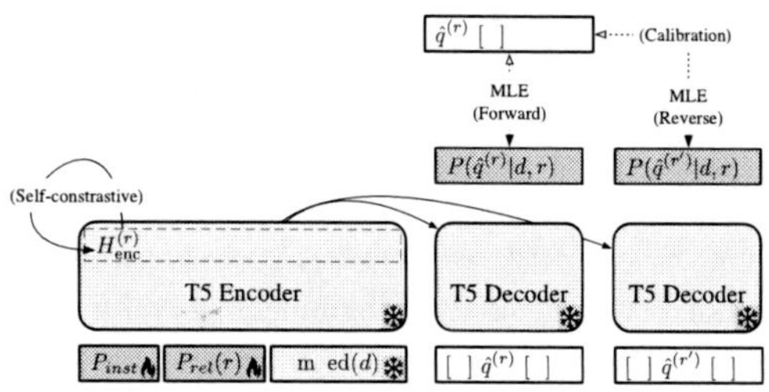

Figure 3: The relevance-aware diverse query generation.

3.1 Overview

As illustrated in the first block of Figure 2, we introduce a novel data augmentation approach, **Re**levance-**a**ware **d**iverse **Q**uery **G**eneration (ReadQG). We generate multiple synthetic queries for each documents in the targeted unseen[2] domains. These queries enables us to construct high-quality docuemnt-centric training pairs (See example in the last block in Fig. 2). By leveraging these training data, we can efficienctly transform general text re-ranking models into domain-adaptive ones as shown in second block of the figure.

3.2 ReadQG: Relevance-aware Diverse Query Generation

Unlike common studies with relevant query generation, we generate a set of relevance-aware queries $Q = [q^{(r_1)}, q^{(r_2)}, ..., q^{(r_n)}]$ for each unseen document $d \in \mathcal{D}$ as illustrated in the Figure 2. Specifically, we aim to generate the positive (relevant) query and the *hard negative* queries.[3] To achieve this, we develop a controllable query generator with diversity text generation objectives.

[2] Here, we regard MSMARCO as the source domain; thus, the retrieval tasks in BEIR are considered as unseen domains.

[3] The term hard negative query refers to less-relevant queries, as oppose to the random (negative) query.

3.2.1 Controllable Query Generation

Here we propose to parameterize such document-to-queries generation process via soft prompt-tuning (Lester et al., 2021). Our focus is specifically on learning such process of *relevance dynamic* from a rich-resource domain (i.e., MS-MARCO) with relatively smaller models instead of directly prompting LLMs. Thus, we leave the attempts of in-context prompting with larger causal LLMs as our future works. Here, we propose to parameterize such a document-to-queries generation process via soft prompt-tuning (Lester et al., 2021). Our focus is specifically on learning the process of *relevance dynamic* from a rich-resource domain (i.e., MSMARCO) with relatively smaller models instead of directly prompting LLMs. Thus, we leave the attempts of in-context prompting with larger causal LLMs as our future work.

Soft prompt-tuning with relevance. As depicted in Figure 3, we employ soft embedding prompts to control the relevance-aware query generation process. These prompts act as the composite input for documents and relevance scores. Simply put, the generator G is expected to generate a query conditioned on the given docuemnt d and also the specified relevance r. To achieve, we include two learnable embedding prompts: an instruction prompt P_{inst} and the relevance prompt $\mathrm{P}_{rel}(r)$. Thus, we can formulate the relevance-aware query generation as:

$$\hat{q}^{(r)} \leftarrow G(\mathrm{P}_{inst}; \mathrm{P}_{rel}(r); d); \quad \forall r \in [0, 1], \quad (1)$$

where the relevance r is a re-scaled continuous variable score ranging from 0 to 1 (See Section 4 for more details). It is worth noting that we only consider the prompts as trainable parameters, encouraging to leverage the inherent capabiltiy of instruction-tuned language models.

Prompt initialization. To inherit the merits of language model pretraining, we initialize P_{inst} with natural-language instructions.[4] While the relevance prompt $\mathrm{P}_{rel}(r)$ is a function of a continuous relevance score r:

$$\begin{bmatrix} r & 1-r \\ \vdots & \vdots \\ r & 1-r \end{bmatrix} \times \begin{bmatrix} \mathrm{P}^{+}_{rel} \leftarrow E(\texttt{true} \ \ldots) \\ \mathrm{P}^{-}_{rel} \leftarrow E(\texttt{false} \ \ldots) \end{bmatrix}.$$

This is basically a linear combination of P^{+}_{rel} and P^{-}_{rel} with respect to relevance. In addition, we initiliaize them with embeddings of "`true`" and "`false`" tokens before fine-tuning.

Encoder-decoder architecture. As our composite input and expected output are highly correlated syntactically, we choose the encoder-decoder architecture, Flan-T5 (Chung et al., 2022) as our backbone model. Formally, the inner flow of hidden states during training is as follow

$$\begin{aligned} H^{(r)}_{enc} &= G_{enc}(\mathrm{P}_{inst}; \mathrm{P}_{rel}(r); d); \\ H^{(r)}_{dec} &= G_{dec}(q_t | q_{<t}; H^{(r)}_{enc}), \end{aligned}$$

where H_{enc} and H_{dec} indicate the hidden states of encoder outputs and decoder outputs respectively. To optimize the parameterized embedding prompts P, we adopt the standard training recipe of teacher-forcing and maximum likelihood estimation (MLE):

$$\mathcal{L}_{mle} = -\log P\Big((H^{(r)}_{dec})^{T}\mathbf{W}\Big), \tag{2}$$

where $\mathbf{W}$ is the projection layer of LM head.

3.2.2 Learning to Diverse Generation

As negative relevance of document-to-queries is intricate, we impose two objectives to encourage sequence generation diversity.

In-batch self-contrastive loss. By treating the generator's encoder G_{enc} as an independant (document) encoder, we can leverage the similar softmax objectives with mini-batch like DPR (Karpukhin et al., 2020). We define the hidden states of encoder output $H^{(r)}_{enc}$ itself as positive and the others in mini-batch as random negatives. Thus, the self-contrastive loss of document d_i with relevance r_j is as follow

$$\mathcal{L}_{\mathrm{sc}} = \frac{\exp\Big(\phi(H^{(r_j),i}_{enc}, H^{(r_j),i}_{enc})/\tau\Big)}{\sum_{i' \in \mathbf{B}, j' \in 2m} \exp\Big(\phi(H^{(r_j),i}_{enc}, H^{(r_{j'}),i'}_{enc})/\tau\Big)}, \tag{3}$$

where $\phi(x, y)$ represents the cosine similarity scores between x and y after average pooling, and τ is the temperature. $2m$ refers to the indices of collected relevance-query samples: $\{(r_j, q^{(r_j)})\}^{2m}_{j}$ for each document, consisting of m positive queries and m negative ones.[5] Intuitively, the semantic distance between arbitrary relevance-aware document representations H_{enc} would propogate gradient to the relevant prompts. Therefore, this loss will guide encoder G_{enc} to comprehend differently across different documents and relevance simultaneously.

Calibrated sequence likelihood. Since negative queries could be infinite, the models will tend to generate random trivial queries or non-scene texts (Welleck et al., 2020; Holtzman et al., 2020). Thus, we specifically control the sequence likelihoods of positive and negative query generation to avoid such degeneration. Inspired by sequence calibration (Zhao et al., 2023), which leverages multiple references to calibrate the sequence likelihood, we treat the relevance-contradicted query as a reference to calibrate the likelihood of the relevance-entailed query, as illustrated in Figure 3.

Specifically, for each composite input of document and relevance, we regard the likelihood of *relevance-entailed* query generation as $\log P_{fw} = \log P(q^{(r)}|d, r)$, indicating the "forward" generation. On the contrary, we calculate the "reverse" likelihood by substituting the decoder input with the contradicted one, denoted as $\log P_{rev} = \log P(q^{(r')}|d, r)$. This implies the likelihood of generating *relevance-contradicted* queries. Both the adjustments can be done efficiently within the batch; we simply swap the decoder inputs between the forward one and the reverse one as demonstrated in Figure 3. The calibration loss for each relevance-aware query generation is as follows:

[4] Among a few preliminary zero-shot tests, we cherry-picked a better one: "`Generate a question for this passage with the labels:`" as initialization.

[5] As we fix the number of sampled queries per document d, we here ignore the docuemnt dependency and replace the notations of r_{ji}, m_i by r_j, m for brevity.

$$\mathcal{L}_{cal} = \sum_{(r,r')} \max\left(0, \epsilon - \log P_{\text{fw}} + \log P_{\text{rev}}\right);$$

$$(\hat{q}^{(r)}, \hat{q}^{(r')}) \in \left([R_d^+; R_d^-], [R_d^-; R_d^+]\right), \quad (4)$$

where ϵ is a fixed margin that provides tolerances when forward-reverse gap is large enough. R_d^+ and R_d^- are the available postive and negative query samples and their corresponding relevance scores (Section 4). In particular, the intuition behind this loss is to increase the discrepancy between positive and negative query generation along with the given relevance distribution.

3.3 Domain-adaptative Passage Re-ranking

Afterward, as depicted in the second block in Figure 2, we can generate diverse relevance-aware queries $\hat{q}^{(r)}$ via ReadQG by feeding the document with different relevance scores. We then use these queries to construct special synthetic training pairs, each comprising a document d, a positive query $\hat{q}$, and a negative one $\hat{q}^-$.[6] These examples, especially the query-query pair, serve as additional domain-adaptive learning signals for downstream text ranking models.

Cross-encoder for relevance classification. We choose cross-encoder architecture and passage re-ranking task as the experimental testbed. And we use binary cross-entropy (BCE) loss for training cross-encoders, similar to the point-wise ranking (Nogueira and Cho, 2020), In addition, we adopt the common in-batch negative sampling (Karpukhin et al., 2020) to obtain a random negative document d^- and formuate the loss $\mathcal{L}_{bce}$ as:

$$\frac{1}{2|\mathcal{D}_{\mathbf{B}}|} \sum_{d}^{\mathcal{D}_{\mathbf{B}}} -\log P_F(\hat{q}, d) + \log P_F(\hat{q}, d^-), \quad (5)$$

where d^- is sampled from documents other than the d (i.e., the positive one) within the same mini-batch $\mathcal{D}_{\mathbf{B}}$; we choose the one with the highest predicted relevance as the negative document sample. Note that this is not a hard negative mining startegy (Xiong et al., 2020); it is only for avoiding underlying overfiting caused by imbalanced labels.

[6]We treat $\hat{q}^{(r=0)}$ as the hard negative query and leave the exploration of other interpolated ones as our future work.

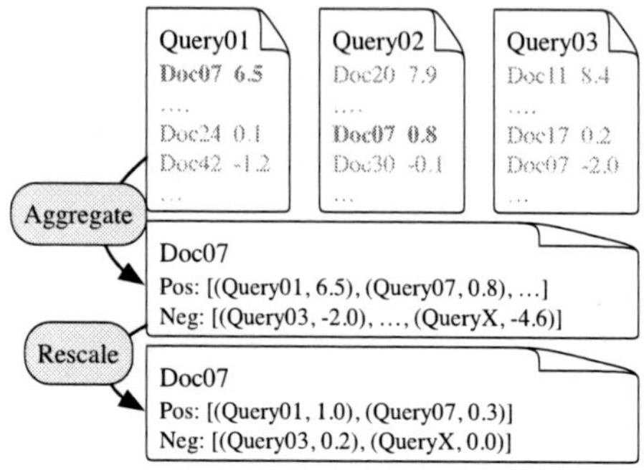

Figure 4: Construct semi-supervised document-centric pairs with MSMARCO and pseudo relevance scores. Once the documents are sorted, we aggregate queries for each document and rescale the relevance scores as document-centric pairs.

Dual learning with query-based objectives. In addition, we include query-based learning with synthetic positive and negative query pairs. The purpose is to enhance domain-specific knowledge through learning from query-query similarity. We hypothesize that the hard negative query could provide a misunderstanding comprehension of the document, offering another view of negative relevance, and thereby steering the ranking model to familiarize itself with unseen domains. Here, we adopt the margin ranking loss with query-query similarity as follows:

$$\mathcal{L}_{mr} = \sum_{d}^{\mathcal{D}_{\mathbf{B}}} \max\left(0, F(\hat{q}, \hat{q}^-) - F(\hat{q}, d)\right). \quad (6)$$

The intuition is that the relevance of the hard negative query should not be greater than the query-document relevance, providing extra gradient for relevance classification. Finally, we fine-tune domain-adaptive cross-encoders in a few-shot manner with the two objectives in Eq.(5) and Eq. (6).

4 Semi-supervised MSMARCO Document-centric Pairs

To fine-tune ReadQG, we collect training pairs for query generation using the MSMARCO passage ranking dataset (Bajaj et al., 2018). We utilize this dataset, along with the pseudo-relevance of BM25 hard negatives[7], which are predicted by the off-the-shelf ranking model, MiniLM.[8] This cross-

[7]`https://huggingface.co/datasets/sentence-transformers/msmarco-hard-negatives`

[8]`https://huggingface.co/cross-encoder/ms-marco-MiniLM-L-6-v2`

encoder is fine-tuned on MS MARCO triplets. The procedure is illustrated in Figure 4.

Query-centric to document-wise aggregation. First, we sort the (query-centric) rank list by pseudo-relevance, as shown at the top of Figure 4. We also define the relevance boundary of positive and negative as 0 since MiniLM was fine-tuned with a regression-like objective. Next, we aggregate queries in a document-wise manner. For example, "Doc07" in Figure 4 appears in three ranking lists. We then re-sort the pseudo-relevance across these three lists and categorize them as positive or negative with the boundary of 0, resulting in semi-supervised document-to-queries pairs.

Re-scaling and sampling. In addition, for each pair, we rescale the relevance scores of the aggregated query set using `MinMaxScaler`.[9] The purpose of this step is to align the scores with the relevance prompt function in Eq. (1). Finally, for each document, we collect positive queries with the top-m highest relevance scores into R_d^+. Conversely, queries with the bottom-m lowest scores are considered negative query samples. Documents with fewer than 2m queries are discarded, resulting in approximately 4.7M document-centric training pairs for ReadQG.

5 Experimental Setups

We will first report the setup of the two stages in the proposed pipeline: data augmnetation using ReadQG (Section 3.2), and domain adaptive passage re-ranking (Section 3.3) fine-tuned on the synthetic training data.

5.1 Training and Inference Setups

Stage I: Data augmentation. Our ReadQG is initialized with Flan-T5 base checkpoint.[10] with only a few tunable parameters of embedding prompts (Section 3.2). We set the length of instruction and relevance prompt as 10 and 5, respectively, ensuring the lightweight training and inference overhead. The generator is then fine-tuned on the semi-supervised training pairs (See Section 4 for details) for 20K steps with a constant learning rate 1e-2. The maximum sequence length of input (document) and target (query) are 128 and 16. We use batch size of 32, comprising 4 documents and $m = 4$, for each positive and negative query samples.

During inference, to control the generation of positive and *hard* negative query, we specify the relevance scores as $r = 1$ and $r = 0$, respectively. We then construct the composite input for positive and negative query generation as described in Eq. (1). The maximum sequence length of input and output are 384 and 64 with top-k ($k = 10$) decoding strategies (Fan et al., 2018). We also analyze greedy and beam search decoding strategy in Section 6.2.

Stage II: Domain-adaptative passage re-ranking Once we have the synthetic training pairs, we use them to fine-tune domain-adaptive passage ranking models. We initialize the models with MiniLM pre-trained on MSMARCO passage ranking, the same model used for pseudo-relevance labels in Section 4. Then, we fine-tune the model with batch size 8 for 2 epoch[11] with learning rate 7e-6. An epoch of training steps is defined as the corpus size divided by batch size, as we only generate one query pair per document. We set the maximum length as 384. Other training hyperparameters follow the default setups of SentenceBERT cross-encoder.[12]

5.2 Evaluation Setups

BEIR benchmark. We experiment on BEIR and select several tasks with corpus size is less than 100K for evaluation, including NFCorpus (NFC, 3.6K), FiQA (FQA, 57.6K), ArguAna (ARG, 8.7K), SCIDOCS (SCD, 25.7K), and SciFact (SCF, 5.2K). For brevity, we will use these abbreviations henceforth. We first validate the domain adaptation capability by out-of-domain text ranking effectiveness nDCG@10, the official metric in BEIR. We used the fixed candidates from BM25 top-100 retrieved results and foucsed on the re-ranking effectiveness for simpler comparison.

Performance metrics. We also investigate the unique charateristic of generated queries directly from an IR perspective. Specifically, by using the off-the-shelf bi-encoders and cross-encoders, we can analyze the useful properties of synthetic query. We introduce the following:

1. **Diversity.** We regard the generated queries Q from an unseen document as different texts.

[9] `https://scikit-learn.org`

[10] `https://huggingface.co/google/flan-t5-base`

[11] We found there is no improvement after the second.

[12] `https://github.com/UKPLab/sentence-transformers`

#	Retrieval + Re-ranking (synthetic data)	Objectives $(\hat{q}, d)$	$(\hat{q}, d, \hat{q}^-)$	Params (M) Gen./Rank	nDCG@10 NFC	FQA	ARG	SCD	SCF	Avg.
	BM25	-	-	-	32.5	23.6	41.4	15.8	66.5	36.0
(0)	BM25 + MiniLM-MS			- / 0.2M	35.0	34.7	41.7	16.6	68.8	39.4
(1)	BM25 + MiniLM-MS (InPars-v2 data)	✓	✗	6B / 0.2M	35.4	**35.2**	42.3	16.6	69.8	39.8
(2)	BM25 + MiniLM-MS (ReadQG)	✓	✗	220M / 0.2M	35.4	34.0	42.8	15.7	71.4	39.8
(3)	BM25 + MiniLM-MS (ReadQG)	✓	✓	220M / 0.2M	**35.5**	34.4	**49.6**	**16.7**	**71.6**	**41.6**

Table 1: The Out-of-domain text re-ranking effectivenss (nDCG@10) with top-100 candidates retrieved using BM25. The third and forth columns indicate learning objectives of Eq. (3) and Eq. (6).

Thus, we first encode n_Q queries with off-the-shelf bi-encoders[13] E^*. Then, we compute the average pairwise angular distance (Cer et al., 2018) across n query embeddings as follow:

$$\frac{2}{n_Q^2 - n_Q} \sum_{i=1}^{n_Q} \sum_{j=i+1} \Omega\left(E^*(q_i), E^*(q_j)\right),$$

where we set $n_Q = 11$ and indicate relevance scores $r \in \{0, 0.1, ..., 1.0\}$. $\Omega(u, v)$ indicates the angular distance between vectors u and v.

2. **Relevancy.** In addition, we feed the document with our generated positive and negative query into another effective cross-encoder model. We use monoT5-3B-InPars-v2 (Jeronymo et al., 2023) as we assume the predicted scores of the larger model can accurately reflect the true relevance between query and document. These metrics include

$$\begin{aligned} \text{rel}^+ &= F^*(\hat{q}^{(r=1)}, d); \\ \text{rel}^- &= F^*(\hat{q}^{(r=0)}, d); \\ \Delta\text{rel} &= \text{rel}^+ - \text{rel}^-. \end{aligned}$$

Note that all metrics will first be calculated per document and then take the average across documents in our later results.

6 Empirical Results

In this section, we first validate the text ranking effectiveness using the synthetic data constructed by ReadQG. Then, we explore the query generation effectiveness via the aforementioned three performance metrics.

6.1 Main Results

Out-of-domain text ranking. Table 1 shows that the domain-adaptive text ranking models fine-tuned with an additional negative query from ReadQG (condition #(3)) increase the average nDCG@10 by approximately two points compared to the initial zero-shot one (i.e., #(0)). This indicates the positive query together with the *hard negative* query can transfer useful signals during learning. Moreover, condition #(3) outperforms our baseline #(2), the condition used only positive queries. This implies the role of negative relevance in Eq. (6) can guide models to accurately estimate the relevancy of queries and documents.

#	Div.	(rel$^+$/rel$^-$/Δrel)	nDCG@10
(a) $\mathcal{L}_{mle}$	.218	(.970/.859/.111)	.707
(b) + $\mathcal{L}_{sc}$	.154	(.957/.938/.019)	.709
(c) + $\mathcal{L}_{cal}$	.269	(.967/.732/.235)	.706
(d) + $\mathcal{L}_{sc} + \mathcal{L}_{cal}$	.219	(.973/.935/.037)	.716

Table 2: Quality of generated query with different diversity learning objectives. We use SCIFACT as example. The reported metrics are diversity (Div.) and relevancy and nDCG@10.

We also compare with the generated query from InPars-v2 (Jeronymo et al., 2023) by fine-tuning the synthetic pairs with identical settings. Note that we here exclude negative documents in the released data[14] for a fair comparison. We also align the amounts of training pairs by random sampling. By comparing conditions #(1) and #(2), we observe the positive queries generated by ReadQG can perform on par with InPars-v2's[15] with a smaller generator (i.e., 220M parameters), demonstrating an efficient alternative to transfer knowledge from rich-resource MSMARCO dataset (Bajaj et al., 2018).

Generation Quality. To better understand generated queries, we compare the variants of our proposed learning objectives in Section 3.2, as shown in different rows in Table 2. We fixed all the settings of query generation, including prompt length

[13]We use GTE encoder (Li et al., 2023) as it has been pretrained on scientific corpora.

[14]https://huggingface.co/datasets/inpars/generated-data

[15]For a fair comparison, we shuffle the generated queries and sample the same size as ours. And we only used the positive query-document pairs.

$\lvert P_{\text{rel}} \rvert$	Div.	($\text{rel}^+/\text{rel}^-/\Delta\text{rel}$)	nDCG@10
1	.204	(.972/.916/.056)	70.4
5	.219	(.973/.935/.037)	71.6
10	.192	(.986/.944/.042)	70.4

Table 3: The impacts of different length of relevance soft prompts. We use the SCIFACT dataset as an example.

Decode	NFC	FQA	ARG	SCD	SCF	Avg.
Beams= 1	35.6	33.8	50.1	16.6	71.6	41.5
Beams= 3	35.5	33.5	52.8	16.6	71.7	42.0
Top-k(10)	35.5	34.4	49.6	16.7	71.6	41.6

Table 4: The impacts of different sequence decoding strategy. The reported scores are nDCG@10.

as 5 and greedy decoding. We observe there is no single metric solely related to the ranking effectiveness. However, one interesting finding is that the condition #(d) (i.e., MLE + two diverse generation losses) and condition #(a) (MLE only) have similar diversity, but their relevance scores of negative queries (i.e., rel^-) differ; condition #(d) has .935 but #(a) is .859. This highlights the unique characteristic of harder negative query – high diversity but also high relevance (Div. $\uparrow$; rel^- $\uparrow$) – with the same document. This also shows that calibration loss with self-contrastive loss can complement each other and produce better relevance-aware diver queries. The high diversity sometimes hurts text ranking effectiveness such as condition #(c), meaning that the negative query is too trivial (i.e., random negative query).

6.2 ReadQG Analysis

Length of relevance prompt. In Table 3, we investigate different lengths of soft relevance prompts as many studies have claimed the impact of prompt length is significant (Li and Liang, 2021; Lester et al., 2021). We train generators with fixed learning objectives and inference with the same greedy decoding. Comparing the first two rows (lengths of 1 and 5), we observe the improvement is attributed to the better expression capability with longer prompts, enabling to parameterize more nonlinearity of query-document relevance. However, further increasing prompt length may not significantly increase the diversity of generated queries and result in lower diversity (Div. $\downarrow$). Moreover, the retrieval effectiveness would be limited when the prompt length is too long even though the relevance of the negative query is higher (rel^- $\uparrow$). This finding aligns with our observation in Table 1 that the informative *hard* negative query is meaningful when exhibits both high diversity and relevance.

Decoding strategies. Table 4 demonstrates the different decoding strategies. Intuitively, we consider beam search as the most effective option for negative query generation. However, the top-k sampling is the better strategy considering the efficiency. It can balance diversity and efficiency. However, since we only test the *hard* negative with relevance score $r = 0$, it required more investigation for interpolated query and the corresponding learning design of text ranking. We hypothesize the diverse generated queries can similarly benefit the dense retrieval models like Lin et al. (2023), which we leave it as our future work.

7 Conclusion

In this study, we present relevance-aware diverse queries generation and validate several setups for constructing more informative queries. The generation of negative query can benefit from appropriate soft-prompt tuning and diverse generation constraints, resulting in a more effective learning process of text ranking models. Thus, we consider the negative query generation as a potential research direction. There are several other avenues for future work, including (1) scaling up ReadQG or prompting larger LLMs for negative queries; (2) mining hard negative documents with hard negative query; (3) fine-tuning bi-encoders dense retrieval with an additional negative query; (4) exploreing more complicated learning tehcniques (Ren et al., 2021; Li et al., 2021) that can fully exploit interpolated negative queries. Regarding the domain adaptation, we suspect the query distribution will be another important factor, as seen in promptagator (Dai et al., 2023) boost the performance with few in-domain data. More empirical evaluation on other benchmarks like Massive Textual Evaluation Benchmark (mteb) can also provide deeper insights of the usefulness of hard negative queries.

Acknowledgements

This research was partially supported by the Hybrid Intelligence Center, a 10-year program funded by the Dutch Ministry of Education, Culture and Science through the Netherlands Organisation for Scientific Research, `https://hybrid-intelligence-centre.nl`.

References

Payal Bajaj, Daniel Campos, Nick Craswell, Li Deng, Jianfeng Gao, Xiaodong Liu, Rangan Majumder, Andrew McNamara, Bhaskar Mitra, Tri Nguyen, Mir Rosenberg, Xia Song, Alina Stoica, Saurabh Tiwary, and Tong Wang. 2018. Ms marco: A human generated machine reading comprehension dataset.

Max Bartolo, Tristan Thrush, Robin Jia, Sebastian Riedel, Pontus Stenetorp, and Douwe Kiela. 2021. Improving question answering model robustness with synthetic adversarial data generation. In *Proceedings of the 2021 Conference on Empirical Methods in Natural Language Processing*, pages 8830–8848, Online and Punta Cana, Dominican Republic. Association for Computational Linguistics.

Luiz Bonifacio, Hugo Abonizio, Marzieh Fadaee, and Rodrigo Nogueira. 2022. Inpars: Unsupervised dataset generation for information retrieval. In *Proceedings of the 45th International ACM SIGIR Conference on Research and Development in Information Retrieval*, SIGIR '22, page 2387–2392, New York, NY, USA. Association for Computing Machinery.

Samuel R. Bowman, Luke Vilnis, Oriol Vinyals, Andrew Dai, Rafal Jozefowicz, and Samy Bengio. 2016. Generating sentences from a continuous space. In *Proceedings of the 20th SIGNLL Conference on Computational Natural Language Learning*, pages 10–21, Berlin, Germany. Association for Computational Linguistics.

Tom Brown, Benjamin Mann, Nick Ryder, Melanie Subbiah, Jared D Kaplan, Prafulla Dhariwal, Arvind Neelakantan, Pranav Shyam, Girish Sastry, Amanda Askell, Sandhini Agarwal, Ariel Herbert-Voss, Gretchen Krueger, Tom Henighan, Rewon Child, Aditya Ramesh, Daniel Ziegler, Jeffrey Wu, Clemens Winter, Chris Hesse, Mark Chen, Eric Sigler, Mateusz Litwin, Scott Gray, Benjamin Chess, Jack Clark, Christopher Berner, Sam McCandlish, Alec Radford, Ilya Sutskever, and Dario Amodei. 2020a. Language models are few-shot learners. In *Advances in Neural Information Processing Systems*, volume 33, pages 1877–1901. Curran Associates, Inc.

Tom Brown, Benjamin Mann, Nick Ryder, Melanie Subbiah, Jared D Kaplan, Prafulla Dhariwal, Arvind Neelakantan, Pranav Shyam, Girish Sastry, Amanda Askell, et al. 2020b. Language models are few-shot learners. *Advances in neural information processing systems*, 33:1877–1901.

Daniel Cer, Yinfei Yang, Sheng yi Kong, Nan Hua, Nicole Limtiaco, Rhomni St. John, Noah Constant, Mario Guajardo-Cespedes, Steve Yuan, Chris Tar, Yun-Hsuan Sung, Brian Strope, and Ray Kurzweil. 2018. Universal sentence encoder.

Jaemin Cho, Minjoon Seo, and Hannaneh Hajishirzi. 2019. Mixture content selection for diverse sequence generation. In *Proceedings of the 2019 Conference on Empirical Methods in Natural Language Processing and the 9th International Joint Conference on Natural Language Processing (EMNLP-IJCNLP)*, pages 3121–3131, Hong Kong, China. Association for Computational Linguistics.

Hyung Won Chung, Le Hou, Shayne Longpre, Barret Zoph, Yi Tay, William Fedus, Yunxuan Li, Xuezhi Wang, Mostafa Dehghani, Siddhartha Brahma, Albert Webson, Shixiang Shane Gu, Zhuyun Dai, Mirac Suzgun, Xinyun Chen, Aakanksha Chowdhery, Alex Castro-Ros, Marie Pellat, Kevin Robinson, Dasha Valter, Sharan Narang, Gaurav Mishra, Adams Yu, Vincent Zhao, Yanping Huang, Andrew Dai, Hongkun Yu, Slav Petrov, Ed H. Chi, Jeff Dean, Jacob Devlin, Adam Roberts, Denny Zhou, Quoc V. Le, and Jason Wei. 2022. Scaling instruction-finetuned language models.

Zhuyun Dai, Vincent Y Zhao, Ji Ma, Yi Luan, Jianmo Ni, Jing Lu, Anton Bakalov, Kelvin Guu, Keith Hall, and Ming-Wei Chang. 2023. Promptagator: Few-shot dense retrieval from 8 examples. In *The Eleventh International Conference on Learning Representations*.

Angela Fan, Mike Lewis, and Yann Dauphin. 2018. Hierarchical neural story generation. In *Proceedings of the 56th Annual Meeting of the Association for Computational Linguistics (Volume 1: Long Papers)*, pages 889–898, Melbourne, Australia. Association for Computational Linguistics.

Luyu Gao, Xueguang Ma, Jimmy Lin, and Jamie Callan. 2022. Precise zero-shot dense retrieval without relevance labels.

Suchin Gururangan, Ana Marasović, Swabha Swayamdipta, Kyle Lo, Iz Beltagy, Doug Downey, and Noah A. Smith. 2020. Don't stop pretraining: Adapt language models to domains and tasks. In *Proceedings of the 58th Annual Meeting of the Association for Computational Linguistics*, pages 8342–8360, Online. Association for Computational Linguistics.

Ari Holtzman, Jan Buys, Li Du, Maxwell Forbes, and Yejin Choi. 2020. The curious case of neural text degeneration. In *International Conference on Learning Representations*.

Vitor Jeronymo, Luiz Bonifacio, Hugo Abonizio, Marzieh Fadaee, Roberto Lotufo, Jakub Zavrel, and Rodrigo Nogueira. 2023. Inpars-v2: Large language models as efficient dataset generators for information retrieval.

Vladimir Karpukhin, Barlas Oğuz, Sewon Min, Patrick Lewis, Ledell Wu, Sergey Edunov, Danqi Chen, and Wen tau Yih. 2020. Dense passage retrieval for open-domain question answering.

Dong Bok Lee, Seanie Lee, Woo Tae Jeong, Donghwan Kim, and Sung Ju Hwang. 2020. Generating diverse and consistent QA pairs from contexts with information-maximizing hierarchical conditional VAEs. In *Proceedings of the 58th Annual*

Meeting of the Association for Computational Linguistics, pages 208–224, Online. Association for Computational Linguistics.

Brian Lester, Rami Al-Rfou, and Noah Constant. 2021. The power of scale for parameter-efficient prompt tuning. In *Proceedings of the 2021 Conference on Empirical Methods in Natural Language Processing*, pages 3045–3059, Online and Punta Cana, Dominican Republic. Association for Computational Linguistics.

Xiang Lisa Li and Percy Liang. 2021. Prefix-tuning: Optimizing continuous prompts for generation. In *Proceedings of the 59th Annual Meeting of the Association for Computational Linguistics and the 11th International Joint Conference on Natural Language Processing (Volume 1: Long Papers)*, pages 4582–4597, Online. Association for Computational Linguistics.

Yizhi Li, Zhenghao Liu, Chenyan Xiong, and Zhiyuan Liu. 2021. More robust dense retrieval with contrastive dual learning. In *Proceedings of the 2021 ACM SIGIR International Conference on Theory of Information Retrieval*, ICTIR '21, page 287–296, New York, NY, USA. Association for Computing Machinery.

Zehan Li, Xin Zhang, Yanzhao Zhang, Dingkun Long, Pengjun Xie, and Meishan Zhang. 2023. Towards general text embeddings with multi-stage contrastive learning.

Sheng-Chieh Lin, Akari Asai, Minghan Li, Barlas Oguz, Jimmy Lin, Yashar Mehdad, Wen tau Yih, and Xilun Chen. 2023. How to train your dragon: Diverse augmentation towards generalizable dense retrieval.

Yixin Liu, Pengfei Liu, Dragomir Radev, and Graham Neubig. 2022. BRIO: Bringing order to abstractive summarization. In *Proceedings of the 60th Annual Meeting of the Association for Computational Linguistics (Volume 1: Long Papers)*, pages 2890–2903, Dublin, Ireland. Association for Computational Linguistics.

Chenyang Lyu, Lifeng Shang, Yvette Graham, Jennifer Foster, Xin Jiang, and Qun Liu. 2021. Improving unsupervised question answering via summarization-informed question generation. In *Proceedings of the 2021 Conference on Empirical Methods in Natural Language Processing*, pages 4134–4148, Online and Punta Cana, Dominican Republic. Association for Computational Linguistics.

Ji Ma, Ivan Korotkov, Yinfei Yang, Keith Hall, and Ryan McDonald. 2021. Zero-shot neural passage retrieval via domain-targeted synthetic question generation. In *Proceedings of the 16th Conference of the European Chapter of the Association for Computational Linguistics: Main Volume*, pages 1075–1088, Online. Association for Computational Linguistics.

Sewon Min, Julian Michael, Hannaneh Hajishirzi, and Luke Zettlemoyer. 2020. AmbigQA: Answering ambiguous open-domain questions. In *Proceedings of the 2020 Conference on Empirical Methods in Natural Language Processing (EMNLP)*, pages 5783–5797, Online. Association for Computational Linguistics.

Rodrigo Nogueira and Kyunghyun Cho. 2020. Passage re-ranking with bert.

Rodrigo Nogueira, Wei Yang, Jimmy Lin, and Kyunghyun Cho. 2019. Document expansion by query prediction.

Barlas Oguz, Kushal Lakhotia, Anchit Gupta, Patrick Lewis, Vladimir Karpukhin, Aleksandra Piktus, Xilun Chen, Sebastian Riedel, Scott Yih, Sonal Gupta, and Yashar Mehdad. 2022. Domain-matched pre-training tasks for dense retrieval. In *Findings of the Association for Computational Linguistics: NAACL 2022*, pages 1524–1534, Seattle, United States. Association for Computational Linguistics.

Ruiyang Ren, Shangwen Lv, Yingqi Qu, Jing Liu, Wayne Xin Zhao, QiaoQiao She, Hua Wu, Haifeng Wang, and Ji-Rong Wen. 2021. Pair: Leveraging passage-centric similarity relation for improving dense passage retrieval. In *Findings of the Association for Computational Linguistics: ACL-IJCNLP 2021*. Association for Computational Linguistics.

Abigail See, Peter J. Liu, and Christopher D. Manning. 2017. Get to the point: Summarization with pointer-generator networks. In *Proceedings of the 55th Annual Meeting of the Association for Computational Linguistics (Volume 1: Long Papers)*, pages 1073–1083, Vancouver, Canada. Association for Computational Linguistics.

Nandan Thakur, Nils Reimers, Andreas Rücklé, Abhishek Srivastava, and Iryna Gurevych. 2021. BEIR: A heterogeneous benchmark for zero-shot evaluation of information retrieval models. In *Thirty-fifth Conference on Neural Information Processing Systems Datasets and Benchmarks Track (Round 2)*.

Kexin Wang, Nandan Thakur, Nils Reimers, and Iryna Gurevych. 2022. GPL: Generative pseudo labeling for unsupervised domain adaptation of dense retrieval. In *Proceedings of the 2022 Conference of the North American Chapter of the Association for Computational Linguistics: Human Language Technologies*, pages 2345–2360, Seattle, United States. Association for Computational Linguistics.

Sean Welleck, Ilia Kulikov, Stephen Roller, Emily Dinan, Kyunghyun Cho, and Jason Weston. 2020. Neural text generation with unlikelihood training. In *International Conference on Learning Representations*.

Lee Xiong, Chenyan Xiong, Ye Li, Kwok-Fung Tang, Jialin Liu, Paul Bennett, Junaid Ahmed, and Arnold Overwijk. 2020. Approximate nearest neighbor negative contrastive learning for dense text retrieval.

Yao Zhao, Mikhail Khalman, Rishabh Joshi, Shashi Narayan, Mohammad Saleh, and Peter J Liu. 2023. Calibrating sequence likelihood improves conditional language generation. In *The Eleventh International Conference on Learning Representations*.

Learning from Others: Similarity-based Regularization for Mitigating Dataset Bias

Reda Igbaria **Yonatan Belinkov**
Technion - Israel Institute of Technology
redaigbaria@technion.ac.il belinkov@technion.ac.il

Abstract

Common methods for mitigating spurious correlations in natural language understanding (NLU) usually operate in the output space, encouraging a main model to behave differently from a bias model by down-weighing examples where the bias model is confident. While improving out-of-distribution (OOD) performance, it was recently observed that the internal representations of the presumably debiased models are actually more, rather than less biased. We propose SimReg, a new method for debiasing internal model components via similarity-based regularization, in representation space: We encourage the model to learn representations that are either similar to an unbiased model or different from a biased model. We experiment with three NLU tasks and different kinds of biases. We find that SimReg improves OOD performance, with little in-distribution degradation. Moreover, the representations learned by SimReg are less biased than in other methods.[1]

1 Introduction

Recent studies (McCoy et al., 2019; Geirhos et al., 2020, *inter alia*) show that in many cases neural models tend to exploit spurious correlations (a.k.a dataset biases, artifacts[2]) in datasets and learn shortcut solutions rather than the intended function. For example, in MNLI—a popular Natural Language Understanding dataset—there is a high correlation between negation words such as "not, don't" and the *contradiction* label (Gururangan et al., 2018). Thus models trained on MNLI confidently predict contradiction whenever there is a negation word in the input without considering the whole meaning of the sentence. As a result of relying on such shortcuts, models fail to generalize and perform poorly when tested on out-of-distribution data (OOD) in which such associative patterns are not present (McCoy et al., 2019); these models are commonly known as 'biased' models. Moreover, this behavior limits their practical applicability in cases where the real-world data distribution differs from the training distribution.

Recent efforts to mitigate learning spurious correlations (a.k.a debiasing methods) perform the debiasing extrinsically, i.e., operating on the output space of the model and dictating how its output should look like. Typically, by downweigh the importance of training samples that contain such correlations, effectively performing data reweighting (Schuster et al., 2019; Utama et al., 2020a; Sanh et al., 2021; Cadene et al., 2019). One might expect that such an *extrinsic* debiasing would lead to "suppressing the model from capturing non-robust features" (Du et al., 2023). However, Mendelson and Belinkov (2021) showed a counter-intuitive trend: a higher accuracy of such models on OOD challenge sets is correlated with a higher representation bias,[3] i.e.,the more extrinsically de-biased a model is, the stronger its intrinsic bias. Such superficial debiasing is problematic as the bias may reappear when the model is used in another setting (Orgad et al., 2022), such as fine-tuned on more data or transferred to other similar tasks.

Inspired by this finding, we investigate whether debiasing the model intrinsically (i.e., operating in the representation space) leads to better models both extrinsically and intrinsically. To this end, we develop SimReg, a new debiasing method based on similarity-regularization. SimReg encourages a model to learn unbiased internal representations by either pushing the learned representations towards a model with *good* (unbiased) representations, or pushing it away from a model with biased representations. Our approach is different from previous

[1]Our code is available at: github.com/simreg/SimReg

[2]We use these words interchangeably.

[3]Representation bias is measured by how easy it is to classify whether a given representation stems from a biased sample or not.

Proceedings of the 9th Workshop on Representation Learning for NLP (RepL4NLP-2024), pages 37–50
August 15, 2024 ©2024 Association for Computational Linguistics

methods, in that we push the model to learn the "good" behavior from other models, while other approaches usually focus on learning to be different from biased models (Utama et al., 2020a; Sanh et al., 2021; Clark et al., 2019; Nam et al., 2020).

We evaluate our approach on three tasks—natural language inference, fact checking, and paraphrase identification—and multiple spurious correlations attested in the literature: lexical overlap, partial inputs, and unknown biases from weak models (see Section 2.1). We demonstrate that our approach improves performance on out-of-distribution (OOD) challenge sets, while incurring little degradation in in-distribution (ID) performance. Finally, we design an experiment to test the bias remaining in the representations, and find that SimReg models tend to have better performance compared to other debiasing methods.

2 Related Work

A growing body of work has revealed that models tend to exploit spurious correlations found in their training data (Geirhos et al., 2020). Spurious correlations are correlations between certain features of the input and certain labels, which are not causal. Models tend to fail when tested on out-of-distribution data, where said correlations do not hold. We briefly mention several relevant cases and refer to Du et al. (2023) for a recent overview of shortcut learning and its mitigation in natural language understanding.

2.1 Dataset bias

Partial-input bias. A common spurious correlation in sentence-pair classification tasks, like natural language inference (NLI), is **partial-input bias** – the association between words in one of the sentences and certain labels. For example, negation words are correlated with a 'contradiction' label when present in the hypothesis in NLI datasets (Gururangan et al., 2018; Poliak et al., 2018) and with a 'refutes' label when present in the claim in fact verification datasets (Schuster et al., 2019). A common approach for revealing the presence of such spurious correlations is to train a partial-input baseline (Feng et al., 2019). When such a model performs well despite having access only to a part of the input, it indicates that that part has spurious correlations.

Lexical overlap bias. Another common bias is when certain labels are associated with **lexical overlap** between the two input sentences. McCoy et al. (2019) found that high lexical-overlap between the premise and hypothesis correlates with 'entailment' in NLI datasets. As a result, NLI models fail when evaluated on HANS, a challenge set where that correlation does not hold. Similarly, Zhang et al. (2019) found that models trained on a paraphrase identification dataset fail to predict 'non-duplicate' questions that have high lexical-overlap.

Unknown biases. Identifying the preceding biases assumes prior knowledge of the type of bias existing in the dataset. A few studies have used weak learners to identify biases in the dataset without an prior assumption(Sanh et al., 2021; Utama et al., 2020b). Utama et al. (2020b) proposes to train a model on limited number of samples, the hypothesis is that pre-trained models "operate as a rapid surface learners", and will learn the bias in the beginning of the training (i.e., with small number of samples). On the other hand, Sanh et al. (2021) proposed to train a limited capacity models such as Tiny-BERT, where the limited capacity tends the learn and recover previously known biases in the literature.

2.2 Debiasing methods

Spurious correlation mitigation can be performed on different levels: Data-based mitigation, where the data is augmented with samples that do not align with the bias found in the dataset (Wang and Culotta, 2021; Kaushik et al., 2020, inter alia). Model/training-based mitigation, where the either the model or the training procedure is modified. A common strategy in this approach is to train a *bias model*, which latches on the bias in the dataset, and use its outputs to train the final, debiased, *main model*. (He et al., 2019) and (Clark et al., 2019) used variants of product-of-experts (**PoE**) to combine the outputs of the biased and main model during training to encourage the main model to "ignore" biased samples. (Utama et al., 2020a) proposed *confidence regularization* (**ConfReg**), where they perform self-distillation with re-weighted teacher outputs using bias-weighted scaling, i.e., they induce the model to be less confident on biased samples. These methods can be viewed as data reweighting methods, similar to (Liu et al., 2021), who proposed to up-weigh examples that are miss-classified by the biased model, i.e., hard examples. Similarly, Yaghoobzadeh et al. (2021) proposed to perform additional fine-tuning on *forgettable* samples after training to increase the robustness ($\mathcal{F}_{\text{BOW}}/\mathcal{F}_{\text{HANS}}$). All these methods work in the output space (extrinsically), while we work in representation space.

Most relevant to our work, Bahng et al. (2020) debias vision models by learning representations that are statistically independent from those of a biased model, by minimizing a statistical independence measure (HSIC) in a min-max optimization objective. We propose a simpler objective function, based on similarity regularization, which can easily be trained by SGD. Additionally, while they focus only on learning representations independent of a biased model, we propose learning representations that are either dissimilar from biased models or similar to unbiased ones.

2.3 Knowledge Distillation

Our approach shares some similarity with Knowledge-Distillation (KD) methods, which transfer knowledge from a teacher model to a (typically smaller) student model. In our framework, we utilize such transfer to improve the robustness of a model. Aguilar et al. (2020) perform KD using internal representations, by minimizing the cosine similarity between the representations of the two models. They compare the similarity of the classification token *(CLS)* whereas we compare all the tokens. Additionally we use second-order isomorphism methods, whereas they use first-order methods.

To our best knowledge, second-order isomorphism methods were previously mainly used for comparing representations and behaviors of models. Our work is one of the first to utilize them to regularize models during training.

3 Methodology

The key idea of our approach is to guide the representation learning of the model in a coarse-grained manner. We achieve this by encouraging the model to learn representations that are either similar to those of an unbiased model or dissimilar from those of a biased model. We design a three-stage procedure (Figure 1):

1. We train a bias model, f_b, on the original training set, $\mathcal{D}$. This model is meant to capture dataset biases, as explained in Section 3.1. In the case of decreasing similarity, we use f_b as our target model, f_g, and continue directly to Stage 3.

2. In order to obtain an unbiased guidance model, we filter the training set based on the predictions of f_b and train a target model f_g on the unbiased part of the training set, $\mathcal{D}^{\mathcal{U}}$ (Section 3.2).

3. We train the main model on $\mathcal{D}$ while encouraging its representations to be (dis)similar to those of f_g (Section 3.3).

3.1 Training a biased model

To mitigate a specific bias (known-bias), we use a bias-specific model, f_b, which is designed to capture that intended bias. For example, to mitigate lexical-overlap bias we use the model proposed in Clark et al. (2019): an MLP whose input features are the ratio of overlap between the two parts of the input, and the average of the minimum cosine similarity between the embeddings of each word from the two sentences. To mitigate unknown-biases, we follow Sanh et al. (2021) and use limited capacity models, such as TinyBert (Turc et al., 2020) and Bag-of-Words (BOW).

In the case of decreasing dissimilarity from a biased model, we use this f_b as the target model, i.e., $f_g = f_b$, and proceed to Stage 3 (Section 3.3). In the case of increasing similarity to an unbiased model, we cannot use f_b as we need an unbiased model; the next section describes how to obtain it.

3.2 Obtaining an unbiased model

To obtain an unbiased guidance model f_g, we run f_b on the training set, $\mathcal{D}$, and exclude samples on which f_b is correct and confident. The remaining samples comprise our unbiased dataset, $\mathcal{D}^{\mathcal{U}}$:

$$\mathcal{D}^{\mathcal{B}} = \{x_i | x_i \in \mathcal{D} \wedge f_b(x) = y_i \wedge c(f_b(x_i)) > c_t\} \tag{1}$$

$$\mathcal{D}^{\mathcal{U}} = \mathcal{D} \setminus \mathcal{D}^{\mathcal{B}} \tag{2}$$

where c_t is a confidence threshold and $c(\cdot)$ is the models' confidence. Our unbiased model, f_g, is obtained by training a new model on $\mathcal{D}^{\mathcal{U}}$.

Choosing the threshold c_t is performed manually by plotting the confidence of the bias model over the training set. When there is a significant bias signal in the dataset, we see a spike in the number of biased samples. Figure 5 (Appendix A.4) shows an example for claim-only bias in FEVER.

A natural question is the following: *What is the advantage of our framework if we already have*

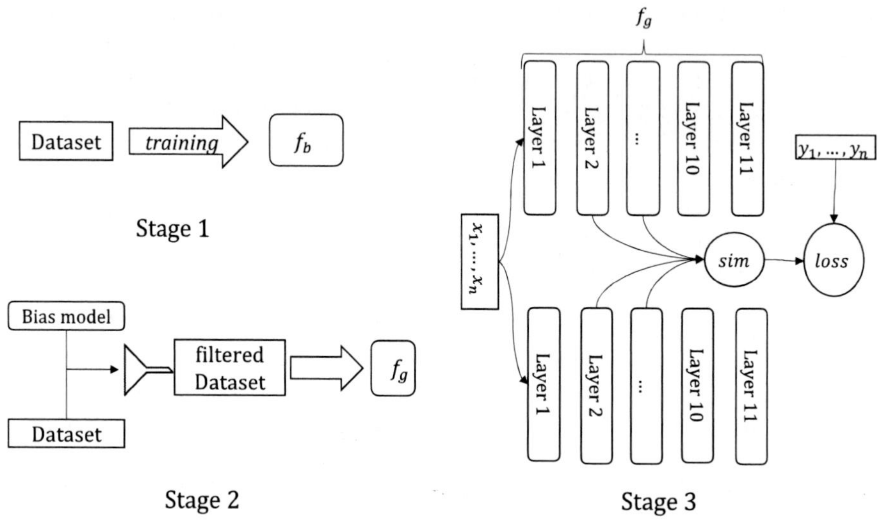

Figure 1: Illustration of SimReg: (1) train a bias model f_b; (2) use its predictions to filter the training set and train a target model f_g; (3) train a main model while guiding its representations to be similar to f_g.

an unbiased model? We emphasize that the unbiased model was trained on $\mathcal{D}^{\mathcal{U}}$, a subset of $\mathcal{D}$, and argue that other samples in $\mathcal{D}$ could also be useful. Indeed, we show experimentally that training a model on the full training set while regularizing it to be similar to the unbiased model leads to a better ID–OOD tradeoff.

3.3 Training the main model

The final step is to train the main model, f_m. We propose two approaches. The first is to encourage the model during training to learn different representations than a biased model, by penalizing its similarity to said biased model, f_b (in this case, $f_g = f_b$). Thus the model would learn different decision boundaries than the biased model. The second approach is to increase the similarity of the learned representations to an unbiased model, f_g. Thus, our model will encode the data in an unbiased manner and its predictions will be less dependant on bias features.

In both cases, we need to compute the similarity between the representations of the main model and those of the target model, f_g. Directly comparing the representations of the models on a single example is not possible, since each model might learn a different latent space for representing the data. Furthermore, the two models might have different architectures and dimensionalities. For instance, in some of our experiments we compare BERT-base (768 dimensions) with TinyBERT (128 dimensions) or with an MLP of 70 dimensions. To overcome these challenges, we use second-order similarity measures, which operate at the batch level (Section 3.3.1).

Formally, we add a similarity regularization term to the batch training loss to promote the similarity/dis-similarity. Given a batch $\mathcal{B}$, we minimize the following objective:

$$\mathcal{L} = \sum_{i \in \mathcal{B}} \mathcal{L}_{CE}(f_m(x_i), y_i) + \lambda \cdot sim(Z, H) \quad (3)$$

where $\mathcal{L}_{CE}$ is the cross-entropy loss, λ is a trade-off hyper-parameter, Z and H are respectively the main and target model representations of the batch, $f(x)$ is the prediction of the model on input x, and sim is a similarity measure. To increase the similarity, we use $\lambda < 0$.

Since we wish the main model, f_m, to resemble or differ from f_g only on biased samples, we apply regularization only on the biased subset, $\mathcal{D}^{\mathcal{B}}$: We stochastically sample a batch either from $\mathcal{D}^{\mathcal{U}}$ and optimize regular cross-entropy, or from $\mathcal{D}^{\mathcal{B}}$ minimizing the objective in Eq. 3. Section 6.3 shows that regularizing only $\mathcal{D}^{\mathcal{B}}$ results in better OOD performance, supporting our intuition.

3.3.1 Models similarity

Different models may represent the same input differently in their learned latent spaces. Directly comparing vectors from different models can be problematic. To address this, we employ second-order isomorphism methods. We assess the similarity of the inputs relative to each other within each modality in a given training batch, then compare the similarity matrices of the two modalities to gauge the resemblance of the model encodings. Specifically, we utilize a well-known similarity measure called Centered Kernel Alignment (CKA; Kornblith et al. 2019) with a linear kernel.

4 Experimental Setup

We run our experiments in two settings: (a) Known-bias settings, where we assume the type of bias existing in the dataset, and can construct targeted biased models; and (b) Unknown-bias settings, where the specific type of bias is not presumed, requiring a more general approach of mitigating unknown-biases.

4.1 Datasets

4.1.1 Natural Language Inference

We train models on MNLI, a popular NLI dataset consisting of $\sim 400k$ English examples in multiple genres (Williams et al., 2018). Each example is a pair of premise and hypothesis sentences, and the task is to predict whether the hypothesis is entailed, contradicted, or neutral w.r.t the premise. MNLI contains several spurious correlations as discussed in Section 2, such as lexical overlap and hypothesis-only biases. We train on the MNLI training set and report ID results on dev-matched.

As OOD test set, we use HANS (McCoy et al., 2019) for evaluation against **lexical overlap bias**. HANS is constructed using structured templates that obey bias heuristics, e.g., the hypothesis overlaps with premise, but with half of the examples having non-entailment labels, as opposed to the bias in MNLI. For **hypothesis-only bias** we use MNLI-hard, a subset of MNLI's dev-mismatched set where a hypothesis-only model failed to classify correctly (Gururangan et al., 2018).

4.1.2 Synthetic MNLI

As a sanity test, we introduce synthetic spurious correlations to MNLI (Synthetic-MNLI), following prior work (He et al., 2019; Sanh et al., 2021; Dranker et al., 2021). We prepend the input with a 'label-token' that correlates highly with the label. We used tokens <*0*>, <*1*>, and <*2*>, corresponding to *entailment*, *neutral*, and *contradiction*. Following (Dranker et al., 2021), we denote the probability of injecting a token to the input as the $prevalence$ of the bias, and the probability of the prepended token being correct as the $strength$ of the bias. Through all our experiments, we used prevalence of 1.0 and strength of 0.95. The subsets of examples containing bias token with wrong and right correlations are denoted *anti_bias* and *bias* subsets, respectively.

The goal of this setting is to demonstrate the viability of the proposed approaches. Thus we use an *oracle unbiased* model as f_g for the case of increasing similarity, i.e., a model trained on regular MNLI (without synthetic bias). For the bias model, f_b, we train a model for a small enough number of steps to capture the bias, judging by the rapid drop of training loss; we found 1k steps sufficient.

4.1.3 Fact Verification

Fact Extraction and VERification (FEVER) (Thorne et al., 2018) is a dataset for fact verification against textual sources. Given evidence and claim sentences, the task is to predict the relation between them: SUPPORTED, REFUTED, or NOT ENOUGH INFO. We followed (Schuster et al., 2019) and trained, evaluated on their processed version of FEVER.

Similar to MNLI, the claim part of the input is spuriously correlated with REFUTES label. We use FEVER-Symmetric (Schuster et al., 2019) for OOD evaluation against **claim-only bias**. The construction of FEVER-Symmetric ensures that there is no correlation between partial input and labels, thus it enables us to evaluate the extent of debiasing on this type of bias.

4.1.4 QQP

Quora Question Pairs (QQP) is a collection of >400K question pairs from the Quora platform. Given a pair of questions, the task is to predict whether they are *duplicate* (paraphrase) or *non-duplicate*. QQP is biased in that question pairs with low **lexical-overlap** between them are correlated with the *non-duplicate* label. We train on the QQP training set and evaluate ID on the development set.

Paraphrase Adversaries from Word Scrambling (PAWS) (Zhang et al., 2019) is a dataset for paraphrase identification that is built in a adversarial manner to lexical-overlap bias. The authors scramble the words of a sentence to generate samples with high lexical-overlap that are not a paraphrase. We use the QQP subset of PAWS as our OOD evaluation set for **lexical-overlap bias**.

	MNLI-Hypothesis		MNLI-Lexical		FEVER		QQP	
	dev	MNLI-HARD	dev	HANS	dev	Sym.	dev	PAWS
BERT	83.9	76.9 ± 0.2	84.2	63.6 ± 1.0	85.6	58.4 ± 1.7	91.0	33.3 ± 0.7
f_g	79.1	78.5 ± 0.5	83.0	70.6 ± 0.8	66.8	61.8 ± 0.2	89.1	39.6 ± 0.1
PoE	82.0	$\mathbf{79.5 \pm 0.4}$	83.2	66.6 ± 3.6	78.0	$\mathbf{63.0 \pm 0.6}$	90.5	34.7 ± 0.3
ConfReg	84.3	78.4 ± 0.6	84.3	66.6 ± 3.9	85.2	61.0 ± 1.7	87.4	37.4 ± 1.8
$\mathcal{F}_{HANS}$	-	-	83.9	69.5 ± 0.9	-	-	-	-
SimReg ↑	84.4	79.2 ± 0.3	83.5	$\mathbf{70.5 \pm 1.9}$	80.9	61.6 ± 0.4	89.8	$\mathbf{41.4 \pm 1.2}$
SimReg ↓	83.0	77.9 ± 0.5	84.0	68.5 ± 0.2	84.1	60.3 ± 1.1	90.8	39.0 ± 0.5

Table 1: Known-bias mitigation.

4.2 Models

We evaluate our approach using BERT (Devlin et al., 2018) as both f_g and the main model. We repeat some of the experiments using DeBERTa-V3 (He et al., 2023) to verify that our method is not specific to BERT. For bias modeling, we used an MLP with lexical features as input following Clark et al. (2019) for lexical-bias modeling. For partial-input bias modeling, we simply train BERT with limited input (only on hypothesis / claim for MNLI / FEVER respectively). In unknown-bias modeling, we use TinyBERT (Turc et al., 2020) for MNLI and QQP, and BOW for FEVER, as our limited-capacity model, following Sanh et al. (2021). For full training details, see Appendix A.1.

5 Results

5.1 Synthetic bias

The results on Synthetic-MNLI are in Table 2. All of the SimReg approaches resulted in an increase compared to the baseline on the *anti-biased* subset, where the synthetic token is mis-aligned with the label. Increasing similarity (↑) performed better than decreasing it (↓). The improvement comes at a cost of a small decrease on the biased subset, which is expected. Compared to an oracle model, which was trained without the synthetic bias, the regularized models perform worse, indicating that they were not able to completely discard the bias.

5.2 Known bias

Tables 1 show the results on known bias cases. All our SimReg models outperform the baseline on the OOD test sets. Increasing similarity (↑) seems to work better than decreasing similarity (↓), consistent with synthetic-bias results. In partial-input bias (MNLI-HARD and FEVER), SimReg performs almost as well as PoE on the challenge sets, while PoE has a greater degradation on ID dev sets. Turning to lexical-overlap bias (QQP and MNLI-HANS), we see a similar pattern: SimReg performs much better than the baseline on HANS and PAWS (the OOD sets), with little or no degradation on the corresponding ID dev sets. In contrast, PoE and ConfReg struggle. Generally, increasing similarity works better than decreasing it.

Model	Biased	Anti-biased
BERT-base	98.5 ± 0.1	41.8 ± 1.1
Oracle	83.8	82.1
SimReg ↑	96.7 ± 0.1	61.0 ± 0.9
SimReg ↓	97.0 ± 0.0	49.0 ± 2.4

Table 2: Results on Synthetic-MNLI.

A telling comparison is between SimReg and the guidance model f_g, which is a model that was trained only on unbiased examples (Section 3.2). In most of the cases, when we increase similarity to this model (rows with ↑), we get models that perform better or similar, on both ID and OOD sets. These results support our hypothesis that increasing similarity to an unbiased model can lead to better representations than those of the unbiased model itself by utilizing more data points.

5.3 Unknown bias

The results of unknown bias mitigation are in Table 3. In this settings, we see similar patterns to known-bias results: SimReg outperforms the baseline and the competitive approaches on challenge sets. Interestingly, in these scenarios, the improvement of SimReg over f_g is more prominent, both in challenge datasets and in ID sets.

	MNLI		FEVER		QQP	
	dev	HANS	dev	Symm.	dev	PAWS
BERT	84.2	63.5 ± 1.0	86.0	58.2 ± 0.6	91.1	33.3 ± 0.7
f_g	77.4	64.1 ± 2.2	84.4	61.3 ± 1.0	82.9	48.7 ± 0.9
ConfReg	83.4	63.2 ± 2.1	86.0	60.0 ± 1.6	88.4	32.3 ± 0.4
POE	81.4	68.8 ± 2.0	82.3	61.1 ± 0.8	89.8	40.8 ± 0.1
$\mathcal{F}_{BOW}$	82.8	70.2 ± 1.2	84.0	59.5 ± 2.5	88.1	41.4 ± 5.2
SimReg↑	81.9	$\mathbf{71.4 \pm 0.8}$	84.3	$\mathbf{62.4} \pm 0.6$	84.4	$\mathbf{50.6} \pm 1.9$

Table 3: Unknown-bias mitigation.

5.4 Results with Stronger Models

In this section we investigate whether our approach improves the performance of stronger models than BERT. While most work tends to compare with BERT as the baseline, it is important to demonstrate that a new debiasing method is effective also when applied to stronger models.[4] We experiment with DeBERTa-V3 (He et al., 2023). As Table 4 shows, SimReg still leads to improvements above the strong DeBERTa-V3. where we see similar patterns to the main results, with SimReg↑ outperforming other approaches. Note that we used here the non-entailment subset of HANS to as our OOD evaluation set in MNLI (Lexical-bias and unknown-bias) to emphasize the improvement on the bias-misaligned subset.

6 Analysis

6.1 Similarity Heat-map Analysis

To investigate whether our similarity-based regularization achieves its goal, we compute the similarity between every layer in the main model and every layer in the (unbiased) guidance model, and likewise the similarity between layers of the baseline model and layers of the guidance model. We expect our similarity regularization to increase the similarity of the main model to the guidance model, compared to that of the baseline model.

Figure 2 (Upper) shows that, without similarity-based regularization, the bottom layers of the baseline and guidance model are already similar, but the top layers are rather different. This is consistent with findings on how fine-tuning affects mostly the top layers (Mosbach et al., 2020; Merchant et al., 2020), as both models started from a pre-trained BERT. Figure 2 (Lower) shows that after our similarity-based regularization, the top layers of the main and guidance models become very similar, as desired. Moreover, the regularization also indirectly affects lower layers (bottom row of the heatmap). We conclude that the similarity regularization is successful and affects large parts of the model even when applied only on a few layers.

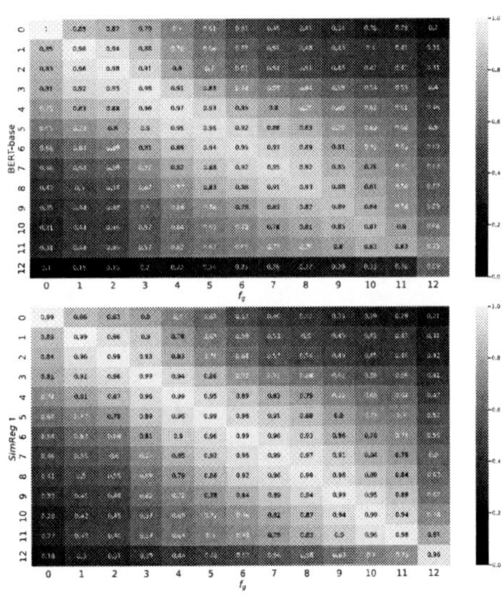

Figure 2: Similarity of an unbiased model, f_g, to either a baseline (Top) or a SimReg model (Bottom). Similarity regularization makes top layers more similar to the unbiased model, as desired.

6.2 Bias recovery

To examine whether representations debiasing does indeed lead to better representations, we designed an experiment to test the bias in the representations. Retraining the classification layer allows us to test to what extent a linear classifier recovers the bias

[4]Bowman (2022) made such a claim about *analyzing* stronger models; we believe it is similarly important to work on *robustifying* stronger models.

	Hypothesis		Lexical	
	ID	HARD	ID	HANS-
baseline	89.9	85.2$\pm$0.1	89.9	56.7$\pm$2.2
ConfReg	90.0	86.3$\pm$0.2	90.3	61.8$\pm$1.9
SimReg ↑	89.1	**86.5**$\pm$**0.2**	89.5	**72.8**$\pm$**0.5**
SimReg ↓	89.4	85.8$\pm$0.3	89.8	63.7$\pm$1.5

(a) Known-bias (MNLI)

	MNLI		QQP	
	ID	HANS-	ID	PAWS
baseline	89.9	56.7$\pm$2.2	89.9	55.7$\pm$5.6
ConfReg	90.1	54.5$\pm$2.0	88.8	61.1$\pm$2.0
SimReg ↑	89.1	**66.8**$\pm$**0.7**	86.3	**67.0**$\pm$**2.0**
SimReg ↓	89.4	61.5$\pm$0.2	89.2	54.8$\pm$1.7

(b) Unknown-bias

Table 4: DeBERTa V3 results for MNLI, QQP biases.

existing in the dataset from the representations. In Table 5, we present the results of retraining the classifier of the debiased models in unknown-bias settings. In all approaches we see a drop in OOD accuracy when retraining the classifier [5], consistent with Mendelson and Belinkov (2021)'s observation that debiased models still encode the bias in their representations. However, in SimReg↑ we generally get the highest performance compared to other methods. This indicates that the representations produced by SimReg↑ have the weakest signal of the spurious correlations. We repeated this experiment on debiased models in known-bias settings in App A.5, and found similar patterns.

	MNLI		FEVER	
	dev	HANS-	dev	Sym
BERT	83.9	30.1 $\pm$1.3	85.4	58.2 $\pm$0.1
ConfReg	84.8	20.5 $\pm$6.2	86.0	59.2 $\pm$1.0
POE	83.0	33.7 $\pm$1.6	83.4	59.1 $\pm$1.5
$\mathcal{F}_{BOW}$	83.1	38.1 $\pm$0.3	84.6	57.0 $\pm$1.5
SimReg↑	83.9	**41.6** $\pm$**4.5**	85.3	**61.3** $\pm$**1.3**

Table 5: Bias recovery: unknown-bias settings. SimReg↑ shows weakest signal of bias when re-training the classifier.

6.3 Ablations

In this section we perform ablations on SimReg↑ on MNLI datasets in unknown-bias settings (using TinyBERT as f_b). Table 6 shows the results of ablating different parts of our method while keeping the reset unchanged.

SimReg↑$_{BOW}$ refers to When using a bag-of-words model as our limited capacity model f_b, SimReg obtains only slightly worse performance (SimReg↑$_{BOW}$ row). However it also shows that the results can depend on the biases that the weak model f_b discovers.

Using a pre-trained BERT as our guidance model (-f_g row) performs poorly. This highlights that the model that is being used to increase similarity to is an important factor in the process, and that indeed the information is being distilled from f_g into the main model.

The last row shows that applying similarity regularization on the entire training set $\mathcal{D}$ performs poorly. This result supports our intuition in regularizing only the biased samples $\mathcal{D}^{\mathcal{U}}$ (Section 3.3).

ablation	dev.	HANS avg.
SimReg↑	81.9	**71.4**
SimReg↑$_{BOW}$	82.8	70.7
- f_g	82.3	58.1
- Bias regularization	84.2	61.3

Table 6: Ablations on SimReg↑ method.

7 Conclusion

In this work, we have introduced SimReg, a new debiasing approach that employs similarity-based regularization at the representation level. We have demonstrated the effectiveness of SimReg across several NLU tasks, where it notably enhances performance on OOD challenge sets with minimal impact on ID sets.

Additionally, we evaluated the representations of SimReg by testing the amount of bias recovered from the debiased models and found that models debiased using SimReg were least biased after retraining their classifier on a dataset that contains bias. Future work may investigate the effect of simultaneously learning from unbiased and biased models. Another interesting direction is to extend our approach to generation tasks, which would require different similarity measures. Moreover, it is

[5]Check Table 10 in the appendix for HANS- evaluation.

worth testing the efficacy of SimReg on other types of biases such as social biases.

Ethics Statement

Our work develops a new approach to mitigate spurious correlations in NLU tasks. These are also known as dataset biases, but are different from social biases such as gender or racial bias. One could use our approach to debias against social biases. However, a malicious actor could use our basic approach to increase such social bias, rather than decrease it, by reversing the optimization.

Limitations

Similar to most debiasing methods, the success of our method relies on the existing of enough non-biased samples in the training set, which is used to guide our learning process. Additionally, a notable limitation is in the case of debiasing against unknown-bias, where one might speculate that a certain weak model captures the bias, however, it could either miss the bias, or be more powerful and capture additional non-biased samples. In this case, an inspection to the predictions of the weak model might help.

Acknowledgements

This research has been supported by an AI Alignment grant from Open Philanthropy, the Israel Science Foundation (grant No. 448/20), and an Azrieli Foundation Early Career Faculty Fellowship.

References

Qoura question pairs dataset. https://quoradata.quora.com/First-Quora-Dataset-Release-Question-Pairs.

Gustavo Aguilar, Yuan Ling, Yu Zhang, Benjamin Yao, Xing Fan, and Chenlei Guo. 2020. Knowledge distillation from internal representations. *Proceedings of the AAAI Conference on Artificial Intelligence*, 34(05):7350–7357.

Hyojin Bahng, Sanghyuk Chun, Sangdoo Yun, Jaegul Choo, and Seong Joon Oh. 2020. Learning de-biased representations with biased representations.

Samuel Bowman. 2022. The dangers of underclaiming: Reasons for caution when reporting how NLP systems fail. In *Proceedings of the 60th Annual Meeting of the Association for Computational Linguistics (Volume 1: Long Papers)*, pages 7484–7499, Dublin, Ireland. Association for Computational Linguistics.

Remi Cadene, Corentin Dancette, Matthieu Cord, Devi Parikh, et al. 2019. Rubi: Reducing unimodal biases for visual question answering. *Advances in Neural Information Processing Systems*, 32:841–852.

Christopher Clark, Mark Yatskar, and Luke Zettlemoyer. 2019. Don't take the easy way out: Ensemble based methods for avoiding known dataset biases. In *Proceedings of the 2019 Conference on Empirical Methods in Natural Language Processing and the 9th International Joint Conference on Natural Language Processing (EMNLP-IJCNLP)*, pages 4069–4082, Hong Kong, China. Association for Computational Linguistics.

Jacob Devlin, Ming-Wei Chang, Kenton Lee, and Kristina N. Toutanova. 2018. Bert: Pre-training of deep bidirectional transformers for language understanding.

Yana Dranker, He He, and Yonatan Belinkov. 2021. IRM—when it works and when it doesn't: A test case of natural language inference. In *Advances in Neural Information Processing Systems*.

Mengnan Du, Fengxiang He, Na Zou, Dacheng Tao, and Xia Hu. 2023. Shortcut learning of large language models in natural language understanding. *Commun. ACM*, 67(1):110–120.

Shi Feng, Eric Wallace, and Jordan Boyd-Graber. 2019. Misleading failures of partial-input baselines. In *Proceedings of the 57th Annual Meeting of the Association for Computational Linguistics*, pages 5533–5538, Florence, Italy. Association for Computational Linguistics.

R. Geirhos, J.-H. Jacobsen, C. Michaelis, R. Zemel, W. Brendel, M. Bethge, and F. A. Wichmann. 2020. Shortcut learning in deep neural networks. *Nature Machine Intelligence*, 2(11):665–673.

Suchin Gururangan, Swabha Swayamdipta, Omer Levy, Roy Schwartz, Samuel Bowman, and Noah A. Smith. 2018. Annotation artifacts in natural language inference data. In *Proceedings of the 2018 Conference of the North American Chapter of the Association for Computational Linguistics: Human Language Technologies, Volume 2 (Short Papers)*, pages 107–112, New Orleans, Louisiana. Association for Computational Linguistics.

He He, Sheng Zha, and Haohan Wang. 2019. Unlearn dataset bias in natural language inference by fitting the residual. In *Proceedings of the 2nd Workshop on Deep Learning Approaches for Low-Resource NLP (DeepLo 2019)*, pages 132–142, Hong Kong, China. Association for Computational Linguistics.

Pengcheng He, Jianfeng Gao, and Weizhu Chen. 2023. DeBERTav3: Improving deBERTa using ELECTRA-style pre-training with gradient-disentangled embedding sharing. In *The Eleventh International Conference on Learning Representations*.

Divyansh Kaushik, Eduard Hovy, and Zachary C Lipton. 2020. Learning the difference that makes a difference with counterfactually augmented data. *International Conference on Learning Representations (ICLR)*.

Simon Kornblith, Mohammad Norouzi, Honglak Lee, and Geoffrey Hinton. 2019. Similarity of neural network representations revisited. In *Proceedings of the 36th International Conference on Machine Learning*, volume 97 of *Proceedings of Machine Learning Research*, pages 3519–3529. PMLR.

Evan Z Liu, Behzad Haghgoo, Annie S Chen, Aditi Raghunathan, Pang Wei Koh, Shiori Sagawa, Percy Liang, and Chelsea Finn. 2021. Just train twice: Improving group robustness without training group information. In *Proceedings of the 38th International Conference on Machine Learning*, volume 139 of *Proceedings of Machine Learning Research*, pages 6781–6792. PMLR.

Tom McCoy, Ellie Pavlick, and Tal Linzen. 2019. Right for the wrong reasons: Diagnosing syntactic heuristics in natural language inference. In *Proceedings of the 57th Annual Meeting of the Association for Computational Linguistics*, pages 3428–3448, Florence, Italy. Association for Computational Linguistics.

Michael Mendelson and Yonatan Belinkov. 2021. Debiasing methods in natural language understanding make bias more accessible. In *Proceedings of the 2021 Conference on Empirical Methods in Natural Language Processing*, pages 1545–1557, Online and Punta Cana, Dominican Republic. Association for Computational Linguistics.

Amil Merchant, Elahe Rahimtoroghi, Ellie Pavlick, and Ian Tenney. 2020. What happens to BERT embeddings during fine-tuning? In *Proceedings of the Third BlackboxNLP Workshop on Analyzing and Interpreting Neural Networks for NLP*, pages 33–44, Online. Association for Computational Linguistics.

Marius Mosbach, Anna Khokhlova, Michael A. Hedderich, and Dietrich Klakow. 2020. On the interplay between fine-tuning and sentence-level probing for linguistic knowledge in pre-trained transformers. In *Proceedings of the Third BlackboxNLP Workshop on Analyzing and Interpreting Neural Networks for NLP*, pages 68–82, Online. Association for Computational Linguistics.

Junhyun Nam, Hyuntak Cha, Sungsoo Ahn, Jaeho Lee, and Jinwoo Shin. 2020. Learning from failure: Debiasing classifier from biased classifier. *Advances in Neural Information Processing Systems*, 33:20673–20684.

Hadas Orgad, Seraphina Goldfarb-Tarrant, and Yonatan Belinkov. 2022. How gender debiasing affects internal model representations, and why it matters. In *Proceedings of the 2022 Conference of the North American Chapter of the Association for Computational Linguistics: Human Language Technologies*, pages 2602–2628, Seattle, United States. Association for Computational Linguistics.

Adam Poliak, Jason Naradowsky, Aparajita Haldar, Rachel Rudinger, and Benjamin Van Durme. 2018. Hypothesis only baselines in natural language inference. In *Proceedings of the Seventh Joint Conference on Lexical and Computational Semantics*, pages 180–191, New Orleans, Louisiana. Association for Computational Linguistics.

Victor Sanh, Thomas Wolf, Yonatan Belinkov, and Alexander M Rush. 2021. Learning from others' mistakes: Avoiding dataset biases without modeling them. In *International Conference on Learning Representations*.

Tal Schuster, Darsh Shah, Yun Jie Serene Yeo, Daniel Roberto Filizzola Ortiz, Enrico Santus, and Regina Barzilay. 2019. Towards debiasing fact verification models. In *Proceedings of the 2019 Conference on Empirical Methods in Natural Language Processing and the 9th International Joint Conference on Natural Language Processing (EMNLP-IJCNLP)*, pages 3419–3425, Hong Kong, China. Association for Computational Linguistics.

James Thorne, Andreas Vlachos, Christos Christodoulopoulos, and Arpit Mittal. 2018. FEVER: a large-scale dataset for fact extraction and VERification. In *Proceedings of the 2018 Conference of the North American Chapter of the Association for Computational Linguistics: Human Language Technologies, Volume 1 (Long Papers)*, pages 809–819, New Orleans, Louisiana. Association for Computational Linguistics.

Iulia Turc, Ming-Wei Chang, Kenton Lee, and Kristina Toutanova. 2020. Well-read students learn better: On the importance of pre-training compact models.

Prasetya Ajie Utama, Nafise Sadat Moosavi, and Iryna Gurevych. 2020a. Mind the trade-off: Debiasing NLU models without degrading the in-distribution performance. In *Proceedings of the 58th Annual Meeting of the Association for Computational Linguistics*, pages 8717–8729, Online. Association for Computational Linguistics.

Prasetya Ajie Utama, Nafise Sadat Moosavi, and Iryna Gurevych. 2020b. Towards debiasing NLU models from unknown biases. In *Proceedings of the 2020 Conference on Empirical Methods in Natural Language Processing (EMNLP)*, pages 7597–7610, Online. Association for Computational Linguistics.

Zhao Wang and Aron Culotta. 2021. Robustness to spurious correlations in text classification via automatically generated counterfactuals. *Proceedings of the AAAI Conference on Artificial Intelligence*, 35(16):14024–14031.

Adina Williams, Nikita Nangia, and Samuel Bowman. 2018. A broad-coverage challenge corpus for sentence understanding through inference. In *Proceedings of the 2018 Conference of the North American Chapter of the Association for Computational Linguistics: Human Language Technologies, Volume 1*

(Long Papers), pages 1112–1122. Association for Computational Linguistics.

Thomas Wolf, Lysandre Debut, Victor Sanh, Julien Chaumond, Clement Delangue, Anthony Moi, Pierric Cistac, Tim Rault, Remi Louf, Morgan Funtowicz, Joe Davison, Sam Shleifer, Patrick von Platen, Clara Ma, Yacine Jernite, Julien Plu, Canwen Xu, Teven Le Scao, Sylvain Gugger, Mariama Drame, Quentin Lhoest, and Alexander Rush. 2020. Transformers: State-of-the-art natural language processing. In *Proceedings of the 2020 Conference on Empirical Methods in Natural Language Processing: System Demonstrations*, pages 38–45, Online. Association for Computational Linguistics.

Yadollah Yaghoobzadeh, Soroush Mehri, Remi Tachet des Combes, T. J. Hazen, and Alessandro Sordoni. 2021. Increasing robustness to spurious correlations using forgettable examples. In *Proceedings of the 16th Conference of the European Chapter of the Association for Computational Linguistics: Main Volume*, pages 3319–3332, Online. Association for Computational Linguistics.

Yuan Zhang, Jason Baldridge, and Luheng He. 2019. PAWS: Paraphrase adversaries from word scrambling. In *Proceedings of the 2019 Conference of the North American Chapter of the Association for Computational Linguistics: Human Language Technologies, Volume 1 (Long and Short Papers)*, pages 1298–1308, Minneapolis, Minnesota. Association for Computational Linguistics.

A Appendix

A.1 Training details

We used pre-trained *bert-base-uncased* from HuggingFace models (Wolf et al., 2020) for both the main model training and the guidance model in SimReg↑. Trained for 5 epochs with batch size of 64, for better similarity estimation. For MNLI, QQP we used learning rate of $5e-5$ and $2e-5$ for FEVER, that warms up for 3k steps and decays linearly to 0. The reported results in the tables are the mean and standard deviation of 3 different random seeds. This is true also for competitive methods.

For computing the similarity, we use the mean token representation per layer as the representation of each layer, then we aggregate the similarities of the layers by summing them. We applied the similarity regularization on multiple layers. For increasing similarity we used the last 3 layers from f_g and the main model, following insights from Section A.2.

For decreasing similarity, f_g had a different architecture, we used a combination of layers that ranged across the models. for example, in FEVER claim bias we used first layer, middle layer and last two layers from both f_b and the main model.

As for the threshold c_t, we used 0.8 for unknown-bias experiments, for known bias we used 0.65 except for FEVER claim-bias where we used 0.8. With $\lambda = 100$ for SimReg↑ and $\lambda = 10$ for SimReg↓.

A.2 Layers

In the main experiments, we regularized multiple layers together, as described in Appendix A.1. Our choice of layers is based on Figure 3, where we performed SimReg↑ debiasing on Synthetic-MNLI across layers. The results indicate that deeper layers have the most effect on the debiasing, thus in our main experiments we choose layers 10-12 for regularization in SimReg↑. In decreasing representation similarity, individual layers are not effective, as opposed to regularizing multiple layers as in the main experiments. Thus we chose to regularize in a wide manner over multiple layers.

A.3 Synthetic Bias

In this section we present more detailed results for synthetic-MNLI. In Table 7 we show wider range of configuration for the case of increasing similarity. Note that higher λ values for resulted in models

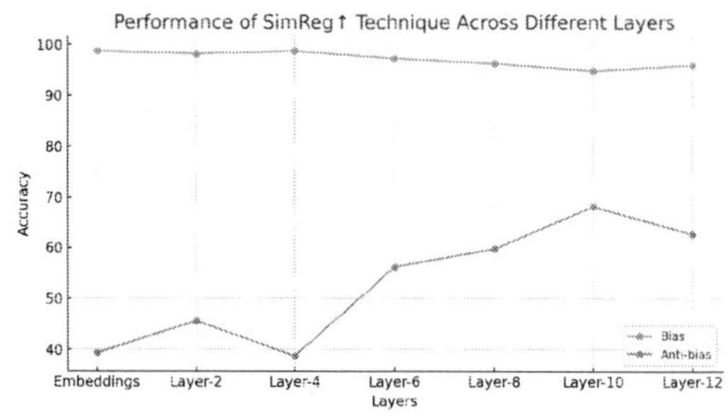

Figure 3: SimReg↑ on Synthetic-MNLI, regularizing one layer at a time.

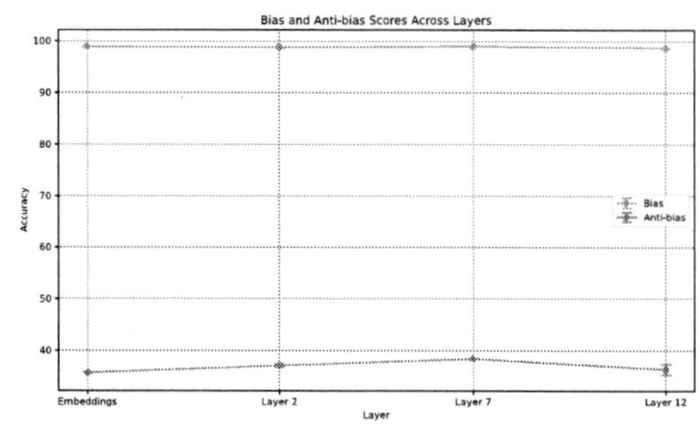

Figure 4: SimReg↓ on Synthetic-MNLI, regularizing one layer at a time.

with better performance on the anti-biased set. Bert-base is BERT trained on Synthetic-MNLI, while BERT (Oracle) is trained on MNLI. In Table 8 we present the case of decreasing similarity. Where we see that in this case, $\lambda = 10$ is a sweet spot, between not changing much ($\lambda = 1$) and changing to much to the level of collapse ($\lambda = 100$).

A.4 Threshold choosing

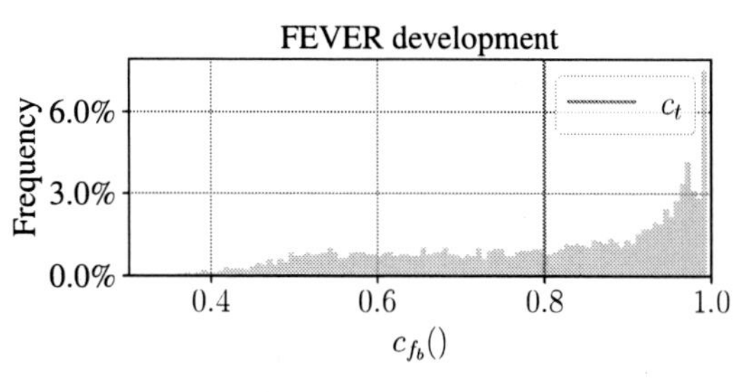

Figure 5: Confidence distribution of a claim-only model (f_b) on FEVER; here $c_t = 0.8$.

A.5 Bias recovery

In Table 9, we present an additional results of our bias-recovery experiments. Where we re-train the

	Biased	Anti-biased	Unbiased
Bert	98.5 ± 0.1	41.8 ± 1.1	78.0 ± 0.4
Oracle	83.5 ± 0.3	82.0 ± 0.9	84.0 ± 0.3
$\lambda = 1$	97.3 ± 0.0	57.7 ± 0.1	83.3 ± 0.2
$\lambda = 10$	96.8 ± 0.1	60.2 ± 0.4	83.6 ± 0.3
$\lambda = 100$	96.7 ± 0.1	61.0 ± 0.9	83.2 ± 0.2

Table 7: SimReg$\uparrow$: Synthetic-MNLI with prevalence=1 and strength=0.95.

Model	Biased	Anti-biased	Unbiased
Bert-base	98.5 ± 0.1	41.8 ± 1.1	78.0 ± 0.4
f_b	99.9	05.7	64.3
$\lambda = 1$	99.6 ± 0.1	12.2 ± 17.3	53.4 ± 25.6
$\lambda = 10$	96.8 ± 0.2	49.8 ± 2.3	72.4 ± 1.5
$\lambda = 100$	33.5 ± 1.6	32.3 ± 0.4	32.3 ± 1.7

Table 8: SimReg$\downarrow$: Synthetic-MNLI with prevalence=1 and strength=0.95.

classification layer of the model on the dataset, to test the amount of biased recovered when evaluating the re-trained classifier + model on the OOD challenge sets. Note that on MNLI we evaluate on the bias-misaligned subset of HANS (the non-entailment subset). For results of the models on these subsets before retraining, check Table 10.

We observe that SimReg$\uparrow$ generally retains high performance on challenge sets after re-training their classifier on the whole dataset $\mathcal{D}$ (with the spurious correlations).

A.6 HANS subsets

Table 10 contains the evaluation of debiasing methods on HANS subsets (non-entailment and entailment).

	IID	HANS -
BERT	83.9 ±0.1	30.1 ±1.3
ConfReg	84.5 ±0.1	7.0 ±2.7
POE	83.6 ±0.1	40.5 ±4.4
SimReg↑	84.0 ±0.1	**42.5 ±1.3**

(a) MNLI Lexical-overlap bias

	dev	FEVER-Sym.
BERT	85.4 ±0.1	58.2 ±0.1
ConfReg	82.1 ±0.4	59.5 ±2.0
POE	79.2 ±0.1	**61.1 ±1.9**
SimReg↑	83.2 ±0.3	60.7 ±0.2

(b) FEVER claim bias

	dev	MNLI-hard
BERT	83.9 ±0.1	76.9 ±0.2
ConfReg	84.5 ±0.2	77.4 ±0.1
POE	83.0 ±0.2	**79.3 ±0.1**
SimReg↑	83.0 ±0.3	79.1 ±0.4

(c) MNLI hypothesis bias

	dev	PAWS
BERT	88.4 ±0.1	28.2 ±2.2
ConfReg	88.0 ±0.1	33.42 ±1.9
POE	90.0 ±0.1	34.1 ±0.1
SimReg↑	90.6 ±0.1	**42.1 ±1.4**

(d) QQP lexical-overlap bias

Table 9: Bias recovery in known-bias settings.

	dev	ent.	non-ent.
BERT	84.2	99.1 ± 0.1	28.1 ± 2.0
f_g	83.0	86.0	55.4
PoE	83.2	77.7 ± 9.8	55.4 ± 7.2
ConfReg	84.3	72.3 ± 8.5	60.9 ± 6.6
$\mathcal{F}_{HANS}$	83.9	–	–
SimReg ↑	83.5	86.4 ± 2.3	54.6 ± 1.6
SimReg ↓	84.0	92.1 ± 0.8	44.8 ± 1.3

(a) Known-bias debiasing.

	dev	ent.	non-ent.
BERT	84.2	99.1 ± 0.1	28.1 ± 2.0
f_g	77.4	53.0 ± 11	75.2 ± 7.4
PoE	81.4	81.1	56.4
ConfReg	83.4	90.0 ± 3.7	36.3 ± 3.7
$\mathcal{F}_{BOW}$	83.0	94.4 ± 1.5	45.9 ± 1.2
SimReg ↑	81.9	78.0 ± 2.5	64.8 ± 1.1
SimReg ↓	82.9	85.6 ± 4.2	41.4 ± 2.5

(b) Unknown-bias debiasing.

Table 10: HANS subsets

Prior Knowledge-Guided Adversarial Training

Lis Kanashiro Pereira[1], Fei Cheng[2], Wan Jou She[3]
Masayuki Asahara[4], Ichiro Kobayashi[5]
[1]National Institute of Information and Communications Technology (NICT), Japan
[2]Kyoto University, Japan
[3]Kyoto Institute of Technology, Japan
[4]National Institute for Japanese Language and Linguistics (NINJAL), Japan
[5]Ochanomizu University, Japan
liskanashiro@nict.go.jp, feicheng@i.kyoto-u.ac.jp, wjs2004@kit.ac.jp
masayu-a@ninjal.ac.jp, koba@is.ocha.ac.jp

Abstract

We introduce a simple yet effective **P**rior **K**nowledge-**G**uided **ADV**ersarial Training (**PKG-ADV**) algorithm to improve adversarial training for natural language understanding. Our method simply utilizes task-specific label distribution to guide the training process. By prioritizing the use of prior knowledge of labels, we aim to generate more informative adversarial perturbations. We apply our model to several challenging temporal reasoning tasks. Our method enables a more reliable and controllable data training process than relying on randomized adversarial perturbation. Albeit simple, our method achieved significant improvements in these tasks. To facilitate further research, we will release the code and models.

1 Introduction

Class imbalance, a classification setting where one or multiple classes (minority classes) are considerably less frequent than others (majority classes), is a common yet challenging problem in natural language processing (NLP) (Henning et al., 2023). The uneven distribution of target categories often leads to lower performance for minority classes. Despite that, NLP research often overlooks the importance of incorporating methods for addressing it, and finding effective solutions remains an open research challenge (Henning et al., 2023). While deep learning models have been successful in various NLP tasks, they are sensitive to changes in the input data distribution.

We explore the use of adversarial training techniques to enhance model performance on such scenarios. More specifically, our proposed approach incorporates the knowledge of task-specific label distribution into the adversarial training process. Typically, the perturbation direction is chosen to mislead the model to flip the current model prediction away from the correct label. However, this strategy might not be optimal because it does not make use of the knowledge of task-specific label distribution during the training process. We hypothesize that such information might indicate which category a model is more likely to misclassify as another category. We focus on temporal reasoning tasks. These tasks are essential for NLP, for timing events, for estimating their duration, frequencies, ordering, etc. Due to the nature of the task, classes are highly imbalanced, as shown in Figure 1 and Table 2. Even the performance of recent large language models (LLMs), such as ChatGPT, is still underperformed by a large margin by simpler and smaller models such as BERT and RoBERTa (Yuan et al., 2023; Chan et al., 2024), indicating the inherent challenge of temporal reasoning tasks. For instance, on the TB-Dense dataset (Cassidy et al., 2014), due to the high label imbalance, the model might misclassify the samples with the true label “VAGUE” as “BEFORE” or "AFTER", as these labels occur more often in the dataset, as shown in Figure 1. Our model, PKG-ADV , can intentionally attack those vulnerable categories and learn how to better distinguish each label class, improving the model performance.

Our experimental results show that, despite its simplicity, our proposed model outperforms standard fine-tuning and a strong adversarial training method on several challenging temporal reasoning tasks. Moreover, our model can outperform ChatGPT-based models with a large gap. Our findings contribute to the understanding and improvement of adversarial training in NLP and can help enhance model performance in scenarios with imbalanced classes, such as temporal reasoning tasks.

2 Adversarial Training for NLP

Standard training objectives seek to learn a function (a classifier) $f(x;\theta) : x \rightarrow C$, parametrized by θ, where C is the class label set. Given a training dataset D of input-output pairs (x, y)

Proceedings of the 9th Workshop on Representation Learning for NLP (RepL4NLP-2024), pages 51–57
August 15, 2024 ©2024 Association for Computational Linguistics

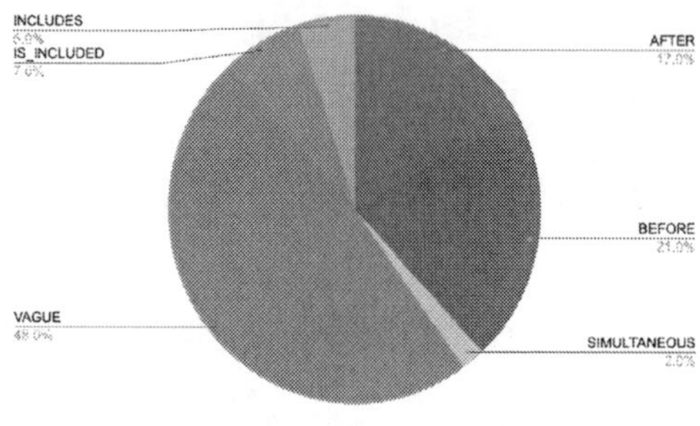

(a) Label Distribution (Train Set)

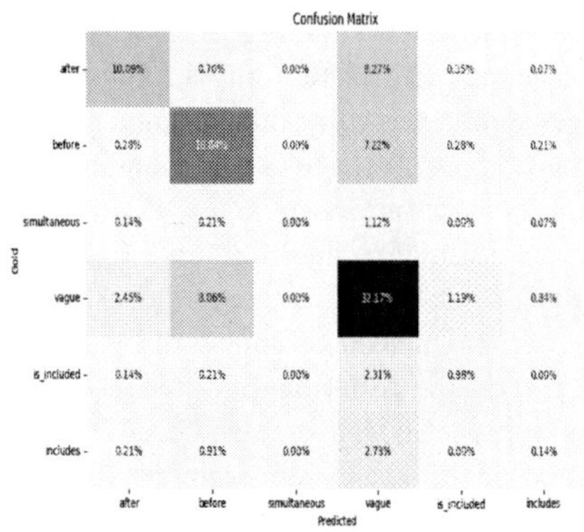

(b) RoBERTa with Standard Fine-Tuning

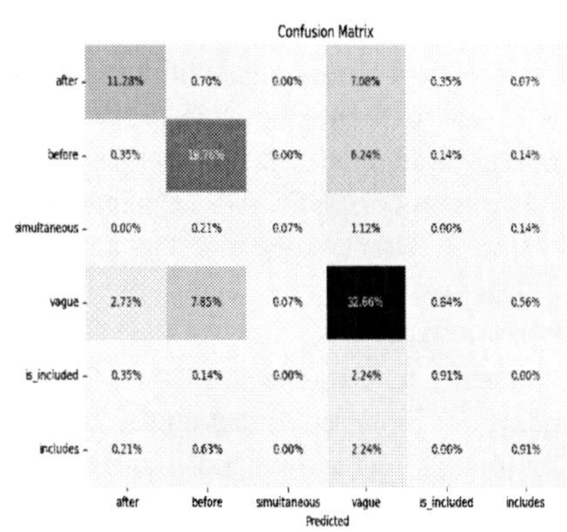

(c) RoBERTa with PKG-ADV Fine-Tuning

Figure 1: a) Label distribution from the TB-Dense (Cassidy et al., 2014) training dataset. b) Confusion matrix obtained after training on the RoBERTa_BASE model. c) Confusion matrix obtained after training on the RoBERTa_BASE model with the PKG-ADV algorithm. X-axis and Y-axis represent the predicted and gold labels, respectively.

and the loss function $l(.,.)$ (e.g., cross entropy), $f(x;\theta)$ is trained to minimize the empirical risk: $\min_\theta \mathbb{E}_{(x,y)\sim D}[l(f(x;\theta),y)]$. While this is effective in training a classifier, it usually suffers from overfitting and poor generalization to unseen cases. Recently, adversarial training has been proven effective in several tasks in nlp (Zhu et al., 2019; Jiang et al., 2019; Pereira et al., 2020). The standard approach is to add the adversarial perturbation to the embeddings. The input is augmented with a small perturbation that maximizes the adversarial loss:

$$\min_\theta \mathbb{E}_{(x,y)\sim D}[\max_\delta l(f(x+\delta;\theta),y)],$$

where the inner maximization can be solved by projected gradient descent (Madry et al., 2017). More recent approaches have explored adding the perturbation to other layers of the model (Pereira et al., 2021). Although these adversarial training algorithms substantially enhance model performance and generalization, such methods adopt *non-targeted* attacks, where the model prediction is not driven towards a specific incorrect label, i.e., such attacks lack a specific target. This might not be optimal, since many natural language processing (NLP) tasks are naturally imbalanced, as some labels occur much more frequently than others. In Figure 1, we illustrate this typical label imbalance scenario with the MATRES dataset (Ning et al., 2018a). Thus, there are consistently classes where the trained classifier may exhibit a higher error rate. This information can highlight the models' weaknesses. Our goal is to incorporate this prior knowledge to enhance model performance.

3 Prior Knowledge Guided Adversarial Training

In our work, we propose to enhance the ALICE (Pereira et al., 2020) algorithm. ALICE is an adversarial training algorithm that combines the two approaches to estimate the perturbation δ: one that uses the label y (Zhu et al., 2019) and another that uses the model prediction $f(x;\theta)$, i.e., a "virtual" label (Miyato et al., 2018; Jiang et al., 2019). The first goal is to improve the robustness of our target label by preventing an increase in error for unperturbed inputs. The second goal is to enforce model smoothness, ensuring the model's output does not change significantly when a small perturbation is injected to the input. The formula of ALICE is shown below:

Algorithm 1 PKG-ADV : We explore incorporating the knowledge of task-specific label distribution into the adversarial training process. The two lines in blue color are the only changes from ALICE.

Input: T: the total number of iterations, $\mathcal{X} = \{(x_1, y_1), \ldots, (x_n, y_n)\}$: the dataset, $f(x;\theta)$: the machine learning model parametrized by θ, σ^2: the variance of the random initialization of perturbation δ_1 and δ_2, δ_{1_r} and δ_{2_r}: the perturbations added to the embedding vector, ϵ: perturbation bound, K: the number of iterations for perturbation estimation, η: the step size for updating perturbation, τ: the global learning rate, α: the smoothing proportion of adversarial training in the augmented learning objective, Π: the projection operation and C: the classes.

1: **for** $t = 1, .., T$ **do**
2:   **for** $(x, y) \in \mathcal{X}$ **do**
3:     $\delta_1 \sim \mathcal{N}(0, \sigma^2 I)$
4:     $\delta_2 \sim \mathcal{N}(0, \sigma^2 I)$
5:     $y_t = sample(C_{\setminus y})$
6:     **for** $m = 1, .., K$ **do**
7:       $g_{adv} \leftarrow \nabla_{\delta_1} l(f(x + \delta_1; \theta), y_t)$
8:       $\delta_1 \leftarrow \Pi_{\|\delta_1\|_\infty \leq \epsilon}(\delta_1 - \eta g_{adv})$
9:       $g_{adv} \leftarrow \nabla_{\delta_2} l(f(x + \delta_2; \theta), f(x; \theta))$
10:       $\delta_2 \leftarrow \Pi_{\|\delta_2\|_\infty \leq \epsilon}(\delta_2 + \eta g_{adv})$
11:     **end for**
12:     $g_\theta \leftarrow \nabla_\theta l(f(x + \delta_1; \theta), y) + \alpha \nabla_\theta l(f(x + \delta_2; \theta), f(x; \theta))$
13:     $\theta \leftarrow \theta - \tau g_\theta$
14:   **end for**
15: **end for**

Output: θ

$$\min_\theta \mathbb{E}_{(x,y)\sim D}[\max_{\delta_1} l(f(x + \delta_1; \theta), y) + \alpha \max_{\delta_2} l(f(x + \delta_2; \theta), f(x; \theta))], \quad (1)$$

where δ_1 and δ_2 are two different perturbations, bounded by a general l_p norm ball, estimated by a fixed K steps of the gradient-based optimization approach and $p = \infty$. Effectively, the second term encourages smoothness in the input neighborhood, and α is a hyperparameter that controls the trade-off between standard errors and adversarial errors. ALICE has been originally applied for the commonsense reasoning task, however, it is a general algorithm that can be applied to other tasks as well.

We enhance ALICE by modifying the first term of Equation 1, to improve the robustness of our target label. PKG-ADV first samples a label from the class label set (excluding the correct label). This label class is sampled with a probability proportional to its frequency in the training dataset. Intuitively, we would like to focus training on prior knowledge at hand. This knowledge consists of the dataset label information, generated offline.

More specifically, PKG-ADV explicitly picks a target $y_t \neq y$ and tries to steer the model towards y_t. We accomplish this by sampling y_t from $C_{\setminus y} = C - \{y\}$ in proportion to the dataset label distribution. PKG-ADV can flexibly use different prior knowledge, i.e. the dataset label information, as shown in line 5. Then the adversarial sample is estimated by the opposite direction as in line 8. The two lines in blue color are the only changes from ALICE. At last, following Jiang et al. (2019) and Miyato et al. (2018), the adversarial regularizer is added to the standard training objective (e.g., cross-entropy between the correct label and prediction). The algorithm of PKG-ADV is depicted in Algorithm 1.

4 Experiments

We compare PKG-ADV with ALICE (Pereira et al., 2020), a strong adversarial training baseline, and several state-of-the-art temporal reasoning models. We use the standard uncased RoBERTa$_{\text{BASE}}$ model (Liu et al., 2019b) as the text encoder, unless noted otherwise.

4.1 Datasets and Evaluation Metrics

We evaluated our model on the following tasks: temporal ordering prediction task, event duration prediction, and temporal commonsense reasoning. We used the following datasets, respectively: MATRES (Ning et al., 2018b), TimeML (Pan et al., 2006), MC-TACO (Ben Zhou and Roth, 2019), TB-Dense (Cassidy et al., 2014), and MAVEN-ERE (Wang et al., 2022). Details of each dataset are in Appendix A. We evaluate the performance of MATRES and MAVEN-ERE in terms of accuracy and F1-score, and TimeML in terms of accuracy. For the MC-TACO and TB-Dense datasets, we report F1 scores.

4.2 Implementation Details

Our model implementation is based on the MT-DNN framework (Liu et al., 2019a, 2020). We use RoBERTa$_{\text{BASE}}$ (Liu et al., 2019b) as the text encoder. RoBERTa remains a competitive pre-trained model for its size among NLP practitioners. We used ADAM (Kingma and Ba, 2014) as our optimizer with a learning rate in the range $\in \{9 \times 10^{-6}, 1 \times 10^{-5}\}$ and a batch size in the range $\in \{16, 32, 64\}$. The maximum number of epochs was set to 10. A linear learning rate decay schedule with warm-up over 0.1 was used unless stated otherwise. To avoid gradient exploding, we

Model	TimeML	MC-TACO	MATRES		TB-Dense	MAVEN-ERE	
	Acc	F1	Acc	F1	F1	Acc	F1
Standard (RoBERTa$_{BASE}$)	81.46	80.84	72.88	47.83	62.02	76.43	31.68
ALICE (RoBERTa$_{BASE}$)	83.15	82.59	71.57	47.02	63.49	77.06	31.27
Multi-Task (ALBERT-xxlarge) (Kimura et al., 2022)	81.10	80.30	**77.20**	-	-	-	-
ChatGPT (Bian et al., 2023)	-	46.79	-	-	-	-	-
ChatGPT_Prompt (Chan et al., 2024)	-	-	-	35.00	23.30	-	-
ChatGPT_PE (Chan et al., 2024)	-	-	-	27.00	47.90	-	-
ChatGPT_ICL (Chan et al., 2024)	-	-		25.00	44.90	-	-
PKG-ADV (RoBERTa$_{BASE}$)	**84.75**	**83.01**	73.00	**49.93**	**65.59**	**78.09**	**32.06**

Table 1: Test results. The best results are in **bold**. Standard denotes the standard fine-tuning procedure where we fine-tune RoBERTa on each task specific temporal reasoning dataset. PKG-ADV denotes our proposed models. Note that Standard, ALICE, and PKG-ADV models use RoBERTa$_{BASE}$ as the text encoder unless stated otherwise, and for a fair comparison, all these results are produced by ourselves.

clipped the gradient norm within 1. All the texts were tokenized using WordPiece and were chopped to spans no longer than 512 tokens. We also set the dropout rate of all the task-specific layers as 0.3. During adversarial training, we follow Jiang et al. (2019) and set the perturbation size to 1×10^{-5}, the step size to 1×10^{-3}, and to 1×10^{-5} the variance for initializing perturbation. We search the regularization weight α in $\{0.01, 0.1, 1\}$. We set the number of projected gradient steps to 1.

4.3 Main Results

We present our results in Table 1. We compare our model, PKG-ADV , with ALICE and other temporal reasoning models. Overall, the adversarial methods, ALICE and PKG-ADV , were able to outperform the standard fine-tuning approach (Standard) and the other baselines, without using any additional knowledge source, and without using any additional datasets other than the target task datasets. Overall, PKG-ADV was able to outperform the other baselines. Kimura et al. (2022) trains an ALBERT XXLarge v2 model using multi-task learning with several additional temporal datasets. Note that ALBERT XXLarge v2 is around 2x larger than the RoBERTa_BASE model. Except on the MATRES dataset, our PKG-ADV model trained on RoBERTa_BASE can outperform their model, without using any additional dataset. Bian et al. (2023) and Chan et al. (2024) use zero-shot inference and designs prompt templates for different datasets in the ChatGPT and ChatGPT_Prompt baselines. In the ChatGPT_PE baseline, Chan et al. (2024) manually designed a more sophisticated prompt template based on the expert understanding. The ChatGPT_ICL baseline refers to the in-context learning approach (Brown et al., 2020), where a number of input-output exemplars for the prompt were manually selected. We observe that still there is a considerable gap between these models and that of supervised methods. Chan et al. (2024) hypothesizes that the poor performance of ChatGPT might be attributed to inadequate human feedback during the model's training process on temporal features.

5 Conclusion

We have presented a Prior Knowledge Guided Adversarial Training (PKG-ADV) algorithm to improve adversarial training for natural language understanding. Albeit simple and drawn from a simple observation (label imbalance, common in most nlp tasks), incorporating task-specific label distribution into the training process for generating better adversarial perturbations has not yet been explored in the literature. PKG-ADV overall shows superior performance compared to standard fine-tuning, strong adversarial training baselines, and ChatGPT-based baselines. PKG-ADV can be applied to other language models as well by incorporating label distribution information. Other types of knowledge, such as annotator agreement data, might help further enhance the performance, and we leave this for future work.

6 Limitations and Ethical Statement

Although our method is task, model, and language-agnostic, we have conducted experiments only on English classification benchmarks, and using only the RoBERTa model. We focus on sentence-level tasks at this time. Although we focused on temporal reasoning tasks, our model can be generalized to other tasks as well. We plan to expand the scope of the experiments in the future. In our work, we have only used publicly available datasets in our experiments, ensuring that there are no privacy concerns or violations.

Acknowledgments

We thank the reviewers for their helpful feedback. This work has been supported by the project KAKENHI ID: 21K17802.

References

Collin F Baker, Charles J Fillmore, and John B Lowe. 1998. The berkeley framenet project. In *COLING 1998 Volume 1: The 17th International Conference on Computational Linguistics*.

Qiang Ning Ben Zhou, Daniel Khashabi and Dan Roth. 2019. "going on a vacation" takes longer than "going for a walk": A study of temporal commonsense understanding. In *EMNLP*.

Ning Bian, Xianpei Han, Le Sun, Hongyu Lin, Yaojie Lu, and Ben He. 2023. Chatgpt is a knowledgeable but inexperienced solver: An investigation of commonsense problem in large language models. *arXiv preprint arXiv:2303.16421*.

Tom Brown, Benjamin Mann, Nick Ryder, Melanie Subbiah, Jared D Kaplan, Prafulla Dhariwal, Arvind Neelakantan, Pranav Shyam, Girish Sastry, Amanda Askell, et al. 2020. Language models are few-shot learners. *Advances in neural information processing systems*, 33:1877–1901.

Taylor Cassidy, Bill McDowell, Nathanael Chambers, and Steven Bethard. 2014. An annotation framework for dense event ordering. In *Proceedings of the 52nd Annual Meeting of the Association for Computational Linguistics (Volume 2: Short Papers)*, pages 501–506, Baltimore, Maryland. Association for Computational Linguistics.

Chunkit Chan, Cheng Jiayang, Weiqi Wang, Yuxin Jiang, Tianqing Fang, Xin Liu, and Yangqiu Song. 2024. Exploring the potential of ChatGPT on sentence level relations: A focus on temporal, causal, and discourse relations. In *Findings of the Association for Computational Linguistics: EACL 2024*, pages 684–721, St. Julian's, Malta. Association for Computational Linguistics.

Sophie Henning, William Beluch, Alexander Fraser, and Annemarie Friedrich. 2023. A survey of methods for addressing class imbalance in deep-learning based natural language processing. In *Proceedings of the 17th Conference of the European Chapter of the Association for Computational Linguistics*, pages 523–540, Dubrovnik, Croatia. Association for Computational Linguistics.

Haoming Jiang, Pengcheng He, Weizhu Chen, Xiaodong Liu, Jianfeng Gao, and Tuo Zhao. 2019. Smart: Robust and efficient fine-tuning for pretrained natural language models through principled regularized optimization. *arXiv preprint arXiv:1911.03437*.

Mayuko Kimura, Lis Kanashiro Pereira, and Ichiro Kobayashi. 2022. Toward building a language model for understanding temporal commonsense. In *Proceedings of the 2nd Conference of the Asia-Pacific Chapter of the Association for Computational Linguistics and the 12th International Joint Conference on Natural Language Processing: Student Research Workshop*, pages 17–24, Online. Association for Computational Linguistics.

Diederik Kingma and Jimmy Ba. 2014. Adam: A method for stochastic optimization. *arXiv preprint arXiv:1412.6980*.

Xiaodong Liu, Pengcheng He, Weizhu Chen, and Jianfeng Gao. 2019a. Multi-task deep neural networks for natural language understanding. *Proceedings of the 57th Annual Meeting of the Association for Computational Linguistics*, pages 4487–4496.

Xiaodong Liu, Yu Wang, Jianshu Ji, Hao Cheng, Xueyun Zhu, Emmanuel Awa, Pengcheng He, Weizhu Chen, Hoifung Poon, Guihong Cao, and Jianfeng Gao. 2020. The microsoft toolkit of multi-task deep neural networks for natural language understanding. *arXiv preprint arXiv:2002.07972*.

Yinhan Liu, Myle Ott, Naman Goyal, Jingfei Du, Mandar Joshi, Danqi Chen, Omer Levy, Mike Lewis, Luke Zettlemoyer, and Veselin Stoyanov. 2019b. Roberta: A robustly optimized bert pretraining approach. *arXiv preprint arXiv:1907.11692*.

Aleksander Madry, Aleksandar Makelov, Ludwig Schmidt, Dimitris Tsipras, and Adrian Vladu. 2017. Towards deep learning models resistant to adversarial attacks. *arXiv preprint arXiv:1706.06083*.

Takeru Miyato, Shin-ichi Maeda, Masanori Koyama, and Shin Ishii. 2018. Virtual adversarial training: a regularization method for supervised and semi-supervised learning. *IEEE transactions on pattern analysis and machine intelligence*, 41(8):1979–1993.

Qiang Ning, Hao Wu, and Dan Roth. 2018a. A multi-axis annotation scheme for event temporal relations. In *arXiv preprint arXiv:1804.07828*.

Qiang Ning, Hao Wu, and Dan Roth. 2018b. A multi-axis annotation scheme for event temporal relations. In *ACL*.

Feng Pan, Rutu Mulkar-Mehta, and Jerry R Hobbs. 2006. Extending timeml with typical durations of events. In *Proceedings of the Workshop on Annotating and Reasoning about Time and Events*, pages 38–45.

Lis Pereira, Xiaodong Liu, Fei Cheng, Masayuki Asahara, and Ichiro Kobayashi. 2020. Adversarial training for commonsense inference. *arXiv preprint arXiv:2005.08156*.

Lis Kanashiro Pereira, Yuki Taya, and Ichiro Kobayashi. 2021. Multi-layer random perturbation training for improving model generalization efficiently. In *Proceedings of the Fourth BlackboxNLP Workshop on Analyzing and Interpreting Neural Networks for NLP*, pages 303–310, Punta Cana, Dominican Republic. Association for Computational Linguistics.

James Pustejovsky, Patrick Hanks, Roser Sauri, Andrew See, Robert Gaizauskas, Andrea Setzer, Dragomir Radev, Beth Sundheim, David Day, Lisa Ferro, et al. 2003. The timebank corpus. In *Corpus linguistics*, volume 2003, page 40. Lancaster, UK.

Naushad UzZaman, Hector Llorens, Leon Derczynski, James Allen, Marc Verhagen, and James Pustejovsky. 2013. SemEval-2013 task 1: TempEval-3: Evaluating time expressions, events, and temporal relations. In *Second Joint Conference on Lexical and Computational Semantics (*SEM), Volume 2: Proceedings of the Seventh International Workshop on Semantic Evaluation (SemEval 2013)*, pages 1–9, Atlanta, Georgia, USA. Association for Computational Linguistics.

Xiaozhi Wang, Yulin Chen, Ning Ding, Hao Peng, Zimu Wang, Yankai Lin, Xu Han, Lei Hou, Juanzi Li, Zhiyuan Liu, et al. 2022. Maven-ere: A unified large-scale dataset for event coreference, temporal, causal, and subevent relation extraction. *arXiv preprint arXiv:2211.07342*.

Chenhan Yuan, Qianqian Xie, and Sophia Ananiadou. 2023. Zero-shot temporal relation extraction with ChatGPT. In *The 22nd Workshop on Biomedical Natural Language Processing and BioNLP Shared Tasks*, pages 92–102, Toronto, Canada. Association for Computational Linguistics.

Chen Zhu, Yu Cheng, Zhe Gan, Siqi Sun, Thomas Goldstein, and Jingjing Liu. 2019. Freelb: Enhanced adversarial training for language understanding. *arXiv preprint arXiv:1909.11764*.

A Evaluation Datasets

TimeML (Pan et al., 2006): This task involves predicting whether a given event has a duration longer or shorter than a day.

TB-Dense (Cassidy et al., 2014): TB-Dense is a public benchmark for temporal relation extraction (TRE). It was annotated from TimeBank (Pustejovsky et al., 2003) and TempEval (UzZaman et al., 2013). Given a passage and two event points, the task is to classify the relations between events into one of 6 types: BEFORE, AFTER, SIMULTANEOUS, VAGUE, IS_INCLUDED, and INCLUDES. An example of a sentence with two events, e1 and e2 (in bold) that hold the SIMULTANEOUS relation is shown below:

> Nobody **(e1:hurried)** her up. No one **(e2:held)** her back.

MATRES (Ning et al., 2018b): This dataset was annotated from TimeBank (Pustejovsky et al., 2003), AQUAINT, and Platinum documents. The task involves predicting the temporal relation between a pair of input events in a span of text. It originally contains 13,577 pairs of events annotated with a temporal relation (BEFORE, AFTER, EQUAL, VAGUE). The relations named EQUAL and VAGUE are equivalent to SIMULTANEOUS and NONE in TB-Dense. An example of a sentence with two events, e1 and e2 (in bold) that hold the BEFORE relation is shown below:

> At one point , when it **(e1:became)** clear controllers could not contact the plane, someone **(e2:said)** a prayer.

MC-TACO (Ben Zhou and Roth, 2019): This task entirely focuses on temporal commonsense reasoning. It considers five temporal properties, (1) duration (how long an event takes), (2) temporal ordering (typical order of events), (3) typical time (when an event occurs), (4) frequency (how often an event occurs), and (5) stationarity (whether a state is maintained for a very long time or indefinitely). It contains 13k tuples, each consisting of a sentence, a question, and a candidate answer, that should be judged as plausible or not. An example from the dataset is below. The correct answer is in **bold**.

> *Paragraph*: Carl Laemmle, head of Universal Studios, gave Einstein a tour of his studio and introduced him to Chaplin.
>
> *Question*: How long did the tour last?
>
> a) 9 hours
>
> b) **45 minutes**
>
> c) 15 days
>
> d) 5 seconds

MAVEN-ERE (Wang et al., 2022): This is a unified large-scale human-annotated event relation extraction dataset. It was annotated at the document level from Wikipedia and FrameNet (Baker et al., 1998), for four tasks: event coreference, temporal, causal, and subevent relations. In our work, we focus on the sentence level temporal event pair relations. Given a passage and two event points, the task is to classify the relations between

Dataset	#Train	#Test	#Label	Label Distribution		Metrics
				Train	Test	
TimeML	1,248	1,003	2	yes: 789, no: 459	yes: 610, no: 393	Accuracy
MC-TACO	3,783	9,442	2	yes: 1,229, no: 2,554	yes: 3,198, no: 6,244	F1-Score
TB-Dense	4,177	1,426	6	VAGUE: 2015, BEFORE: 885, AFTER: 730, IS_INCLUDED: 275, INCLUDES: 209, SIMULTANEOUS: 63	VAGUE: 638, BEFORE: 380, AFTER: 278, IS_INCLUDED: 52, INCLUDES: 57, SIMULTANEOUS: 22	F1-Score
MATRES	12,740	837	4	BEFORE: 6,425, AFTER: 1,416, VAGUE: 4,481, OVERLAP: 418	BEFORE: 427, AFTER: 271, VAGUE: 30, OVERLAP: 109	Accuracy & F1-score
MAVEN-ERE	44,586	10,488	6	BEFORE: 35273, CONTAINS: 5204, SIMULTANEOUS: 2392, OVERLAP: 1605, BEGINS-ON: 58, ENDS-ON: 54	BEFORE: 8092, CONTAINS: 1426, SIMULTANEOUS: 609, OVERLAP: 346, BEGINS-ON: 6, ENDS-ON: 9	Accuracy & F1-score

Table 2: Summary of the English evaluation datasets.

events into one of 6 types: BEFORE, SIMULTANEOUS, CONTAINS, OVERLAP, ENDS-ON, and BEGINS-ON. Despite its larger size, the authors highlight that the label distribution in the dataset is severely unbalanced, but decided to keep the unbalanced distribution so that the dataset reflects the real-world data distribution (Wang et al., 2022). An example of a sentence with two events, e1 and e2 (in bold) that hold the BEFORE relation is shown below:

> It (**e1: turned**) again to 270 then began an abnormal (**e2: descent**).

IT-Tuning : Parameter Efficient Information Token Tuning for Language Model

Jungu Kim, Hyeoncheol Kim*
Department of of Computer Science and Engineering, Korea University
{antonio97k, harrykim}@korea.ac.kr

Abstract

Recently, language models have demonstrated exceptional performance compared to their predecessors. In this context, attention mechanisms and pre-training significantly contribute to the enhanced performance of modern language models. Additionally, a continuously increasing number of parameters plays a crucial role in these advancements. However, an increase in the number of parameters significantly increases the GPU memory and training time required during fine-tuning of language models, this makes fine-tuning infeasible in environments with limited computing resources. Furthermore, after fine-tuning, the storage space required for deployment increases proportionally with the number of tasks, making it challenging to deploy devices with limited storage capacities. In this study, we propose IT-Tuning, a Parameter Efficient Fine-Tuning method that introduces a new concept called information tokens to address these issues.

1 Introduction

Since the introduction of Transformer(Vaswani et al., 2017) and BERT(Devlin et al., 2019), recent Transformer based pre-trained language models have achieved unprecedented performance, coinciding with an increase in the number of parameters.(Kaplan et al., 2020; Brown et al., 2020; Chowdhery et al., 2024; Touvron et al., 2023) Consequently, research on various applications, such as sentiment analysis, question answering, sentence classification, summarization, and machine translation, has been actively conducted. Although pre-trained language models can be utilized in various tasks using only prompts without fine-tuning, as demonstrated by approaches such as chain-of-thought prompting(Wei et al., 2022) or in-context learning(Dong et al., 2022), fine-tuning often leads to better performance. However, recently introduced language models have billions to tens of billions of parameters(Zhao et al., 2023), resulting in increased GPU memory and extended training time requirements during fine-tuning. In addition, deploying these models after fine-tuning across various tasks requires significant storage space proportional to the size of the model and the number of tasks, which poses a challenge.

In this context, we introduce a new concept called "information token" to address this issue. The information token attends to all tokens within the input sentence during the attention mechanism process, selectively condensing the information of the sentence according to the task and delivering it to the input and output sentences, enabling efficient fine-tuning. Based on these information tokens, we propose a new Parameter Efficient Fine-Tuning (PEFT) method called IT-Tuning, the contributions of which are as follows:

1. We introduce a new concept called information tokens to efficiently fine-tune language models and demonstrate experimental methods to adjust them more efficiently within the model.

2. Using only 0.04% of the total parameters, which is five times less than LoRA(Hu et al., 2021), we surpass LoRA and full fine-tuning in the General Language Understanding Evaluation (GLUE) benchmark(Wang et al., 2018), demonstrating efficiency in Natural Language Understanding (NLU) tasks.

3. We have achieved performance surpassing that of full fine-tuning, Prefix Tuning(Li and Liang, 2021), and LoRA using only 0.09% of the total number of parameters in Natural Language Generation (NLG) tasks, as demonstrated through experiments on the End-to-End Natural Language Generation Challenge (E2E NLG Challenge) dataset(Dušek et al., 2020).

Proceedings of the 9th Workshop on Representation Learning for NLP (RepL4NLP-2024), pages 58–68
August 15, 2024 ©2024 Association for Computational Linguistics

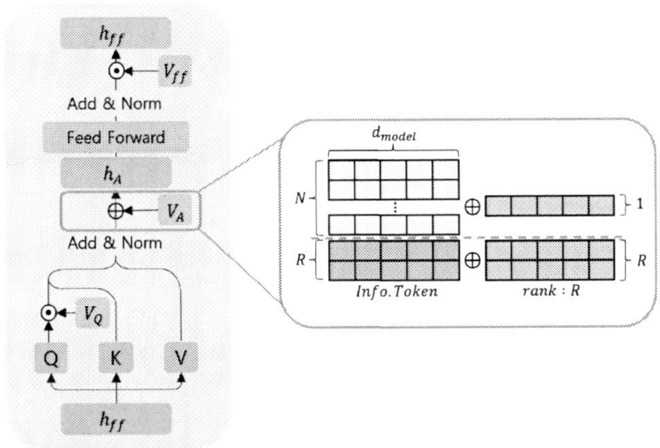

Figure 1: This is the overall architecture of IT-Tuning. As shown in the figure, we perform shifting or scaling after the query vector, the output of the attention, and the feed-forward layer. Additionally, the yellow and red vectors within the green box respectively denote the hidden states of all tokens of the input sentence and the information tokens. N and R(rank) represent the length of the input sentence and the number of additional information tokens. Inside the model, we scale or shift all tokens of the input sentence excluding the information tokens using a single vector to assist the role of information tokens described in Section 3.2. For information tokens, we adjusted each using an equal number of vectors.

2 Related Works

Recently, extensive research has been conducted on PEFT, achieving a performance equivalent to that of full fine-tuning using only 0.1% of the total model parameters.(Hu et al., 2021; Li and Liang, 2021; Liu et al., 2022a; Yang et al., 2023) This approach significantly reduces the size of the GPU memory and training time required. Furthermore, because PEFT requires only a few additional parameters to be stored when a single model is used for various tasks, it saves storage space. In this section, we describe the research on PEFT conducted to date.

Adapter It is a method of inserting multiple adapter modules (MLP modules) into the layers of a language model. Research has continued extensively after the Adapter(Houlsby et al., 2019), and recent studies such as AdapterBias(Fu et al., 2022) and AdaMix(Wang et al., 2022) have significantly improved performance by modifying the structure of the adapter module or proposing the Mixture-of-Adaptation method. Furthermore, adapter-based PEFT methods can adjust the number of parameters used in training by altering the number of parameters in the adapter module, making them applicable to both NLU and NLG tasks.

Trainable Prompt This method involves adding trainable tokens to sentences, with prominent examples of P-Tuning v1 and v2(Liu et al., 2022b, 2021), Prefix Tuning(Li and Liang, 2021), and Prompt Tuning(Lester et al., 2021) . These studies aimed to address the performance gap observed when using sentence-form prompts (discrete prompts) compared with fine-tuned language models by incorporating trainable tokens through fine-tuning rather than nontrainable sentence-form prompts. These studies have demonstrated results achieving equivalent performance to full fine-tuning in NLG(Li and Liang, 2021) tasks and NLU(Liu et al., 2022b, 2021; Lester et al., 2021) tasks.

Low-Rank PEFT methodologies based on low-rank, such as LoRA(Hu et al., 2021) and HiWi(Liao et al., 2023), are gaining attention owing to their robust performance and capability to mitigate the issue of increased inference times associated with additional parameters. However, one of the significant advantages of PEFT is its ability to switch tasks in a multitasking environment, which is compromised by combining model parameters and low-rank parameters to mitigate the increase in inference time. Additionally, there are studies such as $(IA)^3$(Liu et al., 2022a) that achieve better performance with fewer parameters than LoRA in some tasks. Nonetheless, LoRA has proven to be a robust method that is effective in both NLU and NLG tasks. Therefore, we conducted experiments using the LoRA as the baseline.

Direct Update This method directly adjusts the hidden states of the model using the added vectors.

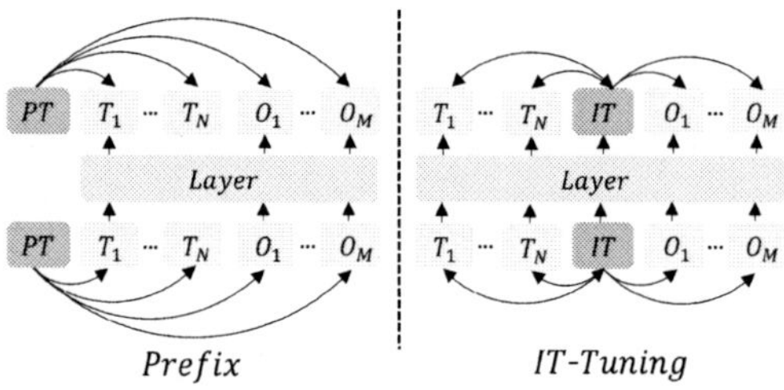

Figure 2: This illustrates the difference in attention mechanisms between Prefix Tuning(Li and Liang, 2021) and IT-Tuning. PT represents additional tokens in Prefix Tuning, IT represents information tokens. The arrows indicate which tokens attend to which tokens.

For PASTA(Yang et al., 2023), only the hidden states of special tokens, such as [CLS] and [SEP], were updated at each layer of the model, resulting in an additional parameter number of 0.02% (0.07M) based on RoBERTa-large(Liu et al., 2019), while achieving a performance equivalent to LoRA on the GLUE dataset. Furthermore, (IA)^3(Liu et al., 2022a) scales only the key and value of the attention operation and the internal parameters of the feed-forward network in each layer, surpassing LoRA in limited-data settings. However, although these approaches are structurally efficient, their inability to adjust the number of trainable parameters renders them unsuitable for tasks requiring more parameters than NLU, such as NLG. IT-Tuning exhibits structural efficiency akin to that observed in two referenced studies. However, by addressing the limitations associated with parameter adjustments through the introduction of information tokens, it also demonstrates applicability to NLG tasks .

3 IT-Tuning

3.1 Model Architecture

Figure 1 illustrates the model structure of IT-Tuning. Our IT-Tuning employs a method that updates the selected tokens using additional parameters. We refer to these selected tokens as information tokens and introduce this concept in Section 3.2. Furthermore, we introduce an efficient structure to enable the efficient update of information tokens within the model in Section 3.3. The operational process of IT-Tuning within the model can be mathematically represented as follows:

$$\begin{aligned} h_Q &= [h_Q^{input} \odot V_Q^1; h_Q^{it} \odot V_Q^2] \\ h_A &= [h_A^{input} \oplus V_A^1; h_A^{it} \oplus V_A^2] \\ h_{ff} &= [h_{ff}^{input} \odot V_{ff}^1; h_{ff}^{it} \odot V_{ff}^2] \end{aligned} \quad (1)$$

In Equation 1, $h_Q, h_A, h_{ff} \in \mathbb{R}^{d_{model} \times (N+R)}$ represent the hidden state of the query vector and output of the attention and feedforward layer containing information tokens, respectively. $h_Q^{input}, h_A^{input}, h_{ff}^{input} \in \mathbb{R}^{d_{model} \times N}$ represent the inputs of the model, excluding the information tokens, and $h_Q^{it}, h_A^{it}, h_{ff}^{it} \in \mathbb{R}^{d_{model} \times R}$ represent the hidden states of the information tokens $V_Q^1, V_A^1, V_{ff}^1 \in \mathbb{R}^{d_{model}}$ are vectors added to efficiently fine-tune the input tokens, excluding the information tokens; $V_Q^2, V_A^2, V_{ff}^2 \in \mathbb{R}^{d_{model} \times R}$ represent vectors added to efficiently fine-tune the information tokens.

During our experimentation process, we examined the magnitude of backpropagated gradients through learning for scaling vectors V_Q, V_{ff}, as well as for shifting vector V_A. We discovered that the magnitude of gradients for the vectors for scaling, V_Q, V_{ff}, was significantly smaller than the gradients for the vector for shifting, V_A, across all layers. To address this issue, similar to LoRA+(Hayou et al., 2024), we varied the learning rate applied to each vector. To achieve this, we introduced a new parameter, $\alpha \geq 1$, where the magnitude of the learning rate applied to V_Q, V_{ff} is determined based on the value of α. This can be represented mathematically as follows:.

$$\begin{aligned} V_Q &= V_Q - \alpha\eta \times G_{V_Q} \\ V_{ff} &= V_{ff} - \alpha\eta \times G_{V_{ff}} \end{aligned} \quad (2)$$

In equation 2, η represents the learning rate, and G denotes the gradients for each vector.

3.2 Information Token

In this study, we introduce the concept of Information Tokens. Information Tokens are tokens selected or added within a sentence for efficient fine-tuning and are updated by individual vectors. Figure 2 illustrates the differences between the Prefix Tuning(Li and Liang, 2021) and IT-Tuning. As shown on the left side of Figure 2, Prefix Tuning adjusts the tokens added to the beginning of the input according to the task and updates both the input and output by attending to the tokens added within the input sentence. However, the tokens added at the beginning of the input cannot attend to the tokens

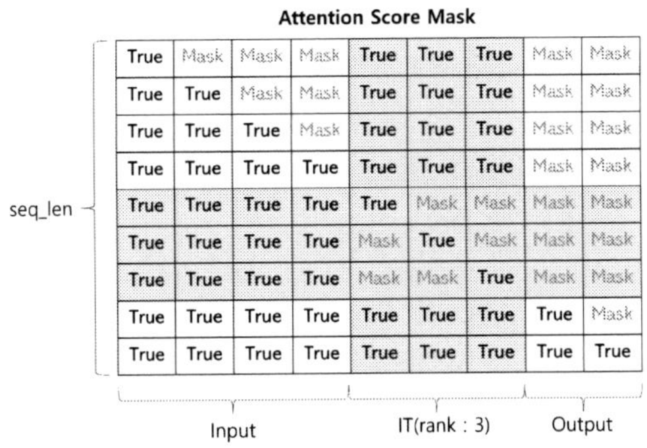

Figure 3: In unidirectional language models like GPT(Radford et al., 2019), we modified the attention score mask to allow each token to attend as shown in Figure 2

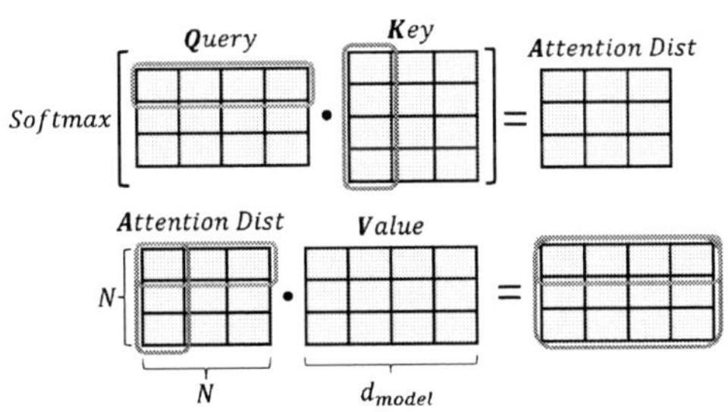

Figure 4: This figure illustrates which hidden states need to be updated for Information Tokens to select and summarize tokens of the input sentence. In the figure, the green box represents hidden states influenced by updating the query vector, while the red box represents hidden states influenced by updating the key vector. For instance, if the key vector is updated as described in $(IA)^3$(Liu et al., 2022a), as illustrated by the attention distribution in the figure, this adjustment alters the extent to which the tokens of the input sentence pay attention to the Information Tokens.

within the input sentence. However, Information Tokens, as shown on the right side of Figure 2, attend to all tokens within the input sentence during the attention operation process; conversely, all tokens within both the input and output sentences can also attend to Information Tokens. Ultimately, Information Tokens select and summarize information from the input sentence according to the task and convey this summarized information to both the input and output sentences.

For Information Tokens to fulfill these roles during the attention process, both bidirectional language models (e.g., BERT(Devlin et al., 2019), RoBERTa(Liu et al., 2019)) and unidirectional language models (e.g., GPT-2(Radford et al., 2019)) must be capable of performing bidirectional attention. Therefore, we modified the attention mask in the unidirectional language model, as shown in Figure 3. In addition, when multiple Information Tokens are added, as shown in Figure 3, each Information Token is prevented from attending to another. This allows each Information Token to attend to the input tokens rather than to each other during the learning process. Thus, we enable Information Tokens to interact with all tokens within a sentence in unidirectional language models, ultimately contributing to the prediction of the next token.

Furthermore, unlike in $(IA)^3$(Liu et al., 2022a), in which update the key vectors, our method involves updating the query vectors. As shown in Figure 4, when updating the key vector of the i-th token, this update adjusts how other tokens select the i-th token, rather than how the i-th token selects other tokens. However, our purpose was to enable the Information Tokens to selectively attend to information in the input sentence according to the task. Therefore, by updating the query vectors of the Information Tokens, as shown in Figure 4, we can enable the Information Tokens to selectively encapsulate important tokens within the input.

3.3 Efficient Structure

In this section, we investigate shifting (addition) and scaling (multiplication) vector operations to adjust the Information Tokens more efficiently within the model. Figure 5 shows the dimensionality reduction of the [CLS] token from the last layer of the BERT model before and after full fine-tuning using the RTE dataset within GLUE(Wang et al., 2018) using t-SNE(Van der Maaten and Hinton, 2008). As is evident from this visualization, language models may seem complex, but in reality, we believe it is a simple process of adjusting the model's parameters through fine-tuning to transform the hidden states into a form that is easily classifiable by the classification layers, as shown in Figure 5. However, rather than fine-tuning the model parameters, our goal was to update the hidden states directly to achieve similar effects, as depicted in Figure 5. To achieve this goal, using both scaling and shifting simultaneously, as in SSF(Lian et al., 2022), is more efficient for transforming vectors compared to the structures of $(IA)^3$ or PASTA(Yang et al., 2023), which utilize only shifting or scaling operations.

To validate our idea, we conducted preliminary

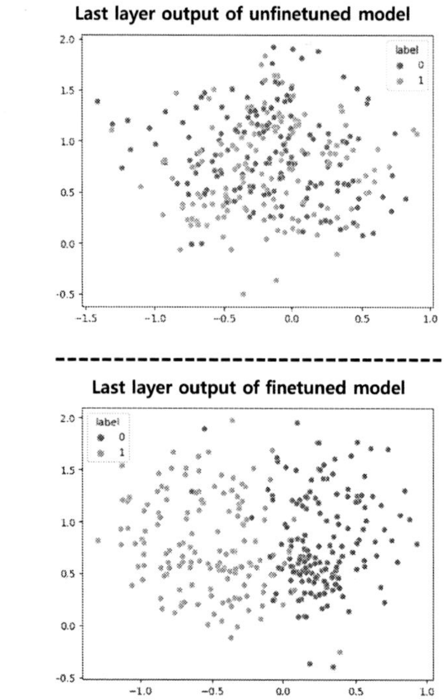

Figure 5: Both the left and right depict visualizations of the [CLS] token from the 12th(last) layer of the BERT-base model when inputting the RTE dataset. The top represents the state after the BERT model has undergone pretraining only, while the down represents the state after conducting full fine-tuning using the RTE dataset.

experiments on tasks within the GLUE dataset before proceeding with the main experiments. Using the BERT-base model, we experimented with five different learning rates for each combination of operations and selected the best-performing. Experimental results, shown in Figure 6, demonstrate that using a combination of one shifting and two scaling operations yields better performance on both large and small datasets than using only shifting or scaling operations. Therefore, we deviate from the framework of previous studies that used single operations to update and enhance IT-Tuning performance by appropriately combining shifting and scaling, as illustrated in Figure 1.

4 Experiment

In this section, experiments are conducted on both NLU and NLG tasks to demonstrate the effectiveness of IT-Tuning. In NLU tasks, we selected the [CLS] token as the information token, while in NLG tasks, we inserted real words such as "summarize", "transformation", "text", "table", etc., between input and output sentences and selected them as information tokens for experimentation.

4.1 NLU

4.1.1 Dataset

In this experiment, we validate the efficiency of IT-Tuning for NLU tasks using the GLUE benchmark. GLUE(Wang et al., 2018) consists of eight datasets: The Corpus of Linguistic Acceptability (CoLA), Stanford Sentiment Treebank (SST-2), Microsoft Research Paraphrase Corpus (MRPC), Semantic Textual Similarity Benchmark (STS-B), Quora Question Pairs (QQP), MultiNLI (MNLI), Question NLI (QNLI), and Recognizing Textual Entailment (RTE). We conducted experiments using these datasets, excluding the WNLI. We used the RoBERTa-large model(Liu et al., 2019) for experimentation, with both rank and α set to 1. Additionally, although the RoBERTa paper suggests using a model pretrained on the MNLI dataset as the initial model when experimenting with small datasets such as RTE, MRPC, and STS-B, we chose not to employ this approach. This is because fine-tuning a pretrained language model on the MNLI dataset is not parameter efficient.

4.1.2 Result

Table 1 presents the results of the experiments with the GLUE dataset using IT-Tuning applied to RoBERTa-large. In Table 1, we report the performance using ACC for the entire validation dataset of the MNLI (matched and mismatched), Matthew's correlation for the CoLA, Pearson's correlation for the STS-B, and ACC for the remaining datasets. Experimental results show that IT-Tuning achieves a performance comparable to that of full fine-tuning and LoRA(Hu et al., 2021) across the GLUE dataset. Notably, IT-Tuning outperforms both full fine-tuning and LoRA using only 0.04% (0.14M) of the parameters of the entire model on the CoLA, MRPC, and RTE datasets with less than 10K training data, excluding STS-B. Moreover, the average IT-Tuning scores surpassed those of both the full fine-tuning and LoRA. Through these experimental results, we demonstrate the high efficiency of IT-Tuning for NLU tasks.

4.2 NLG

4.2.1 Dataset

To demonstrate the effectiveness of IT-Tuning in both NLU and NLG tasks, we conducted exper-

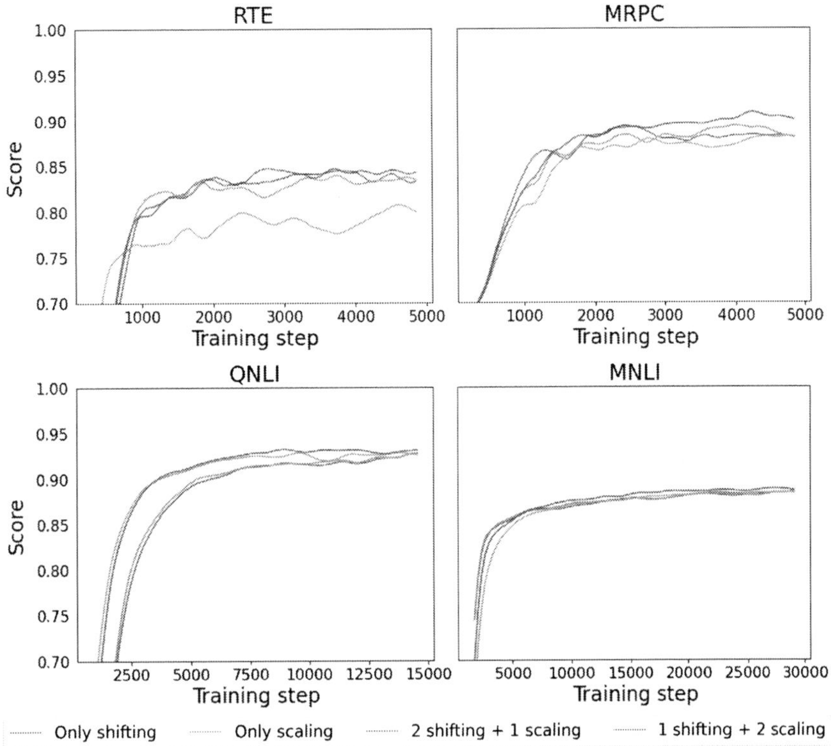

Figure 6: We conducted experiments by updating the hidden states of the query vector, the output of the attention, and the feed-forward layer. In the diagram, "Only shifting" and "Only scaling" represent using only shifting or scaling for all three hidden states, respectively. "2 Shifting + 1 Scaling" applies scaling to the hidden state of the query vector and shifting to the others. "1 Shifting + 2 Scaling" follows the same structure as Figure 1

iments using the E2E NLG Challenge dataset (Dušek et al., 2020). The E2E NLG Challenge dataset comprises approximately 42,000 training instances and 4,600 validation instances for table-to-text evaluation. Each input consisted of slot-value pairs, and the output is a sentence generated based on the input data. We conducted experiments using the GPT2-large model(Radford et al., 2019), with a rank of 4, and an α of 2.

4.2.2 Result

Table 2 presents the results of experiments with the E2E NLG Challenge dataset using IT-Tuning applied to GPT2-large. In Table 2, we evaluated the sentences generated by the model using BLEU(Papineni et al., 2002), NIST(Doddington, 2002), METEOR(Banerjee and Lavie, 2005), ROUGE-L(Lin, 2004), and CIDEr(Vedantam et al., 2015). Experimental results demonstrate the efficiency of our IT-Tuning in both NLU and NLG tasks. Despite using the fewest parameters among all the methods in Table 2, our IT-Tuning has demonstrated astonishing performance surpassing both full fine-tuning and Prefix Tuning(Li and Liang, 2021), as well as LoRA(Hu et al., 2021). Through experiments in NLG tasks, we demonstrated that IT tuning applies not only to NLU but also to NLG. These findings suggest that IT-tuning can serve as a viable alternative to full fine-tuning.

4.3 Ablation Study

4.3.1 Number of Information Token

For our NLU task, we employed one information token, while for NLG tasks, we utilized four information tokens. The ability to adjust the number of information tokens allows us to control the number of parameters used in training, which is one of the significant advantages of IT-Tuning. In this section, we substantiate this aspect. The Table 3 demonstrates the performance variations observed when adjusting the number of information tokens

Model & Method	# Trainable Parameter	CoLA	SST-2	MRPC	STS-B	QQP	MNLI	QNLI	RTE	Avg.
RoB_{large}(FT)*	355.0M	68.0	96.4	<u>90.9</u>	<u>92.4</u>	**92.2**	90.2	94.7	86.6	88.92
RoB_{large}($Adpt^P$)†	3.0M	68.3	96.1	90.2	92.1	91.9	90.2	94.8	83.8	88.42
RoB_{large}($Adpt^P$)†	0.8M	67.8	96.6	89.7	91.9	91.7	<u>90.5</u>	94.8	80.1	87.88
RoB_{large}($Adpt^H$)†	6.0M	66.5	96.2	88.7	91.0	<u>92.1</u>	89.9	94.7	83.4	87.81
RoB_{large}($Adpt^H$)†	0.8M	66.3	96.3	87.7	91.5	91.5	90.3	94.7	72.9	86.40
RoB_{large}(LoRA)†	0.8M	68.2	96.2	<u>90.9</u>	**92.6**	91.6	**90.6**	<u>94.9</u>	<u>87.4</u>	<u>89.05</u>
RoB_{large}(PASTA)††	0.07M	**69.7**	**96.8**	<u>90.9</u>	91.8	89.9	90.4	**95.1**	86.6	88.90
RoB_{large}(ITT)	0.14M	<u>69.5</u>	<u>96.7</u>	**92.2**	91.9	89.7	90.0	94.3	**88.4**	**89.08**

Table 1: RoBERTa-large model performance on GLUE benchmark. In this table, † represents the experimental results of LoRA(Hu et al., 2021), †† indicates the experimental results of PASTA(Yang et al., 2023) **Bold** indicates the best, while <u>underlining</u> indicates the second best.

Model & Method	# Trainable Parameter	BLEU	NIST	MET	ROUGE-L	CIDEr
GPT-2 L (FT)*	774.03M	68.5	8.78	46.0	69.9	2.45
GPT-2 L ($Adpt^L$)†	23.00M	68.9	8.70	46.3	71.3	<u>2.49</u>
GPT-2 L (LoRA)†	0.77M	<u>70.4</u>	**8.89**	<u>46.8</u>	<u>72.0</u>	2.47
GPT-2 L (PrefixTuning)††	0.77M	70.3	<u>8.85</u>	46.2	71.7	2.47
GPT-2 L (ITT)	0.69M	**73.4**	8.75	**49.1**	**76.1**	**2.52**

Table 2: GPT2-large model performance on E2E NLG Challenge dataset. In this table, † represents the experimental results of LoRA(Hu et al., 2021), and †† indicates the experimental results of Prefix Tuning(Li and Liang, 2021) Higher is better for all metrics.

in NLG tasks. Notably, the Table 3 reveals a stark BLEU score of 0.07 when employing only one information token. These experimental findings underscore the critical importance of scalability in IT-Tuning. Furthermore, through our experimentation, we observed that as the rank increases, the rate of decrease in training loss accelerates; however, it also becomes easier to encounter overfitting issues.

4.3.2 Using Key instead of Query

As described in the section 3.2, the roles of key and query within attention are different. We updated the query to focus on selectively condensing the information of input sentences, which is a main role of information tokens. However, to further explore the impact of updating key vectors on the performance of IT-Tuning, we conducted experiments in the same environment as described in Section 4.2. In Table 3, experimental results show a slight decrease in performance when using key vectors, but they still demonstrate efficiency. We believe these experimental results highlight the importance not only of how much information tokens pay attention to the other tokens but also of how much other tokens pay attention to the information tokens. Therefore, we believe that combining and updating query and key appropriately to make IT-Tuning more efficient will also be an interesting future work.

Model & Method	# Trainable Parameter	BLEU	ROUGE-L
GPT-2 L (ITT)			
- rank : 1	0.27M	0.07	7.65
- rank : 2	0.41M	71.9	73.4
- rank : 4	0.69M	**73.4**	**76.1**
- rank : 8	1.24M	73.0	75.4
- rank : 4 & key	0.69M	72.9	75.1

Table 3: In this table, "rank" denotes the number of information tokens utilized in the experiment, while "key" signifies that key was updated instead of query. Other experimental hyperparameters remain consistent with those outlined in Section 4.2

5 Conclusion

In this study, we propose information tokens to efficiently learn various tasks such as prediction, classification, and generation by selectively condensing the information of input sentences according to the task and conveying the condensed information to both input and output sentences. We enabled information tokens to selectively attend to the tokens of input sentences through direct updates of the query vectors of the information tokens in each layer of the model. In addition, we enabled bidirectional operations for information tokens in the attention process in unidirectional language models, such as GPT(Radford et al., 2019), allowing information tokens to fulfill their roles even in unidirectional language models. Furthermore, we enhanced the performance by proposing an efficient structure that combines scaling and shifting within the layers to update the hidden state of the information tokens according to the task requirements.

Ultimately, when conducting experiments using IT-Tuning, we surpassed both full fine-tuning and LoRA(Hu et al., 2021) on the GLUE benchmark(Wang et al., 2018) using only 0.14M parameters, which is five times fewer. Furthermore, unlike existing methods, such as BitFit(Ben Zaken et al., 2022), PASTA(Yang et al., 2023), and $(IA)^3$(Liu et al., 2022a), where the increase or decrease in the number of parameters used for training is fixed and cannot be adjusted, making them applicable only to specific tasks (e.g., NLU tasks), IT-Tuning enables the adjustment of the number of parameters used for training through information tokens. Owing to the scalability of IT-Tuning, when applied to NLG tasks, we achieved a performance surpassing both full fine-tuning and Prefix Tuning(Li and Liang, 2021), as well as LoRA. This demonstrates the wide applicability of IT-Tuning for various tasks.

6 Limitation and Future work

One of the drawbacks of attention architecture is that the computational speed is significantly influenced by the length of the input. In our experiments, for NLU using BERT and RoBERTa, we utilized the existing [CLS] token as the Information Token without adding additional tokens, thus avoiding an increase in input length. However, for NLG tasks using GPT, additional tokens are added to serve as Information Tokens, resulting in an increase in input length. Given that our IT-Tuning has shown remarkably superior performance in NLG tasks, it remains the most efficient operation. However, while the number of parameters used in training is 10% less than LoRA, the training speed has increased by 10%, and the size of GPU memory used during training has increased by 100MB * batch size in the same setting as the experiments. As a future work to address these issues, we propose a method for NLG tasks where Information Tokens are selected from existing input tokens without adding additional tokens, similar to NLU tasks. Furturmore, we provide our implementation of IT-Tuning to support various future work : https://github.com/KU-INI/IT-Tuning.git

Acknowledgements

This work was supported by Institute for Information and Communications Technology Planning and Evaluation (IITP) grant funded by the Korea government (MSIT) (No.2020-0-00368, A Neural-Symbolic Model for Knowledge Acquisition and Inference Techniques).

References

Satanjeev Banerjee and Alon Lavie. 2005. Meteor: An automatic metric for mt evaluation with improved correlation with human judgments. In *Proceedings of the acl workshop on intrinsic and extrinsic evaluation measures for machine translation and/or summarization*, pages 65–72.

Elad Ben Zaken, Yoav Goldberg, and Shauli Ravfogel. 2022. BitFit: Simple parameter-efficient fine-tuning for transformer-based masked language-models. In *Proceedings of the 60th Annual Meeting of the Association for Computational Linguistics (Volume 2: Short Papers)*, pages 1–9, Dublin, Ireland. Association for Computational Linguistics.

Tom Brown, Benjamin Mann, Nick Ryder, Melanie Subbiah, Jared D Kaplan, Prafulla Dhariwal, Arvind Neelakantan, Pranav Shyam, Girish Sastry, Amanda Askell, Sandhini Agarwal, Ariel Herbert-Voss, Gretchen Krueger, Tom Henighan, Rewon Child, Aditya Ramesh, Daniel Ziegler, Jeffrey Wu, Clemens Winter, Chris Hesse, Mark Chen, Eric Sigler, Mateusz Litwin, Scott Gray, Benjamin Chess, Jack Clark, Christopher Berner, Sam McCandlish, Alec Radford, Ilya Sutskever, and Dario Amodei. 2020. Language models are few-shot learners. In *Advances in Neural Information Processing Systems*, volume 33, pages 1877–1901. Curran Associates, Inc.

Aakanksha Chowdhery, Sharan Narang, Jacob Devlin, Maarten Bosma, Gaurav Mishra, Adam Roberts, Paul Barham, Hyung Won Chung, Charles Sutton, Sebastian Gehrmann, Parker Schuh, Kensen Shi, Sashank Tsvyashchenko, Joshua Maynez, Abhishek Rao, Parker Barnes, Yi Tay, Noam Shazeer, Vinodkumar Prabhakaran, Emily Reif, Nan Du, Ben Hutchinson, Reiner Pope, James Bradbury, Jacob Austin, Michael Isard, Guy Gur-Ari, Pengcheng Yin, Toju Duke, Anselm Levskaya, Sanjay Ghemawat, Sunipa Dev, Henryk Michalewski, Xavier Garcia, Vedant Misra, Kevin Robinson, Liam Fedus, Denny

Zhou, Daphne Ippolito, David Luan, Hyeontaek Lim, Barret Zoph, Alexander Spiridonov, Ryan Sepassi, David Dohan, Shivani Agrawal, Mark Omernick, Andrew M. Dai, Thanumalayan Sankaranarayana Pillai, Marie Pellat, Aitor Lewkowycz, Erica Moreira, Rewon Child, Oleksandr Polozov, Katherine Lee, Zongwei Zhou, Xuezhi Wang, Brennan Saeta, Mark Diaz, Orhan Firat, Michele Catasta, Jason Wei, Kathy Meier-Hellstern, Douglas Eck, Jeff Dean, Slav Petrov, and Noah Fiedel. 2024. Palm: scaling language modeling with pathways. *J. Mach. Learn. Res.*, 24(1).

Jacob Devlin, Ming-Wei Chang, Kenton Lee, and Kristina Toutanova. 2019. BERT: Pre-training of deep bidirectional transformers for language understanding. In *Proceedings of the 2019 Conference of the North American Chapter of the Association for Computational Linguistics: Human Language Technologies, Volume 1 (Long and Short Papers)*, pages 4171–4186, Minneapolis, Minnesota. Association for Computational Linguistics.

George Doddington. 2002. Automatic evaluation of machine translation quality using n-gram co-occurrence statistics. In *Proceedings of the second international conference on Human Language Technology Research*, pages 138–145.

Qingxiu Dong, Lei Li, Damai Dai, Ce Zheng, Zhiyong Wu, Baobao Chang, Xu Sun, Jingjing Xu, and Zhifang Sui. 2022. A survey on in-context learning. *arXiv preprint arXiv:2301.00234*.

Ondřej Dušek, Jekaterina Novikova, and Verena Rieser. 2020. Evaluating the state-of-the-art of end-to-end natural language generation: The e2e nlg challenge. *Computer Speech Language*, 59:123–156.

Chin-Lun Fu, Zih-Ching Chen, Yun-Ru Lee, and Hung-yi Lee. 2022. AdapterBias: Parameter-efficient token-dependent representation shift for adapters in NLP tasks. In *Findings of the Association for Computational Linguistics: NAACL 2022*, pages 2608–2621, Seattle, United States. Association for Computational Linguistics.

Soufiane Hayou, Nikhil Ghosh, and Bin Yu. 2024. Lora+: Efficient low rank adaptation of large models. *arXiv preprint arXiv:2402.12354*.

Neil Houlsby, Andrei Giurgiu, Stanislaw Jastrzebski, Bruna Morrone, Quentin De Laroussilhe, Andrea Gesmundo, Mona Attariyan, and Sylvain Gelly. 2019. Parameter-efficient transfer learning for nlp. In *International conference on machine learning*, pages 2790–2799. PMLR.

Edward J Hu, Yelong Shen, Phillip Wallis, Zeyuan Allen-Zhu, Yuanzhi Li, Shean Wang, Lu Wang, and Weizhu Chen. 2021. Lora: Low-rank adaptation of large language models. *arXiv preprint arXiv:2106.09685*.

Jared Kaplan, Sam McCandlish, Tom Henighan, Tom B Brown, Benjamin Chess, Rewon Child, Scott Gray, Alec Radford, Jeffrey Wu, and Dario Amodei. 2020. Scaling laws for neural language models. *arXiv preprint arXiv:2001.08361*.

Brian Lester, Rami Al-Rfou, and Noah Constant. 2021. The power of scale for parameter-efficient prompt tuning. In *Proceedings of the 2021 Conference on Empirical Methods in Natural Language Processing*, pages 3045–3059, Online and Punta Cana, Dominican Republic. Association for Computational Linguistics.

Xiang Lisa Li and Percy Liang. 2021. Prefix-tuning: Optimizing continuous prompts for generation. In *Proceedings of the 59th Annual Meeting of the Association for Computational Linguistics and the 11th International Joint Conference on Natural Language Processing (Volume 1: Long Papers)*, pages 4582–4597, Online. Association for Computational Linguistics.

Dongze Lian, Daquan Zhou, Jiashi Feng, and Xinchao Wang. 2022. Scaling & shifting your features: A new baseline for efficient model tuning. *Advances in Neural Information Processing Systems*, 35:109–123.

Baohao Liao, Yan Meng, and Christof Monz. 2023. Parameter-efficient fine-tuning without introducing new latency. In *Proceedings of the 61st Annual Meeting of the Association for Computational Linguistics (Volume 1: Long Papers)*, pages 4242–4260, Toronto, Canada. Association for Computational Linguistics.

Chin-Yew Lin. 2004. Rouge: A package for automatic evaluation of summaries. In *Text summarization branches out*, pages 74–81.

Haokun Liu, Derek Tam, Mohammed Muqeeth, Jay Mohta, Tenghao Huang, Mohit Bansal, and Colin A Raffel. 2022a. Few-shot parameter-efficient fine-tuning is better and cheaper than in-context learning. *Advances in Neural Information Processing Systems*, 35:1950–1965.

Xiao Liu, Kaixuan Ji, Yicheng Fu, Weng Tam, Zhengxiao Du, Zhilin Yang, and Jie Tang. 2022b. P-tuning: Prompt tuning can be comparable to fine-tuning across scales and tasks. In *Proceedings of the 60th Annual Meeting of the Association for Computational Linguistics (Volume 2: Short Papers)*, pages 61–68, Dublin, Ireland. Association for Computational Linguistics.

Xiao Liu, Kaixuan Ji, Yicheng Fu, Weng Lam Tam, Zhengxiao Du, Zhilin Yang, and Jie Tang. 2021. P-tuning v2: Prompt tuning can be comparable to fine-tuning universally across scales and tasks. *arXiv preprint arXiv:2110.07602*.

Yinhan Liu, Myle Ott, Naman Goyal, Jingfei Du, Mandar Joshi, Danqi Chen, Omer Levy, Mike Lewis, Luke Zettlemoyer, and Veselin Stoyanov. 2019. Roberta: A robustly optimized bert pretraining approach. *arXiv preprint arXiv:1907.11692*.

Kishore Papineni, Salim Roukos, Todd Ward, and Wei-Jing Zhu. 2002. Bleu: a method for automatic evaluation of machine translation. In *Proceedings of the 40th annual meeting of the Association for Computational Linguistics*, pages 311–318.

Alec Radford, Jeffrey Wu, Rewon Child, David Luan, Dario Amodei, Ilya Sutskever, et al. 2019. Language models are unsupervised multitask learners. *OpenAI blog*, 1(8):9.

Hugo Touvron, Louis Martin, Kevin Stone, Peter Albert, Amjad Almahairi, Yasmine Babaei, Nikolay Bashlykov, Soumya Batra, Prajjwal Bhargava, Shruti Bhosale, et al. 2023. Llama 2: Open foundation and fine-tuned chat models. *arXiv preprint arXiv:2307.09288*.

Laurens Van der Maaten and Geoffrey Hinton. 2008. Visualizing data using t-sne. *Journal of machine learning research*, 9(11).

Ashish Vaswani, Noam Shazeer, Niki Parmar, Jakob Uszkoreit, Llion Jones, Aidan N Gomez, Łukasz Kaiser, and Illia Polosukhin. 2017. Attention is all you need. *Advances in neural information processing systems*, 30.

Ramakrishna Vedantam, C Lawrence Zitnick, and Devi Parikh. 2015. Cider: Consensus-based image description evaluation. In *Proceedings of the IEEE conference on computer vision and pattern recognition*, pages 4566–4575.

Alex Wang, Amanpreet Singh, Julian Michael, Felix Hill, Omer Levy, and Samuel Bowman. 2018. GLUE: A multi-task benchmark and analysis platform for natural language understanding. In *Proceedings of the 2018 EMNLP Workshop BlackboxNLP: Analyzing and Interpreting Neural Networks for NLP*, pages 353–355, Brussels, Belgium. Association for Computational Linguistics.

Yaqing Wang, Sahaj Agarwal, Subhabrata Mukherjee, Xiaodong Liu, Jing Gao, Ahmed Hassan Awadallah, and Jianfeng Gao. 2022. AdaMix: Mixture-of-adaptations for parameter-efficient model tuning. In *Proceedings of the 2022 Conference on Empirical Methods in Natural Language Processing*, pages 5744–5760, Abu Dhabi, United Arab Emirates. Association for Computational Linguistics.

Jason Wei, Xuezhi Wang, Dale Schuurmans, Maarten Bosma, Fei Xia, Ed Chi, Quoc V Le, Denny Zhou, et al. 2022. Chain-of-thought prompting elicits reasoning in large language models. *Advances in neural information processing systems*, 35:24824–24837.

Xiaocong Yang, James Y. Huang, Wenxuan Zhou, and Muhao Chen. 2023. Parameter-efficient tuning with special token adaptation. In *Proceedings of the 17th Conference of the European Chapter of the Association for Computational Linguistics*, pages 865–872, Dubrovnik, Croatia. Association for Computational Linguistics.

Wayne Xin Zhao, Kun Zhou, Junyi Li, Tianyi Tang, Xiaolei Wang, Yupeng Hou, Yingqian Min, Beichen Zhang, Junjie Zhang, Zican Dong, et al. 2023. A survey of large language models. *arXiv preprint arXiv:2303.18223*.

A Appendix

The Table 4 shows detailed hyperparameters used in our experiments.

Model	Dataset	CoLA	SST-2	MRPC	STS-B	QQP	MNLI	QNLI	RTE
	Optimizer	AdamW							
	Warmup rate	0.06							
	LR Schedule	Linear							
RoB_{large}	Batch Size	8	64	8	8	32	32	64	16
	# Epochs	100	20	80	50	10	20	20	80
	Learning Rate	9e-4	7e-4	3e-4	9e-4	7e-4	5e-4	7e-4	5e-4
	IT-Tuning r	1							
	IT-Tuning a	1							
	Max Seq. Len.	128 + r							

Model	Dataset	E2E NLG Challenge
	Optimizer	AdamW
	Warmup rate	0.06
	LR Schedule	Cosine Restarts
$GPT2_{large}$	Batch Size	8
	# Epochs	20
	Learning Rate	5e-3
	IT-Tuning r	4
	IT-Tuning a	2
	Max Seq. Len.	128 + r
	Num Beam	10
	No Repeat Ngram	5
	Length Penalty	1.2

Table 4: The hyperparameters we used for RoBERTa and GPT2.

Bridging the Gap: Transfer Learning from English PLMs to Malaysian English

Mohan Raj[1], **Lay-Ki Soon**[1*], **Ong Huey Fang**[1], **and Bhawani Selvaretnam**[2]
[1]School of Information Technology, Monash University Malaysia
{mohan.chanthran, soon.layki, ong.hueyfang}@monash.edu
[2]Valiantlytix
bhawani@valiantlytix.com

Abstract

Malaysian English is a low resource creole language, where it carries the elements of Malay, Chinese, and Tamil languages, in addition to Standard English. Named Entity Recognition (NER) models underperform when capturing entities from Malaysian English text due to its distinctive morphosyntactic adaptations, semantic features and code-switching (mixing English and Malay). Considering these gaps, we introduce MENmBERT and MENBERT, a pre-trained language model with contextual understanding, specifically tailored for Malaysian English. We have fine-tuned MENmBERT and MENBERT using manually annotated entities and relations from the Malaysian English News Article (MEN) Dataset. This fine-tuning process allows the PLM to learn representations that capture the nuances of Malaysian English relevant for NER and RE tasks. MENmBERT achieved a 1.52% and 26.27% improvement on NER and RE tasks respectively compared to the bert-base-multilingual-cased model. Although the overall performance of NER does not have a significant improvement, our further analysis shows that there is a significant improvement when evaluated by the 12 entity labels. These findings suggest that pre-training language models on language-specific and geographically-focused corpora can be a promising approach for improving NER performance in low-resource settings. The dataset and code published in this paper provide valuable resources for NLP research work focusing on Malaysian English.

1 Introduction

With the recent proliferation of Large Language Models (LLMs), the usage of Pre-trained Language Models (PLMs) like BERT (Devlin et al., 2019), RoBERTa (Liu et al., 2019), XLM-RoBERTa (Conneau et al., 2020), ALBERT (Lan et al., 2020) has been overshadowed. However, PLM has shown some significant improvements when further pre-trained in domain specific (Chalkidis et al., 2020; Lee et al., 2019; Araci, 2019; Huang et al., 2020) or language specific corpus (Martin et al., 2020; Chan et al., 2020; Antoun et al., 2021; Vamvas et al., 2023), and subsequently fine-tuned on NLP tasks. The adaptability of pre-trained language model to diverse languages and dialects has enabled its application to specific linguistic contexts, including Malaysian English, a unique and culturally rich variant of the English language.

Malaysian English is also categorized as a creole language due to its distinct characteristics that include loanwords, compound words, and the derivation of new terms from Malay, Chinese, and Tamil, in addition to the Standard English (Chanthran et al., 2024). Existing state-of-the-art (SOTA) solutions do not produce satisfactory outcomes for downstream tasks performed in Malaysian English (Chanthran et al., 2024). This is mainly due to the morphosyntactic and semantical adaption nature of Malaysian English. Hence, there is a need to improve this SOTA in order to support effective processing of Malaysian English texts.

This work investigates the effectiveness of English pre-trained language models (PLMs) to the low resource language like Malaysian English, in downstream task, particularly Named Entity Recognition (NER), and Relation Extraction (RE) performed on Malaysian English. Our findings contribute to the growing body of research on promoting inclusivity in NLP by exploring the applicability of PLMs to non-standard English varieties.

The contributions of this paper are as follows:

1. Multilingual Pre-trained Model for Malaysian English: We introduce MENmBERT, a BERT-based model pre-trained on a Malaysian English News (MEN) Corpus. MEN Corpus comprises 14,320 articles,

*Corresponding Author.

Proceedings of the 9th Workshop on Representation Learning for NLP (RepL4NLP-2024), pages 69–77
August 15, 2024

facilitating research on applying PLMs to Malaysian English (Chanthran et al., 2024). This model will be made public to develop resources and facilitate NLP research in Malaysian English. The code for this experiment, and dataset have been published in `https://github.com/mohanraj-nlp/MEN-Dataset/tree/pretrained-lm`.

2. Fine-Tuned and Evaluated NER and RE on Malaysian English: We evaluated the effectiveness of fine-tuned MENmBERT for NER and RE tasks on a benchmark MEN-Dataset. MEN-Dataset contains 200 news articles with 6,061 annotated entities and 4,095 relation instances (Chanthran et al., 2024). This analysis demonstrates the applicability of transfer learning from English PLMs to Malaysian English NLP tasks.

This paper is structured as follows. Section 2 explores the utilization of pre-trained language models in both English and non-English scenarios. In Section 3, we dive deeper into the pre-training and fine-tune methodologies of MENmBERT and MENBERT. Section 4 we will discuss on the results of fine-tuned NER and RE. Finally, Section 5 concludes the work and shares potential enhancement as the future work.

2 Related Work

2.1 Pre-Trained Language Model for Non-English Context

Language-specific Pre-trained Language Models (PLMs) are essential to handle complex languages and improve performance on downstream NLP task specific to particular language. Considering this, AraBERT has been proposed to address the morphological and syntactic differences in the Arabic language compared to other languages, as Arabic shares very little with Latin-based languages and has unique characteristics (Antoun et al., 2021). Multilingual models to learn representations for multiple languages simultaneously resulted in little data representation and small language-specific vocabulary for Arabic, hindering performance compared to a single-language model. (Antoun et al., 2021) overcome these challenges, the researchers pre-trained AraBERT specifically for the Arabic language to capture the contextualized representations needed for Arabic NLP tasks. By customizing the model for Arabic and optimizing factors such as data size, vocabulary size, and pre-processing techniques, AraBERT was able to achieve state-of-the-art performance on various Arabic NLP tasks. The pre-training has been completed with 70 million sentences and around 24GB of textual Arabic data. AraBERT performs better in downstream tasks like Sentiment Analysis, Named Entity Recognition (NER), and Question Answering (Antoun et al., 2021). Antoun et al. (2021) compared the AraBERT fine-tuned model to SOTA and M-BERT, the results shows AraBERT performing better than mBERT or SOTA.

Following the success of AraBERT in Arabic NLP, similar approaches can be applied to other low-resource languages with unique characteristics. One such example is KinyaBERT, a recent model specifically designed to address the challenges of Natural Language Processing (NLP) tasks in Kinyarwanda (Nzeyimana and Niyongabo Rubungo, 2022). KinyaBERT has been implemented with a two-tier BERT architecture that token-level morphology encoder and sentence/document level encoder. By dividing the model's processing into these two tiers, KinyaBERT aims to effectively capture both the fine-grained morphological details of individual tokens and the broader contextual information present in the input text. The pre-training task has been completed with 16 million and 2.4GB of Kinyarwanda language texts. KinyaBERT is evaluated on NLP downstream tasks such as NER, News Categorization Task (NEWS) and Machine-Translated GLUE Benchmark. From the evaluation, KinyaBERT has outperformed the baseline model like BERT Base Pre-trained on Kinyarwanda Corpus (BERT BPE), BERT Tokenized by Morphological Analyzer (BERT MORPHO) and XLM-R.

Similarly to AraBERT and KinyaBERT, SwissBERT has been proposed specifically for national languages of Switzerland (Vamvas et al., 2023). SwissBERT trained using a combination of domain adaptation, language adaptation, and multilingual approaches. SwissBERT has been fine-tuned for NER task and it was able to outperform the baseline model which has been further pre-trained. SwissBERT has undergone several key adaptations and additions to make it impact for processing Switzerland-related text, this includes:

1. Multilingual Adaptation: SwissBERT is trained on a corpus of more than 21 million Swiss news articles in the national languages of Switzerland, including German, French,

Italian, and Romansh Grischun.

2. Custom Language Adapters: SwissBERT utilizes custom language adapters in each layer of the transformer encoder for the four national languages of Switzerland.

3. Switzerland-Specific Subword Vocabulary: To further enhance its performance on Switzerland-related text, SwissBERT is equipped with a Switzerland-specific subword vocabulary.

SwissBERT's superior performance in Switzerland-related tasks, such as Named Entity Recognition and Stance Detection, highlights its efficacy in handling diverse linguistic content specific to Switzerland.

Devlin et al. (2019) has further pre-trained multilingual BERT (M-BERT) with 104 languages Wikipedia corpus. Wang et al. (2020) suggests enhancing M-BERT by pre-training with low-resource corpora, as 11 languages are not covered in the current 104 languages. The research found that fine-tuning M-BERT (E-MBERT) on low-resource language corpora enhanced NER task performance. Wu and Dredze (2020) found that multilingual BERT (mBERT in Wu and Dredze (2020)) may not perform well in low-resource languages. This inconsistency may be attributed to the fact that mBERT is trained with a multitude of languages. Pre-training mBERT for a low resource language model can negatively impact the performance compared to training a monolingual BERT model for that language. Findings in related works have inspired us to establish better evaluation and model selection criteria for the development of a pre-trained language model for Malaysian English.

3 MENmBERT and MENBERT

3.1 Overview

Chalkidis et al. (2020) discussed about two possible further pre-training strategies:

1. Continued / Further Pre-training (FP): FP creates domain- or language-specific BERT models. FP utilises pre-trained model parameters, saving time and data (Kalyan et al., 2021).

2. Pre-Training from Scratch (SC): Pre-training from scratch lets you train the model with a lot of data. Pre-training the model from scratch will utilise existing language model architecture and parameters (Kalyan et al., 2021).

The difference between two approach is, FP has been pre-trained with generic corpora like BookCorpus, and English Wikipedia (Devlin et al., 2019) while SC has not been pre-trained with any corpus. With this in mind, we proposed to explore several further pre-training strategies:

1. MENBERT-FP: Further pre-train bert-base-cased model with MEN-Corpus

2. MENmBERT-FP: Further pre-train bert-base-multilingual-cased model with MEN-Corpus

3. MENBERT-SC: We pre-train bert-base-cased from scratch with MEN-Corpus

Malaysian English features loan words, compound blend and derivations of new terms from multiple languages local language, making multilingual BERT an effective model for understanding the contexts of news articles. The need to further pre-train BERT, mBERT and train BERT from scratch stems from our hypothesis that PLM with rich language-based understanding will improve the performance of NER and RE after being fine-tuned. Section 3.2 presents the pre-training setup and hyperparameters used, while Section 3.3 explains the model fine-tuning tasks.

3.2 Further Pre-Training MENmBERT and MENBERT

Python library Transformers (Wolf et al., 2020) has been used to pre-train BERT. For MENmBERT and MENBERT we have used bert-base-multilingual-cased and bert-base-cased respectively. Since MENBERT-SC was trained from scratch, we used bert-base-cased architecture. We generated our own vocabulary using BertWordPieceTokenizer for MENBERT-SC, meanwhile for MENmBERT and MENBERT we have used BertTokenizer. We selected the hyperparameter combination with the lowest training loss. Table 1 lists the important hyperparameters used to train the models. Section 4 details the pre-training results and some analyses.

Hyperparameters	MENBERT-FP	MENmBERT-FP	MENBERT-SC
epoch	30	30	30
batch_size	32	16	32
learning_rate	5e-5	5e-5	5e-5
weight_decay	0.001	0.001	0.001
max_sequence_length	512	512	512

Table 1: Hyperparameters used to train MENBERT-FP, MENmBERT-FP, MENBERT-SC

3.3 Fine-Tuning MENmBERT and MENBERT

Fine-Tune is an adaptation method to train pre-trained model for any NLP downstream task (Kalyan et al., 2021). Three pre-trained model MENBERT-FP, MENmBERT-FP, and MENBERT-SC were fine-tuned for NER and RE using MEN-Dataset. Additionally, we also fine-tuned pre-trained models bert-base-cased and bert-base-multilingual-cased. Fine-tuning on pre-trained and further pre-trained models helps us to compare the performance and validate our hypothesis (see Section 3.1).

3.3.1 Named Entity Recognition

We used the Python library Transformers Wolf et al. (2020), specifically the BertForTokenClassification module, for fine-tuning. As suggested by Devlin et al. (2019), we went through hyperparameter optimization to find an optimal hyperparameter for fine-tuning. We leveraged on WandB (Biewald, 2020) for hyperparameter optimization and logging. We used [2e-5, 5e-5] for the learning_rate, [10, 20, 30] for num_train_epochs, [0.01, 0.001, 0.0001] for weight_decay, and finally [4, 8, 16] for the per_device_train_batch_size.

We used a grid-based search approach to find an optimal hyperparameter with maximum F1-Score and minimum evaluation loss. Table 2 provides the hyperparameters used to fine-tune for NER. The MEN-Dataset is split into training (75%), test (10%) and validation (15%), with total entities of 5065, 453 and 618 respectively. Models fine-tuned with optimal hyperparameter were evaluated using the validation set, and discussed in the following Section 4.2.1.

Hyperparameters	epoch	batch_size	learning_rate	weight_decay
bert-based-cased	20	4	5e-5	0.0001
MENBERT-FP	30	4	5e-5	0.01
mbert-based-cased	30	4	5e-5	0.01
MENmBERT-FP	30	4	5e-5	0.01
MENBERT-SC	30	4	5e-5	0.01

Table 2: Optimal Hyperparameters used to fine-tune bert-base-cased, bert-base-multilingual-cased, MENBERT-FP, MENmBERT-FP, MENBERT-SC for NER

3.3.2 Relation Extraction

To efficiently fine-tune PLM for RE on the MEN-Dataset, we leveraged existing fine-tuning code for document-level relation extraction[1]. We then carefully modified this code to accommodate the specific characteristics and labeling scheme of the MEN-Dataset. Similarly like NER we went through hyperparameter optimization to find an optimal hyperparameter for fine-tuning. We used [2e-5, 5e-5] for the learning_rate, [10, 20, 30] for num_train_epochs, [0.01, 0.001, 0.0001] for weight_decay, and finally [4, 8, 16] for the per_device_train_batch_size. Table 3 provides the hyperparameters used to fine-tune for RE.

Hyperparameters	epoch	batch_size	learning_rate	weight_decay
bert-based-cased	30	4	5e-5	0.1
MENBERT-FP	30	4	5e-5	0.1
mbert-based-cased	30	4	5e-5	0.1
MENmBERT-FP	30	4	5e-5	0.1
MENBERT-SC	30	4	5e-5	0.1

Table 3: Optimal Hyperparameters used to fine-tune bert-base-cased, bert-base-multilingual-cased, MENBERT-FP, MENmBERT-FP, MENBERT-SC for RE

MEN-Dataset has relation labels adapted from prominent RE dataset like DocRED (Yao et al., 2019) and ACE-2005 (Walker, 2005). There are 84 relation labels that are adapted from DocRED, and 16 relation labels from ACE-2005. For this study, we concentrated on the relation labels originating from the DocRED dataset. One of the reason for our decision are due to Label Distribution. The DocRED labels constitute the majority within the MEN-Dataset. Focusing on these prevalent labels allows the model to learn robust representations for the most frequently occurring relation types, leading to potentially better performance on tasks involving these relations. Apart from that, we have also excluded a special relation label "NO_RELATION", as they are used is to indicate entities that might have a relation but not captured by the predefined relation set (Chanthran et al., 2024). Including "NO_RELATION" could introduce noise or ambiguity during model training.

MEN-Dataset has a total of 2,237 relation instances adapted from DocRED relation labels, distributed across training (1,693), testing (267), and validation (277) sets. To ensure a comprehensive representation of relation labels during training, we employed a stratified sampling approach on the MEN-Dataset. While the original split allocates 75%, 10%, and 15% for training, validation, and testing, respectively, our stratified sampling guarantees that all relation labels are present in the training data. The result and analysis of fine-tuned

[1]DocRED_Bert Github Link

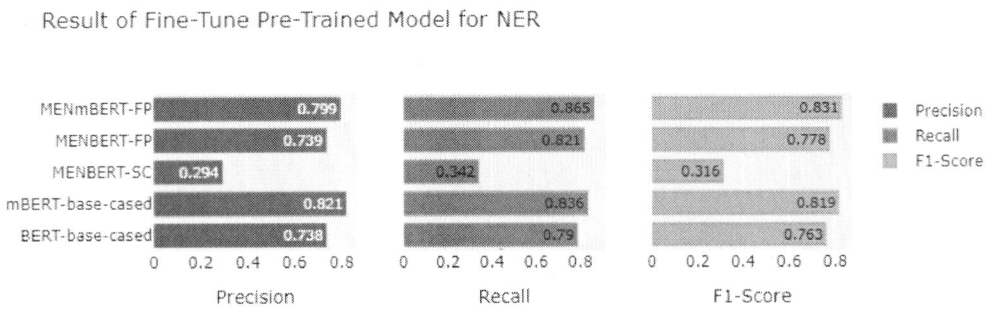

Figure 1: Precision, recall, and F1-score calculated for NER on the MEN-Dataset validation set.

PLM for RE have been discussed in Section 4.2.2.

4 Experiment Result and Analysis

4.1 Further Pre-trained Language Model

(Salazar et al., 2020; Kauf and Ivanova, 2023) suggests a "pseudo-log-likelihood" score calculated by masking tokens individually. The score is computed by summing the log-losses at the different masked positions. However, we are more interested in how accurately the models predict the masked token. This will help us to understand PLM models understanding and contextual awareness. We have collected 100 sentences from Malaysian English news article platform and we have done validation to ensure those sentence not part of our pre-training MEN-Corpus. In the first 70 sentences, one token from the local language, such as Bahasa Malaysia, has been randomly masked. In the remaining 30 sentences, one token of Standard English has been masked. We employ accuracy metrics to assess each model's effectiveness, providing a clear differentiation in their performance. The results demonstrate that additional pretraining on language-specific data significantly enhances the models' predictive capabilities, underscoring the importance of tailored training for improved language understanding.

For each pre-trained model, we calculated the accuracy of correctly predicted masked tokens. We used bert-based-cased and bert-base-multilingual-cased as baseline to investigate the improvement made by further pre-trained model. Based on the result in Figure 2, we have identified that MENmBERT-FP has highest accuracy on predicting masked token from Malaysian English sentence.

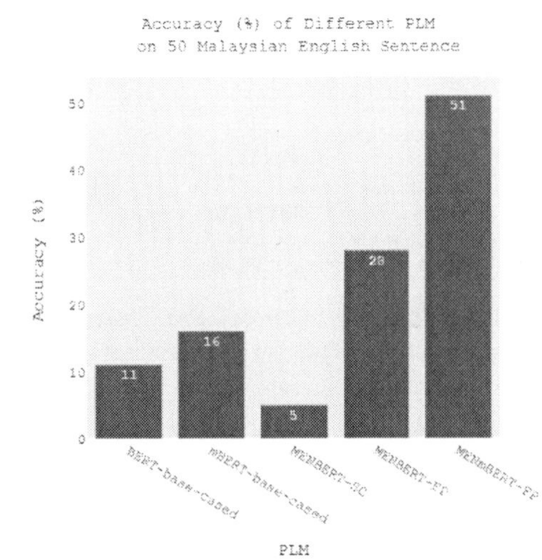

Figure 2: Accuracy of different pre-trained model predicting masked tokens in 50 Malaysian English Sentence.

In Table 4, we present some sample of sentences showcasing how different PLMs perform in predicting masked tokens. Here are the findings obtained from the sample result shown in Table 4:

1. MENmBERT-FP: Even though the model did not predict the exact ground-truth token, in some cases it identified semantically similar tokens. For instance, in the Malaysian context, *Bumiputera* often refers to the *Muslim* community. Here, MENmBERT-FP might predict a token related to ethnicity but not strictly synonymous with *Muslim*. This highlights the model's ability to capture semantic nuances, even when encountering challenging cases.

Masked Sentence	Masked Token	Pretrained Model				
		bert-based -cased	mbert-based -cased	menbert-fp	menbert-sc	menmbert-fp
There are three levels of disaster management, the first involves a locality in a district, secondly when more than two districts of a state is involved and the third involves two or three states. So everyone is aware of this," he told a press conference at <MASK> Sri Muda today.	Taman	the	Sri	the	'	Taman
On the Perlindungan Tenang Voucher, he said all eight million recipients of <MASK> Prihatin Rakyat are eligible to receive the voucher worth RM50 announced in Budget 2021 for the benefit of the B40 group.	Bantuan	the	the	the	the	Anugerah
Ismail Sabri also hoped that ties between Umno and PAS in Bera would remain strong and despite the harsh statement issued by the top leaders of the two parties, priority should be given to unite the Malay Muslims and <MASK>.	Bumiputera	Christians	Muslims	Muslims	,	Muslims
The Ministry of <MASK> Territories (KWP) while ensuring the flood management in Kuala Lumpur is proceeding well.	Federal	New	Protected	Federal	##am	Federal
Hamzah said he had discussed the issue with Inspector-General of Police Tan Sri Acryl Sani <MASK> Sani.	Abdullah	-	.	Abdullah	ser	Abdullah
Hamzah also said police had set up a Tactical Command Centre in <MASK> Langat district in Selangor to coordinate flood relief operations of all units.	Hulu	the	the	Kuala	,	Hulu

Table 4: Some sentences from the MEN-Dataset were used to predict masked tokens using various PLMs. Bold tokens indicate correctly predicted tokens when compared to the ground truth.

2. MENBERT-FP: When we compared the performance of MENBERT-FP with bert-based-cased, we can understand that further-pretraining has improved the performance of language model. The success ratio of bert-based-cased is 0, and once further pre-trained, there is an improvement of +33%.

3. bert-based-cased: Since bert-based-cased has only been trained with English corpus, it was not able to unmask any tokens with compound blend correctly.

4. MENBERT-SC: Based on our observation, MENBERT-SC has produced bad results when unmasking the tokens. Once fine-tune, we will be able to understand better on the performance of the model.

In Section 4.2 we have discussed the performance of pre-trained model once fine-tune them for NER and RE.

4.2 Fine-Tuning Pre-Trained Model

4.2.1 Named Entity Recognition

Figure 1 shows the comparison of Precision, Recall, and F1-Score among five different pre-trained models. To evaluate the performance of further pre-trained models, we also fine-tuned pre-trained model (bert-base-cased, and bert-base-multilingual-cased) as the baseline. Meanwhile in Table 5, we detailed the performance of model by entity labels.

Referring to the results, we observe that MENmBERT-FP achieves the highest F1-Score (0.831), while MENBERT-SC obtains the lowest F1-Score (0.316). Nevertheless, Figure 1 demonstrates an improvement when further pre-training the BERT model, which validated our hypothesis (discussed in Section 3.1). A few other observations from this experiment:

1. MENmBERT-FP has a higher F1-Score (0.831) than mBERT-base-cased (0.819). We observe a +1.52% improvement. Although the improvement is not significant, but when we analyse the F1-Score based on the entity label:

Entity Label	Total Annotated Entity in MEN-Dataset	Total Annotated Entity in Validation Set	bert-based-cased	mbert-based-cased	menbert-fp	menbert-sc	menmbert-fp
PERSON	1646	108	0.74	0.84	0.79	0.17	**0.86**
LOCATION	1157	150	0.86	0.88	0.87	0.48	**0.91**
ORGANIZATION	1624	262	0.81	**0.89**	0.82	0.29	**0.89**
EVENT	386	30	0.67	0.61	0.66	0.13	**0.77**
PRODUCT	72	6	0.24	**0.33**	0.13	0	0.07
FACILITY	208	27	0.24	0.11	**0.47**	0	0.25
ROLE	485	35	**0.39**	0.4	0.37	0.35	0.6
NORP	114	5	0.88	0.6	**0.89**	0.21	0.57
TITLE	300	4	**0.55**	0	0.43	0.18	0.5
LAW	62	5	0.15	0.12	**0.17**	0.1	0.13
LANGUAGE	0	0	0	0	0	0	0
WORK_OF_ART	7	2	0.1	0.15	0.12	0	**0.16**
Total Entities	6061	634					
Overall Micro F1-Score			**0.763**	**0.819**	**0.778**	**0.316**	**0.831**

Table 5: Fine-Tuned model performance (based on F1-Score) calculated based on validation set for each entity labels.

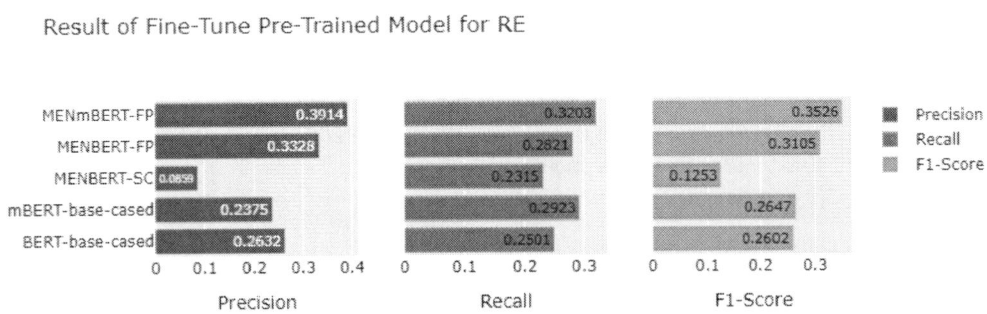

Figure 3: Precision, recall, and F1-score calculated for RE on the MEN-Dataset validation set.

   (a) There is an significant improvement for 6 out of 11 entity labels that are evaluated.
   (b) On average, the difference in F1-Score between MENmBERT-FP and mBERT-base-cased is +10%.
   (c) mBERT-base-cased is only able to achieve on-par in terms of F1-Score with MENmBERT-FP, specifically for entity label ORGANIZATION.

   This in-depth observation proves the significant performance of MENmBERT-FP.

2. MENBERT-FP (F1-Score is 0.778) has a higher F1-Score than bert-based-cased (F1-Score is 0.763), with an improvement of +1.94%. However, after further investigated the performance based on entity labels:
   (a) MENBERT-FP has only improved the performance of only 7 out of 11 entity labels.
   (b) On average, the improvement is only around +2%.
   (c) When compared with MENmBERT-FP, MENBERT-FP is able to outperform in terms of F1-Score for 4 out of 11 entity labels. These include entity labels PRODUCT, FACILITY, NORP and LAW.

3. MENBERT-SC has not shown any improvement in the performance of NER. Our evaluation in Section 4.1 also shows it was not able to unmask the tokens correctly.

The experimental results and findings conclude that our fine-tuned MENmBERT-FP has achieved highest F1-Score compared to other pre-trained models.

MENmBERT-FP could be used to fine-tune for more NLP downstream tasks, involving Malaysian English, for improved performance.

4.2.2 Relation Extraction

Figure 3 shows F1-Scores compared across five PLMs. Like with NER, we used fine-tuned bert-base-cased and bert-base-multilingual-cased as baselines.

MENmBERT-FP achieved the highest F1-score (0.353), indicating a slight improvement over our baseline PLMs. This suggests that further pre-training on MEN-Dataset has been beneficial for RE on Malaysian English context. Here are some of ur observations from the experiment:

1. MENmBERT-FP has made +33.21% improvement in F1-Score compared to baseline approach mBERT-base-cased. This has been proven significant. Our cross-analysis of NER and RE predictions reveals that the TP relation instances have entity pairs correctly classified by the fine-tuned NER model (from previous analysis). This suggests a significant improvement in RE performance due to the model's enhanced entity prediction capabilities.

2. MENBERT-FP (F1-Score is 0.3105) has a higher F1-Score than bert-based-cased (F1-Score is 0.2602), with an improvement of +19.33%. The analysis of the fine-tuned model's predictions did not reveal any surprising or unexpected patterns. This aligns with the observations from the previous point. Meanwhile, for MENBERT-SC was performed badly when fine-tuned for RE task.

Apart from that, it's important to note that our fine-tuned RE models achieved lower performance compared to reported results on other document-level relation extraction datasets like DocRED. For instance, prior work using a fine-tuned BERT model on DocRED (38,269 relation instances) achieved an F1-score of 54.16 (Dev) and 53.20 (Test) (Wang et al., 2019). Compared with our finding, the overall F1-Score could be not significant due to the nature of MEN-Dataset with a small set of annotation instance.

5 Conclusion

This work introduced MENmBERT, a contextualized language model pre-trained on a Malaysian English corpus. Our experiments demonstrated that fine-tuning MENmBERT on language-specific data significantly improves performance on NER tasks with average of +1.74%. For RE, we have achieved average improvement of +26.27% compare our MENmBERT and MENBERT with baseline PLM's. However, the fine-tuned RE models achieved lower performance compared to reported results on other document-level relation extraction datasets. This suggests that while MENmBERT's entity prediction capabilities benefit RE tasks, further exploration is needed to optimize RE performance in the context of our dataset. This has gaps has suggested us for future work, explore several avenues to improve RE performance. One of the approach involve investigating data augmentation techniques to expand our dataset and improve model training. Beyond that, we will extend our experiment do several other downstream NLP task.

6 Acknowledgements

Part of this project was funded by the Malaysian Fundamental Research Grant Scheme (FRGS) FRGS/1/2022/ICT02/MUSM/02/2.

References

Wissam Antoun, Fady Baly, and Hazem Hajj. 2021. Arabert: Transformer-based model for arabic language understanding. *Preprint*, arXiv:2003.00104.

Dogu Araci. 2019. Finbert: Financial sentiment analysis with pre-trained language models. *Preprint*, arXiv:1908.10063.

Lukas Biewald. 2020. Experiment tracking with weights and biases. Software available from wandb.com.

Ilias Chalkidis, Manos Fergadiotis, Prodromos Malakasiotis, Nikolaos Aletras, and Ion Androutsopoulos. 2020. Legal-bert: The muppets straight out of law school. *Preprint*, arXiv:2010.02559.

Branden Chan, Stefan Schweter, and Timo Möller. 2020. German's next language model. *Preprint*, arXiv:2010.10906.

Mohan Raj Chanthran, Lay-Ki Soon, Huey Fang Ong, and Bhawani Selvaretnam. 2024. Malaysian english news decoded: A linguistic resource for named entity and relation extraction. *Preprint*, arXiv:2402.14521.

Alexis Conneau, Kartikay Khandelwal, Naman Goyal, Vishrav Chaudhary, Guillaume Wenzek, Francisco Guzmán, Edouard Grave, Myle Ott, Luke Zettlemoyer, and Veselin Stoyanov. 2020. Unsupervised cross-lingual representation learning at scale. *Preprint*, arXiv:1911.02116.

Jacob Devlin, Ming-Wei Chang, Kenton Lee, and Kristina Toutanova. 2019. Bert: Pre-training of deep bidirectional transformers for language understanding. *Preprint*, arXiv:1810.04805.

Kexin Huang, Jaan Altosaar, and Rajesh Ranganath. 2020. Clinicalbert: Modeling clinical notes and predicting hospital readmission. *Preprint*, arXiv:1904.05342.

Katikapalli Subramanyam Kalyan, Ajit Rajasekharan, and Sivanesan Sangeetha. 2021. Ammus : A survey of transformer-based pretrained models in natural language processing. *Preprint*, arXiv:2108.05542.

Carina Kauf and Anna Ivanova. 2023. A better way to do masked language model scoring. *Preprint*, arXiv:2305.10588.

Zhenzhong Lan, Mingda Chen, Sebastian Goodman, Kevin Gimpel, Piyush Sharma, and Radu Soricut. 2020. Albert: A lite bert for self-supervised learning of language representations. *Preprint*, arXiv:1909.11942.

Jinhyuk Lee, Wonjin Yoon, Sungdong Kim, Donghyeon Kim, Sunkyu Kim, Chan Ho So, and Jaewoo Kang. 2019. BioBERT: a pre-trained biomedical language representation model for biomedical text mining. *Bioinformatics*, 36(4):1234–1240.

Yinhan Liu, Myle Ott, Naman Goyal, Jingfei Du, Mandar Joshi, Danqi Chen, Omer Levy, Mike Lewis, Luke Zettlemoyer, and Veselin Stoyanov. 2019. Roberta: A robustly optimized bert pretraining approach. *Preprint*, arXiv:1907.11692.

Louis Martin, Benjamin Muller, Pedro Javier Ortiz Suá rez, Yoann Dupont, Laurent Romary, Éric de la Clergerie, Djamé Seddah, and Benoît Sagot. 2020. CamemBERT: a tasty french language model. In *Proceedings of the 58th Annual Meeting of the Association for Computational Linguistics*. Association for Computational Linguistics.

Antoine Nzeyimana and Andre Niyongabo Rubungo. 2022. KinyaBERT: a morphology-aware Kinyarwanda language model. In *Proceedings of the 60th Annual Meeting of the Association for Computational Linguistics (Volume 1: Long Papers)*, pages 5347–5363, Dublin, Ireland. Association for Computational Linguistics.

Julian Salazar, Davis Liang, Toan Q. Nguyen, and Katrin Kirchhoff. 2020. Masked language model scoring. In *Proceedings of the 58th Annual Meeting of the Association for Computational Linguistics*. Association for Computational Linguistics.

Jannis Vamvas, Johannes Graën, and Rico Sennrich. 2023. Swissbert: The multilingual language model for switzerland. *Preprint*, arXiv:2303.13310.

Christopher Walker. 2005. *Multilingual Training Corpus LDC2006T06. Web Download. Philadelphia: Linguistic Data Consortium.*

Hong Wang, Christfried Focke, Rob Sylvester, Nilesh Mishra, and William Wang. 2019. Fine-tune bert for docred with two-step process. *Preprint*, arXiv:1909.11898.

Zihan Wang, Karthikeyan K, Stephen Mayhew, and Dan Roth. 2020. Extending multilingual BERT to low-resource languages. In *Findings of the Association for Computational Linguistics: EMNLP 2020*, pages 2649–2656, Online. Association for Computational Linguistics.

Thomas Wolf, Lysandre Debut, Victor Sanh, Julien Chaumond, Clement Delangue, Anthony Moi, Pierric Cistac, Tim Rault, Rémi Louf, Morgan Funtowicz, Joe Davison, Sam Shleifer, Patrick von Platen, Clara Ma, Yacine Jernite, Julien Plu, Canwen Xu, Teven Le Scao, Sylvain Gugger, Mariama Drame, Quentin Lhoest, and Alexander M. Rush. 2020. Transformers: State-of-the-art natural language processing. In *Proceedings of the 2020 Conference on Empirical Methods in Natural Language Processing: System Demonstrations*, pages 38–45, Online. Association for Computational Linguistics.

Shijie Wu and Mark Dredze. 2020. Are all languages created equal in multilingual bert? In *Workshop on Representation Learning for NLP*.

Yuan Yao, Deming Ye, Peng Li, Xu Han, Yankai Lin, Zhenghao Liu, Zhiyuan Liu, Lixin Huang, Jie Zhou, and Maosong Sun. 2019. DocRED: A large-scale document-level relation extraction dataset. In *Proceedings of the 57th Annual Meeting of the Association for Computational Linguistics*, pages 764–777, Florence, Italy. Association for Computational Linguistics.

Unified Interpretation of Smoothing Methods for Negative Sampling Loss Functions in Knowledge Graph Embedding

Xincan Feng[†], **Hidetaka Kamigaito**[†], **Katsuhiko Hayashi**[‡], **Taro Watanabe**[†]
[†]Nara Institute of Science and Technology [‡]The University of Tokyo
{feng.xincan.fy2, kamigaito.h, taro}@is.naist.jp
katsuhiko-hayashi@g.ecc.u-tokyo.ac.jp

Abstract

Knowledge Graphs (KGs) are fundamental resources in knowledge-intensive tasks in NLP. Due to the limitation of manually creating KGs, KG Completion (KGC) has an important role in automatically completing KGs by scoring their links with KG Embedding (KGE). To handle many entities in training, KGE relies on Negative Sampling (NS) loss that can reduce the computational cost by sampling. Since the appearance frequencies for each link are at most one in KGs, sparsity is an essential and inevitable problem. The NS loss is no exception. As a solution, the NS loss in KGE relies on smoothing methods like Self-Adversarial Negative Sampling (SANS) and subsampling. However, it is uncertain what kind of smoothing method is suitable for this purpose due to the lack of theoretical understanding. This paper provides theoretical interpretations of the smoothing methods for the NS loss in KGE and induces a new NS loss, Triplet Adaptive Negative Sampling (TANS), that can cover the characteristics of the conventional smoothing methods. Experimental results of TransE, DistMult, ComplEx, RotatE, HAKE, and HousE on FB15k-237, WN18RR, and YAGO3-10 datasets and their sparser subsets show the soundness of our interpretation and performance improvement by our TANS.

1 Introduction

Knowledge Graphs (KGs) represent human knowledge using various entities and their relationships as graph structures. KGs are fundamental resources for knowledge-intensive tasks like dialog (Moon et al., 2019), question answering (Reese et al., 2020), named entity recognition (Liu et al., 2019), open-domain questions (Hu et al., 2022), and recommendation systems (Gao et al., 2020), etc.

However, to create complete KGs, we need to consider a large number of entities and all their possible relationships. Taking into account the explosively large number of combinations between entities, only relying on manual approaches is unrealistic to make complete KGs.

Knowledge Graph Completion (KGC) is a task to deal with this problem. KGC involves automatically completing missing links corresponding to relationships between entities in KGs. To complete the KGs, we need to score each link between entities. For this purpose, current KGC commonly relies on Knowledge Graph Embedding (KGE) (Bordes et al., 2011). KGE models predict the missing relations, named link prediction, by learning structural representations. In the current KGE, models need to complete a link (triplet) (e_i, r_k, e_j) of entities e_i and e_j, and their relationship r_k by answering e_i or e_j from a given query $(?, r_k, e_j)$ or $(e_i, r_k, ?)$, respectively. Hence, KGE needs to handle a large number of entities and their relationships during its training.

To handle a large number of entities and relationships in KGs, Negative Sampling (NS) loss (Mikolov et al., 2013) is frequently used for training KGE models. The original NS loss is proposed to approximate softmax cross-entropy loss to reduce computational costs by sampling false labels from its noise distribution in training. Trouillon et al. (2016) import the NS loss from word embedding to KGE with utilizing uniform distribution as its noise distribution. Sun et al. (2019) extend the NS loss to Self-Adversarial Negative Sampling (SANS) loss for efficient training of KGE. Unlike the NS loss with uniform distribution, the SANS loss utilizes the training model's prediction as the noise distribution. Since the negative samples in the SANS loss become more difficult to discriminate for models in training, the SANS can extract models' potential compared with the NS loss with uniform distribution.

One of the problems left for KGE is the sparsity of KGs. Figure 1 shows the appearance frequency of queries and answers (entities) in the training data of FB15k-237, WN18RR and YAGO3-10 datasets.

Proceedings of the 9th Workshop on Representation Learning for NLP (RepL4NLP-2024), pages 78–98
August 15, 2024 ©2024 Association for Computational Linguistics

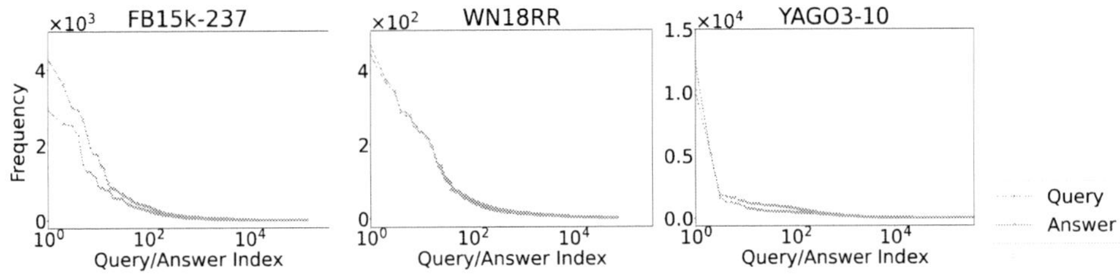

Figure 1: Appearance frequencies of queries and answers (entities) in the training data of FB15k-237, WN18RR, and YAGO3-10. Note that the indices are sorted from high frequency to low.

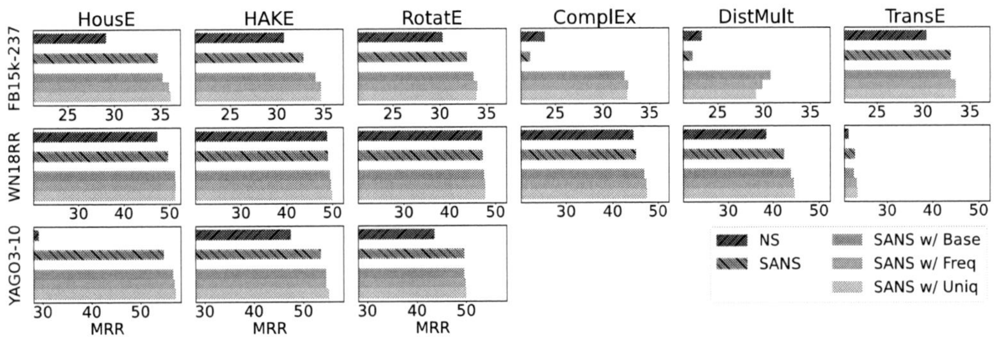

Figure 2: Performances of KGE models HousE, HAKE, RotatE, ComplEx, DistMult, and TransE on datasets FB15k-237, WN18RR, and YAGO3-10 using NS, SANS, and subsampling methods (noted as *Base, Freq, Uniq*).

From the long-tail distribution of this figure, we can understand that both queries and answers necessary for training KGE models may suffer from the sparsity problem.

As a solution, several smoothing methods are used in KGE. Sun et al. (2019) import subsampling from word2vec (Mikolov et al., 2013) to KGE. Subsampling can smooth the appearance frequency of triplets and queries in KGs. Kamigaito and Hayashi (2022a) show a general formulation that covers the basic subsampling of Sun et al. (2019) (Base), their frequency-based subsampling (Freq) and unique-based subsampling (Uniq) for KGE. Kamigaito and Hayashi (2021) indicate that SANS has a similar effect of using label-smoothing (Szegedy et al., 2016) and thus SANS can smooth the frequencies of answers in training. Figure 2 shows the effectiveness of SANS and subsampling in KGC performance. From the figure, since FB15k-237 is more sparse (imbalanced) than WN18RR and YAGO3-10 based on Figure 1, we can understand that strategy in choosing smoothing methods have more considerable influences than models when data is sparse.

While SANS and subsampling can improve model performance by smoothing the appearance frequencies of triplets, queries, and answers, their theoretical relationship is not clear, leaving their capabilities and deficiencies a question. For example, conventional works (Sun et al., 2019; Zhang et al., 2020b; Kamigaito and Hayashi, 2022a)[1] jointly use SANS and subsampling with no theoretical background. Thus, there is a call for further interpretability and performance improvement.

To solve the above problem, we theoretically and empirically study the differences of SANS and subsampling on three common datasets and their sparser subsets with six popular KGE models[2]. Our contributions are as follows:

- By focusing on the smoothing targets, we theoretically reveal the differences between SANS and subsampling and induce a new NS loss, Triplet Adaptive Negative Sampling (TANS), that can cover the smoothing target of both SANS and subsampling.
- We theoretically show that TANS with subsampling can potentially cover the conven-

[1]Note that Sun et al. (2019); Zhang et al. (2020b) use subsampling in their released implementation without referring to it in their paper.

[2]Our code and data are available at https://github.com/xincanfeng/ss_kge.

tional usages of SANS and subsampling.

- We empirically verify that TANS improves KGC performance on sparse KGs in terms of MRR.
- We empirically verify that TANS with subsampling can cover the conventional usages of SANS and subsampling in terms of MRR.

2 Background

In this section, we describe the problem formulation for solving KGC by KGE and explain the conventional NS loss functions in KGE.

2.1 Formulation of KGE

KGC is a research topic for automatically inferring new links in a KG that are likely but not yet known to be true. To infer the new links by KGE, we decompose KGs into a set of triplets (links). By using entities e_i, e_j and their relation r_k, we represent the triplet as (e_i, r_k, e_j). In a typical KGC task, a KGE model receives a query $(e_i, r_k, ?)$ or $(?, r_k, e_j)$ and predicts the entity corresponding to ? as an answer.

In KGE, a KGE model scores a triplet (e_i, r_k, e_j) by using a scoring function $s_\theta(x, y)$, where θ denotes model parameters. Here, using a softmax function, we represent the existence probability $p_\theta(y|x)$ for an answer y of the query x as follows:

$$p_\theta(y|x) = \frac{\exp(s_\theta(x, y))}{\sum_{y' \in Y} \exp(s_\theta(x, y'))}, \quad (1)$$

where Y is a set of entities.

2.2 NS Loss in KGE

To train $s_\theta(x, y)$, we need to calculate losses for the observables $D = \{(x_1, y_1), \cdots, (x_n, y_n)\}$ that follow $p_d(x, y)$. Even if we can represent KGC by Eq. (1), it does not mean we can tractably perform KGC due to the large number of Y in KGs. For the reason of the computational cost, the NS loss (Mikolov et al., 2013) is used to approximate Eq. (1) by sampling false answers.

By modifying that of Mikolov et al. (2013), the following NS loss (Sun et al., 2019; Ahrabian et al., 2020) is commonly used in KGE:

$$\begin{aligned}&\ell_{\text{NS}}(\theta)\\&= -\frac{1}{|D|} \sum_{(x,y) \in D} \Big[\log(\sigma(s_\theta(x, y) + \tau))\\&\quad + \frac{1}{\nu} \sum_{y_i \sim U}^{\nu} \log(\sigma(-s_\theta(x, y_i) - \tau))\Big], \quad (2)\end{aligned}$$

where U is the noise distribution that follows uniform distribution, σ is the sigmoid function, ν is the number of negative samples per positive sample (x, y), and τ is a margin term to adjust the value range decided by $s_\theta(x, y)$.

2.3 Smoothing Methods for the NS Loss in KGE

As shown in Figure 1, KGC needs to deal with the sparsity problem caused by low frequent queries and answers in KGs. Imposing smoothing on the appearance frequencies of queries and answers can mitigate this problem. The following subsections introduce subsampling (Mikolov et al., 2013; Sun et al., 2019; Kamigaito and Hayashi, 2022a) and SANS (Sun et al., 2019), the conventional smoothing methods for the NS loss in KGE.

2.3.1 Subsampling

Subsampling (Mikolov et al., 2013) is a method to smooth the frequency of triplets or queries in the NS loss. Sun et al. (2019) import this approach from word embedding to KGE. Kamigaito and Hayashi (2022b,a) add some variants to subsampling for KGC and theoretically provide a unified expression of them as follows:

$$\begin{aligned}&\ell_{\text{SUB}}(\theta)\\&= -\frac{1}{|D|} \sum_{(x,y) \in D} \Big[A(x, y; \alpha) \log(\sigma(s_\theta(x, y) + \tau))\\&\quad + \frac{1}{\nu} \sum_{y_i \sim U}^{\nu} B(x, y; \alpha) \log(\sigma(-s_\theta(x, y_i) - \tau))\Big], \quad (3)\end{aligned}$$

where α is a temperature term to adjust the frequecy of triplets and queries. Note that we incorporate α into Eq. (3) to consider various loss functions even though Kamigaito and Hayashi (2022b,a) do not consider α. In this formulation, we can consider several assumptions for deciding $A(x, y; \alpha)$ and $B(x, y; \alpha)$. We introduce these assumptions in the following paragraphs:

Base As a basic subsampling approach, Sun et al. (2019) import the one originally used in word2vec (Mikolov et al., 2013) to KGE, defined as follows:

$$A(x, y; \alpha) = B(x, y; \alpha) = \frac{\#(x, y)^{-\alpha} |D|}{\sum_{(x', y') \in D} \#(x', y')^{-\alpha}}, \quad (4)$$

where $\#$ is the symbol for frequency and $\#(x, y)$ represents the frequency of (x, y). In word2vec, subsampling randomly discards a word by a probability $1-\sqrt{t/f}$, where t is a constant value and f is a frequency of a word. This is similar to randomly keeping a word with a probability $\sqrt{t/f}$. Thus, we can understand that Eq. (4) follows the original use in word2vec. Since the actual (x, y) occurs at most once in KGs, when $(x, y) = (e_i, r_k, e_j)$, they approximate the frequency of (x, y) as:

$$\#(x, y) \approx \#(e_i, r_k) + \#(r_k, e_j), \qquad (5)$$

based on the approximation of n-gram language modeling (Katz, 1987).

Freq Kamigaito and Hayashi (2022a) propose frequency-based subsamping (Freq) by assuming a case that (x, y) originally has a frequency, but the observed one in the KG is at most 1.

$$A(x, y; \alpha) = \frac{\#(x, y)^{-\alpha}|D|}{\sum_{(x',y')\in D} \#(x', y')^{-\alpha}},$$
$$B(x, y; \alpha) = \frac{\#x^{-\alpha}|D|}{\sum_{x'\in D} \#x'^{-\alpha}}. \qquad (6)$$

Uniq Kamigaito and Hayashi (2022a) also propose unique-based subsamping (Uniq) by assuming a case that the originally frequency and the observed one in the KG are both 1.

$$A(x, y; \alpha) = B(x, y; \alpha) = \frac{\#x^{-\alpha}|D|}{\sum_{x'\in D} \#x'^{-\alpha}}. \qquad (7)$$

2.3.2 SANS Loss

SANS is originally proposed as a kind of NS loss to train KGE models efficiently by considering negative samples close to their corresponding positive ones. Kamigaito and Hayashi (2021) show that using SANS is similar to imposing label-smoothing on Eq. (1). Thus, SANS is a method to smooth the frequency of answers in the NS loss. The SANS loss is represented as follows:

$$\ell_{\text{SANS}}(\theta) = -\frac{1}{|D|} \sum_{(x,y)\in D} \Big[\log(\sigma(s_\theta(x, y) + \tau)) + \sum_{y_i\sim U}^{\nu} p_\theta(y_i|x; \beta) \log(\sigma(-s_\theta(x, y_i) - \tau))\Big], \qquad (8)$$

$$p_\theta(y_i|x; \beta) \approx \frac{\exp(\beta s_\theta(x, y_i))}{\sum_{j=1}^{\nu} \exp(\beta s_\theta(x, y_j))}, \qquad (9)$$

where β is a temperature to adjust the distribution of negative sampling. Different from subsampling, SANS uses $p_\theta(y_i|x; \beta)$ that is predicted by a model θ to adjust the frequency of the answer y_i. Since $p_\theta(y_i|x; \beta)$ is essentially a noise distribution, it does not receive any gradient during training.

3 Triplet Adaptive Negative Sampling

In this section, we explain our proposed Triplet Adaptive Negative Sampling (TANS) in detail. We first show the overview of our TANS through the comparison with the conventional smoothing methods of the NS loss for KGE (See §2.3) in §3.1 and after that we explain the details of TANS through its mathematical formulations in §3.2 and §3.3.

3.1 Overview

TANS is fundamentally different from SANS, with SANS only taking into account the conditional probability of negative samples and TANS being a loss function that considers the joint probability of the pair of queries and their answers.

Table 1 shows the characteristics of TANS and the conventional smoothing methods of the NS loss for KGE introduced in §2.3. These characteristics are based on the decomposition of $p_d(x, y)$, the appearance probability for the triplet (x, y), into that of its answer $p_d(y|x)$ and query $p(x)$:

$$p_d(x, y) = p_d(y|x)p_d(x) \qquad (10)$$

In Eq. (10), smoothing both $p_d(y|x)$ and $p_d(x)$ is similar to smoothing $p_d(x, y)$. However, smoothing $p_d(x, y)$ does not ensure smoothing both $p_d(x)$ and $p_d(y|x)$ considering the case of only one of them being smoothed, and the left one being still sparse. Similarly, smoothing only $p_d(x)$ or $p_d(y|x)$ does not ensure $p_d(x, y)$ being smoothed due to the case where one of them is still sparse. In Table 1, we denote such a case where the method can influence the probability, but no guarantee of the probability be smoothed as $\triangle$.

In TANS, we aim to smooth $p_d(x, y)$ by smoothing both $p_d(y|x)$ and $p_d(x)$ based on Eq. (10).

3.2 Formulation

Here, we induce TANS from SANS with targeting to smooth $p_d(x, y)$ by smoothing both $p_d(y|x)$ and $p_d(x)$. First, we assume a simple replacement from $p_\theta(y|x)$ to $p_\theta(x, y)$ in $\ell_{\text{SANS}}(\theta)$ of Eq. (9):

$$-\frac{1}{|D|} \sum_{(x,y)\in D} \Big[\log(\sigma(s_\theta(x, y) + \tau)) + \sum_{y_i\sim U}^{\nu} p_\theta(x, y_i) \log(\sigma(-s_\theta(x, y_i) - \tau))\Big]. \qquad (11)$$

Method		Smoothing			Remarks
		$p(x,y)$	$p(y\|x)$	$p(x)$	
Subsampling	Base	✓	△	△	$p(y\|x)$ and $p(x)$ are influenced by $p(x,y)$.
	Uniq	△	×	✓	$p(x,y)$ is indirectly controlled by $p(x)$.
	Freq	✓	△	✓	$p(y\|x)$ is indirectly controlled by $p(x,y)$ or $p(x)$.
SANS		△	✓	×	$p(x,y)$ is indirectly controlled by $p(y\|x)$.
TANS		✓	✓	✓	

Table 1: The characteristics of each smoothing method for the NS loss in KGE (See §2.3 for the details.) and our proposed TANS. ✓ and △ respectively denote the method smooths the probability directly and indirectly. × denotes the method does not smooth the probability.

However, using Eq. (11) causes an imbalanced loss between the first and second terms since the sum of $p_\theta(x,y_i)$ on all negative samples is not always 1. Thus, Eq. (11) is impractical as a loss function.

As a solution, we focus on the decomposition $p_\theta(x,y) = p_\theta(y|x)p_\theta(x)$ and the fact that the sum of $p_\theta(y|x)$ of all negative samples is always 1. By using $p_\theta(x)$ to make a balance between the first and second loss term, we can modify Eq. (11) and induce our TANS as follows:

$$\begin{aligned}&\ell_{\text{TANS}}(\theta)\\&= -\frac{1}{|D|}\sum_{(x,y)\in D} p_\theta(x;\gamma)\Big[\log(\sigma(s_\theta(x,y)+\tau))\\&+\sum_{y_i\sim U}^{\nu} p_\theta(y_i|x;\beta)\log(\sigma(-s_\theta(x,y_i)-\tau))\Big], \quad (12)\end{aligned}$$

$$\begin{aligned}p_\theta(x;\gamma) &= \sum_{y_i\in D} p_\theta(x,y_i;\gamma),\\ p_\theta(x,y_i;\gamma) &= \frac{\exp(\gamma s_\theta(x,y_i))}{\sum_{(x',y')\in D}\exp(\gamma s_\theta(x',y'))}, \quad (13)\end{aligned}$$

where γ is a temperature to smooth the frequency of queries. Since TANS uses a noise distribution decided by $p_\theta(x;\gamma)$ and $p_\theta(y_i|x;\beta)$, it does not propagate gradients through probabilities for negative samples, and thus, memory usage is not increased.

3.3 Theoretical Interpretation

In this subsection, we discuss the difference and similarities among TANS and other smoothing methods for the NS loss in KGE. As shown in Table 1, the subsampling methods, Base and Freq, can smooth triplet frequencies similar to our TANS. To investigate TANS from the view point of subsampling, we reformulate Eq. (12) as follows:

$$\begin{aligned}&\ell_{\text{TANS}}(\theta)\\&= -\frac{1}{|D|}\sum_{(x,y)\in D}\Big[A(x,y;\gamma)\log(\sigma(s_\theta(x,y)+\tau))\\&+\sum_{y_i\sim U}^{\nu} B(x,y;\beta,\gamma)\log(\sigma(-s_\theta(x,y_i)-\tau))\Big], \quad (14)\end{aligned}$$

$$\begin{aligned}A(x,y;\gamma) &= p_\theta(x;\gamma),\\ B(x,y;\beta,\gamma) &= p_\theta(y_i|x;\beta)p_\theta(x;\gamma). \quad (15)\end{aligned}$$

Apart from the temperature terms, α, β, and γ, we can see that the general formulation of subsampling in Eq. (3) and the above Eq. (14) has the same formulation. Thus, TANS is not merely an extension of SANS but also a novel subsampling method.

Even though their similar characteristic, TANS and subsampling have an essential difference: TANS smooths the frequencies by model-predicted distributions as in Eq. (13), and the subsampling methods smooth them by counting appearance frequencies on the observed data as in Eq. (4), (5), (6), and (7). For instance, TANS can work even when the entity or relations included in the target triplet appear more than once, which is theoretically different from conventional approaches.

Since the superiority of using either model-based or count-based frequencies depends on the model and dataset, we empirically investigate this point through our experiments.

4 Unified Interpretation of SANS and Subsampling

In the previous section, we understand that our TANS can smooth triplets, queries, and answers partially covered by SANS and subsampling methods. On the other hand, TANS only relies on model-predicted frequencies to smooth the frequencies.

Temperature			Induced NS Loss
α	β	γ	
$=0$	$=0$	$=0$	Equivalent to $\ell_{\mathrm{NS}}(\theta)$, the basic NS loss in KGE (Eq. (2))
$=0$	$=0$	$\neq 0$	Currently does not exist
$=0$	$\neq 0$	$=0$	Proportional to $\ell_{\mathrm{SANS}}(\theta)$, the SANS loss (Eq. (9))
$=0$	$\neq 0$	$\neq 0$	Equivalent to our $\ell_{\mathrm{TANS}}(\theta)$, the TANS loss (Eq. (12))
$\neq 0$	$=0$	$=0$	Proportional to $\ell_{\mathrm{NS}}(\theta)$, the basic NS loss in KGE (Eq. (2)) with subsampling in §2.3
$\neq 0$	$=0$	$\neq 0$	Currently does not exist
$\neq 0$	$\neq 0$	$=0$	Proportional to $\ell_{\mathrm{SANS}}(\theta)$, the SANS loss (Eq. (9)) with subsampling in §2.3
$\neq 0$	$\neq 0$	$\neq 0$	Equivalent to our $\ell_{\mathrm{UNI}}(\theta)$, the unified NS loss in KGE (Eq. (16)) and also equivalent to our $\ell_{\mathrm{TANS}}(\theta)$, the TANS loss (Eq. (12)) with subsampling in §2.3

Table 2: The relationship among the loss functions from the viewpoint of the unified NS loss, $\ell_{\mathrm{UNI}}(\theta)$ in Eq. (16).

Neubig and Dyer (2016) point out the benefits of combining count-based and model-predicted frequencies in language modeling. This section integrates smoothing methods for the NS loss in KGE from a unified interpretation.

4.1 Formulation

We formulate the unified loss function by introducing subsampling (Eq. (3)) into our TANS (Eq. (12)) as follows:

$$\begin{aligned}&\ell_{\mathrm{UNI}}(\theta)\\ =&-\frac{1}{|D|}\sum_{(x,y)\in D} p_\theta(x;\gamma)\Big[A(x,y;\alpha)\log(\sigma(s_\theta(x,y)+\tau))\\ &+\eta\sum_{y_i\sim U}^{\nu} B(x,y;\alpha)p_\theta(y_i|x;\beta)\log(\sigma(-s_\theta(x,y_i)-\tau))\Big],\end{aligned} \tag{16}$$

where η is a hyperparamter that can be any value to absorb the difference among the three different subsampling methods, Base, Uniq, and Freq.

Here, we can induce the NS losses shown in our paper from Eq. (16) by changing the temperature parameters α, β, and γ. Table 2 shows the induced losses from our $\ell_{\mathrm{UNI}}(\theta)$. Note that since $p_\theta(x;\gamma)$ only appears in our TANS, canceling $p_\theta(x;\gamma)$ by $\gamma=0$ induces an inequivalent but a proportional relationship to the conventional NS loss.

4.2 Theoretical Interpretation

As shown in Table 2, TANS w/ subsampling has characteristics of all smoothing methods for the NS loss in KGE introduced in this paper. Therefore, we can expect higher performance of TANS w/ subsampling than the combination of conventional methods, the basic NS, SANS, and subsampling. However, because TANS w/ subsampling uses subsampling in §2.3, we need to choose the one from Base, Uniq, and Freq for TANS w/ subsampling. Since this part is out of the scope of theoretical interpretation, we investigate this in the experiments.

5 Experiments

In this section, we investigate our theoretical interpretation in §3.3 and §4.2 through experiments.

5.1 Experimental Settings

Datasets We used three common datasets, FB15k-237 (Toutanova and Chen, 2015), WN18RR, and YAGO3-10 (Dettmers et al., 2018) [3].

Comparison Methods As comparison methods, we used TransE (Bordes et al., 2013), DistMult (Yang et al., 2015), ComplEx (Trouillon et al., 2016), RotatE (Sun et al., 2019), HAKE (Zhang et al., 2020a), and HousE (Li et al., 2022). We followed the original settings of Sun et al. (2019) for TransE, DistMult, ComplEx, and RotatE with their implementation[4], the original settings of Zhang et al. (2020a) for HAKE with their implementation[5], and the original settings of Li et al. (2022) for HousE with their implementation[6]. We tuned temperature γ on the validation split for each dataset.

Metrics We employed conventional metrics in KGC, i.e., MRR, Hits@1 (H@1), Hits@3 (H@3), and Hits@10 (H@10) and reported the average scores and their standard deviations by three different runs with fixed random seeds.

[3]Table 3 in Appendix A shows the dataset statistics.

[4]`https://github.com/DeepGraphLearning/KnowledgeGraphEmbedding`

[5]`https://github.com/MIRALab-USTC/KGE-HAKE`

[6]`https://github.com/rui9812/HousE`

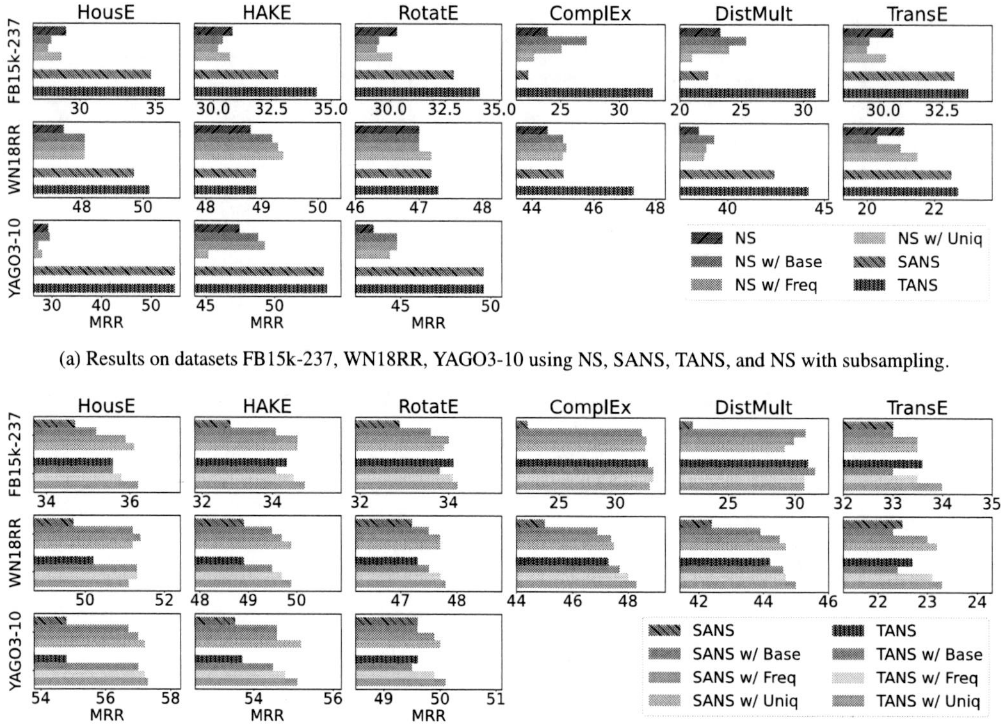

(a) Results on datasets FB15k-237, WN18RR, YAGO3-10 using NS, SANS, TANS, and NS with subsampling.

(b) Results on datasets FB15k-237, WN18RR, YAGO3-10 using SANS, TANS, and those with subsampling.

Figure 3: KGC performance on common KGs (Notations are the same as in Figure 2).

5.2 Results

Since the result tables are large[7], we discuss them individually, focusing on important information in the following subsections.

5.2.1 Effectiveness of TANS

Figure 3a shows the MRR scores of each method. From the result, we can understand the effectiveness of considering triplet information in SANS as conducted in TANS. Thus, the result is along with our expectation in §3.3 that TANS can cover the role of subsampling methods. However, as the result of HAKE on WN18RR shows, there is a case that subsampling methods outperform TANS. As discussed in §3.3, using only TANS does not cover all combinations of NS loss and subsampling. Considering this theoretical fact, we further compare TANS with subsampling and the SANS loss with subsampling in the following section.

[7]The full experimental results are listed in Appendix B. The scores are included in Table 5, 6, and 7 of Appendix B.1. The training loss curves and validation MRR curves for each smoothing method are in Figure 6, 7, and 8 of Appendix B.2.

5.2.2 Validity of the Unified Interpretation

Figure 3b shows the result for each configuration. We can see performance improvements by using subsampling in both SANS and TANS. Furthermore, in almost all cases, TANS with subsampling achieve the highest MRR. This observation is along with the theoretical conclusion in §3.3 that TANS with subsampling can cover the characteristic of other NS loss in terms of smoothing. On the other hand, the results of HAKE on YAGO3-10 show the different tendency that SANS with subsampling achieves the best MRR instead of TANS. Because the model prediction estimates the triplet frequencies, TANS is influenced by the selected model. Therefore, carefully choosing the combination of a loss function and model is still effective in improving KGC performance on the NS loss with subsampling.

6 Analysis

We analyze how TANS mitigates the sparsity problem in imbalanced KGs commonly caused by low frequent triplets in KGC. By considering that all

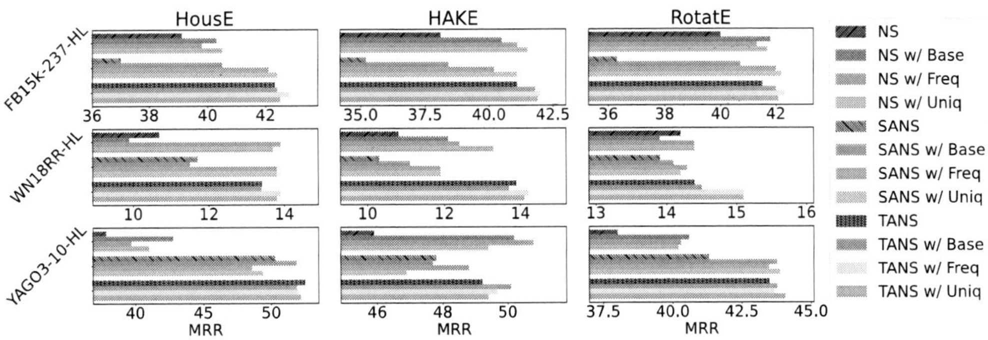

Figure 4: KGC performance on filtered sparser KGs, i.e., FB15k-237-HL, WN18RR-HL, and YAGO3-10-HL (Notations are the same as in Figure 2).

triplets in KGs appear at most once, we focus on queries. We extracted 0.5% triplets with the highest or lowest frequent queries in training, validation, and test splits as the sparser subsets FB15k-237-HL, WN18RR-HL, and YAGO3-10-HL, respectively [8] from original data, for the investigation.

Figure 4 shows MRRs for each model on each sparser dataset. From the result, we can understand that TANS can perform even much better in KGC when KGs get more imbalanced. You can see further detailed results in Table 8, 9, and 10 of Appendix C.3.

7 Related Work

Knowledge Graph Knowledge graphs have important roles in various knowledge-intensive NLP tasks like dialog (Moon et al., 2019), question answering (Reese et al., 2020), named entity recognition (Liu et al., 2019), open-domain questions (Hu et al., 2022), recommendation systems (Gao et al., 2020), and commonsense reasoning (Sakai et al., 2024b), etc. In addition to these text-only tasks, knowledge-intensive vision and language (V&L) tasks such as visual question answering (VQA) (Yue et al., 2023), image generation (Kamigaito et al., 2023), explanation generation (Hayashi et al., 2024), and image review generation (Saito et al., 2024) also require external knowledge. Visual KGs (Zhu et al., 2024) have the potential to contribute to solving these tasks. Therefore, KGs are important materials in various different fields.

Knowlege Graph Completion Even though KGs are useful, their sparsity is a fundamental problem. To solve the sparsity of knowledge graphs, we need to complete them by inferring their unseen links between nodes, which are entities. For that purpose, knowledge graph completion (KGC) and knowledge graph embedding (KGE) (Bordes et al., 2011), which represents KG information as a continuous vector space, are commonly used. As KGE methods, vector space models like TransE (Bordes et al., 2013), DistMult (Yang et al., 2015), ComplEx (Trouillon et al., 2016), RotatE (Sun et al., 2019), HAKE (Zhang et al., 2020a), and HousE (Li et al., 2022), that learn only from task-specific datasets expand this field as pioneers. As well as such approaches, pre-trained language model (PLM)-based approaches like KEPLER (Wang et al., 2021) and SimKGC (Wang et al., 2022) also have an important role in KGC due to their ability to utilize the knowledge obtained in pre-training. However, as pointed out by Sakai et al. (2024a), PLM-based approaches have a leakage issue caused by data contamination in pre-training. Generation-based KGC methods like KGT5 (Saxena et al., 2022) and GenKGC (Xie et al., 2022) are unique in directly generating entity names. In hierarchical text classification (HTC), generation-based approaches contribute to improving performance (Kwon et al., 2023) supported by considering label hierarchies by fusing pre-trained text and label embeddings (Xiong et al., 2021; Zhang et al., 2021) on the decoder. However, Sakai et al. (2024a) point out that commonly used KGC methods conduct link-level prediction, and such generation-based KGC methods make it difficult to use structure information of KGs directly. Thus, their performance gain is limited. This situation requires investigating the benefits of inferring links by generation-based

[8] Note that we show their appearance frequencies of queries and answers in the training data in Figure 5 and detailed statistics in Table 4 of Appendix C.1 and C.2, respectively.

KGC under predefined entities and relationships.

Negative Sampling Mikolov et al. (2013) initially propose the NS loss of the frequent words to train their word embedding model, word2vec. Trouillon et al. (2016) introduce the NS loss to KGE to speed up training. Melamud et al. (2017) use the NS loss to train the language model. In contextualized pre-trained embeddings, Clark et al. (2020a) indicate that a BERT (Devlin et al., 2019)-like model ELECTRA (Clark et al., 2020b) uses the NS loss to perform better and faster than language models. Sun et al. (2019) extend the NS loss to SANS loss for KGE and propose their noise distribution, which is subsampled by a uniformed probability $p_\theta(y_i|x)$. Kamigaito and Hayashi (2021) point out the sparseness problem of KGs through their theoretical analysis of the NS loss in KGE. Furthermore, Kamigaito and Hayashi (2022a,b) reveal that subsampling (Mikolov et al., 2013) can alleviate the sparseness problem in the NS for KGE and conclude three assumptions for subsampling, i.e., Base, Freq, and Uniq. Feng et al. (2023) incorporate their proposed model-based subsampling that estimates frequencies for entities and their relationships by a trained KGE model into the subsampling of the NS loss to mitigate the sparseness issue of counting the frequency by increasing computational cost to train the additional KGE model.

Our Work Through our work, we theoretically clarify the position of the previous works on SANS loss and subsampling from the viewpoint of smoothing methods for the NS loss in KGE. Since our work unitedly interprets SANS loss and subsampling, our proposed TANS inherits the advantages of conventional works and can deal with the sparsity problem in the NS loss for KGE.

8 Conclusion

We reveal the relationships between SANS loss and subsampling for the KG completion task through theoretical analysis. We explain that SANS loss and subsampling under three assumptions, Base, Freq, and Uniq have similar roles to mitigate the sparseness problem of queries and answers of KGs by smoothing the frequencies of queries and answers. Furthermore, based on our interpretation, we induce a new loss function, Triplet Adaptive Negative Sampling (TANS), by integrating SANS loss and subsampling. We also introduce a theoretical interpretation that TANS with subsampling can cover all conventional combinations of SANS loss and subsampling.

We verified our interpretation by empirical experiments in three common datasets, FB15k-237, WN18RR, and YAGO3-10, and six popular KGE models, TransE, DistMult, ComplEx, RotatE, HAKE, and HousE. The experimental results show that our TANS loss can outperform subsampling and SANS loss with many models in terms of MRR as expected by our theoretical interpretation. Furthermore, the combinatorial use of TANS and subsampling achieved comparable or better performance than other combinations and showed the validity of our theoretical interpretation that TANS with subsampling can cover all conventional combinations of SANS loss and subsampling in KGE.

Limitations

Our experiments are conducted exclusively on public datasets, which are relatively well-balanced. Consequently, we anticipate that our TANS will perform better on real-world KGs.

Ethics Statement

We used the publicly available datasets, FB15k-237, WN18RR, and YAGO3-10, to train and evaluate KGE models, and there is no ethical consideration.

Reproducibility Statement

We used the publicly available code to implement KGE models, TransE, DistMult, ComplEx, RotatE, HAKE, and HousE with the author-provided hyperparameters as described in §5.1. Regarding the temperature parameter γ, we tuned it on the validation split for each dataset and reported the values in Table 5, 6, and 7 of Appendix B. Our code and data are available at `https://github.com/xincanfeng/ss_kge`.

Acknowledgements

This work was supported by NAIST Granite, i.e., JST SPRING Grant Number JPMJSP2140.

References

Kian Ahrabian, Aarash Feizi, Yasmin Salehi, William L. Hamilton, and Avishek Joey Bose. 2020. Structure aware negative sampling in knowledge graphs. In *Proceedings of the 2020 Conference on Empirical*

Methods in Natural Language Processing (EMNLP), pages 6093–6101, Online. Association for Computational Linguistics.

Antoine Bordes, Nicolas Usunier, Alberto García-Durán, Jason Weston, and Oksana Yakhnenko. 2013. Translating embeddings for modeling multi-relational data. In *Advances in Neural Information Processing Systems 26: 27th Annual Conference on Neural Information Processing Systems 2013*, pages 2787–2795.

Antoine Bordes, Jason Weston, Ronan Collobert, and Yoshua Bengio. 2011. Learning structured embeddings of knowledge bases. In *Proceedings of the AAAI conference on artificial intelligence*, volume 25, pages 301–306.

Kevin Clark, Minh-Thang Luong, Quoc Le, and Christopher D. Manning. 2020a. Pre-training transformers as energy-based cloze models. In *Proceedings of the 2020 Conference on Empirical Methods in Natural Language Processing (EMNLP)*, pages 285–294, Online. Association for Computational Linguistics.

Kevin Clark, Minh-Thang Luong, Quoc V. Le, and Christopher D. Manning. 2020b. Electra: Pre-training text encoders as discriminators rather than generators. In *International Conference on Learning Representations*.

Tim Dettmers, Pasquale Minervini, Pontus Stenetorp, and Sebastian Riedel. 2018. Convolutional 2d knowledge graph embeddings. In *Proceedings of the Thirty-Second AAAI Conference on Artificial Intelligence, (AAAI-18)*, pages 1811–1818.

Jacob Devlin, Ming-Wei Chang, Kenton Lee, and Kristina Toutanova. 2019. BERT: Pre-training of deep bidirectional transformers for language understanding. In *Proceedings of the 2019 Conference of the North American Chapter of the Association for Computational Linguistics: Human Language Technologies, Volume 1 (Long and Short Papers)*, pages 4171–4186, Minneapolis, Minnesota. Association for Computational Linguistics.

Xincan Feng, Hidetaka Kamigaito, Katsuhiko Hayashi, and Taro Watanabe. 2023. Model-based subsampling for knowledge graph completion. In *Proceedings of the 13th International Joint Conference on Natural Language Processing and the 3rd Conference of the Asia-Pacific Chapter of the Association for Computational Linguistics (Volume 1: Long Papers)*, pages 910–920, Nusa Dua, Bali. Association for Computational Linguistics.

Yang Gao, Yi-Fan Li, Yu Lin, Hang Gao, and Latifur Khan. 2020. Deep learning on knowledge graph for recommender system: A survey.

Kazuki Hayashi, Yusuke Sakai, Hidetaka Kamigaito, Katsuhiko Hayashi, and Taro Watanabe. 2024. Artwork explanation in large-scale vision language models.

Ziniu Hu, Yichong Xu, Wenhao Yu, Shuohang Wang, Ziyi Yang, Chenguang Zhu, Kai-Wei Chang, and Yizhou Sun. 2022. Empowering language models with knowledge graph reasoning for question answering.

Hidetaka Kamigaito and Katsuhiko Hayashi. 2021. Unified interpretation of softmax cross-entropy and negative sampling: With case study for knowledge graph embedding. In *Proceedings of the 59th Annual Meeting of the Association for Computational Linguistics and the 11th International Joint Conference on Natural Language Processing (Volume 1: Long Papers)*, pages 5517–5531, Online. Association for Computational Linguistics.

Hidetaka Kamigaito and Katsuhiko Hayashi. 2022a. Comprehensive analysis of negative sampling in knowledge graph representation learning. In *Proceedings of the 39th International Conference on Machine Learning*, volume 162 of *Proceedings of Machine Learning Research*, pages 10661–10675. PMLR.

Hidetaka Kamigaito and Katsuhiko Hayashi. 2022b. Erratum to: Comprehensive analysis of negative sampling in knowledge graph representation learning. *ResearchGate*.

Hidetaka Kamigaito, Katsuhiko Hayashi, and Taro Watanabe. 2023. Table and image generation for investigating knowledge of entities in pre-trained vision and language models. In *Proceedings of the 61st Annual Meeting of the Association for Computational Linguistics (Volume 2: Short Papers)*, pages 1904–1917, Toronto, Canada. Association for Computational Linguistics.

Slava Katz. 1987. Estimation of probabilities from sparse data for the language model component of a speech recognizer. *IEEE transactions on acoustics, speech, and signal processing*, 35(3):400–401.

Jingun Kwon, Hidetaka Kamigaito, Young-In Song, and Manabu Okumura. 2023. Hierarchical label generation for text classification. In *Findings of the Association for Computational Linguistics: EACL 2023*, pages 625–632, Dubrovnik, Croatia. Association for Computational Linguistics.

Rui Li, Jianan Zhao, Chaozhuo Li, Di He, Yiqi Wang, Yuming Liu, Hao Sun, Senzhang Wang, Weiwei Deng, Yanming Shen, Xing Xie, and Qi Zhang. 2022. House: Knowledge graph embedding with householder parameterization.

Weijie Liu, Peng Zhou, Zhe Zhao, Zhiruo Wang, Qi Ju, Haotang Deng, and Ping Wang. 2019. K-bert: Enabling language representation with knowledge graph.

Oren Melamud, Ido Dagan, and Jacob Goldberger. 2017. A simple language model based on PMI matrix approximations. In *Proceedings of the 2017 Conference on Empirical Methods in Natural Language Processing*, pages 1860–1865, Copenhagen, Denmark. Association for Computational Linguistics.

Tomás Mikolov, Ilya Sutskever, Kai Chen, Greg Corrado, and Jeffrey Dean. 2013. Distributed representations of words and phrases and their compositionality. *CoRR*, abs/1310.4546.

Seungwhan Moon, Pararth Shah, Anuj Kumar, and Rajen Subba. 2019. OpenDialKG: Explainable conversational reasoning with attention-based walks over knowledge graphs. In *Proceedings of the 57th Annual Meeting of the Association for Computational Linguistics*, pages 845–854, Florence, Italy. Association for Computational Linguistics.

Graham Neubig and Chris Dyer. 2016. Generalizing and hybridizing count-based and neural language models. In *Proceedings of the 2016 Conference on Empirical Methods in Natural Language Processing*, pages 1163–1172, Austin, Texas. Association for Computational Linguistics.

Justin Reese, Deepak Unni, Tiffany Callahan, Luca Cappelletti, Vida Ravanmehr, Seth Carbon, Kent Shefchek, Benjamin Good, James Balhoff, Tommaso Fontana, Hannah Blau, Nicolas Matentzoglu, Nomi Harris, Monica Munoz-Torres, Melissa Haendel, Peter Robinson, Marcin Joachimiak, and Christopher Mungall. 2020. Kg-covid-19: a framework to produce customized knowledge graphs for covid-19 response. *Patterns*, 2:100155.

Shigeki Saito, Kazuki Hayashi, Yusuke Ide, Yusuke Sakai, Kazuma Onishi, Toma Suzuki, Seiji Gobara, Hidetaka Kamigaito, Katsuhiko Hayashi, and Taro Watanabe. 2024. Evaluating image review ability of vision language models.

Yusuke Sakai, Hidetaka Kamigaito, Katsuhiko Hayashi, and Taro Watanabe. 2024a. Does pre-trained language model actually infer unseen links in knowledge graph completion? In *Proceedings of the 2024 Conference of the North American Chapter of the Association for Computational Linguistics: Human Language Technologies (Volume 1: Long Papers)*, pages 8091–8106, Mexico City, Mexico. Association for Computational Linguistics.

Yusuke Sakai, Hidetaka Kamigaito, and Taro Watanabe. 2024b. mcsqa: Multilingual commonsense reasoning dataset with unified creation strategy by language models and humans.

Apoorv Saxena, Adrian Kochsiek, and Rainer Gemulla. 2022. Sequence-to-sequence knowledge graph completion and question answering. In *Proceedings of the 60th Annual Meeting of the Association for Computational Linguistics*.

Zhiqing Sun, Zhi-Hong Deng, Jian-Yun Nie, and Jian Tang. 2019. Rotate: Knowledge graph embedding by relational rotation in complex space. In *Proceedings of the 7th International Conference on Learning Representations, ICLR 2019*.

Christian Szegedy, Vincent Vanhoucke, Sergey Ioffe, Jon Shlens, and Zbigniew Wojna. 2016. Rethinking the inception architecture for computer vision. In *Proceedings of the IEEE conference on computer vision and pattern recognition*, pages 2818–2826.

Kristina Toutanova and Danqi Chen. 2015. Observed versus latent features for knowledge base and text inference. In *Proceedings of the 3rd Workshop on Continuous Vector Space Models and their Compositionality*, pages 57–66, Beijing, China. Association for Computational Linguistics.

Théo Trouillon, Johannes Welbl, Sebastian Riedel, Éric Gaussier, and Guillaume Bouchard. 2016. Complex embeddings for simple link prediction. In *Proceedings of the 33nd International Conference on Machine Learning, ICML 2016*, volume 48 of *JMLR Workshop and Conference Proceedings*, pages 2071–2080. JMLR.org.

Liang Wang, Wei Zhao, Zhuoyu Wei, and Jingming Liu. 2022. SimKGC: Simple contrastive knowledge graph completion with pre-trained language models. In *Proceedings of the 60th Annual Meeting of the Association for Computational Linguistics (Volume 1: Long Papers)*, pages 4281–4294, Dublin, Ireland. Association for Computational Linguistics.

Xiaozhi Wang, Tianyu Gao, Zhaocheng Zhu, Zhengyan Zhang, Zhiyuan Liu, Juanzi Li, and Jian Tang. 2021. KEPLER: A unified model for knowledge embedding and pre-trained language representation. *Transactions of the Association for Computational Linguistics*, 9:176–194.

Xin Xie, Ningyu Zhang, Zhoubo Li, Shumin Deng, Hui Chen, Feiyu Xiong, Mosha Chen, and Huajun Chen. 2022. From discrimination to generation: Knowledge graph completion with generative transformer. In *Companion Proceedings of the Web Conference 2022*, WWW '22, page 162–165, New York, NY, USA. Association for Computing Machinery.

Yijin Xiong, Yukun Feng, Hao Wu, Hidetaka Kamigaito, and Manabu Okumura. 2021. Fusing label embedding into BERT: An efficient improvement for text classification. In *Findings of the Association for Computational Linguistics: ACL-IJCNLP 2021*, pages 1743–1750, Online. Association for Computational Linguistics.

Bishan Yang, Wen-tau Yih, Xiaodong He, Jianfeng Gao, and Li Deng. 2015. Embedding entities and relations for learning and inference in knowledge bases. In *Proceddings of the 3rd International Conference on Learning Representations, ICLR 2015*.

Xiang Yue, Yuansheng Ni, Kai Zhang, Tianyu Zheng, Ruoqi Liu, Ge Zhang, Samuel Stevens, Dongfu Jiang, Weiming Ren, Yuxuan Sun, Cong Wei, Botao Yu, Ruibin Yuan, Renliang Sun, Ming Yin, Boyuan Zheng, Zhenzhu Yang, Yibo Liu, Wenhao Huang, Huan Sun, Yu Su, and Wenhu Chen. 2023. Mmmu: A massive multi-discipline multimodal understanding and reasoning benchmark for expert agi.

Ying Zhang, Hidetaka Kamigaito, and Manabu Okumura. 2021. A language model-based generative classifier for sentence-level discourse parsing. In *Proceedings of the 2021 Conference on Empirical Methods in Natural Language Processing*, pages 2432–2446, Online and Punta Cana, Dominican Republic. Association for Computational Linguistics.

Zhanqiu Zhang, Jianyu Cai, Yongdong Zhang, and Jie Wang. 2020a. Learning hierarchy-aware knowledge graph embeddings for link prediction. In *Proceedings of the Thirty-Fourth AAAI Conference on Artificial Intelligence, (AAAI20)*, pages 3065–3072.

Zhiyuan Zhang, Xiaoqian Liu, Yi Zhang, Qi Su, Xu Sun, and Bin He. 2020b. Pretrain-KGE: Learning knowledge representation from pretrained language models. In *Findings of the Association for Computational Linguistics: EMNLP 2020*, pages 259–266, Online. Association for Computational Linguistics.

Xiangru Zhu, Zhixu Li, Xiaodan Wang, Xueyao Jiang, Penglei Sun, Xuwu Wang, Yanghua Xiao, and Nicholas Jing Yuan. 2024. Multi-modal knowledge graph construction and application: A survey. *IEEE Transactions on Knowledge and Data Engineering*, 36(2):715–735.

A Dataset Statistics

Table 3 shows the dataset statistics for dataset FB15k-237, WN18RR, and YAGO3-10, introduced in §5.1.

B Full Experimental Results

B.1 Results Tables

Table 5, 6, and 7 list all results on FB15k-237, WN18RR, and YAGO3-10, explained in §5.2. In these tables, the bold scores are the best results for each subsampling type (e.g. *None*, *Base*, *Freq*, and *Uniq.*), † indicates the best scores for each model, *SD* denotes the standard deviation of the three trials, and γ denotes the temperature chosen by development data.

B.2 Training Loss and Validation MRR Curve

Figure 6, 7, and 8 show the training loss curves and validation MRR curves for each smoothing method. From these figures, we can understand that the convergence of TANS loss is as well as SANS and NS loss on datasets FB15k-237, WN18RR, and YAGO3-10 for each KGE model. Meanwhile, the time complexity of TANS is the same with SANS and NS loss too.

C Sparse Queries

C.1 Appearance Frequencies of Queries and Answers

Figure 5 shows the appearance frequencies of queries and answers in the training set of our filtered sparser data FB15k-237-HL, WN18RR-HL, and YAGO3-10-HL, expained in §6.

C.2 Data Statistics

Table 4 shows detailed statistics of our filtered sparser data FB15k-237-HL, WN18RR-HL, and YAGO3-10-HL, expained in §6.

C.3 Detailed Results

Table 8, 9, and 10 shows the detailed results on our filtered sparser data FB15k-237-HL, WN18RR-HL, and YAGO3-10-HL, expained in §6. Notations are as those described in §B.1.

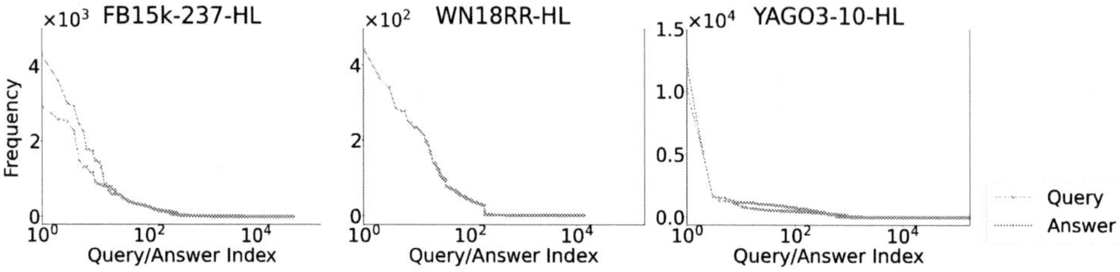

Figure 5: Appearance frequencies of queries and answers (entities) in the training data of the sparser subsets FB15k-237-HL, WN18RR-HL, and YAGO3-10-HL. Note that the indices are sorted from high frequency to low.

Dataset	Split	Tuple	Query	Entity	Relation
FB15k-237	Total	310,116	150,508	14,541	237
	#Train	272,115	138,694	14,505	237
	#Valid	17,535	19,750	9,809	223
	#Test	20,466	22,379	10,348	224
WN18RR	Total	93,003	77,479	40,943	11
	#Train	86,835	74,587	40,559	11
	#Valid	3,034	5,431	5,173	11
	#Test	3,134	5,565	5,323	11
YAGO3-10	Total	1,089,040	372,775	123,182	37
	#Train	1,079,040	371,077	123,143	37
	#Valid	5,000	8,534	7,948	33
	#Test	5,000	8,531	7,937	34

Table 3: Statistics for each public dataset.

Dataset	Split	Tuple	Query	Entity	Relation
FB15k-237-HL	Total	111,631	63,330	11,828	155
	#Train	95,244	55,923	11,600	155
	#Valid	7,571	6,918	4,933	90
	#Test	8,816	7,830	5,406	89
WN18RR-HL	Total	14,697	14,675	12,973	10
	#Train	13,758	13,785	12,275	10
	#Valid	465	619	613	9
	#Test	474	623	619	8
YAGO3-10-HL	Total	366,079	182,274	95,788	29
	#Train	362,728	181,196	95,432	29
	#Valid	1,662	2,316	2,113	13
	#Test	1,689	2,359	2,135	14

Table 4: Statistics of the filtered sparser datasets.

Model	Subsampling Assumption	Loss	MRR Mean	MRR SD	H@1 Mean	H@1 SD	H@3 Mean	H@3 SD	H@10 Mean	H@10 SD	γ
FB15k-237											
ComplEx	None	NS	23.9	0.2	15.8	0.1	26.1	0.3	40.0	0.2	-
		SANS	22.3	0.1	13.8	0.1	24.2	0.0	39.5	0.2	-
		TANS	**32.8**	0.2	**23.2**	0.1	**36.2**	0.2	**52.2**	0.1	-2
	Base	NS	27.2	0.1	19.1	0.1	29.5	0.1	43.0	0.2	-
		SANS	32.3	0.0	23.0	0.1	35.4	0.1	51.2	0.1	-
		TANS	†**33.3**	0.0	†**23.8**	0.1	†**36.9**	0.1	†**52.7**	0.0	-1
	Freq	NS	25.1	0.2	17.1	0.3	27.4	0.2	41.0	0.2	-
		SANS	32.7	0.1	23.6	0.1	36.0	0.1	51.2	0.1	-
		TANS	†**33.3**	0.0	†**23.8**	0.0	**36.8**	0.1	**52.1**	0.2	-0.5
	Uniq	NS	22.8	0.4	14.7	0.5	24.7	0.4	39.0	0.1	-
		SANS	32.6	0.0	**23.5**	0.1	35.8	0.1	51.2	0.1	-
		TANS	**33.0**	0.1	**23.5**	0.1	**36.5**	0.1	**52.1**	0.1	-0.5
DistMult	None	NS	23.3	0.1	15.6	0.1	25.7	0.1	38.4	0.1	-
		SANS	22.3	0.1	14.0	0.2	24.1	0.1	39.2	0.0	-
		TANS	**31.0**	0.1	**21.7**	0.1	**34.0**	0.1	**49.6**	0.1	-1
	Base	NS	25.4	0.1	17.9	0.1	27.6	0.1	40.4	0.1	-
		SANS	30.8	0.1	21.9	0.1	33.6	0.1	48.4	0.1	-
		TANS	†**31.5**	0.1	†**22.4**	0.1	†**34.6**	0.1	†**49.7**	0.0	-0.5
	Freq	NS	24.0	0.1	16.7	0.2	25.9	0.1	38.4	0.1	-
		SANS	29.9	0.0	21.2	0.1	32.8	0.0	47.5	0.1	-
		TANS	**30.7**	0.0	**21.6**	0.0	**34.0**	0.0	**49.0**	0.0	-1
	Uniq	NS	21.0	0.1	13.5	0.2	22.8	0.2	36.3	0.2	-
		SANS	29.2	0.0	20.5	0.1	31.9	0.0	46.7	0.0	-
		TANS	**30.7**	0.1	**21.5**	0.1	**33.8**	0.1	**49.3**	0.1	-2
TransE	None	NS	30.4	0.0	21.3	0.1	33.4	0.1	48.5	0.0	-
		SANS	33.0	0.1	22.9	0.1	37.2	0.1	†**53.0**	0.1	-
		TANS	**33.6**	0.0	**23.9**	0.0	**37.3**	0.0	†**53.0**	0.1	-0.5
	Base	NS	29.4	0.1	20.0	0.1	32.8	0.0	48.1	0.0	-
		SANS	**33.0**	0.1	23.1	0.1	**36.8**	0.1	**52.7**	0.1	-
		TANS	**33.0**	0.0	23.1	0.0	**36.8**	0.1	**52.7**	0.1	-0.1
	Freq	NS	29.3	0.1	20.0	0.1	32.8	0.1	47.8	0.1	-
		SANS	**33.5**	0.0	**23.9**	0.1	**37.2**	0.1	**52.8**	0.1	-
		TANS	**33.5**	0.1	**23.9**	0.1	**37.2**	0.0	**52.8**	0.1	-0.1
	Uniq	NS	30.1	0.1	21.0	0.1	33.6	0.0	48.0	0.0	-
		SANS	33.5	0.0	23.9	0.0	37.3	0.2	52.7	0.1	-
		TANS	†**34.0**	0.1	†**24.5**	0.1	†**37.7**	0.1	†**53.0**	0.1	0.5
RotatE	None	NS	30.3	0.0	21.4	0.1	33.2	0.1	48.4	0.1	-
		SANS	32.9	0.1	22.8	0.1	36.8	0.0	53.1	0.2	-
		TANS	**34.1**	0.1	**24.6**	0.1	**37.7**	0.1	†**53.3**	0.1	-0.5
	Base	NS	29.5	0.0	20.3	0.0	32.7	0.1	47.9	0.0	-
		SANS	33.6	0.1	23.9	0.1	37.3	0.1	**53.1**	0.0	-
		TANS	**33.8**	0.0	**24.2**	0.0	**37.4**	0.0	53.0	0.1	-0.5
	Freq	NS	29.4	0.1	20.2	0.1	32.6	0.1	47.6	0.1	-
		SANS	34.0	0.1	**24.6**	0.0	**37.7**	0.0	53.0	0.0	-
		TANS	**34.1**	0.0	**24.6**	0.0	**37.7**	0.0	**53.1**	0.1	-0.01
	Uniq	NS	30.1	0.0	21.2	0.1	33.3	0.1	47.7	0.1	-
		SANS	33.9	0.1	24.4	0.1	37.6	0.1	52.9	0.1	-
		TANS	†**34.2**	0.0	†**24.7**	0.1	†**37.8**	0.0	**53.1**	0.1	0.5
HAKE	None	NS	30.8	0.1	21.8	0.1	33.8	0.1	48.6	0.1	-
		SANS	32.8	0.2	22.7	0.3	36.9	0.1	52.8	0.1	-
		TANS	**34.4**	0.1	**24.9**	0.1	**37.9**	0.2	**53.6**	0.0	-0.5
	Base	NS	30.4	0.1	21.6	0.1	33.3	0.1	48.2	0.0	-
		SANS	**34.1**	0.1	**24.4**	0.1	**37.9**	0.1	53.6	0.2	-
		TANS	**34.1**	0.0	**24.4**	0.0	**37.9**	0.0	**53.7**	0.0	-0.05
	Freq	NS	30.2	0.1	21.5	0.0	33.1	0.0	47.7	0.1	-
		SANS	**34.7**	0.0	**25.2**	0.1	**38.2**	0.0	**53.8**	0.1	-
		TANS	34.6	0.0	25.0	0.1	**38.2**	0.2	53.7	0.1	0.05
	Uniq	NS	30.7	0.1	22.2	0.1	33.5	0.1	48.0	0.1	-
		SANS	34.7	0.1	25.1	0.1	38.3	0.1	53.9	0.1	-
		TANS	†**34.9**	0.0	†**25.4**	0.0	†**38.6**	0.1	†**54.0**	0.1	0.5
HousE	None	NS	29.1	0.1	20.6	0.1	31.6	0.1	46.3	0.1	-
		SANS	34.7	0.2	24.8	0.2	38.5	0.3	54.4	0.2	-
		TANS	**35.6**	0.1	**26.1**	0.1	**39.4**	0.1	**54.5**	0.1	-1
	Base	NS	28.1	0.1	19.6	0.1	30.9	0.2	45.1	0.2	-
		SANS	35.2	0.2	25.6	0.2	39.0	0.2	54.4	0.3	-
		TANS	**35.6**	0.1	**26.1**	0.1	**39.4**	0.2	**54.5**	0.1	-0.5
	Freq	NS	27.9	0.1	19.2	0.1	30.7	0.2	45.2	0.1	-
		SANS	**35.9**	0.2	**26.4**	0.2	39.5	0.2	**54.7**	0.1	-
		TANS	35.8	0.2	**26.4**	0.2	**39.6**	0.2	**54.7**	0.1	-0.01
	Uniq	NS	28.8	0.1	20.2	0.2	31.9	0.1	45.7	0.0	-
		SANS	36.1	0.1	†**26.7**	0.2	39.8	0.1	†**54.8**	0.2	-
		TANS	†**36.2**	0.1	†**26.7**	0.2	†**39.9**	0.1	†**54.8**	0.1	0.1

Table 5: Results on FB15k-237.

WN18RR											
Model	Subsampling		MRR		H@1		H@3		H@10		γ
	Assumption	Loss	Mean	SD	Mean	SD	Mean	SD	Mean	SD	
ComplEx	None	NS	44.5	0.1	38.1	0.2	48.3	0.2	55.5	0.1	-
		SANS	45.0	0.1	41.0	0.1	46.5	0.3	53.3	0.3	-
		TANS	**47.3**	0.0	**43.3**	0.0	**49.1**	0.1	**55.7**	0.1	-2
	Base	NS	45.0	0.1	38.9	0.1	48.6	0.2	55.7	0.1	-
		SANS	46.9	0.1	42.7	0.2	48.5	0.2	55.5	0.2	-
		TANS	**47.7**	0.2	**43.6**	0.1	**49.3**	0.2	**55.9**	0.3	-2
	Freq	NS	45.1	0.1	38.9	0.1	48.8	0.2	56.0	0.2	-
		SANS	47.4	0.1	43.2	0.1	49.2	0.2	56.0	0.2	-
		TANS	**48.0**	0.1	43.9	0.1	†**49.7**	0.1	**56.1**	0.1	-2
	Uniq	NS	45.0	0.1	38.7	0.1	48.8	0.1	56.0	0.3	-
		SANS	47.5	0.1	43.3	0.1	49.1	0.2	56.2	0.2	-
		TANS	†**48.3**	0.1	†**44.4**	0.2	49.6	0.1	†**56.3**	0.2	-1
DistMult	None	NS	38.5	0.2	30.6	0.3	42.9	0.2	52.5	0.1	-
		SANS	42.4	0.0	38.2	0.1	43.7	0.0	51.0	0.2	-
		TANS	**44.2**	0.1	**40.1**	0.1	**45.3**	0.1	**53.2**	0.2	-2
	Base	NS	39.3	0.2	31.9	0.2	43.3	0.1	53.0	0.2	-
		SANS	43.9	0.1	39.4	0.1	45.2	0.1	53.3	0.2	-
		TANS	**44.6**	0.0	**40.5**	0.2	**45.7**	0.1	**53.9**	0.1	-2
	Freq	NS	39.0	0.2	31.2	0.2	43.2	0.1	52.9	0.2	-
		SANS	44.5	0.1	40.0	0.1	**46.0**	0.1	**54.2**	0.2	-
		TANS	**44.7**	0.1	**40.5**	0.2	45.8	0.0	54.0	0.2	-2
	Uniq	NS	38.8	0.2	30.8	0.2	43.1	0.1	53.0	0.2	-
		SANS	44.7	0.1	40.1	0.1	†**46.2**	0.3	54.3	0.0	-
		TANS	†**45.0**	0.1	†**40.7**	0.1	46.1	0.2	†**54.5**	0.2	-0.5
TransE	None	NS	21.1	0.0	2.1	0.1	36.5	0.2	50.4	0.2	-
		SANS	22.5	0.1	1.7	0.1	**40.2**	0.1	52.5	0.2	-
		TANS	**22.7**	0.0	**2.5**	0.0	39.5	0.2	**53.4**	0.1	0.5
	Base	NS	20.3	0.1	**1.6**	0.1	35.1	0.2	49.9	0.2	-
		SANS	22.3	0.0	1.3	0.1	**40.2**	0.1	52.9	0.1	-
		TANS	**22.4**	0.1	1.4	0.1	40.1	0.1	**53.0**	0.1	0.1
	Freq	NS	21.0	0.1	1.8	0.1	36.4	0.2	51.0	0.2	-
		SANS	23.0	0.0	1.9	0.1	40.9	0.2	53.6	0.0	-
		TANS	**23.1**	0.0	**2.1**	0.0	†**41.0**	0.1	**53.8**	0.0	0.1
	Uniq	NS	21.5	0.1	2.2	0.0	37.2	0.1	51.4	0.2	-
		SANS	23.2	0.0	2.3	0.1	**40.9**	0.2	53.6	0.1	-
		TANS	†**23.3**	0.1	†**3.0**	0.0	40.2	0.2	†**54.4**	0.1	0.5
RotatE	None	NS	47.0	0.1	42.5	0.2	48.6	0.2	55.8	0.3	-
		SANS	**47.2**	0.1	**42.6**	0.1	**49.1**	0.1	**56.7**	0.0	-
		TANS	**47.3**	0.1	**42.6**	0.1	**49.1**	0.1	**56.7**	0.1	-0.01
	Base	NS	47.0	0.0	42.2	0.1	48.7	0.1	56.3	0.1	-
		SANS	**47.5**	0.1	**42.7**	0.2	**49.3**	0.1	**57.2**	0.1	-
		TANS	**47.5**	0.1	**42.7**	0.2	**49.3**	0.1	57.1	0.1	0.01
	Freq	NS	47.1	0.1	42.3	0.1	48.7	0.1	56.4	0.1	-
		SANS	**47.7**	0.1	†**42.9**	0.2	49.6	0.0	**57.4**	0.1	-
		TANS	**47.7**	0.1	42.8	0.2	**49.7**	0.1	**57.4**	0.1	0.1
	Uniq	NS	47.2	0.2	42.7	0.2	48.7	0.1	56.3	0.1	-
		SANS	47.7	0.1	†**42.9**	0.1	49.6	0.1	57.2	0.1	-
		TANS	†**47.8**	0.2	42.8	0.3	†**49.8**	0.1	†**57.6**	0.1	0.5
HAKE	None	NS	48.8	0.1	**44.5**	0.1	50.5	0.2	57.3	0.1	-
		SANS	**48.9**	0.0	**44.5**	0.2	**50.6**	0.3	57.7	0.1	-
		TANS	**48.9**	0.0	44.4	0.1	50.5	0.3	**57.8**	0.1	0.01
	Base	NS	49.2	0.0	44.6	0.1	51.1	0.1	57.9	0.2	-
		SANS	**49.5**	0.1	**45.0**	0.2	51.2	0.2	58.2	0.2	-
		TANS	**49.5**	0.1	**45.0**	0.2	51.2	0.3	**58.4**	0.2	0.1
	Freq	NS	49.3	0.1	44.8	0.1	51.3	0.2	58.0	0.2	-
		SANS	**49.7**	0.1	**45.2**	0.2	51.5	0.1	**58.4**	0.2	-
		TANS	**49.7**	0.0	**45.2**	0.2	**51.6**	0.3	**58.4**	0.2	-0.01
	Uniq	NS	49.4	0.2	44.9	0.2	51.3	0.2	57.8	0.2	-
		SANS	†**49.9**	0.0	45.3	0.1	†**51.8**	0.2	†**58.6**	0.2	-
		TANS	†**49.9**	0.1	†**45.4**	0.1	†**51.8**	0.2	58.5	0.2	0.05
HousE	None	NS	47.4	0.1	41.7	0.1	50.2	0.1	57.3	0.1	-
		SANS	49.7	0.1	44.8	0.2	51.5	0.1	59.5	0.1	-
		TANS	**50.2**	0.1	**45.3**	0.1	**52.0**	0.1	**60.0**	0.1	-0.5
	Base	NS	48.1	0.1	42.4	0.1	50.9	0.1	58.5	0.2	-
		SANS	51.2	0.1	**46.7**	0.1	**53.0**	0.2	60.3	0.1	-
		TANS	**51.3**	0.1	**46.7**	0.2	**53.0**	0.0	**60.4**	0.1	0.05
	Freq	NS	48.1	0.2	42.5	0.3	50.9	0.2	58.5	0.2	-
		SANS	†**51.4**	0.1	†**46.8**	0.1	†**53.2**	0.3	†**60.5**	0.1	-
		TANS	51.3	0.2	46.7	0.2	53.1	0.3	†**60.5**	0.1	0.05
	Uniq	NS	48.1	0.1	42.5	0.1	50.8	0.2	58.1	0.1	-
		SANS	**51.2**	0.2	†**46.8**	0.2	**52.7**	0.1	**60.1**	0.1	-
		TANS	51.1	0.3	46.7	0.5	**52.7**	0.1	60.0	0.1	-0.1

Table 6: Results on WN18RR.

YAGO3-10											
Model	Subsampling		MRR		H@1		H@3		H@10		γ
	Assumption	Loss	Mean	SD	Mean	SD	Mean	SD	Mean	SD	
RotatE	None	NS	43.5	0.1	32.8	0.2	49.1	0.2	63.7	0.3	-
		SANS	**49.6**	0.2	39.9	0.1	55.3	0.3	**67.3**	0.2	-
		TANS	**49.6**	0.2	**40.0**	0.2	**55.4**	0.5	67.2	0.3	-0.05
	Base	NS	44.8	0.1	34.5	0.3	50.0	0.2	64.7	0.2	-
		SANS	**49.6**	0.3	**40.1**	0.3	**55.2**	0.4	**67.4**	0.3	-
		TANS	49.5	0.3	**40.1**	0.3	55.0	0.5	67.3	0.3	-0.05
	Freq	NS	44.8	0.2	34.5	0.3	50.0	0.1	64.7	0.2	-
		SANS	**49.9**	0.2	**40.5**	0.3	**55.5**	0.5	**67.4**	0.3	-
		TANS	**49.9**	0.2	**40.5**	0.3	**55.5**	0.5	**67.4**	0.2	0.01
	Uniq	NS	44.4	0.2	34.0	0.3	49.8	0.2	64.3	0.2	-
		SANS	50.0	0.3	40.6	0.2	55.6	0.3	67.5	0.2	-
		TANS	†**50.1**	0.2	†**40.7**	0.1	†**55.7**	0.3	†**67.6**	0.3	0.05
HAKE	None	NS	47.4	0.3	36.6	0.5	53.9	0.1	67.0	0.1	-
		SANS	53.5	0.2	44.6	0.3	**59.1**	0.4	**69.0**	0.2	-
		TANS	**53.7**	0.1	**45.3**	0.3	59.0	0.1	68.8	0.1	0.05
	Base	NS	48.8	0.3	38.4	0.4	55.0	0.2	68.1	0.3	-
		SANS	**54.6**	0.2	**46.2**	0.3	59.9	0.2	69.6	0.2	-
		TANS	54.5	0.2	45.9	0.3	59.9	0.2	**69.9**	0.1	-0.1
	Freq	NS	49.3	0.2	39.1	0.3	55.4	0.1	68.1	0.2	-
		SANS	54.6	0.4	46.0	0.7	**60.2**	0.1	**69.6**	0.3	-
		TANS	**54.8**	0.2	**46.4**	0.3	60.1	0.1	**69.6**	0.3	0.05
	Uniq	NS	45.2	0.1	34.3	0.1	51.1	0.1	65.8	0.3	-
		SANS	†**55.2**	0.3	†**46.8**	0.5	†**60.5**	0.2	†**70.0**	0.3	-
		TANS	55.1	0.2	†**46.8**	0.3	60.3	0.1	69.9	0.2	-0.1
HousE	None	NS	29.2	0.0	18.3	0.1	33.6	0.2	50.1	0.2	-
		SANS	**54.8**	1.3	46.8	1.3	**59.7**	1.2	**68.9**	1.2	-
		TANS	**54.8**	1.2	**46.9**	1.2	59.6	1.2	68.8	1.1	0.01
	Base	NS	29.6	0.1	19.8	0.1	33.6	0.2	48.9	0.1	-
		SANS	56.7	0.1	48.6	0.2	61.7	0.2	71.3	0.1	-
		TANS	**57.0**	0.2	**49.0**	0.4	**61.9**	0.3	†**71.5**	0.2	-0.1
	Freq	NS	27.3	0.8	17.5	0.9	31.0	0.8	46.6	0.8	-
		SANS	57.0	0.1	49.0	0.2	62.0	0.1	**71.4**	0.1	-
		TANS	**57.2**	0.1	**49.3**	0.1	†**62.3**	0.1	**71.4**	0.1	-0.1
	Uniq	NS	28.1	0.2	18.2	0.4	31.8	0.1	47.6	0.0	-
		SANS	57.2	0.1	49.3	0.2	62.0	0.0	71.4	0.2	-
		TANS	†**57.3**	0.2	†**49.5**	0.3	**62.2**	0.1	†**71.5**	0.1	-0.05

Table 7: Results on YAGO3-10.

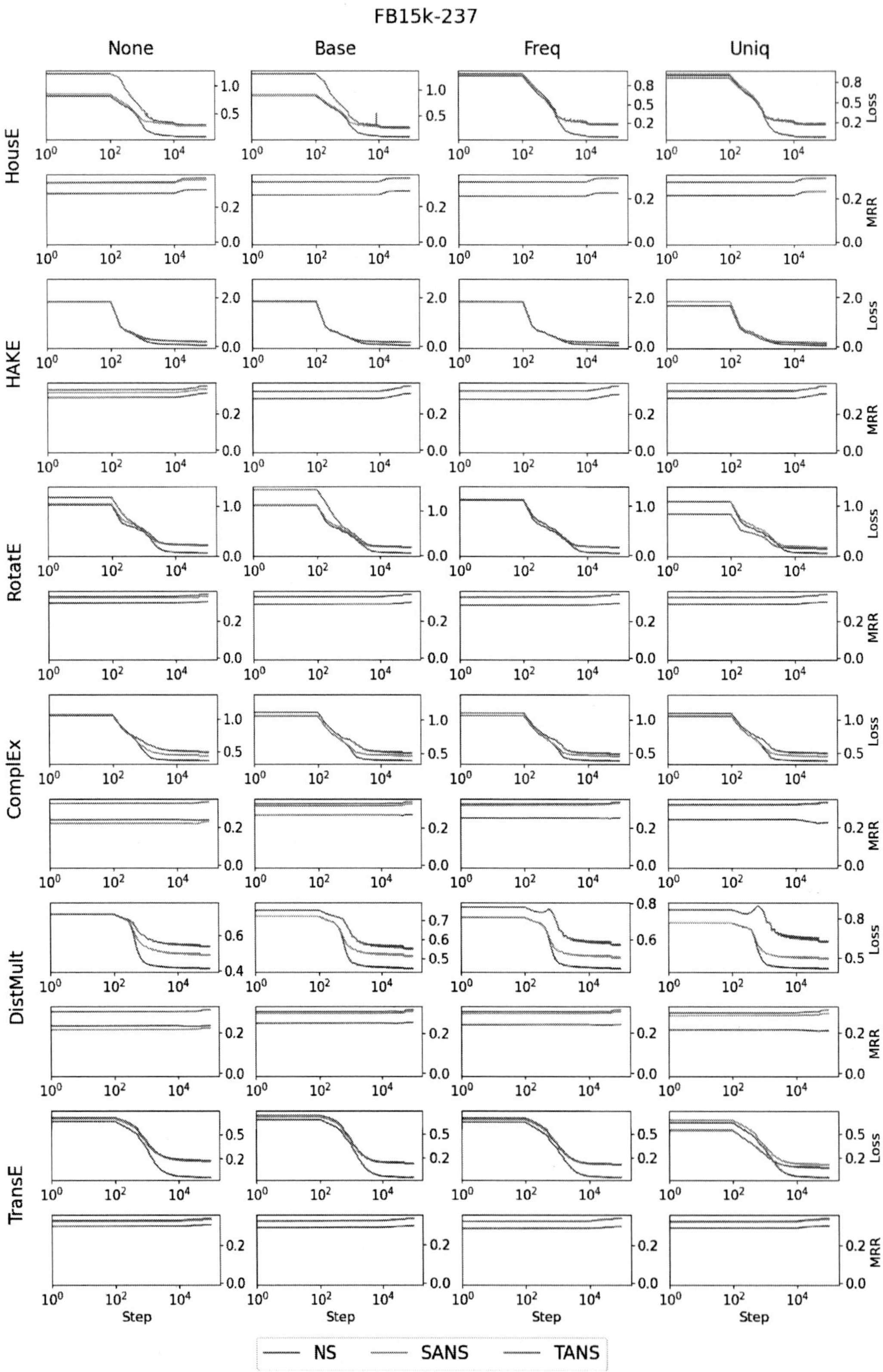

Figure 6: Training loss and validation MRR Curve on FB15k-237.

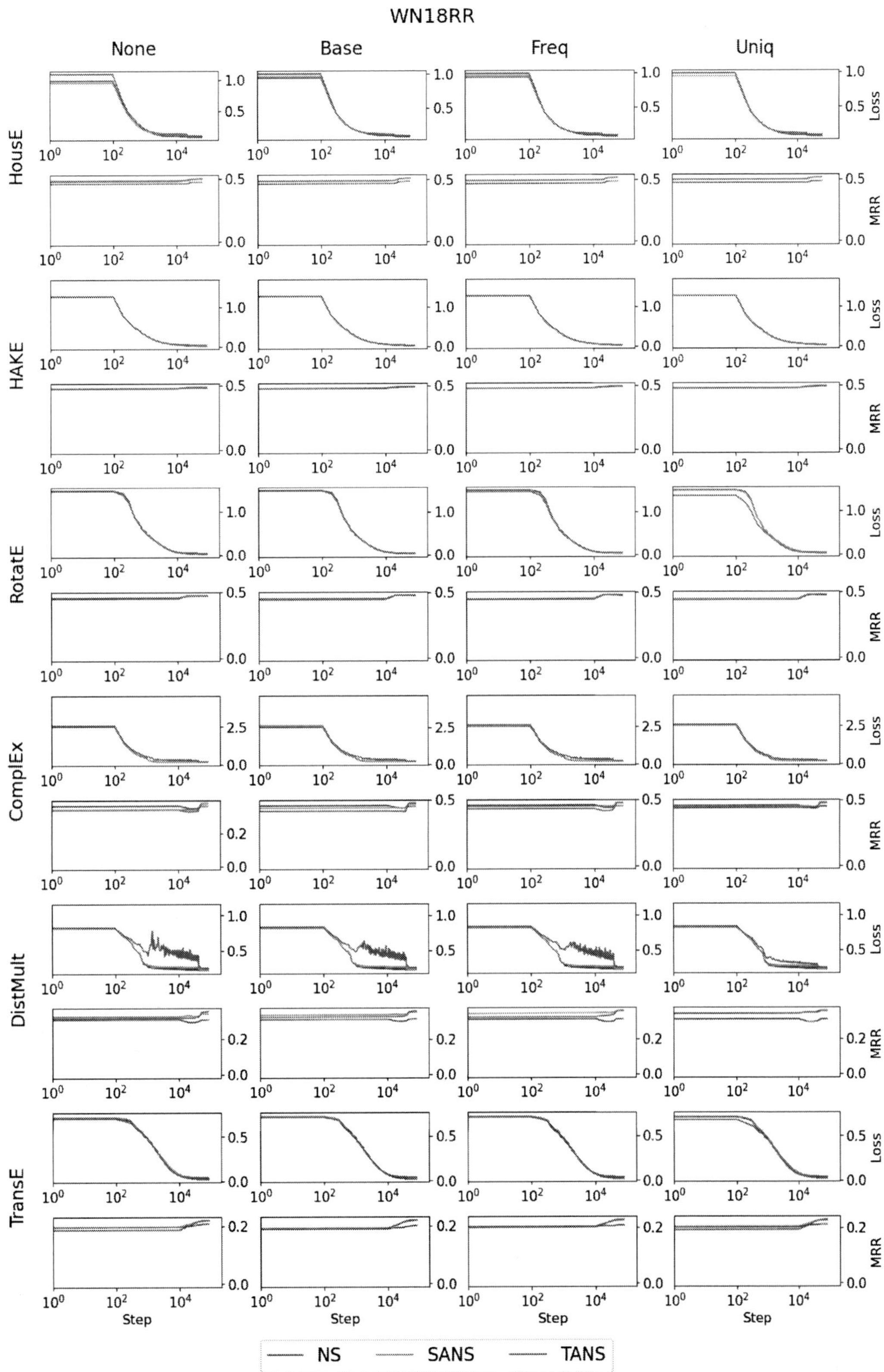

Figure 7: Training loss and validation MRR Curve on WN18RR.

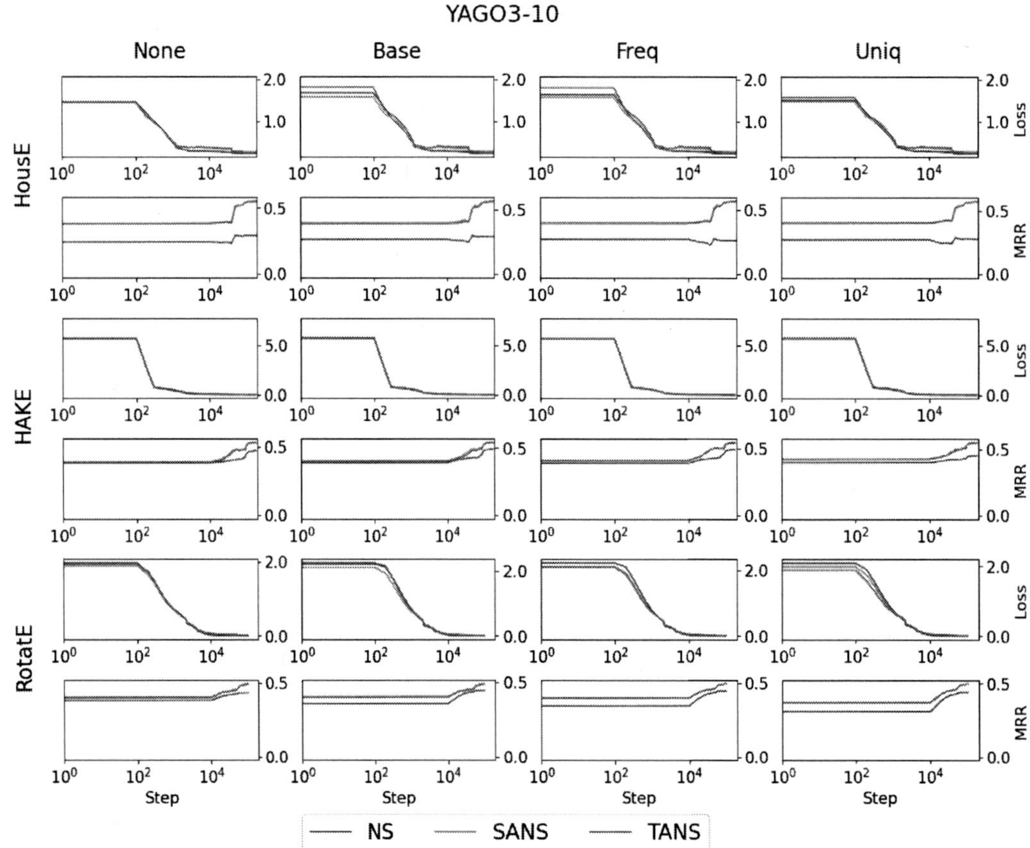

Figure 8: Training loss and validation MRR Curve on YAGO3-10.

FB15k-237-HL							
Model	Subsampling		MRR		H@1		γ
	Assumption	Loss	Mean	SD	Mean	SD	
HAKE	None	NS	38.1	0.3	28.4	0.5	-
		SANS	35.2	0.2	24.5	0.3	-
		TANS	**41.1**	0.1	**33.0**	0.1	-1
	Base	NS	40.5	0.1	31.8	0.2	-
		SANS	38.4	0.2	28.9	0.2	-
		TANS	**41.8**	0.1	**33.6**	0.2	-1
	Freq	NS	41.1	0.1	32.8	0.1	-
		SANS	40.2	0.0	31.5	0.1	-
		TANS	†**42.0**	0.1	†**33.7**	0.1	-1
	Uniq	NS	41.5	0.1	33.2	0.1	-
		SANS	41.1	0.0	32.8	0.0	-
		TANS	**41.9**	0.2	**33.5**	0.2	-0.1
RotatE	None	NS	40.0	0.1	30.8	0.1	-
		SANS	36.3	0.1	25.3	0.2	-
		TANS	**41.5**	0.0	**33.1**	0.1	-1
	Base	NS	41.8	0.1	33.6	0.1	-
		SANS	40.7	0.1	31.7	0.2	-
		TANS	**42.0**	0.1	**33.8**	0.1	-0.5
	Freq	NS	41.3	0.1	33.2	0.1	-
		SANS	42.0	0.2	33.6	0.3	-
		TANS	†**42.3**	0.0	†**34.1**	0.1	-0.5
	Uniq	NS	41.7	0.1	33.7	0.2	-
		SANS	**42.2**	0.1	**33.8**	0.2	-
		TANS	42.1	0.1	**33.8**	0.2	-0.05
HousE	None	NS	39.1	0.2	29.8	0.2	-
		SANS	37.0	0.2	26.2	0.4	-
		TANS	**42.3**	0.1	**34.1**	0.2	-2
	Base	NS	40.3	0.1	31.3	0.2	-
		SANS	40.5	0.4	31.3	0.4	-
		TANS	**42.4**	0.2	**34.2**	0.3	-2
	Freq	NS	39.8	0.3	31.0	0.3	-
		SANS	42.1	0.2	33.8	0.2	-
		TANS	†**42.8**	0.3	†**34.8**	0.4	-1
	Uniq	NS	40.5	0.2	31.9	0.2	-
		SANS	42.4	0.2	34.4	0.2	-
		TANS	**42.5**	0.1	**34.5**	0.0	-1

Table 8: Results on FB15k-237-HL.

WN18RR-HL							
Model	Subsampling		MRR		H@1		γ
	Assumption	Loss	Mean	SD	Mean	SD	
HAKE	None	NS	10.8	0.1	8.7	0.2	-
		SANS	10.3	0.1	7.8	0.1	-
		TANS	**13.9**	0.2	†**12.1**	0.2	-2
	Base	NS	12.1	0.2	9.5	0.3	-
		SANS	11.1	0.1	9.1	0.1	-
		TANS	**13.7**	0.1	**11.7**	0.3	-2
	Freq	NS	12.4	0.1	10.4	0.1	-
		SANS	11.9	0.2	9.5	0.2	-
		TANS	†**14.2**	0.5	**11.9**	0.4	-2
	Uniq	NS	13.3	0.3	11.3	0.3	-
		SANS	11.9	0.2	9.7	0.2	-
		TANS	**14.1**	0.2	**11.7**	0.2	-2
RotatE	None	NS	14.2	0.2	**11.8**	0.3	-
		SANS	13.9	0.3	11.7	0.3	-
		TANS	**14.4**	0.1	**11.8**	0.2	-2
	Base	NS	13.9	0.2	11.5	0.2	-
		SANS	14.1	0.3	**11.7**	0.3	-
		TANS	**14.5**	0.1	**11.7**	0.1	-2
	Freq	NS	14.4	0.1	12.0	0.1	-
		SANS	14.3	0.4	12.0	0.3	-
		TANS	†**15.1**	0.1	**12.2**	0.1	-2
	Uniq	NS	14.4	0.2	12.2	0.1	-
		SANS	14.2	0.2	11.9	0.2	-
		TANS	†**15.1**	0.2	†**12.3**	0.3	-2
HousE	None	NS	10.7	1.8	8.4	1.4	-
		SANS	11.7	1.1	9.5	0.9	-
		TANS	**13.4**	0.4	**11.0**	0.4	-2
	Base	NS	9.9	0.4	8.4	0.4	-
		SANS	11.5	0.2	9.5	0.2	-
		TANS	**13.4**	0.2	**11.3**	0.3	-2
	Freq	NS	†**13.9**	0.1	11.8	0.2	-
		SANS	13.8	0.2	11.9	0.3	-
		TANS	†**13.9**	0.3	†**12.0**	0.2	0.1
	Uniq	NS	13.7	0.1	11.6	0.1	-
		SANS	**13.8**	0.2	11.6	0.2	-
		TANS	**13.8**	0.2	**11.7**	0.3	-0.05

Table 9: Results on WN18RR-HL.

YAGO3-10-HL							
Model	Subsampling		MRR		H@1		γ
	Assumption	Loss	Mean	SD	Mean	SD	
HAKE	None	NS	45.9	0.0	36.9	0.1	-
		SANS	47.8	0.4	**40.0**	0.6	-
		TANS	**49.2**	0.4	39.8	0.7	-0.5
	Base	NS	**50.2**	0.3	**43.0**	0.3	-
		SANS	47.7	0.4	40.5	0.7	-
		TANS	50.1	0.3	41.4	0.3	-0.5
	Freq	NS	[†]**50.8**	0.3	[†]**43.3**	0.2	-
		SANS	48.8	0.1	41.3	0.2	-
		TANS	49.7	0.3	41.0	0.2	-0.5
	Uniq	NS	**49.4**	0.2	**40.8**	0.2	-
		SANS	46.9	0.4	39.8	0.5	-
		TANS	**49.4**	0.6	40.6	0.8	-0.5
RotatE	None	NS	38.0	0.1	28.7	0.3	-
		SANS	41.3	0.1	32.3	0.2	-
		TANS	**43.5**	0.1	**34.8**	0.2	-0.5
	Base	NS	40.6	0.2	31.8	0.5	-
		SANS	**43.8**	0.2	35.1	0.1	-
		TANS	**43.8**	0.2	**35.2**	0.1	-0.05
	Freq	NS	40.3	0.2	31.4	0.4	-
		SANS	43.5	0.2	34.6	0.1	-
		TANS	**43.7**	0.0	**35.1**	0.1	-0.1
	Uniq	NS	40.2	0.0	31.3	0.2	-
		SANS	43.9	0.1	35.1	0.2	-
		TANS	[†]**44.1**	0.1	[†]**35.4**	0.3	-0.1
HousE	None	NS	37.8	0.3	26.9	0.4	-
		SANS	50.3	0.1	40.7	0.3	-
		TANS	[†]**52.5**	0.5	[†]**45.4**	0.3	-0.5
	Base	NS	42.8	1.2	34.3	1.9	-
		SANS	51.9	0.3	44.4	0.2	-
		TANS	**51.9**	0.6	**44.3**	0.8	0.05
	Freq	NS	39.7	0.8	29.9	1.5	-
		SANS	48.6	1.7	40.0	1.4	-
		TANS	**52.0**	0.1	**44.5**	0.3	-1
	Uniq	NS	41.0	0.1	31.6	0.1	-
		SANS	49.4	0.3	41.1	1.1	-
		TANS	**52.2**	0.1	**44.7**	0.1	-0.05

Table 10: Results on YAGO3-10-HL.

How Useful is Continued Pre-Training for Generative Unsupervised Domain Adaptation?

Rheeya Uppaal[1] **Yixuan Li**[1] **Junjie Hu**[1,2]
[1]Department of Computer Sciences,
[2]Department of Biostatistics and Medical Informatics
University of Wisconsin-Madison
{uppaal, jhu, sharonli}@cs.wisc.edu

Abstract

Recent breakthroughs in scale have enabled the emergence of powerful generative language models, and the ability to fine-tune these models on various tasks by casting them into prompts or instructions. In this landscape, the problem of Unsupervised Domain Adaptation (UDA), or the problem of leveraging knowledge from a labeled source domain to an unlabeled target domain, has been left behind, with recent UDA methods still addressing discriminative classification. In particular, two popular UDA approaches, involving Continued Pre-Training (CPT) and learning domain invariant representations, have been under-explored in the generative setting, signaling a gap. In this work, we evaluate the utility of CPT for generative UDA. We first perform an empirical evaluation to measure the trade-offs between CPT and strong methods promoting domain invariance. We further evaluate how well the benefits of CPT extend to different architectures, tuning methods and data regimes. We then motivate the use of CPT by studying to what degree it benefits classification performance on the target domain. Finally, we attempt to understand the mechanism behind which CPT improves classification performance on the unlabeled target domain. Our findings suggest that the model implicitly learns the downstream task while predicting masked words informative to that task. Our work connects the body of UDA research with that of instruction tuning, enabling an initial step towards a wider applicability of modern language models. Our code is available at `https://github.com/Uppaal/cpt-generative-uda`.

1 Introduction

Recent advancements in the pre-training of language models have enabled the widespread use of powerful generative models, which can be leveraged across multiple domains with no training (Brown et al., 2020; Scao et al., 2022; Touvron et al., 2023, *inter alia*). Despite these advancements, these autoregressive models are still fragile under certain kinds of data distribution shifts, making their applications across these domains challenging (Ribeiro et al., 2020; Bajaj et al., 2021; Chuang et al., 2023; Uppaal et al., 2024, *inter alia*). This is addressed, in part, by the concept of instruction tuning with templates (Zhang et al., 2023; Sanh et al., 2022; Ouyang et al., 2022; Wang et al., 2022; Wei et al., 2022), enabling the learning of new tasks without any randomly initialized parameters.

The problem of unsupervised domain adaptation (UDA) leverages learned knowledge from a labeled source domain to an unlabeled target domain (Pan and Yang, 2010; Ganin and Lempitsky, 2015; Long et al., 2015, *inter alia*). It is useful for adaptation to unlabeled domains with high labeling costs, where supervised instruction tuning does not suffice. Despite the pervasive need for models to generalize to such domains, recent UDA methods still address discriminative classification, barring the application of these approaches to recent generative models. In particular, Continued Pre-Training and Domain Invariance-based methods, two widely popular classes of UDA approaches (Ramponi and Plank, 2020), are completely unexplored for UDA in the generative setting.

The Continued Pre-Training (CPT) approach involves extended pre-training on a domain or task, followed by supervised training on the downstream task (Gururangan et al., 2020). This approach has been widely used for adaptation to labeled domains (Gao et al., 2021; Kim et al., 2021; Hung et al., 2023, *inter alia*), and in the UDA setup for unlabeled domains (Han and Eisenstein, 2019; Zhang et al., 2021b; Karouzos et al., 2021; Pfeiffer et al., 2020; Parović et al., 2023). Invariance-based approaches attempt to learn representations that are invariant across domains (Tzeng et al., 2014; Ganin et al., 2016; Wu and Shi, 2022; Guo et al., 2022), with the notion that when the learned representa-

Proceedings of the 9th Workshop on Representation Learning for NLP (RepL4NLP-2024), pages 99–117
August 15, 2024

tions from both domains cannot be distinguished by a classifier and the classifier performs well on the source domain, it will also exhibit strong performance on the target domain. These two classes of methods introduce a trade-off: invariance-based methods suffer from instability issues (Han and Eisenstein, 2019; Kashyap et al., 2021), while continued pre-training requires a larger computational budget. But how would this trade-off extrapolate to the generative setting? For example, invariance-based methods are well motivated in discriminative tasks, where there is a clear decision boundary; however, the same does not hold for generative tasks.

To address these gaps, we introduce the setting of Generative UDA, where an autoregressive model is trained to leverage knowledge from a labeled source domain to an unlabeled target domain, *using only next word prediction as its objective*. We formalize the use of CPT for this setting in Section 2, and then attempt to explore and understand the behaviour of CPT for Generative UDA. We begin by performing an empirical analysis on 40 real-world domain pairs to explore the tradeoff between continued pre-training and invariance-based approaches, and find vanilla CPT to be competitive with and significantly more stable than a state of the art invariance-based approach (Section 3). We then stress test CPT, by applying it across varying model architectures and scales, tuning approaches and data regimes. We find that CPT is robust across these settings, unlike our invariance-based approach (Section 4).

With recent language models being trained across vast corpora which may include domains similar to the target domain, the requirement for continued pre-training may be raised to question. In Section 5, we show that continued pre-training is indeed essential for strong downstream performance on the target domain, and this performance rapidly degrades with limited target domain exposure. Finally, we attempt to shed light on how masking plays a role in improving classification accuracy on the unlabeled target domain in Section 6. We find that the model may implicitly learn the downstream task as it predicts masked words that are informative to the downstream task.

Our work attempts to connect the body of UDA research with recent trends in language modeling, by providing a set of insights into the behaviour of the popular class of continued pre-training approaches, in the Generative UDA setting. We hope this enables an initial step towards a wider applicability of modern language models.

2 Continued Pre-Training for Generative UDA

2.1 Preliminaries: The UDA Problem

We consider a text classification task, where $\mathcal{X}$ is the input space of all text sentences and $\mathcal{Y} = \{1, ...K\}$ is the label space. In the UDA problem, we have access to a source labeled dataset $\mathcal{D}_{\text{src}} = \{(x_i, y_i)\}_{i=1}^{N}$ consisting of samples from a joint distribution P_{src}, and a target unlabeled dataset $\mathcal{D}_{\text{tgt}} = \{x_j\}_{j=1}^{M}$ sampling from a target input distribution $P_{\text{tgt}}^{\mathcal{X}}$. We further denote $P_{\text{src}}^{\mathcal{X}}$ as the marginal distribution of P_{src} on $\mathcal{X}$, where $P_{\text{src}}^{\mathcal{X}} \neq P_{\text{tgt}}^{\mathcal{X}}$. The goal of UDA is to learn a function $f : \mathcal{X} \rightarrow \mathcal{Y}$ that minimizes the error rate $\mathbb{E}_{x \sim P_{\text{tgt}}^{\mathcal{X}}} \mathbb{1}[f(x) \neq y]$.

2.2 CPT for UDA as a Sequence of Prompt Based Tasks

We now formalize the extension of continued pre-training to the setting of generative UDA. We use the traditional two-phase training pipeline from Gururangan et al. (2020)[1]. The first phase uses templates to cast the source and target domain sequences into an autoregressive pre-training task.[2] The second phase applies supervised instruction-tuning of the model on source-labeled data.

Task 1: Autoregressive Continued Pre-training We reuse the input sequences from the source-labeled dataset $\mathcal{D}_{\text{src}}$ as the source-unlabeled dataset, denoted as $\mathcal{D}_{\text{src}}^{\mathcal{X}}$. Next, similar to Raffel et al. (2020); Song et al. (2019), for an unlabeled sequence $x \in \mathcal{D}_{\text{src}}^{\mathcal{X}}$ and $\mathcal{D}_{\text{src}}$, we use a prompt template to convert the sequence x to an input-output sequence pair, i.e., $\mathbb{M}(x) = (\tilde{x}, \tilde{y})$. For masked language modeling (MLM), an instruction is prepended to a randomly masked sequence x to create $\tilde{x}$. The output sequence $\tilde{y}$ is a concatenation of masked words from x. For example, given $x =$*"The movie was so cool! Two hours of fun."*, we construct $\tilde{x} =$*"Fill in the blanks: "The _ cool!*

[1]While we use the two-phase multi-task training pipeline (sequential) in our main experiments, in Appendix I, we show that an equivalent single-phase multi-task training pipeline (joint) results in similar performance.

[2]We investigate mask language modeling for T5 models and switch to causal language modeling for decoder-only models with a few simple template changes. We compare both in Section 4.

Two hours _", and $\tilde{y}$ = "<sep> *movie was so* <sep> *of fun.* <sep>". For causal language modeling (CLM), $\tilde{x} = x$.

Given $(\tilde{x}, \tilde{y})$, we train an autoregressive LM parameterized by θ to minimize the negative log-likelihood loss averaged over output words and the total loss over a corpus $\mathcal{D} = \mathcal{D}_{\text{src}}^{\mathcal{X}} \cup \mathcal{D}_{\text{tgt}}$.

$$\ell(\tilde{x}, \tilde{y}; \theta) = -\frac{1}{|\tilde{y}|} \sum_{t} \log P_{\theta}(\tilde{y}_t | \tilde{x}, \tilde{y}_{1:t-1}) \quad (1)$$

$$\mathcal{L}_{\text{CPT}}(\mathcal{D}; \theta) = \frac{1}{|\mathcal{D}|} \sum_{x \in \mathcal{D}} \ell(\mathbb{M}(x); \theta)$$

Task 2: Source Supervised Instruction-tuning In the second phase, we use labeled data from the source domain to train the model on the downstream classification task. Similar to the first phase, we use prompts[3] to generate input-output sequence pairs: $\mathbb{C}(x, y) = (\tilde{x}, \tilde{y}) \ \forall \ (x, y) \in \mathcal{D}_{\text{src}}$. For example, for sentiment classification, if x = "*I like this movie.*", $y = 1 \Rightarrow \tilde{x}$ = "*[x] Is this sentence positive or negative?*", $\tilde{y}$ = "*Positive*".

Given the augmented sequence pair $(\tilde{x}, \tilde{y})$ and the model trained after the first phase, we compute the same negative log-likelihood loss $\ell(\tilde{x}, \tilde{y}; \theta)$ in Eq. (1). Finally, we define the total loss on the source-labeled dataset in the second phase as:

$$\mathcal{L}_{\text{CLS}}(\mathcal{D}_{\text{src}}; \theta) = \frac{1}{|\mathcal{D}_{\text{src}}|} \sum_{(x,y) \in \mathcal{D}_{\text{src}}} l(\mathbb{C}(x, y); \theta) \quad (2)$$

After training, we follow the practice of Liu et al. (2022) to convert a label string $\tilde{y}$ to its corresponding label y at test time for evaluation.

3 Evaluating the Efficacy of Continued Pre-training for Generative UDA

3.1 Experimental Setup

Datasets We use the MNLI and Amazon Review classification datasets, which are widely used UDA benchmarks (Malik et al., 2023; Karouzos et al., 2021; Guo et al., 2020). The MNLI corpus (Williams et al., 2018) contains sentence pairs across five genres: Travel (T), Fiction (F), Government (G), Slate (S), and Telephone (Te). The task classifies every sentence pair as entailment, neutral, or contradiction. The Multi-Domain Sentiment Analysis Dataset (Blitzer et al., 2007) contains binary sentiment reviews for different types of Amazon products. We use reviews from the Apparel (A), Baby (B), Books (Bo), Cameras (C), and Movies (M) domains. We evaluate a total of 40 pairs of source and target domains, across the two datasets. Appendix A contains more details about the datasets.

Models and Tuning Methods Our main experiments use the T5v1.1 base model and $(IA)^3$ (Liu et al., 2022) PEFT method. T5v1.1 is an improved version of the original T5 model (Raffel et al., 2020), and unlike the original T5 model, it is not trained on any supervised datasets. We then extend our evaluation to different model architectures (T0, GPT-2), tuning methods (full fine-tuning, adapters) and data regimes (Section 4).

Training Each training phase is 30,000 steps long for MNLI and 15,000 steps for the Amazon dataset. We use Adam, a batch size of 8, and a learning rate of 0.003. We set the maximum sequence length to 256 tokens. We use length normalization during evaluation, as proposed by Liu et al. (2022). For each experiment, we report the mean and standard deviation across 3 runs. More details can be found in Appendix B.

Baselines Since our goal is to study the behaviour of CPT for generative UDA, we compare it with a simple supervised baseline, and a state-of-the-art invariance-based approach.

- **Src+Tgt** (All labeled): We fine-tune the model using labeled data from both the source and target domains. This serves as an upper bound on target domain performance.
- **UDAPTER**: Malik et al. (2023) propose an invariance-based method that measures the multi-kernel maximum mean discrepancy (MK-MMD) (Gretton et al., 2012; Bousmalis et al., 2016) between source and target embeddings from each transformer layer and sums them to obtain an aggregate loss $\mathcal{L}_{\text{div}}$. The final loss is the weighted sum of $\mathcal{L}_{\text{div}}$ and the classification loss, i.e., $\mathcal{L} = \lambda \ \mathcal{L}_{\text{cls}} + (1 - \lambda) \ \mathcal{L}_{\text{div}}$, where λ gradually changes from 0 to 1 during training. Here, we use the embeddings from a model as it is being instruction tuned on the downstream classification task. Their method achieves state-of-the-art performance, and outperforms popular UDA approaches like DANN (Ganin et al., 2016) and DSN (Bousmalis et al., 2016); thus we only compare CPT with this approach.

[3]Prompt templates were selected from the Public Pool of Prompts (Bach et al., 2022).

3.2 Continued Pre-training is Competitive with Domain-Invariance Methods

Performance We compare CPT with other baselines over 40 domain pairs of the MNLI and Amazon Review datasets, and report the average accuracies over all pairs in Table 1. We see that CPT is competitive to UDAPTER. (Appendix C contains detailed results over 40 pairs and significance tests to check for competitiveness.) Interestingly, a visualization of sentence embeddings in Figure 8 (Appendix C) suggests that representations learned through CPT are not domain invariant. In addition to the MMD based method of Malik et al. (2023), we also compare CPT on one domain pair with other methods that promote domain invariance (DANN (Ganin et al., 2016), CORAL (Sun et al., 2017)) and weight interpolation (Ilharco et al., 2022) in Appendix C, further confirming the competitiveness of CPT.

Dataset	Src+Tgt	UDAPTER	CPT
Amazon	92.66 (0.45)	89.02 (2.17)	**89.34** (0.48)
MNLI	78.14 (0.25)	70.19 (1.71)	**74.12** (0.68)

Table 1: Avg. target-domain classification accuracy and standard deviation over 3 runs.

Stability CPT performs more stably than UDAPTER, with the invariance-based method often reporting a variance of over 20% across runs (Table 6 in Appendix C). For example, for the MNLI pair Fiction (F) $\rightarrow$ Government (G), minimizing UDAPTER yields a variance of 23.4% across runs. This observation is consistent with existing findings (Kashyap et al., 2021; Han and Eisenstein, 2019) that minimizing divergence measures like MMD, when combined with auxiliary task-specific loss functions, result in training instabilities and vanishing gradients. We discuss this in more detail in Appendix J.

4 How General are the Benefits of CPT?

Instruction tuning for large models is often performed through parameter-efficient fine-tuning (PEFT) on limited data. This tuning also applies to models of different scales and architectures (decoder-only and encoder-decoder). In this section, we evaluate the utility of CPT across these factors, using the A$\rightarrow$M domain pair from the Amazon Reviews dataset.

CPT Helps Decoder-only Models. We extend our analysis from MLM with encoder-decoder language models, to causal language modeling (CLM) with decoder-only language models, using GPT-2 (medium) (Radford et al., 2019). We perform CLM in the first training phase by simply training the model for next-word prediction given the original sequence. Table 2 shows that CPT provides strong improvements on the target domain in comparison to the invariance-based baseline.

Method	Accuracy
Src+Tgt	79.8 (0.3)
UDAPTER	66.0 (1.1)
CPT	**75.8** (0.4)

Table 2: Performance of CPT with causal language modeling for the decoder-only GPT-2 model. CPT significantly outperforms the invariance-based method.

CPT Outweighs Invariance-based Methods for Instruction-tuned Models. We evaluate the performance of CPT over T5v1.1 XL (3B parameters) and the instruction-tuned T0 (3B parameters) (Sanh et al., 2022). Figure 1 (Table 8 of Appendix D) shows a wider gap between UDAPTER and CPT with higher model capacity, and this gap is further increased with instruction tuning. We hypothesize that this gap is due to the vast difference between the objectives of domain invariance and instruction tuning.

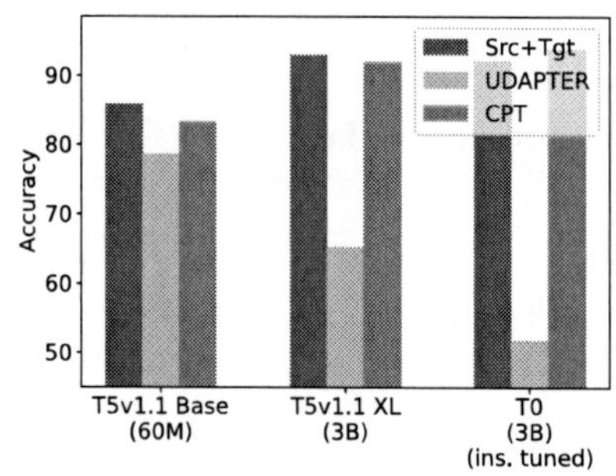

Figure 1: The performance gap between CPT and UDAPTER increases with larger models, from T5v1.1 Base (60M parameters) to T5v1.1 XL (3B parameters), and further increases with instruction tuning (T0 3B).

CPT Benefits are Consistent across Tuning Approaches. PEFT approaches have been shown to introduce resilience to domain shift (Fu et al., 2023). To isolate this effect from the CPT framework, we use T5v1.1 to evaluate CPT in a full fine-tuning setup. Additionally, we compare CPT with two PEFT approaches[4] : Adapters (Houlsby et al., 2019) and (IA)^3 (Liu et al., 2022). We see in Figure 2 (Table 9 in Appendix E) that CPT continues to perform stronger than the domain invariance-based UDAPTER method.

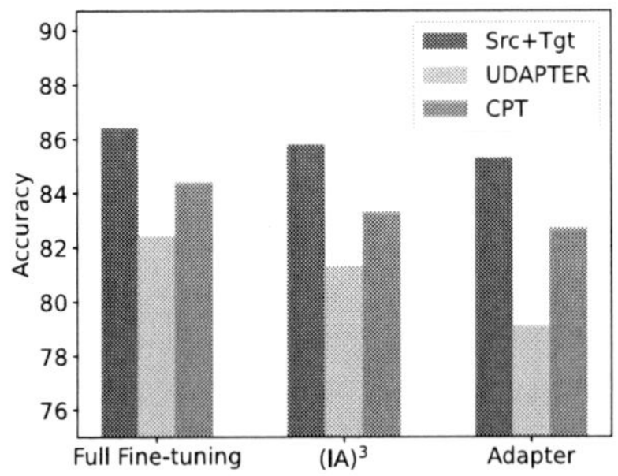

Figure 2: Performance of CPT across different tuning approaches with the T5v1.1 base model. CPT remains more powerful than UDAPTER across all tuning approaches.

CPT Outperforms Invariance-based Methods in Low-data Regimes. In this low-data experiment, we assume access to k labeled source-domain examples. For CPT, we assume access to the full unlabeled dataset in both domains for the first training phase, and k-shot access to labeled source-domain examples for the second phase of supervised training. For a fair comparison, we also introduce a two-phase version of the UDAPTER pipeline—the first phase minimizes MMD between unlabeled source and target domain embeddings (full data access), while the second phase optimizes supervised training on the source domain (k-shot). Figure 3 (Table 10 in Appendix F) showcases CPT clearly outperforming both variants of UDAPTER, across three different models for $k = 256$. Furthermore, Figure 4 (Table 11 in Appendix F) shows CPT providing consistent improvements in as low as 32-shots, unlike the unstable invariance-based approach.

5 To What Extent is Target-Domain Exposure Beneficial?

Given the vast distributions language models are pre-trained on, a natural assumption might be that the model has already been exposed to a domain similar to the target domain during pre-training. This would mean that the model could simply extrapolate the learned downstream task from the source to the target domain, questioning the need for CPT.

In this section, we establish that exposure to the target domain *is* helpful, even when similar domains may have been encountered during pre-training. Table 3 evaluates CPT on the A→M domain pair with the T5v1.1 model. We note that the performance on the target domain is strongly impacted by the presence of target-domain data during the first phase of training.

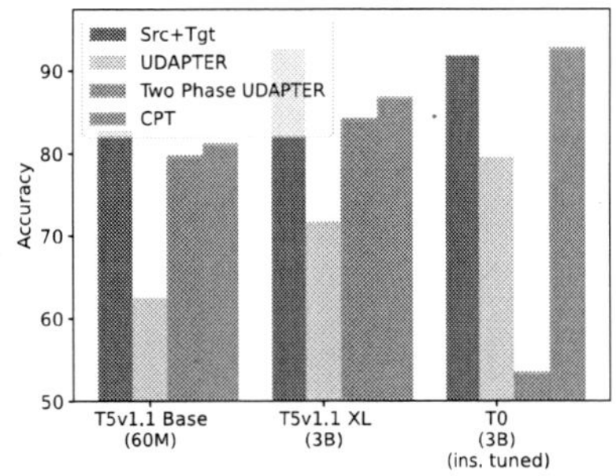

Figure 3: Performance of CPT across different models, in a 256-shot learning setup. Unlike both variants of UDAPTER, CPT is stable and provides consistent benefits across models.

Phase 1 Data	Accuracy	
	Source	Target
Source Only	93.3 (0.1)	76.5 (0.2)
Target Only	92.9 (0.4)	82.3 (0.7)
Source + Target	**93.5** (0.4)	**83.3** (0.5)

Table 3: Comparison of CPT with varying data exposure during the first phase of training. Performance on the target domain strongly benefits more from exposure to target domain, and is boosted further with exposure to the source domain.

For a more fine-grained analysis, we investigate the impact of degree of exposure to the target domain, by varying the masking rates during the first phase of training. While masking 15% of a sequence is considered standard for random masking, previous work has shown that BERT-sized models (Devlin et al., 2019) can learn from as high as 80% masking rates during pre-training followed by adaptation to a labeled task (Wettig et al., 2023). The source-domain performance shown in Figure 5 (Table 12 in Appendix) matches this trend. However,

[4]We choose Adapters because He et al. (2022) present a unified view of PEFT approaches which shows that the operations applied by Adapters are very similar to those of Prefix Tuning (Li and Liang, 2021) and LoRA (Hu et al., 2022). We choose (IA)^3 since it is a state-of-the-art PEFT approach that uses a fraction of the learnable parameters of Adapters (More in Appendix E).

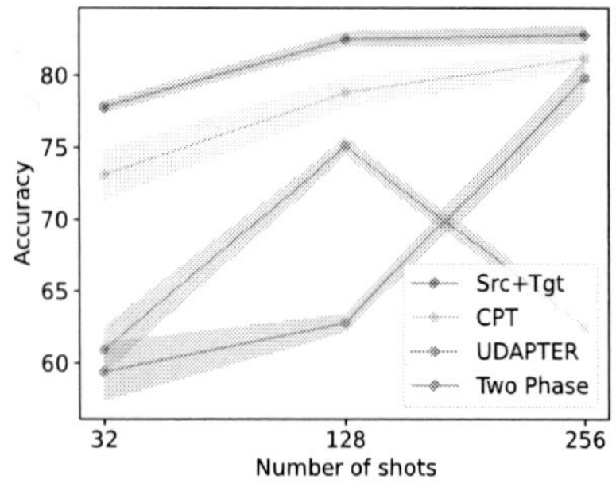

Figure 4: Few-shot performance of CPT, for varying k. Unlike both variants of UDAPTER, CPT is stable and provides consistent benefits across number of shots.

high masking rates effectively reduce the exposure of the model to target data, strongly deteriorating the performance on the target domain[5]. We hypothesize that since the model never sees any labeled data of the target domain, it heavily depends on the signal it gets from the unlabeled data through masking.

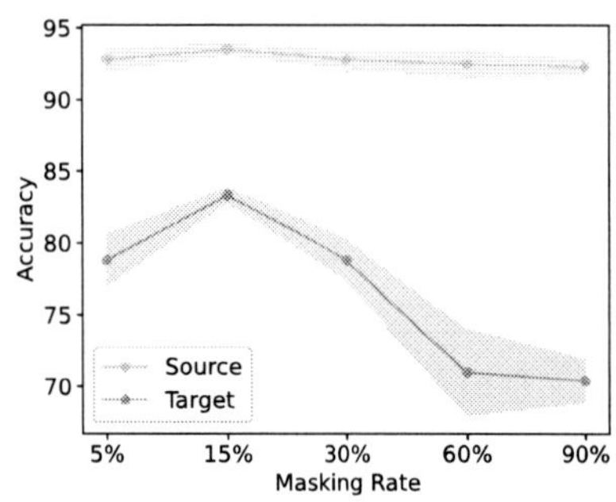

Figure 5: Impact of Masking Rate on CPT. With high masking rates, the performance on the source domain is largely maintained, but the performance on the target domain rapidly deteriorates.

6 Why does Word Prediction Aid Classification for Generative UDA?

In this section, we examine why predicting masked words of the source and target domains through CPT boosts sentence classification on the unlabeled target domain for generative UDA. We hypothesize that by having to predict masked words that are informative to the downstream task during pre-training, the model implicitly learns information about the downstream task. For example, given the masked sentence, *"I really _ the movie, it was a fascinating watch."*, the masked word is indicative of the downstream task, in this case sentiment analysis. The model can only predict this masked word (which would be a positive word like "*loved*" or "*enjoyed*") by using other words informative to the task ("*fascinating*"). Through this process, the model is essentially learning features which are useful to the downstream task, despite having no direct supervision.

To test this hypothesis, we quantize the "informativeness" of each word to a classification task: an informative word is highly correlated with any of the labels in the downstream task.[6] Specifically, we follow Gururangan et al. (2018) and use point-wise mutual information (PMI) (Fano, 1961) of the word with respect to the class label:

$$\text{PMI}(\text{word}, \text{class}) = \log \frac{p(\text{word}, \text{class})}{p(\text{word})p(\text{class})},$$

where we count the frequency of a word-class pair on $\mathcal{D}_{\text{src}}$ to estimate $p(\text{word}, \text{class})$, and similarly count a word and a class individually on $\mathcal{D}_{\text{src}}$ to estimate $p(\text{word})$ and $p(\text{class})$.

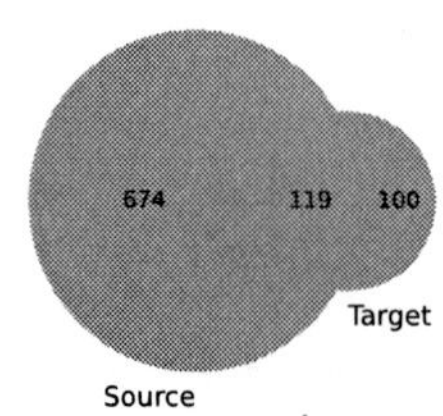

Figure 6: Vocabulary overlap between label-informative words of the source and target domains. The numbers in the Venn diagram indicate the number of words in both sets.

We use two sets of words from a dataset: those with the top $k\%$ (informative) and bottom $k\%$ (uninformative) PMI with any inference label ($k = 15$). We also filter out low-frequency words from the selection.[7] We compute these sets for the source and target domains individually, assuming access to target labels. We use the T5v1.1 model on the A→M pair for our analysis.

[5] With masking rates under the optimal value of 15%, the semantic and background features learned through model prediction of masked words is limited, hurting performance on the target domain.

[6] These informative words are similar to pivot features (Blitzer et al., 2006; Ziser and Reichart, 2018; Ben-David et al., 2020, *inter alia*), with the exception that they are chosen based on information from the source domain only.

[7] Any word that occurs less than 10 times in the entire training corpus is considered to be low frequency.

How Masking helps Learn Classification We first confirm that label-informative words indeed impact the classification performance of the CPT model. We do this by masking informative words from a sentence at inference. Figure 7 (a) shows us that the performance of the model on the source domain is not impacted by masking uninformative words, but drops on masking informative words. However, how do we know how much of this bias towards label informative words was learned during the continued pre-training phase, rather than during supervised fine-tuning? To attempt to disentangle the impact of the training phases, we train the model through selective masking (informative or uninformative) in the first phase of training, and minimize the impact of the second phase by making it a few-shot task. Figure 7 (c) shows us that the model performs best on classification when trained to predict label informative words during masking, indicating that the model does indeed learn features relevant to the downstream task during the first phase of training.

The Interplay between CPT and Classification for Generative UDA We now extend this analysis to the target domain to understand how CPT plays a role in learning features from the unlabeled domain. Figure 7 (d) shows us that informative masking outperforms uninformative masking by a significant gap, once again signaling that the masking process helps the model implicitly learn the downstream task. However, unlike with the source domain, random masking results in the strongest performance. This is due to the domain mismatch: the informative words for the source and target domains are not identical (Figure 6), and the supervised training on the source domain adds a bias towards source-informative words. The mixture of these two sets of words are best predicted through random masking, explaining its strong performance.

This phenomenon also draws the observation that random masking is preferred to selective masking for generative UDA, contrary to single domain settings where informative masking is more useful (Levine et al., 2021; Gu et al., 2020).

7 Discussion

The Computational Trade-off of CPT Our results in Section 3.2 show that continued pre-training and methods promoting domain invariance are competitive with each other. Continued pre-training suffers from the computational drawback of requiring an additional phase of training. Conversely, invariance-based methods are difficult to optimize, possibly requiring more runs to achieve a stable optimum, and having a higher amortized computational cost. Inspired by Karouzos et al. (2021), we introduce a simple single phase variant of continued pre-training which is *equivalent* in performance to its two phase variant, nullifying the additional computational overhead of the approach (more details in Appendix I).

UDA in the Age of LLMs Recent breakthroughs in scale have showcased that large language models (LLMs) are highly powerful, and can perform various downstream tasks with limited or no training. This may raise question on the relevance of the UDA problem as a whole — does a model even require expensive adaptation to a domain it may have already been exposed to during pre-training? In addition to our analysis in Section 5, we argue that the requirement to adapt small models to unseen domains still holds in specific cases. Small supervised models have been shown to be comparable with, or even outperform, zero-shot general-purpose LLMs on various downstream tasks (Huang et al., 2023; Zhu et al., 2023; Tang et al., 2024), serving as lightweight and customizeable (through fine-tuning) alternatives. Safety critical domains like healthcare and finance would benefit more from these models than a generalist LLM. Our study does not address how to better adapt to domains, rather we investigate ways a model may adapt to data unseen during pre-training. This is a question that holds for current LLMs, and will continue to hold as long as models are unable to access infinite data during pre-training.

8 Related Work

UDA through Promoting Domain Invariance A major class of approaches in Model-centric UDA methods (Ramponi and Plank, 2020) aims to minimize $\mathcal{H}\Delta\mathcal{H}$ divergence (Ben-David et al., 2010) between the source and target domain features, through adversarial training (Tzeng et al., 2014; Ganin et al., 2016; Tzeng et al., 2017; Guo et al., 2022, *inter alia*) or through minimizing measures of domain similarity (Bousmalis et al., 2016; Ge et al., 2023). Malik et al. (2023) have shown the minimization of MMD to outperform other invariance-based methods. However, past work has shown that domain-invariance is a weak constraint

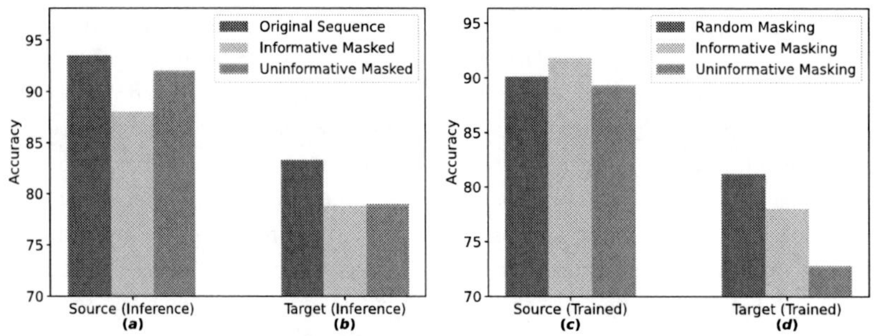

Figure 7: The impact of selective masking on classification performance of a CPT trained model. **Left**: Masking label informative words during inference degrades classification performance, compared to the original unmasked sequence. However, the removal of uninformative words does not impact the model on the source domain. **Right**: The impact of continued pre-training can be partially disentangled from that of supervised training by making the supervised training phase few-shot and training the model to mask informative or uninformative words during the continued pre-training phase. Informative masking is most beneficial for the source domain, indicating that the model learns task relevant features during masking. On the target domain, informative masking still captures some knowledge about the downstream task, however, the supervised training phase adds a bias towards source label informative words. Thus, random masking is most powerful.

for adaptation (Zhao et al., 2019; Karouzos et al., 2021), could introduce domain-specific hyperparameters (Trung et al., 2022), and is also prone to instability issues (Han and Eisenstein, 2019; Sun et al., 2019; Wilson and Cook, 2020; Kashyap et al., 2021).

UDA through Continued Pre-Training The limitations of invariance-based model-centric methods have encouraged the emergence of alternate approaches, based on self-supervised learning through contrastive learning (Kumar et al., 2022; Shen et al., 2022; Long et al., 2022), pseudo-labeling (Zhou and Li, 2005; Ruder and Plank, 2017, *inter alia*) or language model pre-training. Despite not being directly useful to certain downstream tasks (Uppaal et al., 2023), CPT has been used for adaptation to labeled tasks, in both full fine-tuning (Gururangan et al., 2020; Lee et al., 2020; Gao et al., 2021, *inter alia*) and PEFT setups (Kim et al., 2021; Hung et al., 2023). A smaller body of work has explored the utility of CPT in a UDA setup (Han and Eisenstein, 2019; Zhang et al., 2021b; Karouzos et al., 2021; Parović et al., 2023), identifying the class of methods to be more stable than invariance-based methods.

Generative UDA The emergence of large language models (Brown et al., 2020; Scao et al., 2022; Touvron et al., 2023, *inter alia*) introduced the concept of instruction tuning with templates (Zhang et al., 2023; Sanh et al., 2022; Ouyang et al., 2022; Wang et al., 2022; Wei et al., 2022; Gao et al., 2021; Liu et al., 2023), enabling multi-task training without any task specific architectural changes. However, the framework of casting discriminative classification tasks into generative next word prediction tasks has not yet been extended to UDA. The closest work to this setting (Ben-David et al., 2021) uses a generative model to create domain identifier prompts and feed them back into the model, however the final task label prediction is still discriminative. In our work, we focus on gaining insights to extend the powerful class of CPT methods to purely generative UDA, where prediction on the downstream task is treated as a next word prediction task. Through this, we also present novel findings on the impact of CPT to prompt-based classifiers in the UDA framework, countering previous findings from other studies in a single-domain setting (Gu et al., 2020; Levine et al., 2021; Wettig et al., 2023).

9 Conclusion

We introduce the setting of Generative UDA, and perform an investigation on the utility of continued pre-training in this setting. We compare the approach with the popular class of domain-invariance based methods for UDA, showing that CPT is both competitive with, and more stable than invariance-based approaches. Our experiments show that the benefits of CPT extend to different architectures, tuning methods and data regimes. We motivate the need for target domain exposure through CPT by showing that performance on the target domain gradually degrades with increasing masking rate. Finally, we shed light on the interplay between masking and classification performance, and how this aids UDA. Our analysis shows that in predicting masked words that are informative to the downstream task, the model implicitly learns about the downstream task, furthering the benefits of directly learning the task. Our work connects the body of UDA research with that of instruction tuning, enabling an initial step towards a wider applicability of modern language models.

Limitations

Our work presents an investigation into continued pre-training for UDA in a *generative* setting. Since generative UDA is an almost completely unexplored area, we establish a proof of concept by using sentence classification tasks for our analysis. We leave the extending our analysis to more complex tasks to future work.

In our study, we consider a class of PEFT methods that involve inserting learnable parameters between the layers of the model. Other classes of PEFT methods were not considered. However, we use Adapters and He et al. (2022) have shown connections between the method with Prefix Tuning (Li and Liang, 2021) and LoRA (Hu et al., 2022).

Due to the high variance across runs in PEFT-based learning, we note that the performance can vary significantly across random seeds. We attempt to make our findings reproducible by averaging every experiment over 3 seeds. Taking environmental costs into consideration, we reduce our computational budget by running a majority of our experiments with a smaller-sized model. Learning with larger models is discussed in Section 4.

Ethics Statement

Our project aims to extend the problem of unsupervised domain adaptation to the generative setting, matching current needs with large language models. This is an effort towards improving the reliability and safety of language models, which can be fragile under distribution shift (Ribeiro et al., 2020) and incur great costs over incorrect predictions (Ulmer et al., 2020; Zhang et al., 2021a).

Our study does not involve any human subjects or violation of legal compliance. We do not anticipate any potentially harmful consequences to our work. As detailed in Appendix A, all of our experiments are conducted using publicly available datasets. Our code shall be released for reproducibility. Through our study and releasing our code, we hope to raise stronger research and societal awareness toward the problem of unsupervised domain adaptation in natural language processing.

References

Nachman Aronszajn. 1950. Theory of reproducing kernels. *Transactions of the American mathematical society*, 68(3):337–404.

Stephen Bach, Victor Sanh, Zheng Xin Yong, Albert Webson, Colin Raffel, Nihal V Nayak, Abheesht Sharma, Taewoon Kim, M Saiful Bari, Thibault Févry, et al. 2022. Promptsource: An integrated development environment and repository for natural language prompts. In *Proceedings of the 60th Annual Meeting of the Association for Computational Linguistics: System Demonstrations*, pages 93–104.

Ahsaas Bajaj, Pavitra Dangati, Kalpesh Krishna, Pradhiksha Ashok Kumar, Rheeya Uppaal, Bradford Windsor, Eliot Brenner, Dominic Dotterrer, Rajarshi Das, and Andrew Mccallum. 2021. Long document summarization in a low resource setting using pre-trained language models. In *Proceedings of the 59th Annual Meeting of the Association for Computational Linguistics and the 11th International Joint Conference on Natural Language Processing: Student Research Workshop*, pages 71–80.

Eyal Ben-David, Nadav Oved, and Roi Reichart. 2021. Pada: A prompt-based autoregressive approach for adaptation to unseen domains. *arXiv preprint arXiv:2102.12206*, 3.

Eyal Ben-David, Carmel Rabinovitz, and Roi Reichart. 2020. Perl: Pivot-based domain adaptation for pre-trained deep contextualized embedding models. *Transactions of the Association for Computational Linguistics*, 8:504–521.

Shai Ben-David, John Blitzer, Koby Crammer, Alex Kulesza, Fernando Pereira, and Jennifer Wortman Vaughan. 2010. A theory of learning from different domains. *Machine learning*, 79:151–175.

John Blitzer, Mark Dredze, and Fernando Pereira. 2007. Biographies, bollywood, boom-boxes and blenders: Domain adaptation for sentiment classification. In *Proceedings of the 45th annual meeting of the association of computational linguistics*, pages 440–447.

John Blitzer, Ryan McDonald, and Fernando Pereira. 2006. Domain adaptation with structural correspondence learning. In *Proceedings of the 2006 con-*

ference on empirical methods in natural language processing, pages 120–128.

Konstantinos Bousmalis, George Trigeorgis, Nathan Silberman, Dilip Krishnan, and Dumitru Erhan. 2016. Domain separation networks. *Advances in neural information processing systems*, 29.

Tom Brown, Benjamin Mann, Nick Ryder, Melanie Subbiah, Jared D Kaplan, Prafulla Dhariwal, Arvind Neelakantan, Pranav Shyam, Girish Sastry, Amanda Askell, et al. 2020. Language models are few-shot learners. *Advances in neural information processing systems*, 33:1877–1901.

Yun-Shiuan Chuang, Rheeya Uppaal, Yi Wu, Luhang Sun, Makesh Narsimhan Sreedhar, Sijia Yang, Timothy T Rogers, and Junjie Hu. 2023. Evolving domain adaptation of pretrained language models for text classification. In *NeurIPS 2023 Workshop on Distribution Shifts: New Frontiers with Foundation Models*.

Jacob Devlin, Ming-Wei Chang, Kenton Lee, and Kristina Toutanova. 2019. Bert: Pre-training of deep bidirectional transformers for language understanding. In *Proceedings of naacL-HLT*, volume 1, page 2.

Robert M Fano. 1961. Transmission of information: A statistical theory of communications. *American Journal of Physics*, 29(11):793–794.

Zihao Fu, Haoran Yang, Anthony Man-Cho So, Wai Lam, Lidong Bing, and Nigel Collier. 2023. On the effectiveness of parameter-efficient fine-tuning. In *Proceedings of the AAAI Conference on Artificial Intelligence*, volume 37, pages 12799–12807.

Yaroslav Ganin and Victor Lempitsky. 2015. Unsupervised domain adaptation by backpropagation. In *International conference on machine learning*, pages 1180–1189. PMLR.

Yaroslav Ganin, Evgeniya Ustinova, Hana Ajakan, Pascal Germain, Hugo Larochelle, François Laviolette, Mario Marchand, and Victor Lempitsky. 2016. Domain-adversarial training of neural networks. *The journal of machine learning research*, 17(1):2096–2030.

Tianyu Gao, Adam Fisch, and Danqi Chen. 2021. Making pre-trained language models better few-shot learners. In *Proceedings of the 59th Annual Meeting of the Association for Computational Linguistics and the 11th International Joint Conference on Natural Language Processing (Volume 1: Long Papers)*, pages 3816–3830.

Pengfei Ge, Chuan-Xian Ren, Xiao-Lin Xu, and Hong Yan. 2023. Unsupervised domain adaptation via deep conditional adaptation network. *Pattern Recognition*, 134:109088.

Arthur Gretton, Karsten M Borgwardt, Malte J Rasch, Bernhard Schölkopf, and Alexander Smola. 2012. A kernel two-sample test. *The Journal of Machine Learning Research*, 13(1):723–773.

Yuxian Gu, Zhengyan Zhang, Xiaozhi Wang, Zhiyuan Liu, and Maosong Sun. 2020. Train no evil: Selective masking for task-guided pre-training. In *Proceedings of the 2020 Conference on Empirical Methods in Natural Language Processing (EMNLP)*, pages 6966–6974, Online. Association for Computational Linguistics.

Han Guo, Ramakanth Pasunuru, and Mohit Bansal. 2020. Multi-source domain adaptation for text classification via distancenet-bandits. In *Proceedings of the AAAI conference on artificial intelligence*, volume 34, pages 7830–7838.

Xu Guo, Boyang Li, and Han Yu. 2022. Improving the sample efficiency of prompt tuning with domain adaptation. In *Findings of the Association for Computational Linguistics: EMNLP 2022*, pages 3523–3537, Abu Dhabi, United Arab Emirates. Association for Computational Linguistics.

Suchin Gururangan, Ana Marasović, Swabha Swayamdipta, Kyle Lo, Iz Beltagy, Doug Downey, and Noah A Smith. 2020. Don't stop pretraining: Adapt language models to domains and tasks. In *Proceedings of the 58th Annual Meeting of the Association for Computational Linguistics*, pages 8342–8360.

Suchin Gururangan, Swabha Swayamdipta, Omer Levy, Roy Schwartz, Samuel Bowman, and Noah A Smith. 2018. Annotation artifacts in natural language inference data. In *Proceedings of the 2018 Conference of the North American Chapter of the Association for Computational Linguistics: Human Language Technologies, Volume 2 (Short Papers)*, pages 107–112.

Xiaochuang Han and Jacob Eisenstein. 2019. Unsupervised domain adaptation of contextualized embeddings for sequence labeling. In *Proceedings of the 2019 Conference on Empirical Methods in Natural Language Processing and the 9th International Joint Conference on Natural Language Processing (EMNLP-IJCNLP)*, pages 4238–4248.

Junxian He, Chunting Zhou, Xuezhe Ma, Taylor Berg-Kirkpatrick, and Graham Neubig. 2022. Towards a unified view of parameter-efficient transfer learning. In *International Conference on Learning Representations*.

Neil Houlsby, Andrei Giurgiu, Stanislaw Jastrzebski, Bruna Morrone, Quentin De Laroussilhe, Andrea Gesmundo, Mona Attariyan, and Sylvain Gelly. 2019. Parameter-efficient transfer learning for nlp. In *International Conference on Machine Learning*, pages 2790–2799. PMLR.

Edward J Hu, Phillip Wallis, Zeyuan Allen-Zhu, Yuanzhi Li, Shean Wang, Lu Wang, Weizhu Chen, et al. 2022. Lora: Low-rank adaptation of large language models. In *International Conference on Learning Representations*.

Kuan-Hao Huang, I Hsu, Tanmay Parekh, Zhiyu Xie, Zixuan Zhang, Premkumar Natarajan, Kai-Wei Chang, Nanyun Peng, Heng Ji, et al. 2023. A reevaluation of event extraction: Past, present, and future challenges. *arXiv preprint arXiv:2311.09562*.

Chia-Chien Hung, Lukas Lange, and Jannik Strötgen. 2023. Tada: Efficient task-agnostic domain adaptation for transformers. *arXiv preprint arXiv:2305.12717*.

Gabriel Ilharco, Marco Tulio Ribeiro, Mitchell Wortsman, Ludwig Schmidt, Hannaneh Hajishirzi, and Ali Farhadi. 2022. Editing models with task arithmetic. In *The Eleventh International Conference on Learning Representations*.

Constantinos Karouzos, Georgios Paraskevopoulos, and Alexandros Potamianos. 2021. Udalm: Unsupervised domain adaptation through language modeling. In *Proceedings of the 2021 Conference of the North American Chapter of the Association for Computational Linguistics: Human Language Technologies*, pages 2579–2590.

Abhinav Ramesh Kashyap, Devamanyu Hazarika, Min-Yen Kan, and Roger Zimmermann. 2021. Domain divergences: A survey and empirical analysis. In *Proceedings of the 2021 Conference of the North American Chapter of the Association for Computational Linguistics: Human Language Technologies*, pages 1830–1849.

Seungwon Kim, Alex Shum, Nathan Susanj, and Jonathan Hilgart. 2021. Revisiting pretraining with adapters. In *Proceedings of the 6th Workshop on Representation Learning for NLP (RepL4NLP-2021)*, pages 90–99.

Ananya Kumar, Aditi Raghunathan, Robbie Matthew Jones, Tengyu Ma, and Percy Liang. 2022. Fine-tuning can distort pretrained features and underperform out-of-distribution. In *International Conference on Learning Representations*.

Jinhyuk Lee, Wonjin Yoon, Sungdong Kim, Donghyeon Kim, Sunkyu Kim, Chan Ho So, and Jaewoo Kang. 2020. Biobert: a pre-trained biomedical language representation model for biomedical text mining. *Bioinformatics*, 36(4):1234–1240.

Yoav Levine, Barak Lenz, Opher Lieber, Omri Abend, Kevin Leyton-Brown, Moshe Tennenholtz, and Yoav Shoham. 2021. Pmi-masking: Principled masking of correlated spans. In *International Conference on Learning Representations*.

Xiang Lisa Li and Percy Liang. 2021. Prefix-tuning: Optimizing continuous prompts for generation. In *Proceedings of the 59th Annual Meeting of the Association for Computational Linguistics and the 11th International Joint Conference on Natural Language Processing (Volume 1: Long Papers)*, pages 4582–4597.

Haokun Liu, Derek Tam, Mohammed Muqeeth, Jay Mohta, Tenghao Huang, Mohit Bansal, and Colin A Raffel. 2022. Few-shot parameter-efficient fine-tuning is better and cheaper than in-context learning. *Advances in Neural Information Processing Systems*, 35:1950–1965.

Pengfei Liu, Weizhe Yuan, Jinlan Fu, Zhengbao Jiang, Hiroaki Hayashi, and Graham Neubig. 2023. Pre-train, prompt, and predict: A systematic survey of prompting methods in natural language processing. *ACM Computing Surveys*, 55(9):1–35.

Mingsheng Long, Yue Cao, Jianmin Wang, and Michael Jordan. 2015. Learning transferable features with deep adaptation networks. In *International conference on machine learning*, pages 97–105. PMLR.

Quanyu Long, Tianze Luo, Wenya Wang, and Sinno Pan. 2022. Domain confused contrastive learning for unsupervised domain adaptation. In *Proceedings of the 2022 Conference of the North American Chapter of the Association for Computational Linguistics: Human Language Technologies*, pages 2982–2995.

Bhavitvya Malik, Abhinav Ramesh Kashyap, Min-Yen Kan, and Soujanya Poria. 2023. Udapter-efficient domain adaptation using adapters. In *Proceedings of the 17th Conference of the European Chapter of the Association for Computational Linguistics*, pages 2241–2255.

Leland McInnes, John Healy, and James Melville. 2018. Umap: Uniform manifold approximation and projection for dimension reduction. *arXiv preprint arXiv:1802.03426*.

Long Ouyang, Jeffrey Wu, Xu Jiang, Diogo Almeida, Carroll Wainwright, Pamela Mishkin, Chong Zhang, Sandhini Agarwal, Katarina Slama, Alex Ray, et al. 2022. Training language models to follow instructions with human feedback. *Advances in Neural Information Processing Systems*, 35:27730–27744.

Sinno Jialin Pan and Qiang Yang. 2010. A survey on transfer learning. *IEEE Transactions on knowledge and data engineering*, 22(10):1345–1359.

Marinela Parović, Alan Ansell, Ivan Vulić, and Anna Korhonen. 2023. Cross-lingual transfer with target language-ready task adapters. *arXiv preprint arXiv:2306.02767*.

Jonas Pfeiffer, Ivan Vulić, Iryna Gurevych, and Sebastian Ruder. 2020. Mad-x: An adapter-based framework for multi-task cross-lingual transfer. In *Proceedings of the 2020 Conference on Empirical Methods in Natural Language Processing (EMNLP)*, pages 7654–7673.

Alec Radford, Jeffrey Wu, Rewon Child, David Luan, Dario Amodei, Ilya Sutskever, et al. 2019. Language models are unsupervised multitask learners. *OpenAI blog*, 1(8):9.

Colin Raffel, Noam Shazeer, Adam Roberts, Katherine Lee, Sharan Narang, Michael Matena, Yanqi Zhou, Wei Li, and Peter J Liu. 2020. Exploring the limits of transfer learning with a unified text-to-text transformer. *The Journal of Machine Learning Research*, 21(1):5485–5551.

Alan Ramponi and Barbara Plank. 2020. Neural unsupervised domain adaptation in nlp—a survey. In *Proceedings of the 28th International Conference on Computational Linguistics*, pages 6838–6855.

Marco Tulio Ribeiro, Tongshuang Wu, Carlos Guestrin, and Sameer Singh. 2020. Beyond accuracy: Behavioral testing of nlp models with checklist. In *Proceedings of the 58th Annual Meeting of the Association for Computational Linguistics*, pages 4902–4912.

Sebastian Ruder and Barbara Plank. 2017. Learning to select data for transfer learning with bayesian optimization. In *Proceedings of the 2017 Conference on Empirical Methods in Natural Language Processing*, pages 372–382.

Victor Sanh, Albert Webson, Colin Raffel, Stephen Bach, Lintang Sutawika, Zaid Alyafeai, Antoine Chaffin, Arnaud Stiegler, Arun Raja, Manan Dey, et al. 2022. Multitask prompted training enables zero-shot task generalization. In *International Conference on Learning Representations*.

Teven Le Scao, Angela Fan, Christopher Akiki, Ellie Pavlick, Suzana Ilić, Daniel Hesslow, Roman Castagné, Alexandra Sasha Luccioni, François Yvon, Matthias Gallé, et al. 2022. Bloom: A 176b-parameter open-access multilingual language model. *arXiv preprint arXiv:2211.05100*.

Kendrick Shen, Robbie M Jones, Ananya Kumar, Sang Michael Xie, Jeff Z HaoChen, Tengyu Ma, and Percy Liang. 2022. Connect, not collapse: Explaining contrastive learning for unsupervised domain adaptation. In *International Conference on Machine Learning*, pages 19847–19878. PMLR.

Kaitao Song, Xu Tan, Tao Qin, Jianfeng Lu, and Tie-Yan Liu. 2019. Mass: Masked sequence to sequence pre-training for language generation. *arXiv preprint arXiv:1905.02450*.

Baochen Sun, Jiashi Feng, and Kate Saenko. 2017. Correlation alignment for unsupervised domain adaptation. *Domain adaptation in computer vision applications*, pages 153–171.

Yu Sun, Eric Tzeng, Trevor Darrell, and Alexei A Efros. 2019. Unsupervised domain adaptation through self-supervision. *arXiv preprint arXiv:1909.11825*.

Liyan Tang, Philippe Laban, and Greg Durrett. 2024. Minicheck: Efficient fact-checking of llms on grounding documents. *arXiv preprint arXiv:2404.10774*.

Hugo Touvron, Thibaut Lavril, Gautier Izacard, Xavier Martinet, Marie-Anne Lachaux, Timothée Lacroix, Baptiste Rozière, Naman Goyal, Eric Hambro, Faisal Azhar, et al. 2023. Llama: Open and efficient foundation language models. *arXiv preprint arXiv:2302.13971*.

Nghia Ngo Trung, Linh Ngo Van, and Thien Huu Nguyen. 2022. Unsupervised domain adaptation for text classification via meta self-paced learning. In *Proceedings of the 29th International Conference on Computational Linguistics*, pages 4741–4752.

Eric Tzeng, Judy Hoffman, Kate Saenko, and Trevor Darrell. 2017. Adversarial discriminative domain adaptation. In *Proceedings of the IEEE conference on computer vision and pattern recognition*, pages 7167–7176.

Eric Tzeng, Judy Hoffman, Ning Zhang, Kate Saenko, and Trevor Darrell. 2014. Deep domain confusion: Maximizing for domain invariance. *conference on computer vision and pattern recognition*.

Dennis Ulmer, Lotta Meijerink, and Giovanni Cinà. 2020. Trust issues: Uncertainty estimation does not enable reliable ood detection on medical tabular data. In *Machine Learning for Health*, pages 341–354. PMLR.

Rheeya Uppaal, Apratim De, Yiting He, Yiquao Zhong, and Junjie Hu. 2024. Detox: Toxic subspace projection for model editing. *arXiv preprint arXiv:2405.13967*.

Rheeya Uppaal, Junjie Hu, and Yixuan Li. 2023. Is fine-tuning needed? pre-trained language models are near perfect for out-of-domain detection. In *Proceedings of the 61st Annual Meeting of the Association for Computational Linguistics (Volume 1: Long Papers)*.

Yizhong Wang, Swaroop Mishra, Pegah Alipoormolabashi, Yeganeh Kordi, Amirreza Mirzaei, Atharva Naik, Arjun Ashok, Arut Selvan Dhanasekaran, Anjana Arunkumar, David Stap, et al. 2022. Supernaturalinstructions: Generalization via declarative instructions on 1600+ nlp tasks. In *Proceedings of the 2022 Conference on Empirical Methods in Natural Language Processing*, pages 5085–5109.

Jason Wei, Maarten Bosma, Vincent Zhao, Kelvin Guu, Adams Wei Yu, Brian Lester, Nan Du, Andrew M Dai, and Quoc V Le. 2022. Finetuned language models are zero-shot learners. In *International Conference on Learning Representations*.

Alexander Wettig, Tianyu Gao, Zexuan Zhong, and Danqi Chen. 2023. Should you mask 15% in masked language modeling? In *Proceedings of the 17th Conference of the European Chapter of the Association for Computational Linguistics*, pages 2985–3000, Dubrovnik, Croatia. Association for Computational Linguistics.

Adina Williams, Nikita Nangia, and Samuel Bowman. 2018. A broad-coverage challenge corpus for sentence understanding through inference. In *Proceedings of the 2018 Conference of the North American*

Chapter of the Association for Computational Linguistics: Human Language Technologies, Volume 1 (Long Papers), pages 1112–1122.

Garrett Wilson and Diane J Cook. 2020. A survey of unsupervised deep domain adaptation. *ACM Transactions on Intelligent Systems and Technology (TIST)*, 11(5):1–46.

Hui Wu and Xiaodong Shi. 2022. Adversarial soft prompt tuning for cross-domain sentiment analysis. In *Proceedings of the 60th Annual Meeting of the Association for Computational Linguistics (Volume 1: Long Papers)*, pages 2438–2447.

Oliver Zhang, Jean-Benoit Delbrouck, and Daniel L Rubin. 2021a. Out of distribution detection for medical images. In *Uncertainty for Safe Utilization of Machine Learning in Medical Imaging, and Perinatal Imaging, Placental and Preterm Image Analysis*, pages 102–111. Springer.

Rongsheng Zhang, Yinhe Zheng, Xiaoxi Mao, and Minlie Huang. 2021b. Unsupervised domain adaptation with adapter. *Proceedings of the Workshop on Efficient Natural Language and Speech Processing*.

Shengyu Zhang, Linfeng Dong, Xiaoya Li, Sen Zhang, Xiaofei Sun, Shuhe Wang, Jiwei Li, Runyi Hu, Tianwei Zhang, Fei Wu, et al. 2023. Instruction tuning for large language models: A survey. *arXiv preprint arXiv:2308.10792*.

Han Zhao, Remi Tachet Des Combes, Kun Zhang, and Geoffrey Gordon. 2019. On learning invariant representations for domain adaptation. In *International conference on machine learning*, pages 7523–7532. PMLR.

Zhi-Hua Zhou and Ming Li. 2005. Tri-training: Exploiting unlabeled data using three classifiers. *IEEE Transactions on knowledge and Data Engineering*, 17(11):1529–1541.

Wenhao Zhu, Hongyi Liu, Qingxiu Dong, Jingjing Xu, Lingpeng Kong, Jiajun Chen, Lei Li, and Shujian Huang. 2023. Multilingual machine translation with large language models: Empirical results and analysis. *arXiv preprint arXiv:2304.04675*.

Yftah Ziser and Roi Reichart. 2018. Pivot based language modeling for improved neural domain adaptation. In *Proceedings of the 2018 Conference of the North American Chapter of the Association for Computational Linguistics: Human Language Technologies, Volume 1 (Long Papers)*, pages 1241–1251.

A Preparation of Evaluation Benchmarks

We use two classification datasets, with 5 domains each. This results in a total of 40 pairs of source and target domains. For brevity, we include results of 24 domain pairs in the main paper, and the remaining 16 in Appendix C. For both datasets, we use the train, validation and test splits from (Malik et al., 2023). More statistics about each dataset is available in Table 4. The listed datasets are intended for research purposes only. We do not make any commercial use of them.

MNLI The Multigenre Natural Language Inference (MNLI) corpus (Williams et al., 2018) contains sentence pairs across multiple genres: Travel (T), Fiction (F), Government (G), Slate (S) and Telephone (Te). The NLI task involves classifying every premise-hypothesis sentence pair as Entailment, Neutral or Contradiction.

Amazon The Multi Domain Sentiment Analysis Dataset (Blitzer et al., 2007) contains Amazon product reviews for different type of products. We use reviews from the Apparel (A), Baby (B), Books (Bo), Cameras (C) and Movies (M) domains. Each review is labelled as positive or negative.

Dataset	Language	License	Statistics per Domain		
			Train	Val	Test
MNLI	English	cc-by-4.0	69600*	7735**	1945
Amazon	English	cc-by-4.0	1440	160	400

Table 4: Artifacts used in our study. The dataset statistics report the values used in our study.
* All domains contain approximately 69,600 examples. The exception is the Telephone domain, with 75,013 examples.
** All domains contain 7735 validation examples, except for Slate and Telephone, which contain 7731 and 8336 examples respectively.

B Details on Implementation

Models and Implementation We use T5v1.1, T0 and GPT-2 and LLaMA-2 from the HuggingFace library[8], and use PyTorch[9] to train our models.

Training We use the default hyperparameters from Liu et al. (2022), except for batch size and training duration. We perform a grid search for these values. We train each training phase for 30,000 steps on MNLI and 15,000 steps on the Amazon dataset, with a batch size of 8. For the T5v1.1 XL and T0 models (3B parameters each), we use a batch size of 1. We train with Adam and use a learning rate of 0.003. We set the maximum sequence length to 256 tokens. We use length normalization during evaluation, as proposed by Liu et al. (2022). For each experiment, we report the mean and standard deviation across 3 runs.

We choose the number of training steps based on early stopping on the validation set for one domain, and use that number of steps for all domains within that dataset. We report the test set performance after a varying number of training steps in the table below. For example, for the Apparel→Movies domain pair of the Amazon Reviews dataset, the performance saturates at 15,000 steps, as shown in Table 5.

Training Steps	Source Accuracy	Target Accuracy
5,000	93.2 (0.4)	81.9 (0.4)
10,000	93.4 (0.5)	81.6 (0.6)
15,000	93.5 (0.4)	83.3 (0.5)

Table 5: We use early stopping on one domain pair to determine the number of training steps, which we then use for all domain pairs of that dataset. For example, the Apparel→Movies domain pair of the Amazon Reviews dataset shown in the table saturates at 15,000 steps.

Computations Using the $(IA)^3$ PEFT framework, training the T5v1.1 Base model (60 million parameters) for 15,000 steps takes approximately two hours on a single NVIDIA RTX A6000 GPU. The T5v1.1 XL model and T0 model (3 billion parameters) take approximately 8 hours for 15,000 steps of training. For reproducibility, each experiment is repeated thrice, with changing random seeds. In total, we run 540 experiments with the Base model and 72 experiments with the larger models. This results in a total compute time of approximately 2400 GPU hours.

C Detailed results with the Amazon and MNLI Datasets

Table 6 shows the performance of CPT on the Amazon and MNLI datasets.

On the Amazon dataset, CPT is competitive with the state of the art UDAPTER method from Malik et al. (2023) on average. We confirm this by checking for a significant difference in the performance of CPT and UDAPTER on the 20 dataset pairs. The Mann-Whitney U test and Student's t-test both re-

[8]https://github.com/huggingface/transformers
[9]https://pytorch.org/

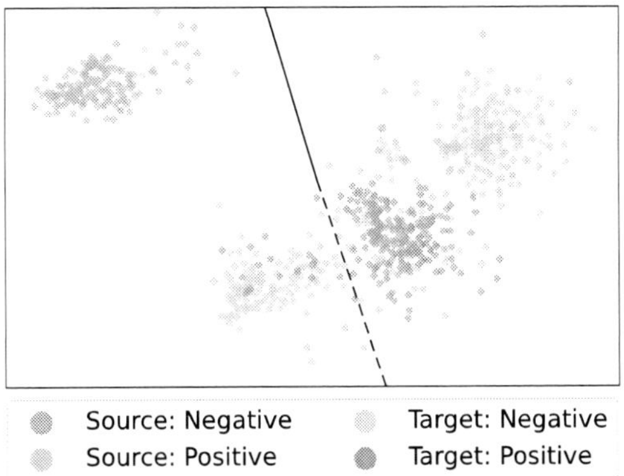

Figure 8: UMap visualizations of sentence embeddings from the Apparel → Movies data pair, using the T5v1.1 base model and $(IA)^3$ PEFT method. Despite not promoting domain-invariance, CPT may be learning sentence embeddings that are separable by class labels, regardless of the domain of these sentences. The classification hyperplane for the source domain has been imagined as a solid line for illustration purposes, and its extension to the target domain is shown as a dashed line.

sulted in non-significant p-values of 0.5516 and 0.8316, confirming the hypothesis that there is no significant difference between CPT and UDAPTER on the Amazon dataset.

However, on the MNLI dataset, where all domains have larger gaps, both significant tests showed a significant difference between CPT and UDAPTER, with CPT being more powerful. This is exemplified through cases like Travel (T) → Government (G), where CPT yields an accuracy of 83.6% on the target domain, equalling the upper bound of the Src+Tgt baseline.

Comparison with other Model Centric Approaches In addition to the MMD based method of Malik et al. (2023), we also compare CPT with other methods that promote domain invariance: 1) DANN (Ganin et al., 2016), which is the most widely used UDA method in NLP (Ramponi and Plank, 2020), but has been shown to be highly unstable; 2) CORAL (Sun et al., 2017), which minimizes second order statistics of the data embeddings. Additionally, with an emerging class of weight interpolation based methods, we make a comparison with task vector arithmetic (Ilharco et al., 2022). The use of task vectors with PEFT methods beyond LoRA (Hu et al., 2022) has been unexplored in the literature, and we find that the method does not work with IA3. With fully fine-tuned models, the method improves in performance, but is still weaker than CPT.

CPT may learn representations that generalize across domains To better understand the improved UDA performance, we visualize the sentence embeddings learned by CPT in Figure 8. Using UMap (McInnes et al., 2018), the figure visualizes embeddings for the Apparel→Movies domain pair from the Amazon Product Review dataset. We see that CPT learns sentence embeddings that generalize across domains. For illustration, we draw a black line that cuts across both source and target domains. Note that the solid line suggests that there exists a classification hyperplane learned on the source labeled data (in blue and green). The same classifier can be potentially used to separate target data (in gray and orange). The visualization suggests that CPT achieves competitive UDA results without having to explicitly promote domain-invariant representations.

D CPT across Model Architectures and Scales

We evaluate the performance of CPT over T5v1.1 XL and the instruction tuned T0 (3B) (Sanh et al., 2022) in Table 8.

E PEFT Frameworks

The framework proposed in Section 2 is general and can be applied to fine-tune all model parameters. Additionally, our CPT framework is compatible with the parameter-efficient fine-tuning approach. The PEFT approach is desirable because it adds only a small amount of learnable parameters ϕ to a pre-trained language model θ, and fine-tunes only ϕ to perform prediction while keeping the other model parameters θ frozen. We use two instantiations in our implementations: Adapters (Houlsby et al., 2019) and $(IA)^3$ (Liu et al., 2022).

$\mathbf{(IA)^3}$ is a state of the art PEFT learning method, and uses around a tenth of learnable parameters compared to popular methods like Adapters. $(IA)^3$ works by element-wise multiplication (i.e. rescaling) of the model's activations against a learned vector. In this case, the set of learnable parameters ϕ is a set of vectors $\{l_v, l_k, l_{ff}\}$ applied to each attention mechanism and feed-forward layer as,

	Amazon				MNLI		
	Src+Tgt	UDAPTER	CPT		Src+Tgt	UDAPTER	CPT
A → B	94.7 (0.2)	93.8 (0.3)	**93.9** (0.3)	T → F	77.2 (0.4)	69.7 (0.8)	**74.1** (0.9)
A → Bo	94.3 (0.4)	**92.5** (1.1)	90.2 (1.2)	T → G	83.6 (0.7)	79.3 (0.5)	**83.6** (0.3)
A → C	95.0 (0.2)	91.8 (0.5)	**92.1** (0.5)	T → S	72.3 (0.5)	69.6 (0.1)	**70.7** (0.6)
A → M	85.8 (0.5)	81.3 (0.6)	**83.3** (0.5)	T → Te	77.8 (0.1)	69.4 (0.8)	**76.8** (0.0)
B → A	93.4 (0.3)	93.3 (0.2)	**93.4** (0.4)	F → T	79.9 (0.1)	**69.9** (0.2)	65.4 (0.8)
B → Bo	94.7 (0.7)	**93.8** (0.3)	92.2 (0.1)	F → G	82.3 (0.1)	54.3 (23.4)	**78.8** (2.5)
B → C	94.7 (0.8)	**93.4** (0.1)	92.1 (0.3)	F → S	72.1 (0.2)	64.6 (1.8)	**65.3** (1.6)
B → M	85.3 (0.2)	81.3 (0.7)	**82.8** (0.2)	F → Te	78.3 (0.6)	64.6 (0.7)	**72.5** (0.2)
Bo → A	94.6 (0.3)	**91.6** (0.5)	91.3 (0.2)	G → T	79.9 (0.4)	**75.9** (0.3)	75.8 (0.6)
Bo → B	94.8 (0.2)	**92.9** (0.6)	90.9 (0.2)	G → F	76.7 (0.1)	69.9 (0.2)	**73.5** (0.2)
Bo → C	94.3 (0.2)	89.8 (0.1)	**90.3** (0.4)	G → S	73.1 (0.0)	**69.4** (0.1)	68.0 (1.8)
Bo → M	85.5 (0.9)	**84.6** (0.7)	80.1 (1.2)	G → Te	78.1 (0.6)	69.9 (0.3)	**73.5** (0.6)
C → A	93.4 (0.4)	92.3 (0.3)	**92.5** (0.6)	S → T	79.5 (0.3)	74.4 (1.7)	**76.8** (0.1)
C → B	95.0 (0.6)	**94.1** (0.1)	92.1 (0.2)	S → F	77.7 (0.2)	**73.1** (0.0)	72.4 (0.5)
C → Bo	93.9 (0.8)	**91.3** (0.5)	89.0 (0.1)	S → G	83.4 (0.2)	**78.2** (0.5)	76.3 (0.9)
C → M	85.8 (0.1)	**81.5** (0.7)	79.7 (1.2)	S → Te	78.5 (0.0)	66.7 (0.2)	**74.8** (0.3)
M → A	94.2 (0.7)	89.1 (1.4)	**90.1** (0.5)	Te → T	79.8 (0.3)	71.4 (0.0)	**76.5** (0.4)
M → B	95.3 (0.5)	81.0 (16.1)	**89.9** (1.2)	Te → F	77.9 (0.1)	69.9 (0.5)	**74.3** (0.5)
M → Bo	94.1 (0.4)	80.5 (18.6)	**91.5** (0.0)	Te → G	82.5 (0.1)	75.6 (1.6)	**82.0** (0.6)
M → C	94.3 (0.5)	**90.5** (0.0)	89.7 (0.3)	Te → S	72.2 (0.0)	68.0 (0.4)	**71.3** (0.5)

Table 6: Comparison of CPT and UDAPTER by target domain classification accuracy on the Amazon Product Review and MNLI datasets. Each row represents a Source→ Target pair. On average, CPT is competitive with UDAPTER, often outperforming it. We use the T5v1.1 base model, and $(IA)^3$ as a PEFT method. The highest values between CPT and UDAPTER have been marked in bold.

Method	Accuracy
CPT	**83.3** (0.9)
UDAPTER	81.3 (0.6)
DANN	52.3 (1.7)
CORAL	80.9 (0.4)
Task Vectors	48.0 (0.7)
Task Vectors (fine-tuning)	69.0 (0.4)

Table 7: Comparison of CPT with more baselines, using the T5v1.1 base model and $(IA)^3$ PEFT method on the Apparel→Movies pair from the Amazon review dataset. For task vectors, we include versions with $(IA)^3$ as well as full fine-tuning. CPT outperforms all baselines.

$$h = \sigma\left(\frac{Q(l_k \odot K^T)}{\sqrt{d_k}}\right)(l_v \odot V)$$

$$h = (l_{ff} \odot \gamma(W_1 x)W_2)$$

Here, K, Q and V are the key, query and value representations used in an attention block, and W_1 and W_2 are the weights in the feed-forward layer following an attention block. $l_k \in \mathbb{R}^{d_k}$, $l_v \in \mathbb{R}^{d_v}$, $l_{ff} \in \mathbb{R}^{d_{ff}}$, σ is the softmax function while γ is any non-linearity.

Model	Src+Tgt	UDAPTER	CPT
T5 v1.1 Base	85.8 (0.5)	78.6 (1.3)	**83.3** (0.5)
T5 v1.1 XL	93.0 (0.5)	65.2 (9.5)	**92.0** (1.5)
T0 3B	92.2 (0.7)	51.8 (0.8)	**93.8** (0.4)

Table 8: The performance gap between CPT and UDAPTER increases with larger models, from T5v1.1 Base (60M parameters) to T5v1.1 XL (3B parameters), and further increases with instruction tuning (T0 3B).

Intuitively, each vector l simply learns weights measuring the importance of each feature in an activation of the pre-trained model, for the specific downstream task the model is trained on.

Adapters are a popularly used and high performing PEFT framework, and He et al. (2022) have shown equivalence in the operations applied by Adapters, Prefix Tuning (Li and Liang, 2021) and LoRA (Hu et al., 2022).

Adapters work by adding small learnable modules between transformer layers. Specifically, down and up projections $W_{\text{down}} \in \mathbb{R}^{d \times r}$ and $W_{\text{up}} \in \mathbb{R}^{r \times d}$ are learnt such that ϕ =

$\{W_{\text{up}}, W_{\text{down}}\}$. A residual connection and non-linearity γ is added at every layer,

$$h = h + \gamma(hW_{\text{down}})W_{\text{up}}$$

Table 9 shows CPT beats UDAPTER across different tuning methods. We also note that fine-tuning yields slightly better performance for all UDA methods.

F CPT in a Few-Shot Setup

Table 10 accompanies Figure 1 (Section 4), showing the 256-shot performance of CPT and other baselines, across model sizes. Similarly, Table 11 accompanies Figure 3, showing the relative performance of all baselines across varying k.

G Impact of Target Domain Exposure

The experiments in this section use the T5v1.1 base model on the Apparel→Movies domain pair of the Amazon reviews dataset.

Table 12 accompanies results from Figure 5, which show the impact of varying masking rates on CPT. Using the T5v1.1 base model, we train CPT using varying random masking rates on the Apparel → Movies domain pair, and report the mean and standard deviation over three runs. With high masking rates, the performance on the source domain is largely maintained, but the performance on the target domain rapidly deteriorates.

H Understanding how CPT aids UDA

Table 13 (accompanies Figure 7) shows the impact of masking sequences at inference, on classification accuracy. Words are selected for masking based on their their "informativeness", measured by their PMI to the inference class label. The performance of the model is best with the original unmasked sequences, indicating the presence of both informative and uninformative words are essential for strong classification performance.

Table 15 accompanies Figure 7 and shows the impact of varying masking strategies on classification performance, in a few-shot setting. We also consider two different few-shot setups: one with access to the full unlabelled datasets in phase 1 pre-training, and another where even the unlabelled data is few-shot.

To isolate any effects of PEFT methods or pre-training data, we repeat the analysis from Table 15 in Table 14 with fine-tuning Flan-T5 in a full data setting, and note similar trends.

I Single Phase CPT Training

Our proposed approach in Section 2 involves two stages of training, which is more expensive than standard single phase UDA approaches. In this section, we propose a single training phase variant to CPT, and show that it performs similarly to the original method. We use the two phase pipeline in our experiments in the main paper, but note that the single and two phase pipelines are interchangeable.

We simply replace the two phase training with a joint multi-task objective as follows,

$$\mathcal{L}(\mathcal{D}, \mathcal{D}_{\text{src}}; \theta) = \frac{1}{|D|}\frac{1}{|D_{\text{src}}|} \sum_{x' \in \mathcal{D}} \sum_{(x,y) \in \mathcal{D}_{\text{src}}} (\lambda\, l(\mathbb{C}(x, y); \theta) + (1 - \lambda)\, l(\mathbb{M}(x'); \theta))$$

where l is the cross-entropy loss defined in Eq. (1), and $\mathbb{M}$ and $\mathbb{C}$ are the templates defined in Section 2. λ is the adaptation factor which gradually changes from 0 to 1 over the course of training. This results in the model being trained almost exclusively on the MLM task early on in training, and the CLS task towards the end of training.

Table 16 compares the performance of the single phase and two phase variants of CPT. We also compare with a vanilla joint single phase objective, where λ is fixed at 0.5 through training (called Single Phase Vanilla). The performance of the single and two phase variants are almost identical, and either can be used interchangeably. In comparison, the vanilla single phase method is significantly weaker on the target domain.

J Instability of Domain Invariance Methods for UDA

The Maximum Mean Discrepancy (MMD) (Gretton et al., 2012) measures the difference between first order moments of variables in a Reproducing Kernel Hilbert Space (Aronszajn, 1950). Multiple lines of work have shown that minimizing divergence measures like MMD, when combined with auxiliary task-specific loss functions, results in training instabilities and vanishing gradients (Kashyap et al., 2021; Han and Eisenstein, 2019).

We also note that as minimizing MMD does not use any label information, there is a possibility for embeddings of the target domain to be aligned with the closest source domain class cluster. For example, Figure 9 shows us a setting where both

Method	Src+Tgt	UDAPTER	CPT
Fine-Tuning	86.4 (0.4)	82.4 (1.6)	**84.4** (0.3)
(IA)3	85.8 (0.5)	81.3 (0.6)	**83.3** (0.5)
Adapters	85.3 (0.5)	79.1 (0.3)	**82.7** (0.5)

Table 9: Performance of CPT across different adaptation methods with the T5v1.1 base model on the Apparel → Movies domain pair. CPT remains more powerful than UDAPTER across all methods.

Model	Src+Tgt	UDAPTER	CPT	Model	Src+Tgt	UDAPTER	Two Phase	CPT
T5v1.1 Base	77.8 (0.4)	60.9 (1.6)	73.1 (1.7)	T5v1.1 Base	82.8 (0.6)	62.5 (0.7)	79.8 (1.4)	81.2 (0.7)
T5v1.1 XL	84.4 (0.1)	84.8 (1.5)	89.9 (1.1)	T5v1.1 XL	92.5 (0.4)	71.7 (7.8)	84.3 (0.9)	86.8 (2.2)
T0 3B	88.3 (0.5)	81.8 (1.3)	93.9 (0.4)	T0 3B	91.8 (0.6)	79.5 (6.7)	53.5 (0.4)	92.8 (0.2)

Table 10: Performance of CPT across different models, in a k-shot learning setup on the Apparel → Movies domain pair. We see CPT retaining strong performance on the target domain across models. **Left**: 32-shot. **Right**: 256-shot.

Number of Shots	Src+Tgt	UDAPTER	Two Phase UDAPTER	CPT
32	77.8 (0.4)	60.9 (1.6)	59.4 (2.0)	73.1 (1.7)
128	82.5 (0.5)	75.1 (0.6)	62.8 (0.6)	78.8 (1.0)
256	82.8 (0.6)	62.5 (0.7)	79.8 (1.4)	81.2 (0.7)

Table 11: Performance of CPT across different number of shots, on the Apparel → Movies domain pair, using the T5v1.1 base model. We see CPT retaining strong performance on the target domain across shots.

Masking Rate	Accuracy	
	Source	Target
5%	92.8 (0.8)	78.8 (1.8)
15%	**93.5** (0.4)	**83.3** (0.5)
30%	92.8 (0.6)	78.8 (1.4)
60%	92.5 (0.9)	71.0 (3.0)
90%	92.3 (0.5)	70.4 (1.5)

Table 12: Impact of Masking Rate on CPT. We train CPT using varying random masking rates on the Apparel → Movies domain pair. With high masking rates, the performance on the source domain is largely maintained, but the performance on the target domain rapidly deteriorates.

Method	Accuracy	
	Source	Target
Original	**93.5**	**83.3**
Informative Masking	88.0	78.8
Uninformative Masking	92.0	79.0

Table 13: Impact of masking at inference. We evaluate CPT on the Apparel → Movies domain pair, and select words for masking based on their "informativeness" to the classification task.

Masking Strategy	Accuracy	
	Source	Target
Random	**95.8** (0.0)	**86.8** (0.3)
Informative	93.9 (0.6)	85.3 (0.3)
Uninformative	95.0 (0.0)	84.8 (0.1)

Table 14: Impact of word selection for masking during training, using Flan-T5 base and no PEFT methods.

Phase 1 Data	Masking Strategy	Accuracy	
		Source	Target
256 Shot	Random	**91.0** (0.9)	**78.1** (2.4)
	Informative	90.4 (0.5)	76.0 (0.7)
	Uninformative	89.6 (1.2)	73.5 (1.6)
Full Data	Random	90.1 (0.5)	**81.2** (0.7)
	Informative	**91.8** (0.5)	78.0 (0.9)
	Uninformative	89.3 (0.5)	72.8 (1.1)

Table 15: Impact of word selection for masking, in a 256-shot learning setup. We evaluate CPT on the Apparel → Movies domain pair, and select words for masking based on their "informativeness" to the classification task. Random masking is most powerful for the target domain, indicating that both semantic and background features are necessary for effective classification on the unlabelled domain. However, informative masking is significantly more useful than uninformative masking.

classes of the target domain (shown in green and gray) are mapped to the cluster of negative class

Method	Accuracy	
	Source	Target
Two Phase	93.7 (0.3)	**83.3** (0.9)
Singe Phase	93.5 (0.4)	**83.3** (0.5)
Singe Phase Vanilla	93.6 (0.1)	75.0 (5.7)

Table 16: Comparison of single and two-phase variants of CPT, on the Apparel → Movies domain pair. The single and two phase variants are almost identical in performance.

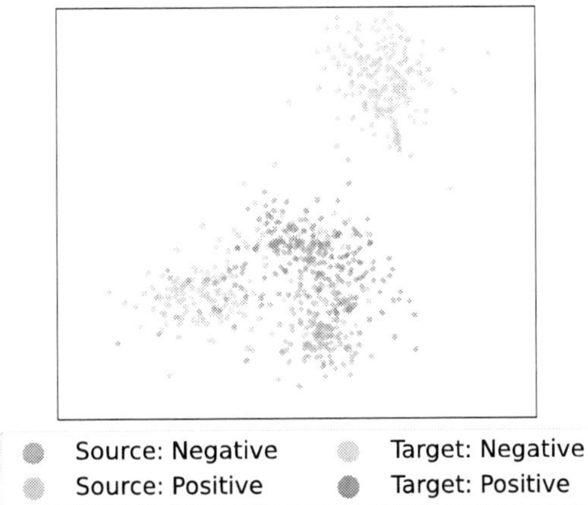

Figure 9: UMap visualizations of sentence embeddings from the Apparel → Movies data pair, using the T5v1.1 base model and $(IA)^3$ PEFT method. Training with UDAPTER risks stability issues, and all embeddings from the target domain can be mapped to the closest source class cluster. This results in poor classification performance on the target domain.

source embeddings (shown in blue).

We compare variants of the UDAPTER method in Table 17 and show that the loss is sensitive to small changes in the loss design. Specifically we compare the UDAPTER method used in the main paper with:

- MMD over Logits: Measures the MMD between the logits of source and target domains, instead of using intermediate model outputs.
- Fixed Weight MMD: Instead of the multi-task loss for the MMD reduction and classification tasks, we use fixed weights for both tasks[10].
- Two Phase MMD: The first training phase is used to minimize MMD between source and target embeddings, while the second phase is used to train the model for classification on the source domain.

CPT remains more powerful than all variants.

Method	Accuracy	
	Source	Target
CPT	93.7 (0.3)	**83.3** (0.9)
UDAPTER	**94.7** (0.3)	81.3 (0.6)
UDAPTER over Logits	95.0 (0.2)	81.3 (0.7)
Fixed Weight MMD	93.4 (0.2)	78.6 (1.3)
Two Phase UDAPTER	90.1 (0.1)	68.7 (2.0)

Table 17: Comparison of variants of minimizing MMD, on the Apparel → Movies domain pair. CPT remains more powerful than all variants.

[10]For the weighted loss, $\mathcal{L}_{\text{CLS}} + 3\ \mathcal{L}_{\text{MMD}}$ was found to be the best performing.

Word Boundary Information Isn't Useful for Encoder Language Models

Edward Gow-Smith[1], **Dylan Phelps**[1], **Harish Tayyar Madabushi**[2],
Carolina Scarton[1] and **Aline Villavicencio**[1]

[1]Department of Computer Science, University of Sheffield
[2]Department of Computer Science, University of Bath

egow-smith1@sheffield.ac.uk

Abstract

All existing transformer-based approaches to NLP using subword tokenisation algorithms encode whitespace (word boundary information) through the use of special space symbols (such as ## or _) forming part of tokens. These symbols have been shown to a) lead to reduced morphological validity of tokenisations, and b) give substantial vocabulary redundancy. As such, removing these symbols has been shown to have a beneficial effect on the processing of morphologically complex words for transformer encoders in the pretrain-finetune paradigm. In this work, we explore whether word boundary information is at all useful to such models. In particular, we train transformer encoders across four different training scales, and investigate several alternative approaches to including word boundary information, evaluating on two languages (English and Finnish) with a range of tasks across different domains and problem set-ups: sentence classification datasets, NER (for token-level classification), and two classification datasets involving complex words (Superbizarre and FLOTA). Overall, through an extensive experimental setup that includes the pretraining of 35 models, we find no substantial improvements from our alternative approaches, suggesting that modifying tokenisers to remove word boundary information isn't leading to a loss of useful information.

1 Introduction

Transformer (Vaswani et al., 2017) pretrained language models for NLP, such as BERT (Devlin et al., 2019) and the GPT family (Brown et al., 2020; Achiam et al., 2023), typically use subword tokenisation algorithms, such as WordPiece (Schuster and Nakajima, 2012), to process text. Previous work (Church, 2020; Park et al., 2021) has shown that such methods have limited alignment with word morphology, resulting in worsened downstream performance for various tasks (Klein and Tsarfaty, 2020; Bostrom and Durrett, 2020; Pinter et al., 2020). In fact, it has been shown that the morphological validity of tokenisation can be improved by removing all whitespace markers (and hence word boundary (WB) information) from the tokenisers (Gow-Smith et al., 2022). However, the full impact of this modification on downstream performance is unknown, and the question of whether WB information is at all useful to models is as yet unanswered. In this work, we first perform a morphological evaluation of WordPiece and WordPiece′, a version which has been modified to have no WB information. We find that WordPiece′ significantly improves the alignment with morphological gold standard references. Then, we evaluate WordPiece and WordPiece′ as tokenisers on downstream tasks. We also introduce models which modify WordPiece′ by including WB information in various ways – either explicitly through the input or implicitly through the pretraining objective. Much interest recently has been in the scaling laws of language models (Kaplan et al., 2020; Hoffmann et al., 2022), and a direction towards training larger models. On the other hand, there has been recent work investigating sample-efficient pretraining on datasets of a developmentally plausible size (Warstadt et al., 2023). In companion to such work, we train our models across four training scales, from approximately 6M params and 250M tokens at the lowest scale to approximately 370M params and 23B tokens at the highest scale.

Across these scales we pretrain all of our models and evaluate in English on four downstream tasks

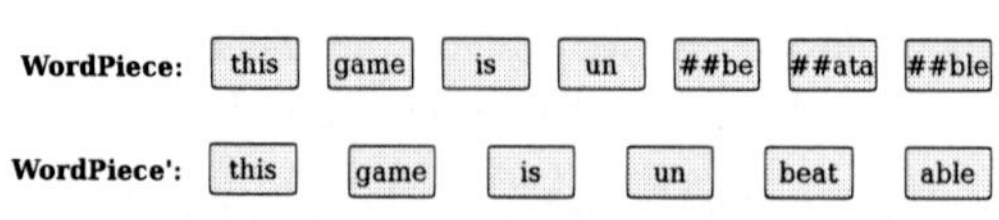

Figure 1: Tokenisations generated by WordPiece and WordPiece′ for the input sequence "this game is unbeatable".

Proceedings of the 9th Workshop on Representation Learning for NLP (RepL4NLP-2024), pages 118–135
August 15, 2024 ©2024 Association for Computational Linguistics

(comprising 16 datasets): Named Entity Recognition (NER), GLUE, and two tasks involving classifying complex words. We additionally train and evaluate in Finnish across two tasks: NER and Sequence Classification.

The findings of our work are as follows: (1) we show that modifying WordPiece to remove WB information (giving WordPiece′) substantially improves the morphological validity of the resulting tokenisations across English and Finnish; (2) across four training scales, we find that WordPiece′ outperforms WordPiece on downstream tasks involving complex words, and gives better performance across most datasets at the lower training scales; (3) we find that none of our methods for including WB information into models, whether implicit or explicit, or through finetuning alone, significantly affects the performance across four downstream tasks and three training scales. Our results indicate that word boundary information isn't providing additional useful information to models, with morphemes being the most important subunit.

2 Tokenisers

One particular design choice of subword tokenisers used by transformer models is the addition of prefixes such as "_" and "##" in order to encode space information, hence representing word boundaries in languages with spaces between words. Previous work (Gow-Smith et al., 2022) has investigated the impact of these prefixes, showing they lead to less morphologically valid tokenisations, and also to a reduced efficiency, since the dual representation of subwords (e.g. "beat" and "_beat") gives a vocabulary redundancy (of approximately 9%). As such, removing these tokens for Unigram (Kudo, 2018) and BPE (Sennrich et al., 2015) has been shown to have a beneficial effect on downstream performance for complex word tasks, whilst retaining equivalent performance in general natural language understanding tasks. We refer readers to Gow-Smith et al. (2022) for a full analysis, but here we focus on WordPiece′ – WordPiece modified such that WB information is removed. We train this model and the default on 1 million sentences from Wikipedia for two languages (English and Finnish). We show an example of the tokenisations generated by this compared to the default for English in Figure 1. We perform a morphological evaluation of WordPiece′ compared to WordPiece across the two languages, shown in Table 2. For English, we use four datasets (LADEC (Gagné et al., 2019), MorphoLex (Sánchez-Gutiérrez et al., 2018), MorphyNet (Batsuren et al., 2021), DagoBERT (Hofmann et al., 2020)), and we average across all four (full breakdown in Table 7). For Finnish, we use the subset of MorphyNet. Here, we follow the evaluation standard from Creutz et al. (2004), reporting precision and F1. Averaging across English and Finnish, we see that WordPiece′ gives 14% shorter sequences, 46% higher precision, and 34% higher F1 compared to WordPiece. We also show examples of English tokenisations for WordPiece and WordPiece′ in Table 1. In general, we can see that WordPiece generates more meaningful tokenisations, but sometimes they are still of limited morphological validity, as for "undesirable" where the prefix is incorrectly split and the base form of the word is lost: we note that WordPiece (like BPE) is a greedy algorithm, meaning it has a tendency to overlengthen the initial token of a word.

WordPiece	WordPiece′
hyp ##ores ##po ##n ##s ##iveness	hypo respons iveness
non ##m ##ult ##ipl ##ayer	non multi player
over ##pr ##iced	over price d
un ##icy ##cle	uni cycle
und ##es ##ira ##ble	und es ira ble

Table 1: Some examples of the tokenisations from WordPiece and WordPiece′.

3 Models

The sequences generated by WordPiece′ have *no word boundary information*, which means some information is lost when using it to encode sequences. We aim to answer the question of whether such information is at all useful to transformer encoders – i.e. can it be incorporated in an alternative way to improve performance? We investigate transformer encoders pretrained using the masked language modelling (MLM) task, and then finetuned on downstream tasks (pretrain-finetune paradigm).

	English			Finnish		
	Len	Precis.	F1	Len	Precis.	F1
WordPiece	3.29	24.8	33.8	3.21	28.3	38.9
WordPiece′	2.75	**42.6**	**52.7**	2.86	**34.7**	**45.0**

Table 2: Performance of WordPiece and WordPiece′ across English and Finnish, showing the average sequence length, precision and F1 score generated following the standard introduced by Creutz et al. (2004).

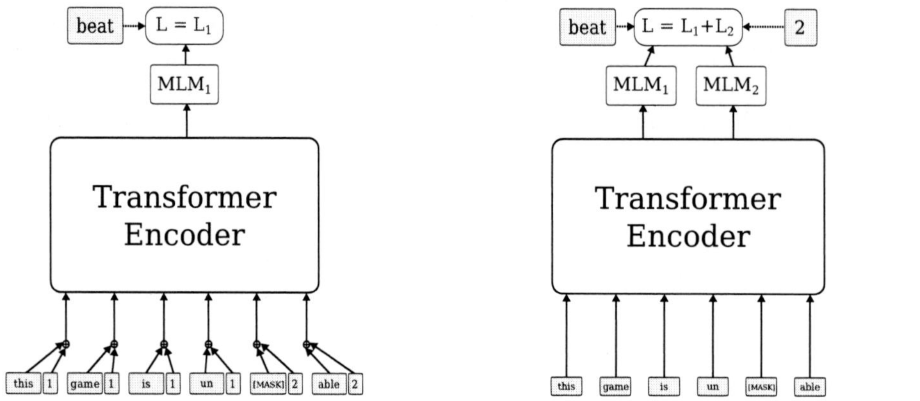

(a) Explicit model, where word boundary embeddings are passed in the input.

(b) Implicit model, with an additional MLM head for predicting word boundaries.

Figure 2: Network diagrams for the modified transformer architectures trained in this work.

We then look to include WB information in two ways, either directly as input (both in pretraining and finetuning), or through a modification of the pretraining task.

3.1 Explicit Model

One approach is to include WB information *explicitly* through the input. Naively, we could add WB tokens in the input sequence, shown in Figure 3. However, this is rather inefficient as it leads to much longer sequences and has been shown to lead to reduced downstream task performance, even when the number of epochs (rather than steps) is matched (Gow-Smith et al., 2022). Nevertheless, we implement this as a baseline. An alternative, and significantly more efficient, way to include this information is to add "word boundary embeddings" to the input, added element-wise with the token embeddings and standard position embeddings, shown in Figure 2a. These embeddings are equivalent to the standard position embeddings in being randomly-initialised and then learned through training.

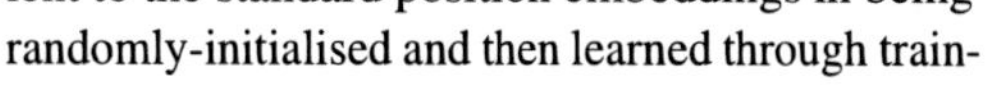

Figure 3: WordPiece′ with word boundary tokens.

We experiment with three methods for indexing the WB embeddings: *binary index*, *word index*, and *subword index*, shown in Figure 4. The *word index* is the position of the word the corresponding token belongs to, whereas the *subword index* is the position within the word. These are chosen to align with how the standard position indices work within transformer architectures, but the *binary index* aligns with how standard WordPiece processes word-initial and word-internal tokens, having a value of 1 if a token appears at the start of the word, and a value of 2 otherwise. The *binary index* is also more parameter-efficient, since it only requires an embedding dimension of 2. In fact, for our experiments the *subword index* gives the most new parameters, since even in our English pretraining corpora (Wikipedia and C4) we encounter large chunks of (e.g. Chinese) text with no whitespace, requiring a high embedding dimension.[1]

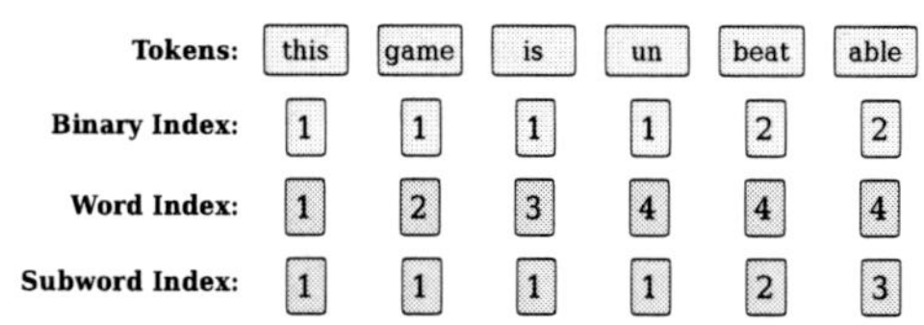

Figure 4: Three alternative indexing methods for the word boundary embeddings.

3.1.1 Finetuning

Alongside including WB information at pretraining, we also experiment with pretraining using the default MLM task and architecture, and then passing the WB information during finetuning only, either with binary index WB embeddings, or WB tokens.

3.2 Implicit Model

One possible drawback of the explicit approach is the reduced difficulty of the MLM task: pass-

[1]We set the embedding dimension at 512, which covers all text encountered for all scales. For the word index, the embedding dimension is set at the max sequence length (256).

	# Articles (M)		Params (M)	Batch Size	# GPUs	Steps (k)
	Eng.	Fin.				
V Low	0.1	0.1	5.8	1024	1	25
Low	0.5	2	21.2	512	1	50
High	6.5	10	98.2	256	1	400
V High	40	-	370.4	128	4	400

Table 3: The four training scales we use to evaluate our models.

ing WB information in the input allows the model to utilise this directly for predicting the masked token, rather than inferring it from context alone. Thus, as an alternative, we modify the architecture with an additional MLM head such that the model has to predict the word boundaries from the input, which we state as *implicitly* using WB information through backpropagation. We show the architecture in Figure 2b. In this set-up, we simply sum the losses from the two MLM heads to give the overall loss.[2]

4 Experiments

We evaluate the two tokenisers (WordPiece and WordPiece′) and our seven explicit and implicit models in the pretrain-finetune paradigm for English and Finnish across three training scales (V Low, Low, High), with an additional scale (V High) for English WordPiece and WordPiece′ (unmodified) – due to the high computational cost of training, we don't train the other models at this scale. Across these scales we vary the number of parameters, batch size, and training steps, shown in Table 3, with further detail in the appendix in Tables 8 and 9. The first three set-ups for English, and the first two for Finnish, take the training data from Wikipedia, whilst the remaining take data from C4 (Raffel et al., 2020). The number of parameters is altered by adjusting the layers, attention heads, and embedding dimension, and a breakdown of this is given in the appendix in Table 10. We train our models in the manner of RoBERTa (Liu et al., 2019) (in comparison to BERT, this involves no next sentence prediction, and dynamic masking is performed), and we mask 15% of tokens. Across all set-ups, we linearly warmup the learning rate to a maximum value of 1e-4, and then linearly decay to 0. We use a sequence length of 256. All training is performed on A100 or H100 GPUs. Training and validation losses for these models are given in the appendix: Figures 7 and 8.

[2]In preliminary experiments we tried weighting the two losses, but no increase in performance was observed.

For these models, we run an evaluation on four downstream tasks. The first two tasks focus on natural language understanding across a broad range of domains:

GLUE We evaluate on 8 GLUE (Wang et al., 2018) tasks (excluding the 9th task of WNLI (Levesque et al., 2012), following previous work, due to its adversarial nature). These tasks all involve sequence classification, and cover a wide range of domains and set-ups: two single-sentence tasks, three similarity and paraphrase tasks, and three inference tasks. We report the average metric across all tasks.

NER We evaluate on three NER datasets from different domains: the English portion of the CoNLL-2003 NER dataset (Tjong Kim Sang and De Meulder, 2003), consisting of sentences taken from the Reuters news corpus (Rose et al., 2002); the NCBI Disease corpus (Doğan et al., 2014), consisting of PubMed abstracts; and the WNUT2017 Shared Task (Derczynski et al., 2017), with training data taken from Twitter, and test data from YouTube.

The final two tasks specifically involve morphologically complex words, where we expect more morphologically valid tokenisations to result in improved performance:

Superbizarre The Superbizarre datasets (Hofmann et al., 2021) involve the binary classification of standalone complex words. We take the two topicality datasets: Arxiv, which involves predicting whether a word comes from the Physics or Computer Science subject areas; Reddit, which involves predicting whether a word comes from an entertainment or discussion subreddit. We report the average macro F1 across the two datasets.

FLOTA The datasets introduced alongside the FLOTA tokenisation method (Hofmann et al., 2022) involve classifying the title of an Arxiv paper into one of 20 subareas for three subject areas (Computer Science, Maths, Physics). We take the small version of the dataset, with a train set of 2 000 titles per subject area. We report the average macro F1 across the three datasets.

4.1 Finnish

In addition to our experiments on English, we train models on Finnish, to see whether our results are transferable to a morphologically complex language – one could hypothesise that with greater

	GLUE				NER				Superbizarre				FLOTA			
	V Low	Low	High	V High	V Low	Low	High	V High	V Low	Low	High	V High	V Low	Low	High	V High
WordPiece	54.7 (.6)	67.7 (1.5)	77.9 (.4)	83.1 (.4)	54.3 (.5)	**68.9 (.4)**	**76.9 (.3)**	81.5 (.4)	65.7 (.1)	66.2 (.1)	67.3 (.1)	68.6 (.1)	19.5 (.8)	31.2 (3.7)	50.4 (.7)	55.0 (1.1)
WordPiece′	**56.2 (.4)**	**69.8 (.5)**	78.0 (.2)	83.7 (1.1)	53.6 (.6)	68.0 (.5)	75.7 (.2)	81.5 (.4)	**66.9 (.1)**	**67.6 (.1)**	**68.4 (.3)**	**69.5 (.2)**	**23.6 (.4)**	**43.1 (.2)**	**52.3 (.5)**	55.2 (1.0)

Table 4: English results across the four tasks and training scales for WordPiece and WordPiece′, with standard deviations in parentheses. Results in bold are those better by more than the combined standard deviation ranges.

	GLUE			NER			Superbizarre			FLOTA		
	V Low	Low	High	V Low	Low	High	V Low	Low	High	V Low	Low	High
WordPiece′	56.2 (.4)	69.8 (.5)	78.0 (.2)	53.6 (.6)	68.0 (.5)	75.7 (.2)	66.9 (.1)	67.6 (.1)	68.4 (.3)	23.6 (.4)	43.1 (.2)	52.3 (.5)
WordPiece′ implicit	56.2 (.3)	69.0 (.2)	77.8 (.8)	55.3 (.3)	69.2 (.2)	75.6 (.4)	66.9 (.1)	67.6 (.1)	68.3 (.1)	23.5 (1.1)	45.1 (.8)	51.8 (1.3)
WordPiece′ explicit binary	55.7 (.4)	70.1 (.2)	78.4 (.5)	54.4 (.4)	68.2 (.8)	75.3 (.4)	66.9 (.1)	67.6 (.1)	68.2 (.1)	24.5 (1.7)	44.5 (.9)	51.8 (.6)
WordPiece′ explicit word	57.2 (.4)	69.2 (.1)	78.8 (.3)	54.9 (.3)	68.4 (.3)	75.4 (.4)	66.8 (.1)	67.6 (.1)	68.4 (.1)	22.3 (.7)	43.2 (1.0)	51.0 (2.7)
WordPiece′ explicit subword	55.6 (.6)	70.3 (.2)	78.1 (.4)	55.0 (.3)	68.1 (.4)	75.4 (.3)	67.0 (.1)	67.7 (.2)	68.2 (.2)	24.3 (1.2)	38.2 (4.9)	51.8 (2.8)
WordPiece′ explicit WB tokens	55.3 (.6)	68.7 (.2)	77.5 (2.0)	52.4 (.5)	67.6 (.2)	74.1 (.2)	66.6 (.1)	67.5 (.1)	68.3 (.2)	23.3 (1.1)	43.5 (.2)	52.3 (.1)
WordPiece′ explicit f/t WB tokens	55.1 (.2)	69.8 (.3)	76.7 (.5)	53.6 (.6)	68.3 (.4)	75.7 (.2)	-	-	-	23.4 (1.5)	43.7 (.7)	52.5 (.8)
WordPiece′ explicit f/t binary	56.2 (.6)	69.9 (.4)	77.8 (.4)	53.6 (.3)	68.6 (.5)	75.4 (.4)	66.9 (.1)	67.5 (.1)	68.1 (.4)	23.4 (1.2)	43.6 (1.5)	52.6 (1.3)

Table 5: English results across the four tasks and three training scales for WordPiece′ and the modified architectures which include word boundary information, with standard deviations in parentheses.

	NER			SeqClass		
	V Low	Low	High	V Low	Low	High
WordPiece	72.2 (.2)	84.2 (.6)	89.9 (.3)	73.1 (.2)	78.7 (.3)	83.6 (.2)
WordPiece′	73.0 (.6)	85.0 (.4)	89.8 (.2)	73.0 (.6)	79.0 (.5)	**84.1 (.3)**

Table 6: Finnish results across the three tasks and training scales for WordPiece and WordPiece′, with standard deviations in parentheses. Results in bold are those better by more than the combined standard deviation ranges.

morphological complexity, word boundary information would be more helpful in disambiguation. We run our experiments on Finnish for WordPiece and WordPiece′ across three training scales, and evaluate on two downstream tasks:

NER We evaluate on the FiNER dataset (Ruokolainen et al., 2020), consisting of news articles annotated with six entity classes, reporting macro F1.

Sequence Classification We look at two sequence classification datasets: the Eduskunta dataset,[3] consisting of ministers' answers to questions from MPs, labelled with the relevant ministry; the FinnSentiment dataset (Lindén et al., 2023), consisting of sentences from social media labelled with their polarity. We report the accuracy over these two datasets.

4.2 Finetuning Procedure

An overview of all datasets is given in Table 11. We finetune on each dataset by updating all parameters, with the following hyperparameters: batch size 32, max sequence length 128, learning rate of 2e-5, warm-up for 5% of steps. We evaluate every epoch on the dev set, taking the best-performing epoch. We train five seeds for every model and report the average metric across these. We also remove outliers which lie more than two standard deviations from the mean, or when very low scores suggest the model failed to train.[4] For the English NER and Complex Words Datasets, and all Finnish datasets, we train for 20 epochs, but for GLUE we limit it to 10 epochs per dataset due to the relatively high training time.

5 Results

We report our full results across all individual datasets for all models in the appendix (Tables 12 and 13). Here, we look at the overall metrics from the four tasks across the training scales, and present our main findings. We note that the plots produced (Figures 5 and 6, and Figures 9 to 12 in the appendix) are approximately logarithmic in training scale, and we reproduce them using a scale factor on the x-axis in the appendix: Figures 15 to 19.

Firstly, we compare WordPiece and WordPiece′ in Table 4 and Figure 5. On GLUE, we see that WordPiece′ performs better than WordPiece across all scales, with a bigger performance difference

[3]`https://github.com/aajanki/eduskunta-vkk`

[4]This occurs for the following. High: one seed of WordPiece′ FLOTA CS (score of 7), one seed of WordPiece′ FLOTA Maths (score of 11), one seed of WordPiece′ f/t WB tokens (score of 3); V High: one seed of WordPiece′ WB tokens CoLA (score of 0), two seeds of WordPiece CoLA (scores of 0 and 8), one seed of WordPiece′ STS-B (score of 2), one seed of WordPiece FLOTA CS (score of 4), one seed of WordPiece FLOTA Maths (score of 3).

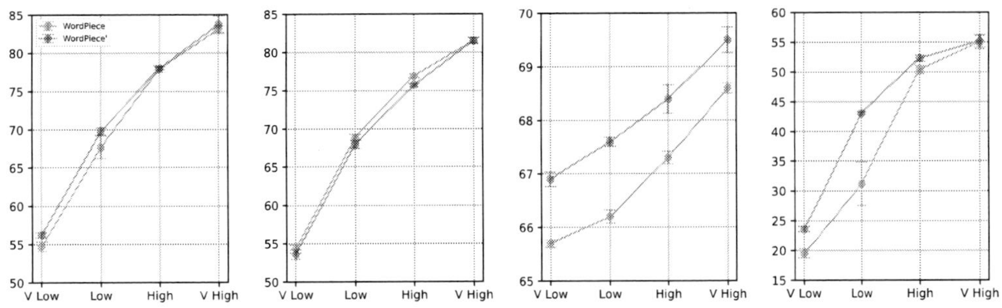

(a) GLUE (b) NER (c) Superbizarre (d) FLOTA

Figure 5: English results for WordPiece and WordPiece′ across four training scales and four tasks.

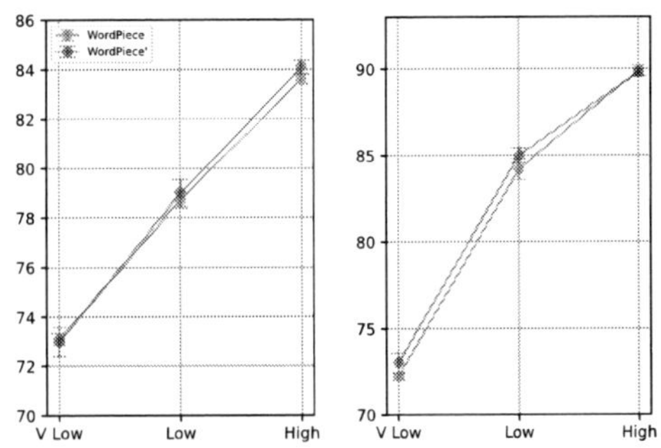

(a) SEQ (b) NER

Figure 6: Finnish results for WordPiece and WordPiece′ across three training scales and two tasks.

at the lower scales (+1.5 and +2.1 for the V Low and Low training scales, respectively). We note that at the higher scales, the differences are within two standard deviations of the baseline, so these results are consistent with those by Gow-Smith et al. (2022). For NER, on the other hand, we find that WordPiece′ performs worse than WordPiece across all training scales except V High, where they perform equivalently. Looking at the individual dataset performances (Table 12 in the appendix) we see that the worse performance on WNUT2017 (-2.5 average decrease across scales) accounts for the worse overall NER performance, with the other two datasets giving similar results (apart from at the V Low scale, where WordPiece′ performs substantially better on them). This dataset involves tagging "unusual, previously-unseen entities", which means morphological composition cannot be leveraged – we hypothesise that the improved ability of WordPiece′ to do this is the cause of the performance drop, due to the futility of composing the meaning of novel surface forms from subunits. Our results on Finnish (Table 6 and Figure 6) show no significant performance difference between WordPiece and WordPiece′ across the sequence classification and NER tasks, apart from for the High training scale on sequence classification, where WordPiece′ outperforms WordPiece.

For the complex word tasks, WordPiece′ substantially outperforms WordPiece: averaging across the training scales, we get 1.1 average increase for Superbizarre, and 4.5 average increase for FLOTA. The relative performance difference is most significant for Superbizarre: at the V Low scale, we would require approximately 20 times the training scale for WordPiece to match WordPiece′ (Figure 15c in the appendix). In general, we find the performance differences to decrease as the training scale increases, as expected,[5] however this effect seems significantly less for Superbizarre, which still has a large performance difference at the V High training scale (+0.9).

Next, we look at the models that attempt to use WB information, with results in Table 5.

Comparing WordPiece′ and the *implicit* variant (shown also in Figure 9 in the appendix), we find that adding the extra loss term gives mixed results across the four tasks and training scales. We do however see that at the V Low and Low training scales, the implicit model improves performance for NER (+1.7 and +1.2, respectively). Since this prediction task is very similar to the finetuning task of token classification, this may explain the effect on performance. The additional MLM head increases the total loss (see Figure 13 in the ap-

[5]Improved morphological validity should matter less when the model capacity is greater, and when morphologically complex and rare words have been encountered more times during pretraining.

pendix), but when we look at the evaluation accuracies for the two MLM heads (Figure 14 in the appendix), we see that the default MLM head has very similar accuracies to the WordPiece′ baseline. We also note that for the Very Low training scale, there is a 3.5% (relative) improvement in default MLM accuracy, which could be contributing to the performance improvement – in a low resource scenario (both compute and data), the extra prediction task may help to leverage additional information.

Next, we look at the *explicit* variants. Naively including the WB information through additional tokens leads to decreased performance across all tasks except for FLOTA, where there is no substantial performance difference (Figure 10 in the appendix). Overall, these differences are small: around 1 for GLUE, 0.5-2 for NER, 0.1-0.3 for Superbizarre. This is despite a significantly lower MLM loss (approximately 60%: Figure 13 in the appendix) due to the high probability of WB tokens, and the fact that this model trains for around 40% fewer epochs (Table 8 in the appendix). We next look at the three variants for WB embeddings (see appendix: Figure 11). Overall, none of these models consistently improve over WordPiece′, and the relative performance of the three indexing methods varies with training scale and task. The subword index model has the greatest number of additional parameters, which might explain why this model performs the best overall at the V Low scale. In this setting this model has 2.3% more parameters than the baseline, compared to 1.1% for the word index model, and 0.01% for the binary index model. The model achieves an average performance across the four tasks of 50.5, compared to 50.3 for the other two variants, and 50.1 for the baseline. However, at the Low training scale, this model actually performs worse than the other two variants (61.1 average compared to 62.6 and 62.1 for binary and word, respectively). At the High training scale they all perform equivalently (68.4 average). Since all three indexing methods are encoding equivalent information through trivial transformations, the performance equivalence is perhaps expected.

Finally, we look at two approaches to including WB information during finetuning only (Figure 12 in the appendix) – with WB tokens or binary index WB embeddings. We find that neither of these approaches improve over the baseline, with the WB tokens approach performing overall slightly worse: averaged across all training scales and datasets, we get 57.5 for default WordPiece′, 57.5 for WordPiece′ f/t binary index, and 57.3 for WordPiece′ f/t WB tokens. This corroborates the results by Abdou et al. (2022), who find that adding position embeddings after pretraining without them does not lead to improved performance. On average, including the WB embeddings during finetuning decreases training stability (increased standard deviation across seeds).

6 Discussion

Overall, we find that *incorporating word boundary information in transformer encoders, either explicitly or implicitly, does not lead to substantial performance improvements*. This suggests that: a) modifying tokenisers such as WordPiece to remove space information does not result in the loss of useful information, b) the default MLM task is sufficient for such models to pretrain effectively.

The pre-tokenisation step of splitting on whitespace prevents tokens from ever crossing word boundaries, which is perhaps a sufficient restriction. Our results indicate the importance of a morpheme compared to a word as the key feature which contributes to meaning.

For English, across all models and training scales, we only see a weak correlation between performance on NER and GLUE – if we compare the difference compared to WordPiece′ for the implicit and explicit models, we find a correlation with Pearson's $\rho = 0.332$.

The Superbizarre task is significantly less affected by model scaling than the other tasks we evaluate on, but much more affected by the choice of tokeniser. This suggests that morphologically valid tokenisation is vital for generating good representations of complex words in the absence of context. This task is also less likely to be dependent on spurious correlations (annotation artefacts) in the data.

All of our models at the High and V High training scales outperform the dev results reported by Hofmann et al. (2022) on the FLOTA ArXiv-S datasets using their tokenisation method. We hypothesise this is likely an effect of hyperparameters, e.g. we use a batch size of 32 rather than their 64, and we use a learning rate scheduler with warm-up, whereas they do not.

7 Related Work

This work aligns with other works that aim to improve the morphological validity of subword tokenisers: Westhelle et al. (2022) introduce Morphologically Informed Segmentation (MIS), a tokeniser based on Morfessor for Portuguese; Hofmann et al. (2022) introduce Few Longest Token Approximation (FLOTA), which preserves the morphology of complex words without necessarily keeping all the characters. Jimenez Gutierrez et al. (2023) introduce a tokeniser for the biomedical domain that is better aligned with morpheme segmentation, and then train their BioVocabBERT model using it. There has also been work looking at the impact of how subword tokens are marked, either with word-initial or word-final prefixes (Jacobs and Pinter, 2022).

There is previous work which has passed additional position indices to transformer models. Jia et al. (2021) introduce a model for neural text-to-speech called PnG BERT which uses word-position embeddings to provide alignment between phonemes and graphemes at the word level. In NLP, Bai et al. (2020) introduce Segatron, a model which modifies the Transformer-XL (Dai et al., 2019) with two additional position embeddings: a sentence index and a paragraph index. They also apply the same modifications to BERT, giving SegaBERT. They find that SegaBERT gives lower validation losses during pre-training, lower language modelling perplexities, and improves upon the GLUE score of BERT. Cheng et al. (2023) include POS tags as additional input embeddings during BERT pretraining, which they find to reduce performance on (Super)GLUE (Wang et al., 2019) and MSGS (Warstadt et al., 2020).

There has also been work which has modified the pretraining objective of transformer models. Yamaguchi et al. (2021) introduce various alternatives to MLM, and pre-train models using them, finding that default MLM is superior in the higher-parameter setting. There have been various works using linguistically-motivated pretraining objectives (Zhou et al., 2019; Levine et al., 2020), with the closest to our work being that by Cui et al. (2022), who find improved performance through simply adding additional MLM heads for linguistic tasks and summing their losses.

8 Conclusion

In this work we investigate whether word boundary information is useful for transformer encoders. In particular, we start with WordPiece′, a version of WordPiece modified to remove word boundary information, and show that it leads to more linguistically meaningful tokenisations, as well as improved performance on tasks involving morphologically complex words, whilst having no significant effect on performance for general domain tasks across English and Finnish. We also investigate modifications to the default model architecture which involve incorporating word boundary information, either explicitly (through the input), or implicitly (through the pretraining task), and through pretraining or finetuning alone. Across all models and training scales, we find that these modifications give no substantial improvements in performance, which suggests transformer encoders can perform well without word boundary information, either in the form of prefixes ("##" or "_"), word boundary tokens, word boundary embeddings, or through a modification to the pretraining task.

Acknowledgements

This work was partially supported by the CDT in Speech and Language Technologies and their Applications funded by UKRI (grant number EP/S023062/1) and the UK EPSRC grant EP/T02450X/1. We appreciate the helpful comments provided by the reviewers.

Limitations

In this work we have only looked at transformer encoder architectures. For encoder-decoder or decoder models, word boundary information needs to be generated in the output – i.e. WordPiece′ is lossy which is problematic for generation. Not including such architectures is a significant limitation of the scope of our work and an important future direction. Despite running pretraining across four scales, we don't look at altering the vocabulary size of our tokenisers, which is another limitation. Whilst we have investigated many approaches to including word boundary information through modified architectures, it is possible that there are alternative approaches which would perform better than these. In addition, whilst we have tried to run experiments on a extensive range of downstream tasks with two languages, it is possible that there are other tasks and languages where the omission of word boundary information would have a significant negative impact on performance.

References

Mostafa Abdou, Vinit Ravishankar, Artur Kulmizev, and Anders Søgaard. 2022. Word order does matter and shuffled language models know it. In *Proceedings of the 60th Annual Meeting of the Association for Computational Linguistics (Volume 1: Long Papers)*, pages 6907–6919, Dublin, Ireland. Association for Computational Linguistics.

Josh Achiam, Steven Adler, Sandhini Agarwal, Lama Ahmad, Ilge Akkaya, Florencia Leoni Aleman, Diogo Almeida, Janko Altenschmidt, Sam Altman, Shyamal Anadkat, et al. 2023. Gpt-4 technical report. *arXiv preprint arXiv:2303.08774*.

He Bai, Peng Shi, Jimmy Lin, Yuqing Xie, Luchen Tan, Kun Xiong, Wen Gao, and Ming Li. 2020. Segatron: Segment-aware transformer for language modeling and understanding. *arXiv preprint arXiv:2004.14996*.

Khuyagbaatar Batsuren, Gábor Bella, and Fausto Giunchiglia. 2021. Morphynet: a large multilingual database of derivational and inflectional morphology. In *Proceedings of the 18th SIGMORPHON Workshop on Computational Research in Phonetics, Phonology, and Morphology*, pages 39–48.

Luisa Bentivogli, Ido Dagan, Hoa Trang Dang, Danilo Giampiccolo, and Bernardo Magnini. 2009. The fifth PASCAL recognizing textual entailment challenge. In *TAC*.

Kaj Bostrom and Greg Durrett. 2020. Byte pair encoding is suboptimal for language model pretraining. In *Findings of the Association for Computational Linguistics: EMNLP 2020*, pages 4617–4624, Online. Association for Computational Linguistics.

Tom Brown, Benjamin Mann, Nick Ryder, Melanie Subbiah, Jared D Kaplan, Prafulla Dhariwal, Arvind Neelakantan, Pranav Shyam, Girish Sastry, Amanda Askell, et al. 2020. Language models are few-shot learners. *Advances in neural information processing systems*, 33:1877–1901.

Daniel Cer, Mona Diab, Eneko Agirre, Iñigo Lopez-Gazpio, and Lucia Specia. 2017. SemEval-2017 task 1: Semantic textual similarity multilingual and crosslingual focused evaluation. In *Proceedings of the 11th International Workshop on Semantic Evaluation (SemEval-2017)*, pages 1–14, Vancouver, Canada. Association for Computational Linguistics.

Ziling Cheng, Rahul Aralikatte, Ian Porada, Cesare Spinoso-Di Piano, and Jackie CK Cheung. 2023. McGill BabyLM shared task submission: The effects of data formatting and structural biases. In *Proceedings of the BabyLM Challenge at the 27th Conference on Computational Natural Language Learning*, pages 207–220, Singapore. Association for Computational Linguistics.

Kenneth Ward Church. 2020. Emerging trends: Subwords, seriously? *Natural Language Engineering*, 26(3):375–382.

Mathias Johan Philip Creutz, Bo Krister Johan Linden, et al. 2004. Morpheme segmentation gold standards for finnish and english. *Publications in Computer and Information Science Report A77*.

Yiming Cui, Wanxiang Che, Shijin Wang, and Ting Liu. 2022. Lert: A linguistically-motivated pre-trained language model. *arXiv preprint arXiv:2211.05344*.

Zihang Dai, Zhilin Yang, Yiming Yang, Jaime Carbonell, Quoc V Le, and Ruslan Salakhutdinov. 2019. Transformer-xl: Attentive language models beyond a fixed-length context. *arXiv preprint arXiv:1901.02860*.

Leon Derczynski, Eric Nichols, Marieke van Erp, and Nut Limsopatham. 2017. Results of the wnut2017 shared task on novel and emerging entity recognition. In *Proceedings of the 3rd Workshop on Noisy User-generated Text*, pages 140–147.

Jacob Devlin, Ming-Wei Chang, Kenton Lee, and Kristina Toutanova. 2019. Bert: Pre-training of deep bidirectional transformers for language understanding. In *Proceedings of the 2019 Conference of the North American Chapter of the Association for Computational Linguistics: Human Language Technologies, Volume 1 (Long and Short Papers)*, pages 4171–4186.

Rezarta Islamaj Doğan, Robert Leaman, and Zhiyong Lu. 2014. Ncbi disease corpus: a resource for disease name recognition and concept normalization. *Journal of biomedical informatics*, 47:1–10.

William B Dolan and Chris Brockett. 2005. Automatically constructing a corpus of sentential paraphrases. In *Proceedings of the International Workshop on Paraphrasing*.

Christina L Gagné, Thomas L Spalding, and Daniel Schmidtke. 2019. Ladec: the large database of english compounds. *Behavior research methods*, 51(5):2152–2179.

Edward Gow-Smith, Harish Tayyar Madabushi, Carolina Scarton, and Aline Villavicencio. 2022. Improving tokenisation by alternative treatment of spaces. *arXiv preprint arXiv:2204.04058*.

Jordan Hoffmann, Sebastian Borgeaud, Arthur Mensch, Elena Buchatskaya, Trevor Cai, Eliza Rutherford, Diego de Las Casas, Lisa Anne Hendricks, Johannes Welbl, Aidan Clark, et al. 2022. Training compute-optimal large language models. *arXiv preprint arXiv:2203.15556*.

Valentin Hofmann, Janet Pierrehumbert, and Hinrich Schütze. 2021. Superbizarre is not superb: Derivational morphology improves BERT's interpretation of complex words. In *Proceedings of the 59th Annual Meeting of the Association for Computational Linguistics and the 11th International Joint Conference on Natural Language Processing (Volume 1: Long Papers)*, pages 3594–3608, Online. Association for Computational Linguistics.

Valentin Hofmann, Janet B Pierrehumbert, and Hinrich Schütze. 2020. Dagobert: Generating derivational morphology with a pretrained language model. *arXiv preprint arXiv:2005.00672*.

Valentin Hofmann, Hinrich Schuetze, and Janet Pierrehumbert. 2022. An embarrassingly simple method to mitigate undesirable properties of pretrained language model tokenizers. In *Proceedings of the 60th Annual Meeting of the Association for Computational Linguistics (Volume 2: Short Papers)*, pages 385–393, Dublin, Ireland. Association for Computational Linguistics.

Cassandra L Jacobs and Yuval Pinter. 2022. Lost in space marking. *arXiv preprint arXiv:2208.01561*.

Ye Jia, Heiga Zen, Jonathan Shen, Yu Zhang, and Yonghui Wu. 2021. Png bert: augmented bert on phonemes and graphemes for neural tts. *arXiv preprint arXiv:2103.15060*.

Bernal Jimenez Gutierrez, Huan Sun, and Yu Su. 2023. Biomedical language models are robust to sub-optimal tokenization. In *The 22nd Workshop on Biomedical Natural Language Processing and BioNLP Shared Tasks*, pages 350–362, Toronto, Canada. Association for Computational Linguistics.

Jared Kaplan, Sam McCandlish, Tom Henighan, Tom B Brown, Benjamin Chess, Rewon Child, Scott Gray, Alec Radford, Jeffrey Wu, and Dario Amodei. 2020. Scaling laws for neural language models. *arXiv preprint arXiv:2001.08361*.

Stav Klein and Reut Tsarfaty. 2020. Getting the ##life out of living: How adequate are word-pieces for modelling complex morphology? In *Proceedings of the 17th SIGMORPHON Workshop on Computational Research in Phonetics, Phonology, and Morphology*, pages 204–209, Online. Association for Computational Linguistics.

Taku Kudo. 2018. Subword regularization: Improving neural network translation models with multiple subword candidates. *arXiv preprint arXiv:1804.10959*.

Hector Levesque, Ernest Davis, and Leora Morgenstern. 2012. The winograd schema challenge. In *Thirteenth international conference on the principles of knowledge representation and reasoning*.

Yoav Levine, Barak Lenz, Or Dagan, Ori Ram, Dan Padnos, Or Sharir, Shai Shalev-Shwartz, Amnon Shashua, and Yoav Shoham. 2020. SenseBERT: Driving some sense into BERT. In *Proceedings of the 58th Annual Meeting of the Association for Computational Linguistics*, pages 4656–4667, Online. Association for Computational Linguistics.

Krister Lindén, Tommi Jauhiainen, and Sam Hardwick. 2023. Finnsentiment: a finnish social media corpus for sentiment polarity annotation. *Language Resources and Evaluation*, 57(2):581–609.

Yinhan Liu, Myle Ott, Naman Goyal, Jingfei Du, Mandar Joshi, Danqi Chen, Omer Levy, Mike Lewis, Luke Zettlemoyer, and Veselin Stoyanov. 2019. Roberta: A robustly optimized bert pretraining approach. *arXiv preprint arXiv:1907.11692*.

Hyunji Hayley Park, Katherine J Zhang, Coleman Haley, Kenneth Steimel, Han Liu, and Lane Schwartz. 2021. Morphology matters: a multilingual language modeling analysis. *Transactions of the Association for Computational Linguistics*, 9:261–276.

Yuval Pinter, Cassandra L. Jacobs, and Jacob Eisenstein. 2020. Will it unblend? In *Findings of the Association for Computational Linguistics: EMNLP 2020*, pages 1525–1535, Online. Association for Computational Linguistics.

Colin Raffel, Noam Shazeer, Adam Roberts, Katherine Lee, Sharan Narang, Michael Matena, Yanqi Zhou, Wei Li, and Peter J Liu. 2020. Exploring the limits of transfer learning with a unified text-to-text transformer. *The Journal of Machine Learning Research*, 21(1):5485–5551.

Pranav Rajpurkar, Jian Zhang, Konstantin Lopyrev, and Percy Liang. 2016. SQuAD: 100,000+ questions for machine comprehension of text. In *Proceedings of EMNLP*, pages 2383–2392. Association for Computational Linguistics.

Tony Rose, Mark Stevenson, and Miles Whitehead. 2002. The Reuters corpus volume 1 -from yesterday's news to tomorrow's language resources. In *Proceedings of the Third International Conference on Language Resources and Evaluation (LREC'02)*, Las Palmas, Canary Islands - Spain. European Language Resources Association (ELRA).

Teemu Ruokolainen, Pekka Kauppinen, Miikka Silfverberg, and Krister Lindén. 2020. A finnish news corpus for named entity recognition. *Language Resources and Evaluation*, 54:247–272.

Claudia H Sánchez-Gutiérrez, Hugo Mailhot, S Hélène Deacon, and Maximiliano A Wilson. 2018. Morpholex: A derivational morphological database for 70,000 english words. *Behavior research methods*, 50(4):1568–1580.

Mike Schuster and Kaisuke Nakajima. 2012. Japanese and korean voice search. In *2012 IEEE international conference on acoustics, speech and signal processing (ICASSP)*, pages 5149–5152. IEEE.

Rico Sennrich, Barry Haddow, and Alexandra Birch. 2015. Neural machine translation of rare words with subword units. *arXiv preprint arXiv:1508.07909*.

Richard Socher, Alex Perelygin, Jean Wu, Jason Chuang, Christopher D Manning, Andrew Ng, and Christopher Potts. 2013. Recursive deep models for semantic compositionality over a sentiment treebank. In *Proceedings of EMNLP*, pages 1631–1642.

Erik F. Tjong Kim Sang and Fien De Meulder. 2003. Introduction to the CoNLL-2003 shared task: Language-independent named entity recognition. In *Proceedings of the Seventh Conference on Natural Language Learning at HLT-NAACL 2003*, pages 142–147.

Ashish Vaswani, Noam Shazeer, Niki Parmar, Jakob Uszkoreit, Llion Jones, Aidan N Gomez, Łukasz Kaiser, and Illia Polosukhin. 2017. Attention is all you need. *Advances in neural information processing systems*, 30.

Alex Wang, Yada Pruksachatkun, Nikita Nangia, Amanpreet Singh, Julian Michael, Felix Hill, Omer Levy, and Samuel Bowman. 2019. Superglue: A stickier benchmark for general-purpose language understanding systems. *Advances in neural information processing systems*, 32.

Alex Wang, Amanpreet Singh, Julian Michael, Felix Hill, Omer Levy, and Samuel Bowman. 2018. GLUE: A multi-task benchmark and analysis platform for natural language understanding. In *Proceedings of the 2018 EMNLP Workshop BlackboxNLP: Analyzing and Interpreting Neural Networks for NLP*, pages 353–355, Brussels, Belgium. Association for Computational Linguistics.

Alex Warstadt, Aaron Mueller, Leshem Choshen, Ethan Wilcox, Chengxu Zhuang, Juan Ciro, Rafael Mosquera, Bhargavi Paranjabe, Adina Williams, Tal Linzen, et al. 2023. Findings of the babylm challenge: Sample-efficient pretraining on developmentally plausible corpora. In *Proceedings of the BabyLM Challenge at the 27th Conference on Computational Natural Language Learning*, pages 1–6.

Alex Warstadt, Amanpreet Singh, and Samuel R. Bowman. 2018. Neural network acceptability judgments. *arXiv preprint 1805.12471*.

Alex Warstadt, Yian Zhang, Xiaocheng Li, Haokun Liu, and Samuel R. Bowman. 2020. Learning which features matter: RoBERTa acquires a preference for linguistic generalizations (eventually). In *Proceedings of the 2020 Conference on Empirical Methods in Natural Language Processing (EMNLP)*, pages 217–235, Online. Association for Computational Linguistics.

Matheus Westhelle, Luciana Bencke, and Viviane P Moreira. 2022. Impact of morphological segmentation on pre-trained language models. In *Brazilian Conference on Intelligent Systems*, pages 402–416. Springer.

Adina Williams, Nikita Nangia, and Samuel R. Bowman. 2018. A broad-coverage challenge corpus for sentence understanding through inference. In *Proceedings of NAACL-HLT*.

Atsuki Yamaguchi, George Chrysostomou, Katerina Margatina, and Nikolaos Aletras. 2021. Frustratingly simple pretraining alternatives to masked language modeling. In *Proceedings of the 2021 Conference on Empirical Methods in Natural Language Processing*, pages 3116–3125, Online and Punta Cana, Dominican Republic. Association for Computational Linguistics.

Junru Zhou, Zhuosheng Zhang, Hai Zhao, and Shuailiang Zhang. 2019. Limit-bert: Linguistic informed multi-task bert. *arXiv preprint arXiv:1910.14296*.

	LADEC			MorphoLex			MorphyNet			DagoBERT			MEAN		
	Len	Precis.	F1	Len	Precis.	F1	Len	Precis.	F1	Len	Precis.	F1	Len	Precis.	F1
WordPiece	3.34	38.0	53.3	2.91	26.0	31.4	3.43	13.2	19.7	3.47	21.9	30.7	3.29	24.8	33.8
WordPiece′	2.66	**53.7**	**67.1**	2.55	**50.0**	**55.1**	2.95	**25.5**	**36.1**	2.85	**41.1**	**52.5**	2.75	**42.6**	**52.7**

Table 7: Performance of WordPiece and WordPiece′ across four English morphological datasets, showing the average sequence length, precision and F1 score generated following the standard introduced by Creutz et al. (2004).

	Base Dataset	# Articles (M)	Examples (M)			Params (M)	Batch Size	# GPUs	Steps (k)	Epochs			Train Time (h)
			WP	WP'	WP' spaces					WP	WP'	WP' Spaces	
V Low	Wikipedia	0.1	1.2	1.1	1.8	5.8	1024	1	25	21.5	23.0	13.9	11.0
Low	Wikipedia	0.5	4.1	3.8	6.3	21.2	512	1	50	6.3	6.7	4.1	19.0
High	Wikipedia	6.5	19.8	18.5	30.2	98.2	256	1	400	5.2	5.5	3.4	29.2
V High	C4	40	88.0	82.2	-	370.4	128	4	400	2.3	2.5	-	70.9

Table 8: The four training scales we use to evaluate our models in English.

	Base Dataset	# Articles (M)	Examples (M)		Params (M)	Batch Size	# GPUs	Steps (k)	Epochs		Train Time (h)
			WP	WP'					WP	WP'	
V Low	Wikipedia	0.1	0.3	0.3	5.8	1024	1	25	78.9	84.8	4.1
Low	Wikipedia	2	1.0	1.0	21.2	512	1	50	24.7	26.6	7.8
High	C4	10	37.6	34.6	98.2	256	1	400	1.4	1.5	78.4

Table 9: The three training scales we use to evaluate our models in Finnish.

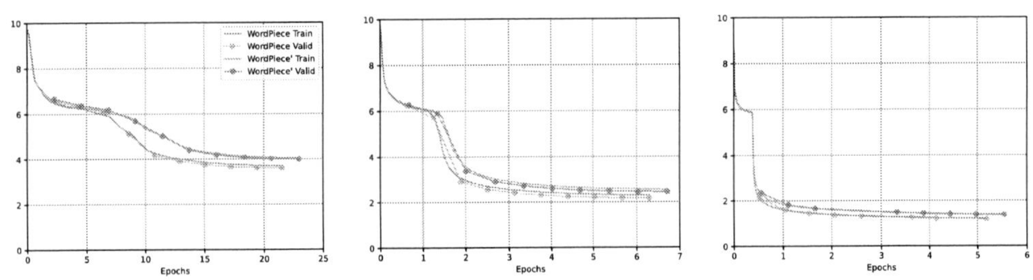

(a) V Low (b) Low (c) High

Figure 7: Training and valid losses for WordPiece and WordPiece′ across three training scales for English.

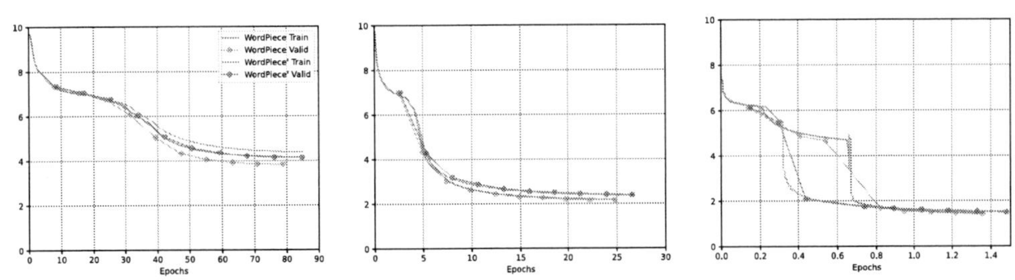

(a) V Low (b) Low (c) High

Figure 8: Training and valid losses for WordPiece and WordPiece′ across three training scales for Finnish.

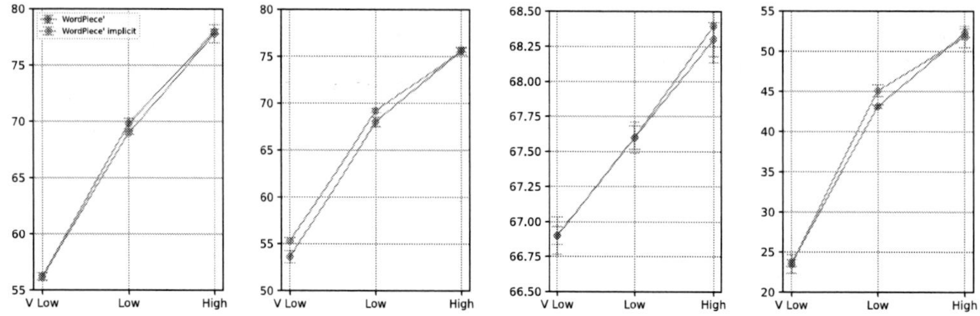

(a) GLUE (b) NER (c) Superbizarre (d) FLOTA

Figure 9: Results for WordPiece′ and WordPiece′ implicit.

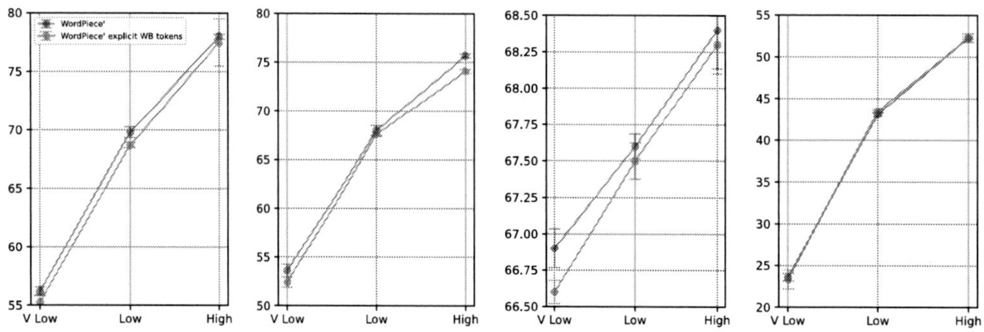

(a) GLUE (b) NER (c) Superbizarre (d) FLOTA

Figure 10: Results for WordPiece′ and WordPiece′ explicit with word boundary tokens.

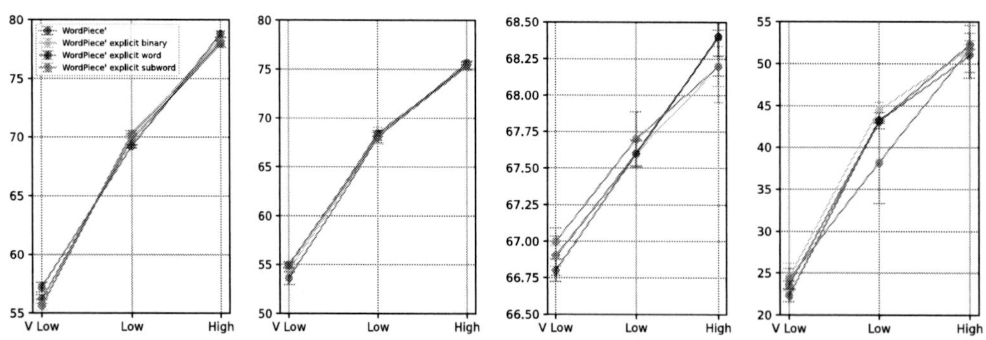

(a) GLUE (b) NER (c) Superbizarre (d) FLOTA

Figure 11: Results for WordPiece′ and WordPiece′ explicit with word boundary embeddings.

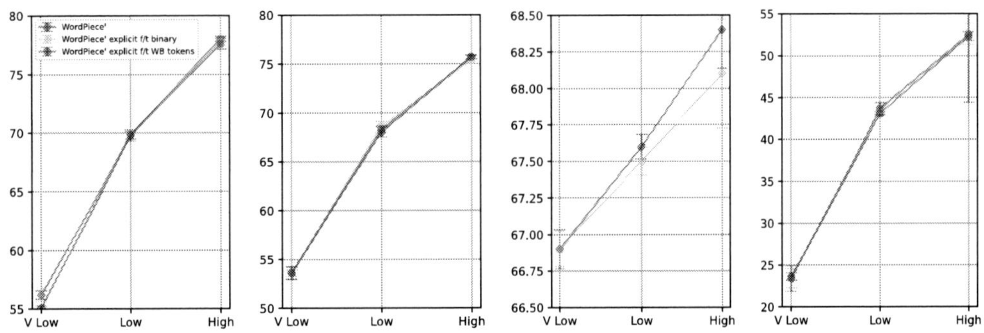

(a) GLUE (b) NER (c) Superbizarre (d) FLOTA

Figure 12: Results for WordPiece′ and WordPiece′ finetuned with either word boundary tokens or binary index word boundary embeddings.

	Layers	Att. Heads	Embed. Dim.
V Low	2	4	256
Low	4	8	512
High	12	12	768
V High	26	16	1024

Table 10: Layers, attention heads, and embedding dimension for the four training scales.

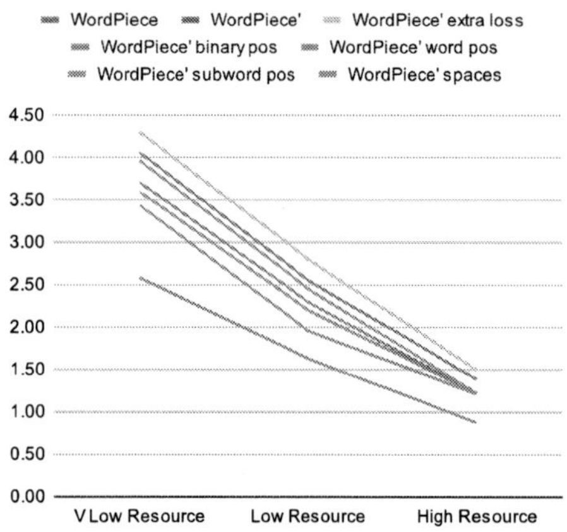

Figure 13: Pretraining MLM losses for all English models across three training scales, averaged across the last 100 steps.

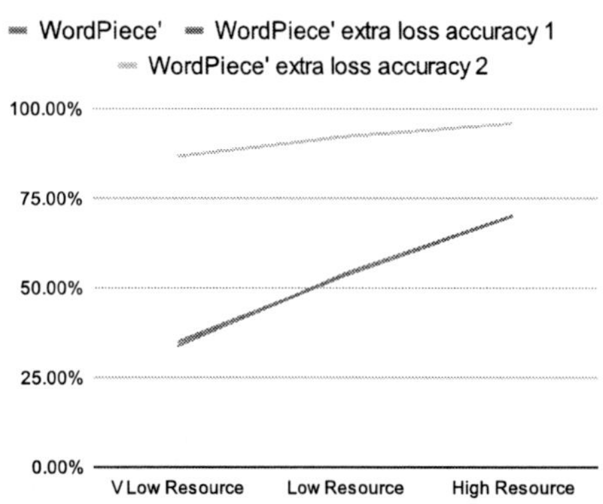

Figure 14: English pretraining evaluation accuracies for WordPiece′ and the two MLM heads for WordPiece′ extra loss.

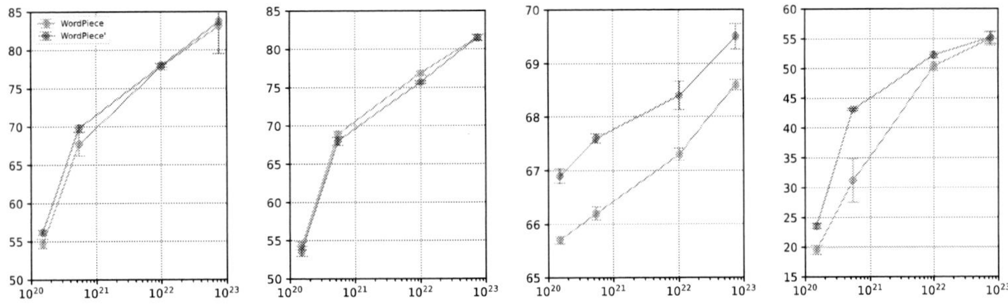

(a) GLUE (b) NER (c) Superbizarre (d) FLOTA

Figure 15: Results for WordPiece and WordPiece′ with log training scale on the x-axis.

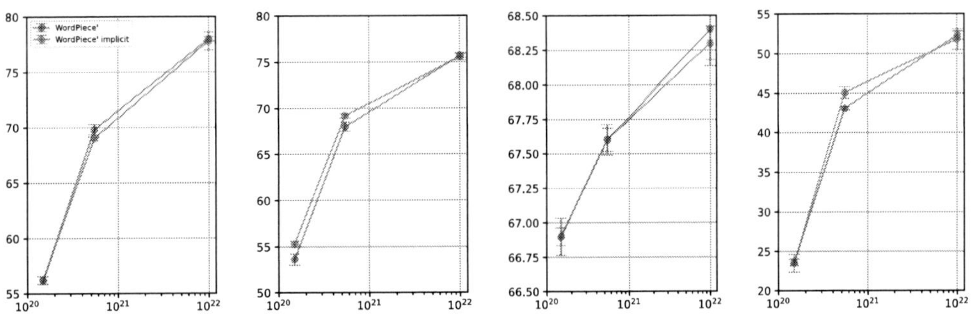

(a) GLUE (b) NER (c) Superbizarre (d) FLOTA

Figure 16: Results for WordPiece′ and WordPiece′ implicit with log training scale on the x-axis.

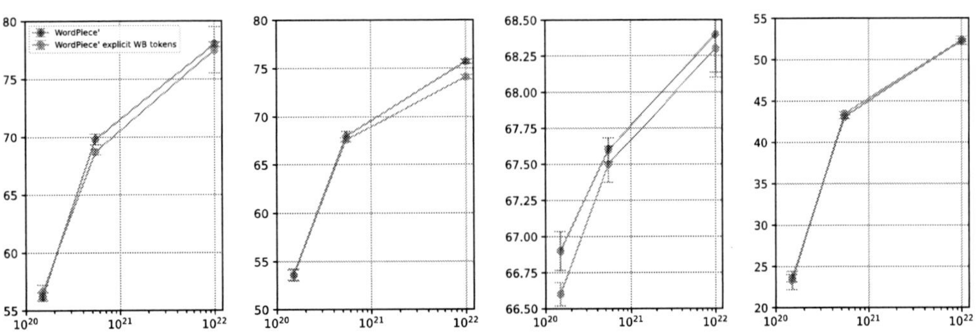

(a) GLUE (b) NER (c) Superbizarre (d) FLOTA

Figure 17: Results for WordPiece′ and WordPiece′ explicit with word boundary tokens with log training scale on the x-axis.

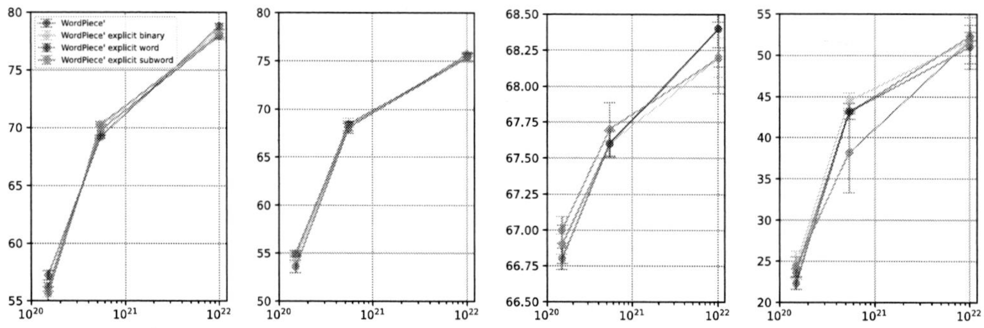

(a) GLUE (b) NER (c) Superbizarre (d) FLOTA

Figure 18: Results for WordPiece′ and WordPiece′ explicit with word boundary embeddings with log training scale on the x-axis.

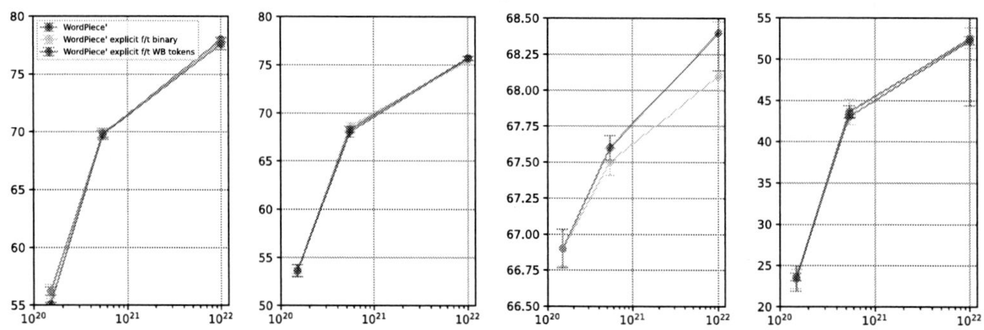

(a) GLUE (b) NER (c) Superbizarre (d) FLOTA

Figure 19: Results for WordPiece′ and WordPiece′ finetuned with either word boundary tokens or binary index word boundary embeddings with log training scale on the x-axis.

	|Train| (k)	|Dev| (k)	Metric	Domain
CoLA (Warstadt et al., 2018)	8.5	1	Matthew's Correlation	Books and Journal Articles
SST-2 (Socher et al., 2013)	67	1	Accuracy	Film Reviews
MRPC (Dolan and Brockett, 2005)	3.7	0.4	F1 / Accuracy	Online News
STS-B (Cer et al., 2017)	5.8	1.5	Pearson / Spearman Correlation	Various
QQP (`https://quoradata.quora.com/First-Quora-Dataset-Release-Question-Pairs`)	364	40	F1 / Accuracy	Quora questions
MNLI (Williams et al., 2018)	393	9.8	Accuracy	Various
QNLI (Rajpurkar et al., 2016)	105	5.5	Accuracy	Wikipedia
RTE (Bentivogli et al., 2009)	2.5	0.3	Accuracy	Wikipedia and News
Superbizarre-Arxiv (Hofmann et al., 2021)	58	19	F1	Arxiv Papers
Superbizarre-Reddit (Hofmann et al., 2021)	51	17	F1	Reddit
FLOTA (Hofmann et al., 2022)	1.2	0.4	F1	Arxiv Paper Titles
FiNER (Ruokolainen et al., 2020)	13.5	1.0	F1	Online News
Eduskunta (`https://github.com/aajanki/eduskunta-vkk`)	49.1	3.0	Accuracy	Parliamentary Questions
FinnSentiment (Lindén et al., 2023)	24.3	2.7	Accuracy	Social Media

Table 11: Information for the datasets we use for evaluation.

										mnli				SB		FLOTA		
		conll	ncbi	wnut17	cola	sst2	mrpc	stsb	qqp	m	mm	qnli	rte	A	R	CS	M	P
V Low	WP	79.5	59.5	24.0	6.9	79.7	76.0	15.7	74.0	59.9	61.1	64.6	54.2	66.1	63.9	20.8	16.9	20.8
	WP′	80.2	60.4	20.4	3.5	80.8	76.2	15.8	77.4	63.8	65.1	67.3	56.0	68.3	65.4	23.0	23.1	24.7
	WP′ extra loss	80.1	61.3	23.0	6.7	80.6	75.6	16.0	76.7	63.3	64.9	65.7	55.3	68.4	65.4	21.6	20.3	28.7
	WP′ binary	79.7	60.8	22.6	7.4	82.7	76.0	15.2	74.7	62.5	63.6	63.6	55.4	68.3	65.4	24.2	21.8	27.4
	WP′ word pos	80.3	60.5	23.9	7.7	81.4	76.1	20.6	78.6	63.7	65.1	68.0	53.8	68.3	65.4	21.7	19.6	25.6
	WP′ subword pos	80.9	62.5	21.6	5.7	82.8	75.9	13.1	74.2	63.0	64.3	65.0	56.0	68.6	65.3	26.0	22.3	24.6
	WP′ spaces	78.0	58.8	20.4	7.3	80.6	76.5	14.4	75.6	62.0	62.6	64.9	53.6	67.8	65.3	20.0	19.9	23.2
	WP′ f/t binary	80.3	60.3	20.1	4.7	81.0	75.5	16.0	77.3	63.8	65.0	66.4	55.7	68.4	65.4	22.1	22.1	25.6
	WP′ f/t spaces	80.2	60.4	20.4	1.9	81.4	76.5	14.0	74.4	63.3	64.6	65.2	54.9	-	-	22.3	21.9	26.0
Low	WP	89.3	78.0	39.5	11.9	85.0	78.2	66.1	85.2	71.9	72.2	82.0	56.7	68.1	64.4	30.3	28.7	34.7
	WP′	89.9	77.0	37.3	16.9	85.3	79.0	78.0	85.6	72.2	72.7	81.6	56.6	69.3	66.0	44.1	38.7	46.6
	WP′ extra loss	90.7	77.6	39.3	15.5	84.6	77.3	75.2	85.2	72.6	73.1	81.2	56.3	69.2	65.9	46.3	41.0	48.1
	WP′ binary	89.9	77.5	37.2	18.5	87.1	77.0	76.3	85.3	73.4	73.4	82.7	57.3	69.1	66.0	44.6	41.7	47.3
	WP′ word pos	89.7	77.1	38.3	16.3	84.2	78.0	76.4	84.8	71.4	72.0	81.8	57.5	69.2	66.0	42.9	39.4	47.4
	WP′ subword pos	90.0	77.0	37.1	18.4	86.3	78.9	77.5	85.6	72.8	73.0	82.5	58.1	69.5	66.0	40.2	33.6	40.8
	WP′ spaces	89.1	76.3	37.5	16.3	84.3	76.0	74.3	85.0	72.0	72.2	80.0	58.1	69.2	65.7	43.2	40.4	47.0
	WP′ f/t binary	90.0	77.3	38.6	16.0	84.9	79.1	77.5	85.5	72.4	73.0	82.3	58.6	69.3	65.8	44.0	40.6	46.1
	WP′ f/t spaces	90.0	76.9	38.1	16.3	84.3	78.2	79.6	85.3	71.9	72.9	81.4	57.1	-	-	45.8	39.3	46.0
High	WP	95.0	83.7	52.1	34.7	90.0	87.2	85.6	88.9	80.3	80.4	89.1	65.1	69.5	65.2	51.6	47.6	52.0
	WP′	94.9	83.7	48.6	40.2	90.8	87.3	85.7	88.6	79.9	80.0	87.1	62.8	70.3	66.5	53.2	49.8	53.8
	WP′ extra loss	94.9	83.2	48.7	34.6	90.4	87.2	85.7	88.5	79.5	80.0	88.5	65.6	70.6	66.1	53.5	48.5	53.3
	WP′ binary	94.6	84.0	47.4	40.4	90.5	87.6	85.7	88.7	79.9	80.3	88.5	64.3	70.1	66.2	52.0	48.1	53.0
	WP′ word pos	94.6	83.1	48.5	40.0	90.7	88.2	86.3	88.7	80.5	80.4	88.2	66.1	70.3	66.5	51.9	49.0	54.7
	WP′ subword pos	94.4	83.7	48.1	38.4	90.4	86.5	85.7	88.8	80.4	80.6	87.9	63.8	70.0	66.4	47.3	46.3	51.0
	WP′ spaces	93.8	83.8	44.6	38.0	90.2	86.6	84.9	88.3	79.3	79.5	86.4	64.3	70.3	66.2	54.0	49.6	53.2
	WP′ f/t binary	94.8	83.3	48.2	39.0	90.9	87.1	85.8	88.5	79.9	80.0	87.0	61.9	70.1	66.0	51.6	51.6	54.7
	WP′ f/t WB tokens	94.9	83.7	48.6	36.3	90.5	87.1	85.7	88.4	80.1	80.6	86.7	63.3	-	-	52.9	49.9	54.7
V High	WP	95.6	86.1	62.9	61.3	92.3	89.2	89.0	89.9	85.6	85.7	91.2	63.9	70.6	66.5	59.2	51.4	54.3
	WP′	95.7	86.5	62.2	61.3	93.1	90.9	89.4	90.0	85.2	85.3	90.9	67.1	71.6	67.4	60.4	49.4	55.6

Table 12: Full English results across all datasets, training scales, and models.

		FiNER	Eduskunta	FinnSentiment
V Low	WP	72.2	64.6	81.6
	WP′	73.0	65.2	80.9
Low	WP	84.2	71.3	86.3
	WP′	85.0	71.1	86.8
High	WP	89.9	75.9	91.3
	WP′	89.8	75.3	92.9

Table 13: Full Finnish results across all datasets, training scales, and models.

Beyond Link Prediction: On Pre-Training Knowledge Graph Embeddings

Daniel Ruffinelli and **Rainer Gemulla**
University of Mannheim
Germany
{druffinelli, rgemulla}@uni-mannheim.de

Abstract

Knowledge graph embeddings (KGEs) provide low-dimensional representations of the entities and relations in a knowledge graph (KG) in order to reason about the KG and to inject structured knowledge into various downstream applications. Most prior work, however, focuses almost exclusively on training and evaluating KGE models for the task of link prediction. In this work, we explore KGE models as general-purpose representations of KGs and study their suitability (i) for more generally capturing properties of the KG and (ii) for downstream tasks such as entity classification and regression. For (i), we designed a new set of graph-structure prediction tasks to assess whether models capture different structures in the graph. For (ii), we investigate whether models provide useful features for a variety of downstream tasks. We found that strong link prediction performance was neither an indication that models generally capture patterns in the graph, nor that they were more useful in downstream tasks. As a result, we included our proposed graph-structure prediction tasks as additional training objectives and found that models trained with this multi-task approach generally, but not always, performed better at both graph-structure prediction and downstream tasks. However, the most suitable choice of pre-training tasks varies across KGE models and types of downstream tasks, suggesting opportunities for more research into the relation between pre-training KGE models and their usability on downstream applications.

1 Introduction

Knowledge graph embeddings (KGE) provide representations of the entities and relations in a knowledge graph (KG). Although a large number of KGE models have been proposed, e.g. Ge et al. (2023); Xiao et al. (2022); Bai et al. (2022), most prior work focuses on the task of link prediction, i.e., answering questions such as *(Austin, capitalOf, ?)* by reasoning over an incomplete KG. In addition to link prediction, it is often argued that KGEs can provide representations that capture semantic properties of the entities (Wang et al., 2022a; Ji et al., 2021; Wang et al., 2017; Nickel et al., 2015; Bordes et al., 2013, 2011) and, indeed, pre-trained KGE models have been used to inject structured knowledge into recommender systems (El-Kishky et al., 2022; Wang et al., 2018), question answering systems (Ilyas et al., 2022) and other types of downstream applications (Ji et al., 2021).

Despite their use as KG representations in downstream applications, the question of whether pre-trained KGE models are generally useful representations of KGs—i.e. representations that are useful beyond the link prediction task—remains largely unexplored. Specifically, it is not well-understood how different pre-training settings affect these representations. This stands in contrast with representation learning of natural language, where representations are intrinsically tested for known linguistic properties (Mikolov et al., 2013) and extrinsically on their usability in downstream applications (Devlin et al., 2019; Radford et al., 2018), and where different pre-training settings are known to improve performance (Raffel et al., 2020; Liu et al., 2019).

In this work, we study the suitability of KGE models as general-purpose KG representations. First, we intrinsically assess whether KGE models capture known properties of the graph, by evaluating their performance on basic graph-structure prediction tasks. We focus on new tasks that are similar to link prediction, but that test different forms of structural knowledge, such as predicting the relation of a triple (e.g., the relationship between *Austin* and *Texas*), the domain and range of a relation (e.g., whether *Austin* is a capital), and the entity and relation neighborhood of an entity (e.g., which entities are related to *Austin*). We found that commonly trained KGE models often performed poorly on such tasks, challenging the intuition that KGE models preserve the structure of a KG.

Proceedings of the 9th Workshop on Representation Learning for NLP (RepL4NLP-2024), pages 136–162
August 15, 2024 ©2024 Association for Computational Linguistics

Second, we extrinsically evaluate whether KGE models are useful pre-trained representations for node-level downstream tasks such as entity classification (e.g., the profession of a person) or regression (e.g., the rating of a movie). We conduct an empirical study using 35 downstream tasks on three different KGs. We found that KGE models often perform decent on these tasks, almost always exceeding the performance of graph neural networks that train directly on the downstream task, such as KE-GCN (Yu et al., 2021). However, the KGE models with best downstream task performance were often not the best-performing models for link prediction. For example, the basic TransE model (Bordes et al., 2013) can be superior to KGE models with stronger performance on link prediction, such as ComplEx (Trouillon et al., 2016) or RotatE (Sun et al., 2019). This suggests that good link prediction performance is not necessarily indicative of good downstream task performance.

Both of these findings suggest that the focus on link prediction tasks is too narrow for pre-training KGE models, i.e., to provide generally useful representations of a KG. We thus included the graph-structure prediction tasks discussed above as additional training objectives. The resulting multi-task KGE models had significantly better overall performance for graph-structure prediction tasks, suggesting that the learned representations capture more information about the graph, at the cost of a small drop in link prediction performance.

Perhaps more importantly, when using pre-trained KGEs in downstream tasks, we found that multi-task training often (but not always) improved downstream performance, especially as data becomes scarce. In fact, excluding the link prediction task during pre-training resulted in better downstream performance more often than not. However, capturing more information about the graph did not directly translate to better downstream performance, as the best performing models in downstream applications were often those that were not pre-trained using all possible tasks. In general, the best choice of pre-training tasks depends on the dataset, KGE model, and type of downstream task, suggesting opportunities for more research to better understand how to pre-train KGE models so they provide generally useful KG representations. We provide all of our resources[1] to promote future work in this direction.

[1] Available at https://github.com/uma-pi1/kge-pretraining.

2 Preliminaries and Related Work

We briefly describe KGE models, training and evaluation methods for link prediction, as well as prior work on other tasks. For a more comprehensive discussion, please see surveys from Nickel et al. (2015); Wang et al. (2017); Ji et al. (2021).

Link prediction. A *knowledge graph* $\mathcal{G} \subseteq \mathcal{E} \times \mathcal{R} \times \mathcal{E}$ is a collection of *(subject, predicate, object)*-triples over a set $\mathcal{E}$ of entities and a set $\mathcal{R}$ of relations. Triples represent known facts such as *(Austin, capitalOf, Texas)*. In the KGE literature, the *link prediction* task is defined as predicting the subject or object to questions of the form *(?, capitalOf, Texas)* and *(Austin, capitalOf, ?)*, resp.

KGE models. KGE models represent each entity and each relation of a KG with a low-dimensional embedding. Each model has a *scoring function* $s : \mathcal{E} \times \mathcal{R} \times \mathcal{E} \rightarrow \mathbb{R}$ that maps each possible triple to a real-valued score. Intuitively, high scores indicate plausible triples, low scores implausible triples. For example, TransE (Bordes et al., 2013) is a translation-based model with $s(i, k, j) = -\|\boldsymbol{e}_i + \boldsymbol{r}_k - \boldsymbol{e}_j\|$, where $\boldsymbol{e}_i \in \mathbb{R}^d$ and $\boldsymbol{r}_k \in \mathbb{R}^d$ are entity and relation embeddings, resp. Scoring functions can be more involved, e.g., based on transformers (Chen et al., 2021a).

Standard training. KGE models are commonly trained on the link prediction task. For each training triple (s, p, o), models are trained such that score $s(s, p, o)$ is high (a known positive) but score $s(s, p, o')$ is low for (pseudo-)negative triples (s, p, o'), where $o' \neq o \in \mathcal{E}$; similarly for subjects $s' \in \mathcal{E}$ with negative triple (s', p, o). Different training objectives exist, all of which follow this approach, but otherwise differ in other hyperparameters; for details, see Ali et al. (2021).

Standard evaluation. The most common evaluation protocol is *entity ranking* (ER), and it is also based on link prediction. Given test triple (s, p, o), models answer the link prediction queries $(s, p, ?)$ and $(?, p, o)$ by ranking all possible answers to each query by their scores, after filtering other known answers. Metrics such as mean reciprocal rank (MRR) and Hits@K are then computed based on the rank of the answers s and o, resp. As an evaluation method, entity ranking has been questioned in prior work (Zhou et al., 2022; Tiwari et al., 2021; Safavi and Koutra, 2020; Wang et al., 2019). In this work, we focus mostly on other evaluation tasks.

Other training approaches. Nickel et al. (2011) and Li et al. (2021) trained on the *reconstruction* task, which aims at reconstructing the training set using cost functions such as $\sum_{t \in \mathcal{G}_{\text{train}}} ||I[(t)] - s(s,p,o)||_2^2$, for training set $\mathcal{G}_{\text{train}}$ and where $I[\cdot]$ is a 0/1 indicator. We do not consider such methods due to excessive training costs. Chen et al. (2021b) augmented the link prediction task with *relation prediction* during training (but not evaluation). We extend this work by including additional pre-training tasks and by focusing on graph-structure prediction and downstream task performance instead.

Other evaluation approaches. Some works evaluate KGE models using *triple classification* (Socher et al., 2013; Lin et al., 2015; Wang et al., 2022b). We do not consider this task because performance estimates are typically overly optimistic and misleading unless hard negatives are used (Safavi and Koutra, 2020); such hard negatives are generally not available. Chang et al. (2020) evaluated KGE models on the relation prediction task, which we also consider as one evaluation task in this work. There is also work on probing KGE models (Meilicke et al., 2018; Allen et al., 2021; Rim et al., 2021), which focus on link prediction performance across different types of relations, e.g. symmetric. In contrast, we focus on studying whether models provide useful representations, i.e. we focus on embedding quality, not just on link prediction performance. In addition, pre-trained KGE models have been used as components in language models (He et al., 2020; Zhang et al., 2019), visual models (Baier et al., 2017), recommender systems (El-Kishky et al., 2022; Wang et al., 2018), or question answering systems (Ilyas et al., 2022). Similarly, some studies have evaluated pre-trained KGE models for entity classification or regression tasks (Pezeshkpour et al., 2018; Jain et al., 2021), as we do. We extend this line of work with a larger set of downstream tasks, and by being the first (to our knowledge) to study the impact of different pre-training methods on downstream task performance.

3 Graph Structure Prediction

In this section, we describe the new graph-structure tasks used in our study. Specifically, how we use them to test whether KGE models preserve known properties in a KG, and how we adapted KGEs to efficiently train on these tasks.

3.1 Graph-Structure Tasks

An example and summary of the graph-structure tasks that we use in our study is given in Table 1. We describe the *queries* for each task as a triple such as $(s, ?, *)$, where s or o denote input entities, p denotes an input relation, ? denotes the prediction target, and $*$ acts as a wildcard. Using this notation, we consider the following tasks and queries:

- **Link prediction** (LP): Given a relation and a subject, predict the object (denoted $(s, p, ?)$). Likewise, given a relation and an object, predict the subject (denoted $(?, p, o)$).
- **Relation prediction** (REL, Chang et al. (2020); Chen et al. (2021b)): Given two entities s and p, predict the relation between them (denoted $(s, ?, o)$).
- **Domain prediction** (DOM): Given a relation, predict its domain (denoted $(?, p, *)$) or its range (denoted $(*, p, ?)$).
- **Entity neighborhood prediction** (NBE): Given a subject entity, predict related objects (denoted $(s, *, ?)$). Likewise, given an object, predict related subjects (denoted $(?, *, o)$).
- **Relation neighborhood prediction** (NBR): Given a entity, predict the relations where it occurs as subject (denoted $(s, ?, *)$) and where it occurs as object (denoted $(*, ?, o)$).

Note that we use the wildcard to denote existential quantification. For example, given a ground-truth KG $\mathcal{G}$ and domain prediction query $(?, p, *)$, an entity $s \in \mathcal{E}$ is a correct answer if there exists an entity $o \in \mathcal{E}$ such that $(s, p, o) \in \mathcal{G}$. We illustrate these new tasks in Figure 2 in Appendix A.

We chose this particular set of tasks because they are simple, they capture basic information about the graph structure beyond link prediction, and they only have one prediction target (an entity or a relation). The latter property allows efficient pre-training and evaluation, as discussed below. For this reason, we exclude tasks such as entity-pair prediction (Wang et al., 2019) (denoted $(?, p, ?)$) or reconstruction (Nickel et al., 2011) (denoted $(?, ?, ?)$). In our experimental study in Sec. 4, we found that the exclusion of some of the above pre-training tasks (e.g., LP) often improves downstream task performance. The optimal choice of tasks depends on dataset, KGE model, and downstream task, however. We leave the exploration of task selection as well as on exploring additional pre-training tasks to future work.

Knowledge graph	Task	Example query	Some answers
(Dallas, locatedIn, Texas)	Link (LP)	*(Austin, locatedIn, ?)*	*Texas, USA*
(Texas, locatedIn, USA)		*(?, locatedIn, Texas)*	*Austin, Dallas*
(Austin, capitalOf, Texas)	Relation (REL)	*(Austin, ?, Texas)*	*locatedIn, capitalOf*
(Austin, locatedIn, Texas)	Domain (DOM)	*(*, locatedIn, ?)*	*Texas, USA, North A.*
(Arkansas, borders, Texas)		*(?, locatedIn, *)*	*Dallas, Texas, USA*
(USA, locatedIn, North A.)	Entity neighb. (NBE)	*(Austin, *, ?)*	*Texas, USA*
(Austin, locatedIn, USA)		*(?, *, Texas)*	*Dallas, Arkansas*
	Relation neighb. (NBR)	*(Austin, ?, *)*	*capitalOf, locatedIn*
		(, ?, Texas)*	*borders, capitalOf*

Table 1: Graph-structure prediction tasks used for self-supervised pre-training and evaluation along with example queries. Here ? denotes the prediction target and $*$ acts as a wildcard.

3.2 Multi-Task Ranking

To intrinsically evaluate whether KGE models preserve properties that are known to exist in a KG, we use the set of graph-structure prediction tasks described above to generalize the entity ranking (ER) protocol for link prediction (see Sec. 2) to a multi-task ranking (MTR) protocol. Intuitively, for each of the nine queries (LP/REL/DOM/NBE/NBR for both subject and object targets), we construct a query from each test triple, obtain a ranking of the prediction targets that do not already occur in the training/validation/test data (filtered setting), and use metrics such as MRR or Hits@K. The final metric is the micro-average over all nine queries.

We now describe how to obtain task-specific rankings. First, for a REL query of form $(s, ?, o)$, we proceed as in Chang et al. (2020) and rank all $p' \in \mathcal{R}$ such that $(s, p', o) \notin \mathcal{G}_{\text{train}}$ in descending order of their scores $s(s, p', o)$. For the other tasks, which involve wildcards, it is not immediately clear how to perform prediction using a KGE model. We first discuss scoring and ranking, then filtering of data for evaluation. Consider for example the NBR query $(s, ?, *)$, where our goal is to rank relations. The perhaps simplest approach to obtain a relation ranking is to first rank all triples of form (s, p', o'), where $p' \in \mathcal{R}$ and $o' \in \mathcal{E}$, and then rank relations by their first appearance (e.g., the relation of the highest-scoring triple is ranked at the top). Generally, we make use of an *extended score function* that accepts wildcards (described in Algorithm 2 in Appendix A). The approach just described corresponds to using $s(s, p', *) = \max_{o' \in \mathcal{E}} s(s, p', o')$, i.e, the score of a relation p' is the score of its most plausible triple. Although other aggregation functions are feasible, we only consider max-aggregation because it does not make any additional assumptions on the scoring function. To filter training/validation/test data during model evaluation (as done in the literature), we remove all relations p' such that $(s, p', o') \in \mathcal{G}_{\text{train}}$ for some $o' \in \mathcal{E}$; i.e., we remove all prediction targets that are already implied by the filtering splits. We proceed similarly for all other tasks involving wildcards. Note that the number of score computations needed to predict entity targets for queries without wildcards is $O(|\mathcal{E}|)$, whereas the one for queries with wildcards is $O(|\mathcal{E}||\mathcal{R}|)$. Similarly, predicting target relations costs $O(|\mathcal{R}||\mathcal{E}|)$ and $O(|\mathcal{R}|)$ with and without wildcards, respectively. We discuss in the next section how to reduce the additional cost of using wildcards to $O(|\mathcal{E}|)$ or $O(|\mathcal{R}|)$.

3.3 Multi-Task Training

We generalize standard KGE model training to all of the graph-structure prediction tasks, called multi-task training (MTT). Our goal is to be able to train KGE models on multiple tasks simultaneously, while keeping training and prediction cost low. We do this by constructing a task-specific cost function for each individual task first; the final cost function is then given as a weighted linear combination of the task-specific costs (and additional regularization terms), where the weights are hyperparameters (costs increase only linearly in the number of tasks, see Table 12). We formalize the MTT training objective in Appendix A.

The task-specific cost functions for link prediction and relation prediction are obtained as in standard training (Sec. 2): for each positive triple $(s, p, o) \in \mathcal{G}$, we construct a set of negatives according to the query (i.e., by perturbing the position of the prediction target) and then apply the loss function (e.g., cross entropy). For our proposed tasks involving wildcards, we proceed differently. Instead of performing some form of (costly) score aggregation during training, we "convert" these tasks with wildcards into tasks without wildcards. To do so, we make use of three virtual *wildcard objects*—one for subjects (any_S), one for relations (any_R), and one for objects (any_O)—and learn embeddings for these objects. During training, we conceptually replace wildcards by their corresponding wildcard entity and proceed as before. For example, for training triple (s, p, o) and NBR query $(s, ?, *)$, we consider the virtual triple (s, p, any_O) along with query $(s, ?, any_O)$. By doing so, we convert the NBR task into a REL task. We also use these wildcard embeddings during inference in the same way; e.g., we set $s(s, p', *) = s(s, p', any_O)$. Instead of performing score aggregation, the model thus directly learns extended scores at the same cost (per task) as standard link prediction, i.e. $O(|\mathcal{E}|)$ for target entities, and $O(|\mathcal{R}|)$ for target relations.

4 Experimental Study

To our knowledge, no prior work has studied the impact that different training objectives have on KG embedding quality, despite this being common practice, e.g. in language models (Raffel et al., 2020; Liu et al., 2019). We conducted a large experimental study with the following goals: (i) to assess whether KGE models capture various properties of a KG by intrinsically evaluating their performance on new graph-structure prediction tasks, (ii) to determine whether (and by how much) KGEs improve their performance on these tasks when simultaneously trained for them, and (iii) to assess the impact that different pre-training approaches have on downstream tasks by extrinsically evaluating pre-trained KGE models. We briefly describe our experimental setup here, for details, see Sec. B.1.

Pre-Training Setup. For training and evaluating KGEs, we closely follow Ruffinelli et al. (2020). We implemented everything in LibKGE (Broscheit et al., 2020), used four benchmark datasets commonly used in recent work (Ge et al., 2023; Xiao et al., 2022; Zhu et al., 2022), all models were trained under the same conditions (as much as possible) and tuned with a large hyperparameter space using random search. For MTT training, we used all tasks in Table 1 (LP, REL, DOM, NBE, NBR), and evaluated models on each of these tasks using filtered MRR, and aggregated these metrics into multi-task ranking MRR (MTR). We selected standard (STD) models with LP and MTT models with both the LP and MTR task, all on validation.

Choice of KGE models. We focused on models that provide entity representations, so we may test their quality in downstream tasks, as done in the industry (El-Kishky et al., 2022; Ilyas et al., 2022). We chose four popular models: TransE (Bordes et al., 2013), DistMult (Yang et al., 2015), RotatE (Sun et al., 2019) and ComplEx (Trouillon et al., 2016). These are not the latest KGE models, but they are common baselines in recent work (Ge et al., 2023; Gui et al., 2022; Chao et al., 2021), and are common choices for pre-trained models (Zhu et al., 2022; El-Kishky et al., 2022; Ilyas et al., 2022). They can also reach SOTA performance with reasonable embedding sizes (Ruffinelli et al., 2020), allowing us to scale our study, and with larger embedding size (Lacroix et al., 2018) and additional training objectives (Chen et al., 2021b), ComplEx outperforms more involved models, e.g. the transformer-based HittER model (Chen et al., 2021a). Some recent models achieve better performance on link prediction, but focus exclusively on that task and do not directly provide entity representations for downstream tasks, e.g. HittER (Chen et al., 2021a) and NBFNet (Zhu et al., 2021).

Downstream Tasks Setup. To extrinsically evaluate our pre-trained models, we collected/created data for 35 downstream tasks on FB15K-237, YAGO3-10 and WIKI5M (examples in Table 2). For downstream models, we used scikit-learn (Pedregosa et al., 2011) models that use only entity embeddings from pre-trained KGE models as input features. We used multilayer perceptrons (MLP), logistic regression, KNN, and random forests for classification, and linear regression and MLP for regression, and treated the choice of downstream model as a hyperparameter. For entity classification, we report *weighted F1* (as Jain et al. (2021)) aggregated across all classification tasks (denoted EC). For regression, we chose relative squared error (RSE) (defined in Sec. B.2), as it allows meaningful averaging across different regression tasks (denoted REG, lower values are better). We report mean and standard deviation over 3 training runs. As baseline, we included KE-GCN (Yu et al., 2021), a state-of-the-art GNN for entity classification. In contrast to KGEs, this model is directly trained on the downstream task (i.e., no pre-training) and uses the KG for inference. Tuning, training, evaluation was done as with KGEs and downstream models.

	Benchmark	Name	Train Size
EC	FB15K-237	Entity Type	6 719
		Profession	2 537
	YAGO3-10	Entity Type	69 592
		Player Type	33 928
REG	FB15K-237	Birth Year	3 538
		Latitude	2 568
	YAGO3-10	Born on Year	60 409
		Created on Year	23 896

Table 2: Some datasets for entity classification (EC) and regression (REG) downstream tasks used to evaluate pre-trained KGEs. See Appendix B for a complete list.

4.1 Results on Graph-Structure Prediction

In Table 3, we report test MRR of graph-structure prediction tasks using standard (STD) and MTT training. We report both training approaches with LP for model selection, as we found this to often produce better downstream performance with MTT (such "cross-over" selection was not useful for STD training, see Table 11). We report MTT with MTR for model selection, and results for WNRR and WIKI5M in Appendix C (Tables 13 and 14, resp.)

Every model is able to capture more information about the KG when trained on multiple tasks simultaneously. For a given model, the improvement can be large, often by a factor of 2x and up to 10x depending on model, task and dataset (or even larger when MTT is used with MTR for model selection, see Table 13). This suggests that, unless trained for it, **KGE models often fail to capture graph structure beyond what is necessary to perform link prediction**. MTT models had slightly lower performance on LP, but the decrease was often small and outweighed by significantly improved performance on other tasks. Moreover, the best models for LP with STD training are often far outperformed on other tasks by other STD models with lower LP performance, suggesting that good LP performance is not indicative of general KG representation. For example, the best LP performance on FB15K-237 is ComplEx STD, but RotatE STD outperforms it considerably on REL and TransE STD on DOM. Similar observations also hold for the best models on MTR, but the compromise on other tasks is significanly smaller. **In general, MTT improved significantly on STD for graph structure prediction and can thus be used so models simultaneously learn more properties in a KG.** Note that our performance on LP, even with MTT, is comparable and sometimes better than recently published works that use comparable embedding sizes (Yang et al., 2022; Dong et al., 2022), or even larger embedding sizes (Gui et al., 2022).

Discussion. From a training perspective, these results are not surprising, as STD training only focuses on the LP task. However, these results do challenge studies that describe KGEs as generally capturing semantic properties of a KG (Ge et al., 2023; Xiao et al., 2022; Gui et al., 2022; Nickel et al., 2015; Bordes et al., 2013), which were likely inspired by work on capturing properties of words despite not directly training for it (Mikolov et al., 2013; Bordes et al., 2013). In addition, some of the new tasks are similar enough to link prediction that the results are indeed unexpected. For example, a good link prediction model may be able to answer *(Austin, capital of, ?)* and *(?, capital of, Texas)*, yet it may not be able to predict that *capital of* is a relation connected to Austin and/or Texas (NBR). Similar arguments can be made for other tasks. Generally, if the goal is *purely* link prediction, STD training is more suitable. But we show empirically in Sec. 4.3 that the choice of training objective has an impact on the learned representations and that including the LP task during pre-training is often detrimental for downstream performance.

4.2 Results on Downstream Tasks

Table 3 also reports downstream performance using models pre-trained with STD and MTT. The EC column reports mean weighted F1 across all classification datasets, and REG column reports mean RSE across all regression datasets. We report on individual downstream tasks in Appendix C.

The best overall downstream task performance across all KGE models was achieved by MTT in all cases, and often combined with LP for model selection. While the margin compared to STD was sometimes small (e.g., EC on YAGO3-10) and sometimes large (e.g., REG on FB1K-237), training only for link prediction (STD) resulted in worse average downstream performance compared to MTT more often than not (especially when considering MTT with MTR selection, see Table 13). Nevertheless, for a given KGE model, STD training did perform better at times. In addition, we found that the best models for both LP and MTR are often not the best models in downstream applications. Perhaps more importantly, **the best downstream performance often comes from models with weaker LP**

Dataset	Model	Train.	Sel.	LP	REL	DOM	NBE	NBR	MTR	EC (↑)	REG (↓)
				Graph-structure prediction (↑)						*Downstream tasks*	
FB15K-237	ComplEx	STD	LP	**.346**	.805	.423	.016	.046	.274	.844±.008	.447±.051
		MTT	LP	.336	.964	.557	**.195**	.794	.525	.858±.005	**.394±.057**
	DistMult	STD	LP	.342	.388	.045	.009	.036	.139	.873±.009	.551±.062
		MTT	LP	.334	.944	.557	.139	.818	.516	.865±.005	.472±.026
	RotatE	STD	LP	.312	.919	.581	.051	.136	.342	.868±.003	.797±.286
		MTT	LP	.319	**.965**	.758	.136	**.880**	**.572**	**.890±.003**	.573±.062
	TransE	STD	LP	.330	.900	.624	.038	.054	.332	.873±.015	.742±.287
		MTT	LP	.317	.963	.653	.152	.855	.547	.855±.007	.795±.257
	KE-GCN			–	–	–	–	–	–	.829±.526	.501±.001
YAGO3-10	ComplEx	STD	LP	**.550**	.900	.120	.215	.517	.411	.712±.008	.589±.023
		MTT	LP	.538	.941	.836	.591	**.978**	.759	.729±.005	.466±.017
	DistMult	STD	LP	.539	.881	.010	.327	.613	.429	.734±.003	.519±.019
		MTT	LP	.536	**.945**	**.861**	.581	**.978**	**.762**	**.746±.006**	.472±.029
	RotatE	STD	LP	.436	.809	.046	.400	.656	.432	.701±.002	.696±.018
		MTT	LP	.509	.918	.011	**.609**	.366	.434	.708±.002	.659±.059
	TransE	STD	LP	.504	.860	.178	.287	.175	.349	.742±.002	.447±.036
		MTT	LP	.462	.940	.037	.476	.338	.396	.723±.004	.441±.029
	KE-GCN			–	–	–	–	–	–	.700±.223	**.398±.008**

Table 3: Performance on test data of graph-structure prediction and downstream tasks. Bold entries show performance per task and dataset. Underlined entries show best performance between STD and MTT.

performance (e.g. RotatE on EC in FB15K-237) or weaker MTR performance (e.g. ComplEx on REG in FB15K-237). This is more clearly visible in Table 15 in Appendix C. **This is problematic, as it suggests that MTR and, perhaps more importantly, LP are often inadequate tasks to guide the choice of the more suitable KGE models for downstream applications.** Ultimately, we conclude that the choice of pre-training objective clearly has an impact on downstream performance, but it is unclear how to make this choice in order to maximize downstream performance.

Downstream Baseline Performance. Compared to KE-GCN, KGE models clearly outperform KE-GCN almost every time (except in REG on YAGO3-10) These results suggest that the information captured by KGE models during pre-training is useful for simple downstream models to be competitive with, and even outperform, more involved downstream models that train directly on the task.

4.3 Impact of Pre-Training Task Selection

Table 4 summarizes our results about the impact that pre-training task selection has on downstream tasks. To keep computational costs feasible, we focused on FB15K-237. We explored performance using MTT without either the LP, REL, DOM, NBE, or NBR pre-training task, and without LP+REL or without DOM+NBR. We report models and sets of tasks relevant for our discussion. For details, see Table 16.

Impact on Graph-Structure Tasks. We found that for graph-structure predictions, excluding a task generally led to lower performance on that task, as expected. It may also, however, lead to a boost in performance on other tasks. For example, RotatE performs best on DOM when the standard LP task is excluded from the training objective.

Impact on Downstream Tasks. For downstream performance, the choice of pre-training tasks has a significant impact, but good choices differ between KGE models and the type of downstream task. For example, compared to full MTT training, using a subset of tasks led to improvements almost every time. Surprisingly, excluding the LP task during pre-training improved downstream performance half of the time compared to STD and full MTT training, suggesting that pre-training with LP can often be detrimental to downstream performance.

	Train.	*Sel.*	*Graph-structure prediction* (↑)						*Downstream tasks*	
			LP	REL	DOM	NBE	NBR	MTR	EC (↑)	REG (↓)
ComplEx	STD	LP	**.346**	.805	.423	.016	.046	.274	.844±.008	.447±.051
	MTT	MTR	.331	**.977**	.773	**.210**	.925	**.606**	.843±.002	**.412±.037**
	w/o LP	MTR	.154	.972	.831	.200	.932	.579	.870±.002	.512±.044
	w/o NBE	MTR	.315	.958	**.850**	.005	.936	.575	.856±.002	.562±.038
	w/o LP+REL	MTR	.001	.009	.843	.177	**.939**	.436	.849±.011	.542±.054
RotatE	STD	LP	.312	.919	.581	.051	.136	.342	.868±.003	.797±.286
	MTT	MTR	.314	.964	.813	.160	.922	.598	.847±.001	.704±.060
	w/o LP	MTR	.204	.914	.842	.126	.928	.568	.874±.000	.661±.043
	w/o DOM	MTR	.319	.965	.661	.170	.883	.559	**.898±.001**	.593±.078
	w/o NBR	MTR	.318	.964	.710	.168	.673	.522	.863±.007	.552±.035

Table 4: Performance on test data of graph-structure and downstream tasks for FB15K-237 of STD and various MTT objectives. Objectives such as w/o LP are MTT objectives with all tasks in Table 1 except one, e.g. LP.

4.4 Data Efficiency Tests

To see whether KGE models that capture more information during pre-training are more beneficial as downstream data becomes scarce, we tested models in a few-shot scenario. For classification, we sampled n positive and n negative examples per class, where $n \in \{3, 5, 10\}$. Figure 1 shows the results for the YAGO3-10 classification tasks (higher is better). We found that as less data becomes available, the average performance of STD models becomes considerably lower compared to pre-trained MTT models, except TransE, where performance difference is not as significant. We observed the same pattern in FB15K-237 (see Fig. 3).

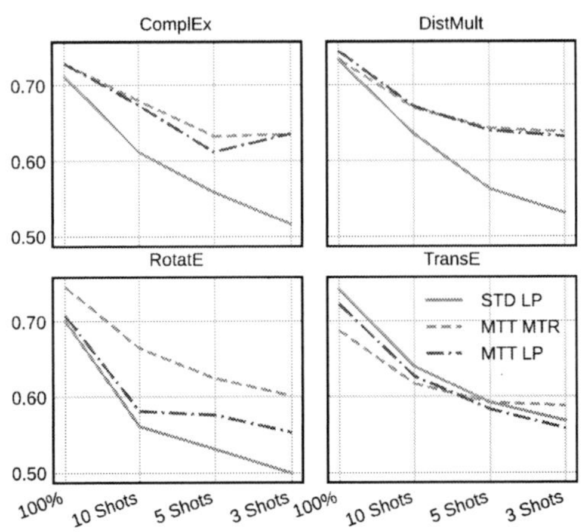

Figure 1: Few-shot performance of entity classification tasks for YAGO3-10 (higher is better). Each n-shot training set consists of n sampled positive and negative examples for each class.

The few-shot scenario applied to regression tasks produced unsatisfactory models almost every time. We thus constructed a different scenario with scarce training data. We randomly sampled $n\%$ of the training set, where again $n \in \{3, 5, 10\}$ (see Figures 5 and 7 in Appendix C, lower is better). For most models, the trend observed with a complete training set is mostly maintained, suggesting that pre-trained MTT models are not always more beneficial with less training data. Still, at no point do models pre-trained with STD become a better choice. **Overall, although not every time, we observed the clear trend that MTT models are more data efficient than STD models, especially for the classification tasks in our tests.**

5 Conclusion

To explore KGE models as general-purpose representions of KGs, we designed a new set of graph-structure prediction tasks for intrinsic evaluation. We found that standard KGE models are not good at predicting simple structures in the graph, challenging the intuition that these models generally capture properties in a KG. In addition, we extrinsically evaluated pre-trained KGE models on several entity-level downstream tasks. We found that link prediction was not indicative of good downstream performance, and that multi-task pre-training was generally better for downstream tasks, often when excluding link prediction during pre-training. However, the best choice of pre-training tasks depends on both KGE model and downstream task, suggesting more research is needed into pre-training KGEs to obtain generally-useful KG representations.

6 Limitations

In our study, we explored the use of different self-supervised tasks for training KGE models. However, as a first step, we tested models using only a limited set of simple pre-training tasks. Aside from the link prediction task that is almost exclusively used in the literature, we also included the relation prediction task (as already done by Chen et al. (2021b)), as well a new set of tasks that we proposed (see Table 1). However, other pre-training tasks are possible and should be explored, e.g. self-supervised tasks such as predicting the n-hop neighborhood of an entity, or even objectives that resemble downstream tasks, such as predicting the size of a neighborhood. It is also possible to combine such objectives with supervised training objectives during training, as already done in previous work (Aribandi et al., 2022).

Another limitation of our work is the small variety in types of downstream tasks. While we focused on entity-level classification and regression tasks, the impact of different pre-training approaches on more involved downstream applications should be explored. Some examples would be testing the use of pre-trained KGEs in recommender systems as in El-Kishky et al. (2022), or question answering systems as in Ilyas et al. (2022).

Finally, while we take the first steps into exploring alternatives for pre-training KGE models, our work does not find a concrete solution to the problem, which may indeed by challenging, as models need to encode hundreds or thousands of different, and often uncorrelated, relation types between entities. We observed the impact that different pre-training tasks have both on capturing properties of a graph, as well as in downstream application performance. In particular, we found that training with more tasks is beneficial for capturing more properties of a KG, and often for improving downstream performance. However, we have no concrete suggestions on how to pre-train KGE models more generally. Different pre-training tasks should be explored in the context of different types of downstream tasks, so that we may better understand the relation between pre-training KGEs and their quality as KG representations in downstream applications. As part of our work, we provide all of our code as well as our collection of downstream task data, to create opportunities for future research into this unexplored question.

References

Mehdi Ali, Max Berrendorf, Charles Tapley Hoyt, Laurent Vermue, Sahand Sharifzadeh, Volker Tresp, and Jens Lehmann. 2021. PyKEEN 1.0: A python library for training and evaluating knowledge graph embeddings. *J. Mach. Learn. Res.*

Carl Allen, Ivana Balazevic, and Timothy Hospedales. 2021. Interpreting knowlege graph relation representation from word embeddings. In *Ninth International Conference on Learning Representations 2021.*

Vamsi Aribandi, Yi Tay, Tal Schuster, Jinfeng Rao, Huaixiu Steven Zheng, Sanket Vaibhav Mehta, Honglei Zhuang, Vinh Q Tran, Dara Bahri, Jianmo Ni, et al. 2022. ExT5: Towards extreme multi-task scaling for transfer learning. In *International Conference on Learning Representations.*

Jiaxin Bai, Zihao Wang, Hongming Zhang, and Yangqiu Song. 2022. Query2particles: Knowledge graph reasoning with particle embeddings. *Findings of the Association for Computational Linguistics: NAACL 2022-Findings.*

Stephan Baier, Yunpu Ma, and Volker Tresp. 2017. Improving visual relationship detection using semantic modeling of scene descriptions. In *ISWC.*

James Bergstra and Yoshua Bengio. 2012. Random search for hyper-parameter optimization. *Journal of machine learning research.*

Antoine Bordes, Nicolas Usunier, Alberto Garcia-Duran, Jason Weston, and Oksana Yakhnenko. 2013. Translating embeddings for modeling multi-relational data. In *Advances in neural information processing systems.*

Antoine Bordes, Jason Weston, Ronan Collobert, and Yoshua Bengio. 2011. Learning structured embeddings of knowledge bases. In *Proceedings of the AAAI conference on artificial intelligence.*

Samuel Broscheit, Daniel Ruffinelli, Adrian Kochsiek, Patrick Betz, and Rainer Gemulla. 2020. LibKGE-a knowledge graph embedding library for reproducible research. In *Proceedings of the 2020 Conference on Empirical Methods in Natural Language Processing: System Demonstrations.*

David Chang, Ivana Balažević, Carl Allen, Daniel Chawla, Cynthia Brandt, and Richard Andrew Taylor. 2020. Benchmark and best practices for biomedical knowledge graph embeddings. In *Proceedings of the conference. Association for Computational Linguistics. Meeting.*

Linlin Chao, Jianshan He, Taifeng Wang, and Wei Chu. 2021. Pairre: Knowledge graph embeddings via paired relation vectors. In *Proceedings of the 59th Annual Meeting of the Association for Computational Linguistics and the 11th International Joint Conference on Natural Language Processing (Volume 1: Long Papers)*, pages 4360–4369.

Sanxing Chen, Xiaodong Liu, Jianfeng Gao, Jian Jiao, Ruofei Zhang, and Yangfeng Ji. 2021a. HittER: Hierarchical transformers for knowledge graph embeddings. In *Proceedings of the 2021 Conference on Empirical Methods in Natural Language Processing*.

Yihong Chen, Pasquale Minervini, Sebastian Riedel, and Pontus Stenetorp. 2021b. Relation prediction as an auxiliary training objective for improving multi-relational graph representations. In *3rd Conference on Automated Knowledge Base Construction*.

Tim Dettmers, Pasquale Minervini, Pontus Stenetorp, and Sebastian Riedel. 2018. Convolutional 2d knowledge graph embeddings. In *Proceedings of the AAAI conference on artificial intelligence*.

Jacob Devlin, Ming-Wei Chang, Kenton Lee, and Kristina Toutanova. 2019. BERT: Pre-training of deep bidirectional transformers for language understanding. In *Proceedings of the 2019 Conference of the North American Chapter of the Association for Computational Linguistics: Human Language Technologies, Volume 1 (Long and Short Papers)*.

Yao Dong, Lei Wang, Ji Xiang, Xiaobo Guo, and Yuqiang Xie. 2022. Rotatect: Knowledge graph embedding by rotation and coordinate transformation in complex space. In *Proceedings of the 29th International Conference on Computational Linguistics*, pages 4918–4932.

Ahmed El-Kishky, Thomas Markovich, Serim Park, Chetan Verma, Baekjin Kim, Ramy Eskander, Yury Malkov, Frank Portman, Sofía Samaniego, Ying Xiao, and Aria Haghighi. 2022. TwHIN: Embedding the twitter heterogeneous information network for personalized recommendation. In *Proceedings of the 28th ACM SIGKDD Conference on Knowledge Discovery and Data Mining*.

Alberto García-Durán, Sebastijan Dumancic, and Mathias Niepert. 2018. Learning sequence encoders for temporal knowledge graph completion. In *EMNLP*.

Xiou Ge, Yun Cheng Wang, Bin Wang, and C-C Jay Kuo. 2023. Compounding geometric operations for knowledge graph completion. In *Proceedings of the 61st Annual Meeting of the Association for Computational Linguistics*.

Xiangyu Gui, Feng Zhao, Langjunqing Jin, and Hai Jin. 2022. Optice: A coherence theory-based model for link prediction. In *Proceedings of the 29th International Conference on Computational Linguistics*.

Bin He, Di Zhou, Jinghui Xiao, Xin Jiang, Qun Liu, Nicholas Jing Yuan, and Tong Xu. 2020. BERT-MK: Integrating graph contextualized knowledge into pre-trained language models. In *Findings of the Association for Computational Linguistics: EMNLP 2020*.

Han Huang, Leilei Sun, Bowen Du, Chuanren Liu, Weifeng Lv, and Hui Xiong. 2021. Representation learning on knowledge graphs for node importance estimation. In *Proceedings of the 27th ACM SIGKDD Conference on Knowledge Discovery & Data Mining*.

Ihab F Ilyas, Theodoros Rekatsinas, Vishnu Konda, Jeffrey Pound, Xiaoguang Qi, and Mohamed Soliman. 2022. Saga: A platform for continuous construction and serving of knowledge at scale.

Nitisha Jain, Jan-Christoph Kalo, Wolf-Tilo Balke, and Ralf Krestel. 2021. Do embeddings actually capture knowledge graph semantics? In *European Semantic Web Conference*.

Shaoxiong Ji, Shirui Pan, Erik Cambria, Pekka Marttinen, and S Yu Philip. 2021. A survey on knowledge graphs: Representation, acquisition, and applications. *IEEE Transactions on Neural Networks and Learning Systems*.

Timothée Lacroix, Nicolas Usunier, and Guillaume Obozinski. 2018. Canonical tensor decomposition for knowledge base completion. In *International Conference on Machine Learning*.

Zelong Li, Jianchao Ji, Zuohui Fu, Yingqiang Ge, Shuyuan Xu, Chong Chen, and Yongfeng Zhang. 2021. Efficient non-sampling knowledge graph embedding. In *Proceedings of the Web Conference 2021*.

Yankai Lin, Zhiyuan Liu, Maosong Sun, Yang Liu, and Xuan Zhu. 2015. Learning entity and relation embeddings for knowledge graph completion. In *Twenty-ninth AAAI conference on artificial intelligence*.

Yinhan Liu, Myle Ott, Naman Goyal, Jingfei Du, Mandar Joshi, Danqi Chen, Omer Levy, Mike Lewis, Luke Zettlemoyer, and Veselin Stoyanov. 2019. Roberta: A robustly optimized bert pretraining approach. *arXiv preprint arXiv:1907.11692*.

Farzaneh Mahdisoltani, Joanna Biega, and Fabian Suchanek. 2014. Yago3: A knowledge base from multilingual wikipedias. In *7th biennial conference on innovative data systems research*.

Christian Meilicke, Manuel Fink, Yanjie Wang, Daniel Ruffinelli, Rainer Gemulla, and Heiner Stuckenschmidt. 2018. Fine-grained evaluation of rule-and embedding-based systems for knowledge graph completion. In *International semantic web conference*.

Tomáš Mikolov, Wen-tau Yih, and Geoffrey Zweig. 2013. Linguistic regularities in continuous space word representations. In *Proceedings of the 2013 conference of the north american chapter of the association for computational linguistics: Human language technologies*.

Maximilian Nickel, Kevin Murphy, Volker Tresp, and Evgeniy Gabrilovich. 2015. A review of relational machine learning for knowledge graphs. *Proceedings of the IEEE*.

Maximilian Nickel, Volker Tresp, and Hans-Peter Kriegel. 2011. A three-way model for collective learning on multi-relational data. In *ICML*.

F. Pedregosa, G. Varoquaux, A. Gramfort, V. Michel, B. Thirion, O. Grisel, M. Blondel, P. Prettenhofer, R. Weiss, V. Dubourg, J. Vanderplas, A. Passos, D. Cournapeau, M. Brucher, M. Perrot, and E. Duchesnay. 2011. Scikit-learn: Machine learning in Python. *Journal of Machine Learning Research*.

Pouya Pezeshkpour, Liyan Chen, and Sameer Singh. 2018. Embedding multimodal relational data for knowledge base completion. In *Empirical Methods in Natural Language Processing (EMNLP)*.

Alec Radford, Karthik Narasimhan, Tim Salimans, and Ilya Sutskever. 2018. Improving language understanding by generative pre-training.

Colin Raffel, Noam Shazeer, Adam Roberts, Katherine Lee, Sharan Narang, Michael Matena, Yanqi Zhou, Wei Li, and Peter J Liu. 2020. Exploring the limits of transfer learning with a unified text-to-text transformer. *The Journal of Machine Learning Research*.

Wiem Ben Rim, Carolin Lawrence, Kiril Gashteovski, Mathias Niepert, and Naoaki Okazaki. 2021. Behavioral testing of knowledge graph embedding models for link prediction. In *3rd Conference on Automated Knowledge Base Construction*.

Daniel Ruffinelli, Samuel Broscheit, and Rainer Gemulla. 2020. You can teach an old dog new tricks! on training knowledge graph embeddings. In *International Conference on Learning Representations*.

Tara Safavi and Danai Koutra. 2020. CoDEx: A Comprehensive Knowledge Graph Completion Benchmark. In *Proceedings of the 2020 Conference on Empirical Methods in Natural Language Processing (EMNLP)*.

Richard Socher, Danqi Chen, Christopher D Manning, and Andrew Ng. 2013. Reasoning with neural tensor networks for knowledge base completion. In *NIPS*.

Zhiqing Sun, Zhi-Hong Deng, Jian-Yun Nie, and Jian Tang. 2019. RotatE: Knowledge graph embedding by relational rotation in complex space. In *International Conference on Learning Representations*.

Sudhanshu Tiwari, Iti Bansal, and Carlos R Rivero. 2021. Revisiting the evaluation protocol of knowledge graph completion methods for link prediction. In *Proceedings of the Web Conference 2021*.

Kristina Toutanova and Danqi Chen. 2015. Observed versus latent features for knowledge base and text inference. In *Proceedings of the 3rd workshop on continuous vector space models and their compositionality*.

Théo Trouillon, Johannes Welbl, Sebastian Riedel, Éric Gaussier, and Guillaume Bouchard. 2016. Complex embeddings for simple link prediction. In *International conference on machine learning*.

Theo Van Veen. 2019. Wikidata. *Information technology and libraries*.

Feiyang Wang, Zhongbao Zhang, Li Sun, Junda Ye, and Yang Yan. 2022a. Dirie: knowledge graph embedding with dirichlet distribution. In *Proceedings of the ACM Web Conference 2022*, pages 3082–3091.

Hongwei Wang, Fuzheng Zhang, Xing Xie, and Minyi Guo. 2018. DKN: Deep knowledge-aware network for news recommendation. In *Proceedings of the 2018 world wide web conference*.

Quan Wang, Zhendong Mao, Bin Wang, and Li Guo. 2017. Knowledge graph embedding: A survey of approaches and applications. *IEEE Transactions on Knowledge and Data Engineering*.

Xiaozhi Wang, Tianyu Gao, Zhaocheng Zhu, Zhengyan Zhang, Zhiyuan Liu, Juanzi Li, and Jian Tang. 2021. KEPLER: A unified model for knowledge embedding and pre-trained language representation. *Transactions of the Association for Computational Linguistics*.

Xintao Wang, Qianyu He, Jiaqing Liang, and Yanghua Xiao. 2022b. Language models as knowledge embeddings. In *Proceedings of the International Joint Conference on Artificial Intelligence (IJCAI 2022)*.

Yanjie Wang, Daniel Ruffinelli, Rainer Gemulla, Samuel Broscheit, and Christian Meilicke. 2019. On evaluating embedding models for knowledge base completion. In *RepL4NLP@ACL*.

Huiru Xiao, Xin Liu, Yangqiu Song, Ginny Y. Wong, and Simon See. 2022. Complex hyperbolic knowledge graph embeddings with fast fourier transform. In *Proceedings of the 2022 Conference on Empirical Methods in Natural Language Processing, EMNLP 2022, Abu Dhabi, United Arab Emirates, December 7-11, 2022*.

Bishan Yang, Scott Wen-tau Yih, Xiaodong He, Jianfeng Gao, and Li Deng. 2015. Embedding entities and relations for learning and inference in knowledge bases. In *Proceedings of the International Conference on Learning Representations (ICLR) 2015*.

Jinfa Yang, Xianghua Ying, Yongjie Shi, Xin Tong, Ruibin Wang, Taiyan Chen, and Bowei Xing. 2022. Knowledge graph embedding by adaptive limit scoring loss using dynamic weighting strategy. In *Findings of the Association for Computational Linguistics: ACL 2022*.

Donghan Yu, Yiming Yang, Ruohong Zhang, and Yuexin Wu. 2021. Knowledge embedding based graph convolutional network. In *Proceedings of the Web Conference 2021*.

Zhengyan Zhang, Xu Han, Zhiyuan Liu, Xin Jiang, Maosong Sun, and Qun Liu. 2019. ERNIE: Enhanced language representation with informative entities. In *Proceedings of the 57th Annual Meeting of the Association for Computational Linguistics*.

Ying Zhou, Xuanang Chen, Ben He, Zheng Ye, and Le Sun. 2022. Re-thinking knowledge graph completion evaluation from an information retrieval perspective. In *Proceedings of the 45th International ACM SIGIR Conference on Research and Development in Information Retrieval*.

Yushan Zhu, Wen Zhang, Mingyang Chen, Hui Chen, Xu Cheng, Wei Zhang, and Huajun Chen. 2022. Dualde: Dually distilling knowledge graph embedding for faster and cheaper reasoning. In *Proceedings of the Fifteenth ACM International Conference on Web Search and Data Mining*.

Zhaocheng Zhu, Zuobai Zhang, Louis-Pascal Xhonneux, and Jian Tang. 2021. Neural bellman-ford networks: A general graph neural network framework for link prediction.

A Multi-Task Training and Evaluation

We illustrate how training objectives are constructed using more than one training task, i.e. query. To this end, we define both the standard training objective (STD) based on link prediction and our proposed multi-task objective (MTT) as follows. Let $T_o = \{(t,l)\}$ be the set of relevant positive and negative examples t and corresponding label l induced by the link prediction query $(s,p,?)$ in a given training set. Let T_s be the analogous set of examples for query $(?,p,o)$. For some loss function L, the STD training approach optimizes the following objective function (we omit the penalty term for brevity):

$$f(\theta) = \operatorname*{argmin}_{\theta} \left(\frac{1}{|T_s|} \sum_{(t,l)\in T_s} L(s(t),l) + \frac{1}{|T_o|} \sum_{(t,l)\in T_o} L(s(t),l) \right) \quad (1)$$

where s is a KGE score function parameterized by model parameters θ. We generalize this objective to define the following multi-task training (MTT) objective:

$$f(\theta) = \operatorname*{argmin}_{\theta} \frac{1}{N} \sum_{T_i \in \mathcal{T}} \sum_{(t,l)\in T_i} \lambda_i L(s(t),l) \quad (2)$$

where $\mathcal{T} = \{T_1, T_2, \ldots\}$ is a superset of training examples for queries T_i, N is the sum of the cardinalities of each T_i and λ_i a hyperparameter that controls the impact of query i in the training objective. Chen et al. (2021b) have already followed this training approach by adding the relation prediction task, i.e. $(i,?,j)$ to Eq. 1. They set $\lambda_s = \lambda_o = 1$ and tune λ_r. Note that Equations 1 and 2 do not describe the exact training objective with some loss functions, e.g. some losses require a positive and corresponding set of negatives to compute a loss value. However, the MTT objective can be reformulated for every loss function commonly used to train KGE models. We provide such a general description of the MTT approach in Algorithm 1. As with loss functions, the MTT approach is agnostic to the choice of model and training task.

W.r.t. to evaluation, Algorithm 2 describes the extended score function described in Section 3.2.

B Experimental Settings

B.1 Experimental Setup: Pre-Training KGEs

Knowledge graphs. We chose four commonly used benchmark datasets for evaluating KGE models: FB15K-237 (Toutanova and Chen, 2015), WNRR (Dettmers et al., 2018), YAGO3-10 (Mahdisoltani et al., 2014), and WIKIDATA5M (WIKI5M) (Wang et al., 2021). Each dataset is associated with a training, a validation and a test split. FB15K-237 and WNRR are designed to be harder benchmarks for link prediction. YAGO3-10 and WIKI5M are considerably larger. Dataset statistics are summarized in Table 5.

KGE training. We used LibKGE (Broscheit et al., 2020) for *STD training* (LP only) as a baseline and added MTT/MTR model training/evaluation. All KGE models were trained for a maximum of 200 epochs with early stopping on validation MRR checked every 10 epochs. We used cross-entropy as loss function, as it systematically outperformed other losses in most prior studies. We used *1vsAll* training with FB15K-237 and WNRR (to achieve good results) and *NegSamp* with YAGO3-10 and WIKI5M to scale to these larger datasets. Models were selected w.r.t. performance (MRR) on the validation data. We selected STD models with LP task and MTT models with the MTR task. For MTT training, we used all tasks in Table 1.

KGE evaluation. As with training, we evaluate KGE models with respect to each of the five graph-structure prediction tasks in Table 1 (LP, REL, DOM, NBE, NBR) using filtered MRR on test data. We also aggregate these metrics into the multi-task ranking MRR (MTR).

KGE hyperparameters. We closely follow the approach of the experimental study of Ruffinelli et al. (2020) to perform hyperparameter selection.

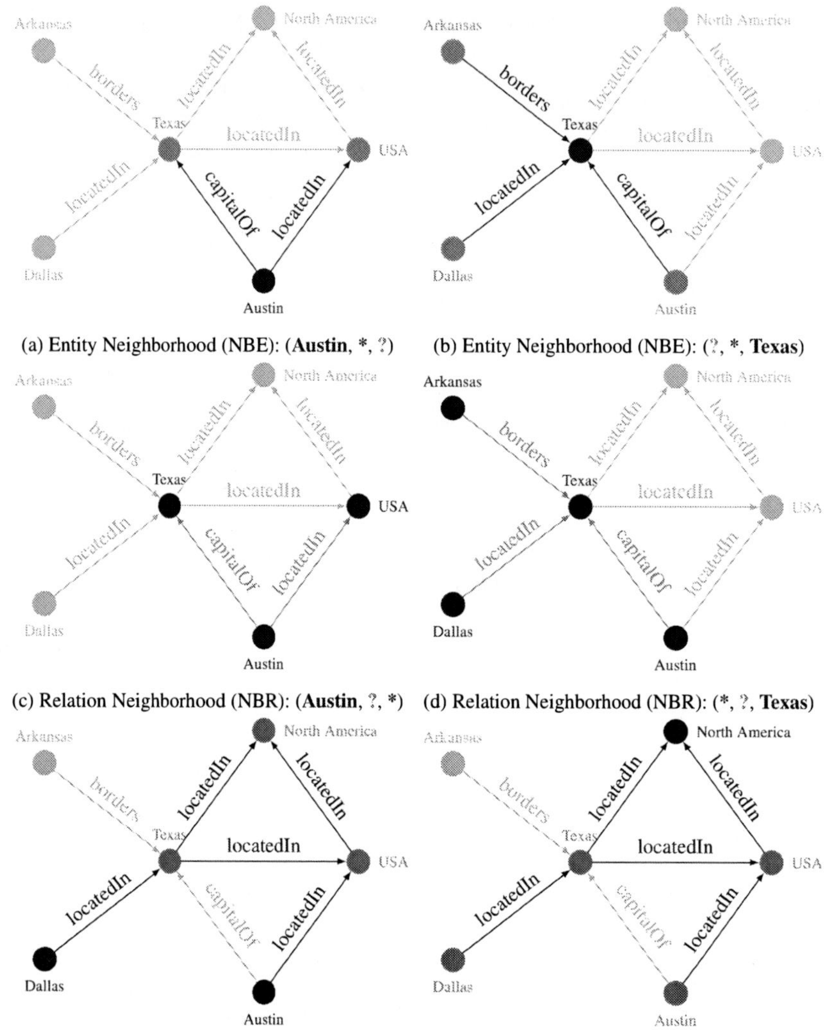

(a) Entity Neighborhood (NBE): (**Austin**, *, ?)

(b) Entity Neighborhood (NBE): (?, *, **Texas**)

(c) Relation Neighborhood (NBR): (**Austin**, ?, *)

(d) Relation Neighborhood (NBR): (*, ?, **Texas**)

(e) Domain (DOM): (*, **locatedIn**, ?)

(f) Domain (DOM): (?, **locatedIn**, *)

Figure 2: Visualization of all proposed prediction tasks that use wildcards introduced in Table 1.

Algorithm 1: Multi-task Training (MTT)

Require: $\mathcal{T}$: set of training triples,
$\mathcal{E}$: set of entities in knowledge graph $\mathcal{K}$
θ: model parameters,
$\mathcal{Q}$: set of (q, w) pairs of training queries and corresponding weights

Ensure: Updated model parameters θ

foreach $q, w \in \mathcal{Q}$ **do**
- $N \leftarrow$ construct set of negatives for q using $\mathcal{T}$
- $\mathcal{T}_{\text{all}} \leftarrow \mathcal{T} \cup N$
- $s_{\text{all}} \leftarrow \text{COMPUTE\_SCORES}(\mathcal{T}_{\text{all}})$
- $l_q \leftarrow w * \text{COMPUTE\_LOSS}(s_{\text{all}}, \mathcal{T}_{\text{all}})$ // loss weighted by w
- $\theta \leftarrow \text{UPDATE\_PARAMETERS}(\theta, l_q)$

Algorithm 2: Extended Score Function (accepts wildcards)

```
Require: t: (i, k, j) triple to compute score
         q: task query, e.g. (i, k, *)
         s: model score function
         C: set of candidates for wildcard slot
Ensure: Score of given triple t
max_score ← 0
if q does not have a wildcard then
    max_score ← s(t)
else
    foreach c ∈ C do
        candidate_t = (i, k, c)                          // e.g. for q = (i, k, *)
        candidate_score = s(candidate_t)
        if candidate_score ≥ max_score then
            max_score ← candidate_score
return max_score
```

Dataset	Entities	Relations	Train	Valid	Test
FB15K-237	14 505	237	272 115	17 535	20 466
YAGO3-10	123 182	37	1 079 040	5 000	5 000
WNRR	40 559	11	86 835	3 034	3 134
WIKIDATA5M	4 818 679	828	21 343 681	5 357	5 321

Table 5: Statistics of benchmark datasets for pre-training knowledge graph embeddings.

We performed 30 random trials using SOBOL sampling (Bergstra and Bengio, 2012) over a large search space to tune several hyperparameters, e.g. regularization, embedding size, batch size, dropout, initialization, and task weights (each in $[0.1, 10.0]$, log scale). To keep our study feasible, we reduced the maximum batch and embedding size for larger datasets and expensive models. The full search space can be found in Table 6.

B.2 Relative Squared Error

For evaluating regression performance, we chose relative squared error (RSE), defined as follows:

$$\text{RSE} = \frac{\sum_{i=1}^{N}(y_i - \hat{y}_i)^2}{\sum_{i=1}^{N}(y_i - \bar{y})^2} \quad (3)$$

where N is the number of evaluation examples, y_i are targets to predict, $\hat{y}_i$ are model predictions, and $\bar{y} = \frac{1}{N}\sum_n y_i$, i.e. the mean of targets to predict. We chose RSE because it is interpretable and allows meaningful averaging across the different regression tasks (denoted REG). An RSE value of 1 is equivalent to the performance of a model that predicts the average of the dependent variable in the evaluation data; lower values are better.

B.3 Experimental Setup: Downstream Tasks

Downstream tasks. We collected or created data for 35 downstream tasks on FB15K-237, YAGO3-10 or WIKI5M (see Tables 7 and 8). This includes the datasets of Jain et al. (2021) for entity classification on FB15K-237 and YAGO3-10, which aim to predict the types of entities at different granularities. For regression, we use the datasets of Pezeshkpour et al. (2018) for YAGO3-10, which consist of temporal prediction tasks (e.g., the year an event took place), and the dataset of Huang et al. (2021) for node importance prediction. We also created several regression tasks for FB15K-237 from the multimodal data of García-Durán et al. (2018) by predicting literals associated to entities (e.g., a date, a person's height, the rating of a movie). To create regression tasks for WIKI5M, we followed the same approach using numerical relations extracted from Wikidata (Van Veen, 2019). Datasets statistics are given in Tables 7 and 8.

Hyperparameter	Values
Embedding size[†]	$\{128, 256, 512\}$
Training type	{NegSamp (YAGO3-10), 1vsAll (FB15K, WNRR)}
Task Weights (MTT)	$[0.1, 10]$, log scale
No. subject samples (NegSamp)	$[1, 10000]$, log scale
No. object samples (NegSamp)	$[1, 10000]$, log scale
Optimizer	{Adam, Adagrad}
Batch size[*]	$\{128, 256, 512, 1024$(except on YAGO3-10)$\}$
Learning rate	$[10^{-4}, 1]$, log scale
LR scheduler patience	$[0, 10]$
L_p regularization	{L1, L2, L3, None}
Entity emb. weight	$[10^{-20}, 10^{-5}]$
Relation emb. weight	$[10^{-20}, 10^{-5}]$
Frequency weighting	{True, False}
Embedding normalization (TransE)	
Entity	{True, False}
Relation	{True, False}
Dropout	
Entity embedding	$[0.0, 0.5]$
Relation embedding	$[0.0, 0.5]$
Embedding initialization	{Normal, Unif, XvNorm, XvUnif}
Std. deviation (Normal)	$[10^{-5}, 1.0]$
Interval (Unif)	$[-1.0, 1.0]$
Gain (XvNorm)	1.0
Gain (XvUnif)	1.0

[†] For RotatE, embedding size is fixed 128 on WNRR and set to either 128 or 256 for YAGO3-10. For Transe, this is set to either 128 or 256 for FB15K-237 and fixed to 128 for WNRR and 1024 for YAGO3-10.
[*] For RotatE, batch size is fixed to 256 in YAGO3-10 and to 128 on FB15K-237 and WNRR. For Transe, this is set to either 128 or 256 on YAGO3-10.

Table 6: Hyperparameter search space for pre-training KGE models. Restrictions for RotatE and TransE are due to higher memory consumption and runtime.

Benchmark	Name	Train	Validation	Test
FB15K-237	Entity Type	6 719	–	1 680
	Profession	2 537	–	635
	Organization Type	342	–	86
	Writer Type	136	–	34
YAGO3-10	Entity Type	69 592	–	17 398
	Player Type	33 928	–	8 483
	Profession	14 480	–	3 621
	Writer Type	4 870	–	1 218
	Scientist Type	2 041	–	511
	Organization Type	1 248	–	312
	Artists Type	520	–	130
	Waterbody Type	195	–	49

Table 7: Statistics of datasets for entity classification downstream tasks used to evaluate pre-trained KGEs. All datasets were created by Jain et al. (2021), they are split into trainining and test only and each consists of predicting entity types at different levels of the entity hierarchy.

Benchmark	Name	Train	Validation	Test
FB15K-237	Node Importance	9 877	1 380	2 823
	Birth Year	3 538	442	444
	Latitude	2 568	321	322
	Longitude	2 560	320	322
	Person Height	2 295	287	288
	Size Area	1 731	216	218
	Population	1 543	193	193
	Film Release Year	1 493	186	188
	Org Year Founded	985	123	124
	Film Rating	591	73	75
YAGO3-10	Born on Year	60 409	–	6 730
	Created on Year	23 896	–	2 638
	Died on Year	13 582	–	1 513
	Destroyed on Year	1 630	–	186
	Happened on Year	749	–	73
WIKI5M	Date of Birth	992 126	124 015	124 017
	Album Publication	29 156	3 644	3 645
	Asteroid Magnitude	16 722	2 090	2 091
	River Length	10 092	1 261	1 262
	Airport Elevation	9 054	1 131	1 133
	Sports Season Start	7 631	953	955
	Village Population	3 691	461	462
	Municipality Area	3 158	394	396

Table 8: Statistics of datasets for regression downstream tasks used to evaluate pre-trained KGEs. YAGO3-10 datasets were created by Pezeshkpour et al. (2018). All FB15K-237 and WIKI5M datasets were created by us, except node importance, created by Huang et al. (2021).

KGE models. Since we are interested in pre-trained KGE models, we used the KGE models trained for the experiments discussed in Sec. 4.1. Thus, no information from downstream tasks was used for KGE model training and selection; i.e. the same KGE model is used for all downstream tasks in each experiment. For model selection, we selected STD models with LP task (the standard approach), but combined MTT models with the LP task or the MTR task. Further improvements may be made by using downstream tasks during training (Aribandi et al., 2022) at the cost, perhaps, of obtaining less general representations; we leave such exploration to future work.

Downstream models. We use scikit-learn (Pedregosa et al., 2011) using only the node embeddings of the pre-trained KG model as input features. For classification, we use multilayer perceptrons (MLP), logistic regression, KNN, and random forests. For regression, we use MLP and linear regression.

Downstream training. Each model was trained using 5-fold cross validation and selected based on mean validation performance across folds (see below). We then retrained the selected model on the union of the training and validation split (if present). To tune hyperparameters, we use 10 trials of random search with SOBOL sampling for each downstream model. The search space for each downstream model is given in Table 9. Note that we treat the choice of downstream model as a hyperparameter as well.

Downstream evaluation. For entity classification, we report *weighted F1*, as in Jain et al. (2021), aggregated across all classification tasks (denoted EC). For regression, we chose relative squared error (RSE) because it is interpretable and allows meaningful averaging across the different regression tasks (denoted REG). An RSE value of 1 is equivalent to the performance of a model that predicts the average of the dependent variable in the evaluation data; lower values are better. For each metric, we report the mean and standard deviation over 3 training runs of the downstream model.

Downstream baselines. We include KE-GCN (Yu et al., 2021), a recent GNN with state-of-the-art results for graph alignment and entity classification. In contrast to KGEs, this model is directly trained on the downstream task (i.e., no pre-training) and needs to access the KG to perform predictions. For regression tasks, we use a linear layer after the final convolutional layer of KE-GCN, as this led to better performance in our experiments compared to using a single dimensional output in the final convolution layer as done by Huang et al. (2021). We tune hyperparameters using 30 SOBOL trials (as for KGE models); the search space is shown in Table 9. For training, evaluation, and model selection, we follow the approach for our downstream models (e.g,. 5-fold CV).

C Additional Experimental Results

Model selection using downstream information. To explore whether results can improve by using downstream information to select models, Table 10 reports performance on FB15K-237 of some KGE models using both training approaches in combination with either LP for model selection (which consistently provided better results for these models with both training approaches) or by selecting directly on the metric used to evaluate the downstream task (weighted F1 for entity classification and RSE for regression). We found that model selection with the downstream task metric provides only marginal benefits for both STD and MTT and can in fact be detrimental, likely due to overfitting on validation data. This indicates that model selection without information about downstream tasks—i.e., using LP or MTR—may be preferrable to using downstream information. This is beneficial, as including downstream information during pre-training or model selection would likely make the resulting representations less general.

Overall, we found that full MTT training with LP for model selection was a suitable choice, but further improvements are possible by dataset-, model- and task-specific choices of pre-training task and validation objective, as discussed in the next section.

Further model selection approaches. For completeness, we also explored the impact of further combinations of model selection methods with both STD and MTT training. To explore whether there would be improvements in STD models when selecting them based on performance on the MTR task, Table 11 reports downstream performance of some KGE models using STD training combined with either LP or MTR for model selection. We see that the combination of STD with MTR leads to lower downstream performance almost every time.

Model	Hyperparameter	Values
MLP	Hidden Layer	$\{(100,), (10,),$ $(100, 100), (10, 10)\}$
	Alpha	$[0.00001, 0.001]$
	Learning Rate	$[0.001, 0.01]$
	Solver	[Adam, LBFGS]
Logistic Regression	C	$[100, 100000]$
KNN	n_neighbors	$[1, 10]$
Random Forest	num_estimators	$[10, 50, 100, 200]$
Linear Regression	Alpha	$[0.00001, 0.001]$
KE-GCN	Dimension	$\{16, 32, 64\}$
	Additional Layers	$\{0, 1, 2\}$
	Learning Rate	$\{0.001, 0.005,$ $0.01, 0.05, 0.1\}$
	Alpha	$\{0.3, 0.5\}$

Table 9: Hyperparameter search space for training downstream models. All hyperparameters except those of KE-GCN follow the semantics by scikit-learn.

		Selection Method			
		EC - Weighted F1		*REG - RSE*	
		LP	Weighted F1	LP	RSE
ComplEx	STD	.844	.850	.447	.437
	MTT	.858	.827	.394	**.393**
DistMult	STD	**.873**	.846	.551	.539
	MTT	.865	.864	.472	.476

Table 10: Performance on FB15K-237 downstream tasks for different KGE model training (STD and MTT) and two model selection approaches: LP and weighted F1 (higher is better) or RSE (lower is better). Using downstream task data for model selection provides only marginal gains and is sometimes detrimental to downstream performance, likely due to overfitting on validation data.

		Selection Method			
		EC - Weighted F1		*REG - RSE*	
		LP	MTR	LP	MTR
ComplEx	STD	.844	.858	**.447**	.545
DistMult	STD	**.873**	.836	.551	.686

Table 11: Performance on FB15K-237 downstream tasks for STD training and two model selection approaches: LP and MTR. On both types of tasks, the best performance is obtained by combining STD training with LP model selection.

		Avg. epoch time in seconds			
		FB-237	YAGO	WNRR	WIKI5M
ComplEx	STD	4.92	97.88	2.32	823.80
	MTT	10.83	137.13	8.13	1635.90
TransE	STD	78.76	141.62	98.45	1115.65
	MTT	245.05	219.42	278.60	2124.29

Table 12: Average training epoch time in seconds over first 5 epochs of best models with STD and MTT training. All tests were done with an 11th gen. Intel Core i7-11700K, 64GB of RAM and an NVIDIA GeForce RTX 3090.

		Train.	*Sel.*	*Graph-structure prediction (↑)*						*Downstream tasks*	
				LP	REL	DOM	NBE	NBR	MTR	EC (↑)	REG (↓)
FB15K-237	ComplEx	STD	LP	**.346**	.805	.423	.016	.046	.274	.844±.008	.447±.051
		MTT	LP	.336	.964	.557	.195	.794	.525	.858±.005	**.394±.057**
		MTT	MTR	.331	**.977**	.773	**.210**	**.925**	**.606**	.843±.002	.412±.037
	DistMult	STD	LP	.342	.388	.045	.009	.036	.139	.873±.009	.551±.062
		MTT	LP	.334	.944	.557	.139	.818	.516	.865±.005	.472±.026
		MTT	MTR	.327	.939	.780	.142	.879	.577	.857±.006	.482±.026
	RotatE	STD	LP	.312	.919	.581	.051	.136	.342	.868±.003	.797±.286
		MTT	LP	.319	.965	.758	.136	.880	.572	**.890±.003**	.573±.062
		MTT	MTR	.314	.964	**.813**	.160	.922	.598	.847±.001	.704±.060
	TransE	STD	LP	.330	.900	.624	.038	.054	.332	.873±.015	.742±.287
		MTT	LP	.317	.963	.653	.152	.855	.547	.855±.007	.795±.257
		MTT	MTR	.288	.960	.708	.112	.911	.555	.878±.009	.681±.095
	KE-GCN			–	–	–	–	–	–	.829±.526	.501±.001
YAGO3-10	ComplEx	STD	LP	**.550**	.900	.120	.215	.517	.411	.712±.008	.589±.023
		MTT	LP	.538	.941	.836	.591	**.978**	.759	.729±.005	.466±.017
		MTT	MTR	.538	.930	.836	.591	.940	.749	.729±.005	.459±.020
	DistMult	STD	LP	.539	.881	.010	.327	.613	.429	.734±.003	.519±.019
		MTT	LP	.536	.945	**.861**	.581	**.978**	**.762**	**.746±.006**	.472±.029
		MTT	MTR	.536	.941	**.861**	.581	.967	.759	.735±.004	.466±.021
	RotatE	STD	LP	.436	.809	.046	.400	.656	.432	.701±.002	.696±.018
		MTT	LP	.509	.918	.011	**.609**	.366	.434	.708±.002	.659±.059
		MTT	MTR	.427	.933	.032	.550	.694	.482	**.746±.001**	.470±.017
	TransE	STD	LP	.504	.860	.178	.287	.175	.349	.742±.002	.447±.036
		MTT	LP	.462	.940	.037	.476	.338	.396	.723±.004	.441±.029
		MTT	MTR	.048	**.954**	.686	.046	.798	.457	.688±.005	.680±.026
	KE-GCN			–	–	–	–	–	–	.700±.223	**.398±.008**

Table 13: Performance on test data of graph-structure prediction and downstream tasks. Bold entries show best performance per task and dataset. Underlined entries show best performance between STD and MTT.

		Train.	Sel.	*Graph-structure prediction (↑)*						*Downstream tasks*	
				LP	REL	DOM	NBE	NBR	MTR	EC (↑)	REG (↓)
WNRR	ComplEx	STD	LP	**.474**	.782	.396	.246	.690	.488	–	–
		MTT	MTR	.459	.831	**.593**	.426	.953	**.633**	–	–
	DistMult	STD	LP	.447	.767	.081	.253	.702	.415	–	–
		MTT	MTR	.431	.804	.573	.342	.952	.600	–	–
	RotatE	STD	LP	.469	.794	.311	**.432**	.881	.553	–	–
		MTT	MTR	.431	**.874**	.512	.239	**.955**	.572	–	–
	TransE	STD	LP	.174	.707	.044	.171	.332	.239	–	–
		MTT	MTR	.094	.603	.476	.095	.827	.399	–	–
WIKI5M	ComplEx	STD*	LP	**.288**	–	–	–	–	–	–	.687±.032
		MTT	LP	.204	.680	.028	.130	.197	.200	–	.706±.025
		MTT	MTR	.215	.804	.087	.136	.342	.263	–	.720±.023
	TransE	STD*	LP	**.288**	–	–	–	–	–	–	**.596±.011**
		MTT	LP	**.250**	**.908**	**.185**	**.169**	**.503**	**.347**	–	.636±.025
		MTT	MTR	**.250**	**.908**	**.185**	**.169**	**.503**	**.347**	–	.650±.018
	KE-GCN†			–	–	–	–	–	–	–	–

* Not evaluated on new graph-structure prediction tasks due to high cost.
† GCN-based model by Yu et al. (2021). Not evaluated due to OOM.

Table 14: Performance on test data of graph-structure prediction and downstream tasks with MTT training and two model selection methods: LP and MTR. Due to high cost, we trained only two models for WIKI5M: ComplEx and TransE. Bold entries show best performance per task and dataset. Underlined entries show best performance between STD and MTT. For entity classification (EC) we report weighted F1 (higher is better), and for regression (REG) we report relative squared error (lower is better).

Model Performance Sorted in Decreasing Order for each Pre-Training and Downstream Task

	Graph-structure		*Downstream Tasks*	
	LP (↑)	MTR (↑)	EC (↑)	REG (↓)
FB15K-237	ComplEx STD .346	ComplEx MTT .606	RotatE MTT .890±.003	ComplEx MTT .394±.057
	DistMult STD .342	RotatE MTT .598	TransE MTT .878±.009	ComplEx STD .447±.051
	ComplEx MTT .331	DistMult MTT .577	TransE STD .873±.015	DistMult MTT .472±.026
	TransE STD .330	TransE MTT .555	DistMult STD .873±.009	KE-GCN .501±.001
	DistMult MTT .327	RotatE STD .342	RotatE STD .868±003	DistMult STD .551±.062
	RotatE MTT .314	TransE STD .332	DistMult MTT .865±009	RotatE MTT .573±.062
	RotatE STD .312	ComplEx STD .274	ComplEx MTT .858±005	TransE MTT .681±.095
	TransE MTT .288	DistMult STD .139	ComplEx STD .844±008	TransE STD .742±.287
			KE-GCN .829±.526	RotatE STD .797±.286
YAGO3-10	ComplEx STD .550	DistMult MTT .759	DistMult MTT .746±.006	KE-GCN .398±.008
	DistMult STD .539	ComplEx MTT .749	RotatE MTT .746±.001	TransE MTT .441±.029
	ComplEx MTT .538	RotatE MTT .482	TransE STD .742±.002	TransE STD .447±.036
	DistMult MTT .536	TransE MTT .457	DistMult STD .734±.003	ComplEx MTT .459±.020
	TransE STD .504	RotatE STD .432	ComplEx MTT .729±.005	RotatE MTT .470±.017
	RotatE STD .436	DistMult STD .429	TransE MTT .723±.004	DistMult MTT .472±.029
	RotatE MTT .427	ComplEx STD .411	ComplEx STD .712±.008	DistMult STD .519±.019
	TransE MTT .048	TransE STD .349	RotatE STD .701±.002	ComplEx STD .589±.023
			KE-GCN .700±.223	RotatE STD .696±.018

Table 15: Sorted performance on test data of graph-structure prediction tasks and downstream tasks of all KGE models we tested, as well as KE-GCN by Yu et al. (2021). The ranking of models given by their LP or MTR performance is not the same as the ranking of models given by their downstream performance, which suggests that more work is needed to understand how to pre-train KGE models to optimize downstream performance.

	Train.	*Sel.*	*Graph-structure prediction (↑)*						*Downstream tasks*	
			LP	REL	DOM	NBE	NBR	MTR	EC (↑)	REG (↓)
ComplEx	STD	LP	**.346**	.805	.423	.016	.046	.274	.844±.008	.447±.051
	MTT	MTR	.331	**.977**	.773	**.210**	.925	**.606**	.843±.002	**.412±.037**
	w/o LP	MTR	.154	.972	.831	.200	.932	.579	.870±.002	.512±.044
	w/o REL	MTR	.322	.831	.831	.159	.927	.590	.851±.005	.486±.035
	w/o DOM	MTR	.327	.966	.713	.198	.915	.586	.851±.003	.479±.029
	w/o NBE	MTR	.315	.958	**.850**	.005	.936	.575	.856±.002	.562±.038
	w/o NBR	MTR	.325	.967	.795	.199	.874	.595	.858±.000	.459±.062
	w/o LP+REL	MTR	.001	.009	.843	.177	**.939**	.436	.849±.011	.542±.054
	w/o DOM+NBR	MTR	.330	.970	.074	.199	.107	.266	.856±.001	.415±.029
DistMult	STD	LP	.342	.388	.045	.009	.036	.139	.873±.009	.551±.062
	MTT	MTR	.327	.939	.780	.142	.879	.577	.857±.006	.482±.026
	w/o LP	MTR	.159	.954	.826	.087	.937	.553	.861±.008	.522±.067
	w/o REL	MTR	.323	.857	.827	.057	.932	.571	.868±.008	.536±.077
	w/o DOM	MTR	.323	.948	.703	.106	.914	.560	.849±.002	.478±.027
	w/o NBE	MTR	.316	.928	.848	.003	.937	.571	.844±.002	.524±.047
	w/o NBR	MTR	.325	.956	.801	.112	.775	.554	.859±.002	.493±.043
	w/o LP+REL	MTR	.000	.019	.837	.108	.937	.420	.856±.001	.572±.085
	w/o DOM+NBR	MTR	.307	.955	.136	.147	.279	.299	.839±.001	.545±.060
RotatE	STD	LP	.312	.919	.581	.051	.136	.342	.868±.003	.797±.286
	MTT	MTR	.314	.964	.813	.160	.922	.598	.847±.001	.704±.060
	w/o LP	MTR	.204	.914	.842	.126	.928	.568	.874±.000	.661±.043
	w/o REL	MTR	.272	.887	.846	.137	.924	.583	.862±.003	.692±.079
	w/o DOM	MTR	.319	.965	.661	.170	.883	.559	**.898±.001**	.593±.078
	w/o NBE	MTR	.301	.960	.813	.003	.912	.558	.862±.003	.558±.050
	w/o NBR	MTR	.318	.964	.710	.168	.673	.522	.863±.007	.552±.035
	w/o LP+REL	MTR	.012	.031	.842	.124	.916	.424	.864±.001	.743±.123
	w/o DOM+NBR	MTR	.322	.945	.016	.166	.019	.221	.854±.001	.809±.249
TransE	STD	LP	.330	.900	.624	.038	.054	.332	.873±.015	.742±.287
	MTT	MTR	.288	.960	.708	.112	.911	.555	.878±.009	.681±.095
	w/o LP	MTR	.271	.968	.781	.138	.901	.572	.870±.000	.486±.027
	w/o REL	MTR	.307	.944	.698	.124	.906	.557	.856±.001	.622±.061
	w/o DOM	MTR	.325	.965	.626	.126	.879	.542	.863±.000	.539±.052
	w/o NBE	MTR	.330	.966	.801	.012	.904	.562	.884±.002	.463±.032
	w/o NBR	MTR	.329	.966	.723	.125	.790	.545	.857±.007	.458±.024
	w/o LP+REL	MTR	.149	.930	.821	.116	.924	.550	.860±.001	.594±.032
	w/o DOM+NBR	MTR	.312	.962	.360	.129	.580	.414	.864±.001	.497±.057

Table 16: Performance on test data of graph-structure prediction and downstream tasks for FB15K-237 of STD with LP model selection and various forms of multi-task training, all using MTR for model selection. Objectives such as w/o LP are MTT objectives with all tasks in Table 1 except one, in this case, LP. Our results show that excluding the LP task during pre-training often results in improved downstream performance, and that using all pre-training tasks is often not the best choice.

		FB15K-237 *Entity Classification (Weighted F1 - higher is better)* Type	Profession	Organization	Writer
ComplEx	STD+LP	.986±.001	.808±.011	.921±.021	.661±.000
	MTT+LP	.986±.000	.820±.005	.946±.003	.682±.012
	MTT+MTR	.986±.000	.802±.004	.944±.003	.641±.000
DistMult	STD+LP	.984±.000	.811±.007	.912±.009	.785±.020
	MTT+LP	.987±.000	.810±.016	.974±.002	.690±.000
	MTT+MTR	.986±.000	.785±.006	.890±.000	.768±.018
RotatE	STD+LP	.985±.000	.797±.000	.908±.013	.781±.000
	MTT+LP	.989±.001	.807±.000	.934±.012	.828±.000
	MTT+MTR	.989±.000	.810±.000	.931±.003	.658±.000
TransE	STD+LP	.984±.001	.791±.005	.913±.032	.806±.021
	MTT+LP	.987±.000	.805±.006	.946±.009	.681±.014
	MTT+MTR	.987±.000	.796±.000	.942±.000	.789±.034
KE-GCN		.988±.000	.738±.000	.906±.002	.685±.020

Table 17: Weighted F1 on test data of downstream classifiers (MLP, Logistic Regression, KNN and Random Forest) that use pre-trained KGE embeddings as input to solve entity classification tasks about entities in FB15K-237; and KE-GCN (Yu et al., 2021), a GCN that trains directly on the downstream data. Datasets are sorted by decreasing size of the training set from left to right.

		YAGO3-10 *Entity Classification (Weighted F1 - higher is better)* Type	Player	Profession	Writer	Scientist	Organization	Artist	Waterbody
ComplEx	STD+LP	.994±.000	.918±.001	.753±.004	.575±.006	.518±.013	.789±.005	.480±.018	.673±.015
	MTT+LP	.997±.000	.919±.002	.790±.002	.619±.006	.553±.011	.877±.003	.466±.013	.614±.000
	MTT+MTR	.996±.000	.914±.001	.776±.000	.617±.009	.556±.007	.871±.005	.491±.021	.614±.000
DistMult	STD+LP	.994±.000	.919±.001	.764±.003	.577±.000	.529±.003	.814±.011	.535±.007	.738±.000
	MTT+LP	.996±.000	.919±.002	.789±.002	.634±.019	.556±.003	.890±.010	.495±.010	.691±.000
	MTT+MTR	.996±.000	.918±.002	.776±.000	.622±.006	.539±.009	.876±.005	.462±.006	.691±.000
RotatE	STD+LP	.973±.001	.914±.000	.706±.002	.611±.000	.545±.000	.734±.014	.530±.000	.593±.000
	MTT+LP	.990±.001	.913±.001	.733±.000	.605±.000	.469±.009	.793±.005	.413±.000	.751±.000
	MTT+MTR	.994±.000	.919±.001	.768±.000	.643±.000	.576±.000	.830±.011	.534±.000	.707±.000
TransE	STD+LP	.993±.000	.919±.001	.762±.000	.623±.000	.630±.000	.833±.000	.507±.015	.670±.000
	MTT+LP	.991±.000	.912±.000	.728±.005	.583±.000	.603±.000	.804±.011	.506±.007	.654±.006
	MTT+MTR	.992±.000	.892±.000	.750±.000	.580±.000	.401±.012	.809±.003	.464±.015	.614±.012
KE-GCN		.996±.000	.896±.001	.709±.000	.582±.005	.610±.006	.853±.006	.463±.014	.488±.014

Table 18: Weighted F1 on test data of downstream classifiers (MLP, Logistic Regression, KNN and Random Forest) that use pre-trained KGE embeddings as input to solve entity classification tasks about entities in YAGO3-10; and KE-GCN (Yu et al., 2021), a GCN that trains directly on the downstream data. Datasets are sorted by decreasing size of the training set from left to right.

		FB15K-237				
		Regression (RSE - lower is better)				
		Node Imp.	Birth Year	Latitude	Longitude	Person Height
ComplEx	STD+LP	.870±.048	.601±.239	.172±.013	.089±.010	.678±.010
	MTT+LP	.918±.142	.477±.190	.145±.015	.066±.008	.661±.011
	MTT+MTR	.909±.086	.214±.050	.143±.009	.096±.008	.678±.000
DistMult	STD+LP	.807±.023	.844±.042	.182±.031	.088±.005	.669±.003
	MTT+LP	.788±.006	.827±.065	.143±.001	.083±.013	.651±.009
	MTT+MTR	.802±.049	.701±.052	.232±.053	.070±.006	.691±.000
RotatE	STD+LP	.913±.000	.872±.027	.498±.057	.279±.003	.657±.000
	MTT+LP	.834±.016	.797±.069	.313±.014	.173±.003	.813±.136
	MTT+MTR	.856±.003	.811±.005	.411±.022	.225±.096	.847±.000
TransE	STD+LP	.886±.035	.836±.041	.170±.022	.084±.006	.722±.003
	MTT+LP	.833±.018	.812±.012	.078±.011	.061±.003	.769±.009
	MTT+MTR	.897±.044	.655±.053	.088±.005	.052±.006	.824±.000
KE-GCN		.804±.005	.376±.035	.218±.023	.113±.003	.748±.002

Table 19: Part 1: Relative squared error (RSE) on test data of downstream models (MLP and Linear Regression) that use pre-trained KGE embeddings as input to solve regression tasks about entities in FB15K-237; and KE-GCN (Yu et al., 2021), a GCN that trains directly on the downstream data. Models with RSE above 1 are considered unsatisfactory. Datasets are sorted by decreasing size of the training set from left to right.

		FB15K-237				
		Regression (RSE - lower is better)				
		Size Area	Population	Film Year	Date Founded	Film Rating
ComplEx	STD+LP	.234±.018	.442±.071	.156±.016	.494±.042	.736±.046
	MTT+LP	.046±.026	.260±.064	.138±.007	.431±.047	.795±.058
	MTT+MTR	.049±.021	.493±.097	.126±.003	.605±.033	.804±.065
DistMult	STD+LP	.412±.318	.914±.093	.152±.003	.627±.036	.813±.062
	MTT+LP	.435±.046	.503±.004	.134±.012	.429±.045	.728±.063
	MTT+MTR	.025±.008	.540±.030	.146±.005	.718±.012	.894±.043
RotatE	STD+LP	.700±.223	.463±.429	.176±.004	.618±.024	.792±.089
	MTT+LP	.708±.112	.537±.035	.146±.008	.514±.055	.897±.168
	MTT+MTR	.440±.190	.710±.158	.157±.010	.631±.060	.949±.056
TransE	STD+LP	.326±.075	.906±.574	.153±.019	.499±.046	.839±.045
	MTT+LP	.041±.744	.227±.730	.141±.004	.300±.013	.690±.031
	MTT+MTR	.833±.684	.675±.109	.130±.012	.708±.022	.946±.018
KE-GCN		.754±.0180	.664±.051	.144±.008	.498±.034	.691±.009

Table 20: Part 2: Relative squared error (RSE) on test data of downstream models (MLP and Linear Regression) that use pre-trained KGE embeddings as input to solve regression tasks about entities in FB15K-237; and KE-GCN (Yu et al., 2021), a GCN that trains directly on the downstream data. Models with RSE above 1 are considered unsatisfactory. Datasets are sorted by decreasing size of the training set from left to right.

		Born on Date	Created on Date	Died on Date	Destroyed on Date	Happened on Date
		YAGO3-10 *Regression (RSE - lower is better)*				
ComplEx	STD+LP	.519±.001	.672±.033	.555±.014	.872±.060	.324±.006
	MTT+LP	.345±.025	.603±.009	.377±.005	.709±.009	.296±.036
	MTT+MTR	.363±.010	.643±.016	.406±.023	.605±.029	.277±.023
DistMult	STD+LP	.432±.013	.612±.024	.466±.025	.773±.004	.311±.030
	MTT+LP	.345±.023	.565±.015	.416±.023	.724±.044	.312±.040
	MTT+MTR	.352±.006	.648±.016	.438±.035	.677±.024	.214±.022
RotatE	STD+LP	.689±.027	.800±.009	.849±.000	.913±.000	.227±.055
	MTT+LP	.538±.006	.717±.008	.657±.018	.886±.031	.497±.233
	MTT+MTR	.421±.016	.706±.012	.468±.003	.616±.043	.137±.013
TransE	STD+LP	.422±.018	.647±.008	.351±.037	.513±.057	.300±.059
	MTT+LP	.371±.006	.725±.022	.434±.009	.573±.081	.100±.027
	MTT+MTR	.494±.017	.777±.000	.521±.038	.942±.048	.666±.024
KE-GCN		.256±.009	.611±.008	.299±.011	.657±.045	.167±.001

Table 21: Relative squared error (RSE) on test data of downstream models (MLP and Linear Regression) that use pre-trained KGE embeddings as input to solve regression tasks about entities in YAGO3-10; and KE-GCN (Yu et al., 2021), a GCN that trains directly on the downstream data. Models with RSE above 1 are considered unsatisfactory. Datasets are sorted by decreasing size of the training set from left to right.

		Date of Birth	Album Pub.	Asteroid Mag.	River Length
		WIKIDATA5M *Regression (RSE - lower is better)*			
ComplEx	STD+LP	.475±.003	.760±.009	.436±.014	.559±.022
	MTT+LP	.481±.006	.844±.009	.519±.026	.540±.007
	MTT+MTR	.468±.010	.813±.006	.518±.014	.659±.025
TransE	STD+LP	.373±.002	.555±.004	.377±.015	.444±.016
	MTT+LP	.434±.007	.669±.003	.439±.013	.433±.029
	MTT+MTR	.455±.005	.667±.010	.455±.021	.418±.021

Table 22: Part 1: Relative squared error (RSE) on test data of downstream models (MLP and Linear Regression) that use pre-trained KGE embeddings as input to solve regression tasks about entities in WIKIDATA5M; Models with RSE above 1 are considered unsatisfactory. Datasets are sorted by decreasing size of the training set from left to right.

		Airport Elev.	Season Start	Population	Munic. Area
		WIKIDATA5M *Regression (RSE - lower is better)*			
ComplEx	STD+LP	.849±.007	.596±.002	.019±.197	.801±.000
	MTT+LP	.917±.000	.695±.014	.785±.139	.867±.000
	MTT+MTR	.928±.000	.657±.040	.841±.086	.877±.000
TransE	STD+LP	.734±.019	.546±.029	.928±.000	.811±.000
	MTT+LP	.894±.037	.654±.024	.739±.087	.825±.000
	MTT+MTR	.873±.000	.610±.011	.896±.080	.825±.000

Table 23: Part 2: Relative squared error (RSE) on test data of downstream models (MLP and Linear Regression) that use pre-trained KGE embeddings as input to solve regression tasks about entities in WIKIDATA5M; Models with RSE above 1 are considered unsatisfactory. Datasets are sorted by decreasing size of the training set from left to right.

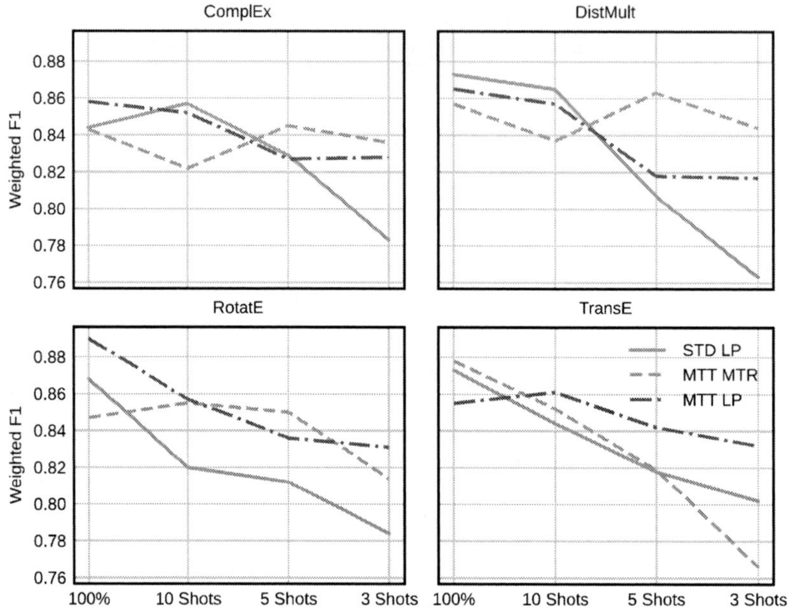

Figure 3: Few-shot performance of entity classification tasks for FB15K-237 (higher is better). Each n-shot training set consists of n sampled positive and negative examples for each class.

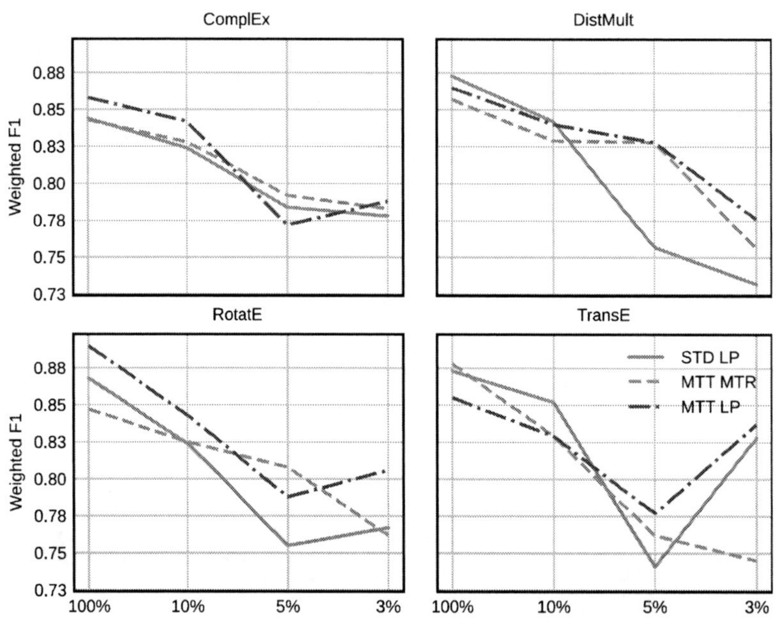

Figure 4: Performance on entity classification for FB15K-237 with downsampled training sets (higher is better). Each training set was constructed by sampling (stratified) a percentage of the training set.

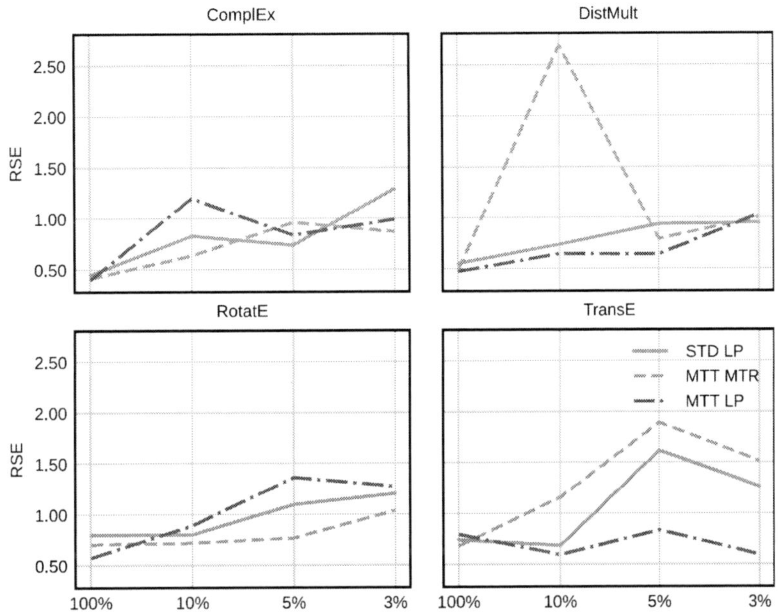

Figure 5: Performance of regression tasks for FB15K-237 with downsampled training sets (lower is better). Each training set was constructed by sampling a percentage of the training set.

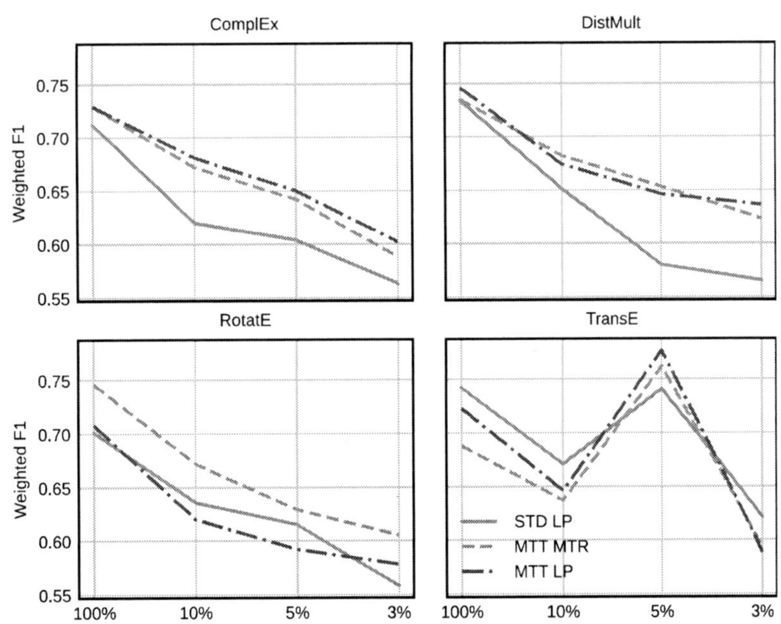

Figure 6: Performance on entity classification for YAGO3-10 with downsampled training sets (higher is better). Each training set was constructed by sampling (stratified) a percentage of the training set.

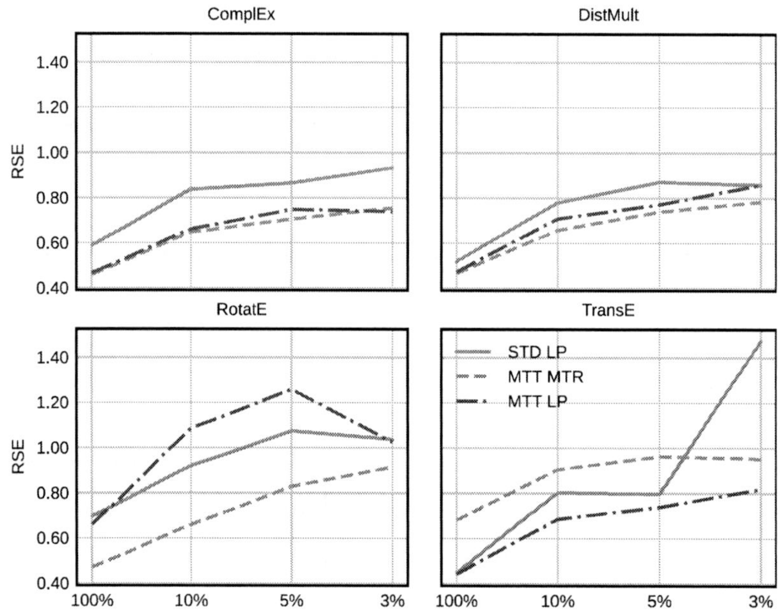

Figure 7: Performance of regression tasks for YAGO3-10 with downsampled training sets (lower is better). Each training set was constructed by sampling a percentage of the training set. The gap in performance between MTT and STD models becomes larger as training data becomes less available.

Learn it or Leave it: Module Composition and Pruning for Continual Learning

Mingyang Wang[1,2,3] **Heike Adel**[4] **Lukas Lange**[1]
Jannik Strötgen[5] **Hinrich Schütze**[2,3]
[1]Bosch Center for Artificial Intelligence, Renningen, Germany
[2]LMU Munich, Germany [3]Munich Center for Machine Learning (MCML)
[4]Hochschule der Medien, Stuttgart, Germany
[5]Karlsruhe University of Applied Sciences, Germany
mingyang.wang2@de.bosch.com

Abstract

In real-world environments, continual learning is essential for machine learning models, as they need to acquire new knowledge incrementally without forgetting what they have already learned. While pretrained language models have shown impressive capabilities on various static tasks, applying them to continual learning poses significant challenges, including avoiding catastrophic forgetting, facilitating knowledge transfer, and maintaining parameter efficiency. In this paper, we introduce MoCL-P, a novel lightweight continual learning method that addresses these challenges simultaneously. Unlike traditional approaches that continuously expand parameters for newly arriving tasks, MoCL-P integrates task representation-guided module composition with adaptive pruning, effectively balancing knowledge integration and computational overhead. Our evaluation across three continual learning benchmarks with up to 176 tasks shows that MoCL-P achieves state-of-the-art performance and improves parameter efficiency by up to three times, demonstrating its potential for practical applications where resource requirements are constrained.

1 Introduction

Continual learning (CL) is a learning paradigm aiming at incrementally acquiring and integrating new knowledge over time without forgetting existing knowledge. This capability is essential for machine learning models to stay effective as they encounter dynamic and evolving real-world environments. While pretrained language models (PLMs) have demonstrated remarkable capabilities on various static tasks, adapting them for continual task learning remains challenging.

In particular, there are three notable challenges for continual learning. (1) Avoiding catastrophic forgetting: The newly learned information should not disrupt and degrade previously acquired knowledge (McCloskey and Cohen, 1989). (2) Facilitating knowledge transfer: The knowledge from past tasks should be reused for efficient learning of new tasks. (3) Maintaining parameter efficiency: The language models need to stay lightweight and effective even if the continual learning sequence scales to hundreds of tasks.

To mitigate catastrophic forgetting, a line of prior works adopt the idea of *parameter isolation* (Razdaibiedina et al., 2022; Wang et al., 2023d,e, 2024), which allocates isolated parameters dedicated for each task to avoid inter-task interference. While parameter isolation typically does not allow knowledge transfer across tasks (Wang et al., 2023d,e), there are attempts to address both challenges of catastrophic forgetting and knowledge transfer at the same time, e.g., by progressively concatenating (Razdaibiedina et al., 2022) or composing task-specific modules (Wang et al., 2024).

Despite their effectiveness in terms of task performance, parameter isolation methods do not scale well with the number of tasks. When the number of tasks in a continual learning sequence is growing into the hundreds, the progressive expansion of task-specific parameters leads to parameter inefficiency and significantly increases computational and storage costs.

In this paper, we address all three continual learning challenges simultaneously and introduce MoCL-P, a lightweight continual learning approach that leverages task representation-guided module composition and adaptive pruning. First, to avoid catastrophic forgetting, MoCL-P continually adds task-specific modules to PLMs for learning new tasks while keeping the modules frozen once the training on the respective tasks is finished. In addition, to enable knowledge transfer across tasks, MoCL-P allows the model to reuse existing knowledge via module composition. Finally, to keep the language model lightweight, MoCL-P adopts an adaptive pruning strategy by removing

Proceedings of the 9th Workshop on Representation Learning for NLP (RepL4NLP-2024), pages 163–176
August 15, 2024

modules with redundant information and retaining only the most salient modules throughout the continual learning process.

In our evaluation on three popular datasets as continual learning benchmarks with up to 176 tasks in the learning sequence, MoCL-P stands out by not only showing state-of-the-art performance but also outperforming prior algorithms in parameter efficiency by up to three times across benchmarks.

To the best of our knowledge, this is the first paper that tackles the three challenges of continual learning simultaneously: MoCL-P avoids catastrophic forgetting, allows knowledge transfer and ensures parameter efficiency. Thus, MoCL-P proposes a sustainable way for continual learning, allowing models to remain lightweight and effective as they evolve with accumulating tasks.

The code base for MoCL is available online.[1]

2 Related Work

2.1 Avoiding Catastrophic Forgetting in Continual Learning

A major challenge in continual learning is known as catastrophic forgetting, where newly learned information disrupts and degrades previously acquired knowledge (McCloskey and Cohen, 1989). Existing approaches to overcome this issue can be broadly divided into three categories (Wang et al., 2023a): (1) *Regularization*-based methods explicitly add regularization terms to the loss function to restrict model updates and preserve existing knowledge (Li and Hoiem, 2017; Kirkpatrick et al., 2017; Aljundi et al., 2018); (2) *Rehearsal*-based methods leverage a memory buffer to store real examples (Rebuffi et al., 2017; Rolnick et al., 2019; Zhang et al., 2022a) or generated pseudo-examples of past tasks for future rehearsal to avoid catastrophic forgetting (Shin et al., 2017; Su et al., 2019); (3) *Parameter isolation*-based methods construct task-specific parameters to prevent inter-task interference by either dynamically expanding model capacity or isolating existing model weights (Madotto et al., 2020; Zhang et al., 2022b; Razdaibiedina et al., 2022; Wang et al., 2023e,d, 2024).

Our method, MoCL-P, belongs to the parameter-isolation based category. We use task representation-guided module composition and adaptive pruning to effectively manage isolated parameters.

[1]https://github.com/boschresearch/MoCL-Pruning

2.2 Transferring Knowledge in Continual Learning

Recent studies in continual learning demonstrate the effectiveness of parameter isolation methods in avoiding catastrophic forgetting (Razdaibiedina et al., 2022; Wang et al., 2023e,d, 2024). However, naive parameter isolation methods do not allow knowledge transfer across tasks, which leads to inefficient learning as the model cannot leverage previously acquired knowledge to facilitate learning new tasks. To address this, Yoon et al. (2017) and Zhu et al. (2022) attempt to first identify reusable modules and only add new parameters when necessary. Ke et al. (2021) and Wang et al. (2022) introduce knowledge-sharing modules to facilitate knowledge transfer while maintaining task-specific parameters to prevent interference. Razdaibiedina et al. (2022) progressively concatenate task-specific modules to incrementally build a composite model that leverages both new and existing knowledge. Wang et al. (2024) introduce a modular and compositional continual learning framework to compose the new module with existing ones based on task module matching.

2.3 Parameter-Efficient Continual Learning

With the ever-increasing number of parameters in PLMs, it becomes increasingly important to develop machine learning systems that are more scalable, practical, and resource-efficient. In the context of continual learning, this necessitates parameter-efficient approaches that can effectively integrate new knowledge without excessive computational and storage costs as the number of tasks in the continual learning sequence increases.

Recent advancements in continual learning integrate parameter isolation with parameter-efficient fine-tuning (PEFT), i.e., they allocate task-specific PEFT modules for learning and inference (Razdaibiedina et al., 2022; Wang et al., 2023e,d, 2024). Various PEFT techniques, such as adapter tuning (Houlsby et al., 2019), prefix tuning (Li and Liang, 2021), and LoRA (Huang, 2022), have been applied in continual learning. Although they reduce the number of training parameters to some extent by freezing the PLM and only updating the PEFT module parameters, it remains challenging to apply them to long-sequence benchmarks that consist of hundreds of tasks. The continuous expansion of task-specific modules leads to significant computational overhead as the number of tasks increases.

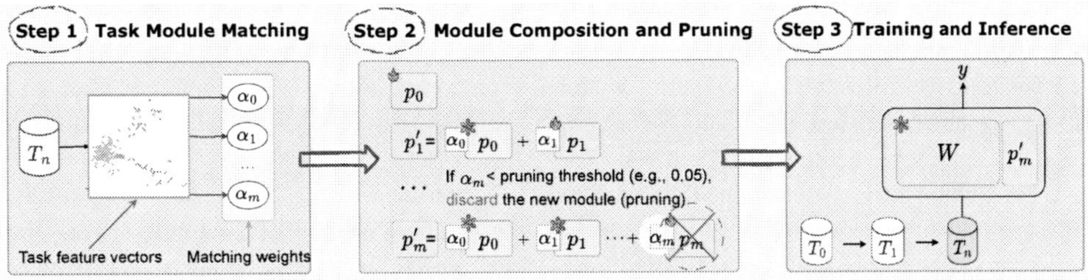

Figure 1: Overview of our proposed method MoCL-P for parameter-efficient continual learning. **Step 1**: We match the n-th task input with task feature vectors to determine the contribution of each existing module for learning the current task. **Step 2**: We compose the newly initialized module with existing ones and perform adaptive module pruning to preserve only the dominant modules. **Step 3**: Finally, we combine the composed module p'_m with the PLM for training and inference.

Our approach builds on the idea of Wang et al. (2024) by utilizing task representations for module composition, ensuring that the model effectively reuses relevant knowledge from previous tasks. Beyond that, we introduce an adaptive pruning strategy to keep the language model lightweight and effective throughout the continual learning process, thus making it scalable for continual learning scenarios with long task sequences.

3 Problem Definition

Continual learning focuses on addressing a series of tasks which arrive in a sequential order. The primary goal is to optimize the model's average performance across all tasks after learning them sequentially. Formally, the sequence of tasks is denoted as $\{T_1, \ldots, T_N\}$. Each task contains a set of input samples $\{(x_n^i, y_n^i)\}$. For the text classification tasks we study in this work, x_n^i is the input text, y_n^i is the ground-truth label, and $n \in \{1, \ldots, N\}$ is the task identity.

In this work, we focus on rehearsal-free continual learning, i.e., data from earlier tasks is not available when training later tasks. Therefore, our model does not suffer from the memory or privacy issues associated with rehearsal-based methods. We assume the task labels are provided during both training and testing, i.e., task-incremental continual learning (Wang et al., 2023a). However, MoCL-P can be adapted for class-incremental learning, where the task labels are not given during testing, with minor modifications following Wang et al. (2024). We leave the exploration of other continual learning settings for future work.

4 Method

In this section, we describe MoCL-P, our proposed CL approach for language models, as illustrated in Figure 1, which tackles catastrophic forgetting and enhances knowledge transfer with superior parameter efficiency at the same time.

4.1 Continual Learning with PEFT

We inherit the idea of parameter isolation with parameter-efficient fine-tuning (PEFT) introduced in prior work (Razdaibiedina et al., 2022; Wang et al., 2023d,e, 2024), which allocates trainable PEFT parameters for each task while keeping other parameters frozen.

We utilize *prefix-tuning* (Li and Liang, 2021) as the PEFT module in consistency with prior works.[2] For each task in the CL sequence, we add a set of trainable PEFT parameters, i.e., a task-specific module, to the pretrained language model (PLM) for downstream task fine-tuning. Instead of updating the whole model, only a small number of the PEFT parameters are optimized. Once training on one given task is completed, the corresponding PEFT module is frozen to preserve the task-specific knowledge in the subsequent training process, thus avoiding catastrophic forgetting.

4.2 Task Representation-Guided Module Matching

In contrast to completely isolating task-specific parameters during continual learning, which excludes knowledge transfer, we follow the idea of

[2]Other PEFT methods like Adapter (Houlsby et al., 2019) and LoRA (Hu et al., 2021) can also be combined with MoCL-P in general. We leave such exploration for future work.

task module composition introduced in Wang et al. (2024) to facilitate knowledge transfer.

To this end, we utilize task representations for task module matching, and consequently for composing old and new modules for learning. The module matching aims to determine the contribution of each existing module to learning the current task, i.e., to what extent previously learned modules can be reused for the current task.

We introduce trainable feature vectors $V \in \mathbb{R}^{N \times D}$ as task representations to capture the features of each task in the CL sequence.[3] We set the dimension of each task feature vector $v \in \mathbb{R}^D$ to the same value as the dimension of the input embeddings $x_n \in \mathbb{R}^D$. Then, we calculate the cosine similarity between the input embeddings x_n and each feature vector v_i up to the current task as the matching score $\alpha_i = \cos(x_n, v_i)$. Consequently, we get the module matching weights $\{\alpha_0, \alpha_1, ...\}$ for module composition (details will be introduced in Section 4.3) to reuse existing knowledge.

4.3 Module Composition with Adaptive Pruning

When the CL learning sequence scales to dozens or hundreds of tasks, the need for efficiency increases. Continuously expanding the module pool to assign a PEFT module to each task, as done in prior works (Wang et al., 2023e; Razdaibiedina et al., 2022; Wang et al., 2024), leads to large computational costs. In contrast, we employ an adaptive pruning strategy to make our approach scalable in scenarios with long task sequences.

In particular, our pruning strategy aims at preserving only those modules that add new and valuable information to the set of already selected modules. Given a set of selected modules $\{P_0, \ldots, P_{m-1}\}$ from previous tasks and a new task T_n, $(m - 1 \ll n)$, we initialize a trainable module P_m and add it temporarily to the model. For each instance[4] x_n^i of the current task T_n, we compute the matching weights $\{\alpha_0, \ldots, \alpha_m\}$ by matching x_n with all task feature vectors $\{v_0, \ldots, v_m\}$ from our current set of modules. Specifically, we calculate the cosine similarity between x_n and $\{v_0, \ldots, v_m\}$ as module matching weights $\alpha_{0:m}$ as detailed in Section 4.2. Then, we compose the new and old modules via a weighted sum: $P'_m = \sum_{k=0}^{m} \alpha_k P_k$. Finally, the composed module P'_m is combined with the PLM, consisting of all the selected module components up to the current task.

After the training on T_n is finished (specifically, the training of the PEFT module P_m and the task feature vector v_m), we compare α_m, the matching weight of the new module P_m, with a threshold[5] to decide whether to prune P_m or leave it in the set of existing modules. The intuition is that large matching weights indicate new and valuable information, while task modules with small matching weights do not contribute new information and, thus can, be discarded.

4.4 Training and Inference

The training objective for the n-th task in the continual learning sequence is to find the PEFT module P_m and the task feature vector v_m that minimize the cross-entropy loss of training examples, and, at the same time, maximize the cosine similarity between the task-specific feature vector v_m and the corresponding task input embeddings x_n:

$$\min_{P_m, v_m} - \sum_{x_n, y_n} \log p(y_n | x_n, P'_n, \theta) - \sum_{x_n} \cos(x_n, v_m)$$

Here $P'_n = \sum_{k=1}^{m} \alpha_k P_k$ is the weighted summation of the new trainable task module and the existing frozen task modules as introduced in Section 4.3. During inference, MoCL-P performs per-instance task module matching and composition. The resulting module is combined with the PLM for inference.

5 Experimental Setup

In this section, we describe datasets, training details and baselines for our experiments.

5.1 Datasets

To evaluate the performance of our method and the effectiveness of its module pruning functionality, we experiment with three continual learning benchmarks, each with long task sequences. Following prior work (Razdaibiedina et al., 2022; Wang et al., 2024), we use MTL15, a multi-task continual learning benchmark comprising 15 classification tasks, and AfriSenti (Muhammad et al., 2023), a multilingual sentiment analysis dataset that includes 12 low-resource African languages. Additionally, we

[3]Note that MoCL-P is agnostic to different types of task representations. In addition to the trainable feature vectors, other static task representations such as task embeddings or Gaussian task distributions can also be combined with MoCL-P. We analyze these options in Section 6.2.

[4]For simplicity, we refer to this as x_n in the following.

[5]The threshold is a tunable hyperparameter.

Method	AfriSenti					WikiAnn				
	AVG	O1	O2	O3	# Params	AVG	O1	O2	O3	# Params
Seq FT (F)	6.17	5.62	6.52	6.30	560M	14.50	3.44	23.36	16.70	110M
Seq FT	49.10	50.05	49.74	47.53	0.4M	67.99	68.25	65.05	70.66	0.1M
Per-task FT	52.41	52.41	52.41	52.41	4.5M	71.22	71.22	71.22	71.22	24.8M
ProgPrompt	49.07	50.16	46.74	50.30	4.5M	73.20	73.24	73.22	73.15	24.8M
EPI	43.10	41.49	42.65	45.16	4.5M	67.34	67.72	67.12	67.18	24.8M
MoCL	59.31	59.56	58.98	59.40	4.5M	73.80	73.78	73.81	73.82	24.9M
MoCL-P (Ours)	**59.41**	59.52	58.97	59.76	2.2M$\pm$0.4	**73.91**	73.94	73.94	73.86	8.0M$\pm$0.1

Table 1: Summary of the continual learning results on two multilingual benchmarks: AfriSenti and WikiAnn NER, with 12 and 176 languages in the task sequence, respectively. We compare MoCL-P with various baseline methods, and show the average model performance (AVG) across different task orders (O1, O2, O3) with the number of trainable parameters (# Params) used by each method. MoCL-P outperforms other methods with significantly fewer parameters, demonstrating its superiority in both model performance and parameter efficiency in long-sequence continual learning scenarios.

include WikiAnn (Pan et al., 2017), a multilingual named entity recognition (NER) dataset covering 176 languages; its long task sequence provides an adequate testbed for the pruning ability of our approach.

We report macro-weighted F1 scores on the AfriSenti benchmark, accuracy on MTL15, and micro-weighted F1 scores on WikiAnn. On the MTL15 benchmark, we select 1000 random samples per class for training each task and hold out 500 samples per class for validation.[6] We explore three task orders for each benchmark, adopting the same multiple task orders as the prior work. Please refer to Appendix A.1 for more details about the benchmarks and task orders.

5.2 Training Details

We deploy three LMs for these datasets, in line with prior work (Razdaibiedina et al., 2022; Wang et al., 2024). We use encoder-based models for AfriSenti and WikiAnn NER (AfroXLM and BERT, respectively), and the encoder-decoder model T5 for MTL15. Prefix-tuning is used as the task-specific modules for all deployed models. All design choices are consistent with previous works to ensure a fair comparison. The reported results represent the average performance after training on all tasks consecutively and are averaged over three random seeds. The detailed experimental settings are provided in Appendix A.2.1.

[6]All design choices of MoCL-P are kept consistent with previous works (Wang et al., 2023b,d, 2024) to ensure a fair comparison.

5.3 Baselines

To compare different CL methods, we include the following baselines: (1) Sequential fine-tuning continuously fine-tunes the language model on the task sequence: (a) **Seq FT (F)** refers to all model parameters are updated (fully fine-tuning), while (b) **Seq FT** only fine-tunes the PEFT parameters; (2) **Per-task FT** trains a separate PEFT module for each task; and the parameter isolation-based methods (3) **ProgPrompt** (Razdaibiedina et al., 2022) assigns task-specific parameters and progressively concatenates modules of all tasks to encourage knowledge transfer; (4) **EPI** (Wang et al., 2023e) introduces a non-parametric task identification technique to select modules for task training and inference; (5) **O-LoRA** (Wang et al., 2023d) learns tasks in different low-rank vector spaces that are kept orthogonal to each other to minimize interference; and (6) **MoCL** (Wang et al., 2024) introduces a modular and compositional framework that progressively expands task-specific modules and composes the new module with existing ones to facilitate knowledge transfer. A detailed description of these methods can be found in Appendix A.2.2.

6 Results and Analysis

In this section, we present and analyze our experimental results.

6.1 Overall Results

Table 1 shows the performance of MoCL-P and other baseline methods on the AfriSenti and WikiAnn benchmarks. MoCL-P consistently outperforms the baselines while significantly reducing the number of trainable parameters. Using only 50% and 30% of the trainable parameters compared to other CL methods on Afrisenti and Wikiann respectively, MoCL-P showcases an exceptional balance of efficiency and performance. In the MTL15 benchmark, as illustrated in Table 2, MoCL-P also shows superior performance. As mentioned in prior work (Wang et al., 2024), tasks in this benchmark share lower similarity compared to AfriSenti and WikiAnn, resulting in weaker reusability of task modules. Therefore, we do not observe a significant drop in the number of trainable parameters here as seen in the other benchmarks. However, we still achieve a 25% reduction in parameter size while maintaining final performance.

Overall, MoCL-P demonstrates its superiority in efficiently managing the continual learning process without the substantial parameter overhead. The competitive performance of MoCL-P across different benchmarks highlights its robust adaptability and scalability to the continual learning sequence up to 176 tasks long.

Method	MTL15				
	AVG	O1	O2	O3	# Params
Seq FT-F	7.4	7.4	7.4	7.5	770M
Seq FT-P	64.7	69.9	58.9	65.1	1.4M
Per-task FT	80.5	80.5	80.5	80.5	21.1M
ProgPrompt	77.9	78.0	77.7	77.9	21.1M
EPI	65.4	62.8	65.3	68.1	21.1M
O-LoRA	69.6	78.0	77.7	77.9	33.8M
MoCL	**82.5**	82.9	82.8	81.9	21.1M
MoCL-P (Ours)	**82.5**	83.0	82.7	81.8	15.6M$\pm$1.1

Table 2: Summary of the continual learning results on the MTL15 benchmark with the T5-large model. MoCL-P achieves the best average performance (AVG) while using fewer parameters (# Params), demonstrating its effectiveness on the multi-task CL benchmark.

6.2 Task Representation Comparison

In this work, we adopt learnable task feature vectors as task representation, and based on these, we perform module composition and pruning. In Section 6.1, we demonstrate the effectiveness of this design choice. While this is not the only option for task representations, in this section, we experiment with two other types of task representation: (1) using Gaussian distributions to model the input embeddings of each task (*w/ Gaussian*) and (2) calculating the mean of the input embeddings of each task for task representations(*w/ Embed mean*).

Table 3 provides the results of using different task representation options for module composition and pruning. A significant performance drop occurs when using Gaussian distributions or the mean of task input embeddings as the task representation. In most cases, their performance is worse than the Per-Task FT baseline, indicating that using these task representations for module composition leads to performance degradation rather than beneficial knowledge transfer across tasks.

	AfriSenti		WikiAnn	
	AVG	# Params	AVG	# Params
Per-task FT	49.10	4.5M	71.22	24.8M
MoCL	59.31	4.5M	73.80	24.9M
w/ Gaussian	42.25	4.5M	67.38	24.8M
w/ Embed mean	52.63	4.5M	70.12	24.8M
MoCL-P (Ours)	**59.41**	2.2M$\pm$0.4	**73.91**	8.0M$\pm$0.1
w/ Gaussian	42.15	4.1M$\pm$0.0	67.46	5.4M$\pm$0.3
w/ Embed mean	52.13	3.9M$\pm$0.2	70.21	20.3M$\pm$0.7

Table 3: Performance comparison of different task representation methods for module composition and pruning. Specifically, we use Gaussian distribution to model the input embeddings of each task (*w/ Gaussian rep*) and calculate the mean of the input embeddings of each task (*w/ Embed mean*). Notably, the use of these variations results in substantially lower performance compared to the original MoCL and MoCL-P which utilizes learnable feature vectors as task representations.

We believe that this degradation is due to the fact that both of these task representations are static and are solely based on the input embeddings. In contrast, MoCL-P utilizes trainable task feature vectors, meaning the model can automatically learn to capture the salient task features necessary for effective module composition. Trainable task representations are a better choice because not all information in the input embedding is relevant for module composition. To effectively capture reusability between task modules, the model must focus on the salient features while ignoring irrelevant ones. Static task representations, which are purely based on input embeddings, fail to achieve this selective focus.

6.3 Ablation Study: Varying the Training Epochs for Task Feature Vectors

To substantiate our assumption introduced in Section 6.2, we additionally conduct ablation experiments on WikiAnn where we vary the training epochs for task feature vectors in MoCL-P. As illustrated in Figure 3, training the task feature vectors for different epochs shows a clear pattern: the model performance improves significantly with the initial increase of the number of training epochs.

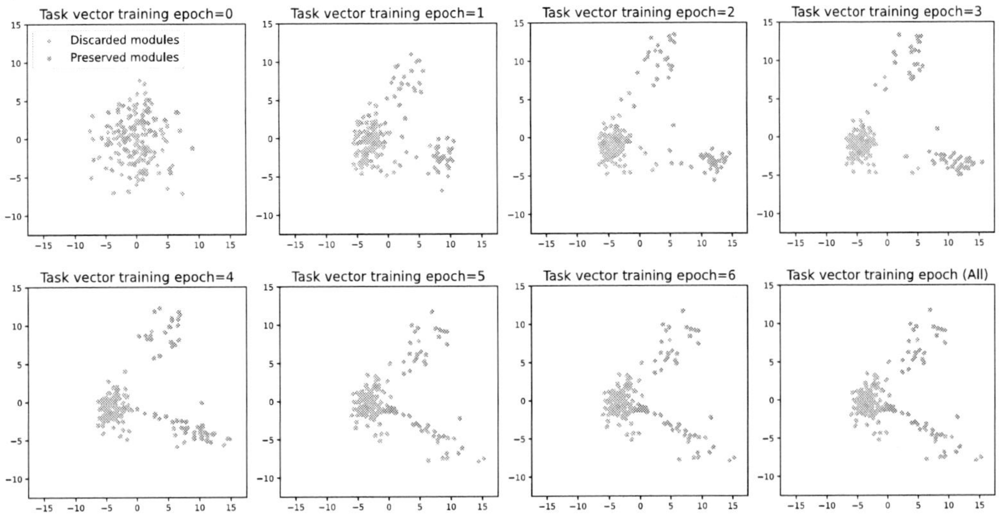

Figure 2: Visualization of task feature vectors on the WikiAnn benchmark using PCA for dimensionality reduction. We vary the training epochs for task feature vectors in MoCL-P. As the training epochs increase, the task feature vectors spread out from the initial dense cluster. Notably, the feature vectors of preserved modules (in orange) are spread across a large area while the discarded modules (in blue) form a dense cluster, indicating their redundancy.

Beyond a certain point (epoch = 4), additional training does not yield further benefits and converges towards a performance plateau. This observation suggests that by allowing the model to adapt these vectors over several epochs, MoCL-P can more accurately identify and leverage the most relevant features for module composition. This underscores the critical importance of the trainable nature of task feature vectors in MoCL-P.

In Figure 2, we visualize the task feature vectors at different training epochs on the WikiAnn dataset, which includes a total of 176 tasks. The colors represent two categories of task modules: those that are eventually discarded (blue) and those that are preserved (orange) through the learning process. Initially (training epoch = 0), the vectors are evenly distributed around the origin since they are uniformly initialized. As the training epochs increase, the task vectors spread out and become more distinct, suggesting that the model captures distinct features of tasks and utilizes them for module pruning. Notably, the feature vectors of preserved modules are spread across a large area, while the discarded modules form a dense cluster, indicating their redundancy. The embeddings of task feature vectors stabilize by epoch 5, indicating a convergence in the task representation learning process. These observed patterns demonstrate the effectiveness of our strategy of using trainable task representations for module composition and pruning, which helps in preserving only the most salient modules for continual learning.

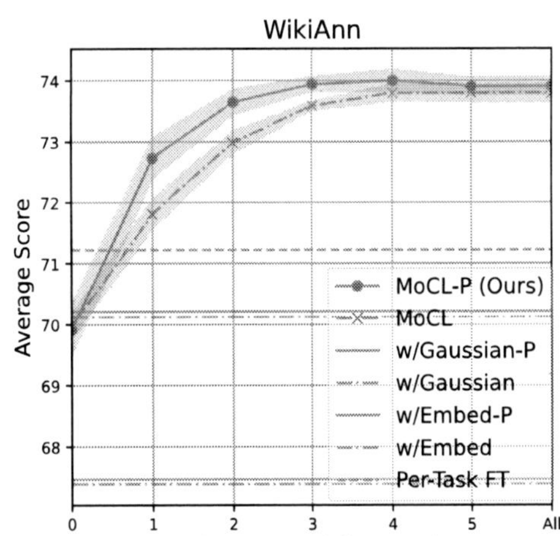

Figure 3: Experimental results with different training epochs for task feature vectors in MoCL-P. The model performance improves rapidly with the initial increase of the number of training epochs and converges towards a performance plateau after epochs > 4. MoCL-P achieves significantly better performance than other task representation options. It highlights the advantage of trainable task representations in capturing salient task features for effective module composition.

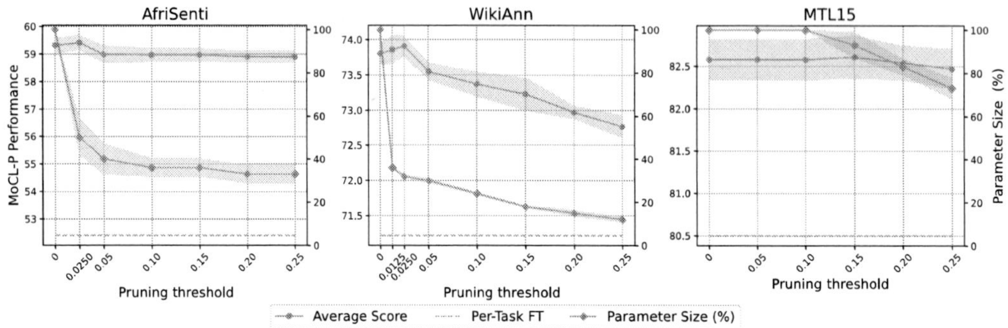

Figure 4: Impact of pruning thresholds on the performance and parameter size of MoCL-P across different benchmarks. The performance of MoCL-P exhibits robustness to different thresholds, with a significant reduction in the number of trainable parameters. This demonstrates that MoCL-P can maintain effective performance despite using fewer parameters.

6.4 Ablation Study: Varying the Pruning Threshold

In this section, we study the impact of using different thresholds on the performance of MoCL-P. As introduced in Section 4.3, we compare the matching weight of the newly initialized task module α_m with the pre-specified threshold α_{ths}, if $\alpha_m < \alpha_{ths}$, then we discard the newly learned module. We vary α_{ths} from 0 to 0.25 for the three benchmarks used in this work.

The results are shown in Figure 4. The figure illustrates how varying the pruning threshold affects both the average performance and the parameter size across different benchmarks.

For the model performance, we observe that the initial increase in the pruning threshold leads to a performance increase on all three benchmarks. This indicates that excluding the redundant modules benefits performance. As the threshold continues to increase, the average performance on AfriSenti and MTL15 remains relatively stable, while the performance on WikiAnn drops, possibly due to the loss of information in potentially useful modules. Additionally, it is worth noting that the performance of MoCL-P is consistently and significantly better than the Per-Task FT baseline, suggesting that MoCL-P achieves effective knowledge transfer at different pruning thresholds.

Furthermore, for the parameter size, a significant reduction is observed as the threshold increases on all three benchmarks. This demonstrates the superiority of MoCL-P on parameter efficiency. We observe that the parameter size decreases more pronounced and faster on AfriSenti and WikiAnn, while it decreases less and more slowly on MTL15. We believe it is due to the characteristics of the benchmarks. As mentioned in Section 6.1, tasks in this benchmark share a lower similarity, therefore, most task modules are highly specialized to these distinct tasks and cannot be discarded.

We choose different pruning thresholds for different benchmarks reported in Table 1. For each benchmark, we select the pruning threshold that best balances performance and parameter size to report the results in Table 1. Specifically, we use $\alpha_{ths} = 0.025$ for AfriSenti and WikiAnn, and $\alpha_{ths} = 0.25$ for MTL15. With these thresholds, MoCL-P achieves equally good performance with only 50%, 30%, and 75% of the number of trainable parameters compared to MoCL without pruning on these three benchmarks, respectively.

7 Conclusion

In this paper, we introduce MoCL-P, a novel continual learning approach that addresses the core challenges of catastrophic forgetting, knowledge transfer, and parameter efficiency in continual learning. We utilize learnable task representations for module composition and adaptive pruning, maintaining a lightweight model while achieving state-of-the-art performance across various benchmarks. Notably, MoCL-P scales effectively to long continual learning sequences, handling up to 176 tasks without compromising performance. These experimental results showcase MoCL-P's potential to enhance practical machine learning applications by effectively managing computational costs, thus providing a scalable and efficient solution for real-world scenarios where minimum resource requirements are crucial.

Limitations

While MoCL-P demonstrates significant advancements in continual learning, our study has some limitations that should be addressed in future work. First, we only use the long sequence multilingual benchmark, i.e., WikiAnn with 176 tasks, in this work due to the lack of existing long sequence multi-task benchmarks. The absence of these benchmarks limits the evaluation of MoCL-P's performance across diverse multi-task scenarios. Building a long sequence multi-task benchmark for continual learning would be an interesting research direction, although it is beyond the scope of this work. Second, as we follow the evaluation setup from prior works, we do not include generative tasks for evaluation. Therefore, we may not capture the potential of MoCL-P in a wider range of continual learning challenges. Including generative tasks in future evaluations would provide a more comprehensive understanding of MoCL-P's capabilities.

References

Rahaf Aljundi, Francesca Babiloni, Mohamed Elhoseiny, Marcus Rohrbach, and Tinne Tuytelaars. 2018. Memory aware synapses: Learning what (not) to forget. In *Proceedings of the European conference on computer vision (ECCV)*, pages 139–154.

Rie Kubota Ando and Tong Zhang. 2005. A framework for learning predictive structures from multiple tasks and unlabeled data. *Journal of Machine Learning Research*, 6:1817–1853.

Galen Andrew and Jianfeng Gao. 2007. Scalable training of L1-regularized log-linear models. In *Proceedings of the 24th International Conference on Machine Learning*, pages 33–40.

Neil Houlsby, Andrei Giurgiu, Stanislaw Jastrzebski, Bruna Morrone, Quentin De Laroussilhe, Andrea Gesmundo, Mona Attariyan, and Sylvain Gelly. 2019. Parameter-efficient transfer learning for nlp. In *International Conference on Machine Learning*, pages 2790–2799. PMLR.

Edward J Hu, Yelong Shen, Phillip Wallis, Zeyuan Allen-Zhu, Yuanzhi Li, Shean Wang, Lu Wang, and Weizhu Chen. 2021. Lora: Low-rank adaptation of large language models. *arXiv preprint arXiv:2106.09685*.

Xiaolei Huang. 2022. Easy adaptation to mitigate gender bias in multilingual text classification. In *Proceedings of the 2022 Conference of the North American Chapter of the Association for Computational Linguistics: Human Language Technologies*, pages 717–723, Seattle, United States. Association for Computational Linguistics.

Zixuan Ke, Hu Xu, and Bing Liu. 2021. Adapting BERT for continual learning of a sequence of aspect sentiment classification tasks. In *Proceedings of the 2021 Conference of the North American Chapter of the Association for Computational Linguistics: Human Language Technologies*, pages 4746–4755, Online. Association for Computational Linguistics.

James Kirkpatrick, Razvan Pascanu, Neil Rabinowitz, Joel Veness, Guillaume Desjardins, Andrei A Rusu, Kieran Milan, John Quan, Tiago Ramalho, Agnieszka Grabska-Barwinska, et al. 2017. Overcoming catastrophic forgetting in neural networks. *Proceedings of the national academy of sciences*, 114(13):3521–3526.

Xiang Lisa Li and Percy Liang. 2021. Prefix-tuning: Optimizing continuous prompts for generation. In *Proceedings of the 59th Annual Meeting of the Association for Computational Linguistics and the 11th International Joint Conference on Natural Language Processing (Volume 1: Long Papers)*, pages 4582–4597.

Zhizhong Li and Derek Hoiem. 2017. Learning without forgetting. *IEEE transactions on pattern analysis and machine intelligence*, 40(12):2935–2947.

Ilya Loshchilov and Frank Hutter. 2017. Decoupled weight decay regularization. *arXiv preprint arXiv:1711.05101*.

Andrew Maas, Raymond E Daly, Peter T Pham, Dan Huang, Andrew Y Ng, and Christopher Potts. 2011. Learning word vectors for sentiment analysis. In *Proceedings of the 49th annual meeting of the association for computational linguistics: Human language technologies*, pages 142–150.

Andrea Madotto, Zhaojiang Lin, Zhenpeng Zhou, Seungwhan Moon, Paul Crook, Bing Liu, Zhou Yu, Eunjoon Cho, and Zhiguang Wang. 2020. Continual learning in task-oriented dialogue systems. *arXiv preprint arXiv:2012.15504*.

Michael McCloskey and Neal J Cohen. 1989. Catastrophic interference in connectionist networks: The sequential learning problem. In *Psychology of learning and motivation*, volume 24, pages 109–165. Elsevier.

Shamsuddeen Hassan Muhammad, Idris Abdulmumin, Abinew Ali Ayele, Nedjma Ousidhoum, David Ifeoluwa Adelani, Seid Muhie Yimam, Ibrahim Sa'id Ahmad, Meriem Beloucif, Saif Mohammad, Sebastian Ruder, et al. 2023. Afrisenti: A twitter sentiment analysis benchmark for african languages. *arXiv preprint arXiv:2302.08956*.

Xiaoman Pan, Boliang Zhang, Jonathan May, Joel Nothman, Kevin Knight, and Heng Ji. 2017. Cross-lingual name tagging and linking for 282 languages.

In *Proceedings of the 55th Annual Meeting of the Association for Computational Linguistics (Volume 1: Long Papers)*, pages 1946–1958, Vancouver, Canada. Association for Computational Linguistics.

Mohammad Sadegh Rasooli and Joel R. Tetreault. 2015. Yara parser: A fast and accurate dependency parser. *Computing Research Repository*, arXiv:1503.06733. Version 2.

Anastasia Razdaibiedina, Yuning Mao, Rui Hou, Madian Khabsa, Mike Lewis, and Amjad Almahairi. 2022. Progressive prompts: Continual learning for language models. In *The Eleventh International Conference on Learning Representations*.

Sylvestre-Alvise Rebuffi, Alexander Kolesnikov, Georg Sperl, and Christoph H Lampert. 2017. icarl: Incremental classifier and representation learning. In *Proceedings of the IEEE conference on Computer Vision and Pattern Recognition*, pages 2001–2010.

David Rolnick, Arun Ahuja, Jonathan Schwarz, Timothy Lillicrap, and Gregory Wayne. 2019. Experience replay for continual learning. *Advances in Neural Information Processing Systems*, 32.

Hanul Shin, Jung Kwon Lee, Jaehong Kim, and Jiwon Kim. 2017. Continual learning with deep generative replay. *Advances in neural information processing systems*, 30.

Xin Su, Shangqi Guo, Tian Tan, and Feng Chen. 2019. Generative memory for lifelong learning. *IEEE transactions on neural networks and learning systems*, 31(6):1884–1898.

Alex Wang, Amanpreet Singh, Julian Michael, Felix Hill, Omer Levy, and Samuel Bowman. 2018. Glue: A multi-task benchmark and analysis platform for natural language understanding. In *Proceedings of the 2018 EMNLP Workshop BlackboxNLP: Analyzing and Interpreting Neural Networks for NLP*, pages 353–355.

Liyuan Wang, Xingxing Zhang, Hang Su, and Jun Zhu. 2023a. A comprehensive survey of continual learning: Theory, method and application. *arXiv preprint arXiv:2302.00487*.

Mingyang Wang, Heike Adel, Lukas Lange, Jannik Strötgen, and Hinrich Schuetze. 2023b. GradSim: Gradient-based language grouping for effective multilingual training. In *Proceedings of the 2023 Conference on Empirical Methods in Natural Language Processing*, Singapore.

Mingyang Wang, Heike Adel, Lukas Lange, Jannik Strötgen, and Hinrich Schuetze. 2024. Rehearsal-free modular and compositional continual learning for language models. In *Proceedings of the 2024 Conference of the North American Chapter of the Association for Computational Linguistics: Human Language Technologies (Volume 2: Short Papers)*, Mexico City, Mexico. Association for Computational Linguistics.

Mingyang Wang, Heike Adel, Lukas Lange, Jannik Strötgen, and Hinrich Schütze. 2023c. NLNDE at SemEval-2023 task 12: Adaptive pretraining and source language selection for low-resource multilingual sentiment analysis. In *Proceedings of the 17th International Workshop on Semantic Evaluation (SemEval-2023)*, pages 488–497, Toronto, Canada. Association for Computational Linguistics.

Xiao Wang, Tianze Chen, Qiming Ge, Han Xia, Rong Bao, Rui Zheng, Qi Zhang, Tao Gui, and Xuan-Jing Huang. 2023d. Orthogonal subspace learning for language model continual learning. In *Findings of the Association for Computational Linguistics: EMNLP 2023*, pages 10658–10671.

Zhicheng Wang, Yufang Liu, Tao Ji, Xiaoling Wang, Yuanbin Wu, Congcong Jiang, Ye Chao, Zhencong Han, Ling Wang, Xu Shao, and Wenqiu Zeng. 2023e. Rehearsal-free continual language learning via efficient parameter isolation. In *Proceedings of the 61st Annual Meeting of the Association for Computational Linguistics (Volume 1: Long Papers)*, pages 10933–10946, Toronto, Canada. Association for Computational Linguistics.

Zifeng Wang, Zizhao Zhang, Sayna Ebrahimi, Ruoxi Sun, Han Zhang, Chen-Yu Lee, Xiaoqi Ren, Guolong Su, Vincent Perot, Jennifer Dy, et al. 2022. Dual-prompt: Complementary prompting for rehearsal-free continual learning. In *European Conference on Computer Vision*, pages 631–648. Springer.

Jaehong Yoon, Eunho Yang, Jeongtae Lee, and Sung Ju Hwang. 2017. Lifelong learning with dynamically expandable networks. *arXiv preprint arXiv:1708.01547*.

Xiang Zhang, Junbo Zhao, and Yann LeCun. 2015. Character-level convolutional networks for text classification. *Advances in neural information processing systems*, 28.

Yanzhe Zhang, Xuezhi Wang, and Diyi Yang. 2022a. Continual sequence generation with adaptive compositional modules. In *Proceedings of the 60th Annual Meeting of the Association for Computational Linguistics (Volume 1: Long Papers)*, pages 3653–3667, Dublin, Ireland. Association for Computational Linguistics.

Yanzhe Zhang, Xuezhi Wang, and Diyi Yang. 2022b. Continual sequence generation with adaptive compositional modules. *arXiv preprint arXiv:2203.10652*.

Qi Zhu, Bing Li, Fei Mi, Xiaoyan Zhu, and Minlie Huang. 2022. Continual prompt tuning for dialog state tracking. In *Proceedings of the 60th Annual Meeting of the Association for Computational Linguistics (Volume 1: Long Papers)*, pages 1124–1137, Dublin, Ireland. Association for Computational Linguistics.

A Appendix

A.1 Dataset Information

Here we provide detailed information on the datasets used in this work. The MTL15 benchmark consists of 15 classification tasks, combining five datasets from the standard CL benchmark MTL5 (AG News, Amazon reviews, Yelp reviews, DBpedia, and Yahoo Answers) (Zhang et al., 2015), four tasks from the GLUE benchmark (MNLI, QQP, RTE, SST2) (Wang et al., 2018), five tasks from the SuperGLUE benchmark (WiC, CB, COPA, MultiRC, BoolQ), and the IMDB movie reviews dataset (Maas et al., 2011). Details of the MTL15 benchmark are provided in Table 4. Following Wang et al. (2024), we use AfriSenti (Muhammad et al., 2023; Wang et al., 2023c), a multilingual sentiment analysis dataset covering 12 low-resource African languages, including Amharic (am), Algerian Arabic (dz), Hausa (ha), Igbo (ig), Kinyarwanda (kr), Moroccan Arabic (ma), Nigerian Pidgin (pcm), Mozambican Portuguese (pt), Swahili (sw), Xitsonga (ts), Twi (twi), and Yoruba (yo). Additionally, to further evaluate the module pruning capability of MoCL-P, we include WikiAnn, a multilingual named entity recognition (NER) dataset that covers 176 languages. The long task sequence in WikiAnn provides an adequate testbed for evaluating the pruning functionality of MoCL-P. Due to space constraints, we do not list the names of the 176 languages and their corresponding abbreviations. The specific language information is available at https://huggingface.co/datasets/wikiann.

We use different task orders for each dataset to evaluate the robustness of continual learning methods against changing task orders. For the MTL15 and AfriSenti benchmarks, we follow the task orders used in prior works, while for the WikiAnn benchmarks, we generate three random task orders for evaluation. The task orders used are summarized in Table 6.

A.2 Experiment Details

In this section, we provide the implementation details for the experiments and a detailed description of the baseline methods used in this work.

A.2.1 Implementation Details

We use the AdamW optimizer (Loshchilov and Hutter, 2017) for all experiments. We choose the same maximum sequence length and prefix length as prior work (Razdaibiedina et al., 2022; Wang et al., 2023e). Table 5 provides detailed hyperparameter choices for MoCL-P across different datasets. The training was performed on Nvidia A100 GPUs.[7]

A.2.2 Baseline Methods

In Section 6, we evaluate MoCL-P and prior continual learning methods on different benchmark datasets. Here, we provide a more detailed description of the baseline methods used in this work.

ProgPrompt (Razdaibiedina et al., 2022): A parameter isolation-based continual learning method that assigns task-specific parameters to avoid catastrophic forgetting. During continual learning, ProgPrompt progressively concatenates all task-specific modules to encourage forward transfer.

EPI (Wang et al., 2023e): A parameter isolation-based method applicable to the class-incremental learning setting (CIL), where task identities are not given during inference. EPI introduces a non-parametric task identification module that identifies tasks during testing. Given reliable task identification, the CIL performance of EPI could be comparable to TIL, where the ground truth task identities are given during inference.

O-LoRA (Wang et al., 2023d): A parameter isolation-based method that learns tasks in different low-rank vector spaces that are kept orthogonal to each other to minimize interference. It mitigates catastrophic forgetting by constraining the gradient update of the current task to be orthogonal to the gradient space of past tasks. However, the orthogonality of the gradient subspace for individual tasks also limits knowledge transfer between tasks.

MoCL (Wang et al., 2024): Introduces a modular and compositional continual learning framework to compose the new module with existing ones based on task module matching. This compositional strategy enables effective knowledge transfer by considering task interaction.

As discussed in Section 2, we build on the idea of MoCL (Wang et al., 2024) by utilizing task representations for module composition, ensuring that the model effectively reuses relevant knowledge from previous tasks. Beyond that, we introduce an adaptive pruning strategy to keep the language model lightweight and effective throughout the continual learning process, making it scalable for continual learning scenarios with long task sequences.

[7] All experiments ran on a carbon-neutral GPU cluster.

Dataset name	Category	Task	Domain
Yelp	MTL5	sentiment analysis	Yelp reviews
Amazon	MTL5	sentiment analysis	Amazon reviews
DBpedia	MTL5	topic classification	Wikipedia
Yahoo	MTL5	QA	Yahoo Q&A
AG News	MTL5	topic classification	news
MNLI	GLUE	NLI	various
QQP	GLUE	paraphrase detection	Quora
RTE	GLUE	NLI	news, Wikipedia
SST2	GLUE	sentiment analysis	movie reviews
WiC	SuperGLUE	word sense disambiguation	lexical databases
CB	SuperGLUE	NLI	various
COPA	SuperGLUE	QA	blogs, encyclopedia
BoolQ	SuperGLUE	boolean QA	Wikipedia
MultiRC	SuperGLUE	QA	various
IMDB	Other	sentiment analysis	movie reviews

Table 4: The details of 15 datasets used in the MTL15 benchmark. NLI denotes natural language inference, and QA denotes questions and answers task.

	Hyperparameters		
	AfriSenti-AfroXLMR	WikiAnn-BERT	MTL15-T5
Epochs	40	5	40
Early stop patience	5	N/A	5
Batch size	8	32	8
Learning rate	2e-4	1e-3	5e-2
Max. sequence length	256	128	512
Prefix length	16	8	10

Table 5: Hyperparameters used in this work across different CL experiments.

Table 6: The different orders of task sequences used for continual learning experiments.

Dataset	Order	Model	Task Sequence
AfriSenti	1	AfroXLMR	am → dz → ha → ig → kr → ma → pcm → pt → sw → ts → twi → yo
	2	AfroXLMR	ma → pcm → kr → pt → ig → sw → ha → ts → dz → twi → am → yo
	3	AfroXLMR	am → dz → ha → ma → ig → kr → sw → ts → twi → yo → pcm → pt
MTL15	1	T5	mnli → cb → wic → copa → qqp → boolq → rte → imdb → yelp → amazon → sst2 → dbpedia → ag → multirc → yahoo
	2	T5	multirc → boolq → wic → mnli → cb → copa → qqp → rte → imdb → sst2 → dbpedia → ag → yelp → amazon → yahoo
	3	T5	yelp → amazon → mnli → cb → copa → qqp → rte → imdb → sst2 → dbpedia → ag → yahoo → multirc → boolq → wic
WikiAnn	1	BERT	ga → fi → sco → bs → co → pnb → eu → vls → os → de → hy → mwl → ca → or → wa → rw → simple → tl → crh → lij → min → ko → scn → an → mk → hi → ug → ext → sl → sw → nap → et → wuu → uz → mzn → ast → jv → su → ilo → csb → cdo → tk → ckb → lv → ur → th → am → kn → pms → ba → tt → pl → vec → ru → cs → ne → bn → es → fy → fiu-vro → bo → mt → fr → mr → nn → bar → ang → no → fo → el → qu → fa → eml → kk → tr → pt → km → dv → hsb → rm → ta → fur → war → frr → ps → io → da → zh-yue → ms → cv → diq → mn → lb → cy → sa → ig → oc → hu → arc → ln → ku → hr → nds → az → ar → ce → lt → zea → it → zh-classical → be-x-old → mi → ia → is → la → sv → nl → gd → pa → xmf → ksh → zh-min-nan → lmo → tg → sh → eo → zh → te → he → vep → as → yi → cbk-zam → yo → ro → ace → id → jbo → nov → bg → map-bms → be → sr → sah → ml → my → vo → so → gu → br → gl → ka → li → pdc → ky → bat-smg → als → mg → szl → gn → ceb → vi → sq → mhr → ay → en → bh → uk → gan → sk → si → hak → af → ja → arz → sd

Continued on next page

Table 6 – continued from previous page

Dataset	Order	Model	Task Sequence
	2	BERT	wuu → cy → mwl → eu → gn → scn → ka → pdc → it → ro → pnb → ig → tl → sah → is → ga → ml → wa → vo → simple → hr → dv → mn → csb → sl → gl → fy → bn → tg → fr → th → vls → arz → zh-classical → ln → tr → su → min → si → ur → sr → et → eo → sh → li → fiu-vro → rw → no → mg → mr → oc → nap → yi → pa → lt → ug → co → tt → sv → uk → so → ext → ky → ru → kk → sa → la → el → hsb → be-x-old → bg → pt → bh → br → mt → ne → id → te → cv → fo → cdo → bs → lij → sw → he → ceb → hak → es → kn → mk → am → or → ms → az → als → my → ce → os → ca → tk → diq → zh → fi → jbo → mhr → ay → pms → rm → zea → en → zh-yue → sco → ang → bo → ar → ia → zh-min-nan → ckb → fa → crh → as → yo → szl → fur → hi → eml → mi → lb → de → bat-smg → uz → lv → nov → ast → cs → hy → sk → sq → be → xmf → af → ps → qu → da → ja → vep → ku → mzn → nl → vec → map-bms → ace → io → gu → bar → ilo → km → arc → cbk-zam → pl → ksh → war → gd → ba → lmo → gan → ko → an → frr → vi → hu → jv → sd → nds → nn → tas
	3	BERT	tl → sah → ckb → qu → az → ast → mr → eo → wa → zh-classical → fiu-vro → eu → nl → map-bms → id → szl → mi → io → lt → war → my → bat-smg → jv → en → zh-min-nan → sh → su → frr → am → hu → hy → zh → ps → hi → tg → pl → nov → dv → min → jbo → diq → ksh → gn → vec → nds → lij → pdc → os → rw → als → sq → fi → da → sr → ru → uz → fr → scn → tt → bh → bn → mwl → et → hsb → kn → rm → nn → mhr → bg → sd → ko → la → ka → de → he → pt → cs → hr → tk → cy → co → or → csb → bar → mt → vo → oc → simple → ml → bs → km → sk → ang → br → xmf → ay → zea → ln → sco → ku → ilo → lv → mzn → zh-yue → gan → ta → gl → ca → hak → mg → ne → ur → cbk-zam → uk → mn → fy → ba → nap → kk → yo → tr → so → fo → ug → ace → fur → pa → lmo → it → be-x-old → sa → arc → ig → lb → ms → th → cv → arz → bo → el → eml → gd → pnb → cdo → ky → af → vls → be → ga → es → yi → si → ext → gu → mk → ja → is → no → ceb → ro → sv → ar → an → te → sl → sw → wuu → pms → fa → vi → as → ce → vep → li → ia → crh

Text-Guided Alternative Image Clustering

Andreas Stephan[1,2,7], **Lukas Miklautz**[1], **Collin Leiber**[5,6], **Pedro Henrique Luz de Araujo**[1,2], **Dominik Répás**[1], **Claudia Plant**[1,3] and **Benjamin Roth**[1,3,4]
[1] Faculty of Computer Science, [2] UniVie Doctoral School Computer Science,
[3] ds:UniVie, [4] Faculty of Philological and Cultural Studies,
University of Vienna, Vienna, Austria
[5] LMU Munich, Germany
[6] Munich Center for Machine Learning, Munich, Germany
[7]andreas.stephan@univie.ac.at

Abstract

Traditional image clustering techniques only find a single grouping within visual data. In particular, they do not provide a possibility to explicitly define multiple types of clustering. This work explores the potential of large vision-language models to facilitate alternative image clustering. We propose Text-Guided Alternative Image Consensus Clustering (TGAICC), a novel approach that leverages user-specified interests via prompts to guide the discovery of diverse clusterings. To achieve this, it generates a clustering for each prompt, groups them using hierarchical clustering, and then aggregates them using consensus clustering. TGAICC outperforms image- and text-based baselines on four alternative image clustering benchmark datasets. Furthermore, using count-based word statistics, we are able to obtain text-based explanations of the alternative clusterings. In conclusion, our research illustrates how contemporary large vision-language models can transform explanatory data analysis, enabling the generation of insightful, customizable, and diverse image clusterings. [1]

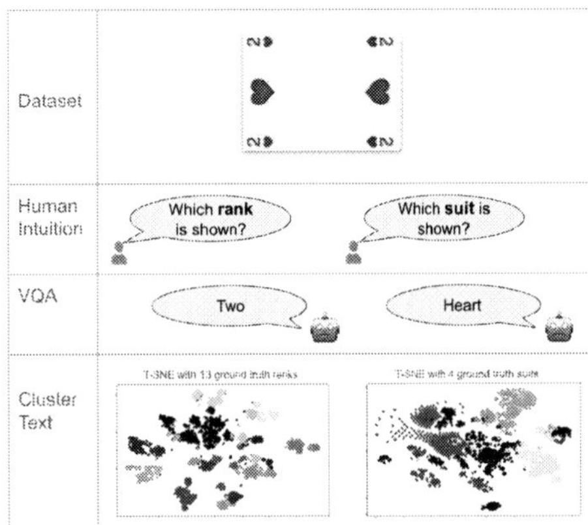

Figure 1: Assume we have an image of a card depicting a "heart two". Given two different user queries, the VQA model gives different responses. Clustering the generated text based on different prompts results in alternative clusterings that satisfy different needs. The colors in the figure represent the ground truths of "rank" and "suit" for different generated texts.

1 Introduction

Exploratory data analysis (EDA) is crucial in the comprehension and analysis of data (Tukey, 1970). Clustering arises as a cornerstone EDA methodology, facilitating the grouping of similar data objects into coherent groups. A dataset of images, for example, can be clustered based on semantic similarities between the shown objects. Nevertheless, within applied contexts, variations in user requirements or foci demand distinct clustering formations. One might, for instance, cluster a dataset of cards by rank or by suit (see Figure 1). In such circumstances, it is advantageous to derive multifaceted insights into a dataset from diverse perspectives.

Current approaches in alternative image clustering either rely on image-based features (Mautz et al., 2018; Miklautz et al., 2020) or utilize text through image-text bi-encoders, often with architectures resembling CLIP (Radford et al., 2021; Yao et al., 2024). These methods, while powerful, neglect the rich insights that can be extracted by models explicitly trained to retrieve specific aspects of information from images using text (e.g., visual question answering (VQA) models (Antol et al., 2015)). Stephan et al. (2024) demonstrate the effectiveness of using generated text descriptions to improve standard image clustering tasks, i.e. in scenarios where a single clustering structure is expected.

We aim to use image-to-text models to obtain alternative clusterings. By encoding visual content into text, similarity dimensions beyond the visual features can be explored, potentially revealing interpretable relationships. We introduce *TGAICC*

[1]Code available at `https://github.com/AndSt/alternative_image_clustering`.

Proceedings of the 9th Workshop on Representation Learning for NLP (RepL4NLP-2024), pages 177–190
August 15, 2024

(Text-Guided Alternative Image Consensus Clustering), a clustering method that uses the output of multiple image-to-text models to obtain alternative clusterings. TGAICC incorporates VQA models to generate multiple textual descriptions of images and then clusters the images based on the generated natural language descriptions. We identify similar clusterings using their mutual information, group them using hierarchical clustering and aggregate them using consensus clustering to form refined, alternative clusterings.

Our experimental setup employs four widely used alternative image clustering datasets, each possessing two or three ground truth labelings (e.g., playing cards clustered by rank or suit). We compare TGAICC against baselines for alternative clustering using image-only features and baselines that make use of the generated text. Our experiments demonstrate the following key findings: methods clustering the generated text outperform methods based on image features on these alternative clustering datasets, underscoring the power of textual representations in capturing diverse aspects of similarity. Further, TGAICC, on average, achieves superior results across the evaluated datasets and metrics when compared to all other methods, highlighting the effectiveness of our framework in leveraging image-to-text models to uncover alternative and insightful clusterings. Lastly, we can better interpret the clusterings by explaining the content using word statistics. Our case study on the cards dataset shows that text provides an opportunity to obtain an informative overview of the data.

In summary, our research provides the following contributions:

1. We introduce a prompt-based setup to obtain alternative image clusterings.

2. We introduce TGAICC, a method that combines ideas from multi-modality, hierarchical clustering, and consensus clustering to obtain alternative clusterings.

3. Our experiments on four common alternative image clustering datasets show that TGAICC outperforms baseline algorithms.

4. Our methodology enables the ability to generate textual cluster explanations, offering a clear overview of the unique content captured within each alternative clustering.

2 Related Work

This work builds upon image clustering, consensus clustering, and alternative clustering approaches. We provide a brief overview of these relevant areas and describe the necessary background.

2.1 Image Clustering

Research in image clustering has addressed several standard issues, and a variety of techniques have been developed to tackle them. (Ezugwu et al., 2022) provide a survey on clustering approaches. Classic approaches like k-means (Lloyd, 1982) have demonstrated effectiveness but often struggle with complex or high-dimensional image data. To address these limitations, more recent work has explored deep clustering methods such as DEC (Xie et al., 2016) and IDEC (Guo et al., 2017). In addition to these core techniques, representation learning and more specifically, self-supervised learning (Jaiswal et al., 2021) has emerged as a vital aspect of image clustering (Lehner et al., 2023; Adaloglou et al., 2023). In Contrastive Clustering (Li et al., 2021), the authors use one loss contrasting image features and another loss contrasting clustering features, i.e., the predicted cluster of two augmentations of the same image. A different approach is used in Text-Guided Image Clustering (Stephan et al., 2024). This paradigm leverages image-to-text models and subsequently cluster text. The observation that text often outperforms image-based features motivates this work.

2.2 Consensus Clustering

Variability in clustering results arises from different clustering algorithms or variations in their initializations. Given that different clusterings potentially reveal different insights (e.g., accurately identifying a cluster representing "hearts"). Consensus clustering methods aim to aggregate results from multiple base clustering algorithms to produce a more robust and stable final clustering. The problem was formalized by (Strehl and Ghosh, 2002) and the authors introduce the Cluster-based Similarity Partitioning Algorithm (CSPA), HyperGraph Partitioning Algorithm (HGPA), and the Meta-CLustering Algorithm (MCLA). All three methods employ similarity functions, e.g. Normalized Mutual Information (NMI), to construct a similarity graph and use graph theory to obtain a consensus clustering. In (Li and Ding, 2008), non-negative matrix factorization (NMF) is used to obtain a consensus clustering.

The Hybrid Bipartite Graph Formulation (HBGF) (Fern and Brodley, 2004) employs a bipartite graph representation. In (Miklautz et al., 2022), the authors introduce DECCS, a deep learning-based consensus method, which learns a representation on which heterogeneous clustering algorithms share a consensus on the obtained clusterings.

2.3 Alternative Clustering

Clustering methods usually focus on finding a single optimal clustering solution. Motivated by the fact that there may be multiple meaningful ways to group data points, alternative clustering approaches aim to uncover multiple, diverse clustering structures within the same data (Yu et al., 2024; Müller et al., 2012).

Cui et al. (2007) first apply a traditional clustering algorithm and then transform the dataset into a feature space orthogonal to the current clustering. Two strategies are proposed: orthogonal clustering (orth1) and clustering in orthogonal subspaces (orth2). In contrast, Non-redundant K-means (Nr-Kmeans) (Mautz et al., 2018) simultaneously identifies multiple clusterings within a dataset by iteratively rotating the feature space and assigning features to specific clusterings. ENRC (Miklautz et al., 2020) is a deep non-redundant clustering method that learns multiple clusterings from a dataset by (soft-)assigning each dimension of the embedded space to a clustering. In (Kwon et al., 2024), the authors provide initial text criteria, e.g., suits and ranks, and use image-to-text models to extract information, and then GPT-4 to obtain cluster names and classify images into clusters. Thus, this approach is expensive. In concurrent work, (Yao et al., 2024) use GPT-4 to generate cluster name candidates and contrastively fine-tune CLIP (Radford et al., 2021).

2.4 Image-To-Text Models

Recently, the development of multimodal models has seen rapid advancement. Image-to-text models, in particular, learn to associate visual content with corresponding textual descriptions, which is useful for, e.g., visual question-answering (VQA) (Yin et al., 2023; Antol et al., 2015).

Flamingo (Alayrac et al., 2022) allows interleaving images and text by using Perceiver Resamplers on top of pre-trained models. BLIP and BLIP2 (Li et al., 2022, 2023a) employ a frozen image encoder along with a frozen LLM to generate text. LLaVA and LLaVA-NeXT(Liu et al., 2023b,a) convert image patches into token embeddings using a fixed Vision Transformer encoder followed by a trained MLP. These tokens then become the input for the LLM, enhancing the descriptive results.

In this work, we use LLaVA to extract relevant information from images. More specifically, we frame the image-to-text generation as a VQA task: we prompt LLaVA with an image and corresponding questions about it to generate natural language descriptions of the image.

3 TGAICC

We use image-to-text models, specifically models that are able to describe specific aspects of information from images in order to obtain different clusterings. Thus, we design prompts to perform VQA. It is well known (Bach et al., 2022; Sclar et al., 2024) that responses to seemingly semantically equal prompts might vary heavily. Thus, we use multiple formulations of each prompt and aggregate their clusterings afterward. Figure 2 gives an overview of the process.

Setup. The input to TGAICC is a dataset of k datapoints, t initial prompts, and, as common in the alternative-clustering literature, the number of clusters in the ground truth clusterings $\{z_1, \dots, z_t\}, z_i \in \mathbb{N}$. E.g., $\{2, 4\}$ means the algorithm should return one clustering with 2 and one clustering with 4 clusters. Note that the difference between the traditional alternative clustering setup and ours is that we assume additional initial prompts. The output is comprised of t clusterings where the k data points are grouped into $z_1, \dots, z_t$ clusters.

3.1 Initialization

The initialization encompasses step 1 to step 4 in Figure 2 and returns a set of clusterings.

Prompt Design In Step 1, we write a query and ask GPT-4 (OpenAI et al., 2024) to automatically generate additional questions. The specific prompt is '*Generate three diverse paraphrases for the following question: {initial question}*'. Further, we generate a variation of each prompt by appending the directive "Write concisely.", aiming to reduce the verbosity of the responses. The output is depicted in Step 2. This is based on the observation that image clusters are often described by succinct short descriptors, e.g., the datasets in our experiments or ImageNet-based (Deng et al., 2009) clustering datasets. Thus, these prompts align with our knowledge about the clustering tasks.

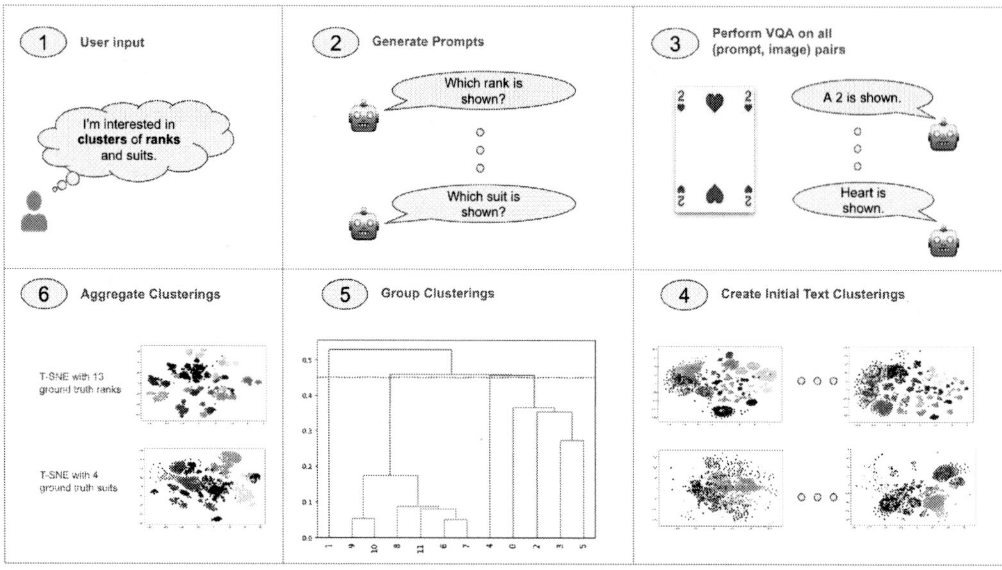

Figure 2: An overview of our methodology. In 1) a user provides text, indicating his interest in the data. In 2) a LLM generates a set of prompts tailored to extract specific information from images, and in 3) VQA is performed for each prompt on each data sample. In 4) the texts generated per prompt are clustered (colors resemble ground truth "rank" and "suit"). In 5) a hierarchy of similar clusterings is built. Based on a threshold (dotted line), multiple groups of clusterings (green and orange) are identified and in 6) aggregated to obtain the final alternative clusterings.

Initial Clustering In Step 3, we perform VQA for each pair of images and prompts, generating responses relevant to the visual content. Next, in Step 4, we create text representations using both traditional TF-IDF (Sparck Jones, 1988) and an advanced sentence embedding model, namely *gte-large* (Li et al., 2023b). Finally, we apply k-means to these text representations and obtain a clustering for each prompt and each representation.

3.2 Grouping

The input to the grouping stage are n pairs of prompt and corresponding clustering $(p_i, \pi_i), i \in [n]$ and the number of ground truth clustering sizes $\{z_1, \ldots, z_t\}, z_i \in \mathbb{N}$, e.g. $\{2, 4\}$. The goal is to obtain groups of clusterings to later find consensus between the individual clusterings explaining the data from a similar perspective. This is displayed in Step 5 of Figure 2. Specifically, we aim to connect semantically similar clusterings and detect potential outlier clusterings, which are caused by prompts leading to unexpected or inconsistent VQA outcomes and are not useful for our final clustering. Find examples of generated text in Table 6.

Therefore, we compute the similarity of two clusterings using Adjusted Mutual Information (AMI) (Vinh et al., 2010). We choose AMI as it is a standard clustering metric based on information theory. Then, we use a spanning-tree-based hierarchical clustering (Müllner, 2011) algorithm[2] to systematically group similar prompts, facilitating a structured analysis of clustering behavior (see Step 5 of Figure 2). The basic idea is that for a threshold $\tau \in (0, 1)$, two clusterings A, B are connected if their distance is less than τ, i.e. $AMI(A, B) < \tau$. Here, we use two strategies, which we call "min" and "max". For "min", we find a minimum threshold such that the resulting number of groups is equal to the number of expected groupings t. For "max", we find a maximum threshold such that this constraint is fulfilled. We use the trivial solution to iterate over all thresholds in $\tau \in (0, 1)$ in steps of 0.02 as the runtime is negligible.

3.3 Aggregation

In the end, we synthesize each group of clusterings. Given that we aggregate potentially very different clusterings, it is beneficial to use different aggregation schemes. Therefore, we apply multi-

[2]Algorithm is readily available in the Scipy library (Virtanen et al., 2020): `https://docs.scipy.org/doc/scipy/reference/generated/scipy.cluster.hierarchy.fcluster.html`

ple consensus clustering algorithms for each group and choose the instance with the lowest clustering loss. Specifically, we employ MCLA, HBGF, CSPA, and NMF (Strehl and Ghosh, 2002; Li and Ding, 2008) to aggregate the clusterings within the groups[3]. Thereby, we aim to use consensus clustering to combine the strength of multiple clusterings. In our ablation analysis we also test the simple solution where we concatenate the generated text of the prompts in each clustering group and perform k-means on the concatenated string.

4 Experiments

In this section, we introduce the experimental setup. Afterwards, we discuss the main results obtained, highlighting the performance of TGAICC and text-based methods. Additionally, we provide an ablation study, systematically analyzing the impact of various components and prompts on the overall performance. Finally, we perform a simple cluster explainability method to get a textual overview of the data.

Dataset	#samples	#clusters	Size
Fruits-360	4856	4; 4	100x100
Cards	8029	3; 4	224x224
GTSRB	6720	4; 2	15x15 to 250x250
NR-Objects	10000	6; 2; 3	100x100

Table 1: Overview of statistics of the dataset. The third column contains the number of clusters in the ground truth clusterings.

4.1 Experimental Setup

In this section, we outline the key components of our experimental setup, including the evaluation metrics, data representations, and models used. All experiments were run on a single A100 GPU. VQA took approximately 24 hours, and TGAICC experiments took about the same amount of time. Embedding text and running consensus clustering are the most time-consuming elements. Each algorithm is executed 10 times with different random states, and we report the average performance across these runs.

4.1.1 Metrics

We employ two widely used metrics to assess the performance of our clustering models. The Adjusted Rand Index (ARI) (Rand, 1971) measures the similarity between the predicted cluster assignments and the ground truth labels, adjusting for chance agreement. The Adjusted Mutual Information (AMI) (Vinh et al., 2010) quantifies the shared information between the predicted clusters and the true labels. We multiply by 100 to increase readability.

4.1.2 Representations

We utilize image- and text-based representations to capture different aspects of the data.

Image Embeddings: We utilize the LLaVA-NeXT model (Liu et al., 2023a), which incorporates the image encoder of a frozen CLIP model. This allows us to directly use the image embeddings learned during the contrastive pre-training of CLIP (Radford et al., 2021) for our clustering tasks.

Statistical text embeddings: We employ Term Frequency-Inverse Document Frequency (TF-IDF) embeddings, a standard word frequency-based technique for representing documents.

Neural text embeddings: To better capture semantic relationships, we employ the "gte-large"[4] model (Li et al., 2023b), a state-of-the-art sentence encoder.

4.1.3 Datasets

In the following, we briefly describe the used datasets. Table 1 summarizes the relevant statistics for all datasets. More details about datasets and corresponding prompts are given in Appendix A.

Cards[5] This dataset is primarily used for classification tasks but contains attributes suitable for clustering based on the suit and rank of the cards.

Fruits-360 (Mureșan and Oltean, 2018) The dataset is composed of images that can be clustered by fruit type (citrus, berries, etc.) and color.

NR-Objects (Miklautz et al., 2020) The dataset contains images of objects (e.g., cubes), which can be clustered by shape, material, or color.

German Traffic Sign Recognition (GTSRB) (Houben et al., 2013) This dataset contains traffic signs and can be clustered by color and traffic sign type.

[3]We used the library Cluster Ensembles: https://github.com/GGiecold-zz/Cluster_Ensembles

[4]Model is available on Hugging Face (https://huggingface.co/thenlper/gte-large, and is used via the Sentence-BERT (SBERT) library (Reimers and Gurevych, 2019)

[5]https://www.kaggle.com/datasets/gpiosenka/cards-imagedatasetclassification

Dataset	Type		Image k-means	Image orth-1	Image orth-2	Image Nr-Kmeans	Image ENRC	TF-IDF Avg. Prompt	TF-IDF Concatenate	SBERT Avg. Prompt	SBERT Concatenate	TGAICC
Fruits-360	fruit	ARI	27.40	31.50	30.80	**35.40**	26.00	14.80	20.10	15.10	17.20	18.60
		AMI	41.30	42.10	42.90	**50.60**	36.70	24.80	32.20	25.00	28.60	26.90
	colour	ARI	33.20	35.40	33.50	40.90	39.70	40.00	54.60	47.40	51.60	**54.70**
		AMI	47.30	53.30	51.70	55.50	54.90	50.70	**65.50**	56.90	60.80	64.80
GTSRB	type	ARI	41.70	46.80	46.80	22.70	38.20	45.10	**61.00**	49.70	57.50	58.00
		AMI	51.50	55.50	55.50	38.60	**72.50**	52.40	67.90	55.50	63.20	64.60
	colour	ARI	23.00	0.10	0.10	49.00	55.90	79.20	87.40	88.50	**90.00**	88.00
		AMI	33.40	0.10	0.10	43.30	28.30	73.70	82.30	82.70	**84.50**	83.00
Cards	rank	ARI	30.10	29.70	26.70	35.70	33.10	24.30	24.70	33.00	**50.70**	34.70
		AMI	47.80	47.60	41.70	55.20	52.40	41.30	41.60	50.00	**68.40**	50.20
	suit	ARI	25.90	1.10	3.80	10.60	14.30	19.70	29.60	25.90	28.30	**29.70**
		AMI	34.40	1.20	8.20	16.60	19.80	27.40	37.10	33.60	35.40	**38.30**
NR-Objects	shape	ARI	95.30	94.40	94.40	76.00	72.70	65.70	94.50	75.90	95.00	**100.00**
		AMI	96.20	95.10	95.10	82.20	82.70	71.30	96.50	79.40	95.80	**100.00**
	material	ARI	0.00	26.70	30.60	30.70	**31.60**	9.20	1.60	14.80	0.00	9.00
		AMI	0.00	25.90	38.80	32.70	**39.40**	10.10	1.80	15.00	0.00	17.10
	colour	ARI	9.70	87.00	75.10	50.40	45.70	66.80	91.10	81.20	83.70	**97.80**
		AMI	21.70	93.00	79.00	65.70	66.00	81.20	95.30	88.30	91.40	**97.90**
Avg.		ARI	31.81	39.19	37.98	39.04	39.69	40.53	51.62	47.94	52.67	**54.50**
		AMI	41.51	45.98	45.89	48.93	50.30	48.10	57.80	54.04	58.68	**60.31**

Table 2: Main results table. Best results are in bold, second best results are underlinded.

4.1.4 Baselines

We use multiple image-based alternative clustering baselines and baselines using the generated text. It is important to note that the generated text uses additional information in the form of prompts provided by a user. While this implies that there is no exact comparison between image- and text-based methods, it is also worth noting that it is not possible to incorporate such information into image-based methods trivially. The code is implemented using the ClustPy[6] library (Leiber et al., 2023). Additional details are given in Appendix B.

Orth (Cui et al., 2007) iteratively identifies several clusterings by first clustering using PCA (keeping 90% of the variance) in combination with k-means and then creating a new orthogonal feature space. There are two strategies for orthogonalization: *orthogonal clustering* (orth-1) and *clustering in orthogonal subspaces* (orth-2).

Nr-Kmeans (Mautz et al., 2018) simultaneously optimizes several clusterings by assigning each clustering result a separate subspace in which k-means is executed.

ENRC (Miklautz et al., 2020) is a deep clustering method that assigns multiple clusterings to a dataset by (soft-)assigning each dimension of the embeddings space to a clustering.

Avg. Prompt. We measure the performance of clustering each text generated per prompt and subsequentially report the average performance.

Concat. by Category. We manually group all

[6]https://github.com/collinleiber/ClustPy

			TF-IDF concatenation min	TF-IDF concatenation max	TF-IDF consensus min	TF-IDF consensus max	SBERT concatenation min	SBERT concatenation max	SBERT consensus min	SBERT consensus max
Fruits-360	fruit	ARI	20.80	**24.60**	17.40	19.50	19.60	17.20	15.80	18.60
		AMI	36.60	**39.10**	29.00	32.90	33.00	30.90	23.20	26.90
	colour	ARI	51.80	52.20	51.10	51.90	**58.60**	57.20	54.30	54.70
		AMI	61.70	62.20	60.70	61.40	**71.50**	66.40	64.90	64.80
GTSRB	type	ARI	52.70	**73.20**	49.70	54.10	50.80	58.00	51.60	58.00
		AMI	60.80	**75.40**	56.60	60.40	57.80	64.10	60.00	64.60
	colour	ARI	74.70	74.00	87.10	87.30	73.10	70.20	**88.90**	88.00
		AMI	70.70	70.10	81.60	81.80	70.20	68.60	**83.20**	83.00
Cards	rank	ARI	28.60	28.00	27.00	26.90	40.30	**56.00**	36.30	34.70
		AMI	48.30	47.00	47.60	46.20	58.50	**72.20**	51.30	50.20
	suit	ARI	19.40	20.10	21.60	21.10	19.60	19.90	22.40	**29.70**
		AMI	29.30	28.90	23.60	23.70	30.50	27.30	27.40	**38.30**
NR-Objects	shape	ARI	98.70	98.90	99.30	99.30	**100.00**	**100.00**	**100.00**	**100.00**
		AMI	97.60	97.90	98.90	98.70	**100.00**	**100.00**	**100.00**	**100.00**
	material	ARI	**23.10**	22.40	0.10	1.00	0.00	0.00	9.00	9.00
		AMI	**22.70**	22.20	0.10	1.80	0.00	0.00	17.10	17.10
	colour	ARI	33.30	33.30	80.00	84.10	43.60	43.60	**97.80**	**97.80**
		AMI	65.20	65.20	87.50	90.10	66.60	66.60	**97.90**	**97.90**
Avg.		ARI	44.79	47.41	48.14	49.47	45.07	46.90	52.90	**54.50**
		AMI	54.77	56.44	53.96	55.22	54.23	55.12	58.33	**60.31**

Table 3: An ablation analysis of TGAICC, where "min" and "max" refer to the thresholding strategy, and concatenation and consensus to the aggregation scheme. Consensus-max resembles TGAICC. The best results are in bold, and the second best results are underlined.

prompts together that belong to the same clustering type (e.g., "rank" or "suit"), concatenate all generated text, and cluster it using k-means.

4.2 Main Experiments

The results of our main experiments are shown in Table 2. They reveal that, on average, text-based methods, including TGAICC, outperform image-based methods. Further, we observe that TGAICC, on average, demonstrates superiority over average prompting and concatenation baselines. In addition, we can see that clustering by material in the NR-Objects dataset does not work in the text domain. See Table 6 for VQA examples. The main take-

	Prompt	TF-IDF ARI	TF-IDF AMI	SBERT ARI	SBERT AMI
suit	Can you tell me the suit of the playing card shown in the picture?	25.42	31.25	25.42	31.25
	What suit does the playing card in the image belong to?	25.59	33.53	25.59	33.53
	Could you identify the suit of the playing card depicted in the photo?	**29.29**	33.64	**29.29**	33.64
	Can you tell me the suit of the playing card shown in the picture? Answer concisely.	24.25	**37.32**	24.25	**37.32**
	What suit does the playing card in the image belong to? Answer concisely.	<u>28.97</u>	<u>36.35</u>	<u>28.97</u>	<u>36.35</u>
	Could you identify the suit of the playing card depicted in the photo? Answer concisely.	21.85	29.71	21.85	29.71
rank	Can you tell me the rank of the card shown in the picture?	26.76	43.33	26.76	43.33
	What is the numerical or face value of the card displayed in the image?	32.06	47.36	32.06	47.36
	What level or position does the card in the photo hold?	31.52	47.28	31.52	47.28
	Can you tell me the rank of the card shown in the picture? Answer concisely.	<u>37.48</u>	<u>55.42</u>	<u>37.48</u>	<u>55.42</u>
	What is the numerical or face value of the card displayed in the image? Answer concisely.	**38.79**	**56.09**	**38.79**	**56.09**
	What level or position does the card in the photo hold? Answer concisely.	31.15	50.44	31.15	50.44

Table 4: Ablation study comparing the clustering performance of individual prompts. Here we show a case study based on the Cards dataset. The best results are in bold, and the second-best results are underlined.

away is that, in many cases, the VQA model provides too much information, even information that should be used for a different clustering, e.g., color or shape. This highlights a core limitation of our methodology. If the text generation does not work sufficiently well, the subsequent clustering can not work. Nevertheless, TGAICC is model-agnostic and can be used with any VQA image-to-text system. In this way, it can use future advancements in VQA models.

4.3 Aggregation ablation

In this ablation study, we investigate the aggregation components of TGAICC. More specifically, we investigate the impact of the thresholding and aggregation strategies on clustering performance.

Setup. We ablate the "min" and "max" thresholding strategies, which find the minimum and maximum threshold such that the number of clustering groups corresponds to the expected number of alternative clusterings. We experiment with the consensus-clustering-based aggregation scheme used in TGAICC and compare it to the simple "concatenation" baseline, which concatenates the text of the corresponding clustering groups. Results are shown in Table 3. Note that TGAICC is consensus-max.

Results. Our analysis reveals that consensus clustering outperforms concatenation-based selection. Furthermore, SBERT-based clustering outperforms TF-IDF-based clustering. We observe that the performance of the 'min' and the 'max' strategies are very similar, indicating the stability of the method w.r.t. the thresholding strategy.

Suit Truth	Suit Top Words	Rank Truth	Rank Top Words
heart	heart	ace	ace
diamond	diamond	king	king
club	club	queen	queen
spade	spade	jack	jack
		5	heart
		9	spade
		3	rank
		4	club
		6	diamond
		10	10
		2	twos
		8	8
		7	7

Table 5: This table shows how we are able to explain the datasets by listing the top most used words of the two final clusterings. For each top word, we show the ideal ground truth cluster name assignment.

4.4 Individual prompt analysis

TGAICC is based on the aggregation of multiple clusterings, which in turn are based on generated texts using different VQA prompts. As known from other tasks (Sclar et al., 2024), different prompts potentially result in high-performance variance.

Setup. In Table 4 we analyze the clustering performance per prompt on the case study of the Cards dataset. Note that again, we execute k-means 10 times and present the average results.

Results. In the case study, the addition of the prompt "Answer concisely" mostly yields similar clustering results to the original version, with a slight performance advantage when the "Answer

Material	Image	Question	Generated Text
Rubber	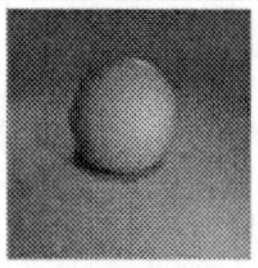	What substance is the item in the picture made of? Answer concisely.	Plastic
		What substance is the item in the picture made of?	The item in the picture appears to be a sphere made of a smooth, shiny material that could be plastic, metal, or a similar synthetic material. It's difficult to determine the exact material without more information or a closer inspection.
Metal	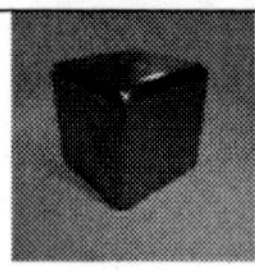	What substance is the item in the picture made of? Answer concisely.	The item in the picture is made of metal.
		Can you identify the material used in the object shown in the image? Answer concisely.	The object in the image appears to be made of a shiny, reflective material, possibly metal or a metal-like material.
		What is the composition of the object depicted in the photo? Answer concisely.	The object in the photo is a 3D rendering of a red cube.

Table 6: Some VQA examples on the NR-Objects dataset. While all answers are reasonable, they often provide too much information, such as information about the shape, or make statements about the ambiguity of the underlying material.

concisely" prompt is included. Furthermore, we note a significant variation in clustering performance across different prompts.

4.5 Explainability

Our cluster explainability aims to provide insights into the different clustering possibilities. This understanding is essential for interpreting and validating clustering outcomes. We use a simple word frequency-based algorithm to explain the data.

Setup. For a specific final clustering of TGAICC, we concatenate all generated texts belonging to the prompts used to obtain this clustering. The resulting text is changed to lowercase and made singular. Finally, to explain a final clustering, we determine the z most frequently occurring words, where z is the number of clusters of the respective clustering. For instance, for the suit clustering $z = 4$. Table 5 shows the resulting words for the Cards dataset. We reorder the ground truth cluster names suitably.

Analysis. Notably, the explainability method effectively identifies the "suits" cluster names, providing a comprehensive description of this clustering type, even though clustering performance has an AMI of less than 40%. Additionally, the frequency analysis exposed many of the card types in the dataset. However, suit names are also assigned as cluster names for the expected card ranking clusters (e.g., "heart" as the top word of the "5" cluster). Figure 6 presents concrete examples demonstrating that VQA models often provide additional information, such as suit, thereby explaining the inclusion of suits as rank names.

5 Discussion

5.1 Text-driven data interaction

Textual data, as a fundamental form of human communication, offers a natural and intuitive interface for interacting with complex datasets. Our method capitalizes on this inherent connection by utilizing textual prompts for VQA models to guide alternative clusterings. This approach aligns with real-world scenarios where users possess domain knowledge and seek answers to specific questions. We envision a future where users can explore datasets from diverse perspectives and test emerging hypotheses interactively using text. This research contributes towards this vision.

5.2 Domain Expertise

Our approach incorporates domain expertise, recognizing that users often either have specific questions or some knowledge about their data. This stands in contrast to the traditional clustering setup, which typically operates without user input. By leveraging domain knowledge, our approach aligns with real-world scenarios and allows for more targeted and insightful data exploration.

6 Conclusion

In conclusion, this research introduces TGAICC (Text-Guided Alternative Image Consensus Clustering), a novel approach that leverages prompting to inject domain knowledge and human intuition into the clustering process. The experiments on four common alternative image clustering benchmarks demonstrate that TGAICC outperforms competitive image- and text-based baselines. Furthermore, the inherent explainability of text enables a deeper understanding of the underlying data cluster formations.

By utilizing textual prompts, we can explicitly guide the clustering process from various angles simultaneously, aligning with human intuition. This approach offers a more comprehensive and flexible way to analyze visual data, revealing insights that might be missed by traditional clustering methods.

7 Acknowledgements

This research was funded by the WWTF through the project "Knowledge-infused Deep Learning for Natural Language Processing" (WWTF Vienna Research Group VRG19-008) and through the project "Transparent and Explainable Models" (WWTF ICT19-041).

References

Nikolas Adaloglou, Felix Michels, Hamza Kalisch, and Markus Kollmann. 2023. Exploring the limits of deep image clustering using pretrained models. In *34th British Machine Vision Conference 2023, BMVC 2023, Aberdeen, UK, November 20-24, 2023*. BMVA.

Jean-Baptiste Alayrac, Jeff Donahue, Pauline Luc, Antoine Miech, Iain Barr, Yana Hasson, Karel Lenc, Arthur Mensch, Katherine Millican, Malcolm Reynolds, Roman Ring, Eliza Rutherford, Serkan Cabi, Tengda Han, Zhitao Gong, Sina Samangooei, Marianne Monteiro, Jacob L Menick, Sebastian Borgeaud, Andy Brock, Aida Nematzadeh, Sahand Sharifzadeh, Mikoł aj Bińkowski, Ricardo Barreira, Oriol Vinyals, Andrew Zisserman, and Karén Simonyan. 2022. Flamingo: a visual language model for few-shot learning. In *Advances in Neural Information Processing Systems*, volume 35, pages 23716–23736. Curran Associates, Inc.

Stanislaw Antol, Aishwarya Agrawal, Jiasen Lu, Margaret Mitchell, Dhruv Batra, C. Lawrence Zitnick, and Devi Parikh. 2015. Vqa: Visual question answering. In *Proceedings of the IEEE International Conference on Computer Vision (ICCV)*.

Stephen H. Bach, Victor Sanh, Zheng-Xin Yong, Albert Webson, Colin Raffel, Nihal V. Nayak, Abheesht Sharma, Taewoon Kim, M Saiful Bari, Thibault Fevry, Zaid Alyafeai, Manan Dey, Andrea Santilli, Zhiqing Sun, Srulik Ben-David, Canwen Xu, Gunjan Chhablani, Han Wang, Jason Alan Fries, Maged S. Al-shaibani, Shanya Sharma, Urmish Thakker, Khalid Almubarak, Xiangru Tang, Xiangru Tang, Mike Tian-Jian Jiang, and Alexander M. Rush. 2022. Promptsource: An integrated development environment and repository for natural language prompts.

Ying Cui, Xiaoli Z. Fern, and Jennifer G. Dy. 2007. Non-redundant multi-view clustering via orthogonalization. In *Proceedings of the 7th IEEE International Conference on Data Mining (ICDM 2007), October 28-31, 2007, Omaha, Nebraska, USA*, pages 133–142. IEEE Computer Society.

Jia Deng, Wei Dong, Richard Socher, Li-Jia Li, Kai Li, and Li Fei-Fei. 2009. Imagenet: A large-scale hierarchical image database. In *2009 IEEE Conference on Computer Vision and Pattern Recognition*, pages 248–255.

Absalom E. Ezugwu, Abiodun M. Ikotun, Olaide O. Oyelade, Laith Abualigah, Jeffery O. Agushaka, Christopher I. Eke, and Andronicus A. Akinyelu. 2022. A comprehensive survey of clustering algorithms: State-of-the-art machine learning applications, taxonomy, challenges, and future research prospects. *Engineering Applications of Artificial Intelligence*, 110:104743.

Xiaoli Zhang Fern and Carla E. Brodley. 2004. Solving cluster ensemble problems by bipartite graph partitioning. In *Proceedings of the Twenty-First International Conference on Machine Learning*, ICML '04, page 36, New York, NY, USA. Association for Computing Machinery.

Xifeng Guo, Long Gao, Xinwang Liu, and Jianping Yin. 2017. Improved deep embedded clustering with local structure preservation. In *Proceedings of the Twenty-Sixth International Joint Conference on Artificial Intelligence, IJCAI 2017, Melbourne, Australia, August 19-25, 2017*, pages 1753–1759. ijcai.org.

Sebastian Houben, Johannes Stallkamp, Jan Salmen, Marc Schlipsing, and Christian Igel. 2013. Detection of traffic signs in real-world images: The german traffic sign detection benchmark. In *The 2013 International Joint Conference on Neural Networks (IJCNN)*, pages 1–8.

Ashish Jaiswal, Ashwin Ramesh Babu, Mohammad Zaki Zadeh, Debapriya Banerjee, and Fillia Makedon. 2021. A survey on contrastive self-supervised learning. *Technologies*, 9(1).

Sehyun Kwon, Jaeseung Park, Minkyu Kim, Jaewoong Cho, Ernest K. Ryu, and Kangwook Lee. 2024. Image clustering conditioned on text criteria. In *The Twelfth International Conference on Learning Representations*.

Johannes Lehner, Benedikt Alkin, Andreas Fürst, Elisabeth Rumetshofer, Lukas Miklautz, and Sepp Hochreiter. 2023. Contrastive tuning: A little help to make masked autoencoders forget. *arXiv preprint arXiv:2304.10520*.

Collin Leiber, Lukas Miklautz, Claudia Plant, and Christian Böhm. 2023. Benchmarking deep clustering algorithms with clustpy. In *2023 IEEE International Conference on Data Mining Workshops (ICDMW)*, pages 625–632. IEEE.

Junnan Li, Dongxu Li, Silvio Savarese, and Steven Hoi. 2023a. Blip-2: Bootstrapping language-image pre-training with frozen image encoders and large language models.

Junnan Li, Dongxu Li, Caiming Xiong, and Steven Hoi. 2022. BLIP: Bootstrapping language-image pre-training for unified vision-language understanding and generation. In *Proceedings of the 39th International Conference on Machine Learning*, volume 162 of *Proceedings of Machine Learning Research*, pages 12888–12900. PMLR.

Tao Li and Chris Ding. 2008. *Weighted Consensus Clustering*, pages 798–809.

Yunfan Li, Peng Hu, Zitao Liu, Dezhong Peng, Joey Tianyi Zhou, and Xi Peng. 2021. Contrastive clustering. In *Proceedings of the AAAI Conference on Artificial Intelligence*, volume 35, pages 8547–8555.

Zehan Li, Xin Zhang, Yanzhao Zhang, Dingkun Long, Pengjun Xie, and Meishan Zhang. 2023b. Towards general text embeddings with multi-stage contrastive learning. *arXiv preprint arXiv:2308.03281*.

Haotian Liu, Chunyuan Li, Yuheng Li, and Yong Jae Lee. 2023a. Improved baselines with visual instruction tuning.

Haotian Liu, Chunyuan Li, Qingyang Wu, and Yong Jae Lee. 2023b. Visual instruction tuning. In *NeurIPS*.

Stuart P. Lloyd. 1982. Least squares quantization in PCM. *IEEE Trans. Inf. Theory*, 28(2):129–136.

Dominik Mautz, Wei Ye, Claudia Plant, and Christian Böhm. 2018. Discovering non-redundant k-means clusterings in optimal subspaces. In *Proceedings of the 24th ACM SIGKDD International Conference on Knowledge Discovery & Data Mining, KDD 2018, London, UK, August 19-23, 2018*, pages 1973–1982. ACM.

Lukas Miklautz, Dominik Mautz, Muzaffer Can Altinigneli, Christian Böhm, and Claudia Plant. 2020. Deep embedded non-redundant clustering. *Proceedings of the AAAI Conference on Artificial Intelligence*, 34(04):5174–5181.

Lukas Miklautz, Martin Teuffenbach, Pascal Weber, Rona Perjuci, Walid Durani, Christian Böhm, and Claudia Plant. 2022. Deep clustering with consensus representations. In *2022 IEEE International Conference on Data Mining (ICDM)*, pages 1119–1124.

Emmanuel Müller, Stephan Günnemann, Ines Färber, and Thomas Seidl. 2012. Discovering multiple clustering solutions: Grouping objects in different views of the data. In *Proceedings of the 28th ICDE, Washington, DC, USA, 1-5 April, 2012*, pages 1207–1210.

Horea Mureşan and Mihai Oltean. 2018. Fruit recognition from images using deep learning. *Acta Universitatis Sapientiae, Informatica*, 10:26–42.

Daniel Müllner. 2011. Modern hierarchical, agglomerative clustering algorithms.

OpenAI, Josh Achiam, Steven Adler, Sandhini Agarwal, Lama Ahmad, Ilge Akkaya, Florencia Leoni Aleman, Diogo Almeida, Janko Altenschmidt, Sam Altman, Shyamal Anadkat, Red Avila, Igor Babuschkin, Suchir Balaji, Valerie Balcom, Paul Baltescu, Haiming Bao, Mohammad Bavarian, Jeff Belgum, Irwan Bello, Jake Berdine, Gabriel Bernadett-Shapiro, Christopher Berner, Lenny Bogdonoff, Oleg Boiko, Madelaine Boyd, Anna-Luisa Brakman, Greg Brockman, Tim Brooks, Miles Brundage, Kevin Button, Trevor Cai, Rosie Campbell, Andrew Cann, Brittany Carey, Chelsea Carlson, Rory Carmichael, Brooke Chan, Che Chang, Fotis Chantzis, Derek Chen, Sully Chen, Ruby Chen, Jason Chen, Mark Chen, Ben Chess, Chester Cho, Casey Chu, Hyung Won Chung, Dave Cummings, Jeremiah Currier, Yunxing Dai, Cory Decareaux, Thomas Degry, Noah Deutsch, Damien Deville, Arka Dhar, David Dohan, Steve Dowling, Sheila Dunning, Adrien Ecoffet, Atty Eleti, Tyna Eloundou, David Farhi, Liam Fedus, Niko Felix, Simón Posada Fishman, Juston Forte, Isabella Fulford, Leo Gao, Elie Georges, Christian Gibson, Vik Goel, Tarun Gogineni, Gabriel Goh, Rapha Gontijo-Lopes, Jonathan Gordon, Morgan Grafstein, Scott Gray, Ryan Greene, Joshua Gross, Shixiang Shane Gu, Yufei Guo, Chris Hallacy, Jesse Han, Jeff Harris, Yuchen He, Mike Heaton, Johannes Heidecke, Chris Hesse, Alan Hickey, Wade Hickey, Peter Hoeschele, Brandon Houghton, Kenny Hsu, Shengli Hu, Xin Hu, Joost Huizinga, Shantanu Jain, Shawn Jain, Joanne Jang, Angela Jiang, Roger Jiang, Haozhun Jin, Denny Jin, Shino Jomoto, Billie Jonn, Heewoo Jun, Tomer Kaftan, Łukasz Kaiser, Ali Kamali, Ingmar Kanitscheider, Nitish Shirish Keskar, Tabarak Khan, Logan Kilpatrick, Jong Wook Kim, Christina Kim, Yongjik Kim, Jan Hendrik Kirchner, Jamie Kiros, Matt Knight, Daniel Kokotajlo, Łukasz Kondraciuk, Andrew Kondrich, Aris Konstantinidis, Kyle Kosic, Gretchen Krueger, Vishal Kuo, Michael Lampe, Ikai Lan, Teddy Lee, Jan Leike, Jade Leung, Daniel Levy, Chak Ming Li, Rachel Lim, Molly Lin, Stephanie Lin, Mateusz Litwin, Theresa Lopez, Ryan Lowe, Patricia Lue, Anna Makanju, Kim Malfacini, Sam Manning, Todor Markov, Yaniv Markovski, Bianca Martin, Katie Mayer, Andrew Mayne, Bob McGrew, Scott Mayer McKinney, Christine McLeavey, Paul McMillan, Jake McNeil, David Medina, Aalok Mehta, Jacob Menick, Luke Metz, Andrey Mishchenko, Pamela Mishkin, Vinnie Monaco, Evan Morikawa, Daniel Mossing, Tong Mu, Mira Murati, Oleg Murk, David Mély, Ashvin Nair, Reiichiro Nakano, Rajeev Nayak, Arvind Neelakantan, Richard Ngo, Hyeonwoo Noh, Long Ouyang, Cullen O'Keefe, Jakub Pachocki, Alex Paino, Joe Palermo, Ashley Pantuliano, Giambattista Parascandolo, Joel Parish, Emy Parparita, Alex Passos, Mikhail Pavlov, Andrew Peng, Adam Perelman, Filipe de Avila Belbute Peres, Michael Petrov, Henrique Ponde de Oliveira Pinto, Michael, Pokorny, Michelle Pokrass, Vitchyr H. Pong, Tolly Powell, Alethea Power, Boris Power, Elizabeth Proehl,

Raul Puri, Alec Radford, Jack Rae, Aditya Ramesh, Cameron Raymond, Francis Real, Kendra Rimbach, Carl Ross, Bob Rotsted, Henri Roussez, Nick Ryder, Mario Saltarelli, Ted Sanders, Shibani Santurkar, Girish Sastry, Heather Schmidt, David Schnurr, John Schulman, Daniel Selsam, Kyla Sheppard, Toki Sherbakov, Jessica Shieh, Sarah Shoker, Pranav Shyam, Szymon Sidor, Eric Sigler, Maddie Simens, Jordan Sitkin, Katarina Slama, Ian Sohl, Benjamin Sokolowsky, Yang Song, Natalie Staudacher, Felipe Petroski Such, Natalie Summers, Ilya Sutskever, Jie Tang, Nikolas Tezak, Madeleine B. Thompson, Phil Tillet, Amin Tootoonchian, Elizabeth Tseng, Preston Tuggle, Nick Turley, Jerry Tworek, Juan Felipe Cerón Uribe, Andrea Vallone, Arun Vijayvergiya, Chelsea Voss, Carroll Wainwright, Justin Jay Wang, Alvin Wang, Ben Wang, Jonathan Ward, Jason Wei, CJ Weinmann, Akila Welihinda, Peter Welinder, Jiayi Weng, Lilian Weng, Matt Wiethoff, Dave Willner, Clemens Winter, Samuel Wolrich, Hannah Wong, Lauren Workman, Sherwin Wu, Jeff Wu, Michael Wu, Kai Xiao, Tao Xu, Sarah Yoo, Kevin Yu, Qiming Yuan, Wojciech Zaremba, Rowan Zellers, Chong Zhang, Marvin Zhang, Shengjia Zhao, Tianhao Zheng, Juntang Zhuang, William Zhuk, and Barret Zoph. 2024. Gpt-4 technical report.

F. Pedregosa, G. Varoquaux, A. Gramfort, V. Michel, B. Thirion, O. Grisel, M. Blondel, P. Prettenhofer, R. Weiss, V. Dubourg, J. Vanderplas, A. Passos, D. Cournapeau, M. Brucher, M. Perrot, and E. Duchesnay. 2011. Scikit-learn: Machine learning in Python. *Journal of Machine Learning Research*, 12:2825–2830.

Alec Radford, Jong Wook Kim, Chris Hallacy, Aditya Ramesh, Gabriel Goh, Sandhini Agarwal, Girish Sastry, Amanda Askell, Pamela Mishkin, Jack Clark, Gretchen Krueger, and Ilya Sutskever. 2021. Learning transferable visual models from natural language supervision. In *Proceedings of the 38th International Conference on Machine Learning*, volume 139 of *Proceedings of Machine Learning Research*, pages 8748–8763. PMLR.

William M Rand. 1971. Objective criteria for the evaluation of clustering methods. *Journal of the American Statistical association*, 66(336):846–850.

Nils Reimers and Iryna Gurevych. 2019. Sentence-bert: Sentence embeddings using siamese bert-networks. In *Proceedings of the 2019 Conference on Empirical Methods in Natural Language Processing*. Association for Computational Linguistics.

Melanie Sclar, Yejin Choi, Yulia Tsvetkov, and Alane Suhr. 2024. Quantifying language models' sensitivity to spurious features in prompt design or: How i learned to start worrying about prompt formatting. In *The Twelfth International Conference on Learning Representations*.

Karen Sparck Jones. 1988. *A statistical interpretation of term specificity and its application in retrieval*, page 132–142. Taylor Graham Publishing, GBR.

Andreas Stephan, Lukas Miklautz, Kevin Sidak, Jan Philip Wahle, Bela Gipp, Claudia Plant, and Benjamin Roth. 2024. Text-guided image clustering. In *Proceedings of the 18th Conference of the European Chapter of the Association for Computational Linguistics (Volume 1: Long Papers)*, pages 2960–2976, St. Julian's, Malta. Association for Computational Linguistics.

Alexander Strehl and Joydeep Ghosh. 2002. Cluster ensembles - a knowledge reuse framework for combining multiple partitions. *Journal of Machine Learning Research*, 3:583–617.

J.W. Tukey. 1970. *Exploratory Data Analysis*. Number v. 1 in Exploratory Data Analysis. Addison Wesley Publishing Company.

Nguyen Xuan Vinh, Julien Epps, and James Bailey. 2010. Information theoretic measures for clusterings comparison: Variants, properties, normalization and correction for chance. *Journal of Machine Learning Research*, 11(95):2837–2854.

Pauli Virtanen, Ralf Gommers, Travis E. Oliphant, Matt Haberland, Tyler Reddy, David Cournapeau, Evgeni Burovski, Pearu Peterson, Warren Weckesser, Jonathan Bright, Stéfan J. van der Walt, Matthew Brett, Joshua Wilson, K. Jarrod Millman, Nikolay Mayorov, Andrew R. J. Nelson, Eric Jones, Robert Kern, Eric Larson, C J Carey, İlhan Polat, Yu Feng, Eric W. Moore, Jake VanderPlas, Denis Laxalde, Josef Perktold, Robert Cimrman, Ian Henriksen, E. A. Quintero, Charles R. Harris, Anne M. Archibald, Antônio H. Ribeiro, Fabian Pedregosa, Paul van Mulbregt, and SciPy 1.0 Contributors. 2020. SciPy 1.0: Fundamental Algorithms for Scientific Computing in Python. *Nature Methods*, 17:261–272.

Junyuan Xie, Ross B. Girshick, and Ali Farhadi. 2016. Unsupervised deep embedding for clustering analysis. In *Proceedings of the 33nd International Conference on Machine Learning, ICML 2016, New York City, NY, USA, June 19-24, 2016*, volume 48 of *JMLR Workshop and Conference Proceedings*, pages 478–487. JMLR.org.

Jiawei Yao, Qi Qian, and Juhua Hu. 2024. Multi-modal proxy learning towards personalized visual multiple clustering. *arXiv preprint arXiv:2404.15655*.

Shukang Yin, Chaoyou Fu, Sirui Zhao, Ke Li, Xing Sun, Tong Xu, and Enhong Chen. 2023. A survey on multimodal large language models. *arXiv preprint arXiv:2306.13549*.

Guoxian Yu, Liangrui Ren, Jun Wang, Carlotta Domeniconi, and Xiangliang Zhang. 2024. Multiple clusterings: Recent advances and perspectives. *Computer Science Review*, 52:100621.

A Datasets

In addition to the dataset description presented in Section 4.1, we provide the following supplementary materials to enhance the reader's understanding. Table 7 shows examples of images from each dataset. Furthermore, Table 7 provides all prompts generated by GPT-4, paired with their corresponding ground truth cluster names for each clustering type. Together, they give a good insight into the datasets and a textual interaction with them.

B Baselines

In the following, additional details for the baselines are given. We employ all of the following ones on the image embedding of the CLIP encoder of LLaVA-NeXT:

K-means. For all k-means runs, we utilize the k-means++ initialization strategy and set the number of initializations to 1. The code was implemented using scikit-learn (Pedregosa et al., 2011).

Nr-Kmeans. We set a limit of 300 maximum iterations.

Orth 1/2. We set the explained variance parameter to 90%.

ENRC. We try the learning rates $lr = 0.001, 0.0001$, use NR-Kmeans as initialization, a batch size of 128, and optimize for 200 epochs.

Dataset	Type	Cluster Names	Prompts
Fruits-360	fruit	apple, banana, cherry, grape	What kind of produce is shown in the picture? Can you identify the type of produce depicted in the image? What category of produce does the image represent? What kind of produce is shown in the picture? Answer concisely. Can you identify the type of produce depicted in the image? Answer concisely. What category of produce does the image represent? Answer concisely.
	colour	burgundy, green, red, yellow	Can you tell me the color of the fruits and vegetables shown in the picture? What color is the produce displayed in the photo? What hue are the items in the picture? Can you tell me the color of the fruits and vegetables shown in the picture? Answer concisely. What color is the produce displayed in the photo? Answer concisely. What hue are the items in the picture? Answer concisely.
GTSRB	type	70_limit, dont_overtake, go_right, go_straight	What kind of traffic sign is shown in the picture? Can you identify the category of the traffic sign displayed in the image? What class of traffic sign is depicted in the photo? What kind of traffic sign is shown in the picture? Answer concisely. Can you identify the category of the traffic sign displayed in the image? Answer concisely. What class of traffic sign is depicted in the photo? Answer concisely.
	colour	blue, red	What color is the traffic sign shown in the picture? Can you tell me the color of the traffic sign depicted in the image? What hue is the traffic sign in the photograph? What color is the traffic sign shown in the picture? Answer concisely. Can you tell me the color of the traffic sign depicted in the image? Answer concisely. What hue is the traffic sign in the photograph? Answer concisely.
NR-Objects	shape	cube, cylinder, sphere	Can you identify the form of the object shown in the picture? What form does the object in the picture take? Could you tell me the configuration of the object depicted in the image? Can you identify the form of the object shown in the picture? Answer concisely. What form does the object in the picture take? Answer concisely. Could you tell me the configuration of the object depicted in the image? Answer concisely.
	material	metal, rubber	What substance is the item in the picture made of? Can you identify the material used in the object shown in the image? What is the composition of the object depicted in the photo? What substance is the item in the picture made of? Answer concisely. Can you identify the material used in the object shown in the image? Answer concisely. What is the composition of the object depicted in the photo? Answer concisely.
	colour	blue, gray, green, purple, red, yellow	What color is the item shown in the picture? Can you tell me the color of the object depicted in the image? What hue does the object in the photo have? What color is the item shown in the picture? Answer concisely. Can you tell me the color of the object depicted in the image? Answer concisely. What hue does the object in the photo have? Answer concisely.
Cards	rank	ace, eight, five, four, jack, king, nine, queen, seven, six, ten, three, two	Can you tell me the rank of the card shown in the picture? What is the numerical or face value of the card displayed in the image? What level or position does the card in the photo hold? Can you tell me the rank of the card shown in the picture? Answer concisely. What is the numerical or face value of the card displayed in the image? Answer concisely. What level or position does the card in the photo hold? Answer concisely.
	suit	clubs, diamonds, hearts, spades	Can you tell me the suit of the playing card shown in the picture? What suit does the playing card in the image belong to? Could you identify the suit of the playing card depicted in the photo? Can you tell me the suit of the playing card shown in the picture? Answer concisely. What suit does the playing card in the image belong to? Answer concisely. Could you identify the suit of the playing card depicted in the photo? Answer concisely.

Table 7: Overview of the datasets, the names of their ground truth clusterings, and all generated prompts.

dataset	Image 1	Image 2	Image 3
Fruits-360	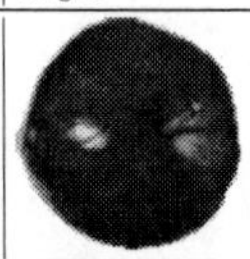	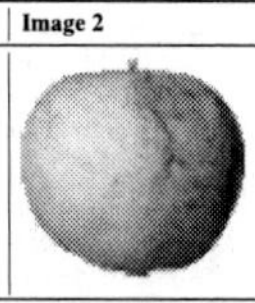	
GTSRB			
NR-Objects	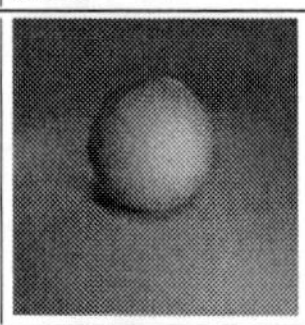	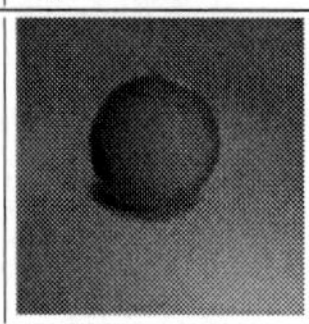	
Cards	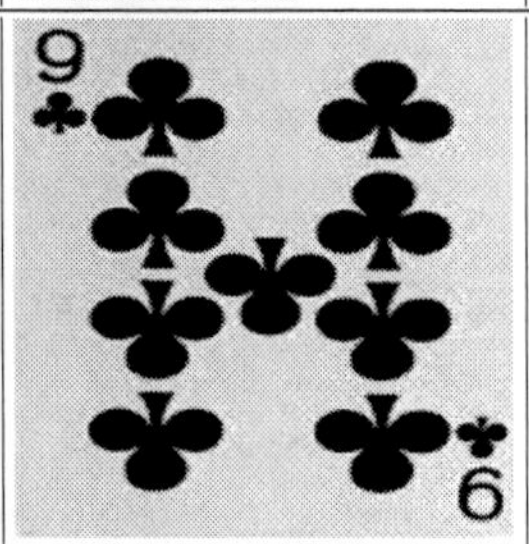		

Table 8: A few example images for each dataset.

QAVSA: Question Answering using Vector Symbolic Algebras

Ryan Laube and **Chris Eliasmith**
University of Waterloo, ON, Canada
{rlaube,celiasmith}@uwaterloo.ca

Abstract

With the advancement of large pretrained language models (PLMs), many question answering (QA) benchmarks have been developed in order to evaluate the reasoning capabilities of these models. Augmenting PLMs with external knowledge in the form of Knowledge Graphs (KGs) has been a popular method to improve their reasoning capabilities, and a common method to reason over KGs is to use Graph Neural Networks (GNNs). As an alternative to GNNs to augment PLMs, we propose a novel graph reasoning module using Vector Symbolic Algebra (VSA) graph representations and a k-layer MLP. We demonstrate that our VSA-based model performs as well as QA-GNN, a model combining a PLM and a GNN-module, on 3 multiple-choice question answering (MCQA) datasets. Our model has a simpler architecture than QA-GNN and also converges 39% faster during training.

1 Introduction

Models that perform question answering tasks require some amount of knowledge, whether it is structured or implicit, about the concepts to be reasoned over. Modern large pretrained language models (PLMs), linguistic knowledge is implicit in the token embeddings that have been learned using a self-attention mechanism on large text corpuses to perform next-token prediction (Vaswani et al., 2017). With enough model parameters and training data, these PLMs have been successful in a wide range of question-answering and reasoning benchmarks. However, when analyzing deductive reasoning performance, i.e. the ability to learn and generalize from logic rules, smaller PLMs like BERT and RoBERTa demonstrate inconsistent performance (Yuan et al., 2023).

As a result, there have been many studies that work to integrate external, structured knowledge and reasoning modules with PLMs to perform more reliable logical reasoning. One type of knowledge structure that is commonly used are knowledge graphs (KG), due to their suitability for symbolic reasoning (Lan et al., 2021). Graph Neural Networks (GNNs) are deep learning networks that have gained popularity for reasoning over graph-structured data. Consequently, methods that integrate KGs with PLMs often also use GNNs (Ye et al., 2022). One recent approach to combining these techniques is captured by the QA-GNN (Yasunaga et al., 2021), which is able to answer multiple-choice questions by scoring the plausibility of each question answer.

Rather than using GNNs to model structured data, our model, QAVSA, uses a lesser known method, Vector Symoblic Algebras (VSAs; also known as Vector Symbolic Architectures), to represent and combine high-dimensional concept vectors in a structured way. The integration of PLMs and VSAs has not been previously proposed, to our knowledge. As a result, the focus of this paper is to perform a comparison between our VSA-based method and the GNN-based method of QA-GNN for improving reasoning capabilities of PLMs in the context of multiple-choice question answering.

Specifcally, we compare the performance of QAVSA and QA-GNN on CommonsenseQA (Talmor et al., 2019), OpenbookQA (Mihaylov et al., 2018), and MedQA-USMLE (Jin et al., 2021), with the first two datasets being focused on commonsense reasoning, and the latter focusing on domain-specific medical questions.

The main contributions of this paper are: 1) a novel combination of PLM text encoders and VSAs that performs as well as an analgous GNN-based method on three MCQA datasets while training faster; 2) a comparative evaluation of different VSAs and PLMs used in the model; 3) a study on ablation and variations of the model architecture and graph embedding representations; and 4) a new VSA-specific method of analyzing model

Proceedings of the 9th Workshop on Representation Learning for NLP (RepL4NLP-2024), pages 191–202
August 15, 2024 ©2024 Association for Computational Linguistics

explainability.

2 Related Work

Many of the top performing models on MCQA benchmarks involving reasoning are larger 10B or 100B+ parameter PLMs. High performance can come from fine-tuning on MCQA datasets as has been shown with UnifiedQA (Khashabi et al., 2020) and UNICORN Lourie et al. (2021). High performance with these models has also been shown to be achievable with prompting techniques including few-shot prompting (Anil et al., 2023), Chain-of-Thought prompting with self-consistency (Huang et al., 2023a), and ensemble refinement (Singhal et al., 2023).

More relevant to our research, several approaches have been proposed to integrate external knowledge graphs with PLMs in order to make use of more domain-specific structured knowledge. These include KEAR (Xu et al., 2022) and DEKCOR (Xu et al., 2021), which use a PLM and knowledge retrieved from an external KG and Wiktionary to train an attention mechanism on these external knowledge bases and PLM representations to improve commonsense reasoning.

Similarly, KagNet (Lin et al., 2019) performs commonsense reasoning by grounding the concepts within each question-answer (QA) pair of multiple-choice datasets to extract subgraphs from an external knowledge graph. KagNet then uses a combination of Graph Convolutional Networks, LSTM-based relational path encodings, and a path-based attention mechanism to identify important reasoning paths to generate graph vector encodings for each QA pair to subsequently score them. Adopting similar graph preprocessing to KagNet, MHGRN (Feng et al., 2020) performs multi-hop, multi-relation reasoning by using multi-hop message passing from Relational Graph Convolutional Networks, structured relational attention, and node attention pooling to generate its graph representations and score QA pairs.

Another family of models that also use the same graph processing above stem from the QA-GNN (Yasunaga et al., 2021) model. QA-GNN fuses a PLM representation of the QA context as a node into the QA subgraphs. Using a Graph Attention Network (GAT), QA-GNN updates the subgraph concept embeddings, including the QA context node and edge weights. The initial PLM QA context representation, along with the final graph representation of the QA context and graph concept attention pooling is used to score the QA pairs. This method is refined in GreaseLM (Zhang et al., 2021) in which the PLM token and graph node modalities of the QA context are mixed over several layers to simultaneously update the PLM and GNN concept embeddings. Further refinements are made in DRAGON (Yasunaga et al., 2022a), where the cross-modal encoder from GreaseLM is pre-trained in a self-supervised fashion to perform both masked language modeling and KG link prediction. Our QAVSA model uses similar pre-processing to QA-GNN but with a different representation of the graph. Consequently, most of our direct comparisons are to QA-GNN.

There exist other models that use external KGs but are not GNN-based, such as GSC (Wang et al., 2022) and MVP-Tuning (Huang et al., 2023b). GSC uses a simple graph neural counter to reduce the node and embeddings to one dimension and performs GNN-like embedding updates on these single values. MVP-Tuning makes use of semantically similar QA pairs in the training set to improve knowledge retrieval and tunes prompt tokens of the PLM by using the QA context and retrieved KG triplets as input to the PLM.

3 Vector Symbolic Algebras

Vector Symbolic Algebras (VSAs) are defined by a set of three vector operations that are useful for building up structured vector representations. These include the similarity, bundling (or collecting), and binding operations. There are a wide variety of possible choices for these operations, but we consider only two sets of operators, those for Holographic Reduced Representations (Plate, 1995) and for Vector-derived Transformation Bindings (Gosmann and Eliasmith, 2019).

A similarity operation is necessary to compare different vectors within the VSA space, and it is often computed with a normalized vector dot product, i.e., cosine similarity. For two VSA-encoded vectors $\mathbf{x}, \mathbf{y} \in \mathbb{R}^d$, this is defined as $s(\mathbf{x}, \mathbf{y}) = \frac{<\mathbf{x},\mathbf{y}>}{\|\mathbf{x}\| \cdot \|\mathbf{y}\|}$. Both HRRs and VTBs use this similarity operator.

A bundling operation is used to represent a set of objects and is usually defined by element-wise addition. Thus, the bundling of $\mathbf{x}, \mathbf{y} \in \mathbb{R}^d$ can by defined by $S(\mathbf{x}, \mathbf{y}) = \mathbf{x} + \mathbf{y}$. In a VSA, this operation should result in a new vector that is similar to both $\mathbf{x}$ and $\mathbf{y}$, as is the case with element-wise addition. Both HRRs and VTBs use this bundling operator.

A binding operation, is used to combine two symbols together in a single representation, which is often used to represent slot-filler pairs. In HRRs, circular convolution is used as a binding operator, defined by

$$(\mathbf{x} \circledast \mathbf{y})_i := \sum_{j=1}^{d} x_j y_{((i-j) mod\, d)+1}, i \in \{1, 2, ..., d\}.$$

A desired property of a binding operator is that the resulting vector from $\mathbf{x} \circledast \mathbf{y}$ should be dissimilar to both $\mathbf{x}$ and $\mathbf{y}$. Also, an unbinding operation, or a pseudo-inverse to binding should exist. With circular convolution, this is done by binding the pseudo-inverse of the given operand: $(\mathbf{x} \circledast \mathbf{y}) \circledast^{-1} \mathbf{y} \approx \mathbf{x} \circledast \mathbf{y} \circledast \mathbf{y}^{+} \approx \mathbf{x}$. For HRRs the approximate inverse to $\mathbf{y}$ is $\mathbf{y}^{+} := (y_1, y_d, y_{d-1}, ..., y_2)^{\top}$ (Plate, 1995).

Since circular convolution is commutative, there is no directional relation to two bound vectors in the HRR VSA. In contrast, VTB has a non-associative and non-commutative binding operation defined on vectors $\mathbf{x}, \mathbf{y} \in \mathbb{R}^d$. Specifically, given $d^{\frac{1}{2}} = d' \in \mathbb{N}_{>0}$, we have

$$\mathbf{x} \circledast \mathbf{y} := \mathbf{V_y x} = \begin{bmatrix} \mathbf{V_y'} & 0 & 0 \\ 0 & \mathbf{V_y'} & 0 \\ 0 & 0 & \ddots \end{bmatrix} \mathbf{x}$$

, where

$$\mathbf{V_y'} = d^{\frac{1}{4}} \begin{bmatrix} y_1 & y_2 & \cdots & y_{d'} \\ y_{d'+1} & y_{d'+2} & \cdots & y_{2d'} \\ \vdots & \vdots & \ddots & \vdots \\ y_{d-d'+1} & y_{d-d'+2} & \cdots & y_d \end{bmatrix}.$$

The approximate inverse to $\mathbf{y}$ is $\mathbf{y}^{+}$, where the elements of $\mathbf{y}$ are permuted such that $\mathbf{V_{y^+}} = \mathbf{V_y^{\top}}$.

The VTB binding operation has only right inverses and identities, so there exists an alternative Transposed VTB (TVTB) algebra, with two-sided inverses and identities with the following binding operation:

$$\mathbf{x} \circledast \mathbf{y} := \mathbf{V_y^{\top} x} = \begin{bmatrix} \mathbf{V_y'^{\top}} & 0 & 0 \\ 0 & \mathbf{V_y'^{\top}} & 0 \\ 0 & 0 & \ddots \end{bmatrix} \mathbf{x}$$

where $\mathbf{V_y'}$ is the same as in VTB.

Plate (1995) initially proposed the HRR VSA in order to represent complex compositional structures, specifically ones used for language processing and reasoning, with distributed representations like neural networks. Jackendoff proposed four linguistic challenges involving how to neurally represent the compositional structure and rules of language that previously divided linguistic theory and connectionist cognitive neuroscience. VSAs solve these four problems (Gayler, 2004), which supports the idea that VSAs are useful in studying linguistics and reasoning within the context of neural networks. For example, VSAs have been used in neural models to represent lexical relations and recursively structured sentences successfully (Crawford et al., 2016). The quality of structural representation and mathematical ability to query information from these VSA representations naturally lends this method to QA tasks where representing and extracting relational information pertaining to a set of concepts is necessary.

As a simple example, a scene of a dog holding a stick could be represented with VSAs in a slot-filler fashion as: $\mathbf{scene} = \mathbf{subject} \circledast \mathbf{dog} + \mathbf{verb} \circledast \mathbf{holds} + \mathbf{object} \circledast \mathbf{stick}$, given the slot vectors $\mathbf{subject}, \mathbf{verb}, \mathbf{object} \in \mathbb{R}^d$ and filler vectors $\mathbf{dog}, \mathbf{holds}, \mathbf{stick} \in \mathbb{R}^d$. One could then query the subject of the scene with unbinding: $\mathbf{scene} \circledast \mathbf{subject}^{+} \approx \mathbf{dog} + noise$, which can be cleaned up to the exact $\mathbf{dog}$ vector by finding the VSA vector in the vocabulary with the highest similarity to the result. We use these techniques for representing structure to capture concept relations in a knowledge graph to propose a novel question answering neural network model.

4 Methods

Given a multiple-choice question q and an answer option a, as in QA-GNN (Yasunaga et al., 2021), the purpose of the model is to score the plausibility of each (q, a) pair from the set of all answer options by performing joint reasoning using a (q, a) context, $\mathbf{z}$, generated from a PLM text encoder, and a working graph G_w that contains relations and concepts pertaining to each specific (q, a) pair. In QA-GNN, the graph reasoning portion of the model consists of a specific type of GNN called a Graph Attention Network (GAT; Velickovic et al. (2018)). As a replacement for the GAT in QAVSA, a single VSA vector representation of the (q, a) graph is generated. This representation is used as input to a simple k-layer MLP to realize the graph reasoning portion of QAVSA. Using this learned MLP along with the PLM (q, a) context embeddings, the (q, a) pair is scored, as shown in Figure 1.

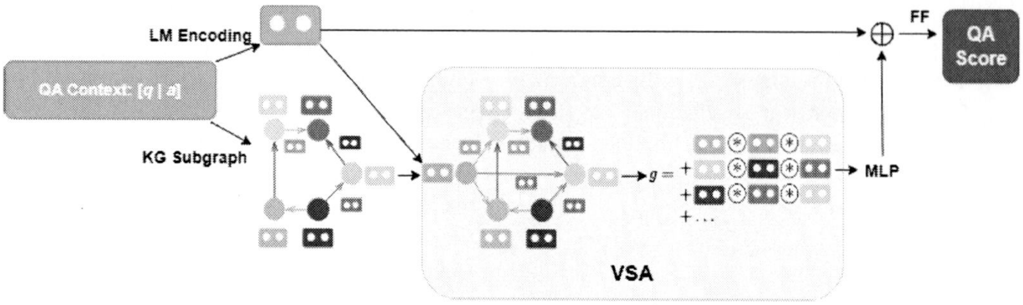

Figure 1: QAVSA model outline. The QA context, $[q|a]$, is inputted to a PLM to generate an LM Encoding for the context and is also used to generate a KG subgraph. The LM encoded QA context is added to the graph, and the graph is converted to a single vector using VSA. The VSA representation is feed through a k-layer MLP, concatenated with the original QA context encoding, and passed through a single FF layer to score the QA pair.

4.1 Graph Data Pre-processing

To generate the working graph G_w, we follow the exact pre-processing technique described in Lin et al. (2019). The external domain-specific or world knowledge relevant to the answer question task is defined by a knowledge graph $G = (V, E)$ made up of a set of nodes, V, and a set of directed edges to capture relations, $E \subseteq V \times R \times V$, connecting the nodes with relation types from the set R.

The nodes of the working subgraph G_w are selected by first linking the concepts from the question, V_q, and from the answer, V_a, to nodes in G, where $V_q \cup V_a = V_{q,a} \subset V$. All of the nodes on a 2-hop path between the nodes in $V_{q,a}$, i.e., all nodes in V related to two of the nodes in $V_{q,a}$ are also included in the working graph, producing V_w. Finally, V_w is pruned down to 200 nodes by scoring the relevance of each node to the (q, a) pair using a PLM as described in Yasunaga et al. (2021). All of the edges connecting each pair of nodes in V_w, defined as $E_w \subset E$, are included in the final working graph, $G_w = (V_w, E_w)$.

Following Yasunaga et al. (2021), the initial 1024-dimensional embeddings of these nodes are defined by feeding each triple composed of a head, relation and tail entity, $(h, r, t) \in V_w \times R \times V_w$, as a sentence into a PLM text encoder. The representations for each concept are pooled using the corresponding portion of each triple that they appear in. Computing relation embeddings r in Yasunaga et al. (2021) in this way was unnecessary, as they represent the relation type as a one-hot vector for their GNN module. However, in our approach, each relation is a distributed representation, r, so we use an initial vector embedding computed in the same way as each graph concept embedding is computed.

Feng et al. (2020) provide embeddings computed for each concept in the graphs used. However, these embeddings do not include relations. As a result, we computed all embeddings following the process defined in Lin et al. (2019).

4.2 Model

Given the working graph for a (q, a) pair, $G_w = (V_w, E_w)$, and initial concept and relation embeddings $\mathbf{v_i}, i \in [0, 1, \ldots, |V_w|]$, $\mathbf{r_j}, j \in [0, 1, \ldots, |R|]$, the VSA representation of a given triple can be computed as follows. For triple $triple_k = (h_k, e_k, t_k), k \in [0, 1, \ldots, |E_w|]$, where h_k, e_k, t_k specifies the type of entity for the head, relation, and tail of the triple, respectively, we bind each of the elements together using the binding operation of the given VSA: $\mathbf{triple_{k_{vsa}}} = \mathbf{v_{h_k}} \circledast \mathbf{r_{e_k}} \circledast \mathbf{v_{t_k}}$. The working graph VSA representation can be calculated by adding up all the triple VSA representations in the graph:

$$\mathbf{g_{vsa}} = \sum_{k=1}^{|E_w|} \mathbf{triple_{k_{vsa}}} = \sum_{k=1}^{|E_w|} \mathbf{v_{h_k}} \circledast \mathbf{r_{e_k}} \circledast \mathbf{v_{t_k}}.$$

Since circular convolution is commutative, $\mathbf{triple_{k_{vsa}}}$ does not contain information on the direction of the relation, so a specific permutation σ can be applied to either the head or tail element of each triple to specify the directionality of the relation. To query this triple for a permuted concept, σ^{-1} is applied after unbinding.

Given a QA input for question q and answer option a, an LM representation of the context is generated with a pretrained encoder to generate $LM(q|a) = \mathbf{z}$. We can also integrate $\mathbf{z}$ into $\mathbf{g_{vsa}}$, analogous to Yasunaga et al. (2021), by forming new triples that bind $\mathbf{z}$ with two new defined relation SPs, **IsAnswerConcept** and **IsQuestionConcept**, along with the corresponding answer and question concepts in $\mathbf{g_{vsa}}$. These triples are then added to $\mathbf{g_{vsa}}$ like usual.

For example, the question in the CSQA dataset "What is the primary purpose of cars?" has the answer options {cost money, slow down, move people, turn right}, with the correct answer being "move people". The subgraph for the QA context [What is the primary purpose of cars? move people] has question concepts V_q = {PURPOSE, CAR, PRIMARY, CARS}, answer concepts V_a = {PEOPLE, MOVE, MOVE_PEOPLE}, and many intermediate concepts, along with a set of triples, E = {(MOVE, ANTONYM, STOP), (CAR, CAPABLEOF, GO_FAST), ... }. The graph VSA vector is computed as

$$\mathbf{g_{vsa}} = (\mathbf{MOVE} \circledast \mathbf{ANTONYM} \circledast \mathbf{STOP})_{\mathbf{vsa}} + (\mathbf{CAR} \circledast \mathbf{CAPABLEOF} \circledast \mathbf{GO\_FAST})_{\mathbf{vsa}} + \ldots$$

$\mathbf{g_{vsa}}$ is then used as the input to a k-layer MLP with dropout and layer normalization, $MLP(\mathbf{g_{vsa}}) = \mathbf{g^*_{vsa}}$, and is responsible for learning to update the VSA representations within the graph vectors to solve the task (see Figure 1).

A plausibility score, i.e. the probability of answer a being correct, is computed with $p(a|q) \propto \exp(FF(\mathbf{z} \bigoplus \mathbf{g^*_{vsa}}))$, where the initial QA context $\mathbf{z}$ is concatenated with the final graph VSA representation, $\mathbf{g^*_{vsa}}$, and is passed through a final feedforward layer.

During training, the cross entropy between the plausibility scores of all answer options are computed, and are backpropagated through both the LM and VSA MLP components of the model.

5 Experiments

In order to perform a comparison to QA-GNN, we evaluate QAVSA on the same three datasets that were used to evaluate QA-GNN in Yasunaga et al. (2021). However, we hyperparameter tune our model rather than keeping parameters the same as those used in QA-GNN to maximize accuracy on the benchmark development splits.

5.1 Datasets

CommonsenseQA (CSQA) (Talmor et al., 2019) is a 5-way multiple choice commonsense reasoning task that requires different types of commonsense knowledge. The dataset has 12,102 questions, and the inhouse train/dev/test split is adapted from Lin et al. (2019) as 8500/1221/1241.

OpenbookQA (OBQA) (Mihaylov et al., 2018) is a 4-way multiple choice dataset aiming to assess human understanding of a subject in an openbook setting. The dataset consists of a list of 1326 science facts along with 5957 elementary school science questions with a train/dev/test split of 4957/500/500.

MedQA-USMLE (MedQA) (Jin et al., 2021) is a 4-way multiple choice dataset based on questions from the United States Medical License Exams (USMLE). The english version of the dataset has 12,723 questions, with a train/dev/test split of 10178/1272/1273.

For CSQA and OBQA, the external KG used is ConceptNet (Speer et al., 2017). ConceptNet consists of 799,273 common words or phrases connected by edges of 17 different merged relation types, after preprocessing. The method to initialize the concept and relation embeddings for ConceptNet are also described in Section 4.1, and uses PLMs BERT-large or RoBERTa-Large. Following Yasunaga et al. (2021), RoBERTa-Large is he PLM used to encode the QA contexts in QAVSA for CSQA, and AristoRoBERTa (Clark et al., 2020) is used for the QA contexts for OBQA.

The external KG used for MedQA is the Unified Medical Language System (UMLS; Bodenreider (2004)), a popular biomedical knowledge base with 300K nodes, 1M edges, and 98 relation types. The PLM encoder used to generate concept and relation vector embeddings is BioLinkBERT, following Yasunaga et al. (2022a), which is a specific version of LinkBERT that utilizes medical document hyperlinks. BioLinkBERT is pretrained on PubMed with citation links to perform both masked language modeling and document relation prediction (Yasunaga et al., 2022b).

5.2 Implementation and Training Details

Because we had to recompute concept embeddings for ConceptNet and UMLS, we reproduced results from QA-GNN with these new embeddings as a baseline. The LM and MLP learning rates and learning schedule for QA-GNN are kept to their

Model	IH Dev. Acc.	IH Test Acc. (%)
RoBERTa-Large* (w/o KG)	76.27 (±0.45)	70.23 (±0.80)
+QA-GNN*	75.97 (±0.64)	**71.88 (±1.11)**
+QAVSA	**76.61 (±0.54)**	70.56 (±0.72)

Table 1: Accuracy and standard deviation on CSQA inhouse dev. and test splits. Reproduced results (*) use reproduced node embeddings and all results are averaged over 5 different seeds.

Model	Dev. Acc. (%)	Test Acc. (%)
AristoRoBERTa* (w/o KG)	81.32 (±0.61)	81.00 (±0.65)
+QA-GNN*	**81.92 (±0.78)**	80.36 (±1.63)
+QAVSA	81.76 (±1.41)	**81.92 (±0.88)**

Table 2: Test accuracy on OBQA. Reproduced results (*) use reproduced node embeddings and all results are averaged over 5 different seeds.

original values for all three datasets since their model training proved to be unstable with the parameters that were optimized for QAVSA. The number of training epochs for QA-GNN are 15, 40, and 30 for CSQA, OBQA, and MedQA, respectively, to match the original amount epochs, whereas QAVSA is trained for 15 epochs on each dataset. As a baseline to both QA-GNN and QAVSA model results, we reran our model consisting of only the PLM encoder and final layer scoring components, with all other parameters remaining unchanged.

Hyperparameter tuning was done using a Tree-structured Parzen Estimater as a sampler for both OBQA and CSQA. The variables optimized during tuning and final model parameter values are shown in Appendix A.1 in Tables 7 and 6, respectively.

Although the QA-context embedding, $\mathbf{z}$, is added to the graph in Figure 1, the QAVSA results in Section 6.1 are produced from a version of QAVSA that uses working graphs without adding $\mathbf{z}$ to them.

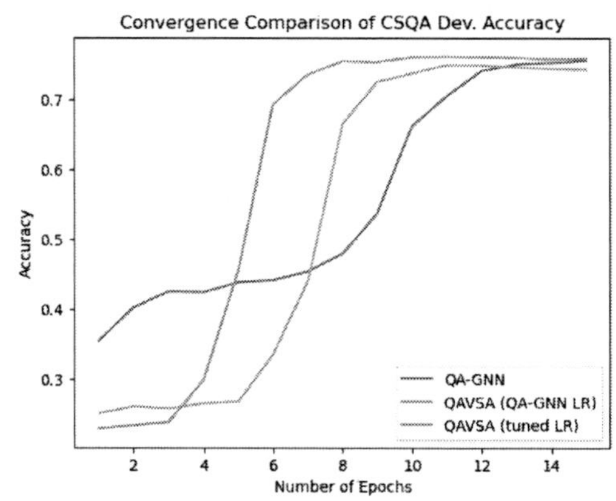

Figure 2: Mean accuracy of QA-GNN, QAVSA using our tuned LR schedule, and QAVSA using the LR schedule of QA-GNN on the CSQA dev. split for each epoch, averaged over 5 seed runs.

6 Results

6.1 Main Results

As shown in Table 1, QAVSA has an improvement in mean accuracy of 0.34% and 0.61% compared to QA-GNN and RoBERTa-Large, respectively, on the CSQA inhouse dev. split. On the inhouse test split however, QA-GNN outperforms QAVSA by a difference of 1.32% and improves upon the baseline by 1.65%.

On the OBQA dataset, QA-GNN has the best performance on the dev. split with a mean accuracy of 81.92%, as seen in Table 2. QAVSA is close behind with a mean accuracy of 81.76%, which is a 0.44% increase compared to the AristoRoBERTa baseline. However, on the test split QAVSA outperforms QA-GNN by a larger margin with a mean accuracy of 81.92%, which is a 0.92% improvement on the AristoRoBERTa baseline and a 1.56% improvement over QA-GNN.

As shown in Table 3, QAVSA outperforms QA-GNN and the BioLinkBERT baseline on MedQA by a mean accuracy of 0.37% and 0.61%, respectively, on the dev. split and by 0.42% and 1.16%, respectively, on the test split.

Also, as shown in Figure 2, QAVSA converges faster during training. On average, it takes 11.2, 8.8, and 6.8 epochs to reach within 5% of each run's maximum accuracy for QA-GNN, QAVSA (QA-GNN LR schedule), and QAVSA (our LR sched-

Model	Dev. Acc. (%)	Test Acc. (%)
BioLinkBERT* (w/o KG)	43.55 ($\pm$0.08)	43.96 ($\pm$0.12)
+QA-GNN*	43.79 ($\pm$0.31)	44.7 ($\pm$0.47)
+QAVSA	**44.16 ($\pm$0.57)**	**45.12 ($\pm$0.70)**

Table 3: Test accuracy and standard deviation on MedQA. Reproduced results are denoted with * and all results are averaged over 3 runs.

ule), respectively. Demonstrating that QAVSA can be trained 39% faster than QA-GNN.

Overall, these results suggest that QAVSA performs similarly to QA-GNN, but has a significantly faster convergence time during training.

6.2 Model Variations and Ablation

Results of several QAVSA model variations on the OBQA benchmark are shown in Table 4, with all other architecture parameters in Table 6 kept constant. The QAVSA result in Table 4 corresponds to the results of one of the five seeds from Table 2. Including the QA context into the working graph drops the dev. and test accuracy by $\sim 3\%$, suggesting that for this parameter configuration, dynamically updating the graph representation in this way either muddles the original graph representation, or creates a VSA representation that is more difficult to learn by the neural network.

Introducing directionality in the VSA triples by means of permutation on the head or tail entities in the triple does not improve accuracy, which indicates that binding through circular convolution stores enough semantic information from the graph for the task. Furthermore, the HRR VSA is superior to other non-commutative algebras like VTB and TVTB with this architecture, with improvements of 1.6% and 2.2% in dev. accuracy and 3.2% and 1.4% in test accuracy, compared to VTB and TVTB, respectively.

Applying normalization to the graph VSA vectors only drops performance when the concept vectors are also normalized. This indicates that including some type of information of the magnitude of either the graphs or concepts in the VSA vectors is useful for question answering. Not normalizing both graphs and concepts resulted in graph VSA vectors with too wide of a magnitude range for stable training.

Also, BERT performs fairly similarly to RoBERTa in initializing concept and relation embeddings (Section 4.1), with a drop in accuracy only on the dev. split.

Results for an ablation study on the OBQA benchmark are shown in Table 5. Replacing BERT-encoded relation embeddings with random unit-length 1024-D vectors, with a maximum similarity to the concept vocabulary of 0.3, dropped the test accuracy by 2%. However, the dev. accuracy remained fairly consistent, suggesting that the dissimilarity of the relation vectors may be enough to properly represent the semantics of the graph.

Removing node pruning, so that all the nodes and respective edges are included subgraph rather than just the top 200 nodes, dropped test accuracy the most significantly, which may suggest that the extra nodes included in the graph vectors did not add triples useful to reasoning over the question and answer concepts.

Layer normalization between the VSA MLP layers also seems to be important for learning over these graph representations, as seen in the 1.8% drop in dev. and test accuracy when it is removed.

6.3 Explainable Graph VSA Representations

We can analyze the effectiveness of the MLP portion of QAVSA by computing the similarities of each triple VSA vector in a graph to the initial graph vector, $\mathbf{g}_{\mathbf{vsa}}$, and the final graph vector, $\mathbf{g}^*_{\mathbf{vsa}} = MLP(\mathbf{g}_{\mathbf{vsa}})$ using the similarity operator defined in Section 3. Such similarities can be used to determine which triples become the most prominent in the graph vector through the MLP transformation. In the top 20 most similar triples from the initial graph representation in Section 4.2, we find triples relating to the concept CAR, such as (CAR, RELATEDTO, DRIVE), (MOTOR, RELATEDTO, CAR), and (STOP, RELATEDTO, CAR), but it does not contain any triple relating the answer "move people". After the MLP, however, in the top 20 most similar triples to $\mathbf{g}^*_{\mathbf{vsa}}$, the triples (STREET, USEDFOR, TRANSPORTATION), (TRANSPORTATION, RELATEDTO, CAR), and (STREET, RELATEDTO, CARS) appear. Given that the concept TRANSPORTATION is closely related to the answer "move people" and does not appear in the most similar initial triples, we can see that the $\mathbf{g}^*_{\mathbf{vsa}}$ attends more to

Model Version	Dev. Acc. (%)	Test Acc. (%)
QAVSA	82.6	**83.4**
+ QA-context	79.8	80.2
+ Permutation (head)	81.8	82.6
+ Permutation (tail)	81.6	83.2
+ Graph norm	81.6	82.4
+ Graph norm - Concept not norm	**83.0**	82.8
RoBERTa Embeddings	81.0	**83.4**
VTB	81	80.2
TVTB	80.4	82.0

Table 4: Accuracy of different model variations on dev. and test splits of OBQA.

Model Version	Dev. Acc. (%)	Test Acc. (%)
QAVSA	**82.6**	**83.4**
– BERT rels	82.4	81.4
– Node Pruning	82	80.4
– Layer Norm	80.8	81.6

Table 5: Accuracy on OBQA of ablation study. The minus sign (–) indicates what was removed.

concepts and reasoning paths necessary for answering the question. Since the learned graph transformations are not perfect, some unrelated triples do appear in $\mathbf{g}^*_{\mathbf{vsa}}$, such as (CHROME, RELATEDTO, METAL) and (FERRY, RELATEDTO, MOVE).

This method of analysis can also explain incorrect answers produced by the model. For the question from the CSQA dev. split, "What do audiences clap for?", QAVSA predicted the answer to be "hockey game" rather than the correct label "show". Looking at the 20 most similar triples in $\mathbf{g}^*_{\mathbf{vsa}}$ for the answer option "show", there are triples relating to AUDIENCE and SHOW, like (AUDIENCE, RELATEDTO, THEATRE) and (PROGRAM, RELATEDTO, SHOW), but there are no triples related to CLAP. Looking at the 20 most similar triples to $\mathbf{g}^*_{\mathbf{vsa}}$ for the answer option "hockey game", a reasoning path can be drawn with (SPORT, RELATEDTO, PLAY), (PLAY, RELATEDTO, EVENT), (BEAT, RELATEDTO, EVENT), and (CLAP, HAS_SUB_EVENT, BEAT). Two different definitions of BEAT are used in the prior triples, making the reasoning path illogical. The concept "CLAP" appears in 3 out of the top 20 triples for answer option, thus potentially leading QAVSA to choose this option as the most correct answer. With this particular example, this VSA-style analysis suggests that QAVSA may attend to multiple meanings of the same concept incorrectly, which could be useful information for finetuning the method further or applying it to other tasks.

7 Discussion

On the CSQA and OBQA datasets, there is no definitive top performer between QA-GNN and QAVSA due to the fact that both models have the best performance on one of the dataset splits. The accuracy of QA-GNN is slightly lower than PLM baseline for the CSQA inhouse dev. split and the OBQA test split, and this is most likely due to a combination of larger variance of model accuracy between seeds along with the fact that the model learning rate was not tuned for our recomputed concept embeddings.

For MedQA however, QAVSA slightly outperforms QA-GNN on both the dev. and test splits. MedQA is a significantly harder than CSQA and OBQA due to the nature of the in-depth medical questions asked. This is evidenced by the difference in accuracy of more than 30% compared to CSQA and OBQA. This more consistent performance increase may suggest that the increased semantic complexity of the concepts and relations in UMLS benefit more from the structured VSA representations generated and reasoned over in QAVSA rather than using multi-relational GNNs to update concept embeddings.

Although QAVSA does not consistently outperform QA-GNN, the architecture is much simpler than the Graph Attention Network in QA-GNN as it feeds VSA vectors into standard MLP layers. There is no requirement to use node embeddings matrices during computation along with linear and non-linear transformations on node and relation type embeddings to perform message passing between concepts. Also, there is no requirement to use graph attention layers to create attention weights on the relations between concepts. In QAVSA, the attention on the relational edges within the graph arises naturally and can be analyzed as shown in Section 6.3.

Additionally, the QAVSA memory requirements for its graph representation is constant at the dimensionality of the VSA vector, d. This compares favorable to GNNs that require an $N \times d$ node embedding matrix and an $N \times N$ adjacency matrix. For these benchmarks, QA-GNN requires graphs with exactly 200 nodes for each QA pair. If one wanted to scale up the number of nodes in the graph significantly, the memory resources required would grow quadratically. In contrast, with an increase in the number of graph nodes and edges, the memory requirements for QAVSA are constant.

8 Conclusion

We presented QAVSA, a new type of model that leverages VSA-represented knowledge graphs along with general linguistic knowledge from PLMs to perform reasoning on MCQA benchmarks. Through a direct comparison to the GNN-based model QA-GNN, we exhibit the ability of QAVSA to perform similarly to QA-GNN on three datasets, while using a simpler k-layer MLP reasoning module. We also demonstrate faster convergence during training than QA-GNN and highlight the explainability of our model outputs through our VSA graph representations.

For future study, our method of representing knowledge graphs with VSAs could be useful in a wide variety of knowledge graph QA tasks involving information retrieval, like multi-hop reasoning (Lan et al., 2021). There are many other ways that KGs are integrated into LLMs, such as using them to augment LLM input or using them as training objectives during LLM pretraining, so having an efficient VSA representation of these KGs may be beneficial to these methods (Pan et al., 2024). GNNs are also widespread for tasks outside of natural language processing, such object detection, chemical reaction prediction, and disease classification, and it is worthwhile to determine if our VSA-based approach is useful for representing structures that are not linguistic (Zhou et al., 2020).

Limitations

Our method depends on already constructed knowledge graphs (i.e., ConceptNet, UMLS), and specifically with these benchmarks, a predefined subgraph generation process. Thus, the quality of our graph VSA representations for question answering tasks is dependent on the quality of the initial graph construction.

Similarly, the quality of the intitial concept and relation embeddings is of great importance. If the concept vector embeddings are too low-dimensional, have large variance in their magnitude, or are too similar to each other, the individual triple or graph VSA representations may not be able to contain many graph triples.

Ethical Concerns

Our proposed model uses pretrained language models, and because of this, any biases or stereotypes in their training data may be reflected in model outputs.

Broader Impact

The augmentation of PLMs with GNNs is widespread, so many further studies could be conducted to compare this VSA-based method to any of these models. Also, this paper encourages the exploration of augmenting large language models using VSAs outside the context of KGs and GNNs.

Acknowledgements

The authors would like to thank the members of the Computational Neuroscience Research Group (CNRG) for discussions that helped improve this paper. This work was supported by CFI (52479-10006) and OIT (35768) infrastructure funding as well as the Canada Research Chairs program, and NSERC Discovery grant 261453.

References

Rohan Anil, Andrew M. Dai, Orhan Firat, Melvin Johnson, Dmitry Lepikhin, Alexandre Passos, Siamak Shakeri, Emanuel Taropa, Paige Bailey, Zhifeng Chen, Eric Chu, Jonathan H. Clark, Laurent El Shafey, Yanping Huang, Kathy Meier-Hellstern, Gaurav Mishra, Erica Moreira, Mark Omernick, Kevin Robinson, Sebastian Ruder, Yi Tay, Kefan Xiao, Yuanzhong Xu, Yujing Zhang, Gustavo Hernandez Abrego, Junwhan Ahn, Jacob Austin, Paul Barham, Jan Botha, James Bradbury, Siddhartha Brahma, Kevin Brooks, Michele Catasta, Yong Cheng, Colin Cherry, Christopher A. Choquette-Choo, Aakanksha Chowdhery, Clément Crepy, Shachi Dave, Mostafa Dehghani, Sunipa Dev, Jacob Devlin, Mark Díaz, Nan Du, Ethan Dyer, Vlad Feinberg, Fangxiaoyu

Feng, Vlad Fienber, Markus Freitag, Xavier Garcia, Sebastian Gehrmann, Lucas Gonzalez, Guy Gur-Ari, Steven Hand, Hadi Hashemi, Le Hou, Joshua Howland, Andrea Hu, Jeffrey Hui, Jeremy Hurwitz, Michael Isard, Abe Ittycheriah, Matthew Jagielski, Wenhao Jia, Kathleen Kenealy, Maxim Krikun, Sneha Kudugunta, Chang Lan, Katherine Lee, Benjamin Lee, Eric Li, Music Li, Wei Li, YaGuang Li, Jian Li, Hyeontaek Lim, Hanzhao Lin, Zhongtao Liu, Frederick Liu, Marcello Maggioni, Aroma Mahendru, Joshua Maynez, Vedant Misra, Maysam Moussalem, Zachary Nado, John Nham, Eric Ni, Andrew Nystrom, Alicia Parrish, Marie Pellat, Martin Polacek, Alex Polozov, Reiner Pope, Siyuan Qiao, Emily Reif, Bryan Richter, Parker Riley, Alex Castro Ros, Aurko Roy, Brennan Saeta, Rajkumar Samuel, Renee Shelby, Ambrose Slone, Daniel Smilkov, David R. So, Daniel Sohn, Simon Tokumine, Dasha Valter, Vijay Vasudevan, Kiran Vodrahalli, Xuezhi Wang, Pidong Wang, Zirui Wang, Tao Wang, John Wieting, Yuhuai Wu, Kelvin Xu, Yunhan Xu, Linting Xue, Pengcheng Yin, Jiahui Yu, Qiao Zhang, Steven Zheng, Ce Zheng, Weikang Zhou, Denny Zhou, Slav Petrov, and Yonghui Wu. 2023. PaLM 2 Technical Report. ArXiv:2305.10403 [cs].

Olivier Bodenreider. 2004. The Unified Medical Language System (UMLS): integrating biomedical terminology. *Nucleic Acids Research*, 32(Database issue):D267–D270.

Peter Clark, Oren Etzioni, Daniel Khashabi, Tushar Khot, Bhavana Dalvi Mishra, Kyle Richardson, Ashish Sabharwal, Carissa Schoenick, Oyvind Tafjord, Niket Tandon, Sumithra Bhakthavatsalam, Dirk Groeneveld, Michal Guerquin, and Michael Schmitz. 2020. From F to A on the New York Regents Science Exams — An Overview of the Aristo Project. *AI Magazine*, 41(4):39–53.

Eric Crawford, Matthew Gingerich, and Chris Eliasmith. 2016. Biologically plausible, human-scale knowledge representation. *Cognitive science*, 40(4):782–821.

Yanlin Feng, Xinyue Chen, Bill Yuchen Lin, Peifeng Wang, Jun Yan, and Xiang Ren. 2020. Scalable Multi-Hop Relational Reasoning for Knowledge-Aware Question Answering. In *Proceedings of the 2020 Conference on Empirical Methods in Natural Language Processing (EMNLP)*, pages 1295–1309, Online. Association for Computational Linguistics.

Ross W. Gayler. 2004. Vector symbolic architectures answer jackendoff's challenges for cognitive neuroscience. *ArXiv*, abs/cs/0412059.

Jan Gosmann and Chris Eliasmith. 2019. Vector-Derived Transformation Binding: An Improved Binding Operation for Deep Symbol-Like Processing in Neural Networks. *Neural Computation*, 31(5):849–869.

Jiaxin Huang, Shixiang Gu, Le Hou, Yuexin Wu, Xuezhi Wang, Hongkun Yu, and Jiawei Han. 2023a. Large Language Models Can Self-Improve. In *Proceedings of the 2023 Conference on Empirical Methods in Natural Language Processing*, pages 1051–1068, Singapore. Association for Computational Linguistics.

Yongfeng Huang, Yanyang Li, Yichong Xu, Lin Zhang, Ruyi Gan, Jiaxing Zhang, and Liwei Wang. 2023b. MVP-Tuning: Multi-View Knowledge Retrieval with Prompt Tuning for Commonsense Reasoning. In *Proceedings of the 61st Annual Meeting of the Association for Computational Linguistics (Volume 1: Long Papers)*, pages 13417–13432, Toronto, Canada. Association for Computational Linguistics.

Di Jin, Eileen Pan, Nassim Oufattole, Wei-Hung Weng, Hanyi Fang, and Peter Szolovits. 2021. What Disease Does This Patient Have? A Large-Scale Open Domain Question Answering Dataset from Medical Exams. *Applied Sciences*, 11(14):6421. Number: 14 Publisher: Multidisciplinary Digital Publishing Institute.

Daniel Khashabi, Sewon Min, Tushar Khot, Ashish Sabharwal, Oyvind Tafjord, Peter Clark, and Hannaneh Hajishirzi. 2020. UNIFIEDQA: Crossing Format Boundaries with a Single QA System. In *Findings of the Association for Computational Linguistics: EMNLP 2020*, pages 1896–1907, Online. Association for Computational Linguistics.

Yunshi Lan, Gaole He, Jinhao Jiang, Jing Jiang, Wayne Xin Zhao, and Ji-Rong Wen. 2021. A Survey on Complex Knowledge Base Question Answering: Methods, Challenges and Solutions. In *Proceedings of the Thirtieth International Joint Conference on Artificial Intelligence*, pages 4483–4491, Montreal, Canada. International Joint Conferences on Artificial Intelligence Organization.

Bill Yuchen Lin, Xinyue Chen, Jamin Chen, and Xiang Ren. 2019. KagNet: Knowledge-Aware Graph Networks for Commonsense Reasoning. In *Proceedings of the 2019 Conference on Empirical Methods in Natural Language Processing and the 9th International Joint Conference on Natural Language Processing (EMNLP-IJCNLP)*, pages 2829–2839, Hong Kong, China. Association for Computational Linguistics.

Nicholas Lourie, Ronan Le Bras, Chandra Bhagavatula, and Yejin Choi. 2021. UNICORN on RAINBOW: A Universal Commonsense Reasoning Model on a New Multitask Benchmark. *Proceedings of the AAAI Conference on Artificial Intelligence*, 35(15):13480–13488. Number: 15.

Todor Mihaylov, Peter Clark, Tushar Khot, and Ashish Sabharwal. 2018. Can a Suit of Armor Conduct Electricity? A New Dataset for Open Book Question Answering. ArXiv:1809.02789 [cs].

Shirui Pan, Linhao Luo, Yufei Wang, Chen Chen, Jiapu Wang, and Xindong Wu. 2024. Unifying large language models and knowledge graphs: A roadmap. *IEEE Transactions on Knowledge and Data Engineering*.

T.A. Plate. 1995. Holographic reduced representations. *IEEE Transactions on Neural Networks*, 6(3):623–641. Conference Name: IEEE Transactions on Neural Networks.

Karan Singhal, Tao Tu, Juraj Gottweis, Rory Sayres, Ellery Wulczyn, Le Hou, Kevin Clark, Stephen Pfohl, Heather Cole-Lewis, Darlene Neal, Mike Schaekermann, Amy Wang, Mohamed Amin, Sami Lachgar, Philip Mansfield, Sushant Prakash, Bradley Green, Ewa Dominowska, Blaise Aguera y Arcas, Nenad Tomasev, Yun Liu, Renee Wong, Christopher Semturs, S. Sara Mahdavi, Joelle Barral, Dale Webster, Greg S. Corrado, Yossi Matias, Shekoofeh Azizi, Alan Karthikesalingam, and Vivek Natarajan. 2023. Towards Expert-Level Medical Question Answering with Large Language Models. ArXiv:2305.09617 [cs].

Robyn Speer, Joshua Chin, and Catherine Havasi. 2017. ConceptNet 5.5: An Open Multilingual Graph of General Knowledge. *Proceedings of the AAAI Conference on Artificial Intelligence*, 31(1). Number: 1.

Alon Talmor, Jonathan Herzig, Nicholas Lourie, and Jonathan Berant. 2019. CommonsenseQA: A Question Answering Challenge Targeting Commonsense Knowledge. ArXiv:1811.00937 [cs].

Ashish Vaswani, Noam Shazeer, Niki Parmar, Jakob Uszkoreit, Llion Jones, Aidan N Gomez, Ł ukasz Kaiser, and Illia Polosukhin. 2017. Attention is All you Need. In *Advances in Neural Information Processing Systems*, volume 30. Curran Associates, Inc.

Petar Velickovic, Guillem Cucurull, Arantxa Casanova, Adriana Romero, Pietro Liò, and Yoshua Bengio. 2018. Graph Attention Networks. In *International Conference on Learning Representations*.

Kuan Wang, Yuyu Zhang, Diyi Yang, Le Song, and Tao Qin. 2022. GNN is a Counter? Revisiting GNN for Question Answering. In *International Conference on Learning Representations*.

Yichong Xu, Chenguang Zhu, Shuohang Wang, Siqi Sun, Hao Cheng, Xiaodong Liu, Jianfeng Gao, Pengcheng He, Michael Zeng, and Xuedong Huang. 2022. Human Parity on CommonsenseQA: Augmenting Self-Attention with External Attention. In *Proceedings of the Thirty-First International Joint Conference on Artificial Intelligence, IJCAI-22*, volume 3, pages 2762–2768. ISSN: 1045-0823.

Yichong Xu, Chenguang Zhu, Ruochen Xu, Yang Liu, Michael Zeng, and Xuedong Huang. 2021. Fusing Context Into Knowledge Graph for Commonsense Question Answering. In *Findings of the Association for Computational Linguistics: ACL-IJCNLP 2021*, pages 1201–1207, Online. Association for Computational Linguistics.

Michihiro Yasunaga, Antoine Bosselut, Hongyu Ren, Xikun Zhang, Christopher D. Manning, Percy S. Liang, and Jure Leskovec. 2022a. Deep Bidirectional Language-Knowledge Graph Pretraining. *Advances in Neural Information Processing Systems*, 35:37309–37323.

Michihiro Yasunaga, Jure Leskovec, and Percy Liang. 2022b. LinkBERT: Pretraining Language Models with Document Links. In *Proceedings of the 60th Annual Meeting of the Association for Computational Linguistics (Volume 1: Long Papers)*, pages 8003–8016, Dublin, Ireland. Association for Computational Linguistics.

Michihiro Yasunaga, Hongyu Ren, Antoine Bosselut, Percy Liang, and Jure Leskovec. 2021. QA-GNN: Reasoning with Language Models and Knowledge Graphs for Question Answering. In *Proceedings of the 2021 Conference of the North American Chapter of the Association for Computational Linguistics: Human Language Technologies*, pages 535–546, Online. Association for Computational Linguistics.

Zi Ye, Yogan Jaya Kumar, Goh Ong Sing, Fengyan Song, and Junsong Wang. 2022. A Comprehensive Survey of Graph Neural Networks for Knowledge Graphs. *IEEE Access*, 10:75729–75741. Conference Name: IEEE Access.

Zhangdie Yuan, Songbo Hu, Ivan Vulić, Anna Korhonen, and Zaiqiao Meng. 2023. Can Pretrained Language Models (Yet) Reason Deductively? In *Proceedings of the 17th Conference of the European Chapter of the Association for Computational Linguistics*, pages 1447–1462, Dubrovnik, Croatia. Association for Computational Linguistics.

Xikun Zhang, Antoine Bosselut, Michihiro Yasunaga, Hongyu Ren, Percy Liang, Christopher D. Manning, and Jure Leskovec. 2021. GreaseLM: Graph REASoning Enhanced Language Models. In *International Conference on Learning Representations*.

Jie Zhou, Ganqu Cui, Shengding Hu, Zhengyan Zhang, Cheng Yang, Zhiyuan Liu, Lifeng Wang, Changcheng Li, and Maosong Sun. 2020. Graph neural networks: A review of methods and applications. *AI Open*, 1:57–81.

A Appendix

A.1 Model Parameters

Final model and training parameters are shown in Table 6. The parameters optimized for OBQA are also used for MedQA. k specifies how many layers the MLP will have. LR schedule cycles defines how many cosine periods are in the LR schedule. The encoder learning rate (LR) specifies the LR for whatever PLM is in use to encode the QA context, and the decoder LR applies to all other components of the model. The unfreeze epoch defines after how many epochs do the PLM weights unfreeze. The ranges for these variables during hyperparameter tuning are shown in Table 7.

Variable	CSQA Value	OBQA Value	MedQA Value
k	5	4	4
Epochs	15	15	15
LR Schedule	cosine w/ restarts	cosine w/ restarts	cosine w/ restarts
LR Schedule Cycles	1	2	1
Warmup Steps	200	200	200
Batch Size	64	64	64
Mini Batch Size	8	8	2
Encoder LR	1.77e-5	4.17e-5	4.17e-5
Decoder LR	3.71e-2	3.41e-2	3.41e-2
Unfreeze epoch	3	3	3
Dropout (VSA MLP)	0.2	0.4	0.4
Dropout (final layer)	0.4	0.8	0.8

Table 6: Model parameter values on all experiment datasets.

Variable	Range
k	{3, 4, 5}
LR Schedule Cycles	{1, 2, 3}
Encoder LR	[1e-7, 5e-4]
Decoder LR	[1e-5, 5e-2]
Unfreeze epoch	{0, 3, 6}
Dropout (VSA MLP)	{0.2, 0.4, 0.6, 0.8}
Dropout (final layer)	{0.2, 0.4, 0.6, 0.8}

Table 7: Variable ranges for hyperparameter tuning for CSQA and OBQA.

Tracking linguistic information in transformer-based sentence embeddings through targeted sparsification

Vivi Nastase[1] and **Paola Merlo**[1,2]
[1]Idiap Research Institute, Martigny, Switzerland
[2]University of Geneva, Swizerland
vivi.a.nastase@gmail.com, Paola.Merlo@unige.ch

Abstract

Analyses of transformer-based models have shown that they encode a variety of linguistic information from their textual input. While these analyses have shed a light on the relation between linguistic information on one side, and internal architecture and parameters on the other, a question remains unanswered: how is this linguistic information reflected in sentence embeddings? Using datasets consisting of sentences with known structure, we test to what degree information about chunks (in particular noun, verb or prepositional phrases), such as grammatical number, or semantic role, can be localized in sentence embeddings. Our results show that such information is not distributed over the entire sentence embedding, but rather it is encoded in specific regions. Understanding how the information from an input text is compressed into sentence embeddings helps understand current transformer models and help build future explainable neural models.

1 Introduction

In the quest for understanding transformer-based models, much work has been dedicated to uncover what kind of information is encoded in the model's various layers and parameters. These analyses have provided several enlightening insights: (i) different types of linguistic information – e.g. parts of speech, syntactic structure, named entities – are selectively more evident at different layers of the model (Tenney et al., 2019a; Rogers et al., 2020), (ii) subnetworks can be identified that seem to encode particular linguistic functionalities (Csordás et al., 2021), and (iii) fine-tuning for specific tasks can be focused on very small subsets of parameters, on different parts of a model's layers (Panigrahi et al., 2023). While these analyses and probes have focused on the insides of the models, mostly their parameters and layers, testing their impact is usually done by using the output of the model, namely token or sentence embeddings, to solve specific tasks. The link between the inside of the model and its outputs is usually not explicitly investigated.

We ask several facets of this question here: how are the internally-detected information types and structures reflected in the model's output? And how are arbitrarily long and complex sentences encoded systematically in a fixed-sized vector?

Understanding what kind of information the sentence embeddings encode, and how, has multiple benefits: (i) it connects internal changes in the model parameters and structure with changes in its outputs; (ii) it contributes to verifying the robustness of models and whether or not they rely on shallow or accidental regularities in the data; (iii) it narrows down the field of search when a language model produces wrong outputs, and (iv) it helps maximize the use of training data for developing more robust models from smaller textual resources.

Transformer-based models usually use a token-focused learning objective, and have a weaker supervision signal at the sentence level – e.g. a next sentence prediction (Devlin et al., 2018), or sentence order information (Lan et al., 2019). Despite this focus, high performance in a variety of tasks (using raw or fine-tuned sentence embeddings) as well as direct probing shows that sentence representations encode a variety of linguistic information (Conneau et al., 2018). On the other hand, direct exploration of BERT sentence embeddings has also shown that they contain mostly shallow information, related to sentence length and lexical variation, and that many of their dimensions are correlated, indicating that either information is redundantly encoded, or that not all dimensions encode useful information (Nikolaev and Padó, 2023). Some of this preexisting work assumes that sentence embeddings encode information in an overt manner, for example, each principal component dimension is responsible for encoding some type of information.

We adopt the different view that information in

Proceedings of the 9th Workshop on Representation Learning for NLP (RepL4NLP-2024), pages 203–214
August 15, 2024 ©2024 Association for Computational Linguistics

sentence embeddings may be encoded in merged layers, in a manner similar to audio signals being composed of overlapping signals of different frequencies. We hypothesize that each such layer may encode different types of information. We aim to test this hypothesis and check (i) whether we can separate such layers, and (ii) investigate whether information about specific chunks in a sentence –noun,verb, or prepositional phrases– is encoded in different layers and parts of a sentence embedding.

We perform our investigation in an environment with data focused on specific grammatical phenomena, while displaying lexical, structural and semantic variation, and a previously developed system that has been shown to detect the targeted phenomena well (Nastase and Merlo, 2024). The system is a variational encoder-decoder, with an encoder that compresses the information in the input into a very low-dimensional latent vector. Nastase and Merlo (2024) have shown that the sentence embeddings, and their compressed representations on the latent layer, encode information about chunks – noun, verb, prepositional phrases – and their linguistic properties.

The current study investigates the general hypothesis indicated above by specifically exploring two new research questions in this setting:

1. Whether a targeted sparsification of the system maintains a high performance on the task, indicating that information about chunks in the sentence is localizable.

2. Contingent on the answer to the first question, we trace back the signal from the latent layer to the input sentence embeddings, and analyze how specific differences in chunk properties – different number of chunks, or chunks that differ from each other only on one property (e.g. grammatical number) – are localized and reflected in the sentence embeddings.

The code and data are available at https://github.com/CLCL-Geneva/BLM-SNFDisentangling.

2 Related work

Sentence embeddings Transformer models induce contextual token embeddings by passing the embedding vectors through successive layers using multi-head attention that allows for tokens to influence each other's representation at each successive step (Vaswani et al., 2017). The model focuses on the token embeddings, as the tokens expected on the output layer provide the training signal. There are numerous variations on the BERT (Devlin et al., 2018) transformer model[1], that vary in the way the models are trained (Liu et al., 2019), how they combine (or not) the positional and token embeddings (He et al., 2020), how the input is presented to the model (Liu et al., 2019; Clark et al., 2020). With regards to the sentence-level supervision signal, BERT (Devlin et al., 2018) uses the next sentence prediction objective, ALBERT (Lan et al., 2019), aiming to improve coherence, uses sentence order prediction. It is more common to further train or fine-tune a pre-trained model to produce sentence embeddings fitting specific tasks, such as story continuation (Ippolito et al., 2020) or sentence similarity (Reimers and Gurevych, 2019).

Electra (Clark et al., 2020) does not have a sentence-level objective, but it relies on replaced token detection, which relies on the sentence context to determine whether a (number of) token(s) in the given sentence were replaced by a generator sample. This leads to sentence embeddings that perform well on tasks such as Question Answering, or detecting verb classes (Yi et al., 2022).

Probing embeddings and models for linguistic information Most work investigating the kind of knowledge captured by transformer-based models have focused on analysing the architecture of the model (Tenney et al., 2019b; Rogers et al., 2020) to determine the localization and flow of information through the model's layers. There is also much work on analyzing the induced token embeddings to determine what kind of linguistic information they encode, such as sentence structure (Hewitt and Manning, 2019), predicate argument structure (Conia et al., 2022), subjecthood and objecthood (Papadimitriou et al., 2021), among others. Testing whether sentence representation contain specific types of linguistic information has been done using task (or information)-specific classifiers (Adi et al., 2017; Conneau et al., 2018; Goldberg, 2019; Wilson et al., 2023). Opitz and Frank (2022) aim to map subsets of dimensions of fine-tuned sentence embeddings to semantic features.

Sparsification Deep learning models have billions of parameters. This makes them not only incomprehensible, but also expensive to train. The

[1] https://huggingface.co/docs/transformers/en/model_summary

lottery ticket hypothesis (Frankle and Carbin, 2018) posits that large networks can be reduced to subnetworks that encode efficiently the functionality of the entire network. Detecting functional subnetworks can be done *a posteriori*, over a pre-learned network to investigate the functionality of detected subnetworks (Csordás et al., 2021), the potential compositionality of the learned model (Lepori et al., 2023), or where task-specific skills are encoded in a fine-tuned model (Panigrahi et al., 2023).

Instead of learning a sparse network over a pre-learned model, Cao et al. (2021) use a pruning-based approach to finding subnetworks in a pre-trained model that performs some linguistic task. Pruning can be done at several levels of granularity: weights, neurons, layers. Their analyses confirm previous investigations of the types of information encoded in different layers of a transformer (Conneau et al., 2018). Conmy et al. (2023) introduce the Automatic Circuit DisCovery (ACDC) algorithm, which adapts subnetwork probing and head importance score for pruning to discover circuits that implement specific linguistic functions.

Sparsification can also be achieved using L_0 regularization, as the pruning would be done directly during training by encouraging weights to become exactly zero. Louizos et al. (2018); Savarese et al. (2020), among others, implement solutions to the issue that L_0 regularization is non-differentiable, and test it on image classification.

The cited work focuses on the parameters of the model, and sparsification approaches aiming to detect the subnetworks to which specific skills or linguistic information can be ascribed. Our focus, instead, is the output of transformer-based models, in particular sentence embeddings, which we investigate using targeted sparsification.

3 Approach overview

We investigate whether we can identify specific sentence properties in sentence embeddings. Nastase and Merlo (2024) have shown that using an encoder-decoder architecture, sentence embeddings can be compressed into a latent representation that preserves information about chunks in a sentence, and their properties necessary to solve a specific linguistic task.

We first test whether we can sparsify this architecture in a targeted manner, such that each region of the sentence embedding contributes a signal to only one unit of the latent layer. This allows us to isolate different parts of the sentence embedding.

After establishing that sparsification does not lead to a dramatic drop in performance, we trace back the signal from the latent layer to the sentence embeddings, and test whether we can localize information about how different numbers of chunks, or chunks with different properties, are encoded.

In the final step, we use the sparse encoder-decoder sentence compression system as the first in a two-layer system used to solve language tasks – called Blackbird Language Matrices (Merlo, 2023) – that require chunk and chunk properties information. The first layer will compress each sentence into a very small latent vector, and this representation is then used on the second layer to solve a pattern detection problem that relies on information about chunks in a sentence and their pattern across a sequence of sentences.

4 Data

We use two data types: (i) a dataset of sentences with known chunk structure and chunk properties, (ii) two datasets representing two multiple-choice problems, whose solution requires understanding the chunk structure and chunk properties of the sentences in each instance.

4.1 A dataset of sentences

We start with an artificially-created set of sentences built from noun, prepositional and verb phrases. Each sentence has one of the following structures: NP [PP_1 [PP_2]] VP , where the parentheses surround optional structure. Each chunk can have singular or plural form, with agreement between the first NP (the subject) and the VP. This leads to 14'336 sentences with one of 14 patterns.

The dataset consists of ordered pairs of one input sentence and N (=7) output sentences, extracted from the set described above. Only one of the output sentences has the same chunk pattern as the input sentence, and is considered as the correct output. We select 4004 instances uniformly distributed over the 14 patterns, which are split into train:dev:test – 2576:630:798.

4.2 Multiple Choice Problems: Blackbird Language Matrices

Blackbird Language Matrices (BLMs) (Merlo, 2023) are language versions of the visual Raven Progressive Matrices (RPMs). Like the RPMs, they are multiple-choice problems. The input is a sequence of 7 sentences built using specific rules, and

BLM agreement problem

CONTEXT TEMPLATE			
NP-sg	PP1-sg		VP-sg
NP-pl	PP1-sg		VP-pl
NP-sg	PP1-pl		VP-sg
NP-pl	PP1-pl		VP-pl
NP-sg	PP1-sg	PP2-sg	VP-sg
NP-pl	PP1-sg	PP2-sg	VP-pl
NP-sg	PP1-pl	PP2-sg	VP-sg

ANSWER SET	
NP-sg PP1-sg et NP2 VP-sg	Coord
NP-pl PP1-pl NP2-sg VP-pl	correct
NP-sg PP1-sg VP-sg	WNA
NP-pl PP1-pl NP2-pl VP-sg	AE_V
NP-pl PP1-sg NP2-pl VP-sg	AE_N1
NP-pl PP1-pl NP2-sg VP-sg	AE_N2
NP-pl PP1-sg PP1-sg VP-pl	WN1
NP-pl PP1-pl PP2-pl VP-pl	WN2

BLM verb alternation problem

CONTEXT TEMPLATE			
NP-Agent	Verb	NP-Loc	PP-Theme
NP-Theme	VerbPass	PP-Agent	
NP-Theme	VerbPass	PP-Loc	PP-Agent
NP-Theme	VerbPass	PP-Loc	
NP-Loc	VerbPass	PP-Agent	
NP-Loc	VerbPass	PP-Theme	PP-Agent
NP-Loc	VerbPass	PP-Theme	

ANSWER SET	
NP-Agent Verb NP-Theme PP-Loc	CORRECT
NP-Agent *VerbPass NP-Theme PP-Loc	AGENTACT
NP-Agent Verb NP-Theme *NP-Loc	ALT1
NP-Agent Verb *PP-Theme PP-Loc	ALT2
NP-Agent Verb *[NP-Theme PP-Loc]	NOEMB
NP-Agent Verb NP-Theme *PP-Loc	LEXPREP
*NP-Theme Verb NP-Agent PP-Loc	SSM1
*NP-Loc Verb NP-Agent PP-Theme	SSM2
*NP-Theme Verb NP-Loc PP-Agent	AASSM

Figure 1: Structure of two BLM problems, in terms of chunks in sentences and sequence structure.

the correct answer fits within the sequence defined by these rules. The incorrect options are built by corrupting some of the underlying generating rules of the input sentence sequence. Solving the problem requires identifying the entities (the chunks), their relevant attributes (their morphological or semantic properties) and their connecting operators.

We use two BLM datasets: (i) BLM-AgrF – subject verb agreement in French (An et al., 2023), and (ii) BLM-s/lE – the spray-load verb alternations in English[2] (Samo et al., 2023). The structure of these datasets – in terms of the sentence chunks and sequence structure – is shown in Figure 1.

Datasets statistics Table 1 shows the datasets statistics. Each set is split 90:10 into train:test subsets, and then we randomly sample 2000 instances as train data. 20% of the train data is used for development. Types I, II, III correspond to different amounts of lexical variation within an instance.

	Subj.-verb agr.	Verb alternations	
		ALT-ATL	ATL-ALT
Type I	2000:252	2000:375	2000:375
Type II	2000:4866	2000:1500	2000:1500
Type III	2000:4869	2000:1500	2000:1500

Table 1: Train:Test statistics for the two BLM problems.

To solve a BLM instance, the system processes the input sentence sequence and outputs a sentence representation that will be compared to the representation of the sentences in the answer set. The candidate answer closest to the generated sentence representation will be considered the correct one.

[2]Agent-Location-Theme (ALT) – Agent-Theme-Location (ATL)

We run the experiments on the BLMs for agreement and on the verb alternation BLMs. While the information necessary to solve the agreement task is more structural, solving the verb alternation task requires not only structural information on chunks, but also semantic information, as syntactically similar chunks play different roles in a sentence.

5 Experiments

We present a progression of experiments.

1. Using the dataset of sentences with known chunk structure, we test whether a sparse variational encoder-decoder system can distill information about the chunk structure of a sentence from its embedding.
2. We analyze the sparse model, and trace the information from the latent layer back to the sentence embedding to understand where in the sentence embeddings these differences are encoded.
3. We combine the sparsified variational encoder-decoder with another VAE-like layer to solve the BLM tasks, and test whether the latent layer sentence encodings maintain information useful for the tasks.

All experiments use Electra (Clark et al., 2019)[3]. We use as sentence representations the embedding of the [CLS] token, reshaped as a two dimensional array with shape 32x24.

[3]Electra pretrained model: google/electra-base-discriminator

The experiments are analyzed through the output of the system, in terms of average F1 score over three runs. For the investigations of the sentence embeddings, we also analyze the compressed vectors on the latent layer, to determine whether chunk patterns are encoded in these vectors. If these vectors cluster by the chunk pattern of the corresponding sentences it will indicate that sentence chunk patterns were indeed detected and are encoded differently in the latent layer.

5.1 Sparsification

Nastase and Merlo (2024) have shown that sentence embeddings contain information about the chunk structure and their properties using an encoder-decoder architecture that compresses the relevant information into a small latent layer. They build on Nastase and Merlo (2023) who show that reshaping a sentence embedding from the commonly used one-dimensional array to a two-dimensional representation allows grammatical information to become more readily accessible.

We adopt the system of (Nastase and Merlo, 2024), with the same architecture (including number of CNN channels and kernel size), and sparsify it, to determine whether specific information can be localized in sentence embeddings. The encoder of the system consists of a CNN layer followed by a FFNN, that compresses the information into a latent layer, as illustrated in Figure 2.

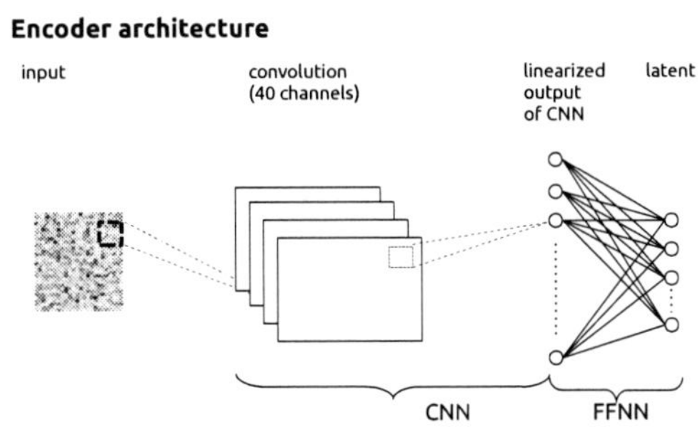

Figure 2: Details of the encoder architecture

The CNN layer in the encoder detects a different pattern in the sentence representation on each of its 40 channels. The linear layer compresses the linearized output of the CNN into a very small latent layer (length 5). A vector is sampled from this, and then decoded into a sentence representation using a decoder which is a mirror of the encoder.

An instance consists of an input sentence s, and 7 output sentences, only one of which has the same chunk structure as the input and is considered the correct one (section 4.1). The aim is to guide the system to capture information about the chunk structure of the sentences in the latent layer, by using a max-margin loss function that assigns a higher score to the correct option relative to the others. Formally, if e_s is the embedding of the input sentence s, $\hat{e}_s$ is the embedding output by the decoder, e_c is the embedding of the correct option and e_i, $i = 1, 6$ are the embeddings of the other options, and mm is the maxmargin function, then:

$$loss(s) = mm(\hat{e}_s, e_c, \{e_i|i = 1, 6\}) + KL(z_s||\mathcal{N}(0, 1))$$

$$mm(\hat{e}_s, e_c, e_i) = max(0, 1 - score(\hat{e}_s, e_c) + \sum_{i=1}^{6} score(\hat{e}_s, e_i)/6)$$

We want to sparsify this network in a targeted way: we enforce that each output unit from the CNN layer will contribute to only one unit in the latent layer. Figure 3 illustrates the process.

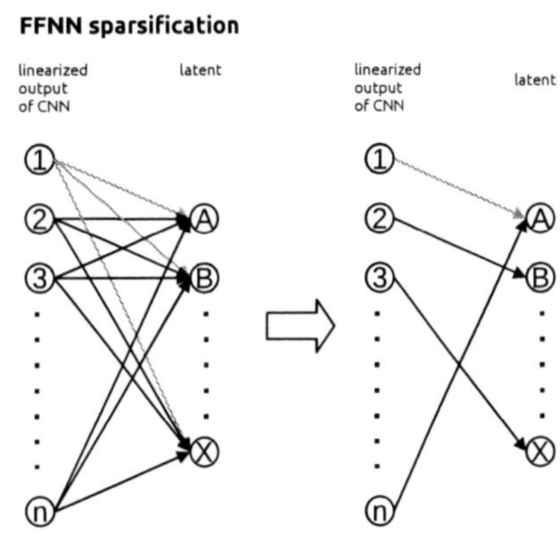

Figure 3: Separating linguistic signals by masking the one-layer FFNN

To enforce this behaviour, we use an approach inspired from sparsification (Savarese et al., 2020) and subnetworking (Lepori et al., 2023). Instead of considering the output of the CNN as the input layer of a linear network, we make each CNN output unit the input of a separate linear network, connected to the latent layer. We apply a mask m to the weights W of this network, and compute a masked weight matrix $W_m = W \times softmax(M/\tau)$, where τ is a temperature parameter used to push the softmax function towards a one-hot vector.

We use a kernel 15x15[4] and equal stride (15x15) to have a very clear separation of the information flow from the sentence embedding to the latent

[4]We adopt the size of the kernel from previous work.

layer. This will ensure our sparsification desideratum, and the learned network will have a particular configuration: if N_{CNN} is the set of output nodes from the CNN, and N_L are the nodes on the latent layer, then the sets of CNN output nodes connected to each of the latent units are disjunct:

$$\forall n_l \in N_L, S^l_{CNN} = \{n_c \in N_{CNN} | W_m(n_l, n_c) > 0\}$$

$$\text{and if } i \neq j \text{ then } S^i_{CNN} \cap S^j_{CNN} = \varnothing$$

Sparsification results Despite the fact that this type of sparsification is very harsh, and channels the information from the sentence embedding into very few paths on the way to the latent layer, the results in terms of average F1-score/standard deviation over three runs without 0.997 (0.0035) and with sparsification 0.977 (0.0095) are close. While this difference is rather small, we notice a bigger difference in the latent layer. Figure 5 shows the TSNE projections of the latent layers. As can be seen, while the full network shows a very clear and crisp separation of latents that encode different chunk patterns – with a 0.9928/0.0101 F1 macro-average/standard deviation – when sparsifying the information is slightly less crisp in the 2D TSNE projection, but still high F1 macro-average/standard deviation (0.9886/0.0038)

5.2 Localizing linguistic information in sentence embeddings

We approach the isolation of linguistic information with the following intuition: on each channel, the CNN discovers different patterns in various regions of the sentences. Some combination of these patterns – i.e. some combinations of signals from the CNN output – encode specific properties of the sentences. These signals eventually reach the latent layer. Previous experiments have shown that this latent layer contains information about chunks and their properties. Working backwards from the latent layer to the sentence embedding – through the CNN output layer, the different channels and sentence embedding regions – helps us trace back where the biggest changes are when the input sentences have different properties.

To verify whether specific linguistic information, like different number of chunks, or different chunk properties, is encoded in different regions of the sentence embeddings, we analyse the distribution of values in each network node in the encoder, namely the CNN output nodes N_{CNN} and the latent nodes N_L.

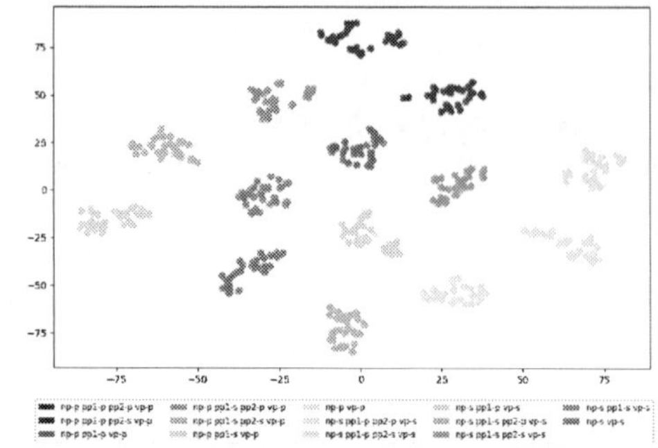

Figure 4: TSNE projection of the latent layer for encoder-decoder with full network connections.

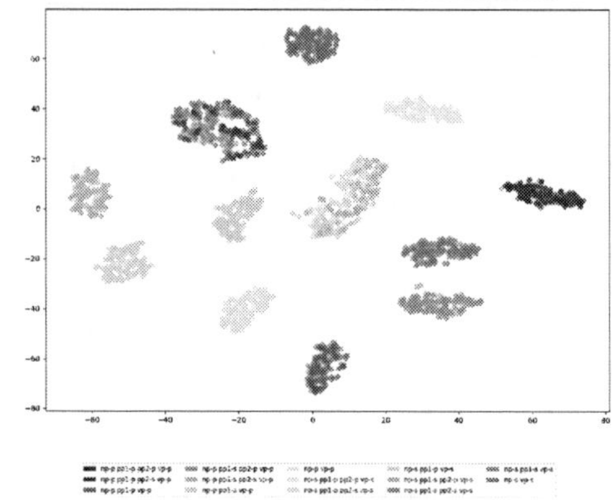

Figure 5: TSNE projection of the latent layer for sparsified encoder-decoder.

We denote S_p the set of input sentences that share the same chunk pattern p (for instance, p = "NP-s VP-s"). We pass their sentence embeddings through the learned encoder, and gather the values in each CNN output node:

$$V^p_{CNN} = \{V^p_{CNN}(n_c) | n_c \in N_{CNN}\}$$
$$V^p_{CNN}(n_c) = \{val_{n_c}(s) | s \in S_p\}$$

and $val_{n_c}(s)$ is the value in the CNN output node n_c when the input is the embedding of sentence s.

To check for differences in how sentence with different patterns are encoded, we will look at sets of sentences S_{p_1} and S_{p_2} where p_1 and p_2 are patterns that differ minimally. We consider three such minimal differences:

length one pattern has an extra (or one less) chunk than the other but are otherwise identical (*np-s vp-s* vs. *np-s ppl-s vp-s*),

grammatical number the two patterns have the same number of chunks, but one (and only one) chunk has a different grammatical number than the other (*np-s ppl-s vp-s* vs. *np-s ppl-p vp-s*),

subject-verb number alternation the two patterns are identical except in the grammatical number of the subject and verb (*np-s̲ pp1-s vp-s̲* vs. *np-p̲ pp1-s vp-p̲*).

To compare how chunk information is encoded in sentences that have different patterns p_1 and p_2, we compare the sets of values in each CNN output node n_c: $V^{p_1}_{CNN}(n_c)$ and $V^{p_2}_{CNN}(n_c)$. If these value distributions are very different, this is an indication that the area of a sentence embedding where the signal to n_c is coming from is involved in encoding the type of information that is different between p_1 and p_2.

We perform this analysis in two steps: (i) a filtering step that eliminates from the analysis the CNN output nodes that do not encode differences in behaviour between patterns, and (ii) a quantification of the differences in the values in the node for different patterns.

The filtering step is performed using a two-sample Kolmogorov-Smirnov test (Hodges, 1958),[5] which provides information whether two samples come from the same distribution. As we are interested in the CNN output nodes where the value distributions are different when the inputs are sentences with different patterns, we will filter out from the analysis the nodes n_c where the sets of values $V^{p}_{CNN}(n_c)$ come from the same distribution for all patterns p represented in the data.

For the remaining CNN output nodes, we project the value distributions onto the same set of bins, and then quantify the difference using cosine distance. Specifically, we determine the range of values for V^{p}_{CNN} for all patterns p – $min_{V_{CNN}}, max_{V_{CNN}}$, and split it into 100 bins. For each CNN output node n_c and pattern p we make a value distribution vector $v^{p}_{n_c}$ from the node's set of values $V^{p}_{CNN}(n_c)$, w.r.t. the 100 bins.

We then compute a score for every pair of minimally different patterns p_1, p_2 for each node n_c as the cosine distance:

$score_{n_c}(p_1, p_2) = 1 - cos(v^{p_1}_{n_c}, v^{p_2}_{n_c})$

This score quantifies how different a region of the sentence embedding is when encoding sentences with different chunk patterns.

Localization results A first clue that information related to chunk patterns in a sentence is localized is the fact that the filtering step using the two-sample Kolmogorov-Smirnov test leads to the removal of 83 CNN output nodes out of the 240 (34%).

For the remaining nodes where differences in value distributions between different sentence patterns exist, we compute the cosine distance between pairs of minimally different patterns with respect to grammatical number, length and subject-verb number alternations. Figure 6 shows the differences in value distributions in each CNN output nodes from each channel – channels are reprezented on the y-axis, and the 5 latent units on the x-axis in different colours. A stronger colour indicates a stronger effect. More detailed plots are included in Figure 9 in the appendix.

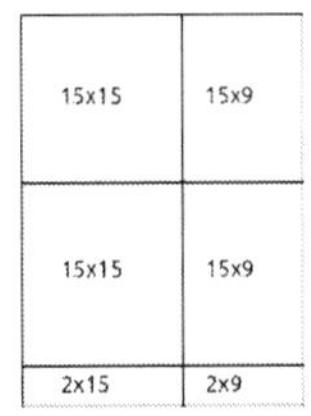

These plots indicate that there are few channel-sentence region combinations that encode differences in chunk structure in the input sentences. While in the figure the sentence areas are illustrated with equal sizes, the regions are presented transposed for space considerations, and they have the shapes shown in the adjacent figure. The chunks and the chunk information seems to be encoded in the bottom part of the sentence embedding, and much of it in the bottom 2x24 area.

5.3 BLM tasks

To further test whether task specific information is robust to sparsification, we use the two-level variational encoder-decoder depicted in Figure 8.

An instance for a BLM task consists of a tuple, comprising a sequence of sentences $S = \{s_i | i = 1, 7\}$ as input, and an answer set with one correct answer a_c, and several incorrect answers a_{err}. The sentence level of the 2-level encoder-decoder compresses the sentence embeddings of each of the sentences in the input sequence into a small latent vector. The sampled latent representations are then used as the representations of the sentences in the input sequence. This sequence representation is passed as input to the BLM-level encoder-decoder, it is compressed into a new latent layer, and the sampled vector is then decoded into a sentence representation that best matches the representation of the correct answer.

BLM task results We evaluate the performance of the sparsified 2-level VAE on the BLM tasks. Only the first level of the VAE, the one processing individual sentences, is sparsified as described

[5]We use the ks_2samp test in the scipy Python package

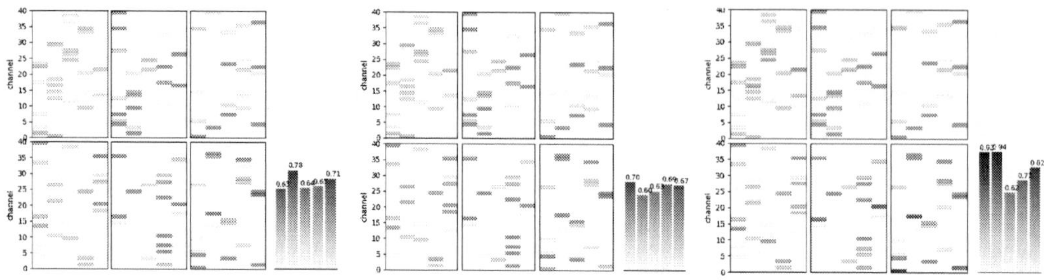

Figure 6: Average cosine distance between value distributions in each CNN output node (i.e. each node corresponding to the application of the kernel from each channel on the sentence embeddings, according to the kernel size and stride) for sets of sentences with minimally different patters: (left) patterns differ in only one grammatical number attribute for one chunk, (middle) patterns differ only in length, (right) patterns differ only in the number of the subject and verb. Each panel corresponds to one region of the sentence embedding the size of the kernel. The y-axis represents the channels of the CNN. The x-axis represents the latent units in different colours (the stronger the color, the higher the value, max = 1), and the pairs of compared patterns represented as adjacent rectangles.

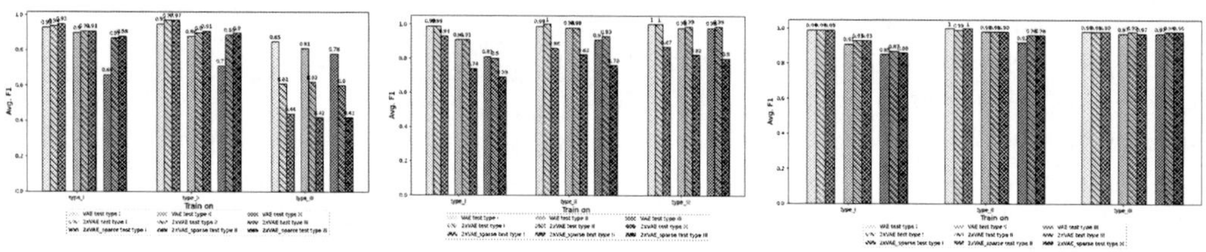

Figure 7: Results in term of average F1 scores over 3 runs, for the BLM agreement (1) and verb alternations ALT-ATL (2) and ATL-ALT (3)

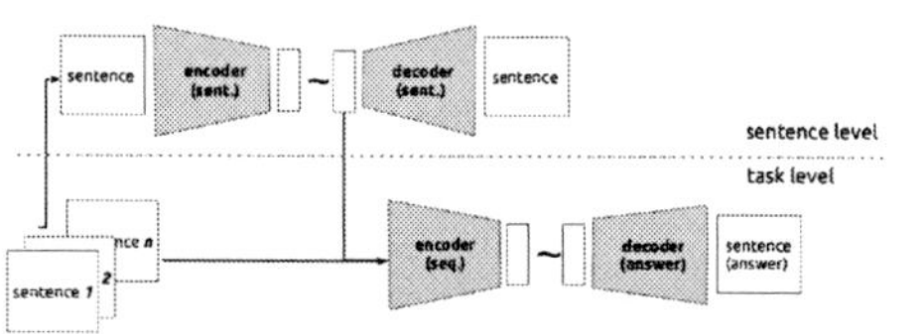

Figure 8: A two-level variational encoder-decoder: the top level compresses the sentence embeddings into a latent layer, and the bottom level uses the compressed sentence representations to solve the BLM tasks.

in section 5.1. Figure 7 shows the performance of three system variations: (i) a one-level VAE that processes the input sequence of sentences and produces a sentence representation, (ii) the two-level VAE described in more detail in (Nastase and Merlo, 2024), (iii) the sparsified version of the sentence level VAE in the two-level VAE. As in the previous experiments, sparsification does not cause harsh drops in performance for either of the two BLM tasks. The reason for this is the same reason we chose this particular data for experiments: solving the task relies on the system having information about the chunks in the sentence, and their properties. As long as that type of information is preserved, the tasks can be solved successfully.

We note two main changes however. In the agreement task, the sparsified system registers a drop in performance when trained on maximally lexically different data (type III). The two-level system without sparsification also registers such a drop in comparison with the baseline one-level encoder decoder. Both these effects may be due to the ambiguous supervision signal at the sentence level of the system: while using type I and type II data with little lexical variation, it is easier for the system to focus on structural differences between the correct and incorrect output options. When using type III data with much lexical variation, it is not clear for the system what is the relevant dimension of difference between the output options.

In the verb alternation task, previous results on predicting the Agent-Theme-Location or the Agent-Location-Theme alternation produced very similar results. This is not the case here, but understanding why this happens requires additional analysis.

6 Conclusions

Our aim was to understand how information is encoded in sentence embedding, given that previous work has shown that various types of linguistic information is encoded in a model's layers and parameters. We investigated this question using a dataset of sentences with specific chunk structure, and two multiple-choice problems that require information about sentence chunks and their properties to be solved successfully. We have shown that using a sparsified encoder-decoder system, the sentence representations can be compressed into a latent layer that encodes chunk structure properties. We then traced back the signal from the latent layer to the sentence embedding, to detect which areas of the sentence embeddings change the most when comparing sentences with different chunk patterns. This analysis shows that such information is captured by a small number of channel-sentence area combinations. Further experiments with the two multiple-choice tasks have confirmed that chunk information and their grammatical properties (for the agreement BLM) and chunk information and their semantic role properties (for the verb alternation BLM) are captured by the sparsified sentence compression level. We envision further analyses to see where the differences between chunk patterns that have different semantic roles are encoded, and get closer to decoding the sentence embeddings.

7 Limitations

We have explored sentence embeddings using an artificially constructed dataset with simple chunk structure. To check how this kind of information is localized, we started from a previously developed system that showed high performance in distinguishing the patterns of interest. We have not changed the system's parameters (such as the kernel size of the CNNs), and have not performed additional parameter search to narrow down the locations to smaller regions. We plan to address sentence complexity issues and parameters for narrower localization of information in future work.

References

Yossi Adi, Einat Kermany, Yonatan Belinkov, Ofer Lavi, and Yoav Goldberg. 2017. Fine-grained analysis of sentence embeddings using auxiliary prediction tasks. In *5th International Conference on Learning Representations, ICLR 2017, Toulon, France, April 24-26, 2017, Conference Track Proceedings*. OpenReview.net.

Aixiu An, Chunyang Jiang, Maria A. Rodriguez, Vivi Nastase, and Paola Merlo. 2023. BLM-AgrF: A new French benchmark to investigate generalization of agreement in neural networks. In *Proceedings of the 17th Conference of the European Chapter of the Association for Computational Linguistics*, pages 1363–1374, Dubrovnik, Croatia. Association for Computational Linguistics.

Steven Cao, Victor Sanh, and Alexander Rush. 2021. Low-complexity probing via finding subnetworks. In *Proceedings of the 2021 Conference of the North American Chapter of the Association for Computational Linguistics: Human Language Technologies*, pages 960–966, Online. Association for Computational Linguistics.

Kevin Clark, Urvashi Khandelwal, Omer Levy, and Christopher D. Manning. 2019. What does BERT look at? an analysis of BERT's attention. In *Proceedings of the 2019 ACL Workshop BlackboxNLP: Analyzing and Interpreting Neural Networks for NLP*, pages 276–286, Florence, Italy. Association for Computational Linguistics.

Kevin Clark, Minh-Thang Luong, Quoc V. Le, and Christopher D. Manning. 2020. ELECTRA: Pre-training text encoders as discriminators rather than generators. In *ICLR*.

Simone Conia, Edoardo Barba, Alessandro Scirè, and Roberto Navigli. 2022. Semantic role labeling meets definition modeling: Using natural language to describe predicate-argument structures. In *Findings of the Association for Computational Linguistics: EMNLP 2022*, pages 4253–4270, Abu Dhabi, United Arab Emirates. Association for Computational Linguistics.

Arthur Conmy, Augustine Mavor-Parker, Aengus Lynch, Stefan Heimersheim, and Adrià Garriga-Alonso. 2023. Towards automated circuit discovery for mechanistic interpretability. In *Advances in Neural Information Processing Systems*, volume 36, pages 16318–16352. Curran Associates, Inc.

Alexis Conneau, German Kruszewski, Guillaume Lample, Loïc Barrault, and Marco Baroni. 2018. What you can cram into a single $&!#* vector: Probing sentence embeddings for linguistic properties. In *Proceedings of the 56th Annual Meeting of the Association for Computational Linguistics (Volume 1: Long Papers)*, pages 2126–2136, Melbourne, Australia. Association for Computational Linguistics.

Róbert Csordás, Sjoerd van Steenkiste, and Jürgen Schmidhuber. 2021. Are neural nets modular? inspecting functional modularity through differentiable weight masks. In *Int. Conf. on Learning Representations (ICLR)*, Virtual only.

Jacob Devlin, Ming-Wei Chang, Kenton Lee, and Kristina Toutanova. 2018. BERT: pre-training of deep bidirectional transformers for language understanding. *CoRR*, abs/1810.04805.

Jonathan Frankle and Michael Carbin. 2018. The lottery ticket hypothesis: Training pruned neural networks. *CoRR*, abs/1803.03635.

Yoav Goldberg. 2019. Assessing bert's syntactic abilities. *arXiv preprint arXiv:1901.05287.*

Pengcheng He, Xiaodong Liu, Jianfeng Gao, and Weizhu Chen. 2020. Deberta: Decoding-enhanced BERT with disentangled attention. *CoRR*, abs/2006.03654.

John Hewitt and Christopher D. Manning. 2019. A structural probe for finding syntax in word representations. In *Proceedings of the 2019 Conference of the North American Chapter of the Association for Computational Linguistics: Human Language Technologies, Volume 1 (Long and Short Papers)*, pages 4129–4138, Minneapolis, Minnesota. Association for Computational Linguistics.

Joseph L. Hodges. 1958. The significance probability of the smirnov two-sample test. *Arkiv für Matematik*, 3:469–486.

Daphne Ippolito, David Grangier, Douglas Eck, and Chris Callison-Burch. 2020. Toward better storylines with sentence-level language models. In *Proceedings of the 58th Annual Meeting of the Association for Computational Linguistics*, pages 7472–7478, Online. Association for Computational Linguistics.

Zhenzhong Lan, Mingda Chen, Sebastian Goodman, Kevin Gimpel, Piyush Sharma, and Radu Soricut. 2019. ALBERT: A lite BERT for self-supervised learning of language representations. *CoRR*, abs/1909.11942.

Michael Lepori, Thomas Serre, and Ellie Pavlick. 2023. Break it down: Evidence for structural compositionality in neural networks. *Advances in Neural Information Processing Systems*, 36:42623–42660.

Yinhan Liu, Myle Ott, Naman Goyal, Jingfei Du, Mandar Joshi, Danqi Chen, Omer Levy, Mike Lewis, Luke Zettlemoyer, and Veselin Stoyanov. 2019. Roberta: A robustly optimized bert pretraining approach. *arXiv preprint arXiv:1907.11692.*

Christos Louizos, Max Welling, and Diederik P. Kingma. 2018. Learning sparse neural networks through l_0 regularization. In *6th International Conference on Learning Representations, ICLR 2018, Vancouver, BC, Canada, April 30 - May 3, 2018, Conference Track Proceedings*. OpenReview.net.

Paola Merlo. 2023. Blackbird language matrices (BLM), a new task for rule-like generalization in neural networks: Motivations and formal specifications. *ArXiv*, cs.CL 2306.11444.

Vivi Nastase and Paola Merlo. 2023. Grammatical information in BERT sentence embeddings as two-dimensional arrays. In *Proceedings of the 8th Workshop on Representation Learning for NLP (RepL4NLP 2023)*, pages 22–39, Toronto, Canada. Association for Computational Linguistics.

Vivi Nastase and Paola Merlo. 2024. Are there identifiable structural parts in the sentence embedding whole?

Dmitry Nikolaev and Sebastian Padó. 2023. The universe of utterances according to BERT. In *Proceedings of the 15th International Conference on Computational Semantics*, pages 99–105, Nancy, France. Association for Computational Linguistics.

Juri Opitz and Anette Frank. 2022. SBERT studies meaning representations: Decomposing sentence embeddings into explainable semantic features. In *Proceedings of the 2nd Conference of the Asia-Pacific Chapter of the Association for Computational Linguistics and the 12th International Joint Conference on Natural Language Processing (Volume 1: Long Papers)*, pages 625–638, Online only. Association for Computational Linguistics.

Abhishek Panigrahi, Nikunj Saunshi, Haoyu Zhao, and Sanjeev Arora. 2023. Task-specific skill localization in fine-tuned language models. In *International Conference on Machine Learning*, pages 27011–27033. PMLR.

Isabel Papadimitriou, Ethan A. Chi, Richard Futrell, and Kyle Mahowald. 2021. Deep subjecthood: Higher-order grammatical features in multilingual BERT. In *Proceedings of the 16th Conference of the European Chapter of the Association for Computational Linguistics: Main Volume*, pages 2522–2532, Online. Association for Computational Linguistics.

Nils Reimers and Iryna Gurevych. 2019. Sentence-BERT: Sentence embeddings using Siamese BERT-networks. In *Proceedings of the 2019 Conference on Empirical Methods in Natural Language Processing and the 9th International Joint Conference on Natural Language Processing (EMNLP-IJCNLP)*, pages 3982–3992, Hong Kong, China. Association for Computational Linguistics.

Anna Rogers, Olga Kovaleva, and Anna Rumshisky. 2020. A primer in BERTology: What we know about how BERT works. *Transactions of the Association for Computational Linguistics*, 8:842–866.

Giuseppe Samo, Vivi Nastase, Chunyang Jiang, and Paola Merlo. 2023. BLM-s/lE: A structured dataset of English spray-load verb alternations for testing generalization in LLMs. In *Findings of the 2023 Conference on Empirical Methods in Natural Language Processing*.

Pedro Savarese, Hugo Silva, and Michael Maire. 2020. Winning the lottery with continuous sparsification. In *Proceedings of the 34th International Conference on Neural Information Processing Systems*, NIPS'20, Red Hook, NY, USA. Curran Associates Inc.

Ian Tenney, Dipanjan Das, and Ellie Pavlick. 2019a. BERT rediscovers the classical NLP pipeline. In *Proceedings of the 57th Annual Meeting of the Association for Computational Linguistics*, pages 4593–4601, Florence, Italy. Association for Computational Linguistics.

Ian Tenney, Patrick Xia, Berlin Chen, Alex Wang, Adam Poliak, R Thomas McCoy, Najoung Kim, Benjamin

Van Durme, Samuel R Bowman, Dipanjan Das, et al. 2019b. What do you learn from context? probing for sentence structure in contextualized word representations. In *The Seventh International Conference on Learning Representations (ICLR)*, pages 235–249.

Ashish Vaswani, Noam Shazeer, Niki Parmar, Jakob Uszkoreit, Llion Jones, Aidan N Gomez, Łukasz Kaiser, and Illia Polosukhin. 2017. Attention is all you need. *Advances in neural information processing systems*, 30.

Michael Wilson, Jackson Petty, and Robert Frank. 2023. How abstract is linguistic generalization in large language models? experiments with argument structure. *Transactions of the Association for Computational Linguistics*, 11:1377–1395.

David Yi, James Bruno, Jiayu Han, Peter Zukerman, and Shane Steinert-Threlkeld. 2022. Probing for understanding of English verb classes and alternations in large pre-trained language models. In *Proceedings of the Fifth BlackboxNLP Workshop on Analyzing and Interpreting Neural Networks for NLP*, pages 142–152, Abu Dhabi, United Arab Emirates (Hybrid). Association for Computational Linguistics.

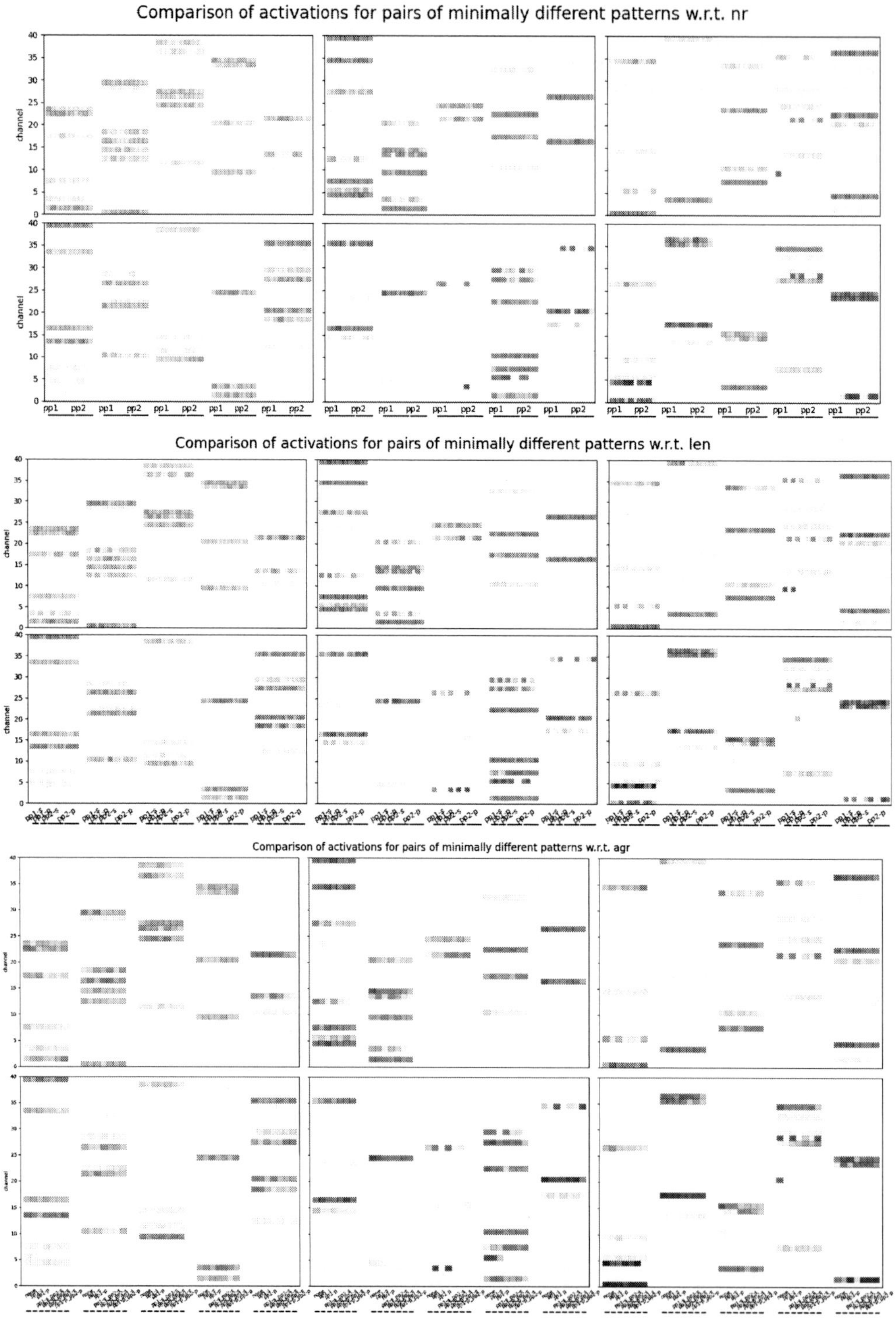

Figure 9: Differences between value distributions in each CNN output node (i.e. each node corresponding to the application of the kernel from each channel on the sentence embeddings, according to the kernel size and stride) for sets of sentences with minimally different patters: (top) patterns differ in only one grammatical number attribute for one chunk, (bottom) patterns differ only in length. Each panel corresponds to one region of the sentence embedding the size of the kernel. The y-axis represents the channels of the CNN. The x-axis represents the latent units in different colours (the stronger the color, the higher the value, max = 1), and the pairs of compared patterns represented as adjacent rectangles. The difference between the patterns is written below the x-axis.

Learning New Tasks from a Few Examples with Soft-Label Prototypes

Avyav Kumar Singh[1], **Ekaterina Shutova**[2], **Helen Yannakoudakis**[1]
[1]Department of Informatics, King's College London, United Kingdom
[2]ILLC, University of Amsterdam, the Netherlands
avyav_kumar.singh@kcl.ac.uk, e.shutova@uva.nl,
helen.yannakoudakis@kcl.ac.uk

Abstract

Existing approaches to few-shot learning in NLP rely on large language models (LLMs) and/or fine-tuning of these to generalise on out-of-distribution data. In this work, we propose a novel few-shot learning approach based on *soft-label prototypes* (SLPs) designed to collectively capture the distribution of different classes across the input domain space. We focus on learning previously unseen NLP tasks from very few examples (4, 8, 16) per class and experimentally demonstrate that our approach achieves superior performance on the majority of tested tasks in this data-lean setting while being highly parameter efficient. We also show that our few-shot adaptation method can be integrated into more generalised learning settings, primarily meta-learning, to yield superior performance against strong baselines.

1 Introduction

Humans have a remarkable ability to adapt knowledge gained in one domain and apply it in another setting, and to identify or disambiguate objects after observing only a handful of examples (Lake et al., 2015). This has inspired research in few-shot learning that aims to build models that can learn a new task using only a small number of examples per class. Early few-shot learning in NLP relied on interventions at the data level, such as dataset augmentation (Clark et al., 2018) or generation of adversarial examples from few-shot datasets (Miyato et al., 2016), while more recent approaches (van der Heijden et al., 2021; Langedijk et al., 2022) utilise meta-learning (Finn et al., 2017; Snell et al., 2017) to optimise model parameters such that models adapt quickly to new tasks using past experience (Dou et al., 2019; Holla et al., 2020; van der Heijden et al., 2021). The advent of large language models (LLMs) has led to a plethora of further methods, including fine-tuning on different target tasks (Sun et al., 2020; Zhou and Srikumar, 2022), creating prompt-enhanced few-shot datasets for training (Gao et al., 2020; Schick and Schütze, 2020; Lester et al., 2021) as well as parameter-efficient fine-tuning methods for very large language models, with parameters running into billions (Hu et al., 2022; Dettmers et al., 2023).

In this paper, we propose a simple and effective approach to few-shot learning based on *soft-label prototypes* (SLPs) that capture the distribution of different classes across the input domain space, inspired by previous work on generating compact representations of input training data (Sucholutsky et al., 2021). Our contributions are summarised as follows: 1) We develop a novel neural framework for few-shot learning via soft-label prototypes that has a very small computational and memory footprint, and achieves state-of-the-art results in limited-resource settings. Our approach (DeepSLP) does not rely on (expensive) LLM parameter updates or auxiliary training data. 2) We focus on few-shot learning of new, unseen NLP tasks using as little as 4 examples per class, and demonstrate that we outperform strong baselines on the majority of test tasks. 3) We demonstrate that our approach can also be effectively adapted (MetaSLP) in high-resource settings when auxiliary training data is available for few-shot learning, and performs competitively when compared against strong baselines. 4) We release our code and data to facilitate further research in the field.[1]

2 Related work

Early few-shot learning approaches in NLP include data augmentation and semi-supervised learning; e.g., augmentation with adversarial examples (Miyato et al., 2016), interpolation of training data into a learnable higher dimensional embedding space (Chen et al., 2020), and consistency training to

[1]https://github.com/avyavkumar/meta-learned-lines

Proceedings of the 9th Workshop on Representation Learning for NLP (RepL4NLP-2024), pages 215–236
August 15, 2024 ©2024 Association for Computational Linguistics

make models more resistant to noise (Xie et al., 2019). Recent research efforts on large-scale pre-training of language models (Devlin et al., 2019; Radford et al., 2019; Brown et al., 2020; Touvron et al., 2023; BigScience Workshop, 2023; OpenAI, 2024) reduce the amount of data required for their subsequent fine-tuning or utilisation in a given task. Instruction tuning and in-context learning (Brown et al., 2020; Gao et al., 2020; Sanh et al., 2021; Liu et al., 2021; Min et al., 2022; Sun et al., 2024; Zhou et al., 2024) show that natural language instructions or prompts can enhance a model's few-shot learning abilities by leveraging the language (instruction) understanding abilities of the given pretrained LLM (Zhao et al., 2021; Liu et al., 2022). To fine-tune extremely large language models (with billions of parameters) efficiently, a host of parameter-efficient fine-tuning techniques have also been developed (Hu et al., 2022; Dettmers et al., 2023), which leverage pre-trained LLMs and produce superior results on tasks such as question answering, reasoning, text summarisation, coding, etc. (Kotitsas et al., 2024; Jiaramaneepinit et al., 2024; Yang et al., 2024; Ding et al., 2023).

However, the search space over LLMs, prompt templates and few-shot learning is so great that there is yet to be an established standard. Different models require different styles of (few-shot) prompting, and certain prompt templates may work better with specific LLMs and datasets rather than universally across the board (e.g., Davis et al. (2024)). Furthermore, evaluating robustness of state-of-the-art / generative LLMs on new, unseen tasks (OOD generalisation) presents a significant challenge due to their vast and unknown training data, resulting in artificially inflated performance as a result of data leakage (Yang et al., 2023).

Previous work has also tackled few-shot learning within the meta-learning paradigm of *"learning to learn"* (Schmidhuber, 1987; Bengio et al., 1990; Thrun and Pratt, 1998), utilising methods that are trained to adapt quickly (in a few gradient steps) to new tasks and from a small number of examples, using past experience. Meta-learning has emerged as a promising technique for a range of tasks (Finn et al., 2017; Koch et al., 2015; Ravi and Larochelle, 2017), including NLP such as natural language inference, text classification, etc. (Obamuyide and Vlachos, 2019a,b; Holla et al., 2020; Bansal et al., 2020b; Nooralahzadeh et al., 2020; Wang et al., 2020; Langedijk et al., 2022; Mueller et al., 2023).

In a similar spirit to parameter-efficient fine-tuning (Hu et al., 2022; Dettmers et al., 2023), our work shifts away from the aforementioned paradigms that suffer from lack of standardisation (LLM few-shot prompting) and increased computational complexity for fine-tuning (e.g., fine-tuning extremely large language models such as GPT (OpenAI, 2024). We present a novel, parameter-efficient few-shot learning framework (DeepSLP) based on soft-label prototypes (SLPs), which we show to be effective on a range of tasks in limited and high-resource settings, while having a substantially smaller computational and memory footprint. While DeepSLP does not rely on LLM fine-tuning or auxiliary training data, we present a variant (MetaSLP) that can be used for few-shot learning via auxiliary data and fine-tuned encoders.

We target few-shot learning of new, unseen tasks (i.e., tasks and classes not previously trained on) (a) in limited-resource settings, without access to auxiliary training data, and with frozen model parameters, and (b) in high-resource settings, with access to auxiliary training data, which are used to update model parameters. For the latter, our work is similar to Bansal et al. (2020a). The authors target few-shot learning of unseen tasks via meta-learning, utilising auxiliary training data.

3 Approach: few-shot learning with Soft-Label Prototypes (SLPs)

A soft label is defined as a vector Y representing a data point's simultaneous membership to several classes (Sucholutsky and Schonlau, 2021), essentially denoting a point's partial association to different classes. Using this definition, a soft-label prototype (SLP) is defined as $(\vec{X}, Y)$, where $\vec{X}$ is a point in input space (e.g., an input feature vector) and Y is its corresponding soft label. The underlying idea in Sucholutsky and Schonlau (2021)'s work is that a small set of soft-label prototypes can be used to accurately represent a training set. We build on this idea and reframe SLPs for the task of few-shot learning of new, unseen tasks where very small amounts of data are available per class.

3.1 Generating soft-label prototypes

Soft-label prototypes assign soft labels to every point in the input domain; therefore, a soft-label prototype at point $\vec{X}$ represents the class distribution (determined from the training data) at $\vec{X}$. The fundamental idea behind a "soft-label" is that, unlike hard labels, which are one-hot encoded la-

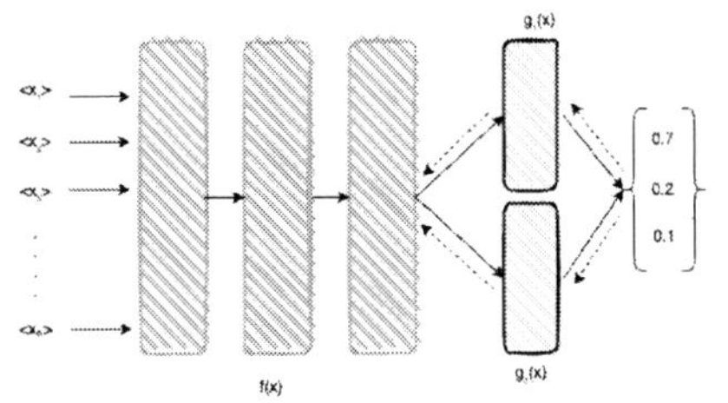

Figure 1: Learning soft-label prototypes using two trainable linear layers (yellow): example for a 3-class prototype. Dotted lines indicate backpropagation.

bels, soft-labels contain a distribution of probabilistic label values at a particular point in a high-dimensional embedding space.

The process of generating soft-label prototypes from training data can be split into a two step process (Sucholutsky et al., 2021): (1) finding lines that connect the class centroids in the training data, where each line connects some of the centroids, and every centroid belongs to one line; and (2) using linear constraints to derive soft-label prototypes capturing the class distribution at the ends of each line. The two steps are presented in detail below.

3.1.1 Finding lines connecting all centroids

Here we seek to find classes that lie on the same manifold. First, we compute the centroid of each class in the input training data. Then, we find and fit class centroids on the minimum number of lines using recursive regression (Sucholutsky et al., 2021). This method clusters centroids hierarchically to group similar (interval) centroids together, and fits a regression line on the centroids. The similarity of centroids within a single cluster is judged by how well all the centroids fit on a regression line. If the Euclidean distance of a particular centroid is beyond a pre-defined tolerance threshold ϵ from a line, it is removed from that cluster and assigned to another one. We use this method for all our experiments, as we experimentally find (on our dev data) that it performs well on high-dimensional data spread across many classes such as the ones we test here. In Appendix A.1, Figure 3a, we present an example set of lines connecting all centroids.

3.1.2 Learning soft-label prototypes

Once we find the lines, we use the endpoints of each line as the location of soft-label prototypes. Therefore, for l lines fitted on n centroids we have $2l$ prototypes. Then, we need to find the class distribution at each end point / soft-label prototype. We develop and experiment with two different approaches to finding the class distributions, one based on constraint optimisation (*constraintSLP*), and another based on gradient descent (*DeepSLP*).

Learning via linear constraints (constraintSLP) One way in which we can approach this is via constraint optimisation and, specifically, an optimisation problem that consists of two main sets of constraints (Sucholutsky et al., 2021): (i) the target class at each centroid has the maximum influence amongst all classes at certain points along the line (endpoint of the line and midpoints between classes); and (ii) the difference between the influence of the target class and the sum of the influences of all other classes along the line is maximised. In order to make this approach powerful enough for large, high-dimensional NLP data, we require an optimiser that scales on such complex data. To this end, we use the MOSEK solver for linear programming (MOSEK ApS, 2019) in the CVXPY library (Diamond and Boyd, 2016) to perform the required computations to generate the soft-label prototype class distributions. The output of this is then a set of soft-label prototypes which "sit" at the ends of each line (i.e., $\vec{X}$) as shown in Appendix A.1, Figure 3b.

Learning via gradient descent (DeepSLP) Rather than use linear constraints to generate soft-label prototypes, we develop a novel gradient-based approach to generate soft labels as a function of an input x by minimising training loss on a few-shot dataset. After generating lines connecting all class centroids (Section 3.1.1), we set two soft-label prototypes at the ends of the lines. Each soft-label prototype p_i is denoted by $g_i(f(x))$ where g is a neural network parameterised by θ_i and $f(x)$ is a point in the input space. The neural network consists of a fixed BERT (Devlin et al., 2019) encoder[2] given by $f(x)$, and a trainable linear layer which returns the soft-label probability distribution at any point x given by $g_i(x)$. Figure 1 presents a visual representation of our model. Compared to constraintSLP where we find soft-label probability distributions via linear constraint optimisation, we now parameterise our soft-label probability distribution with a neural network.

[2]We use BERT as our encoder given its comparatively higher computational efficiency, and do not include LLMs such as Llama and the GPT family as they have already been pre-trained on our test tasks (found here) and hence suffer from data contamination.

Algorithm 1: DeepSLP

$\lambda \leftarrow$ set of lines connecting all centroids
f_{θ_l} is the network parameterised by θ_l for the left-end prototype on a line
f_{θ_r} is the network parameterised by θ_r for the right-end prototype on a line
$\mathcal{J} \leftarrow$ loss function
$D \leftarrow$ training data
Require $\lambda \neq \emptyset$
for $i \in \lambda$ **do**
    for *epoch* $1.....N$ **do**
        $p_{il} \leftarrow$ location of left prototype
        $p_{ir} \leftarrow$ location of right prototype
        for $x \in minibatch(D)$ **do**
            $d_1 \leftarrow ||p_{il} - x||$
            $d_2 \leftarrow ||p_{ir} - x||$
            $pred.append\left(\frac{f_{\theta_{il}}(x)}{d_1} + \frac{f_{\theta_{ir}}(x)}{d_2}\right)$
        end
        $d\_loss \leftarrow \mathcal{J}(pred, D)$
        $loss_1 \leftarrow \frac{d_2}{d_1+d_2} * d\_loss$
        $loss_2 \leftarrow \frac{d_1}{d_1+d_2} * d\_loss$
        $\theta_{il} \leftarrow \theta_{il} - \eta\nabla_{\theta_{il}} loss_1$
        $\theta_{ir} \leftarrow \theta_{ir} - \eta\nabla_{\theta_{ir}} loss_2$
    end
end

Crucially, the encoder parameters are frozen as we need our input data points to have an unchanged location in the input space – changing their position might result in class centroids that were previously lying on a straight line to no longer lie on the line. The model is optimised using both soft-label prototypes along a line (see Algorithm 1 below and Section 3.2, Equation 1). Specifically, a higher distance between a data point x and a prototype leads to a correspondingly smaller effect of the prototype on the final classification; therefore, we want to penalise the prototype that is closer to x more if there is an incorrect classification. Each prototype is therefore assigned a fraction of the total loss that is proportional to the other prototype's Euclidean distance from x. This way, the closer prototype's weights are corrected more in case of a misclassification. The complete algorithm can be seen in Algorithm 1, while an example optimisation is presented in Figure 2.

We use cross entropy loss which gives a measure of the difference between the true and predicted labels. We initialise the weights of $g_1(x)$ and $g_2(x)$ using a uniform Xavier initialisation (Glorot and Bengio, 2010) and use warmup steps to adjust the learning rate. Epochs vary based on the number of classes in the classifier head (between 15 and 25; see datasets used in Section 4): preliminary experiments on the development data show that more epochs are needed when a higher number of classes lie along a line.

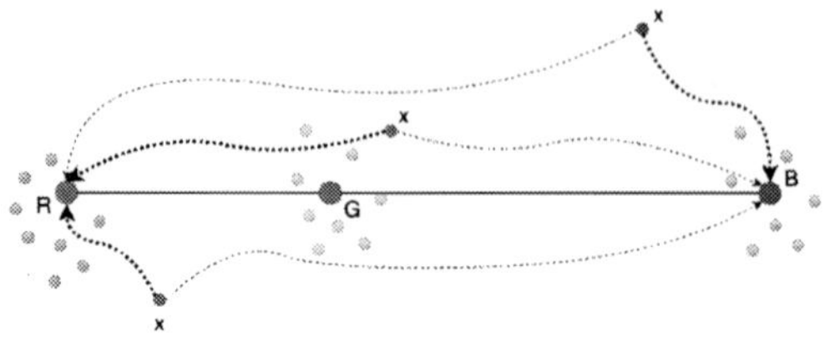

Figure 2: Training soft-label prototypes in DeepSLP. Class centroids are represented with large circles that lie on a line (**R**ed, **G**reen, **B**lue), while training set examples are represented with smaller circles of the same colour. Dotted lines represent the backpropagation error, of which the bolded ones represent a larger error per soft-label prototype. Predictions for x are based on the prototypes at each end of the line.

3.2 Classification with soft-label prototypes

Given M soft-label prototypes representing the input distribution of N classes, we define $S = (\vec{X}_1, Y_1), ..., (\vec{X}_M, Y_M)$ to be our set of prototypes, where $\vec{X}_i$ is the location of the ith prototype in the input feature space and Y_i is a matrix of dimension $[N \times 1]$ denoting the soft labels. Given a test datapoint $\vec{x}$, we calculate the Euclidean distances $D = (\vec{X}_i, \vec{x})_{i=1,2...M}$ from each prototype to $\vec{x}$. We then sort S in ascending order of distances using D, weigh the probability distribution of the ith nearest prototype inversely by its distance to $\vec{x}$, and select the line containing the closest prototype to get Y^* (Sucholutsky et al., 2021):

$$Y^* = \sum_{i=1}^{k} \frac{Y_i}{d(\vec{X}_i, \vec{x})} \tag{1}$$

As we consider the two nearest neighbours / prototypes, we set k to 2. $\vec{x}$ is then assigned the class $C^{SLP}(\vec{x}) = \underset{j}{\text{argmax}} Y_j^*$ where Y_j^* is the jth element of Y^*. In other words, we sum over the k-nearest soft-label prototypes (i.e., vectors) to $\vec{x}$, and weigh each prototype inversely proportional to its distance from $\vec{x}$. $\vec{x}$ is then assigned the class with the largest value in the resulting vector (see Appendix A.1 for a toy classification example).

3.3 Meta-training DeepSLP (MetaSLP)

We further test the suitability of soft-labels in high-resource settings, tuning our text encoder using auxiliary training data. This is similar to the work of (Bansal et al., 2020a) that develop a meta-learning approach for few-shot learning of new, unseen tasks while utilising auxiliary training data. We employ a similar approach for rapid generalisation by utilising first-order meta-learning algorithms (which we describe in detail in Appendix A.2). Our model architecture is similar to DeepSLP – it comprises a BERT encoder with two linear layers on top. We train only the last v layers of our encoder to reduce computational overhead, where v is a hyperparameter (See Appendix A.6). We denote the encoder by $f_\theta(x)$, and each soft-label prototype at the end of a line by g_1 and g_2, parameterised by θ_1 and θ_2 respectively. The difference between DeepSLP and MetaSLP is that MetaSLP is trained using meta-learning (using auxiliary data described in Section 4), and the encoder $f_\theta(x)$ in MetaSLP is fine-tuned (as opposed to being fixed in DeepSLP), following previous work (Bansal et al., 2020a).

Inner-loop training We optimise the soft-label prototypes in the same manner as DeepSLP; i.e., we use Algorithmn 1 to few-shot train the linear layers $g_1(x)$ and $g_2(x)$ parameterised by θ_1 and θ_2 respectively. However, meta-learning requires a large set of diverse and balanced meta-learning tasks for effective learning (Holla et al., 2020). To ameliorate this, we split the auxiliary datasets (Section 4) used for meta-learning into multiple pairwise tasks to meta-train MetaSLP (Bansal et al., 2020a). This means that, during training, we now consider a large number of two-class problems, as opposed to a small number of multi-class problems where the number of classes $n \geq 2$. Such a setting also enables fine-tuning of our encoder $f_\theta(x)$. In general, allowing the physical location of encodings to change (in this case via meta-learning's inner-loop training process), may result in centroids originally connected by a line to no longer be connected by that line (i.e., in the next inner-loop optimisation step). However, if we only meta-train on tasks that focus on two classes at a time, this can trivially ensure that the same line is utilised each time. Our inner-loop optimisation process is given in Algorithm 3 in Appendix A.4.

Outer-loop training We perform meta-learning using the updated parameters in the inner-loop training process. We experiment with both Reptile (Nichol et al., 2018) and FOMAML (Finn et al., 2017) as our meta-learning algorithms. Reptile can be considered a simpler variant to MAML-based meta-learning algorithms. We present our outer-loop process in Algorithm 4, Appendix A.4.

Meta-testing We construct lines for the test sets using the trained MetaSLP model, and fine-tune them on the few-shot adaptation training data for each test task. We then use these lines for classification as described in Section 3.2.

4 Experimental settings and datasets

Experimental settings We experiment with two settings in terms of amounts of available data. The first is a limited-resource setting where we only train / fine-tune our models in a few-shot manner on small amounts of training data (i.e., in the absence of auxiliary training data). The other setting is a high-resource setting where we assume that auxiliary training data is available for additional training / fine-tuning.

Datasets We tackle few-shot learning of previously unseen tasks (i.e., not seen during training/fine-tuning), and so our work is similar to Bansal et al. (2020a). For our high-resource setting, we train and test our models on the same data as Bansal et al. (2020a) to ensure direct comparability. For our limited-resource setting, we test in the same way but do not utilise any auxiliary training data; i.e., we only utilise few-shot fine-tuning data for unseen tasks (i.e., only using a very small set of training/fine-tuning examples for the test tasks).

High-resource setting auxiliary training data Similar to Bansal et al. (2020a), we use GLUE (Wang et al., 2018) to train our models in the high-resource setting. This dataset consists of a range of natural language tasks such as entailment, classification and textual similarity, which are used for model training and evaluation. We use only the training split for meta-learning. Similar to Bansal et al. (2020a), the MNLI (Williams et al., 2018) and SNLI (Bowman et al., 2015) entailment tasks, which are three-label classification problems, are split in a pairwise manner such that they are included as multiple two-label datasets during training. Following Bansal et al. (2020a), we also train for detecting the sentiment contained within phrases of a sentence by using the phrase-level annotations in SST2 (Wang et al., 2018). We utilise the same validation sets – labelled Amazon review data from music, toys and videos for sentiment classification (Blitzer et al., 2007). We provide dataset and training details in Appendix A.5.

Evaluation data We use the same test datasets and evaluation setting as Bansal et al. (2020a) for both the high-resource and low-resource settings. These cover a variety of text classification tasks: (a) *Entity typing* – the CoNLL-2003 (Tjong Kim Sang and De Meulder, 2003) and MIT-Restaurant (Liu et al., 2013) datasets; (b) *Review rating classification* – review ratings from Amazon Reviews (Blitzer et al., 2007) with a three-way classification; (c) *Text classification* – scraped social media data from crowdflower comprising sentiment and emotion classification in a range of domains, as well as political bias detection; and (d) *Natural language inference* in the scientific domain – the SciTail dataset (Khot et al., 2018). We use the same data splits, which are publicly available. During evaluation, Bansal et al. (2020a) fine-tune their models using a small few-shot (support) training set per test task (using a k-shot setting of $4, 8, 16$ examples per class), and then evaluate performance on each task's dedicated, unseen test set. As model performance can be affected by the k examples chosen for training/fine-tuning, for each task and for every k, they sample 10 few-shot training sets and report the mean and standard deviation, which we also adopt in our experiments.

5 Baselines

Our aim is to determine how well our models – DeepSLP and MetaSLP – perform in the low and high-resource setting respectively, compared to strong baselines when given the same few-shot adaptation sets. Our focus is on (a) evaluating in an extreme few-shot learning scenario where no auxiliary data is available (using DeepSLP), and (b) evaluating in a high-resource setting when additional (auxiliary) training data is available (MetaSLP). We use BERT (Devlin et al., 2019) as our text encoder throughout to facilitate model comparisons. We report DeepSLP and MetaSLP$_{\text{REPTILE}}$ (i.e., using Reptile as our meta-learning algorithm) in our main table of results (given their effectiveness), and present additional baselines as well as hyperparameters and training details in Appendix A.6.

We use BERT (Devlin et al., 2019) as our encoder as it is a text encoder that allows us to get passage-level encodings, it is computationally lightweight compared to decoder-based LLMs such as Llama (Touvron et al., 2023) and GPT (OpenAI, 2024) (and we can carry out full fine-tuning) and, crucially, it does not suffer from data contamination as, in contrast to the more recent LLMs, it has not been pre-trained on our test data[3].

5.1 Low-resource setting baselines

BERT$_{\text{fine-tuned}}$ We use BERT$_{\text{fine-tuned}}$ reported in Bansal et al. (2020a), which is fine-tuned (all layers) on the few-shot training set of each test task.

LORA$_{\text{BERT}}$ LORA (Hu et al., 2022) decomposes a fine-tuned weight matrix to two low-rank matrices, which – when multiplied and added to the original weights – reproduce the fine-tuned weights. This is advantageous as, instead of fine-tuning all parameters, we fine-tune these two matrices with a low computational cost, as they are much smaller individually compared to fully fine-tuned weights.

constraintSLP We use constraintSLP as a baseline to evaluate the effectiveness of soft-label prototypes that are based on linear constraints.

5.2 High-resource setting baselines

Reptile We train a meta-learning Reptile (Nichol et al., 2018) model on our auxiliary data and use it as another baseline. This allows us to directly assess the added advantage of utilising SLPs in MetaSLP$_{\text{REPTILE}}$.

Prototypical Networks We use ProtoNet (Snell et al., 2017) as another baseline *for both* the high and low-resource settings. ProtoNets use Euclidean distance as a measure of similarity between points and clusters, which is similar to DeepSLP and MetaSLP that assign test points to the closest line.

LEOPARD Bansal et al. (2020a) present LEOPARD, a meta-learning algorithm that achieves the best performance across most test tasks for entity typing, ratings classification and text classification, and which we also use.

We do not include HSMLMT (Bansal et al., 2020b) as a baseline as it is pretrained on semi-supervised meta-training tasks in addition to supervised learning and therefore it is not directly comparable.

[3]https://github.com/iesl/leopard/tree/master/data/json

Category (Classes)	Shot	LORA$_{BERT}$	BERT$_{\text{fine-tuned}}$*	DeepSLP	LEOPARD*	Reptile	MetaSLP$_{REPTILE}$
Political Bias (2)	4	52.75 ± 4.33	54.57 ± 5.02	53.251 ± 4.042	60.49 ± 6.66	58.82 ± 4.31	60.96 ± 6.13
	8	53.66 ± 4.25	56.15 ± 3.75	58.209 ± 5.198	61.74 ± 6.73	59.43 ± 3.79	63.65 ± 4.57
	16	59.21 ± 2.27	60.96 ± 4.25	61.479 ± 2.974	65.08 ± 2.14	62.21 ± 0.72	66.05 ± 1.57
Emotion (13)	4	7.56 ± 2.93	09.20 ± 3.22	9.076 ± 1.108	11.71 ± 2.16	11.65 ± 3.21	11.94 ± 1.95
	8	9.02 ± 2.36	08.21 ± 2.12	8.041 ± 2.797	12.90 ± 1.63	10.56 ± 2.85	13.42 ± 1.46
	16	10.29 ± 1.67	13.43 ± 2.51	10.919 ± 1.615	13.38 ± 2.20	11.62 ± 3.11	14.03 ± 2.35
Sentiment Books (2)	4	51.27 ± 2.75	54.81 ± 3.75	58.67 ± 4.753	82.54 ± 1.33	76.95 ± 1.03	83.22 ± 0.95
	8	58.16 ± 3.3	53.54 ± 5.17	64.78 ± 2.615	83.03 ± 1.28	77.49 ± 1.08	83.8 ± 0.8
	16	59.16 ± 2.59	65.56 ± 4.12	67.453 ± 3.085	83.33 ± 0.79	77.88 ± 0.56	83.8 ± 1.59
Rating DVD (3)	4	31.65 ± 4.91	32.22 ± 08.72	39.566 ± 5.086	49.76 ± 9.80	45.91 ± 9.85	45.2 ± 8.91
	8	37.69 ± 3.16	36.35 ± 12.50	38.788 ± 4.449	53.28 ± 4.66	47.23 ± 9.22	58.38 ± 2.9
	16	38.63 ± 5.52	42.79 ± 10.18	40.53 ± 4.375	53.52 ± 4.77	48.49 ± 8.88	57.41 ± 4.71
Rating Electronics (3)	4	31.66 ± 2.94	39.27 ± 10.15	39.977 ± 5.959	51.71 ± 7.20	44.47 ± 8.25	45.34 ± 7.22
	8	38.72 ± 5.95	28.74 ± 08.22	41.926 ± 3.985	54.78 ± 6.48	49.1 ± 6.81	55.10 ± 5.12
	16	39.15 ± 6.6	45.48 ± 06.13	44.917 ± 3.164	58.69 ± 2.41	50.68 ± 6.8	59.47 ± 2.29
Rating Kitchen (3)	4	36.63 ± 4.68	34.76 ± 11.20	39.624 ± 6.787	50.21 ± 09.63	45.38 ± 10.96	45.20 ± 8.78
	8	39.69 ± 6.22	34.49 ± 08.72	41.081 ± 6.777	53.72 ± 10.31	46.71 ± 9.84	54.53 ± 9.9
	16	38.17 ± 7.14	47.94 ± 08.28	45.801 ± 4.562	57.00 ± 08.69	52.87 ± 9.52	58.94 ± 7.58
Political Audience (2)	4	49.75 ± 1.03	51.02 ± 1.72	51.741 ± 2.827	52.60 ± 3.51	52.45 ± 4.26	54.1 ± 3.66
	8	54.05 ± 2.54	52.80 ± 2.72	54.506 ± 3.274	54.31 ± 3.95	52.87 ± 4.31	56.01 ± 3.65
	16	55.39 ± 3.66	58.45 ± 4.98	56.956 ± 3.045	57.71 ± 3.52	55.6 ± 1.85	58.57 ± 2.04
Sentiment Kitchen (2)	4	53.02 ± 1.54	56.93 ± 7.10	60.76 ± 4.426	78.35 ± 18.36	69.81 ± 14.58	81.96 ± 3.73
	8	55.54 ± 3.47	57.13 ± 6.60	65.733 ± 3.198	84.88 ± 1.12	75.76 ± 1.13	83.33 ± 1.99
	16	58.59 ± 4.83	68.88 ± 3.39	69.18 ± 2.589	85.27 ± 1.31	76.41 ± 0.66	84.33 ± 1.81
Disaster (2)	4	56.02 ± 6.35	55.73 ± 10.29	54.252 ± 9.843	51.45 ± 4.25	49.76 ± 4.73	55.03 ± 8.73
	8	57.46 ± 6.9	56.31 ± 09.57	61.3 ± 7.961	55.96 ± 3.58	52.17 ± 5.17	57.77 ± 6.40
	16	65.79 ± 2.03	64.52 ± 08.93	69.28 ± 2.358	61.32 ± 2.83	55.37 ± 4.53	65.18 ± 4.41
Airline (3)	4	24.36 ± 5.42	42.76 ± 13.50	50.987 ± 4.936	54.95 ± 11.81	57.11 ± 14.16	57.39 ± 7.83
	8	52.31 ± 7.89	38.00 ± 17.06	55.209 ± 6.049	61.44 ± 03.90	64.37 ± 3.49	65.67 ± 4.82
	16	54.1 ± 8.57	58.01 ± 08.23	60.247 ± 4.577	62.15 ± 05.56	66.31 ± 2.55	69.48 ± 2.06
Rating Books (3)	4	34.69 ± 2.12	39.42 ± 07.22	42.116 ± 4.725	54.92 ± 6.18	56.57 ± 8.17	55.79 ± 5.61
	8	39.36 ± 6.33	39.55 ± 10.01	42.156 ± 4.608	59.16 ± 4.13	57.33 ± 7.63	65.74 ± 5.58
	16	41.23 ± 5.32	43.08 ± 11.78	46.513 ± 3.036	61.02 ± 4.19	63.26 ± 3.59	67.87 ± 3.45
Political Message (9)	4	12.16 ± 1.46	15.64 ± 2.73	14.421 ± 1.095	15.69 ± 1.57	14.58 ± 1.78	18.84 ± 1.82
	8	15.71 ± 2.04	13.38 ± 1.74	16.919 ± 1.756	18.02 ± 2.32	15.13 ± 2.16	20.09 ± 2.71
	16	15.53 ± 2.55	20.67 ± 3.89	18.319 ± 1.74	18.07 ± 2.41	16.38 ± 2.15	23.22 ± 1.17
Sentiment DVD (2)	4	50.77 ± 0.78	54.98 ± 3.96	55.003 ± 2.936	80.32 ± 1.02	72.03 ± 11.61	80.97 ± 1.21
	8	52.24 ± 1.54	55.63 ± 4.34	57.527 ± 3.562	80.85 ± 1.23	75.79 ± 1.62	81.85 ± 1.79
	16	52.6 ± 2.09	58.69 ± 6.08	60.76 ± 2.944	81.25 ± 1.41	76.69 ± 0.8	83.48 ± 1.01
Scitail (2)	4	43.36 ± 4.74	58.53 ± 09.74	54.101 ± 3.759	69.50 ± 9.56	59.13 ± 10.58	53.48 ± 5.59
	8	54.29 ± 5.25	57.93 ± 10.70	56.341 ± 5.786	75.00 ± 2.42	62.63 ± 10.85	60.79 ± 4.6
	16	52.68 ± 3.0	65.66 ± 06.82	59.692 ± 4.227	77.03 ± 1.82	68.03 ± 1.57	61.67 ± 3.61
Restaurant (8)	4	10.56 ± 1.36	49.37 ± 4.28	47.634 ± 5.237	49.84 ± 3.31	13.37 ± 2.25	27.00 ± 2.61
	8	20.92 ± 2.4	49.38 ± 7.76	55.912 ± 4.494	62.99 ± 3.28	16.83 ± 3.42	35.66 ± 2.39
	16	29.37 ± 4.05	69.24 ± 3.68	61.716 ± 2.208	70.44 ± 2.89	16.0 ± 3.44	37.20 ± 2.68
CoNLL (4)	4	21.48 ± 2.71	50.44 ± 08.57	52.724 ± 5.84	54.16 ± 6.32	31.31 ± 5.32	40.79 ± 3.40
	8	29.84 ± 3.28	50.06 ± 11.30	60.374 ± 3.731	67.38 ± 4.33	33.17 ± 5.1	41.25 ± 5.21
	16	37.18 ± 3.32	74.47 ± 03.10	67.496 ± 4.551	76.37 ± 3.08	34.04 ± 3.59	45.96 ± 4.75

Table 1: Classification performance (accuracy) of our methods (DeepSLP and MetaSLP) and baselines. * refers to the baselines as reported in Bansal et al. (2020a). The best performing models for each setting (without and with auxiliary data) are highlighted in gray and green respectively. Double lines group similar tasks together: the first set contains intent classification tasks, the second focuses on natural language inference, and the last contains entity typing tasks.

6 Results and Discussion

Due to space restrictions, we present and discuss our best models in Table 1. All other baselines and results are discussed in Appendix A.7.

Low-resource setting In the low-resource setting with no auxiliary data (left side of Table 1), DeepSLP outperforms all baselines, including BERT$_{\text{fine-tuned}}$ in $31/48$ tasks and LORA$_{\text{BERT}}$ in $45/48$ tasks, achieving a new state-of-the-art result. Our results demonstrate the usefulness of soft-label prototypes and their superiority over strong baselines (i.e., LLM fine-tuning and LORA / low-rank adaptation) in the low-resource setting.

Unlike BERT$_{\text{fine-tuned}}$, DeepSLP and LORA$_{\text{BERT}}$ do not fine-tune the encoder. Specifically, we only need to fine-tune $1500-10K$ parameters (based on the number of classes) for each line with two soft-label prototypes for DeepSLP, compared to $50K-100K$ parameters for LORA$_{\text{BERT}}$ with $rank = 2$, and $> 10^8$ parameters for BERT$_{\text{fine-tuned}}$. We also note that DeepSLP is lightweight and does not require a GPU. LORA$_{\text{BERT}}$ mostly achieves accuracies within 90% of BERT$_{\text{fine-tuned}}$, in line with previous work (Hu et al., 2022; Dettmers et al., 2023) (even outperforming BERT$_{\text{fine-tuned}}$ in $15/48$ tasks), except for entity-typing tasks where LORA$_{\text{BERT}}$ struggles to generalise and achieves substantially lower performance compared to BERT$_{\text{fine-tuned}}$.

On the other hand, constraintSLP, a simpler variant of DeepSLP (see Appendix A.7, Table 5 for results) is one of the lower performing baselines, together with ProtoNet. We find that constraintSLP exhibits a substantial weakness (see further details in Theorem A.2, Appendix A.3): given Euclidean distance, constraintSLP does not always select the nearest class centroid to a test point. This violates our inductive bias that points located closest to a class centroid are assigned to that class. If we consider the case where $N = 2$, constraintSLP essentially acts as a 1-NN with soft labels trivially at $[1, 0]$ and $[0, 1]$, with class centroids acting as the nearest neighbour. However, when generalising beyond this setting, the model's stability is affected. constraintSLP optimises soft labels using the geometric properties of a line and does not consider each (training) data point individually – the soft labels produced by SLP are constants. DeepSLP, on the other hand, learns from training data and produces soft labels as a function of the input; therefore, it has the ability to output soft labels based on the location of an input (test) point (with the location of the prototypes being fixed).

High-resource setting MetaSLP$_{\text{REPTILE}}$ has the highest performance overall in text classification and entailment tasks (Tasks 1-14), with the best accuracy in $33/42$ tasks/settings. LEOPARD, on the other hand, achieves the highest score in only $8/42$. Interestingly, we find that all models in the high-resource setting have lower performance for *Disaster* compared to the models in the low-resource setting. We surmise this to be due to the auxiliary data and the fact that the meta-training distribution differs substantially from the test distribution.

For entity typing tasks (CoNLL and Restaurant), LEOPARD outperforms all models, with MetaSLP$_{\text{REPTILE}}$ and Reptile performing comparatively poorly, even outperformed by the low-resource methods (DeepSLP and BERT$_{\text{fine-tuned}}$). It should be noted that there seems to be little benefit of meta-learning with auxiliary data when tackling entity typing tasks, even for LEOPARD, as the difference between LEOPARD and BERT$_{\text{fine-tuned}}$ is not substantial. We surmise this to be due to the fact that the meta-training distribution (i.e., GLUE tasks) is different from the test distribution for entity typing tasks which degrades performance for the test tasks. Note that we do not meta-train the entire model (only top 4 layers for Reptile and MetaSLP$_{\text{REPTILE}}$), unlike LEOPARD.

Overall, MetaSLP$_{\text{REPTILE}}$ outperforms all models and baselines, including Reptile in $42/48$ tasks and LEOPARD in 34/48 tasks. Specifically, MetaSLP$_{\text{REPTILE}}$ consistently outperforms Reptile, demonstrating the effectiveness of our approach over its meta-learning variant (i.e., Reptile) that does not use SLPs. In Appendix A.8 we present detailed analyses of DeepSLP and show that it displays several desirable properties of ensemble methods which drive its performance, in addition to it being a computationally efficient approach that only utilises a small number of parameters.

7 Conclusion and future work

We presented a novel few-shot learning paradigm that is based on soft-label prototypes capturing the simultaneous membership of data points over several classes, and demonstrated its effectiveness in low and high-resource settings. We evaluated our approach on 48 different tasks / settings and showed that it outperforms a range of strong baselines. In the future, we plan to use meta-learning algorithms such as PACMAML (Ding et al., 2021) and Bayesian MAML (Kim et al., 2018) that relax assumptions with respect to train–test set distributions and thus alleviate this current limitation in our work.

8 Ethics

To the best of our knowledge, there are no ethical concerns involved in this research. We conduct our work using publicly available English datasets and tasks, and models pre-trained on English text. Our results may not generalise to other languages. To facilitate further research in the field, we release our source code and models.

References

Taiga Abe, Estefany Kelly Buchanan, Geoff Pleiss, Richard Zemel, and John P Cunningham. 2022. Deep ensembles work, but are they necessary? In *Advances in Neural Information Processing Systems*, volume 35, pages 33646–33660. Curran Associates, Inc.

Antreas Antoniou, Harrison Edwards, and Amos Storkey. 2019. How to train your MAML. In *International Conference on Learning Representations*.

Arsenii Ashukha, Alexander Lyzhov, Dmitry Molchanov, and Dmitry Vetrov. 2020. Pitfalls of in-domain uncertainty estimation and ensembling in deep learning. *arXiv preprint arXiv:2002.06470*.

Trapit Bansal, Rishikesh Jha, and Andrew McCallum. 2020a. Learning to few-shot learn across diverse natural language classification tasks. In *Proceedings of the 28th International Conference on Computational Linguistics*, pages 5108–5123, Barcelona, Spain (Online). International Committee on Computational Linguistics.

Trapit Bansal, Rishikesh Jha, Tsendsuren Munkhdalai, and Andrew McCallum. 2020b. Self-supervised meta-learning for few-shot natural language classification tasks.

Yoshua Bengio, Samy Bengio, and Jocelyn Cloutier. 1990. *Learning a synaptic learning rule*. Citeseer.

BigScience Workshop. 2023. Bloom: A 176b-parameter open-access multilingual language model.

John Blitzer, Mark Dredze, and Fernando Pereira. 2007. Biographies, Bollywood, boom-boxes and blenders: Domain adaptation for sentiment classification. In *Proceedings of the 45th Annual Meeting of the Association of Computational Linguistics*, pages 440–447, Prague, Czech Republic. Association for Computational Linguistics.

Samuel R. Bowman, Gabor Angeli, Christopher Potts, and Christopher D. Manning. 2015. A large annotated corpus for learning natural language inference.

Tom B. Brown, Benjamin Mann, Nick Ryder, Melanie Subbiah, Jared Kaplan, Prafulla Dhariwal, Arvind Neelakantan, Pranav Shyam, Girish Sastry, Amanda Askell, Sandhini Agarwal, Ariel Herbert-Voss, Gretchen Krueger, Tom Henighan, Rewon Child, Aditya Ramesh, Daniel M. Ziegler, Jeffrey Wu, Clemens Winter, Christopher Hesse, Mark Chen, Eric Sigler, Mateusz Litwin, Scott Gray, Benjamin Chess, Jack Clark, Christopher Berner, Sam McCandlish, Alec Radford, Ilya Sutskever, and Dario Amodei. 2020. Language models are few-shot learners.

Jiaao Chen, Zichao Yang, and Diyi Yang. 2020. Mixtext: Linguistically-informed interpolation of hidden space for semi-supervised text classification.

Kevin Clark, Minh-Thang Luong, Christopher D. Manning, and Quoc V. Le. 2018. Semi-supervised sequence modeling with cross-view training.

Christopher Davis, Andrew Caines, Øistein Andersen, Shiva Taslimipoor, Helen Yannakoudakis, Zheng Yuan, Christopher Bryant, Marek Rei, and Paula Buttery. 2024. Prompting open-source and commercial language models for grammatical error correction of english learner text.

Tim Dettmers, Artidoro Pagnoni, Ari Holtzman, and Luke Zettlemoyer. 2023. Qlora: Efficient finetuning of quantized llms. In *Advances in Neural Information Processing Systems*, volume 36, pages 10088–10115. Curran Associates, Inc.

Jacob Devlin, Ming-Wei Chang, Kenton Lee, and Kristina Toutanova. 2019. BERT: Pre-training of deep bidirectional transformers for language understanding. In *Proceedings of the 2019 Conference of the North American Chapter of the Association for Computational Linguistics: Human Language Technologies, Volume 1 (Long and Short Papers)*, pages 4171–4186, Minneapolis, Minnesota. Association for Computational Linguistics.

Steven Diamond and Stephen Boyd. 2016. CVXPY: A Python-embedded modeling language for convex optimization. *Journal of Machine Learning Research*, 17(83):1–5.

Thomas G. Dietterich. 2000. Ensemble methods in machine learning. In *Multiple Classifier Systems*, pages 1–15, Berlin, Heidelberg. Springer Berlin Heidelberg.

Nan Ding, Xi Chen, Tomer Levinboim, Sebastian Goodman, and Radu Soricut. 2021. Bridging the gap between practice and pac-bayes theory in few-shot meta-learning. In *Advances in Neural Information Processing Systems*, volume 34, pages 29506–29516. Curran Associates, Inc.

Ning Ding, Xingtai Lv, Qiaosen Wang, Yulin Chen, Bowen Zhou, Zhiyuan Liu, and Maosong Sun. 2023. Sparse low-rank adaptation of pre-trained language models. In *Proceedings of the 2023 Conference on Empirical Methods in Natural Language Processing*, pages 4133–4145, Singapore. Association for Computational Linguistics.

William B. Dolan and Chris Brockett. 2005. Automatically constructing a corpus of sentential paraphrases. In *Proceedings of the Third International Workshop on Paraphrasing (IWP2005)*.

Zi-Yi Dou, Keyi Yu, and Antonios Anastasopoulos. 2019. Investigating meta-learning algorithms for low-resource natural language understanding tasks. In *Proceedings of the 2019 Conference on Empirical Methods in Natural Language Processing and the 9th International Joint Conference on Natural Language Processing (EMNLP-IJCNLP)*, pages 1192–1197, Hong Kong, China. Association for Computational Linguistics.

Chelsea Finn, Pieter Abbeel, and Sergey Levine. 2017. Model-agnostic meta-learning for fast adaptation of deep networks. In *Proceedings of the 34th International Conference on Machine Learning*, volume 70 of *Proceedings of Machine Learning Research*, pages 1126–1135. PMLR.

Tianyu Gao, Adam Fisch, and Danqi Chen. 2020. Making pre-trained language models better few-shot learners.

Danilo Giampiccolo, Hoa Trang Dang, Bernardo Magnini, Ido Dagan, Elena Cabrio, and William B. Dolan. 2008. The fourth pascal recognizing textual entailment challenge. In *Text Analysis Conference*.

Xavier Glorot and Yoshua Bengio. 2010. Understanding the difficulty of training deep feedforward neural networks. In *Proceedings of the Thirteenth International Conference on Artificial Intelligence and Statistics*, volume 9 of *Proceedings of Machine Learning Research*, pages 249–256, Chia Laguna Resort, Sardinia, Italy. PMLR.

Nithin Holla, Pushkar Mishra, Helen Yannakoudakis, and Ekaterina Shutova. 2020. Learning to learn to disambiguate: Meta-learning for few-shot word sense disambiguation. In *Findings of the Association for Computational Linguistics: EMNLP 2020*, pages 4517–4533, Online. Association for Computational Linguistics.

Edward J Hu, yelong shen, Phillip Wallis, Zeyuan Allen-Zhu, Yuanzhi Li, Shean Wang, Lu Wang, and Weizhu Chen. 2022. LoRA: Low-rank adaptation of large language models. In *International Conference on Learning Representations*.

Boonnithi Jiaramaneepinit, Thodsaporn Chay-intr, Kotaro Funakoshi, and Manabu Okumura. 2024. Extreme fine-tuning: A novel and fast fine-tuning approach for text classification. In *Proceedings of the 18th Conference of the European Chapter of the Association for Computational Linguistics (Volume 2: Short Papers)*, pages 368–379, St. Julian's, Malta. Association for Computational Linguistics.

Tushar Khot, Ashish Sabharwal, and Peter Clark. 2018. Scitail: A textual entailment dataset from science question answering. In *AAAI*.

Taesup Kim, Jaesik Yoon, Ousmane Dia, Sungwoong Kim, Yoshua Bengio, and Sungjin Ahn. 2018. Bayesian model-agnostic meta-learning.

Gregory Koch, Richard Zemel, and Ruslan Salakhutdinov. 2015. Siamese neural networks for one-shot image recognition. In *ICML deep learning workshop*, volume 2. Lille.

Sotiris Kotitsas, Panagiotis Kounoudis, Eleni Koutli, and Haris Papageorgiou. 2024. Leveraging fine-tuned large language models with LoRA for effective claim, claimer, and claim object detection. In *Proceedings of the 18th Conference of the European Chapter of the Association for Computational Linguistics (Volume 1: Long Papers)*, pages 2540–2554, St. Julian's, Malta. Association for Computational Linguistics.

Brenden M. Lake, Ruslan Salakhutdinov, and Joshua B. Tenenbaum. 2015. Human-level concept learning through probabilistic program induction. *Science*, 350(6266):1332–1338.

Balaji Lakshminarayanan, Alexander Pritzel, and Charles Blundell. 2017. Simple and scalable predictive uncertainty estimation using deep ensembles. In *Advances in Neural Information Processing Systems*, volume 30. Curran Associates, Inc.

Anna Langedijk, Verna Dankers, Phillip Lippe, Sander Bos, Bryan Cardenas Guevara, Helen Yannakoudakis, and Ekaterina Shutova. 2022. Meta-learning for fast cross-lingual adaptation in dependency parsing. In *Proceedings of the 60th Annual Meeting of the Association for Computational Linguistics (Volume 1: Long Papers)*, pages 8503–8520, Dublin, Ireland. Association for Computational Linguistics.

Stefan Lee, Senthil Purushwalkam, Michael Cogswell, David Crandall, and Dhruv Batra. 2015. Why m heads are better than one: Training a diverse ensemble of deep networks.

Brian Lester, Rami Al-Rfou, and Noah Constant. 2021. The power of scale for parameter-efficient prompt tuning.

Jiachang Liu, Dinghan Shen, Yizhe Zhang, Bill Dolan, Lawrence Carin, and Weizhu Chen. 2022. What makes good in-context examples for GPT-3? In *Proceedings of Deep Learning Inside Out (DeeLIO 2022): The 3rd Workshop on Knowledge Extraction and Integration for Deep Learning Architectures*, pages 100–114, Dublin, Ireland and Online. Association for Computational Linguistics.

Jingjing Liu, Panupong Pasupat, Scott Cyphers, and Jim Glass. 2013. Asgard: A portable architecture for multilingual dialogue systems. In *2013 IEEE International Conference on Acoustics, Speech and Signal Processing*, pages 8386–8390.

Pengfei Liu, Weizhe Yuan, Jinlan Fu, Zhengbao Jiang, Hiroaki Hayashi, and Graham Neubig. 2021. Pre-train, prompt, and predict: A systematic survey of prompting methods in natural language processing. *ACM Computing Surveys*, 55:1 – 35.

Ilya Loshchilov and Frank Hutter. 2017a. Decoupled weight decay regularization.

Ilya Loshchilov and Frank Hutter. 2017b. SGDR: stochastic gradient descent with warm restarts. In *5th International Conference on Learning Representations, ICLR 2017, Toulon, France, April 24-26, 2017, Conference Track Proceedings*. OpenReview.net.

Sewon Min, Xinxi Lyu, Ari Holtzman, Mikel Artetxe, Mike Lewis, Hannaneh Hajishirzi, and Luke Zettlemoyer. 2022. Rethinking the role of demonstrations: What makes in-context learning work? In *Proceedings of the 2022 Conference on Empirical Methods in Natural Language Processing*, pages 11048–11064, Abu Dhabi, United Arab Emirates. Association for Computational Linguistics.

Takeru Miyato, Andrew M. Dai, and Ian Goodfellow. 2016. Adversarial training methods for semi-supervised text classification.

MOSEK ApS. 2019. *The MOSEK optimization toolbox for MATLAB manual. Version 9.3.*

Aaron Mueller, Kanika Narang, Lambert Mathias, Qifan Wang, and Hamed Firooz. 2023. Meta-training with demonstration retrieval for efficient few-shot learning. In *Findings of the Association for Computational Linguistics: ACL 2023*, pages 6049–6064, Toronto, Canada. Association for Computational Linguistics.

Alex Nichol, Joshua Achiam, and John Schulman. 2018. On first-order meta-learning algorithms.

Farhad Nooralahzadeh, Giannis Bekoulis, Johannes Bjerva, and Isabelle Augenstein. 2020. Zero-shot cross-lingual transfer with meta learning.

Abiola Obamuyide and Andreas Vlachos. 2019a. Meta-learning improves lifelong relation extraction. In *Proceedings of the 4th Workshop on Representation Learning for NLP (RepL4NLP-2019)*, pages 224–229, Florence, Italy. Association for Computational Linguistics.

Abiola Obamuyide and Andreas Vlachos. 2019b. Model-agnostic meta-learning for relation classification with limited supervision. In *Proceedings of the 57th Annual Meeting of the Association for Computational Linguistics*, pages 5873–5879, Florence, Italy. Association for Computational Linguistics.

OpenAI. 2024. Gpt-4 technical report.

Alec Radford, Jeff Wu, Rewon Child, David Luan, Dario Amodei, and Ilya Sutskever. 2019. Language models are unsupervised multitask learners.

Sachin Ravi and Hugo Larochelle. 2017. Optimization as a model for few-shot learning. In *International Conference on Learning Representations*.

Sashank J. Reddi, Satyen Kale, and Sanjiv Kumar. 2018. On the convergence of adam and beyond. In *International Conference on Learning Representations*.

Victor Sanh, Albert Webson, Colin Raffel, Stephen H. Bach, Lintang Sutawika, Zaid Alyafeai, Antoine Chaffin, Arnaud Stiegler, Teven Le Scao, Arun Raja, Manan Dey, M Saiful Bari, Canwen Xu, Urmish Thakker, Shanya Sharma Sharma, Eliza Szczechla, Taewoon Kim, Gunjan Chhablani, Nihal Nayak, Debajyoti Datta, Jonathan Chang, Mike Tian-Jian Jiang, Han Wang, Matteo Manica, Sheng Shen, Zheng Xin Yong, Harshit Pandey, Rachel Bawden, Thomas Wang, Trishala Neeraj, Jos Rozen, Abheesht Sharma, Andrea Santilli, Thibault Fevry, Jason Alan Fries, Ryan Teehan, Tali Bers, Stella Biderman, Leo Gao, Thomas Wolf, and Alexander M. Rush. 2021. Multitask prompted training enables zero-shot task generalization.

Timo Schick and Hinrich Schütze. 2020. It's not just size that matters: Small language models are also few-shot learners.

Jurgen Schmidhuber. 1987. Evolutionary principles in self-referential learning. *On learning how to learn: The meta-meta-... hook.) Diploma thesis, Institut f. Informatik, Tech. Univ. Munich*, 1(2).

Jake Snell, Kevin Swersky, and Richard S. Zemel. 2017. Prototypical networks for few-shot learning.

Richard Socher, Alex Perelygin, Jean Wu, Jason Chuang, Christopher D. Manning, Andrew Ng, and Christopher Potts. 2013. Recursive deep models for semantic compositionality over a sentiment treebank. In *Proceedings of the 2013 Conference on Empirical Methods in Natural Language Processing*, pages 1631–1642, Seattle, Washington, USA. Association for Computational Linguistics.

Ilia Sucholutsky, Nam-Hwui Kim, Ryan P. Browne, and Matthias Schonlau. 2021. One line to rule them all: Generating LO-shot soft-label prototypes. In *2021 International Joint Conference on Neural Networks (IJCNN)*. IEEE.

Ilia Sucholutsky and Matthias Schonlau. 2021. 'less than one'-shot learning: Learning n classes from m < n samples. *Proceedings of the AAAI Conference on Artificial Intelligence*, 35(11):9739–9746.

Chi Sun, Xipeng Qiu, Yige Xu, and Xuanjing Huang. 2020. How to fine-tune bert for text classification?

Simeng Sun, Yang Liu, Shuohang Wang, Dan Iter, Chenguang Zhu, and Mohit Iyyer. 2024. PEARL: Prompting large language models to plan and execute actions over long documents. In *Proceedings of the 18th Conference of the European Chapter of the Association for Computational Linguistics (Volume 1: Long Papers)*, pages 469–486, St. Julian's, Malta. Association for Computational Linguistics.

Sebastian Thrun and Lorien Pratt. 1998. Learning to learn: Introduction and overview. In *Learning to learn*, pages 3–17. Springer.

Erik F. Tjong Kim Sang and Fien De Meulder. 2003. Introduction to the CoNLL-2003 shared task: Language-independent named entity recognition. In *Proceedings of the Seventh Conference on Natural Language Learning at HLT-NAACL 2003*, pages 142–147.

Hugo Touvron, Thibaut Lavril, Gautier Izacard, Xavier Martinet, Marie-Anne Lachaux, Timothée Lacroix, Baptiste Rozière, Naman Goyal, Eric Hambro, Faisal Azhar, Aurelien Rodriguez, Armand Joulin, Edouard Grave, and Guillaume Lample. 2023. Llama: Open and efficient foundation language models.

Niels van der Heijden, Helen Yannakoudakis, Pushkar Mishra, and Ekaterina Shutova. 2021. Multilingual and cross-lingual document classification: A meta-learning approach. In *Proceedings of the 16th Conference of the European Chapter of the Association for Computational Linguistics: Main Volume*, pages 1966–1976, Online. Association for Computational Linguistics.

Alex Wang, Amanpreet Singh, Julian Michael, Felix Hill, Omer Levy, and Samuel Bowman. 2018. GLUE: A multi-task benchmark and analysis platform for natural language understanding. In *Proceedings of the 2018 EMNLP Workshop BlackboxNLP: Analyzing and Interpreting Neural Networks for NLP*, pages 353–355, Brussels, Belgium. Association for Computational Linguistics.

Zhiguo Wang, Wael Hamza, and Radu Florian. 2017. Bilateral multi-perspective matching for natural language sentences.

Zirui Wang, Zachary C. Lipton, and Yulia Tsvetkov. 2020. On negative interference in multilingual models: Findings and a meta-learning treatment. In *Proceedings of the 2020 Conference on Empirical Methods in Natural Language Processing (EMNLP)*, pages 4438–4450, Online. Association for Computational Linguistics.

Alex Warstadt, Amanpreet Singh, and Samuel R Bowman. 2018. Neural network acceptability judgments. *arXiv preprint arXiv:1805.12471*.

Adina Williams, Nikita Nangia, and Samuel Bowman. 2018. A broad-coverage challenge corpus for sentence understanding through inference. In *Proceedings of the 2018 Conference of the North American Chapter of the Association for Computational Linguistics: Human Language Technologies, Volume 1 (Long Papers)*, pages 1112–1122, New Orleans, Louisiana. Association for Computational Linguistics.

Andrew G Wilson and Pavel Izmailov. 2020. Bayesian deep learning and a probabilistic perspective of generalization. In *Advances in Neural Information Processing Systems*, volume 33, pages 4697–4708. Curran Associates, Inc.

Qizhe Xie, Zihang Dai, Eduard Hovy, Minh-Thang Luong, and Quoc V. Le. 2019. Unsupervised data augmentation for consistency training.

Adam Yang, Maxime Robeyns, Xi Wang, and Laurence Aitchison. 2024. Bayesian low-rank adaptation for large language models. In *Socially Responsible Language Modelling Research*.

Linyi Yang, Yaoxian Song, Xuan Ren, Chenyang Lyu, Yidong Wang, Jingming Zhuo, Lingqiao Liu, Jindong Wang, Jennifer Foster, and Yue Zhang. 2023. Out-of-distribution generalization in natural language processing: Past, present, and future. In *The 2023 Conference on Empirical Methods in Natural Language Processing*.

Zihao Zhao, Eric Wallace, Shi Feng, Dan Klein, and Sameer Singh. 2021. Calibrate before use: Improving few-shot performance of language models. In *Proceedings of the 38th International Conference on Machine Learning*, volume 139 of *Proceedings of Machine Learning Research*, pages 12697–12706. PMLR.

Kun Zhou, Yifan Li, Xin Zhao, and Ji-Rong Wen. 2024. Diffusion-NAT: Self-prompting discrete diffusion for non-autoregressive text generation. In *Proceedings of the 18th Conference of the European Chapter of the Association for Computational Linguistics (Volume 1: Long Papers)*, pages 1438–1451, St. Julian's, Malta. Association for Computational Linguistics.

Yichu Zhou and Vivek Srikumar. 2022. A closer look at how fine-tuning changes BERT. In *Proceedings of the 60th Annual Meeting of the Association for Computational Linguistics (Volume 1: Long Papers)*, pages 1046–1061, Dublin, Ireland. Association for Computational Linguistics.

A Appendix

A.1 Deriving soft-label prototypes using constraintSLP

Finding lines connecting all centroids

In Figure 3a, we present an example set of lines connecting all class centroids. For further details on recursive regression, we refer the reader to Sucholutsky et al. (2021).

Deriving soft-label prototypes by optimising for linear constraints

Example soft-label prototypes which are "set" at the ends of each line are shown in Figure 3b.

Classification with constraintSLP: A toy example

Figure 4 presents an example classification with soft-label prototypes. Given the class centroids for *blue*, *green* and *yellow* are located at $(0, 0)$, $(1.5, 0)$ and $(3, 0)$ respectively, two soft-label prototypes are defined by a line connecting *yellow* and *blue*, and are thus located at $(3, 0)$ and $(0, 0)$ respectively. The soft labels in Figure 4a contain

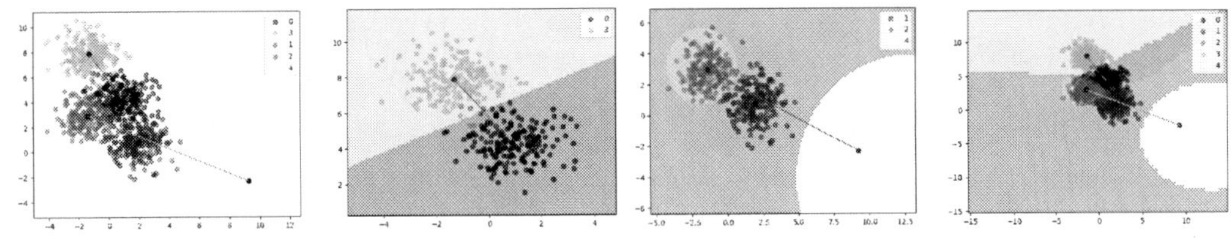

a Computing lines b Generating soft-label prototypes c The decision landscape

Figure 3: Generating and classifying data with soft-label prototypes.

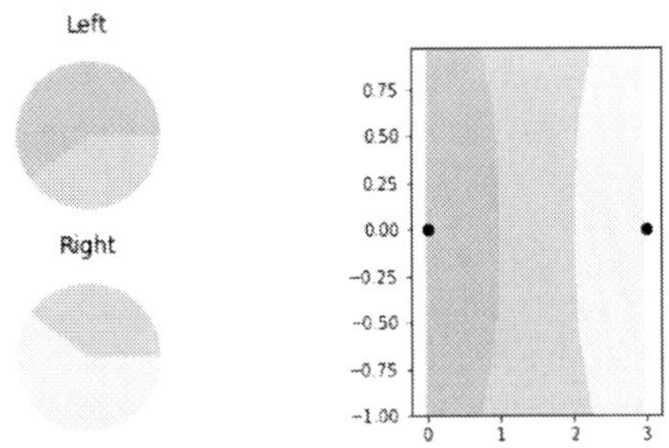

a b

Figure 4: Classification example with constraintSLP (figure from Sucholutsky and Schonlau (2021)).

the per-class probability distribution derived by the constraintSLP method; for example, $p(x = blue) = 0.6$ and $p(x = green) = 0.4$ for the left prototype, and $p(x = green) = 0.4$ and $p(x = yellow) = 0.6$ for the right prototype. When a new test instance x located at $(1.5, 0.8)$ is presented, we make predictions as follows: we find the nearest line to x and consider its distance from the two prototypes at the ends of the line and multiply the class distribution of each prototype by the inverse distance as per Eq. 1.

Since x is equidistant from both prototypes, the distance between the x and each prototype is 1.5. Therefore, the values for *blue* and *yellow* (given both soft-label prototypes) become $soft\_label(x = blue) = \frac{0.6}{1.5} + \frac{0}{1.5} = 0.4$ and $soft\_label(x = yellow) = \frac{0}{1.5} + \frac{0.6}{1.5} = 0.4$ respectively. In contrast, for *green*, which is directly informed by both prototypes (i.e., no zero values in the numerator), the probability distribution becomes $soft\_label(x = green) = \frac{0.4}{1.5} + \frac{0.4}{1.5} = 0.53$. Therefore x is classified as green. This decision boundary can be seen in Figure 4b.

A.2 Meta-learning

For encoder-based models, meta-learning has emerged as a viable methodology for few-shot learning. In the meta-learning paradigm, the training and test sets, referred to as $\mathcal{D}_{\text{meta-train}}$ and $\mathcal{D}_{\text{meta-test}}$, are split into episodes. Each episode encompasses a task $\mathcal{T}_{\text{i}}$ and consists of a support set $\mathcal{D}^{(i)}{}_{\text{support}}$ and a query set $\mathcal{D}^{(i)}{}_{\text{query}}$. Meta-learning algorithms initially fit the model on the support set of the episode (inner-loop optimisation) and then achieve generalisation across episodes by optimising performance on the query sets of the episodes (outer-loop optimisation). For evaluation, the model is first fine-tuned on the support set and then evaluated on the query set for each task $\mathcal{T}_{\text{i}} \in \mathcal{D}_{\text{meta-test}}$. We describe the process algorithmically in Algorithm 2 and describe the *MetaUpdate* process for different algorithms subsequently.

Algorithm 2: Meta-learning

```
α, β ← learning rates
Sample batch of tasks {T_i} ~ p(T)
Initialise θ'_i ← θ
for T_i ~ p(T) do
    Partition T_i into D_i^s and D_i^q
    θ'_i ← θ − α∇_θ L^s_{D_i}(f_θ) for k steps
end
θ ← MetaUpdate(θ_i, D_i^q, β)
```

Model Agnostic Meta-Learning MAML (Finn et al., 2017) is an *optimisation-based* meta-learning approach which incorporates generalisability across tasks in its cost function. The task loss $\mathcal{L}^q_{\mathcal{T}_i}$ is computed on the query examples in each episode, using this task-specific model. The initial model parameters θ are then updated so as to minimize the sum of the losses of all tasks in a batch, leading to improved generalisation across tasks. The *MetaUpdate* step is thus defined as

$$\theta \leftarrow \theta - \beta \nabla_\theta \sum_{T_i \sim p(T)} \mathcal{L}^q_{\mathcal{D}_i}(f_{\theta'_i})$$

Note that the *MetaUpdate* expression calculates the gradients of each θ_i with respect to θ, thus necessitating the computation of second-order gradients. To ease computation, we use a first-order approximation of MAML (FOMAML) wherein the gradients of each θ_i are calculated with respect to θ_i and reduce the *MetaUpdate* term to

$$\theta \leftarrow \theta - \beta \nabla_{\theta_i} \sum_{T_i \sim p(T)} \mathcal{L}^q_{\mathcal{D}_i}(f_{\theta'_i})$$

LEOPARD Bansal et al. (2020a) employ meta-learning for diverse NLP tasks in an approach inspired from MAML which integrates a text encoder model with a meta-learned parameter generator to tailor task-specific initialisations for the classification head. Their inner-loop update learns the parameter generator for the task, adapts task-specific model parameters and the *MetaUpdate* step adapts model parameters as done in MAML. They show that their method, LEOPARD, outperforms multi-task trained models as well as a range of other meta-learning methods.

Reptile This meta-learning algorithm, introduced by Nichol et al. (2018), is computationally simple compared to MAML and LEOPARD - the *MetaUpdate* step simply moves the model parameters towards inner-loop fine-tuned model parameters, thus assuming the form:

$$\theta \leftarrow \theta + \beta \frac{1}{|\{T_i\}|} \sum_{T_i \sim p(T)} (\theta_i - \theta)$$

Despite it's simplicity, it reports strong performance on a variety of few-shot learning tasks (Dou et al., 2019).

Prototypical Networks Unlike optimisation-driven meta-learning methods, Prototypical Networks (Snell et al., 2017) is a metric-based meta-learning method that uses an embedding function f_θ to encode training support samples and compute a high-dimensional vector μ_c that is the arithmetic mean of the training data points of class c. It then uses a distance function d to compute the similarity between a query instance x and the mean vector of each class to get the class distribution as:

$$p(y = c|x) = softmax(-d(f_\theta(x), \mu_c)) = \frac{exp(-d(f_\theta(x), \mu_c))}{\sum_{c' \in C} exp(-d(f_\theta(x), \mu'_c))}$$

Model optimisation is done using the loss function $J(\theta) = -log(p(y = c^*|x, \theta))$.

A.3 Analysis of soft-labels derived from linear constraints: constraintSLP

Theorem A.1. *The soft-label value of each class within a single soft-label prototype generated using constraintSLP is inversely proportional to its distance from the soft-label prototype along the line connecting all classes captured by it.*

Proof of Theorem A.1 (Informal) Consider a line l connecting three class centroids (while we focus on a three class system, the conclusions generalise to $n > 3$ classes too). The class centroids are represented by A, B and C. The soft-label prototypes at ends A and C contain the values $[a_1, a_2, a_3]$ and $[c_1, c_2, c_3]$ respectively. Consider a support example $x \in A$ at a distance d_a and d_b from A and C respectively. Directly using the constraints in Algorithm 4 of Sucholutsky et al. (2021), we state that the influence of A (i.e., the distance-weighted sum of the soft-labels at x) should be more than the sum of the influence of the other two classes. Thus, we need to maximise:

$$\frac{a_1}{d_a} + \frac{c_1}{d_b} > \left(\frac{a_2}{d_a} + \frac{c_2}{d_b}\right) + \left(\frac{a_3}{d_a} + \frac{c_3}{d_b}\right) \quad (2)$$

As we move x further towards A, $d_a \rightarrow 0$ and the influence of $[a_1/d_1, a_2/d_2, a_3/d_3]$ increases thus $\sum_{i=2}^{i=3} c_i/d_b <<< \sum_{i=2}^{i=3} a_i/d_a$. Therefore we have the approximation:

$$\frac{a_1}{d_a} > \frac{a_2}{d_a} + \frac{a_3}{d_a} \implies a_1 > a_2 + a_3 \quad (3)$$

If we take a support example $x \in C$, by symmetry as x is moved towards C, $d_b \rightarrow 0$, we can also write:

$$\frac{c_3}{d_b} > \frac{c_2}{d_b} + \frac{c_1}{d_b} \implies c_3 > c_2 + c_1 \quad (4)$$

Furthermore, consider a point x in the middle of l equidistant from A and C (by a distance d) – such a point will always be classified as $x \in B$. Thus, the influence of B should be higher than both A and C. Thus we have:

$$\frac{a_2}{d} + \frac{c_2}{d} > \frac{a_1}{d} + \frac{c_1}{d} \quad \& \quad \frac{a_2}{d} + \frac{c_2}{d} > \frac{a_3}{d} + \frac{c_3}{d}$$
$$\implies a_2 + c_2 > a_1 + c_1 \quad \& \quad a_2 + c_2 > a_3 + c_3$$

From Equation 3 and Equation 4 we can replace a_1 and c_3 and get:

$$a_2 + c_2 > a_2 + a_3 + c_1 \implies c_2 > c_1$$
$$a_2 + c_2 > a_3 + c_2 + c_1 \implies a_2 > a_3$$

Therefore, we have:

$$a_1 > a_2 > a_3 \quad \& \quad c_3 > c_2 > c_1$$

This is an intuitive result as the soft-label value of each class decreases as the distance of the class centroid increases from the prototype location – the class nearest to the prototype has the highest soft-label value and the class furthest away has the lowest soft-label value.

Recall that $\sum_{i=1}^{3} a_i = 1$ and $\sum_{i=1}^{3} c_i = 1$ and $a_i, c_i \geq 0 \; \forall i = \{1, 2, 3\}$ otherwise the optimisation problem becomes unbounded. Therefore, the ranges of values for $[a_1, a_2, a_3]$ and $[c_1, c_2, c_3]$ are:

$$a_3 \in [0, a_2), \; a_2 \in (a_3, a_1), \; a_1 \in (a_2, 1]$$
$$c_3 \in (c_2, 1], \; c_2 \in (c_1, c_3), \; c_1 \in [0, c_2)$$

Using Algorithm 4 in Sucholutsky et al. (2021), we see that there are multiple constraints for a_1 and a_2 which require them to be maximised, but there are none for a_3. Thus, to maximise Equation 3, a_3 adjusts to the minimum value it can get:

$$a_3 = min(0, a_2) = \epsilon \simeq 0$$

By symmetry, we can also conclude that:

$$c_1 = min(0, c_2) = \epsilon \simeq 0$$

These approximations are also generalisable to multiple classes connected by a line, for example, if a line connects only two centroids, the soft-labels at each end are derived as $[0, 1]$ and $[1, 0]$ - the same as a "hard" label. These findings are substantiated experimentally in Table 2 where we examine the soft-labels generated by DeepSLP and constraintSLP using a few-shot training support set of the task *airline* with 8 examples per class – the constraintSLP soft label corresponding to the furthest class from the prototype location drops to almost zero compared to other soft label values. On the other hand, DeepSLP prevents overfitting on the nearest classes and produces a more generalised distribution of soft-labels. This is a trend generally observed in other tasks and classes as well. We further use this theorem to prove the main theorem given by Theorem A.2.

Theorem A.2. *The constant soft-labels in constraintSLP do not always select the closest class centroid to a test point.*

#	constraintSLP	DeepSLP(x)
1	$5.6422e-01$	$9.7887e-01$
	$4.3577e-01$	$2.0995e-02$
	$9.7973e-16$	$1.3500e-04$
2	$5.3090e-13$	$2.5240e-02$
	$4.3212e-01$	$9.7475e-01$
	$5.6787e-01$	$1.0000e-05$

Table 2: Soft labels derived using constraintSLP and DeepSLP. # denotes the index of the soft-label prototype lying on the line. Soft labels are constant for constraintSLP, however, they are a function of input point x for DeepSLP, thus allowing more flexibility.

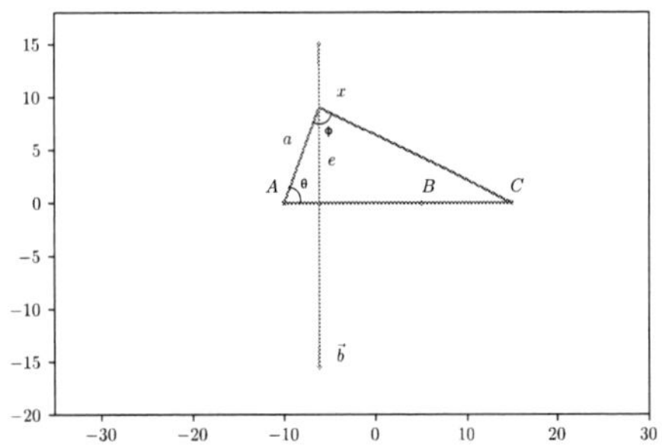

Figure 5: Schematic diagram for ascertaining θ with class centroids $A = (-10, 0)$, $B = (5, 0)$ and $C = (15, 0)$.

Proof of Theorem A.2 (Informal) Furthermore, consider a line b perpendicular to l – it intersects l between A and B. We select θ such that $\phi = \pi/2$. We denote the complete setup diagrammatically in Figure 5.

Consider the distance weighted influences at x for class A. We have the influence as $\frac{a_1 sin\theta}{e} + \frac{c_1 cos\theta}{e} = \frac{a_1 sin\theta}{e}$ as $c_1 \simeq 0$. Similarly, for class B, we have the weighted influence as $\frac{a_2 sin\theta}{e} + \frac{c_2 cos\theta}{e}$. To calculate values of θ where the weighted influence of B is more than the weighted influence of A, we get:

$$\frac{a_2 sin\theta}{e} + \frac{c_2 cos\theta}{e} > \frac{a_1 sin\theta}{e}$$
$$\implies a_2 sin\theta + c_2 cos\theta > a_1 sin\theta$$
$$\implies c_2 cos\theta - (a_1 - a_2) sin\theta > 0$$
$$\implies \frac{c_2 cos\theta - (a_1 - a_2) sin\theta}{\sqrt{c_2^2 + (a_1 - a_2)^2}} > 0$$
$$\implies cos(\theta + \alpha) > 0$$

where $\alpha = tan^{-1}\left(\frac{a_1 - a_2}{c_2}\right)$. Since $cos(\theta + \alpha) > 0$

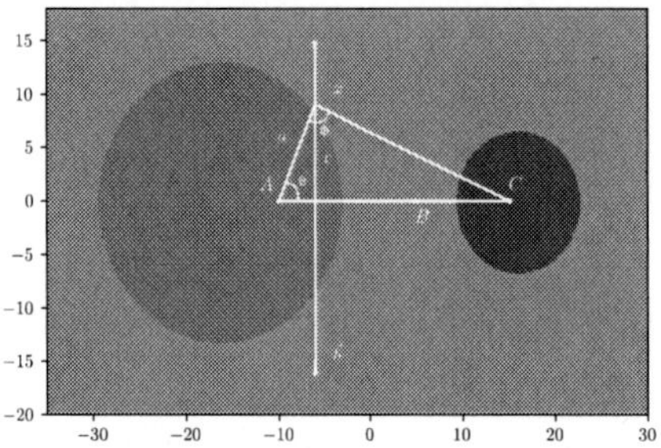

a Denoting the decision boundaries calculated with constraintSLP. Green represents points classified as class A, pink represents the points classified as class B, and brown represents the points classified as C.

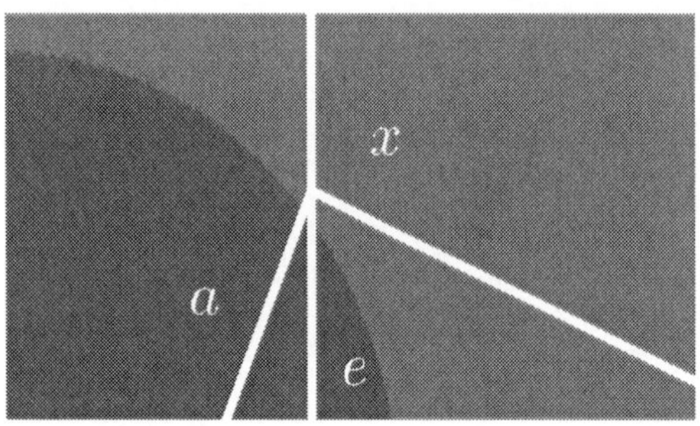

b Zooming in at point x. We can see that it is classified as B.

Figure 6: The soft-labels of the linear constraint system at A and C using constraintSLP are calculated as $[0.5963, 0.4036, 0.0001]$ and $[0.0001, 0.4495, 0.5504]$. We also get $\theta = 66.84°$. Using these soft-labels, we calculate the decision boundaries for points in this area. We use θ to calculate the coordinates of x. Zooming in, we can visually inspect that x is classified to class B. For x, the Euclidean distance of x from A and B is 9.847 and 14.338 respectively. From the figure, we can see that constraintSLP classifies x as B even though the Euclidean distance of x from A is shorter.

we have $(\theta + \alpha) \in (-\pi/2, \pi/2)$ and since $\theta > 0$, thus for $\theta \in [0, \pi/2 - \alpha)$, the weighted influence of B is more than the weighted influence of A.

However, it is worth observing the result for θ derived above can contain points closer to A (using Euclidean distance) which are *actually* classified as B. We can easily demonstrate this with a counter example explained in Figure 6.

Therefore, for points closer to A compared to B using an Euclidean measure, constraintSLP can still return a higher value for the influence at B compared to A. This adversely affects performance in classifiers where we rely on selection of the closest class centroid for classification – such as

Algorithm 3: Inner-loop training of MetaSLP

$\mathcal{T}_i \leftarrow$ meta-training task
$\mathcal{L} \leftarrow$ line connecting both centroids of a task
$\alpha \leftarrow$ inner-loop learning rate
$\mathcal{S} \leftarrow$ inner-loop optimisation steps
Initialise $g_1x(x)$ and $g_2(x)$ randomly
while $s < \mathcal{S}$ **do**
  Sample support examples X^s for $\mathcal{T}_i$
  Calculate locations of each soft-label prototype in $\mathcal{L}$
  Use Equation 1 to classify $x \in X^s$
  Calculate $\nabla \mathcal{L}_{\mathcal{T}_i}(f_\theta(x), g_1(x), g_2(x))$
  Scale $\nabla_\phi \mathcal{L}_{\mathcal{T}_i}(g_1(x))$ and $\nabla_\omega \mathcal{L}_{\mathcal{T}_i}(g_2(x))$ by the distances from the soft-label prototypes
  $\theta'_i \leftarrow \theta - \alpha \nabla_\theta \mathcal{L}_{\mathcal{T}_i}(f_\theta(x))$
  $\theta'_{1_i} \leftarrow \theta_1 - \alpha \nabla_\phi \mathcal{L}_{\mathcal{T}_i}(g_1(x))$
  $\theta'_{2_i} \leftarrow \theta_2 - \alpha \nabla_\omega \mathcal{L}_{\mathcal{T}_i}(g_2(x))$
end

1-NN, Prototypical Networks, and constraintSLP – and we believe this is the reason behind the poor performance of constraintSLP for cases where the total classes is greater than two.

A.4 Training algorithms for MetaSLP

Inner-loop training Our inner-loop training algorithm for MetaSLP is presented in Algorithm 3. The inner-loop encoder optimisation can be understood as updating the parameters of the encoder to "push" different classes away from each other and "pull" points belonging to the same class together; i.e., increase inter-class distance and decrease intra-class distance which leads to well-defined clusters per class. We present this process in Figure 7.

Outer-loop training Our outer-loop training algorithm is presented in Algorithm 4.

A.5 Meta-training details

GLUE (Wang et al., 2018) tasks and their details are provided in Table 3. These tasks include MNLI (Williams et al., 2018), SST2 (Socher et al., 2013), CoLA (Warstadt et al., 2018), MRPC (Dolan and Brockett, 2005), QQP (Wang et al., 2017), QNLI (Wang et al., 2018), RTE (Giampiccolo et al., 2008) and SNLI (Bowman et al., 2015). We employ the same tasks as Bansal et al. (2020a) to ensure direct comparability. Note that the datasets and

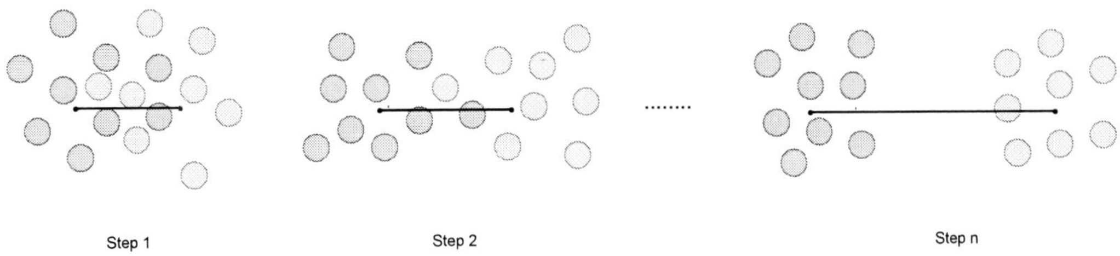

Figure 7: Inner-loop training – note that inter-class embeddings are pushed further away, and intra-class embeddings are pushed closer together across n steps. The endpoints of the line mark the location of the soft-label prototypes.

Algorithm 4: Outer-loop training of MetaSLP

$\mathcal{T} \leftarrow$ batch of meta-training tasks, $|\mathcal{T}| = n$
$\mathcal{M} \leftarrow$ batch of distinct inner-loop optimised models parameterised by θ_i, $|\mathcal{M}| = n$
$\beta \leftarrow$ outer-loop learning rate
for $\mathcal{T}_i,\ \mathcal{M}_i \in \mathcal{T},\ \mathcal{M}$ **do**
  if *FOMAML* **then**
    Sample query examples X^q for $\mathcal{T}_i$, $X^s \cap X^q = \Phi$
    Use Equation 1 to classify $x \in X^q$
    Calculate $\nabla_{\theta'_i} \mathcal{L}_{\mathcal{T}_i}(f_{\theta'_i}(x), g_{\phi'_i}(x), h_{\omega'_i}(x))$
    Update $\nabla_{\theta} \mathcal{L}_{\mathcal{T}_i}(f_{\theta}(x)) += \nabla_{\theta'_i} \mathcal{L}_{\mathcal{T}_i}(f_{\theta'_i}(x), g_{\phi'_i}(x), h_{\omega'_i}(x))$
  end
  if *Reptile* **then**
    Update $\nabla_{\theta} \mathcal{L}_{\mathcal{T}_i}(f_{\theta}(x)) += \theta - \theta_i$
  end
end
Update $\theta \leftarrow \theta - \frac{\beta}{n} \sum_{i=1}^{n} \nabla_{\theta} \mathcal{L}_{\mathcal{T}_i}(f_{\theta}(x))$

classes in GLUE are completely different from the datasets used for evaluating the model - thus the final model fine-tunes on unseen few-shot data and learns classes it has previously not encountered.

To train our model to detect the sentiment contained within phrases of a sentence by using the annotations for phrases within sentences for SST2, we append a separator token and the annotated phrase for each sentence at the end of the sentence in the form "[CLS] <sentence_1> [SEP] <sentence_2> [SEP]" and obtain the passage level embedding for training.

Dataset	Labels	Training Size	Validation Size	Test Size
CoLA	2	8551	1042	-
MRPC	2	3669	409	-
QNLI	2	104744	5464	-
QQP	2	363847	40431	-
RTE	2	2491	278	-
SNLI	3	549368	9843	-
SST-2	2	67350	873	-
MNLI	3	392703	19649	-

Table 3: Details of GLUE tasks used for meta-training.

A.6 Hyperparameters

Generating lines The hyperparameters used to generate lines are: (a) ϵ, which is a control factor used to denote the maximum tolerance between a centroid and the line assigned to it using Euclidean distance—we use a tolerance value of $1e-1$; and (b) l, which denotes the maximum number of lines used to connect all centroids. We experiment with a range of values ($l \in \{0.25n, 0.5n, 0.75n, n-1\}$, where n is the number of centroids), but find $l = \lceil n/2 \rceil$ to give the best accuracy on the validation data with the minimum number of lines required.[4]

DeepSLP For DeepSLP, we find that more epochs are needed to train models with a higher number of soft labels (i.e., a higher number of classes in the output of the classifier head) - essentially, 3 classes fitted on a line need more epochs compared to 2 classes fitted on a line. We use *AdamW* (Loshchilov and Hutter, 2017a) as our optimiser and perform hyperparameter tuning on the validation set. We only need a few epochs (5 to 10) to generalise well depending on the training task. We fix a random seed, train our models and evaluate performance on the test tasks. We repeat

[4]The right choice of hyperparameters is key as the optimisation process fails when it is not possible to connect n centroids with l lines.

Parameter	Search Space	MetaSLP$_{\text{REPTILE}}$	MetaSLP$_{\text{FOMAML}}$	Reptile
Tunable layers (v)	$[1, 2, 3, 4]$	4	4	4
K-shot	$[8, 16, 32]$	16	16	16
Batch size	$[8, 16, 32]$	16	16	16
Steps	$[3, 5, 7]$	5	5	5
α_f	$[5e-3, 1e-3, 1e-4]$	$5e-3$	Learnable	$1e-3$
$\alpha_g,\ \alpha_h$	$[5e-3, 1e-3, 1e-4, 1e-2]$	$5e-3$	Learnable	$1e-3$
Nesterov	$[True, False]$	$True$	$True$	$True$
Momentum	$[0.5, 0.7, 0.9]$	0.9	0.9	$True$
β_{initial}	$[1e-5, 2e-5, 5e-5]$	$5e-5$	$2e-5$	$1e-5$
β_{final}	$[1e-5, 2e-5, 5e-6]$	$2e-5$	$2e-5$	$1e-5$
Task sampling	[*square root, uniform*]	*square root*	*square root*	*square root*

Table 4: Meta-training hyperparameters.

this process across three different seeds and report the mean and standard deviation. Hyperparameters for all baselines in this setting can be found online in our code repository[5].

Meta-training For inner-loop optimisation, we use SGD as an optimiser with Nesterov and a momentum factor. We use a cosine annealing learning rate scheduler (Loshchilov and Hutter, 2017b) on our outer-loop learning rate to decay the learning rate from a starting rate to an end rate without restarts across one epoch for MetaSLP$_{\text{REPTILE}}$. We use AdamW (Loshchilov and Hutter, 2017a) as our outer-loop optimiser with AMSGrad (Reddi et al., 2018). We employ early stopping and stop training if our model does not improve it's validation set accuracy over 100 batches. We use learnable inner-loop learning rates for MetaSLP$_{\text{FOMAML}}$ per parameter group for better optimisation as indicated by previous literature (Antoniou et al., 2019). All meta-training hyperparameters can be found in Appendix A.6, Table 4.

Meta-testing Similar to inner-loop optimisation at meta-training, we use SGD with Nesterov and the same optimiser hyperparameters. However, we decay the learning rate using a cosine scheduler across all fine-tuning epochs to prevent overfitting on the few-shot (support) training set per task for MetaSLP$_{\text{REPTILE}}$.

A.7 Results

The complete set of results of all models and baselines can be seen in Table 5 for the low-resource setting and DeepSLP, and Table 6 for the high-resource setting and MetaSLP.

[5]<anon-url>

DeepSLP Our results (Table 5) demonstrate that DeepSLP$_{\text{BERT}}$ outperforms BERT$_{\text{fine-tuned}}$ in $31/48$ tasks, constraintSLP$_{\text{BERT}}$ in $43/48$ tasks and LORA$_{\text{BERT}}$ in $45/48$ tasks, demonstrating the usefulness of soft-label prototypes and superiority over the "standard" LLM fine-tuning paradigm, as well as the simpler constraintSLP variant. constraintSLP$_{\text{BERT}}$, on the other hand, fares worse than BERT$_{\text{fine-tuned}}$ and LORA, outperforming the former in only $19/48$ tasks and the latter in $25/48$ tasks, while exhibiting high standard deviations which can be explained by Theorem A.2, as constraintSLP can behave erratically and not select the closest point to the class centroid. Overall, DeepSLP is the best performing method, demonstrating the highest accuracy in $31/48$ tasks, while being on-par with the second best model (BERT$_{\text{fine-tuned}}$) on the remaining tasks ($15/48$ tasks). Fine-tuned BERT is, overall, the next best model with $13/48$ tasks while constraintSLP achieves the best performance amongst all methods in only $1/48$ tasks. ProtoNet's comparatively lower performance can be explained by the fact that meta-learning approaches tend to require a large number of diverse and structured meta-training tasks for effective learning — thus not making them readily suited for (extreme) few-shot learning settings.

MetaSLP In Table 6, MetaSLP$_{\text{REPTILE}}$ outperforms all baselines achieving the highest performance in $33/48$ tasks. LEOPARD is the next best model with the highest performance in $11/48$ tasks. Interestingly, MetaSLP$_{\text{FOMAML}}$ does not fare as well as MetaSLP$_{\text{REPTILE}}$ and achieves the highest performance in only $1/48$ tasks while outperforms LEOPARD in only $6/48$ tasks. MetaSLP$_{\text{FOMAML}}$ nevertheless outperforms

MetaSLP$_{\text{REPTILE}}$ and Reptile in natural language inference tasks – demonstrating the usefulness of learnable inner-loop learning rates across multiple task distributions while meta-training.

A.8 Ensemble properties of DeepSLP

In this study, we compare and contrast DeepSLP to ensembles and draw similarities between the two, shedding further light into the effectiveness of our approach. Each prediction decision by DeepSLP is the result of two soft-label prototypes – those that lie on each end of the line nearest to a test point x. An analogy can then be drawn between the prototypes used at prediction time and those individual (albeit independent) models that are utilised by an ensemble when producing the final classification.

While DeepSLP prototypes are not independent but are rather trained jointly (and share the same encoder), in what follows, we demonstrate that they display several properties of ensemble methods, while being computationally efficient and utilising a small number of parameters. For the analyses below, we consider the tasks Airline and Disaster using an 8-shot setting and evaluate on the test data for each. However, we find the below properties to generalise across all tasks.

A.8.1 Individual vs joint prediction

In a similar way as an ensemble exhibits superior performance to the individual models it utilises, we seek to assess whether the joint utilisation of prototypes at prediction time is indeed more effective than utilising each prototype individually. To evaluate this, we measure the probability distribution of each setting on the test data using negative log-likelihood:

$$NLL(\mathbf{f}(\mathbf{x}), y) \triangleq -log(\mathbf{f}^{(\mathbf{y})}(\mathbf{x}))$$

Following Abe et al. (2022), for a strictly convex function such as NLL, we use Jensen's inequality:

$$NLL(\mathbf{F}(\mathbf{x}), y) \;\leq\; \mathbb{E}[NLL(\mathbf{f}(\mathbf{x}), y)]$$

where $F(x)$ is the ensemble and $f(x)$ are the constituent models. The idea is that the probability distribution of the ensemble fits the target distribution more closely than the corresponding expected probability distributions of its constituent models. For joint soft-label prototypes parameterised by g_1 and g_2 and located at p_1 and p_2, we have:

$$NLL\left(softmax\left(\frac{g_1(f(x))}{||f(x)-p_1||}) + \frac{g_2(f(x))}{||f(x)-p_2||}\right), y\right)$$
$$= -\sum log\left(softmax\left(\frac{g_1^y(f(x))}{||f(x)-p_1||}) + \frac{g_2^y(f(x))}{||f(x)-p_2||}\right)\right)$$

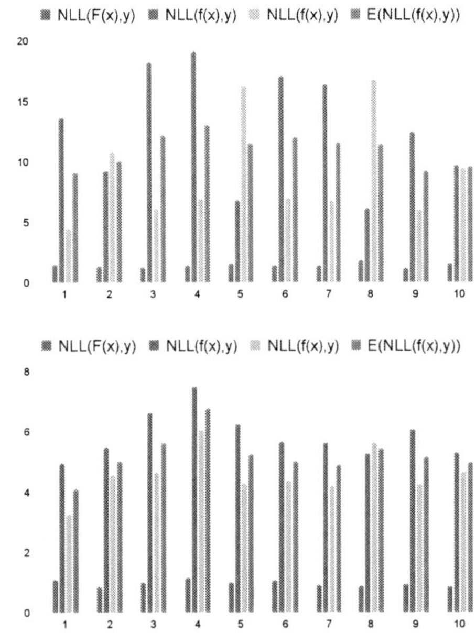

Figure 8: $NLL(\mathbf{F}(\mathbf{x}), y)$ vs. $\mathbb{E}[NLL(\mathbf{f}(\mathbf{x}), y)]$ for Disaster (top) and Airline (bottom). The ith subscript refers to the ith soft-label prototype.

For the individual soft-label prototypes, weighing the outputs by distance does not change the final softmax probability distribution; therefore, we can define $\mathbb{E}[NLL(\mathbf{f}(\mathbf{x}), y)]$ as their average:

$$-\frac{1}{2}\sum log(softmax(g_1^y(f(x)) + log(softmax(g_2^y(f(x))$$

We plot the negative log likelihoods for Airline and Disaster on the test set after fine-tuning each model on ten subsets of few-shot training data (as explained before in Section 4) in Figure 8 to assess whether DeepSLP exhibits this property of ensemble methods. We find that $NLL(\mathbf{F}(\mathbf{x}), y)$ is much lower than $\mathbb{E}[NLL(\mathbf{f}(\mathbf{x}), y)]$, which confirms that the joint utilisation of prototypes results in better predictions than if they were to be used individually. Our experiments confirm that this is a general trend we observe across tasks. In the following sections, we investigate the reasons behind the high values observed for $\mathbb{E}[NLL(\mathbf{f}(\mathbf{x}), y)]$, and compare the jointly trained prototypes against a strong baseline, the fine-tuned BERT baseline.

A.8.2 Jointly utilised soft-label prototypes improve diversity

Diversity in ensemble classifications refers to the difference in the probability distribution on out-of-distribution (ood) data for classifications between

Category (Classes)	Shot	LORA$_{\text{BERT}}$	ProtoNet	constraintSLP$_{\text{BERT}}$	BERT$_{\text{fine-tuned}}$*	DeepSLP$_{\text{BERT}}$
Political Bias (2)	4	52.75 ± 4.33	51.15 ± 2.454	53.447 ± 3.281	54.57 ± 5.02	53.251 ± 4.042
	8	53.66 ± 4.25	56.568 ± 4.228	55.824 ± 3.725	56.15 ± 3.75	58.209 ± 5.198
	16	59.21 ± 2.27	59.183 ± 4.706	58.277 ± 4.128	60.96 ± 4.25	61.479 ± 2.974
Emotion (13)	4	7.56 ± 2.93	8.953 ± 2.052	8.662 ± 6.213	09.20 ± 3.22	9.076 ± 1.108
	8	9.02 ± 2.36	10.857 ± 3.436	8.16 ± 3.266	08.21 ± 2.12	8.041 ± 2.797
	16	10.29 ± 1.67	11.479 ± 2.96	8.115 ± 3.66	13.43 ± 2.51	10.919 ± 1.615
Sentiment Books (2)	4	51.27 ± 2.75	55.53 ± 4.097	59.89 ± 5.385	54.81 ± 3.75	58.67 ± 4.753
	8	58.16 ± 3.3	58.97 ± 4.909	64.34 ± 2.565	53.54 ± 5.17	64.78 ± 2.615
	16	59.16 ± 2.59	65.5 ± 7.026	66.36 ± 2.183	65.56 ± 4.12	67.453 ± 3.085
Rating DVD (3)	4	31.65 ± 4.91	37.665 ± 7.184	32.298 ± 16.263	32.22 ± 08.72	39.566 ± 5.086
	8	37.69 ± 3.16	37.008 ± 5.118	32.644 ± 16.016	36.35 ± 12.50	38.788 ± 4.449
	16	38.63 ± 5.52	39.123 ± 6.004	35.587 ± 17.445	42.79 ± 10.18	40.53 ± 4.375
Rating Electronics (3)	4	31.66 ± 2.94	33.696 ± 5.55	35.188 ± 16.211	39.27 ± 10.15	39.977 ± 5.959
	8	38.72 ± 5.95	37.297 ± 5.938	29.624 ± 12.876	28.74 ± 08.22	41.926 ± 3.985
	16	39.15 ± 6.6	43.825 ± 5.946	29.836 ± 12.753	45.48 ± 06.13	44.917 ± 3.164
Rating Kitchen (3)	4	36.63 ± 4.68	35.914 ± 6.678	28.253 ± 15.907	34.76 ± 11.20	39.624 ± 6.787
	8	39.69 ± 6.22	38.46 ± 11.124	24.397 ± 11.961	34.49 ± 08.72	41.081 ± 6.777
	16	38.17 ± 7.14	46.546 ± 8.394	31.926 ± 18.29	47.94 ± 08.28	45.801 ± 4.562
Political Audience (2)	4	49.75 ± 1.03	50.976 ± 1.84	51.305 ± 2.68	51.02 ± 1.72	51.741 ± 2.827
	8	54.05 ± 2.54	52.022 ± 3.964	53.104 ± 3.669	52.80 ± 2.72	54.506 ± 3.274
	16	55.39 ± 3.66	54.024 ± 3.071	53.888 ± 3.305	58.45 ± 4.98	56.956 ± 3.045
Sentiment Kitchen (2)	4	53.02 ± 1.54	55.24 ± 3.427	61.96 ± 4.594	56.93 ± 7.10	60.76 ± 4.426
	8	55.54 ± 3.47	62.28 ± 5.103	64.83 ± 3.983	57.13 ± 6.60	65.733 ± 3.198
	16	58.59 ± 4.83	66.9 ± 5.441	68.21 ± 3.298	68.88 ± 3.39	69.18 ± 2.589
Disaster (2)	4	56.02 ± 6.35	51.474 ± 8.848	52.77 ± 10.803	55.73 ± 10.29	54.252 ± 9.843
	8	57.46 ± 6.9	60.661 ± 4.991	56.888 ± 11.139	56.31 ± 09.57	61.3 ± 7.961
	16	65.79 ± 2.03	63.893 ± 6.62	65.907 ± 3.691	64.52 ± 08.93	69.28 ± 2.358
Airline (3)	4	24.36 ± 5.42	44.167 ± 10.752	36.243 ± 22.607	42.76 ± 13.50	50.987 ± 4.936
	8	52.31 ± 7.89	50.148 ± 13.429	44.972 ± 22.584	38.00 ± 17.06	55.209 ± 6.049
	16	54.1 ± 8.57	54.8 ± 10.49	29.238 ± 17.494	58.01 ± 08.23	60.247 ± 4.577
Rating Books (3)	4	34.69 ± 2.12	37.715 ± 5.801	25.562 ± 15.207	39.42 ± 07.22	42.116 ± 4.725
	8	39.36 ± 6.33	38.518 ± 5.327	34.026 ± 14.123	39.55 ± 10.01	42.156 ± 4.608
	16	41.23 ± 5.32	44.694 ± 7.797	32.509 ± 16.132	43.08 ± 11.78	46.513 ± 3.036
Political Message (9)	4	12.16 ± 1.46	13.888 ± 2.076	12.438 ± 1.799	15.64 ± 2.73	14.421 ± 1.095
	8	15.71 ± 2.04	16.155 ± 2.316	15.08 ± 2.925	13.38 ± 1.74	16.919 ± 1.756
	16	15.53 ± 2.55	18.324 ± 2.011	13.121 ± 3.294	20.67 ± 3.89	18.319 ± 1.74
Sentiment DVD (2)	4	50.77 ± 0.78	51.06 ± 3.302	56.06 ± 2.408	54.98 ± 3.96	55.003 ± 2.936
	8	52.24 ± 1.54	55.19 ± 3.298	56.98 ± 3.299	55.63 ± 4.34	57.527 ± 3.562
	16	52.6 ± 2.09	59.45 ± 3.84	58.95 ± 2.813	58.69 ± 6.08	60.76 ± 2.944
Scitail (2)	4	43.36 ± 4.74	50.227 ± 5.69	52.296 ± 4.366	58.53 ± 09.74	54.101 ± 3.759
	8	54.29 ± 5.25	54.196 ± 6.678	55.964 ± 5.705	57.93 ± 10.70	56.341 ± 5.786
	16	52.68 ± 3.0	57.744 ± 5.696	59.675 ± 4.033	65.66 ± 06.82	59.692 ± 4.227
Restaurant (8)	4	10.56 ± 1.36	18.161 ± 2.822	24.932 ± 17.102	49.37 ± 4.28	47.634 ± 5.237
	8	20.92 ± 2.4	32.146 ± 5.785	29.787 ± 9.573	49.38 ± 7.76	55.912 ± 4.494
	16	29.37 ± 4.05	40.435 ± 3.348	29.154 ± 13.537	69.24 ± 3.68	61.716 ± 2.208
CoNLL (4)	4	21.48 ± 2.71	35.438 ± 7.324	27.02 ± 7.346	50.44 ± 08.57	52.724 ± 5.84
	8	29.84 ± 3.28	44.259 ± 4.886	31.296 ± 17.487	50.06 ± 11.30	60.374 ± 3.731
	16	37.18 ± 3.32	52.116 ± 5.354	22.923 ± 7.933	74.47 ± 03.10	67.496 ± 4.551

Table 5: Classification performance (accuracy) of our methods (constraintSLP and DeepSLP) and baselines in the low-resource setting. Entries in grey indicate the best model out of all; * refers to the baseline as reported in Bansal et al. (2020a). Subscripts for constraintSLP and DeepSLP refer to the (non-fine-tuned) encoder used. Each set of results is separated by a double line. The first set of results contains intent classification tasks, the second set has a natural language inference task and the last set contains entity typing tasks.

Category (Classes)	Shot	ProtoNet	LEOPARD*	Reptile	MetaSLP$_{REPTILE}$	MetaSLP$_{FOMAML}$
Political Bias (2)	4	56.33 ± 4.37	60.49 ± 6.66	58.82 ± 4.31	60.96 ± 6.13	55.06 ± 5.9
	8	58.87 ± 3.79	61.74 ± 6.73	59.43 ± 3.79	63.65 ± 4.57	58.97 ± 5.5
	16	57.01 ± 4.44	65.08 ± 2.14	62.21 ± 0.72	66.05 ± 1.57	63.63 ± 4.74
Emotion (13)	4	09.18 ± 3.14	11.71 ± 2.16	11.65 ± 3.21	11.94 ± 1.95	11.03 ± 2.98
	8	11.18 ± 2.95	12.90 ± 1.63	10.56 ± 2.85	13.42 ± 1.46	12.38 ± 2.69
	16	12.32 ± 3.73	13.38 ± 2.20	11.62 ± 3.11	14.03 ± 2.35	12.32 ± 1.76
Sentiment Books (2)	4	73.15 ± 5.85	82.54 ± 1.33	76.95 ± 1.03	83.22 ± 0.95	74.51 ± 5.25
	8	75.46 ± 6.87	83.03 ± 1.28	77.49 ± 1.08	83.8 ± 0.8	79.25 ± 1.97
	16	77.26 ± 3.27	83.33 ± 0.79	77.88 ± 0.56	83.8 ± 1.59	78.41 ± 1.08
Rating DVD (3)	4	47.73 ± 6.20	49.76 ± 9.80	45.91 ± 9.85	45.2 ± 8.91	39.64 ± 5.17
	8	47.11 ± 4.00	53.28 ± 4.66	47.23 ± 9.22	58.38 ± 2.9	52.35 ± 5.27
	16	48.39 ± 3.74	53.52 ± 4.77	48.49 ± 8.88	57.41 ± 4.71	60.4 ± 3.71
Rating Electronics (3)	4	37.40 ± 3.72	51.71 ± 7.20	44.47 ± 8.25	45.34 ± 7.22	39.53 ± 5.76
	8	43.64 ± 7.31	54.78 ± 6.48	49.1 ± 6.81	55.10 ± 5.12	47.83 ± 5.94
	16	44.83 ± 5.96	58.69 ± 2.41	50.68 ± 6.8	59.47 ± 2.29	56.53 ± 4.36
Rating Kitchen (3)	4	44.72 ± 9.13	50.21 ± 09.63	45.38 ± 10.96	45.20 ± 8.78	39.11 ± 7.16
	8	46.03 ± 8.57	53.72 ± 10.31	46.71 ± 9.84	54.53 ± 9.9	50.19 ± 8.36
	16	49.85 ± 9.31	57.00 ± 08.69	52.87 ± 9.52	58.94 ± 7.58	57.63 ± 8.37
Political Audience (2)	4	51.47 ± 3.68	52.60 ± 3.51	52.45 ± 4.26	54.1 ± 3.66	52.03 ± 2.73
	8	51.83 ± 3.77	54.31 ± 3.95	52.87 ± 4.31	56.01 ± 3.65	52.06 ± 2.27
	16	53.53 ± 3.25	57.71 ± 3.52	55.6 ± 1.85	58.57 ± 2.04	54.33 ± 3.14
Sentiment Kitchen (2)	4	62.71 ± 9.53	78.35 ± 18.36	69.81 ± 14.58	81.96 ± 3.73	72.73 ± 7.97
	8	70.19 ± 6.42	84.88 ± 1.12	75.76 ± 1.13	83.33 ± 1.99	76.86 ± 4.46
	16	71.83 ± 5.94	85.27 ± 1.31	76.41 ± 0.66	84.33 ± 1.81	80.78 ± 4.38
Disaster (2)	4	50.87 ± 1.12	51.45 ± 4.25	49.76 ± 4.73	55.03 ± 8.73	52.62 ± 2.71
	8	51.30 ± 2.30	55.96 ± 3.58	52.17 ± 5.17	57.77 ± 6.40	55.04 ± 5.79
	16	52.76 ± 2.92	61.32 ± 2.83	55.37 ± 4.53	65.18 ± 4.41	62.27 ± 4.42
Airline (3)	4	40.27 ± 8.19	54.95 ± 11.81	57.11 ± 14.16	57.39 ± 7.83	51.62 ± 10.53
	8	51.16 ± 7.60	61.44 ± 03.90	64.37 ± 3.49	65.67 ± 4.82	57.47 ± 9.37
	16	48.73 ± 6.79	62.15 ± 05.56	66.31 ± 2.55	69.48 ± 2.06	65.02 ± 5.16
Rating Books (3)	4	48.44 ± 7.43	54.92 ± 6.18	56.57 ± 8.17	55.79 ± 5.61	54.4 ± 5.83
	8	52.13 ± 4.79	59.16 ± 4.13	57.33 ± 7.63	65.74 ± 5.58	57.17 ± 6.77
	16	57.28 ± 4.57	61.02 ± 4.19	63.26 ± 3.59	67.87 ± 3.45	66.66 ± 3.93
Political Message (9)	4	14.22 ± 1.25	15.69 ± 1.57	14.58 ± 1.78	18.84 ± 1.82	14.96 ± 1.94
	8	15.67 ± 1.96	18.02 ± 2.32	15.13 ± 2.16	20.09 ± 2.71	16.09 ± 2.6
	16	16.49 ± 1.96	18.07 ± 2.41	16.38 ± 2.15	23.22 ± 1.17	16.62 ± 2.19
Sentiment DVD (2)	4	74.38 ± 2.44	80.32 ± 1.02	72.03 ± 11.61	80.97 ± 1.21	73.08 ± 7.56
	8	75.19 ± 2.56	80.85 ± 1.23	75.79 ± 1.62	81.85 ± 1.79	76.55 ± 2.9
	16	75.26 ± 1.07	81.25 ± 1.41	76.69 ± 0.8	83.48 ± 1.01	78.19 ± 1.32
Scitail (2)	4	76.27 ± 4.26	69.50 ± 9.56	59.13 ± 10.58	53.48 ± 5.59	61.55 ± 9.11
	8	78.27 ± 0.98	75.00 ± 2.42	62.63 ± 10.85	60.79 ± 4.6	68.03 ± 4.54
	16	78.59 ± 0.48	77.03 ± 1.82	68.03 ± 1.57	61.67 ± 3.61	68.5 ± 3.7
Restaurant (8)	4	17.36 ± 2.75	49.84 ± 3.31	13.37 ± 2.25	27.00 ± 2.61	20.31 ± 2.97
	8	18.70 ± 2.38	62.99 ± 3.28	16.83 ± 3.42	35.66 ± 2.39	27.74 ± 2.29
	16	16.41 ± 1.87	70.44 ± 2.89	16.0 ± 3.44	37.20 ± 2.68	28.57 ± 2.41
CoNLL (4)	4	32.23 ± 5.10	54.16 ± 6.32	31.31 ± 5.32	40.79 ± 3.40	36.07 ± 3.25
	8	34.49 ± 5.15	67.38 ± 4.33	33.17 ± 5.1	41.25 ± 5.21	40.5 ± 2.16
	16	33.75 ± 6.05	76.37 ± 3.08	34.04 ± 3.59	45.96 ± 4.75	43.67 ± 6.92

Table 6: Classification performance (accuracy) of MetaSLP and baselines in the high-resource setting. Entries in green indicate the best model out of all; * refers to the baseline as reported in Bansal et al. (2020a). Each set of results is separated by a double line. The first set of results contains intent classification tasks, the second set has a natural language inference task and the last set contains entity typing tasks.

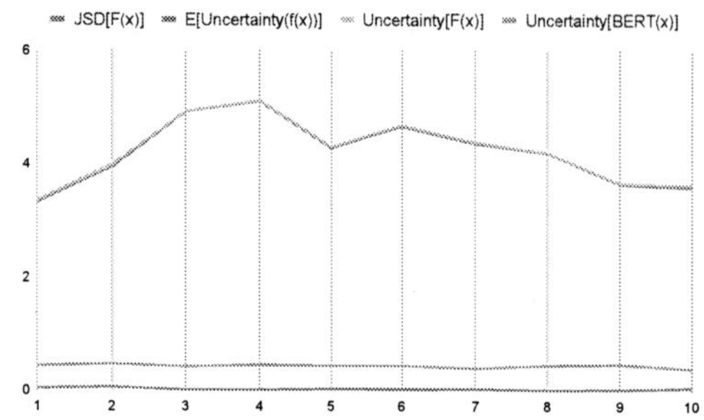

Figure 9: Ensemble uncertainty contrasted against the uncertainty of fine-tuned BERT, where we observe that DeepSLP's uncertainty $F(x)$ (given by yellow) is driven by ensemble diversity, given by $JSD(F(x))$ in blue.

individual models and the ensemble. We use this definition to ascertain the diversity of classifications provided by the jointly utilised soft-label prototypes. Diversity is a desirable property as ensemble predictions are generally more robust due to diversity between the predictions of their individual members (Lee et al., 2015).

Existing work (Ashukha et al., 2020; Lakshminarayanan et al., 2017) defines ensemble uncertainty as the sum of ensemble diversity and the expected average model uncertainty on ood data. Based on Abe et al. (2022), it is calculated as:

$$H([y|F(x)] = \frac{-1}{C}\sum p(y_i|F(x))log(p(y_i|F(x)))$$

If we use the Jenson-Shannon divergence as a diversity measure for an ensemble given by

$$JSD_{p(f)}[y|f(x)] = \frac{1}{M}\sum KL[y|f(x)||y|F(x)]$$

where KL is the average KL divergence between the output distribution of each soft-label prototype and the jointly utilised soft-label prototypes, from Abe et al. (2022), this expression reduces to:

$$H([y|F(x)] = \overbrace{JSD_{p(f)}[y|f(x)]}^{ens.\ diversity} + \overbrace{E_{p(f)}[H[y|f(x)]]}^{avg.\ model\ uncert.}$$

We contrast ensemble uncertainty and single model uncertainty using the fine-tuned BERT model for the task *airline* in Figure 9, but note that similar trends are observed across all tasks. We note that the uncertainty of jointly utilised soft-label prototypes is generally higher than that of the fine-tuned BERT model. As the average model uncertainty of individual soft-label prototypes is negligibly low, the uncertainty in the joint case is driven mainly by the diversity of the ensemble. This is in line with previous work which attributes an increase in uncertainty in ensembles due to diversity (Lakshminarayanan et al., 2017; Dietterich, 2000; Wilson and Izmailov, 2020). Though not strictly an ensemble, our approach exhibits similar properties (higher uncertainty driven by model diversity), as well as a general reduction in standard deviation compared to fine-tuned BERT.

The above provide evidence that our approach as a whole exhibits desirable properties of ensembles which drive a higher performance but which do not lead to higher training time nor compute.

Learned Transformer Position Embeddings Have a Low-Dimensional Structure

Ulme Wennberg
Division of Speech, Music and Hearing
KTH Royal Institute of Technology
`ulme@kth.se`

Gustav Eje Henter
Division of Speech, Music and Hearing
KTH Royal Institute of Technology
`ghe@kth.se`

Abstract

Position embeddings have long been essential for sequence-order encoding in transformer models, yet their structure is underexplored. This study uses principal component analysis (PCA) to quantitatively compare the dimensionality of absolute position and word embeddings in BERT and ALBERT. We find that, unlike word embeddings, position embeddings occupy a low-dimensional subspace, typically utilizing under 10% of the dimensions available. Additionally, the principal vectors are dominated by a few low-frequency rotational components, a structure arising independently across models.

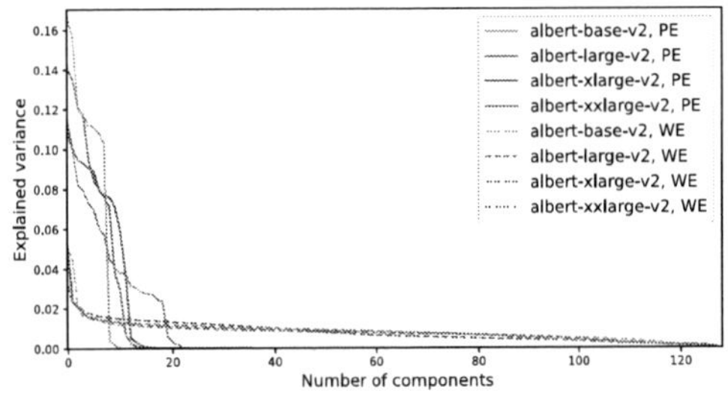

Figure 1: Variance explained by each individual principal component for position (PE, solid lines) and word (WE, dashed) embeddings across four ALBERT models. Each component explains less variance than the previous one by definition. Unlike word embeddings, position embeddings occupy a low-dimensional subspace.

1 Introduction

Transformers, as introduced by Vaswani et al. (2017), have significantly advanced the field of natural language processing, excelling in tasks like machine translation (Lample et al., 2018), question answering (Yamada et al., 2020), information extraction (Wadden et al., 2019; Lin et al., 2020), and text generation (Radford et al., 2018; Brown et al., 2020). The ability to encode positional information is vital in these models, since the transformer architecture otherwise does not take order into account.

Despite their widespread use, the structure of absolute position embeddings in NLP models like BERT (Devlin et al., 2019), RoBERTa (Liu et al., 2019), ALBERT (Lan et al., 2020), and ELECTRA (Clark et al., 2020), as well as vision models like the vision transformer (Dosovitskiy et al., 2021) and BEIT (Bao et al., 2022), remains underexplored. Our research aims to address this gap.

This paper investigates the structure of learned absolute position embeddings in greater detail than before. Specifically, we apply principal components analysis to the learned position embeddings across 12 different transformer-based language models. This yields several novel observations:

- Unlike word embeddings, position embeddings occupy a low-dimensional subspace.
- Variation within this subspace takes the shape of mutually orthogonal periodic components operating pairwise at different frequencies.

These trends are consistent across different models. Our findings resemble mechanisms for mathematical processing recently observed in transformers and suggest new ways in which sequence order can be encoded and learned in transformer models.

2 Background

Transformer-based language models, such as those by Vaswani et al. (2017), have dramatically changed natural language processing by effectively integrating information across long distances in a sequence. Central to the functionality of these models are position embeddings, which enable the encoding of sequence order—an essential aspect in otherwise order-agnostic transformer architectures.

Content embeddings z_i in transformers are constructed as $z_i = e_W(x_i) + e_P(i)$, where x_i is the token at position i, e_W represents word embeddings, and $e_P(i)$ is the position embedding vector of position i; E_P will denote the matrix obtained by stacking all row-vectors e_P. This setup allows the final representation of tokens in a sequence

Proceedings of the 9th Workshop on Representation Learning for NLP (RepL4NLP-2024), pages 237–244
August 15, 2024 ©2024 Association for Computational Linguistics

Table 1: Variance in principal components (PCs) of word and position embeddings for twelve different language models. PCA of sinusoidal position embeddings (Vaswani et al., 2017) is also included for reference.

(a) Position embeddings

Model	Tot. PCs	Top 3	Top 5	Top 10	$N_{50\%}$	(%)
Sinusoidal	128	0.28	0.37	0.52	10	7.8%
albert-base-v1	128	0.50	0.69	0.99	4	3.1%
albert-base-v2	128	0.44	0.67	1.00	4	3.1%
albert-large-v1	128	0.45	0.63	0.95	4	3.1%
albert-large-v2	128	0.40	0.61	0.96	4	3.1%
albert-xlarge-v1	128	0.34	0.51	0.88	5	3.9%
albert-xlarge-v2	128	0.31	0.49	0.89	6	4.7%
albert-xxlarge-v1	128	0.27	0.41	0.68	7	5.5%
albert-xxlarge-v2	128	0.29	0.44	0.72	6	4.7%
bert-base-uncased	512	0.25	0.38	0.62	8	1.6%
bert-base-cased	512	0.28	0.42	0.64	7	1.4%
bert-large-uncased	512	0.23	0.33	0.53	10	2.0%
bert-large-cased	512	0.27	0.41	0.65	7	1.4%

(b) Word embeddings

Model	Tot. PCs	Top 3	Top 5	Top 10	$N_{50\%}$	(%)
albert-base-v1	128	0.07	0.11	0.19	37	28.9%
albert-base-v2	128	0.11	0.15	0.21	39	30.5%
albert-large-v1	128	0.08	0.12	0.20	34	26.6%
albert-large-v2	128	0.09	0.13	0.20	39	30.5%
albert-xlarge-v1	128	0.09	0.13	0.23	27	21.1%
albert-xlarge-v2	128	0.09	0.13	0.21	33	25.8%
albert-xxlarge-v1	128	0.08	0.11	0.18	39	30.5%
albert-xxlarge-v2	128	0.07	0.11	0.18	39	30.5%
bert-base-uncased	768	0.09	0.10	0.12	185	24.1%
bert-base-cased	768	0.05	0.07	0.10	164	21.4%
bert-large-uncased	1024	0.07	0.08	0.10	238	23.2%
bert-large-cased	1024	0.07	0.08	0.11	198	19.3%

to depend on token positions, which is crucial to adequately model contextual effects in text.

While Vaswani et al. (2017) used a fixed, non-learnable encoding scheme for position embeddings, subsequent work has aimed to enhance the expressiveness and efficiency of position encoding. BERT (Devlin et al., 2019) and RoBERTa (Liu et al., 2019) used learnable, data-driven position embeddings to better capture positional dependencies. ALBERT (Lan et al., 2020) refined this approach by introducing factorized embedding parameterizations, reducing model size and complexity while maintaining performance. Research has shown that varying word embedding sizes based on frequency can significantly improve computational efficiency and performance (Grave et al., 2017; Baevski and Auli, 2019; Dai et al., 2019), but varying sizes between word and position embeddings has not been explored, with standard practice being to use the same dimensionality for both.

Most work on position embeddings examines their impact on model performance, not their intrinsic properties. Existing results show that self-attention tends to localize in models using absolute position embeddings (Clark et al., 2019; Htut et al., 2019) and that these embeddings have translation-equivariant structure (Wennberg and Henter, 2021).

3 Dimensionality Analysis of Embeddings

We now analyze the dimensionality of word and position embeddings in transformer-based language models. A deeper dive into into the structure of position embeddings is reserved for Sec. 4.

To understand the structural characteristics of position and word embeddings, we extracted both embedding types from various pre-trained transformer models, specifically twelve different versions of ALBERT and BERT provided by Hugging Face (Wolf et al., 2020). We then applied principal component analysis (PCA) to these embeddings, analyzing each type separately. PCA computes a linear transformation that decomposes high-dimensional data into orthogonal vectors representing the primary axes of variation. Dimensionality reduction is performed by keeping only the k leading principal components (PCs).

Table 1 reports on the results of the PCA analysis. Specifically, it shows how much of the total variance among embedding vectors of each same type that can be explained by the top 3, 5, and 10 principal components, as well as how many components are needed to explain at least 50% of the variation between the vectors (denoted $N_{50\%}$). This allows us to assess and compare the effective dimensionality between position and word embeddings.

From the tables, we see that position embeddings have a significantly lower-dimensional structure compared to word embeddings, suggesting that positional information is encoded more compactly. All ALBERT and BERT models considered have 50% of their variance in the first 1.4–5.5% of the principal components or less, while word embeddings require 19–30% of the PCs to achieve the same result. Figure 1 graphs the variance explained by individual principal components in detail for the ALBERT v2 models, finding that position-embedding vectors lie almost perfectly on a subspace of 10 to 20 dimensions, whereas word embeddings use the entire 128-dimensional space.

4 Analyzing the Principal Components

Having established the low dimensionality of position embeddings, we next explore what the uncovered principal components represent and how they contribute to the embedding structure.

First, we plot (in Figure 2) the leading principal

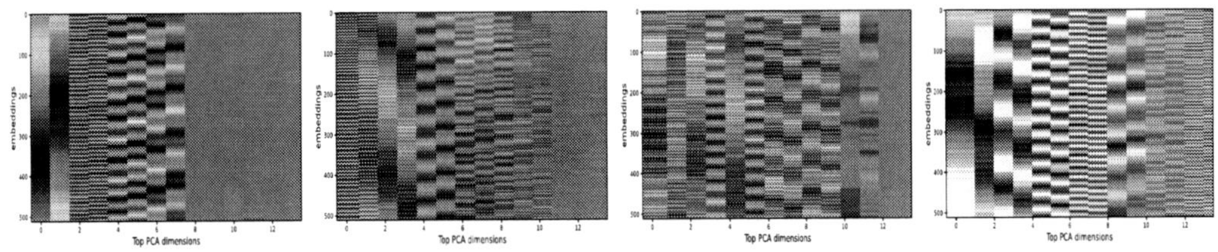

(a) albert-base-v2 (b) albert-large-v2 (c) albert-xlarge-v2 (d) albert-xxlarge-v2

Figure 2: Heatmaps visualizing the top 14 PCs of the position-embedding matrices E_P of the ALBERT v2 models. Best viewed in Adobe Acrobat to avoid blurry rendering. The full matrix with all PCs can be found in Figure 7.

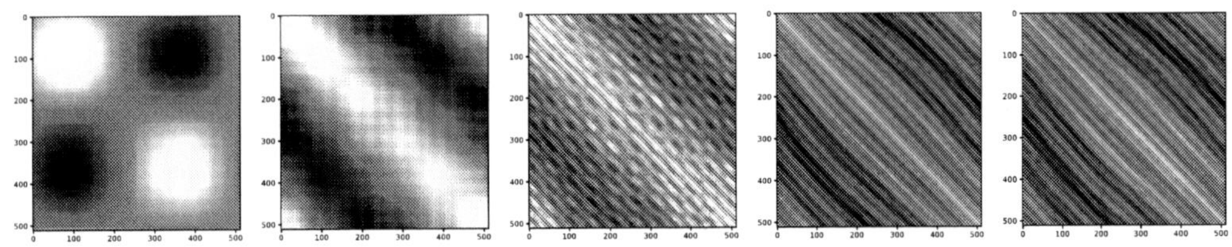

(a) 1 component (b) 2 components (c) 6 components (d) 10 components (e) All components

Figure 3: Heatmaps visualizing the matrix $P = E_P E_P^T$ of position-embedding inner products in albert-base-v2, when E_P is approximated by its top k PCs. The greater the value of the inner product, the lighter the color.

components of a few models to visually interpret the dominant patterns in the position embeddings. This reveals intriguing patterns. In all cases, the first ten components take the form of smooth, periodic oscillations as a function of position, indicative of simple harmonic structure. Although the specific ordering and frequencies change between models, components come in pairs that exhibit similar periodic structure, like sine and cosine representing cyclical motion. For all models except the largest, the highest components plotted appear flat and uniform red (i.e., close to zero), reflecting the limited dimensionality of the position embeddings.

Figure 5 in the appendix demonstrates, through Fourier analysis, that the sequence of principal component scores contains only a few dominant frequencies, which accounts for their periodic appearance. The peak frequencies observed, such as those representing 1, 5, 15, and 49 revolutions as i runs through its full range from 0 to 511 in the case of albert-base-v2, are relatively low. This finding is distinct from the sinusoidal position embeddings described by Vaswani et al. (2017), which utilize 512 sinusoids of equal magnitude. Unlike the principal component scores, these sinusoids are not mutually orthogonal and are designed with different objectives for encoding position in a sequence.

By computing the matrix $E_P E_P^T$, which contains the inner products between all pairs of position embeddings, it has been found that learned position embeddings tend to exhibit translation equivariance (Wennberg and Henter, 2021). In contrast, classic sinusoidal position embeddings display weak inner products between off-diagonal elements, suggesting an absence of such patterns (Wang and Chen, 2020). By repeating this inner-product experiment, but approximating the position-embedding matrix E_P by its top k principal components, we can see how translation-equivariant structure (where each row of the matrix is a translation of the one above it) is rapidly created using only a few principal components for the albert-v2-base model in Figure 3.

Finally, as PCA is a dimensionality-reduction technique, we can visualize all 512 albert-base-v2 position-embedding vectors in two dimensions by means of a scatter plot of their two leading principal components, as shown in Figure 4. We observe a very clear rotational structure, where as the position i goes from 0 to 511, the 2D representation of $e_P(i)$ almost completes a full clockwise turn. Other principal-component pairs show similar patterns, but complete multiple rotations as i runs through the full range of position indices.

Figure 4 exhibits two outliers from the circular pattern, namely vectors 0 and 511 (the first and last). This is likely due to how the model is trained: position embeddings are only ever used after being summed with a word embedding, and the the first and the last sequence positions are always assigned the specific tokens "CLS" and "SEP", respectively.

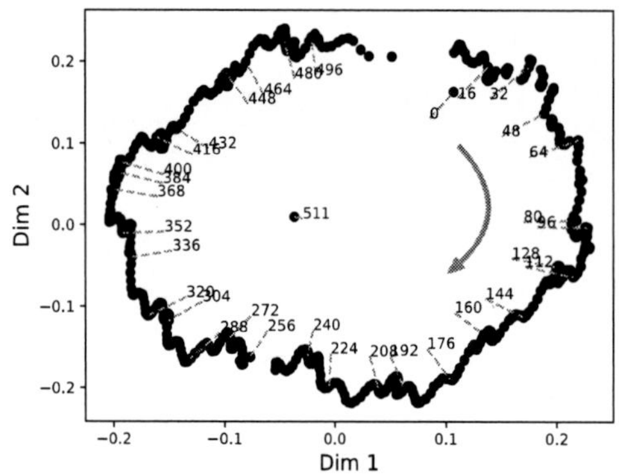

Figure 4: Scatter plot of albert-base-v2 position embeddings reduced to two dimensions using PCA. For clarity, every 16th position is annotated.

This means that, unlike at all other positions, these two vectors are largely arbitrary, e.g., adding any vector v to $e_P(0)$ while subtracting the same vector from $e_W(\text{CLS})$ leads to the exact same z_0.

5 Discussion and Implications

We have demonstrated that position embeddings operate within a significantly lower-dimensional space compared to word embeddings. This likely reflects their role in encoding less complex, but nonetheless essential structural information.

Opportunities for Transformer Models: Intuitively, our findings present an opportunity to streamline embeddings and reduce computational demands without compromising the model's ability to interpret linguistic contexts. For example, one could utilize factorized embedding parametrizations of different dimensionalities for position embeddings versus word embeddings, similar to how ALBERT mentions the possibility to use different embedding dimensionalities for different word tokens (Lan et al., 2020), although they opted not to do so. To further refine model inductive biases based on the patterns we observed, learned position embeddings could be initialized or otherwise incentivized to have rotational structure, e.g., being parameterized by sines and cosines with a learnable frequency. This would differ from the rotational position embeddings (RoPE) of by Su et al. (2024), whose rotational frequencies are not learnable.

We observed a consistently low-dimensional structure of position embeddings among a wide class of transformer models. This supports the soundness of the heuristic approach for creating position embeddings used in Longformer (Beltagy et al., 2020) – where pre-trained RoBERTa position embeddings were used as a starting point for training a new model – and further suggests that re-using learned position embeddings from older models may be useful as a general strategy.

Insights into Embedding Ordered Sequences: Transformers, particularly those like ALBERT models which have undergone extensive training, exhibit an intriguing pattern in their position embeddings. These models often utilize approximately 10 principal components—closely aligning with $2^9 = 512$, the typical maximum sequence length. This choice of dimensionality suggests that each dimension may function akin to a binary system, with each principal component potentially implementing a sine or cosine curve. Such a structure effectively splits the data, allowing for a compact yet robust representation of sequence positions.

This method of embedding sequences as concurrent rotations in low-dimensional spaces indicates a standardized approach to processing sequential data via embeddings. This geometric encoding strategy is echoed in findings across several recent studies. Nanda et al. (2023) noted that transformer models trained on mathematical tasks often use a "clock algorithm" in their latent spaces, enabling modular arithmetic. Similarly, Zhong et al. (2023) and Wennberg and Henter (2024) observed analogous rotational patterns in numerical embeddings, whether trained from scratch on mathematical tasks or using language-modeling techniques.

These observations highlight the potential of using geometric transformations as a unified method to encode sequential information across diverse applications, like time-series analysis, where precision and optimized data representation are crucial.

6 Conclusions and Future Work

We have found that learned position embeddings in a range of transformer language models differ from the behavior of word embeddings, in that position embeddings are confined to a low-dimensional linear subspace. We furthermore find evidence that this subspace takes the form of a few orthogonal rotational components at different frequencies.

Interesting future directions to explore include studying position embeddings in other domains, such as vision, and leveraging our findings to devise more efficient transformer variants with improved inductive biases for modeling sequence data.

Limitations

This study examined a select number of transformer models, using principal component analysis. PCA only considers linear subspaces for dimensionality reduction. Consequently, our analysis can only be interpreted as an upper-bound estimate of the intrinsic dimensionality of the manifold of which position embeddings reside, and may overlook nonlinear relationships within the embeddings. In other words, the actual dimensionality of the position-embedding manifold may be lower than our estimates, if it is nonlinear.

Our analysis is limited to a set of twelve different transformer-based language models that use learned absolute position embeddings. With our focus on absolute position embeddings, we did not study alternative position embeddings such as RoPE (Su et al., 2024). Although including additional position-embedding schemes would indeed be interesting, adapting our analysis methodology to RoPE is not straightforward, since it implements positional dependence differently, and in particular not by summing word embeddings with explicit postion embedding vectors $e_P(i)$. Additionally, it should be said that even though many recent language models utilize RoPE, models in other domains such as computer vision (Dosovitskiy et al., 2021; Bao et al., 2022) still use absolute position embeddings like the ones analyzed in this paper.

Furthermore, our investigation is confined to the input embeddings z_i of the models we study. This means that we cannot tell how the structure and dimensionality of these vectors may change during processing, as they pass through successive internal layers of the models and become increasingly context-dependent.

Finally, our study does not specifically analyze how the low-dimensional manifolds we uncovered influence the transformer self-attention. Investigating this might shed light on why these low-dimensional manifolds emerge in the first place.

Ethics Statement

To the best of our knowledge, this paper, which focuses on the analysis of learned position embeddings in transformer models, does not directly raise any ethical concerns.

References

Alexei Baevski and Michael Auli. 2019. Adaptive input representations for neural language modeling. In *Proc. ICLR*.

Hangbo Bao, Li Dong, Songhao Piao, and Furu Wei. 2022. BEiT: BERT pre-training of image transformers. In *Proc. ICLR*.

Iz Beltagy, Matthew E. Peters, and Arman Cohan. 2020. Longformer: The long-document transformer. *Preprint*, arXiv:2004.05150.

T. Brown, B. Mann, N. Ryder, M. Subbiah, J. D. Kaplan, P. Dhariwal, A. Neelakantan, P. Shyam, G. Sastry, A. Askell, and et al. 2020. Language models are few-shot learners. In *Proc. NeurIPS*, pages 1877–1901.

Kevin Clark, Urvashi Khandelwal, Omer Levy, and Christopher D. Manning. 2019. What does BERT look at? An analysis of BERT's attention. In *Proc. BlackboxNLP@ACL*, pages 276–286.

Kevin Clark, Minh-Thang Luong, Quoc V. Le, and Christopher D. Manning. 2020. Pre-training transformers as energy-based cloze models. In *Proc. EMNLP*, pages 285–294.

Zihang Dai, Zhilin Yang, Yiming Yang, Jaime Carbonell, Quoc V. Le, and Ruslan Salakhutdinov. 2019. Transformer-XL: Attentive language models beyond a fixed-length context. In *Proc. ACL*, pages 2978–2988.

Jacob Devlin, Ming-Wei Chang, Kenton Lee, and Kristina Toutanova. 2019. BERT: Pre-training of deep bidirectional transformers for language understanding. In *Proc. NAACL-HLT*, pages 4171–4186.

Alexey Dosovitskiy, Lucas Beyer, Alexander Kolesnikov, Dirk Weissenborn, Xiaohua Zhai, Thomas Unterthiner, Mostafa Dehghani, Matthias Minderer, Georg Heigold, Sylvain Gelly, Jakob Uszkoreit, and Neil Houlsby. 2021. An image is worth 16x16 words: Transformers for image recognition at scale. In *Proc. ICLR*.

Edouard Grave, Armand Joulin, Moustapha Cissé, David Grangier, and Hervé Jégou. 2017. Efficient softmax approximation for GPUs. In *Proc. ICML*, pages 1302–1310.

Phu Mon Htut, Jason Phang, Shikha Bordia, and Samuel R. Bowman. 2019. Do attention heads in BERT track syntactic dependencies? *Preprint*, arXiv:1911.12246.

Guillaume Lample, Myle Ott, Alexis Conneau, Ludovic Denoyer, and Marc'Aurelio Ranzato. 2018. Phrase-based & neural unsupervised machine translation. In *Proc. EMNLP*, pages 5039–5049.

Zhenzhong Lan, Mingda Chen, Sebastian Goodman, Kevin Gimpel, Piyush Sharma, and Radu Soricut. 2020. ALBERT: A lite BERT for self-supervised learning of language representations. In *Proc. ICLR*.

Ying Lin, Heng Ji, Fei Huang, and Lingfei Wu. 2020. A joint neural model for information extraction with global features. In *Proc. ACL*, pages 7999–8009.

Yinhan Liu, Myle Ott, Naman Goyal, Jingfei Du, Mandar Joshi, Danqi Chen, Omer Levy, Mike Lewis, Luke Zettlemoyer, and Veselin Stoyanov. 2019. RoBERTa: A robustly optimized BERT pretraining approach. *Preprint*, arXiv:1907.11692.

Neel Nanda, Lawrence Chan, Tom Lieberum, Jess Smith, and Jacob Steinhardt. 2023. Progress measures for grokking via mechanistic interpretability. In *Proc. ICLR*.

Alec Radford, Karthik Narasimhan, Tim Salimans, and Ilya Sutskever. 2018. Improving language understanding by generative pre-training. `https://s3-us-west-2.amazonaws.com/openai-assets/research-covers/language-unsupervised/language_understanding_paper.pdf`. Accessed: 2024-05-16.

Jianlin Su, Murtadha Ahmed, Yu Lu, Shengfeng Pan, Wen Bo, and Yunfeng Liu. 2024. RoFormer: Enhanced transformer with rotary position embedding. *Neurocomputing*, 568:127063.

Ashish Vaswani, Noam Shazeer, Niki Parmar, Jakob Uszkoreit, Llion Jones, Aidan N. Gomez, Łukasz Kaiser, and Illia Polosukhin. 2017. Attention is all you need. In *Proc. NeurIPS*, pages 5998–6008.

David Wadden, Ulme Wennberg, Yi Luan, and Hannaneh Hajishirzi. 2019. Entity, relation, and event extraction with contextualized span representations. In *Proc. EMNLP-IJCNLP*, pages 5784–5789.

Yu-An Wang and Yun-Nung Chen. 2020. What do position embeddings learn? An empirical study of pre-trained language model positional encoding. In *Proc. EMNLP*, pages 6840–6849.

Ulme Wennberg and Gustav Eje Henter. 2021. The case for translation-invariant self-attention in transformer-based language models. In *Proc. ACL-IJCNLP*, pages 130–140.

Ulme Wennberg and Gustav Eje Henter. 2024. Exploring internal numeracy in language models: A case study on ALBERT. *Preprint*, arXiv:2404.16574.

Thomas Wolf, Lysandre Debut, Victor Sanh, Julien Chaumond, Clement Delangue, Anthony Moi, Pierric Cistac, Tim Rault, Remi Louf, Morgan Funtowicz, Joe Davison, Sam Shleifer, Patrick von Platen, Clara Ma, Yacine Jernite, Julien Plu, Canwen Xu, Teven Le Scao, Sylvain Gugger, Mariama Drame, Quentin Lhoest, and Alexander Rush. 2020. Transformers: State-of-the-art natural language processing. In *Proc. EMNLP System Demonstrations*, pages 38–45.

Ikuya Yamada, Akari Asai, Hiroyuki Shindo, Hideaki Takeda, and Yuji Matsumoto. 2020. LUKE: Deep contextualized entity representations with entity-aware self-attention. In *Proc. EMNLP*, pages 6442–6454.

Ziqian Zhong, Ziming Liu, Max Tegmark, and Jacob Andreas. 2023. The clock and the pizza: Two stories in mechanistic explanation of neural networks. In *Proc. NeurIPS*, pages 27223–27250.

A Appendix

For the interested reader, this appendix provides supplementary visual data to complement the analyses discussed in the main sections of the paper.

Figure 5 presents the summed frequency magnitude spectrum of the sequence of the principal component scores, based on the position embeddings from ALBERT base-v2, emphasizing dominant frequencies with a normalized Nyquist limit of 0.5 and a logarithmic magnitude scale.

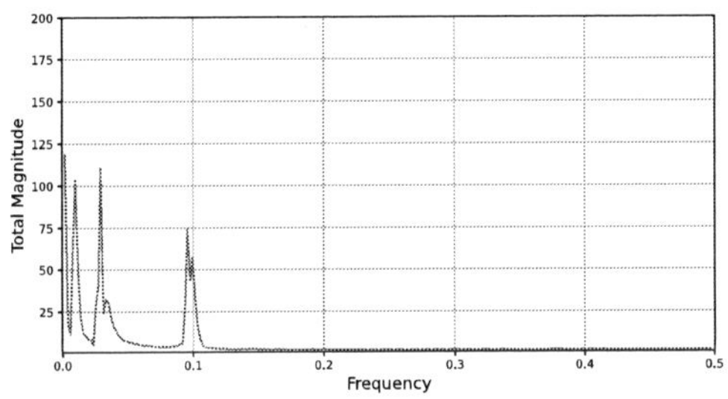

Figure 5: Frequency magnitude spectrum of principal component scores from albert-base-v2. The plot displays the sum of Fourier magnitudes across all the principal components, thus highlighting dominant frequencies. Frequencies are normalized with 0.5 as the Nyquist limit, and the plot uses a logarithmic y-axis.

Furthermore, Figure 6 depicts the frequency magnitude spectrum for each of the top 10 principal components in the sequence of the principal component scores, highlighting the unique spectral contributions of each principal component.

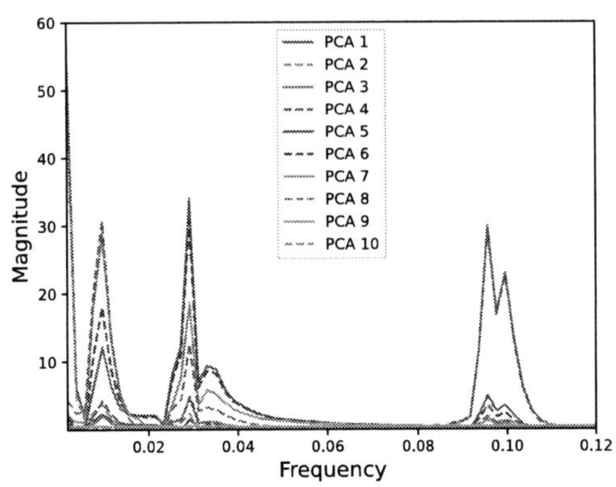

Figure 6: Frequency magnitude spectrum for each of the top 10 principal component scores from albert-base-v2. The plot displays the Fourier magnitudes for each principal component, thus highlighting their individual contributions. Frequencies are normalized with 0.5 as the Nyquist limit.

Figure 7 presents extended heatmaps representing the entirety of the principal component scores analyzed for various ALBERT models. It is easily noticeable that only the leftmost principal components contribute meaningfully to the variability in the data.

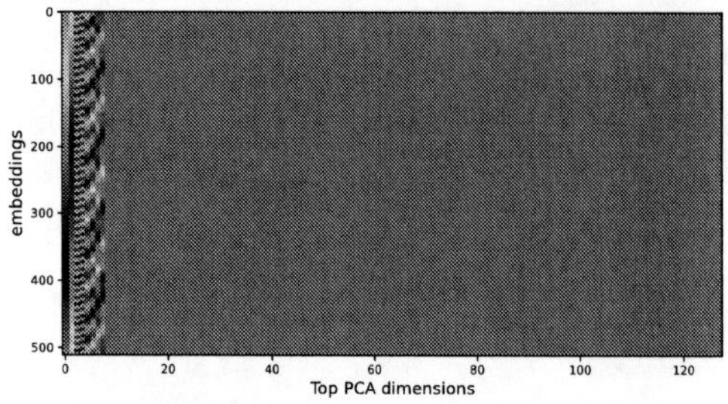

(a) Heatmap of the principal component scores for albert-base-v2, visualizing the matrix of all $k = 128$ principal components.

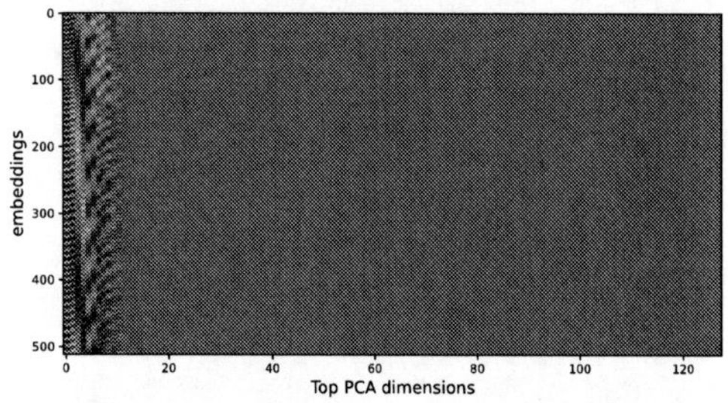

(b) Heatmap of the principal component scores for albert-large-v2, visualizing the matrix of all $k = 128$ principal components.

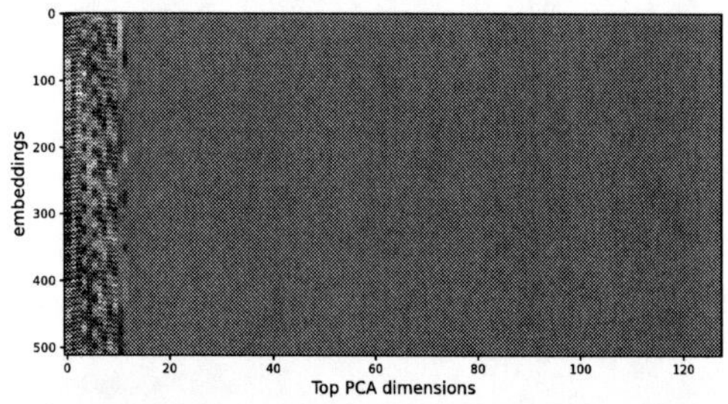

(c) Heatmap of the principal component scores for albert-xlarge-v2, visualizing the matrix of all $k = 128$ principal components.

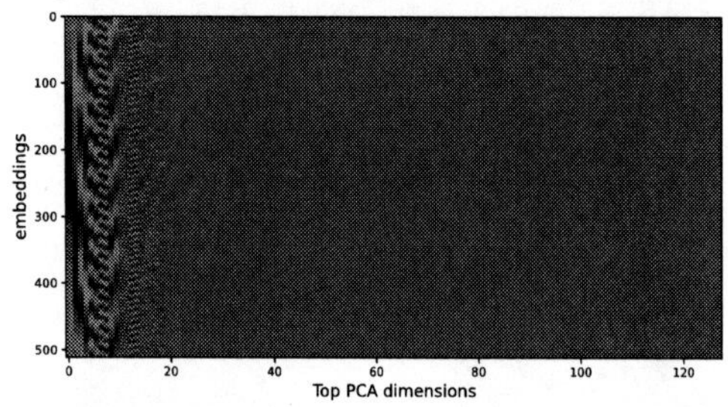

(d) Heatmap of the principal component scores for albert-xxlarge-v2, visualizing the matrix of all $k = 128$ principal components.

Figure 7: Extended heatmaps representing the entirety of the principal component scores analyzed for various ALBERT models, highlighting the contribution of the leftmost components to the variability in the data.

Multi-label Learning with Random Circular Vectors

Ken Nishida*
Hokkaido University

Kojiro Machi
Hokkaido University

Kazuma Onishi
Hokkaido University

Katsuhiko Hayashi
The University of Tokyo

Hidetaka Kamigaito
Nara Institute of Science and Technology

Abstract

The extreme multi-label classification (XMC) task involves learning a classifier that can predict from a large label set the most relevant subset of labels for a data instance. While deep neural networks (DNNs) have demonstrated remarkable success in XMC problems, the task is still challenging because it must deal with a large number of output labels, which make the DNN training computationally expensive. This paper addresses the issue by exploring the use of random circular vectors, where each vector component is represented as a complex amplitude. In our framework, we can develop an output layer and loss function of DNNs for XMC by representing the final output layer as a fully connected layer that directly predicts a low-dimensional circular vector encoding a set of labels for a data instance. We conducted experiments on synthetic datasets to verify that circular vectors have better label encoding capacity and retrieval ability than normal real-valued vectors. Then, we conducted experiments on actual XMC datasets and found that these appealing properties of circular vectors contribute to significant improvements in task performance compared with a previous model using random real-valued vectors, while reducing the size of the output layers by up to 99%.

1 Introduction

Extreme multi-label classification (XMC) problems arise in various domains, such as product recommendation systems (Jain et al., 2016), labeling large encyclopedia (Dekel and Shamir, 2010; Partalas et al., 2015), instance-level image recognition (Deng et al., 2010; Ridnik et al., 2021) and natural language generation (Mikolov et al., 2013). The XMC task involves learning a classifier which can predict from a large label set the most relevant subset of labels for a data instance. Recent work has focused on deep neural network (DNN) models (Liu et al., 2017; You et al., 2019; Chang et al., 2020; Zhang et al., 2021; Dahiya et al., 2023; Jain et al., 2023) that deliver task performances superior to those of early approaches using linear predictors (Babbar and Schölkopf, 2017; Prabhu et al., 2018b).

While DNN models have brought great performance improvements, the XMC task still remains a challenge mainly due to the extremely large output space. Since a large number of output labels make it difficult to train DNN models efficiently, various methods for improving training efficiency have been proposed (Khandagale et al., 2020; Wydmuch et al., 2018; Jiang et al., 2021; Ganesan et al., 2021). Among the previous studies, Ganesan et al. (2021) presented a promising method that employs random real-valued vectors for reducing the output layer size of DNN models. In this approach, a high-dimensional output space vector is replaced with a low-dimensional random vector encoding the relevant label information for a data instance. Then, DNN models are trained to predict the label-encoded vector directly. After the model generates a vector, it can be checked approximately whether a label is encoded in it or not through a vector comparison using the cosine similarity between the output vector and a vector that the label is assigned to. The basic idea of the label encoding and retrieval framework relies on the theory of Holographic Reduced Representations (Plate, 1995), which was developed in the cognitive neuroscience field.

However, random real-valued vectors do not have sufficient ability for representing data instances that belong to many class concepts. As our experiments in § 3 show, the label retrieval accuracy decreases markedly as the number of class labels encoded in a vector increases. To alleviate the issue, this paper presents a novel method that uses *circular* vectors instead of real-valued vectors. Each element of a circular vector takes a complex amplitude as its value; i.e., the vector element is represented by an angle ranging from

*Email: z301067a@gmail.com

Proceedings of the 9th Workshop on Representation Learning for NLP (RepL4NLP-2024), pages 245–255
August 15, 2024 ©2024 Association for Computational Linguistics

$-\pi$ to π. Since an angle can be represented by a real value, the memory cost for the circular vector representation is the same as that for a normal real-valued vector. In spite of this fact, surprisingly, circular vectors have better label encoding and retrieval capacities than real-valued vectors. One of the challenges in applying circular vectors to DNN models is how to adapt the output layer to a circular vector. In § 4, we describe our neural network architecture that uses circular vectors in the output layer. Our experimental results on XMC datasets show that our method based on circular vectors significantly outperforms a previous model using real-valued vectors, while reducing the size of the output layers by up to 99%.

2 Previous Study: Learning with Holographic Reduced Representations

Several vector symbolic architectures have been developed in the field of cognitive neuroscience, including Tensor Product Representations (Smolensky, 1990), Binary Spatter Code (Kanerva, 1996), Binary Sparse Distributed Representations (Rachkovskij, 2001), Multiply-Add-Permute (Gayler, 2004), and Holographic Reduced Representations (HRR) (Plate, 1995). Among them, HRR is a successful architecture for distributed representations of compositional structures. To model complex structured prediction tasks in a vector space that involve key-value stores, sequences, trees and graphs, many prior studies have explored how to use HRR in various machine learning frameworks; Recurrent Neural Networks (Plate, 1992), Tree Kernels (Zanzotto and Dell'Arciprete, 2012), Knowledge Graph Representation Learning (Nickel et al., 2016; Hayashi and Shimbo, 2017), Long-short Term Memory Networks (Danihelka et al., 2016), Transformer Networks (Alam et al., 2023), and among others. In particular, Ganesan et al. (2021) presented a general framework based on the HRR architecture for efficient multi-label learning of DNN models. To clarify the motivation of our study, we will review the framework in more detail in the following subsections.

2.1 Holographic Reduced Representations (HRR)

In the HRR architecture, terms in a domain are represented by real-valued vectors. Here, we assume that each vector is independently sampled from a Gaussian distribution $\mathcal{N}(0, \mathbf{I}_d \cdot d^{-1})$, where d is the vector dimension size and $\mathbf{I}_d$ is the $d \times d$ identity matrix. To bind an association of two terms represented by vectors $\mathbf{a}$ and $\mathbf{b}$, respectively, HRR uses circular convolution, denoted by the mathematical symbol $\otimes$:

$$\mathbf{a} \otimes \mathbf{b} = \mathcal{F}^{-1}(\mathcal{F}(\mathbf{a}) \odot \mathcal{F}(\mathbf{b})) \quad (1)$$

where $\odot$ is element-wise vector multiplication. Note that the circular convolution can be computed by using a fast Fourier transform (FFT) $\mathcal{F}$ and inverse FFT $\mathcal{F}^{-1}$, but they require $\mathcal{O}(d \log d)$ computation time. Given several associations $\mathbf{a} \otimes \mathbf{b}$, $\mathbf{c} \otimes \mathbf{d}$ and $\mathbf{e} \otimes \mathbf{f}$, the vectors can be superposed to represent their combination: $\mathbf{S} = (\mathbf{a} \otimes \mathbf{b}) \oplus (\mathbf{c} \otimes \mathbf{d}) \oplus (\mathbf{e} \otimes \mathbf{f})$, where the "superposition" operator $\oplus$ is just normal vector addition $+$. The HRR architecture also provides the inversion operation $\dagger$:

$$\mathbf{a}^{\dagger} = \mathcal{F}^{-1}(\frac{1}{\mathcal{F}(\mathbf{a})}). \quad (2)$$

The inversion operation can be used to perform "unbinding". For an example, it allows the reconstruction of a noisy version of $\mathbf{d}$ to be recreated from the memory $\mathbf{S}$ and a cue $\mathbf{c}$: $\mathbf{S} \otimes \mathbf{c}^{\dagger} \approx \mathbf{d}$. Finally, the "similarity" operation is defined as the dot-product $\mathbf{a}^{\mathrm{T}}\mathbf{b}$. Using the similarity operation, we can check approximately whether $\mathbf{a}$ exists in a memory $\mathbf{S}$ if $\mathbf{S}^{\mathrm{T}}\mathbf{a} \approx 1$ or not present if $\mathbf{S}^{\mathrm{T}}\mathbf{a} \approx 0$.

2.2 Multi-label Learning with HRR

Ganesan et al. (2021) introduced a novel method using HRR for reducing the computational complexity of training DNNs for XMC tasks. Let L be the number of class labels in an XMC task. The basic idea behind the approach of (Ganesan et al., 2021) is quite intuitive; for efficient DNN training, an L-dimensional output (teacher) vector is replaced with a d-dimensional real-valued vector encoding the relevant label information for a data instance. By assuming $d \ll L$, we can dramatically reduce the output layer size of the DNN model.

In this approach, each class label y is assigned to a d-dimensional vector $\mathbf{c}_y \in \mathbb{R}^d$. Then, the label information for a data instance x is represented as a *label vector* $\mathbf{S}_x \in \mathbb{R}^d$:

$$\mathbf{S}_x = \bigoplus_{p \in \mathcal{Y}_x} \mathbf{p} \otimes \mathbf{c}_p \quad (3)$$

where $\mathcal{Y}_x$ denotes the set of class labels that x belongs to and $\mathbf{p} \in \mathbb{R}^d$ represents the positive class concept.[1] To train a DNN model $f(\mathbf{x})$ that generates $\hat{\mathbf{S}}_x \in \mathbb{R}^d \approx \mathbf{S}_x$, Ganesan et al. (2021) define a loss function:

$$loss = \sum_{p \in \mathcal{Y}_x} (1 - sim((\hat{\mathbf{S}}_x \otimes \mathbf{p}^\dagger), \mathbf{c}_p)). \quad (4)$$

To prevent the model from maximizing the magnitudes of the output vectors, Ganesan et al. (2021) used the cosine similarity as $sim(\cdot,\cdot)$, which is a normalized version of the dot product that ranges from -1 to 1. In the inference phase, labels can also be ranked according to the cosine similarity computed by $sim(\hat{\mathbf{S}}_x \otimes \mathbf{p}^\dagger, \mathbf{c}_p)$ for each label p. Moreover, Ganesan et al. (2021) introduced a novel vector *projection* method to reduce the effect of the variance of the similarity computation:

$$\pi(\mathbf{x}) = \mathcal{F}^{-1}\left(\ldots, \frac{\mathcal{F}(\mathbf{x})_j}{|\mathcal{F}(\mathbf{x})_j|}, \ldots\right). \quad (5)$$

Here, each HRR vector $\mathbf{x}$ is initialized with $\mathbf{x} \overset{\mathrm{d}}{=} \pi\left(\mathcal{N}(0, \mathbf{I}_d \cdot d^{-1})\right)$, which ensures each element of the vector in the frequency domain is unitary; i.e., the complex magnitude is one.

3 Multi-label Representations with Circular Vectors

In this section, we show through experiments that random real-valued vectors actually do not have sufficient ability for representing data instances that belong to many classes. The reason is mainly due to the projection operation in Equation 5. As described in § 2, the projection operation was proposed as a way to reduce the effect of the variance of the similarity computation, but each element of the superposition between two normalized vectors via the projection is no longer unitary. Thus, the effect of the projection decreases when a label vector encodes more class labels. To alleviate the issue, we developed a simple alternative that forces all vector elements to be unitary in the complex domain even after the superposition operation. We describe the details in the following subsection.

3.1 HRR with Circular Vectors

Our idea is to use *circular* vectors instead of real-valued vectors. Circular vectors have a complex amplitude (see Figure 1), which can be represented by a real value ϕ ranging from $-\pi$ to π. However, to force all vector elements to be unitary after any operations, we require a special HRR system for circular vectors. In this paper, we borrow the concept of a circular HRR (CHRR) system from (Plate, 2003).

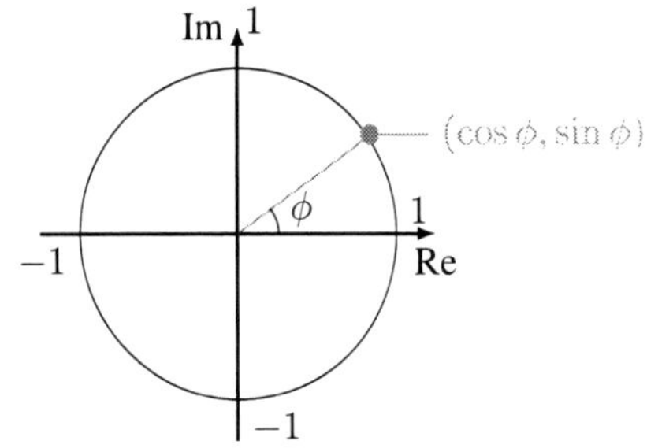

Figure 1: The unit circle in the complex plane with coordinates. The angle ϕ represents an element of the circular vector $\bar{\phi}$.

Table 1 compares the HRR operations of the standard and circular systems. For circular vectors, each element must be sampled from a uniform distribution $\mathcal{U}(-\pi, \pi)$ over $(-\pi, \pi]$. The binding $\otimes$ and inversion $\dagger$ of CHRR are implemented with the standard vector arithmetic operations like addition and subtraction. The similarity of two circular vectors can be simply determined from the sum of the cosines of the differences between angles. On the other hand, superposition is somewhat tricky because in general the sum of unitary complex values does not lie on the unit circle. For each pair of elements ϕ_j and θ_j of two circular vectors $\bar{\phi}$ and $\bar{\theta}$, the result of superposition is $\angle(e^{i \cdot \phi_j} + e^{i \cdot \theta_j})$. Here, $\angle(v)$ extracts an angle of a complex value v and discards the magnitude of v. Since all of these operations do not affect the unitary property of circular vectors, we no longer need the projection normalization process. Our framework also has an advantage in computational cost; we can avoid the FFT and inverse FFT operations, which take $\mathcal{O}(d \log d)$ computation time.

3.2 Retrieval Accuracy Experiment

We experimentally demonstrated CHRR's capacity by comparing its retrieval accuracy with that of HRR. The experiment attempted to verify how accurately the positive class vector can be retrieved from a memory vector. For a data instance x, let $\mathbf{c}_p$ be a vector for a positive class p to which x belongs,

[1] We can encode information on negative labels into a label vector as well as positive ones, but as shown in (Ganesan et al., 2021), the negative label information does not contribute to improving XMC task performance. Thus, in this paper, we will omit discussion on negative labels for notational brevity.

Operation	Real-valued (Ganesan et al., 2021)	Circular
vector	$\mathbf{x} = [x_0, \ldots, x_{d-1}]$	$\phi = [\phi_0, \ldots, \phi_{d-1}]$
random vector	$\mathbf{x} \stackrel{\mathrm{d}}{=} \pi\left(\mathcal{N}(0, \mathbf{I}_d \cdot d^{-1})\right)$	$\phi_j \stackrel{\mathrm{d}}{=} \mathcal{U}(-\pi, \pi)$
binding	$\mathbf{x} \otimes \mathbf{y} = \mathcal{F}^{-1}(\mathcal{F}(\mathbf{x}) \odot \mathcal{F}(\mathbf{y}))$	$\bar{\phi} \otimes \bar{\theta} = [(\phi_0 + \theta_0) \bmod 2\pi, \ldots, (\phi_{d-1} + \theta_{d-1}) \bmod 2\pi]$
unbinding	$\mathbf{x} \otimes \mathbf{y}^{\dagger} = \mathbf{x} \otimes \mathcal{F}^{-1}(\frac{1}{\mathcal{F}(\mathbf{y})})$	$\bar{\phi} \otimes \bar{\theta}^{\dagger} = -\bar{\theta} \otimes \bar{\phi}$
similarity	$sim(\mathbf{x}, \mathbf{y}) = \mathbf{x}^{\mathrm{T}}\mathbf{y}$	$sim(\bar{\phi}, \bar{\theta}) = \frac{1}{d}\sum_j \cos(\phi_j - \theta_j)$
superposition	$\mathbf{x} \oplus \mathbf{y} = \mathbf{x} + \mathbf{y}$	$\bar{\phi} \oplus \bar{\theta} = [\angle(e^{i \cdot \phi_0} + e^{i \cdot \theta_0}), \ldots, \angle(e^{i \cdot \phi_{d-1}} + e^{i \cdot \theta_{d-1}})]$

Table 1: Comparison of HRR operations on real-valued and circular vectors.

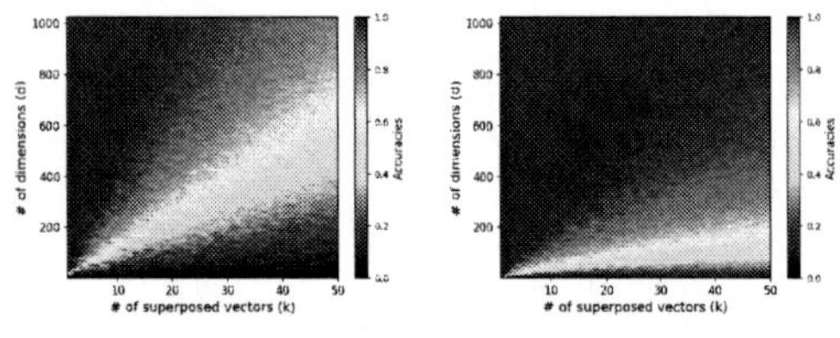

(a) HRR(w/Proj) (b) CHRR

Figure 2: Retrieval accuracies of HRR(w/Proj) and CHRR. The number of dimensions d was $1, \ldots, 1024$ and the number of positive classes k was $1, \ldots, 50$.

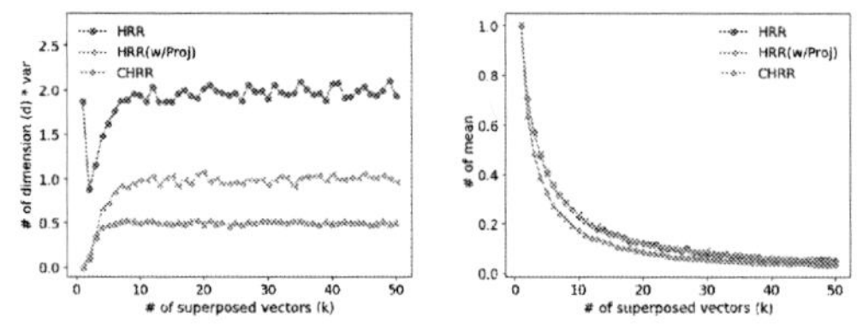

(a) Variance (b) Mean

Figure 3: Variance and mean of the similarities of HRR, HRR(w/Proj), and CHRR. We fixed the number of dimensions d to 400 and varied the number of positive classes k from 1 to 50.

and let $\mathbf{p}$ be a vector for the positive class concept label. The binding and superposition operations allow us to represent all positive classes for x as $\mathbf{R}$:

$$\mathbf{R} = \bigoplus_{p \in \mathcal{Y}_x} (\mathbf{p} \otimes \mathbf{c}_p). \tag{6}$$

In the experiment, we generated a database consisting of $N = 1{,}000$ random d-dimensional vectors ($\mathbf{c}_j \in \mathbb{R}^d$, for all $j \in [1, \ldots, N]$). Then, to create $\mathbf{R}$, we randomly selected k vectors from the database to be $\mathbf{c}_p$ and one vector to be $\mathbf{p}$. As shown in Equation 6, the k associations can be superposed to represent $\mathbf{R}$. To retrieve $\mathbf{c}_p$ from $\mathbf{R}$, we used the unbinding operation to decode a noisy version of the vector $\mathbf{c}_p$ from $\mathbf{R}$, as $\hat{\mathbf{c}}_p = \mathbf{R} \otimes \mathbf{p}^{\dagger}$. For each $j \in [1, \ldots, N]$, we computed the similarity $s_j = sim(\hat{\mathbf{c}}_p, \mathbf{c}_j)$ between the decoded vector $\hat{\mathbf{c}}_p$ and the individual vector $\mathbf{c}_j$. After that, we compiled the top-k label list according to the similarity scores s_j. To evaluate the retrieval accuracy, we measured the percentage of class labels in the list, whose vectors were encoded into the memory $\mathbf{R}$. By varying the number of dimensions $d = 1, \ldots, 1024$ and the number of binding pairs $k = 1, \ldots, 50$, we plotted the accuracies as a heat-map (Figure 2, where warmer colors indicate higher accuracy).[2] The results clearly show that CHRR has better retrieval accuracies than those of HRR. Moreover, the larger the number of superposed vectors (k) is, the bigger the performance difference between CHRR and HRR becomes. Hence, this tendency indicates that CHRR is more suitable than HRR for encoding many labels.

3.3 Variance Comparison Experiment

In § 3.2, we confirmed that CHRR exhibits superior retrieval ability to HRR. There is a possibility that the CHRR's similarity operation reduces the variance more than the projection does. The experiment reported below was conducted to check the numerical stability of the CHRR's similarity operation. To create $\mathbf{R}$ as Equation 6, we generated k random vectors $\mathbf{c}_p$ and $\mathbf{p}$. We extracted a noisy version of $\mathbf{c}_p$ from $\mathbf{R}$ as $\hat{\mathbf{c}}_p = \mathbf{R} \otimes \mathbf{p}^{\dagger}$. For each $j \in [1, \ldots, k]$, we measure the similarity between $\hat{\mathbf{c}}_{\mathbf{p}}$ and $\mathbf{c}_j$ as $s_j = sim(\hat{\mathbf{c}}_p, \mathbf{c}_j)$. We plotted the variances and means of the similarities in Figure 3 (a) and (b), respectively. We fixed the number of dimensions d to 400 and varied the number of binding pairs $k = 1, \ldots, 50$. Our experiments compared three methods, CHRR, HRR proposed in (Plate, 1995), and HRR with the projection of (Ganesan et al., 2021) (HRR(w/Proj)).

Figure 3 (a) shows that as k increases, the vari-

[2] Schlegel et al. (2021) also demonstrated that CHRR has a higher retrieval capacity compared with HRR. Yet, they used all distinct vectors: $\mathbf{R} = (\mathbf{a} \otimes \mathbf{b}) \oplus (\mathbf{c} \otimes \mathbf{d})$, and did not use a fixed $\mathbf{p}$: $\mathbf{R} = (\mathbf{p} \otimes \mathbf{a}) \oplus (\mathbf{p} \otimes \mathbf{b})$. Therefore, we changed their experimental settings to fit the XMC learning with HRR.

ances of all methods tend to converge. However, while the variance converges, the mean also decreases near zero, as shown in Figure 3 (b). Therefore, as the number of superposed vectors k increases, the impact of variance becomes relatively larger. Regarding the variance, we can see the need for the projection, since the HRR(w/Proj) is more suppressed than the original HRR. Yet, we found that CHRR is most suppressed; that is, CHRR is more numerically stable than HRR(w/Proj). As for the mean, the three methods had roughly comparable performances. Although the mean approached zero as k increased, this is not a problem in using similarity for compiling a ranking list of labels.

4 Neural Network Architecture

One of the challenges in adapting CHRR to XMC tasks is how to adapt the output layer of DNN models to a circular vector because it has a cyclic feature; i.e., $\theta = 2\pi n \times \theta$, where $n \in \mathbb{Z}$. To meet it, we developed a neural network for predicting angles that considers the cyclic feature during the training. The key idea was to represent the output in Cartesian coordinates, which can uniquely represent a point on a unit circle. Then, we converted the output into polar coordinates to obtain angles.

4.1 Architecture for Circular Vectors

We used fully connected (FC) networks in all of the experiments. They were each composed of a F-dimensional input layer, two h-dimensional hidden layers with ReLU activation (Agarap, 2018), and a d'-dimensional output layer. That is, they had the same architecture except for the output layer.

We selected two baselines from Ganesan et al. (2021) by using the FC networks. The first baseline had L output nodes and each node is used to binary classification (we refer to it below as FC). The second baseline was the method using HRR as described in § 2.2. It had d output nodes (we refer to it below as HRR).

Our network for CHRR represented a pair of the outputs as a point on a unit circle on Cartesian coordinates; i.e., $(\cos\phi, \sin\phi)$, as shown in Figure 1. Then we converted the point into polar coordinates $(1, \phi)$, and used ϕ as an element of the predicted label vector. Let $\hat{\mathbf{s}} \in \mathbb{R}^{2d}$ be the raw output vector, and $\hat{\mathbf{S}} \in \mathbb{C}^{d}$ be the converted circular vector. We represented d pairs from $\hat{\mathbf{s}}$ in Cartesian coordinates as $a_i = (x_i, y_i)$. Then, we normalized them to satisfy $\|a_i\| = 1$. Although there was a similar work for an angle prediction using a neural network (Heffernan et al., 2015), they used $\arctan \frac{y}{x}$ for the conversion whose range was limited to $[\frac{-\pi}{2}, \frac{\pi}{2}]$. Instead, we used the atan2 function (Organick, 1966), which can convert a (x, y) point to a corresponding angle $(-\pi, \pi]$. Finally, we adapted the atan2 to a_i to obtain $\hat{S}_i$. We named this method as CHRR.

4.2 Impact of Model Architecture

Because the number of the output nodes of CHRR ($2d$) is twice as that of HRR (d), the total model size of CHRR also increases. Therefore, we conducted two different experiments using the same model size as HRR (see § 5.4 for the results). The first experiment changed the network architecture of CHRR. Figure 4 compares the architectures of CHRR and the changed model (CHRR-Half) to illustrate the impact of halving the hidden and output layer sizes on model performance. This adjustment ensures that CHRR-Half has the same number of parameters as HRR, allowing for a fair comparison. We made CHRR-Half by splitting the second hidden layer's nodes and output nodes of CHRR in half. This resulted in two sets of $\frac{h}{2}$ hidden nodes and d output nodes. Then we connected one set of hidden nodes to one set of output nodes, and the other set of hidden nodes to the other set of output nodes. As a result, $2 \times (\frac{h}{2} \times d) = h \times d$ parameters were obtained, which equals the number of parameters between the second hidden layer and the output layer in HRR. The results of the experiment in § 5.4 showed no significant difference in performance between CHRR and this model. Therefore, the increase in the model size is not a big issue. In the second experiment, to demonstrate the advantage of the proposed architecture against naive implementation, we used the same network architecture as HRR, and mapped the real-valued outputs to angles with activation functions. We tried two activation functions, sin and tanh to map the outputs to $[-1, 1]$; then the output was multiplied by π to obtain $(-\pi, \pi]$ outputs. We named these models as CHRR-sin and CHRR-tanh. Both showed more modest levels of performance compared with CHRR.

5 Experiment on XMC Datasets

To examine the advantages of circular vectors, we conducted experiments on several XMC datasets. Note that achieving the state-of-the-art perfor-

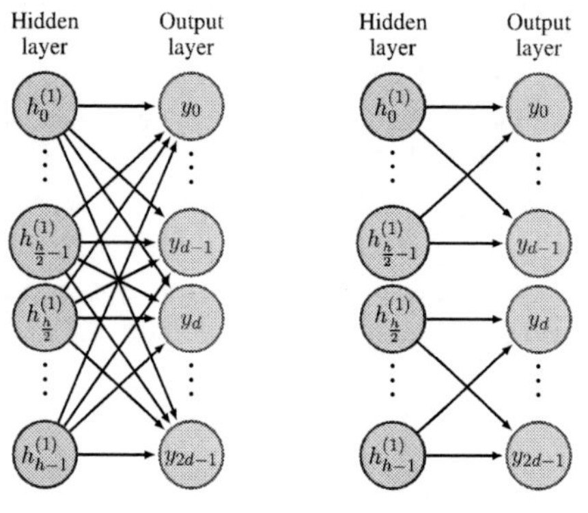

(a) CHRR (b) CHRR-Half

Figure 4: Comparison of CHRR and CHRR-Half architectures.

Dataset	N_{train}	N_{test}	L	$\bar{L}$
Delicious	12,920	3,185	983	311.61
EURLex-4K	15,539	3,809	3,993	25.73
Wiki10-31K	14,146	6,616	101,938	8.52
Delicious-200K	196,606	100,095	205,443	2.29

Table 2: Details of the datasets from Bhatia et al. (2016). Here, N_{train} is the number of training samples, N_{test} is the number of test samples, L is the number of labels, $\bar{L}$ is the average number of samples per label.

mance on XMC datasets was not the goal of this study, which focuses on the efficiency of the learning method with circular vectors. However, to validate the effectiveness of CHRR in the XMC task, we compared our method with several strong baselines. These include tree-based FastXML (Prabhu and Varma, 2014), PfastreXML (Prabhu et al., 2018a), and deep learning based XML-CNN (Zhang et al., 2018), in addition to FC and HRR.

5.1 Datasets

We evaluated our method on the four datasets for text XMC tasks from Bhatia et al. (2016). Table 2 shows the details of the datasets. The features for each sample is a bag-of-words of F words.

5.2 Evaluation Metrics

We evaluated each method by using precision at k (P@$k = \frac{1}{k}\sum_{l\in \text{rank}_k(\hat{\mathbf{y}})} \mathbf{y}_l$) and the propensity score at k (PSP@k), which are commonly used metrics in the XMC task. P@k is the proportion of true labels in the top-k predictions. PSP@k = $\frac{1}{k}\sum_{l\in \text{rank}_k(\hat{\mathbf{y}})} \frac{\mathbf{y}_l}{p_l}$ is a variation of precision that takes into account the relative frequency of each label. Here, $\text{rank}_k(\hat{\mathbf{y}})$ is the ranking of all labels in the predicted $\hat{\mathbf{y}}$ and p_l is the relative frequency of the l-th label. We used $k = 1, 5, 10, 20$ for P@k, and $k = 1, 5, 10, 20$ for PSP@k in the experiments described below.

5.3 Experimental Settings

We compared CHRR to five competitive methods (FC, HRR, FastXML, PfastreXML, XML-CNN) over four datasets. For the implementation of FC and HRR, we used the scripts provided by Ganesan et al. (2021) available at the GitHub URL.[3] We implemented CHRR by using PyTorch (Paszke et al., 2019). The training methods and the model architectures basically followed the scripts provided by Ganesan et al. (2021). The learning rate was set to 1, the batch size was 64, and the number of training epochs was 100. These hyperparameters were chosen based on preliminary experiments to balance training time and model performance. For the EURLex-4K and Wiki10-31K datasets, we also conducted experiments using both BoW (Bag of Words) and pretrained XLNet embeddings (Chang et al., 2020) as features. The dimensionality of BoW is the same as the dimensionality F of the features shown in Table 2, and the dimensionality of XLNet as a feature is $1,024$ dimensions. In CHRR, we varied the dimension of the symbol vectors (d) $\{100, 400, 800, 1000\}$. To investigate the possibility that a larger hidden layer size h improves the learning effect in FCs with large output dimensionality, we conducted experiments with three settings of hidden layer size (h) $\{768, 1024, 2048\}$. For main results, we chose $d = 800$ and $h = 768$ for CHRR and $h = 2048$ for FC. All experiments are conducted with two hidden layers.

5.4 Results and Discussion

Table 3 lists P@1, P@5, PSP@1, and PSP@5 for the CHRR model, with five standard methods. CHRR achieves up to 99% output dimension compression and 62% model size reduction compared to FC, which is comparable or better than other baselines. CHRR+ϕ_{XLNet} with XLNet as a feature showed higher results than the CHRR case with BoW. In particular, it showed significant improvement on the Wiki10-31K dataset. Figure 5 shows the impact of the dimensionality size d of the HRR

[3] https://github.com/NeuromorphicComputationResearchProgram/Learning-with-Holographic-Reduced-Representations

	Delicious (**59%**, **19%**)				Delicious-200K (**61%**, **80%**)			
	P@1	P@5	PSP@1	PSP@5	P@1	P@5	PSP@1	PSP@5
FastXML	69.6	**59.3**	32.3	35.4	43.1	36.2	6.5	8.3
PfastreXML	67.1	58.6	**34.6**	35.9	41.7	35.6	3.2	4.4
FC	70.8	59.2	34.1	**36.1**	35.1	32.1	5.3	7.4
CHRR	**71.2**	**59.3**	34.3	35.9	**43.2**	**37.1**	**6.6**	**8.5**
	EURLex-4K (**61%**, **99%**)				Wiki10-31K (**62%**, **99%**)			
	P@1	P@5	PSP@1	PSP@5	P@1	P@5	PSP@1	PSP@5
FastXML	76.4	52.0	33.2	**42.0**	83.0	57.8	9.8	10.5
PfastreXML	71.4	**50.4**	26.6	39.0	83.6	59.1	**19.0**	**18.4**
XML-CNN	75.3	49.2	32.4	39.5	81.4	56.1	9.4	10.2
FC	**77.4**	47.9	**33.6**	37.3	80.5	46.4	10.5	8.9
FC+ϕ_{XLNet}	73.3	48.8	33.0	40.0	84.0	58.9	10.9	11.5
CHRR	75.2	47.8	28.7	34.9	82.2	58.8	10.2	10.9
CHRR+ϕ_{XLNet}	77.0	50.0	29.8	37.6	**86.8**	**65.1**	11.9	13.0

Table 3: Performance comparisons of CHRR and other competing methods over four benchmark datasets, and the left number in **bold** represents the compression ratio $\left(1 - \frac{(F\times h_C + h_C \times h_C)+(h_C\times 2d + d\times L)}{(F\times h_F + h_F\times h_F)+(h_F\times L)}\right)$ of the CHRR's model size for FC's model size. CHRR is set with $d = 800$ and $h_C = 768$. And the right number in **bold** represents the compression ratio $(1 - \frac{d}{L})$ of the CHRR's output dimensions for FC's output dimensions. For FC, d is set at the number of labels in each dataset (L) and h is set at 2048. FC+ϕ_{XLNet} and CHRR+ϕ_{XLNet} refers to the results obtained using XLNet as the feature representation. We obtained the results for FastXML, PfastreXML, and XML-CNN from (You et al., 2019) and (Yu et al., 2022).

and CHRR on performance, in addition to the FC results. On certain datasets, CHRR outperformed FC even when it had vectors with lower dimensions. These results suggest that CHRR has a higher capacity for learning on datasets with a large number of labels than FC does.

We also compared CHRR with HRR. As shown in Figure 5, CHRR was better than HRR in many cases. In particular, the results for P@20 and PSP@20, where the value of the evaluation index k is large, we confirmed that the difference in performance is significant. As our theoretical experiment in § 3.2 showed, CHRR could represent many labels with high accuracy even for low-dimensional vectors. The results of the theoretical experiments in § 3.2 and the experiment on real datasets in § 5 suggest that the CHRR is able to represent a larger number of correct labels.

5.5 Impact of Model Architecture

This section describes the results of the experiments on the impact of the model architectures in § 4.2. Figure 6 compares the performances of the CHRR variants (CHRR, CHRR-Half, CHRR-sin, and CHRR-tanh) on the Wiki10-31K dataset. As mentioned in § 4.2, there was no significant difference in performance between CHRR and this model. CHRR-sin and CHRR-tanh both obtained similar results that were inferior to those of CHRR and CHRR-Half. While the sin function in CHRR-sin seems to consider the cyclic feature, the results show that it is imperfect at predicting the of the circular-label vector. In short, our developed network architecture is important for the XMC learning with circular vectors, while the increase in the model size is not a big issue.

6 Conclusion

The XMC task still faces challenge of dealing with a large number of output labels. In this paper, we attempted to address this issue by using a low dimensional circular vector to output directly. In theoretical experiments in § 3.2 and § 3.3, we showed that many labels can be accurately encoded by using circular vectors (CHRR) rather than normal real-valued vectors (HRR). Moreover, using actual XMC datasets, we compared CHRR with baseline methods in § 5. CHRR reduced the output layer size by up to 99% compared to FC, while it outperformed other baselines in most results. Comparing HRR and CHRR, CHRR outperformed on most results. In the future, we will incorporate

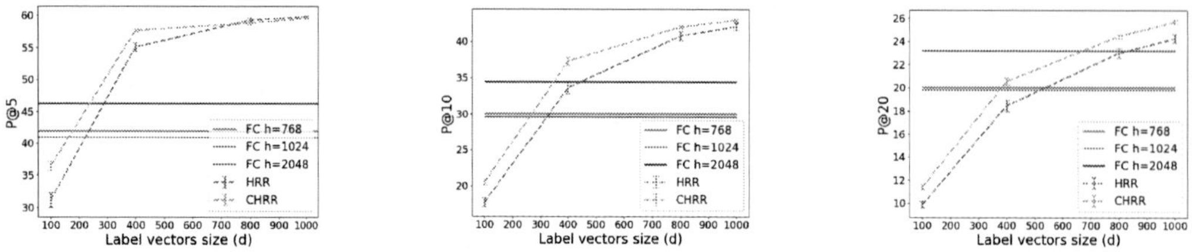

(a) Wiki10-31K P@5 (b) Wiki10-31K P@10 (c) Wiki10-31K P@20

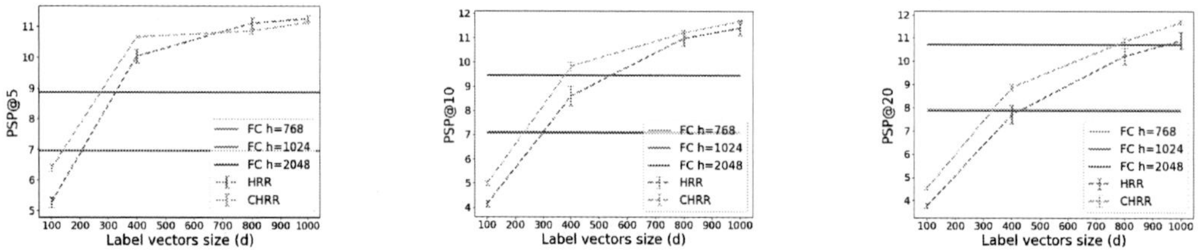

(d) Wiki10-31K PSP@5 (e) Wiki10-31K PSP@10 (f) Wiki10-31K PSP@20

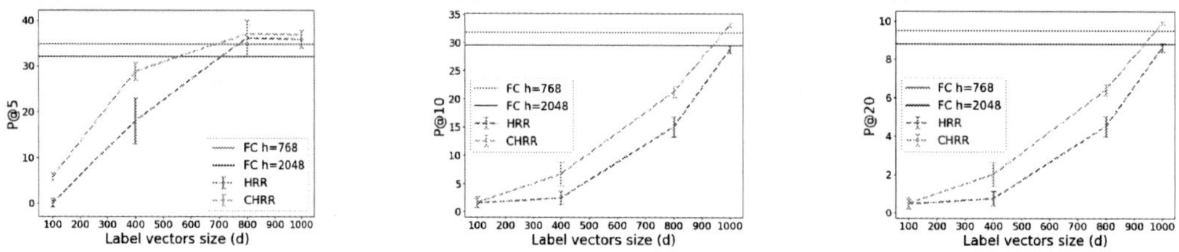

(g) Delicious-200K P@5 (h) Delicious-200K P@10 (i) Delicious-200K P@20

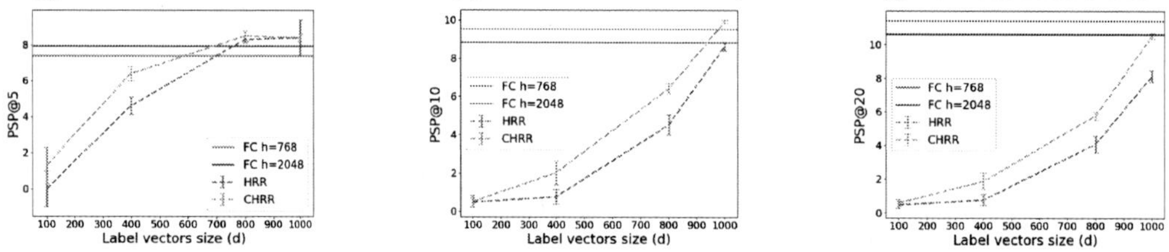

(j) Delicious-200K PSP@5 (k) Delicious-200K PSP@10 (l) Delicious-200K PSP@20

Figure 5: Impact of the number of dimensions (d) on P@5, P@10, P@20, PSP@5, PSP@10, and PSP@20 for Wiki10-31K and Delicious-200K datasets. We used BoW as features in all models.

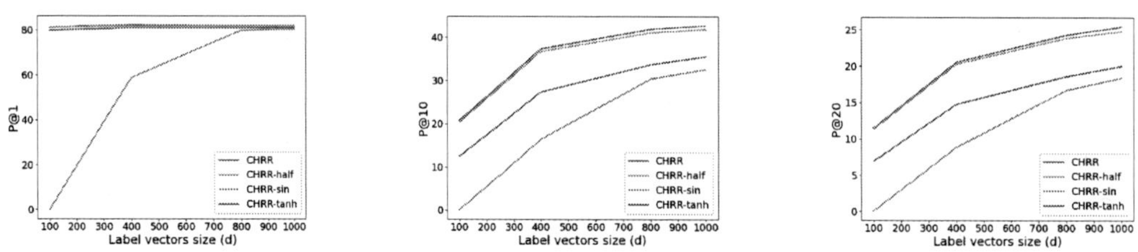

(a) P@1 (b) P@10 (c) P@20

Figure 6: Comparison of CHRR variants (CHRR, -Half, -sin, and -tanh) on the Wiki10-31K dataset.

circular vector systems into other DNN models such as LSTM (Hochreiter and Schmidhuber, 1997) and Transformer (Vaswani et al., 2017), as well as Associative LSTM (Danihelka et al., 2016) and Hrrformer (Alam et al., 2023).

Limitations

Our study has several limitations that should be considered in interpreting the results:

1. **Model Age and Adaptability:** The HRR and CHRR models utilized in our experiments are based on established frameworks that may not incorporate the latest advancements in neural network architectures (Ganesan et al., 2021). Newer models or hybrid approaches might offer improved performance.

2. **Comparison with State-of-the-Art XMC Models:** Our study did not include a comparison with the latest models in the Extreme Multi-label Classification (XMC) domain, such as APLC-XLNet (Ye et al., 2020), LightXML (Jiang et al., 2021), AttentionXML (You et al., 2019), and CascadeXML (Kharbanda et al., 2022). Future research should consider comparing the performance of HRR, HRR(w/Proj), and CHRR against these state-of-the-art models to provide a more comprehensive evaluation of their effectiveness in .

3. **Comparison with LLM:** Our study did not include a comparison with the Large Language Model (LLM) approach, which is currently the state-of-the-art in various NLP tasks. Future research should consider comparing the performance of HRR, HRR(w/Proj), and CHRR against LLMs to further evaluate the effectiveness of these models.

These limitations underscore the need for further research to refine and extend the applicability of the models proposed in this study.

Ethics Statement

We used the publicly available XMC datasets, Delicious, EURLex-4K, Wiki10-31K and Delicious-200K, to train and evaluate DNN models, and there is no ethical consideration.

Reproducibility Statement

As mentioned in § 5.3, we used the publicly available code to implement FC, HRR and CHRR. Our code will be available at `https://github.com/Nishiken1/Circular-HRR`.

References

Abien Fred Agarap. 2018. Deep learning using rectified linear units (relu). *arXiv preprint arXiv:1803.08375.*

Mohammad Mahmudul Alam, Edward Raff, Stella Biderman, Tim Oates, and James Holt. 2023. Recasting self-attention with holographic reduced representations. *arXiv preprint arXiv:2305.19534.*

Rohit Babbar and Bernhard Schölkopf. 2017. Dismec: Distributed sparse machines for extreme multi-label classification. In *Proceedings of the tenth ACM international conference on web search and data mining*, pages 721–729.

K. Bhatia, K. Dahiya, H. Jain, P. Kar, A. Mittal, Y. Prabhu, and M. Varma. 2016. The extreme classification repository: Multi-label datasets and code.

Wei-Cheng Chang, Hsiang-Fu Yu, Kai Zhong, Yiming Yang, and Inderjit S Dhillon. 2020. Taming pretrained transformers for extreme multi-label text classification. In *Proceedings of the 26th ACM SIGKDD international conference on knowledge discovery & data mining*, pages 3163–3171.

Kunal Dahiya, Nilesh Gupta, Deepak Saini, Akshay Soni, Yajun Wang, Kushal Dave, Jian Jiao, Gururaj K, Prasenjit Dey, Amit Singh, et al. 2023. Ngame: Negative mining-aware mini-batching for extreme classification. In *Proceedings of the Sixteenth ACM International Conference on Web Search and Data Mining*, pages 258–266.

Ivo Danihelka, Greg Wayne, Benigno Uria, Nal Kalchbrenner, and Alex Graves. 2016. Associative long short-term memory. *CoRR*, abs/1602.03032.

Ofer Dekel and Ohad Shamir. 2010. Multiclass-multilabel classification with more classes than examples. In *Proceedings of the Thirteenth International Conference on Artificial Intelligence and Statistics*, pages 137–144. JMLR Workshop and Conference Proceedings.

Jia Deng, Alexander C Berg, Kai Li, and Li Fei-Fei. 2010. What does classifying more than 10,000 image categories tell us? In *Computer Vision–ECCV 2010: 11th European Conference on Computer Vision, Heraklion, Crete, Greece, September 5-11, 2010, Proceedings, Part V 11*, pages 71–84. Springer.

Ashwinkumar Ganesan, Hang Gao, Sunil Gandhi, Edward Raff, Tim Oates, James Holt, and Mark McLean. 2021. Learning with holographic reduced representations. *Advances in Neural Information Processing Systems*, 34:25606–25620.

Ross W Gayler. 2004. Vector symbolic architectures answer jackendoff's challenges for cognitive neuroscience. *arXiv preprint cs/0412059.*

Katsuhiko Hayashi and Masashi Shimbo. 2017. On the equivalence of holographic and complex embeddings for link prediction. In *Proceedings of the 55th Annual Meeting of the Association for Computational Linguistics (Volume 2: Short Papers)*, pages 554–559, Vancouver, Canada. Association for Computational Linguistics.

Rhys Heffernan, Kuldip Paliwal, James Lyons, Abdollah Dehzangi, Alok Sharma, Jihua Wang, Abdul Sattar, Yuedong Yang, and Yaoqi Zhou. 2015. Improving prediction of secondary structure, local backbone angles and solvent accessible surface area of proteins by iterative deep learning. *Scientific Reports*, 5(1):11476.

Sepp Hochreiter and Jürgen Schmidhuber. 1997. Long short-term memory. *Neural computation*, 9(8):1735–1780.

Himanshu Jain, Yashoteja Prabhu, and Manik Varma. 2016. Extreme multi-label loss functions for recommendation, tagging, ranking & other missing label applications. In *Proceedings of the 22nd ACM SIGKDD international conference on knowledge discovery and data mining*, pages 935–944.

Vidit Jain, Jatin Prakash, Deepak Saini, Jian Jiao, Ramachandran Ramjee, and Manik Varma. 2023. Renee: End-to-end training of extreme classification models. *Proceedings of Machine Learning and Systems*, 5.

Ting Jiang, Deqing Wang, Leilei Sun, Huayi Yang, Zhengyang Zhao, and Fuzhen Zhuang. 2021. Lightxml: Transformer with dynamic negative sampling for high-performance extreme multi-label text classification. In *Proceedings of the AAAI Conference on Artificial Intelligence*, volume 35, pages 7987–7994.

Pentti Kanerva. 1996. Binary spatter-coding of ordered k-tuples. In *International Conference on Artificial Neural Networks*.

Sujay Khandagale, Han Xiao, and Rohit Babbar. 2020. Bonsai: diverse and shallow trees for extreme multi-label classification. *Machine Learning*, 109:2099–2119.

Siddhant Kharbanda, Atmadeep Banerjee, Erik Schultheis, and Rohit Babbar. 2022. Cascadexml: Rethinking transformers for end-to-end multi-resolution training in extreme multi-label classification.

Jingzhou Liu, Wei-Cheng Chang, Yuexin Wu, and Yiming Yang. 2017. Deep learning for extreme multi-label text classification. In *Proceedings of the 40th international ACM SIGIR conference on research and development in information retrieval*, pages 115–124.

Tomas Mikolov, Kai Chen, Greg Corrado, and Jeffrey Dean. 2013. Efficient estimation of word representations in vector space. *arXiv preprint arXiv:1301.3781*.

Maximilian Nickel, Lorenzo Rosasco, and Tomaso Poggio. 2016. Holographic embeddings of knowledge graphs. In *Proceedings of the AAAI conference on artificial intelligence*, volume 30.

EI Organick. 1966. Some processors also offer the library function called atan2 a function of two arguments (opposite and adjacent). In *A FORTRAN IV Primer*, page 42. Addison-Wesley.

Ioannis Partalas, Aris Kosmopoulos, Nicolas Baskiotis, Thierry Artieres, George Paliouras, Eric Gaussier, Ion Androutsopoulos, Massih-Reza Amini, and Patrick Galinari. 2015. Lshtc: A benchmark for large-scale text classification. *arXiv preprint arXiv:1503.08581*.

Adam Paszke, Sam Gross, Francisco Massa, Adam Lerer, James Bradbury, Gregory Chanan, Trevor Killeen, Zeming Lin, Natalia Gimelshein, Luca Antiga, et al. 2019. Pytorch: An imperative style, high-performance deep learning library. *Advances in neural information processing systems*, 32.

Tony A Plate. 1992. Holographic recurrent networks. *Advances in neural information processing systems*, 5.

Tony A Plate. 1995. Holographic reduced representations. *IEEE Transactions on Neural networks*, 6(3):623–641.

Tony A Plate. 2003. *Holographic Reduced Representation: Distributed representation for cognitive structures*, volume 150. CSLI Publications Stanford.

Y. Prabhu, A. Kag, S. Gopinath, K. Dahiya, S. Harsola, R. Agrawal, and M. Varma. 2018a. Extreme multi-label learning with label features for warm-start tagging, ranking and recommendation. In *Proceedings of the ACM International Conference on Web Search and Data Mining*.

Y. Prabhu and M. Varma. 2014. Fastxml: A fast, accurate and stable tree-classifier for extreme multi-label learning. In *Proceedings of the ACM SIGKDD Conference on Knowledge Discovery and Data Mining*.

Yashoteja Prabhu, Anil Kag, Shrutendra Harsola, Rahul Agrawal, and Manik Varma. 2018b. Parabel: Partitioned label trees for extreme classification with application to dynamic search advertising. In *Proceedings of the 2018 World Wide Web Conference*, pages 993–1002.

D.A. Rachkovskij. 2001. Representation and processing of structures with binary sparse distributed codes. *IEEE Transactions on Knowledge and Data Engineering*, 13(2):261–276.

Tal Ridnik, Emanuel Ben-Baruch, Asaf Noy, and Lihi Zelnik-Manor. 2021. Imagenet-21k pretraining for the masses. *arXiv preprint arXiv:2104.10972*.

Kenny Schlegel, Peer Neubert, and Peter Protzel. 2021. A comparison of vector symbolic architectures. *Artificial Intelligence Review*, 55(6):4523–4555.

Paul Smolensky. 1990. Tensor product variable binding and the representation of symbolic structures in connectionist systems. *Artificial intelligence*, 46(1-2):159–216.

Ashish Vaswani, Noam Shazeer, Niki Parmar, Jakob Uszkoreit, Llion Jones, Aidan N Gomez, Łukasz Kaiser, and Illia Polosukhin. 2017. Attention is all you need. *Advances in neural information processing systems*, 30.

Marek Wydmuch, Kalina Jasinska, Mikhail Kuznetsov, Róbert Busa-Fekete, and Krzysztof Dembczynski. 2018. A no-regret generalization of hierarchical softmax to extreme multi-label classification. *Advances in neural information processing systems*, 31.

Hui Ye, Zhiyu Chen, Da-Han Wang, and Brian D. Davison. 2020. Pretrained generalized autoregressive model with adaptive probabilistic label clusters for extreme multi-label text classification.

Ronghui You, Zihan Zhang, Ziye Wang, Suyang Dai, Hiroshi Mamitsuka, and Shanfeng Zhu. 2019. Attentionxml: Label tree-based attention-aware deep model for high-performance extreme multi-label text classification. *Advances in Neural Information Processing Systems*, 32.

Hsiang-Fu Yu, Kai Zhong, Jiong Zhang, Wei-Cheng Chang, and Inderjit S. Dhillon. 2022. Pecos: Prediction for enormous and correlated output spaces.

Fabio Massimo Zanzotto and Lorenzo Dell'Arciprete. 2012. Distributed tree kernels. In *Proceedings of the 29th International Coference on International Conference on Machine Learning*, pages 115–122.

Jiong Zhang, Wei-Cheng Chang, Hsiang-Fu Yu, and Inderjit Dhillon. 2021. Fast multi-resolution transformer fine-tuning for extreme multi-label text classification. *Advances in Neural Information Processing Systems*, 34:7267–7280.

Wenjie Zhang, Junchi Yan, Xiangfeng Wang, and Hongyuan Zha. 2018. Deep extreme multi-label learning.

Mitigating Semantic Leakage in Cross-lingual Embeddings via Orthogonality Constraint

Dayeon Ki[1*] **Cheonbok Park**[2] **Hyunjoong Kim**[2]
[1]University of Maryland [2]NAVER Cloud
dayeonki@umd.edu

Abstract

Accurately aligning contextual representations in cross-lingual sentence embeddings is key for effective parallel data mining. A common strategy for achieving this alignment involves disentangling semantics and language in sentence embeddings derived from multilingual pre-trained models. However, we discover that current disentangled representation learning methods suffer from *semantic leakage*—a term we introduce to describe when a substantial amount of language-specific information is unintentionally leaked into semantic representations. This hinders the effective disentanglement of semantic and language representations, making it difficult to retrieve embeddings that distinctively represent the meaning of the sentence. To address this challenge, we propose a novel training objective, ORthogonAlity Constraint LEarning (ORACLE), tailored to enforce orthogonality between semantic and language embeddings. ORACLE builds upon two components: intra-class clustering and inter-class separation. Through experiments on cross-lingual retrieval and semantic textual similarity tasks, we demonstrate that training with the ORACLE objective effectively reduces semantic leakage and enhances semantic alignment within the embedding space.[1]

1 Introduction

Parallel datasets play a pivotal role in enhancing neural machine translation (NMT) performance (Michel and Neubig, 2018). However, acquiring high-quality parallel texts is challenging, especially for lower-resourced languages where monolingual data is more abundant (Niu et al., 2018). In this context, effective approaches for mining parallel data are essential for applying NMT in practical scenarios (Artetxe and Schwenk, 2019a).

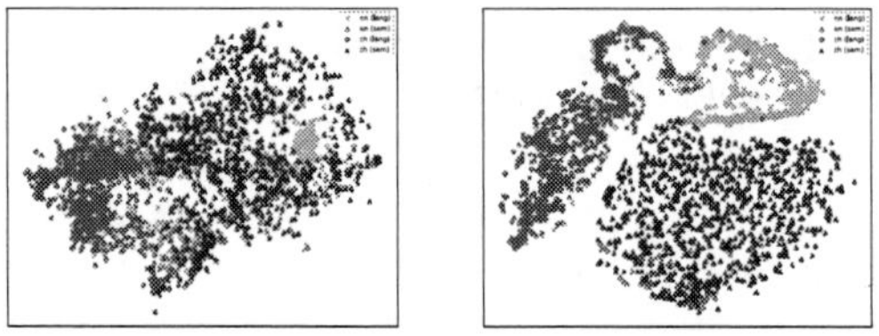

(a) Semantic Leakage (b) ORACLE

Figure 1: Visualization of LaBSE sentence embeddings for 1,000 Chinese-English sentence pairs. Figure 1(a) shows substantial overlap between semantic and language-specific representations. This overlap is effectively mitigated by the proposed ORACLE method, as shown in Figure 1(b).

Recent approaches to this problem utilize cross-lingual sentence embeddings (Schwenk and Douze, 2017; Schwenk, 2018) generated by multilingual pre-trained encoders such as multilingual BERT (Devlin et al. (2019), mBERT) or XLM-RoBERTa (Conneau et al. (2020), XLM-R). These embeddings aim to align semantically similar sentences across languages into a unified latent space, facilitating the extraction of pseudo-parallel pairs (Wang et al., 2022). However, Tiyajamorn et al. (2021) and Kuroda et al. (2022) demonstrate that embeddings of parallel sentences from these encoders form clusters by language rather than by semantics. Building on this, they attempt to disentangle language-specific information from sentence embeddings, thereby distilling language-agnostic semantic embeddings.

In order to achieve this, two premises need to be considered. Given parallel sentence,

(1) How well are the semantic representations **aligned**?
(2) How well are the language-specific representations **separated**?

Prior works have primarily focused on the former, leaving the latter question underexplored. Figure 1 illustrates sentence embeddings of a parallel cor-

*Work done during internship at NAVER Cloud.
[1]Our code and models will be released at publication.

Proceedings of the 9th Workshop on Representation Learning for NLP (RepL4NLP-2024), pages 256–273
August 15, 2024 ©2024 Association for Computational Linguistics

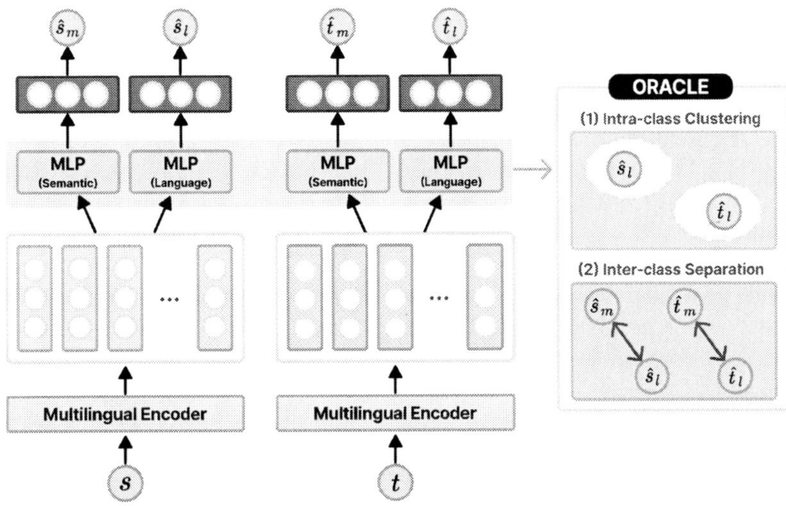

Figure 2: ORACLE objective for training semantic and language MLP networks. ORACLE is composed of two components: **(1) Intra-class clustering** for bringing related components closer in embedding space, **(2) Inter-class separation** for ensuring unrelated components to be distant. s and t represent source and target sentence input respectively. $\hat{s}_m$: source semantic representation; $\hat{s}_l$: source language representation; $\hat{t}_m$: target semantic representation; $\hat{t}_l$: target language representation.

pus pair, indicating that while semantics are well-aligned with previous disentanglement methods, there is still substantial overlap between language-specific and semantic information (Figure 1a). We define this issue as **semantic leakage**, which undermines the effectiveness of cross-lingual embeddings in accurately mining parallel pairs. By constraining orthogonality between semantic and language representations, we facilitate a clearer separation of language-specific information in the embedding space (Figure 1b).

In this work, we introduce **ORACLE** (ORthogonality Constraint LEarning), a training objective aimed at enforcing orthogonality between semantic and language-specific representations. Our goal is to render these two representations independent to each other, thus ensuring their clear differentiation in the embedding space (Mitchell and Steedman, 2015). ORACLE consists of two key components: intra-class clustering and inter-class separation. As shown in Figure 2, intra-class clustering aligns related components more closely, while inter-class separation enforces orthogonality between unrelated components. Our method is designed to be simple and effective, capable of being implemented atop any disentanglement methods.

We explore a range of pre-trained multilingual encoders (LASER (Artetxe and Schwenk, 2019b), InfoXLM (Chi et al., 2021), and LaBSE (Feng et al., 2022)) to generate initial sentence embeddings. Subsequently, we train each semantic and language multi-layer perceptrons (MLPs) with ORACLE to disentangle the sentence embeddings into semantics and language-specific information. Experimental results on both cross-lingual sentence retrieval tasks (Artetxe and Schwenk, 2019b; Zweigenbaum et al., 2017) and the Semantic Textual Similarity (STS) task (Cer et al., 2017) demonstrate higher performance on semantic embeddings and lower performance on language embeddings with ORACLE. This suggests that our method not only resolves semantic leakage but also enhances semantic alignment (§6). Our analysis further reveals that ORACLE leads to robust performance in challenging scenarios such as code-switching (§7.1).

To summarize, our contributions are threefold:
(1) We make the first attempt to address the issue of *semantic leakage*, wherein a substantial amount of language-specific information is leaked into semantic representations.
(2) We mitigate semantic leakage with ORACLE, a simple and effective training objective that improves disentanglement of semantic and language-specific information.
(3) We show that ORACLE leads to robust mining in code-switched scenarios.

2 Related work

2.1 Cross-lingual Sentence Embeddings

Earlier works primarily centered on learning sentence-level representations for mining pseudo-parallel pairs. Initial methods utilized neural machine translation (NMT) systems with a shared encoder (Schwenk and Douze, 2017; Schwenk, 2018). This approach inspired supervised approaches which train neural networks with large parallel datasets. For instance, Lee and Chen (2017) introduced the multilingual Universal Sentence Encoder (mUSE), a dual-encoder model pre-trained on parallel corpora in 16 languages. Similarly, LASER (Artetxe and Schwenk, 2019b) is an encoder-decoder model based on recurrent neural network. More recently, there has been a shift towards using multilingual sentence encoders such as mBERT (Devlin et al., 2019), XLM-R (Conneau et al., 2020), and CRISS (Tran et al., 2020), which are based on single self-attention networks pre-trained on large monolingual datasets. InfoXLM (Chi et al., 2021) extends XLM-R by adding a cross-lingual contrastive pre-training objective to enhance cross-lingual understanding task performance. Subsequently, the Dual Encoder with Anchor Model (DuEAM) (Goswami et al., 2021) incorporates a dual-encoder approach and integrates the word mover's distance to better capture semantic similarity between sentences. LaBSE (Feng et al., 2022) is a state-of-the-art multilingual sentence encoder built upon a dual-encoder framework, pre-trained with both monolingual and bilingual corpora. We leverage several of these multilingual sentence encoders to derive initial cross-lingual sentence embeddings. For our experiments, we specifically focus on three open-source baselines: LASER, InfoXLM, and LaBSE. We investigate the issue of semantic leakage in these encoders and effectively address it by integrating ORACLE.

2.2 Disentangled Representation Learning

A high-quality cross-lingual sentence embedding should effectively align semantically similar sentences from different languages in a shared embedding space (Wang et al., 2022). However, embeddings obtained from multilingual sentence encoders are often highly biased by language-specific information (Tiyajamorn et al., 2021). In this context, previous research has largely focused on learning disentangled representations to separate language-specific elements from semantics (Pires et al., 2019; Libovický et al., 2020; Gong et al., 2021; Zhao et al., 2021). One prevalent method involves training semantic and language networks separately, where the former is responsible for extracting meaning while the latter extracts language-specific information (Tiyajamorn et al., 2021; Kuroda et al., 2022; Wu et al., 2022). Specifically, DREAM (Tiyajamorn et al., 2021) utilize a multi-task training approach with a combination of reconstruction, semantic embedding, and language embedding losses, while MEAT (Kuroda et al., 2022) introduces novel loss combinations for more direct disentanglement. The distinct loss components of both methods are outlined in Table 1.

Decomposer	L_R	L_{CR}	L_S	L_L	L_A
DREAM (Tiyajamorn et al., 2021)	✓		✓	✓	
MEAT (Kuroda et al., 2022)	✓	✓		✓	✓

Table 1: Comparison of loss components in DREAM and MEAT. L_R: Reconstruction loss, L_{CR}: Cross-Reconstruction loss, L_S: Semantic embedding loss, L_L: Language embedding loss, L_A: Adversarial loss.

Although disentangled representation learning has been explored previously, existing methods have primarily focused on aligning semantics. We discover that these approaches suffer from semantic leakage, as evidenced by the high performance of language-specific representations. Our work is the first to address this challenge through ORACLE, which enforces orthogonality between semantic and language representations.

3 Background

3.1 DREAM

DREAM (Tiyajamorn et al., 2021) employs two separate multi-layer perceptron (MLP) networks in an autoencoder setup to learn disentangled semantic and language-specific representations. Given a parallel corpus $C = \{(s^1, t^1), ..., (s^n, t^n)\}$, comprising pairs of sentences from a source and target language, each sentence pair (s^i, t^i) is input into a multilingual pre-trained model (PLM). This generates original embeddings for the source $\mathbf{e}_s^i \in \mathbb{R}^d$ and the target sentences $\mathbf{e}_t^i \in \mathbb{R}^d$, where d represents the dimension of the input sentence embeddings. Semantic and language representations are then extracted from these embeddings using a separate semantic MLP network MLP_m (denoted by m to signify "meaning") and a language MLP network MLP_l.

$$\hat{\mathbf{s}}_m^i = \mathrm{MLP}_m(\mathbf{e}_s^i) \quad (1)$$

$$\hat{\mathbf{s}}_l^i = \mathrm{MLP}_l(\mathbf{e}_s^i) \quad (2)$$

Here, $\hat{\mathbf{s}}_m^i, \hat{\mathbf{s}}_l^i \in \mathbb{R}^d$ represent the semantic and language representations of the source sentence, respectively, and similarly $\hat{\mathbf{t}}_m^i, \hat{\mathbf{t}}_l^i \in \mathbb{R}^d$ for the target sentence. We repeat this process across the entire parallel corpus C.

For each language, the extracted semantic and language representations are element-wise summed to reconstruct the original sentence embedding as the final output. DREAM trains the two MLPs in a multi-task fashion, integrating three loss functions:

$$\mathcal{L}_{\text{DREAM}} = \mathcal{L}_R + \mathcal{L}_S + \mathcal{L}_L \quad (3)$$

where $\mathcal{L}_R$ is the reconstruction loss for reconstructing the original sentence embedding using semantic and language representations. $\mathcal{L}_S$ and $\mathcal{L}_L$ are responsible for extracting semantic and language information, respectively. Furthermore, $\mathcal{L}_L$ comprises both the language embedding loss ($\mathcal{L}_L^m$) and the language classification loss ($\mathcal{L}_L^i$), where $\mathcal{L}_L^m$ minimizes the distance within language embeddings and $\mathcal{L}_L^i$ computes the multi-class cross-entropy loss for the language classification task.

3.2 MEAT

MEAT (Kuroda et al., 2022) builds upon DREAM but incorporates more direct supervision to better disentangle semantic and language representations. MEAT trains the two MLPs with a new combination of four losses:

$$\mathcal{L}_{\text{MEAT}} = \mathcal{L}_R + \mathcal{L}_{CR} + \mathcal{L}_L + \mathcal{L}_A \quad (4)$$

$\mathcal{L}_{CR}$ is the cross-reconstruction loss for reconstructing the original source embedding using semantic from the target and language embedding from the source, and vice versa. $\mathcal{L}_A$ is the adversarial loss designed to reduce language identifiability in semantic representations.

4 ORACLE

The two key ingredients of ORACLE are intra-class clustering (§4.1) and inter-class separation (§4.2). We reformulate the losses originally derived in DREAM and MEAT and impose additional constraints to ensure orthogonality between semantic and language embeddings. Following the setup introduced in Section 3.1, ORACLE also uses semantic (MLP_m) and language MLP (MLP_l) to extract semantics ($\hat{\mathbf{s}}_m^i$, $\hat{\mathbf{t}}_m^i$) and language-specific information ($\hat{\mathbf{s}}_l^i$, $\hat{\mathbf{t}}_l^i$) for each language.

4.1 Intra-class clustering ($\mathcal{L}_{\text{IC}}$)

$\mathcal{L}_{\text{IC}}$ aims to bring relevant representations closer in the multilingual embedding space. As shown in Figure 1a, we notice that previous methods lack a constraint to enforce language embeddings to be clustered within themselves. This causes the language-specific information to leak into the semantics, making it difficult to capture the underlying semantics of the sentence. We constrain this by imposing pairwise cosine distances of each language embeddings:

$$\mathcal{L}_{\text{IC}} = \frac{1}{N}\sum_{i=1}^{N}\left(2 - \phi(\hat{\mathbf{s}}_l^i, \hat{\mathbf{s}}_l^j) - \phi(\hat{\mathbf{t}}_l^i, \hat{\mathbf{t}}_l^j)\right), \quad (5)$$

where $\phi(\cdot)$ denotes pairwise cosine similarity. $\phi(\hat{\mathbf{s}}_l^i, \hat{\mathbf{s}}_l^j)$ and $\phi(\hat{\mathbf{t}}_l^i, \hat{\mathbf{t}}_l^j)$ $(i \neq j)$ measures the pairwise cosine similarity of language embeddings in source and target language respectively. We subtract from 2 to transition each of the similarity metric into distance metric. By minimizing $\mathcal{L}_{\text{IC}}$, we aim to cluster language-specific representation for each language.

4.2 Inter-class separation ($\mathcal{L}_{\text{IS}}$)

Simultaneously, $\mathcal{L}_{\text{IS}}$ enforces irrelevant representations to be clearly separated:

$$\mathcal{L}_{\text{IS}} = \frac{1}{N}\sum_{i=1}^{N}\max(0, \phi(\hat{\mathbf{s}}_m^i, \hat{\mathbf{s}}_l^i) + \max(0, \phi(\hat{\mathbf{t}}_m^i, \hat{\mathbf{t}}_l^i)) \quad (6)$$

where $\phi(\cdot)$ denotes cosine similarity. We impose a minimum value constraint of 0 to ensure the proper enforcement of orthogonality, indicative of unrelatedness, between the source and target language embeddings. Minimizing $\mathcal{L}_{\text{IS}}$ effectively disentangles semantics from language-specific representations by constraining them to be orthogonal in the embedding space.

Combining with the intra-class clustering objective we get the final loss as:

$$\mathcal{L}_{\text{ORACLE}} = \mathcal{L}_{\text{IC}} + \mathcal{L}_{\text{IS}}. \quad (7)$$

We train both MLP networks, MLP_m and MLP_l, with the combined loss $\mathcal{L}_{\text{ORACLE}}$ in a multi-task learning approach. We integrate $\mathcal{L}_{\text{ORACLE}}$ with the existing loss functions of DREAM or MEAT. This is based on our experiments in Section 7.3 where integrating ORACLE with DREAM or MEAT yields better performance than using it as a stand-alone objective.

5 Experimental setup

5.1 Data

We compile a dataset comprising 12 language pairs sourced from publicly available bilingual corpora[2]. English is chosen as the source language for all pairs. We randomly sample 0.5M sentences for each language pair, which is later split into 0.45M for training and 0.05M for testing. In total, we utilize 6M parallel sentences. We select the language pairs based on diversity in language families, semantic similarity to English, and resource availability. Additional details for each language pair are provided in Table 2.

Language	Family	ISO Code	Similarity	Resource level
English	Germanic	en	-	high
German	Germanic	de	0.81	high
Portuguese	Romance	pt	0.84	high
Italian	Romance	it	0.85	high
Spanish	Romance	es	0.86	high
French	Romance	fr	0.86	high
Chinese	Sino-Tibetan	zh	0.81	high
Arabic	Semitic	ar	0.91	high
Japanese	Japonic	ja	0.69	high
Dutch	Germanic	nl	0.80	medium
Romanian	Romance	ro	0.88	medium
Guaraní	Tupi-Guaraní	gn	0.25	low
Aymara	Andean	ay	0.18	low

Table 2: Summary of 12 languages used for training. Similarity refers to the cosine similarity between 1,000 sample of English and target language sentences measured using LaBSE embeddings.

5.2 Baselines

Our study encompasses three open-source multilingual sentence encoders to generate initial sentence embeddings:

- **LASER**: Multilingual enc-decoder model trained on 93 languages (Artetxe and Schwenk, 2019b).
- **InfoXLM**: XLM-R (Conneau et al., 2020) trained with masked language modeling (MLM), translation language modeling (TLM), and cross-lingual contrastive learning task with monolingual and parallel corpora (Chi et al., 2021).
- **LaBSE**: A dual-encoder framework trained with MLM and TLM on both monolingual and bilingual corpora (Feng et al., 2022).

Each multilingual sentence encoder is pre-trained with different combinations of languages. Consequently, the list of seen and unseen languages from our training data varies for each encoder, as summarized in Appendix Table 6.

5.3 Implementation Details

We train the two MLP layers—a semantic embedding layer and a language embedding layer—to distill semantic and language-specific features while keeping the backbone sentence encoder frozen. The output embedding of the [CLS] token is used for sentence embedding. Further details on training process is detailed in Appendix A.3.

5.4 Evaluation task

Cross-lingual Sentence Retrieval. We evaluate our model on two distinct cross-lingual sentence retrieval tasks: held-out test set and Tatoeba[3] (Artetxe and Schwenk, 2019b). Given a list of bilingual sentences, the cross-lingual sentence retrieval task aims to accurately pair sentences that are in a parallel relationship across languages. The dataset consists of up to 1,000 sentences per language along with their English translations. We follow the evaluation setup proposed by Wang et al. (2022), evaluating accuracy in both Tatoeba-14 and Tatoeba-36 settings, each covering 14 languages from LASER and 36 languages from the XTREME benchmark (Hu et al., 2020). We measure retrieval accuracy using both semantic and language-specific representations. Lower language embedding retrieval results suggest reduced semantic leakage in these representations, while higher semantic retrieval accuracy indicates improved semantic alignment in bilingual sentence pairs.

Semantic Textual Similarity. We also report performance on the SemEval-2017 Semantic Textual Similarity (STS) task (Cer et al., 2017). This task involves 7 cross-lingual and 3 monolingual sentence pairs. We aim to achieve high Spearman's rank correlation coefficients (ρ) with semantic representations, indicating better semantic alignment, while expecting lower coefficients with language representations, indicating effective separation.

[2]Our training corpus is obtained from OPUS (https://opus.nlpl.eu/). Details regarding the training corpus for each language pair are outlined in Appendix A.1.

[3]https://tatoeba.org/

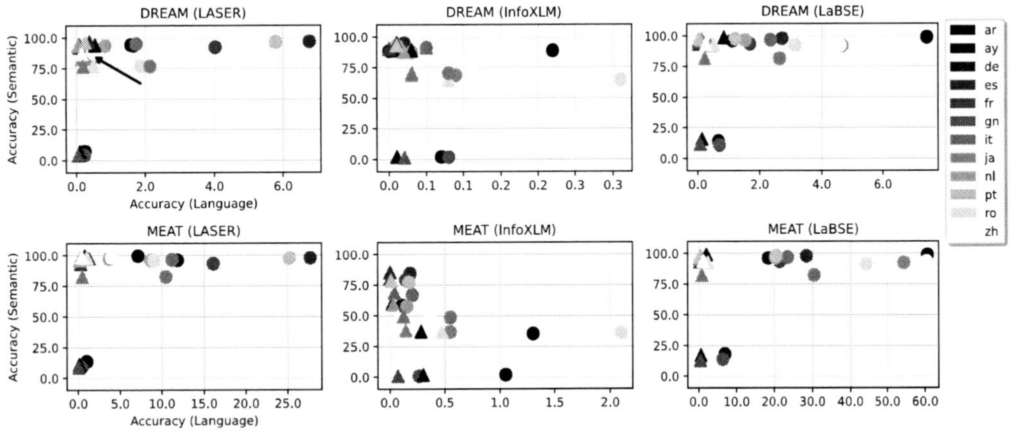

Figure 3: Cross-lingual sentence retrieval performance using our test set, consisting of 0.5M pairs for each language. The optimal representations exhibit high semantic retrieval accuracy and low language embedding retrieval accuracy, aiming for the upper left corner of each plot (indicated by the arrow). ●: vanilla DREAM or MEAT; ▲: with ORACLE objective. Grey: Average accuracy across 12 language pairs. *Top row*: DREAM with each multilingual encoder baselines; *Bottom row*: MEAT with multilingual encoders. Numerical results are in Appendix B.1.

6 Results

6.1 Cross-lingual Sentence Retrieval

Held-out Test Set. Figure 3 illustrates the performance of cross-lingual sentence retrieval on our held-out test set, consisting of 0.5M parallel sentences per language pair. We assess retrieval accuracy using semantic and language-specific representations of these parallel sentences. The optimal representation entails high semantic accuracy and low language embedding accuracy. Notably, applying ORACLE shifts performance towards the upper left quadrant, indicative of higher semantic accuracy and reduced language embedding accuracy across all encoder baselines. We report detailed numerical results in Appendix Table 8.

Tateoba. We draw similar conclusions from another cross-lingual retrieval task, Tatoeba, as shown in Table 3. Utilizing disentangled representations with ORACLE generally yields superior performance compared to representations learned by existing methods such as DREAM and MEAT. One exception is DREAM with LaBSE sentence embeddings, for which the accuracy drops by 0.06 points after integrating ORACLE.

Furthermore, we observe that models exhibit stronger performance from English (EN-XX) than into English (XX-EN) directions. Specifically, for Tatoeba-14, the semantic accuracy difference between the two settings of the vanilla model is smallest for LaBSE at 0.14 points, 0.69 points for LASER, and 15.6 points for InfoXLM on average. We notice a similar trend with the application of ORACLE, with the smallest difference for LaBSE at 0.08 points, 0.22 points for LASER, and 15.78 points for InfoXLM on average. We attribute this to EN-XX setting being similar to our training corpus. We present comprehensive results on Tatoeba in Appendix B.2.

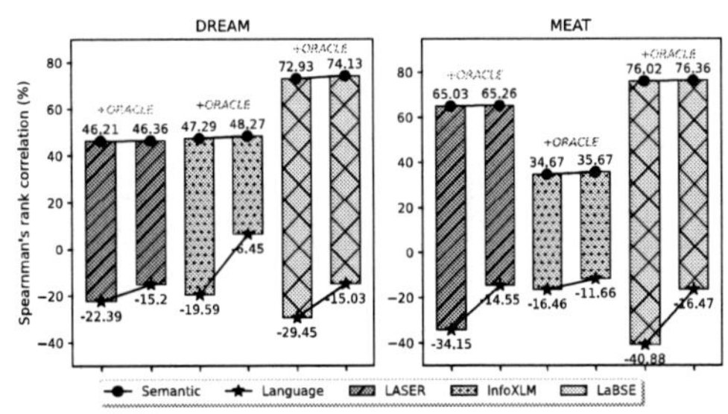

Figure 4: Spearman's rank correlation (%) from the STS task for each multilingual encoder baseline. Length of the bars reflects the performance gap between semantic (●) and language-specific (★) representations. Each set of three bars displays results for LASER, InfoXLM, and LaBSE. Within each color set, the first bar represents the vanilla approach, and the second bar denotes the integration of ORACLE objective.

Seen vs. Unseen. Each multilingual encoder unsurprisingly show lower performance for their unseen target languages, as indicated in Table 6. One exception is the performance of LASER embeddings on Aymara (ay), which shows low per-

Encoder	Objective	Tatoeba-14		Tatoeba-36	
		(En-XX)	(XX-En)	(En-XX)	(XX-En)
Semantic Embedding (↑)					
LASER	DREAM	68.68	69.53	59.94	62.01
	+ORACLE	**68.82**	**69.66**	**60.14**	**62.11**
	MEAT	88.48	89.00	80.56	79.26
	+ORACLE	88.30	87.70	**81.06**	**79.27**
InfoXLM	DREAM	42.20	51.40	39.51	47.10
	+ORACLE	**42.35**	**51.87**	**39.73**	**47.71**
	MEAT	31.50	53.49	28.21	44.53
	+ORACLE	**32.79**	**54.83**	**29.53**	**45.63**
LaBSE	DREAM	95.57	95.76	95.27	95.09
	+ORACLE	**95.69**	95.75	95.26	95.03
	MEAT	95.67	95.76	95.33	95.06
	+ORACLE	**96.06**	**96.16**	**95.58**	**95.48**
Language Embedding (↓)					
LASER	DREAM	1.58	1.35	1.44	1.21
	+ORACLE	**0.17**	**0.27**	**0.20**	**0.26**
	MEAT	12.52	10.93	10.12	7.86
	+ORACLE	**0.34**	**0.36**	**0.37**	**0.41**
InfoXLM	DREAM	0.31	0.27	0.35	0.37
	+ORACLE	**0.12**	**0.12**	**0.14**	**0.14**
	MEAT	0.33	1.92	0.36	2.32
	+ORACLE	**0.14**	**0.18**	**0.17**	**0.20**
LaBSE	DREAM	18.39	18.09	19.33	19.58
	+ORACLE	**1.26**	**1.36**	**1.50**	**1.70**
	MEAT	87.35	36.66	86.51	40.61
	+ORACLE	**8.48**	**7.00**	**9.92**	**8.41**

Table 3: Cross-lingual retrieval accuracy with Tatoeba dataset. We report the accuracy in both directions (from English and into English). **Bold** denotes better performance than the vanilla approach. All improvements are statistically significant with p-value ≤ 0.001.

formance despite being a seen language. Additionally, we note that ORACLE has a greater impact on the semantic embedding accuracy of unseen languages compared to seen languages. When training with ORACLE, the average semantic accuracy of the seen languages increases from 83.32→83.33 for LASER, 84.29→84.63 for InfoXLM, and 95.43→95.61 for LaBSE. The gap is more significant for unseen languages, increasing from 8.73→8.91 for LASER, 1.93→2.43 for InfoXLM, and 12.51→13.96 for LaBSE. This trend suggests that ORACLE helps bridge the performance gap between seen and unseen languages.

6.2 Semantic Textual Similarity

In Figure 4, we present the average Spearman's rank correlation coefficient across 10 STS tasks. The lengths of the bars indicate the performance gap between semantic and language-specific representations. With ORACLE, we observe a stronger positive correlation with STS scores for semantics and a stronger negative correlation for language representations. The extent of improvement in semantic results differs depending on both the encoder and the objective loss function. For DREAM, the highest gain is observed for LaBSE as +1.2 and the lowest for LASER as +0.15. Conversely, for MEAT, the highest gain is observed for InfoXLM as +1.0 and the lowest for LASER as +0.23.

Monolingual vs Cross-lingual. We categorize the STS results into two groups of language pairs: monolingual and cross-lingual. For both DREAM and MEAT, regardless of integrating ORACLE, the semantic embedding performance of monolingual language pairs is superior to that of cross-lingual language pairs. However, while the performance gap between monolingual and cross-lingual language pairs is larger for vanilla DREAM or MEAT, ORACLE can mitigate this gap. When applying ORACLE, the performance gap decreases by approximately 0.73 points for LASER, 1.47 points for InfoXLM, and 0.50 points for LaBSE. We report detailed results for each monolingual and cross-lingual language pairs in Appendix B.3.

7 Detailed Analysis

7.1 Code-switching

We manually create a code-switched dataset using bilingual dictionaries from MUSE (Conneau et al., 2018). For each language pair, we randomly replace words in the source sentence with corresponding translations in the target language. Further implementation details are provided in Appendix 7.1. As illustrated in Appendix Table 11, our results confirm that integrating ORACLE enhances both semantic and language embedding accuracy, even in practical and challenging scenarios likely encountered during parallel mining, such as code-switching.

7.2 Visualization

In Figure 5, we visualize the LaBSE sentence embedding space using 1,000 English-Chinese sentence pairs from our held-out test set. While previous methods ((a) and (c)) effectively align semantic representations, there is still substantial overlap in the language-specific representations. By applying ORACLE ((b) and (d)), we aim to mitigate the semantic leakage issue, distancing the language representations in parallel sentences while maintaining semantic alignment. We show that this trend is consistent across all language pairs through the visualizations in Appendix D.

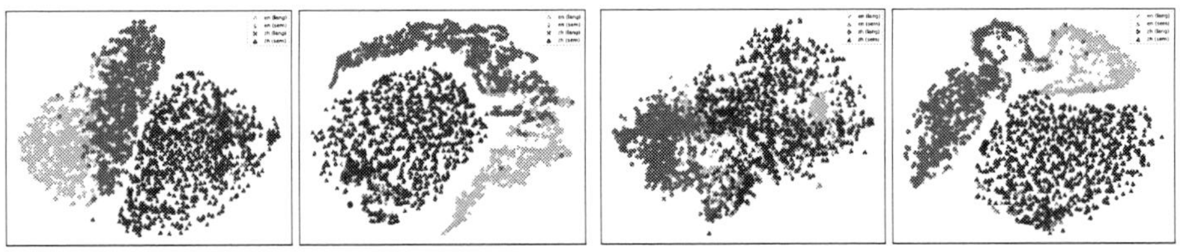

(a) DREAM (b) DREAM + ORACLE (c) MEAT (d) MEAT + ORACLE

Figure 5: Visualization of English-Chinese sentence embeddings from our held-out test set. Orange and green denote language embeddings of English and Chinese respectively. Red and blue represent their semantic counterparts. With ORACLE, we can preserve the semantic alignment and clearly divide the language-specific representations.

7.3 ORACLE Components

ORACLE is a multi-task learning objective consisting of two components: intra-class clustering and inter-class separation. Our analysis in Table 4 reveals the distinct impact of each component. Interestingly, using only the inter-class clustering loss demonstrates competitive performance, highlighting its critical role in the effectiveness of ORACLE. However, employing either intra-class clustering or inter-class separation alone presents trade-offs. Combining both components yields the most balanced performance, with highest semantic and lowest language embedding retrieval accuracy.

Furthermore, we discuss the potential of ORACLE as a stand-alone objective. In Figure 6, we illustrate the performance gap when ORACLE is used alone versus alongside DREAM or MEAT losses. We observe that ORACLE alone effectively mitigates semantic leakage with low language retrieval accuracy. However, this is offset by a decrease in semantic alignment compared to its use with DREAM. Therefore, we opt to integrate ORACLE with previous approaches, making it easily adaptable to various frameworks.

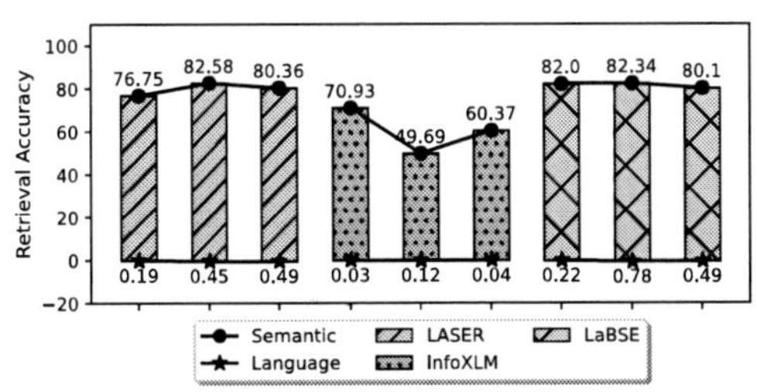

Figure 6: Performance gap between using ORACLE with DREAM (*left*), MEAT (*middle*) or as a stand-alone objective (*right*).

Objective	Tatoeba-14	Tatoeba-36	STS
Semantic Embedding (↑)			
ORACLE	**96.11**	95.53	**74.21**
- $\mathcal{L}_{\text{IC}}$	95.89	95.38	74.13
- $\mathcal{L}_{\text{IS}}$	96.11	**95.54**	72.81
Language Embedding (↓)			
ORACLE	**7.74**	**9.17**	**16.47**
- $\mathcal{L}_{\text{IC}}$	37.78	39.15	30.14
- $\mathcal{L}_{\text{IS}}$	8.07	9.59	18.20

Table 4: Performance change when removing each component of ORACLE from LaBSE sentence embeddings. $\mathcal{L}_{\text{IC}}$: Intra-class clustering; $\mathcal{L}_{\text{IS}}$: Inter-class separation. **Bold** denotes best results for each semantic and language embedding.

8 Conclusion

We explore the issue of semantic leakage, which we define as when language-specific information is leaked into the semantic representations, across various multilingual encoders and objective functions. Addressing this issue is crucial for achieving disentangled semantic and language representations, which is a cornerstone for effective parallel mining. We introduce ORACLE, a simple and effective training objective designed to enforce orthogonality between semantic and language embeddings. Through comprehensive evaluations, we demonstrate that integrating ORACLE not only improves semantic alignment but also ensures clear separation of language representations, as evidenced by embedding space visualization. Further, we conduct detailed analysis to understand the roles of the two key components of ORACLE: intra-class clustering and inter-class separation. While our study primarily focuses on integrating ORACLE with DREAM and MEAT, our method is easily adaptable to various frameworks, offering promising avenues for future work.

9 Limitations

Our work highlights the effectiveness of ORACLE in addressing semantic leakage and improving semantic alignment. While ORACLE demonstrates competitive performance as a stand-alone objective, its integration with DREAM or MEAT losses yields even better results. This limits the usage of ORACLE to be used alongside other methods. This opens many questions for future work to further explore the optimal combination of existing approaches and ORACLE.

Moreover, our study assesses the disentanglement of semantic and language representations in embeddings, focusing on two key aspects: the alignment of semantics in bilingual sentence pairs and the separation of language-specific information. While ORACLE effectively addresses the separation of language-specific information, we notice a trade-off in semantic alignment for certain language pairs. Future works can delve into methods that more efficiently mitigate semantic leakage without compromising semantic representation quality.

Lastly, our experiments are limited to 12 selected language pairs for training. To expand the scope of our study, future work could involve a wider array of language pairs and a broader range of multilingual encoder baselines.

References

Mikel Artetxe and Holger Schwenk. 2019a. Margin-based parallel corpus mining with multilingual sentence embeddings. In *Proceedings of the 57th Annual Meeting of the Association for Computational Linguistics*. Association for Computational Linguistics.

Mikel Artetxe and Holger Schwenk. 2019b. Massively multilingual sentence embeddings for zero-shot cross-lingual transfer and beyond. *Transactions of the Association for Computational Linguistics*, 7:597–610.

Daniel Cer, Mona Diab, Eneko Agirre, Iñigo Lopez-Gazpio, and Lucia Specia. 2017. SemEval-2017 task 1: Semantic textual similarity multilingual and crosslingual focused evaluation. In *Proceedings of the 11th International Workshop on Semantic Evaluation (SemEval-2017)*, pages 1–14, Vancouver, Canada. Association for Computational Linguistics.

Zewen Chi, Li Dong, Furu Wei, Nan Yang, Saksham Singhal, Wenhui Wang, Xia Song, Xian-Ling Mao, Heyan Huang, and Ming Zhou. 2021. InfoXLM: An information-theoretic framework for cross-lingual language model pre-training. In *Proceedings of the 2021 Conference of the North American Chapter of the Association for Computational Linguistics: Human Language Technologies*, pages 3576–3588, Online. Association for Computational Linguistics.

Alexis Conneau, Kartikay Khandelwal, Naman Goyal, Vishrav Chaudhary, Guillaume Wenzek, Francisco Guzmán, Edouard Grave, Myle Ott, Luke Zettlemoyer, and Veselin Stoyanov. 2020. Unsupervised cross-lingual representation learning at scale. In *Proceedings of the 58th Annual Meeting of the Association for Computational Linguistics*, pages 8440–8451, Online. Association for Computational Linguistics.

Alexis Conneau, Guillaume Lample, Marc'Aurelio Ranzato, Ludovic Denoyer, and Hervé Jégou. 2018. Word translation without parallel data.

Jacob Devlin, Ming-Wei Chang, Kenton Lee, and Kristina Toutanova. 2019. BERT: Pre-training of deep bidirectional transformers for language understanding. In *Proceedings of the 2019 Conference of the North American Chapter of the Association for Computational Linguistics: Human Language Technologies, Volume 1 (Long and Short Papers)*, pages 4171–4186, Minneapolis, Minnesota. Association for Computational Linguistics.

Fangxiaoyu Feng, Yinfei Yang, Daniel Cer, Naveen Arivazhagan, and Wei Wang. 2022. Language-agnostic BERT sentence embedding. In *Proceedings of the 60th Annual Meeting of the Association for Computational Linguistics (Volume 1: Long Papers)*, pages 878–891, Dublin, Ireland. Association for Computational Linguistics.

Hongyu Gong, Vishrav Chaudhary, Yuqing Tang, and Francisco Guzmán. 2021. Lawdr: Language-agnostic weighted document representations from pre-trained models.

Koustava Goswami, Sourav Dutta, Haytham Assem, Theodorus Fransen, and John P. McCrae. 2021. Cross-lingual sentence embedding using multi-task learning. In *Proceedings of the 2021 Conference on Empirical Methods in Natural Language Processing*, pages 9099–9113, Online and Punta Cana, Dominican Republic. Association for Computational Linguistics.

Junjie Hu, Sebastian Ruder, Aditya Siddhant, Graham Neubig, Orhan Firat, and Melvin Johnson. 2020. Xtreme: A massively multilingual multi-task benchmark for evaluating cross-lingual generalization. *CoRR*, abs/2003.11080.

Yuto Kuroda, Tomoyuki Kajiwara, Yuki Arase, and Takashi Ninomiya. 2022. Adversarial training on disentangling meaning and language representations for unsupervised quality estimation. In *Proceedings of the 29th International Conference on Computational Linguistics*, pages 5240–5245, Gyeongju, Republic of Korea. International Committee on Computational Linguistics.

Guang-He Lee and Yun-Nung Chen. 2017. MUSE: Modularizing unsupervised sense embeddings. In *Proceedings of the 2017 Conference on Empirical Methods in Natural Language Processing*, pages 327–337, Copenhagen, Denmark. Association for Computational Linguistics.

Jindřich Libovický, Rudolf Rosa, and Alexander Fraser. 2020. On the language neutrality of pre-trained multilingual representations. In *Findings of the Association for Computational Linguistics: EMNLP 2020*, pages 1663–1674, Online. Association for Computational Linguistics.

Paul Michel and Graham Neubig. 2018. MTNT: A testbed for machine translation of noisy text. In *Proceedings of the 2018 Conference on Empirical Methods in Natural Language Processing*, pages 543–553, Brussels, Belgium. Association for Computational Linguistics.

Jeff Mitchell and Mark Steedman. 2015. Orthogonality of syntax and semantics within distributional spaces. In *Proceedings of the 53rd Annual Meeting of the Association for Computational Linguistics and the 7th International Joint Conference on Natural Language Processing (Volume 1: Long Papers)*, pages 1301–1310, Beijing, China. Association for Computational Linguistics.

Xing Niu, Michael Denkowski, and Marine Carpuat. 2018. Bi-directional neural machine translation with synthetic parallel data. In *Proceedings of the 2nd Workshop on Neural Machine Translation and Generation*, pages 84–91, Melbourne, Australia. Association for Computational Linguistics.

Telmo Pires, Eva Schlinger, and Dan Garrette. 2019. How multilingual is multilingual BERT? In *Proceedings of the 57th Annual Meeting of the Association for Computational Linguistics*, pages 4996–5001, Florence, Italy. Association for Computational Linguistics.

Holger Schwenk. 2018. Filtering and mining parallel data in a joint multilingual space. In *Proceedings of the 56th Annual Meeting of the Association for Computational Linguistics (Volume 2: Short Papers)*, pages 228–234, Melbourne, Australia. Association for Computational Linguistics.

Holger Schwenk and Matthijs Douze. 2017. Learning joint multilingual sentence representations with neural machine translation. In *Proceedings of the 2nd Workshop on Representation Learning for NLP*, pages 157–167, Vancouver, Canada. Association for Computational Linguistics.

Nattapong Tiyajamorn, Tomoyuki Kajiwara, Yuki Arase, and Makoto Onizuka. 2021. Language-agnostic representation from multilingual sentence encoders for cross-lingual similarity estimation. In *Proceedings of the 2021 Conference on Empirical Methods in Natural Language Processing*, pages 7764–7774, Online and Punta Cana, Dominican Republic. Association for Computational Linguistics.

Chau Tran, Yuqing Tang, Xian Li, and Jiatao Gu. 2020. Cross-lingual retrieval for iterative self-supervised training.

Yaushian Wang, Ashley Wu, and Graham Neubig. 2022. English contrastive learning can learn universal cross-lingual sentence embeddings. In *Proceedings of the 2022 Conference on Empirical Methods in Natural Language Processing*, pages 9122–9133, Abu Dhabi, United Arab Emirates. Association for Computational Linguistics.

Linjuan Wu, Shaojuan Wu, Xiaowang Zhang, Deyi Xiong, Shizhan Chen, Zhiqiang Zhuang, and Zhiyong Feng. 2022. Learning disentangled semantic representations for zero-shot cross-lingual transfer in multilingual machine reading comprehension. In *Proceedings of the 60th Annual Meeting of the Association for Computational Linguistics (Volume 1: Long Papers)*, pages 991–1000, Dublin, Ireland. Association for Computational Linguistics.

Wei Zhao, Steffen Eger, Johannes Bjerva, and Isabelle Augenstein. 2021. Inducing language-agnostic multilingual representations. In *Proceedings of *SEM 2021: The Tenth Joint Conference on Lexical and Computational Semantics*, pages 229–240, Online. Association for Computational Linguistics.

Pierre Zweigenbaum, Serge Sharoff, and Reinhard Rapp. 2017. Overview of the second BUCC shared task: Spotting parallel sentences in comparable corpora. In *Proceedings of the 10th Workshop on Building and Using Comparable Corpora*, pages 60–67, Vancouver, Canada. Association for Computational Linguistics.

A Implementation Details

A.1 Training Corpus

In this section, we discuss the implementation details of our ORACLE objective. We describe the specific training corpus utilized for each language pair in Table 5.

A.2 Seen vs. Unseen Languages

In Table 6, we present the list of seen and unseen languages for each multilingual sentence encoder baseline, listed in alphabetical order. Across all encoders, Guaraní (gn) is categorized as an unseen language, while Aymara (ay) is classified as an unseen language for InfoXLM and LaBSE.

A.3 Training Details

Size of each MLP layer is embedding size of the encoder (1024 for LASER and 768 for XLM-R and LaBSE) by the number of language pairs (12). For training, we use Adam optimizer with an initial learning rate as 1e-5 and a batch size of 512.

We train the model for 10,000 iterations, evaluating the model's performance on the validation set at the end of each iteration. We implement early stopping to halt training when there is no improvement over 10 consecutive iterations. We find that DREAM converges in approximately 250 iterations and MEAT in 20 iterations.

Training corpus	Language pair
Europarl	en-de, en-es, en-fr, en-it, en-nl, en-pt
Wikimatrix	en-ar, en-ja, en-ro, en-zh
Tatoeba	en-gn
NLLB	en-ay

Table 5: Summary of training corpus for each language pair.

Encoder	Seen	Unseen
LASER	ar, ay, de, en, es, fr, it, ja, nl, pt, ro, zh	gn
InfoXLM	ar, de, en, es, fr, it, ja, nl, pt, ro, zh	ay, gn
LaBSE	ar, de, en, es, fr, it, ja, nl, pt, ro, zh	ay, gn

Table 6: Seen and unseen languages for each pre-trained multilingual encoder. Note that seen refers to languages used during pre-training.

B Detailed Results

B.1 Held-out Test set

In Table 8, we present detailed results for the cross-lingual sentence retrieval task using our held-out test set. The top section shows the performance of the initial sentence embeddings from LASER, InfoXLM, and LaBSE. In the middle section, we detail the accuracy of extracted semantic embeddings, while the bottom rows represent the language embedding accuracy. ORACLE, particularly for LaBSE, notably reduces language embedding accuracy, indicating a mitigation of semantic leakage compared to the vanilla DREAM or MEAT frameworks. Additionally, we observe an improvement in the semantic retrieval accuracy across all encoder baselines on average.

B.2 Tatoeba

In our analysis of the Tatoeba dataset detailed in Table 9, we exclude two language pairs (en-ay and en-gn) as Tatoeba does not support them. We show that a similar trend is observed: training MLP networks with ORACLE not only improves semantic alignment but also effectively addresses the semantic leakage issue in the vanilla DREAM or MEAT. Also, we observe that training LaBSE sentence embeddings with ORACLE yields state-of-the-art semantic retrieval accuracy compared to previous methods.

B.3 Semantic Textual Similarity

We present detailed numerical results for the monolingual and cross-lingual STS benchmark in Table 10. The results support our observation from the cross-lingual retrieval tasks that ORACLE helps address both semantic alignment and the semantic leakage issue.

C Code-switching

C.1 Dataset Construction

For our code-switching evaluation, we utilize bilingual dictionaries sourced from MUSE (Conneau et al., 2018). MUSE provides dictionaries in both the to English (XX-EN) and from English (EN-XX) directions. Specifically, we focus on dictionaries with the XX-EN direction. These dictionaries comprise root words in the source language paired with their corresponding translations in the target language. As noted by Conneau et al. (2018), the translations are generated using an internal translation tool, which accounts for word polysemy, resulting in some root words having multiple translations.

For each language pair listed in Table 3, we randomly substitute words in the source sentences with their corresponding translations in the target language, utilizing the dictionaries from MUSE. We ensure that the selected sentences of our code-switching evaluation contain at least one code-switched word. The resulting dataset comprises 1,000 sentences per language pair. We show examples of the manually created code-switched dataset in Table 7.

C.2 Results

In Table 11, we present the retrieval accuracy achieved on our code-switched dataset. Similar to the trends observed in other tasks, integrating ORACLE consistently improves both semantic and language embedding accuracy across all multilingual encoder baselines.

D Visualizations

From Figures 7 to 16, we provide visualizations of semantic and language embeddings for each language pair, complementing the discussion in Section 7.2. We use LaBSE to generate the initial sen-

Language pair	Code-switched Example
De-En	Source: Wie *long should* Tom *and I* hierbleiben? Target: How long are Tom and I supposed to stay here?
Fr-En	Source: Je *am here* jusqu'à *three* heures. Target: I will stay here till three o'clock.
It-En	Source: Fadil sparò al *dog* di Dania. Target: Fadil shot Dania's dog.
Ro-En	Source: E *traditional* să gates *black* la înmormântare. Target: It is traditional to wear black to a funeral.

Table 7: Examples of code-switched dataset manually created using bilingual dictionaries from MUSE (Conneau et al., 2018). *Italic* represent words that are code-switched in the source sentence.

tence embeddings, with 1,000 parallel sentences sampled from our held-out test set for each language pair. When solely using DREAM or MEAT (depicted in (a) and (c) for each visualization), we observe a notable amount of overlap in language embeddings between the source and target language, indicating semantic leakage. However, the integration of ORACLE effectively mitigates this issue, resulting in clearer separation and reduced overlap in language embeddings (depicted in (b) and (d)). This improvement is consistent across all language pairs.

Encoder	Objective	en-ar	en-ay	en-de	en-es	en-fr	en-gn	en-it	en-ja	en-nl	en-pt	en-ro	en-zh	Avg.
Original Embedding														
LASER	-	99.87	11.36	96.13	97.88	93.38	5.12	96.78	98.86	96.48	97.83	99.34	99.39	82.70
InfoXLM*	-	21.24	1.40	25.53	29.31	28.41	0.69	29.07	10.48	14.72	23.80	15.59	13.06	17.78
LaBSE	-	99.00	16.33	96.16	97.82	93.37	12.82	96.77	92.30	96.21	97.66	87.60	94.05	81.67
Semantic Embedding (↑)														
LASER	DREAM	94.22	7.27	93.85	96.81	92.28	4.33	95.13	82.94	93.46	96.39	77.05	87.10	76.74
	+ORACLE	94.10	7.23	**93.87**	96.79	92.28	4.26	95.13	**82.95**	**93.54**	96.39	**77.27**	**87.13**	**76.75**
	MEAT	99.58	13.50	95.91	97.71	93.18	8.73	96.29	97.20	95.95	97.54	95.82	98.42	82.49
	+ORACLE	**99.78**	11.11	**95.92**	97.71	**93.21**	**8.91**	**96.33**	**97.57**	**96.02**	**97.67**	**98.16**	**98.54**	**82.58**
InfoXLM	DREAM	88.74	2.06	88.61	94.89	90.47	1.80	91.14	68.71	87.44	93.06	64.87	74.96	70.56
	+ORACLE	**89.11**	**2.89**	**89.20**	**95.00**	**90.50**	**1.96**	**91.49**	**69.21**	**87.85**	**93.27**	**65.23**	**75.46**	**70.93**
	MEAT	35.24	1.87	58.32	84.47	79.28	0.79	66.85	36.85	57.57	77.28	35.81	48.18	48.54
	+ORACLE	**37.13**	1.87	**60.09**	**85.46**	**80.35**	**0.87**	**68.79**	**38.02**	**59.00**	**78.80**	**36.92**	**48.96**	**49.69**
LaBSE	DREAM	98.88	14.14	96.20	97.85	93.42	10.87	96.79	91.90	96.50	97.79	92.49	92.52	81.61
	+ORACLE	98.87	**15.94**	**96.22**	97.84	**93.44**	**11.97**	**96.86**	**92.52**	96.46	**97.80**	**92.66**	**93.45**	**82.00**
	MEAT	98.75	17.97	96.14	97.83	93.38	13.85	96.71	92.42	96.53	97.77	91.32	93.30	82.16
	+ORACLE	**99.08**	17.18	**96.29**	**97.87**	**93.41**	12.96	**96.86**	**93.17**	**96.54**	**97.79**	**92.95**	**93.99**	**82.34**
Language Embedding (↓)														
LASER	DREAM	1.58	0.24	1.66	6.76	4.02	0.22	1.74	0.45	0.82	5.78	1.87	0.50	2.14
	+ORACLE	**0.53**	**0.09**	**0.08**	**0.37**	**0.07**	**0.04**	**0.07**	**0.14**	**0.04**	**0.25**	**0.48**	**0.15**	**0.19**
	MEAT	7.13	0.96	11.83	27.65	16.07	0.38	11.20	3.67	8.61	25.16	9.04	3.95	10.47
	+ORACLE	**0.76**	**0.11**	**0.21**	**1.26**	**0.25**	**0.04**	**0.18**	**0.22**	**0.12**	**0.86**	**1.04**	**0.40**	**0.45**
InfoXLM	DREAM	0.22	0.07	0.00	0.02	0.01	0.08	0.05	0.09	0.03	0.01	0.31	0.11	0.08
	+ORACLE	**0.03**	**0.01**	0.01	**0.01**	**0.00**	**0.02**	0.05	**0.03**	**0.02**	0.01	**0.08**	**0.03**	**0.03**
	MEAT	1.30	1.05	0.11	0.18	0.14	0.26	0.20	0.55	0.15	0.17	2.10	0.36	0.55
	+ORACLE	**0.28**	**0.30**	**0.02**	**0.00**	**0.00**	**0.07**	**0.04**	**0.14**	**0.03**	**0.01**	**0.47**	**0.07**	**0.12**
LaBSE	DREAM	7.42	0.66	1.12	2.73	1.68	0.69	2.35	4.65	1.54	1.21	3.15	4.59	2.65
	+ORACLE	**0.85**	**0.13**	**0.04**	**0.03**	**0.03**	**0.08**	**0.13**	**0.40**	**0.10**	**0.03**	**0.52**	**0.26**	**0.22**
	MEAT	60.54	6.84	18.34	28.36	21.33	6.27	23.46	54.32	20.33	20.38	44.17	60.28	30.39
	+ORACLE	**1.98**	**0.50**	**0.18**	**0.22**	**0.22**	**0.38**	**0.31**	**1.59**	**0.35**	**0.16**	**2.36**	**1.14**	**0.78**

Table 8: Cross-lingual sentence retrieval accuracy with our test set, comprising 0.5M pairs for each language. We expect the semantic retrieval accuracy to be higher and lower with language embedding. **Bold** represents when our method surpass the vanilla approach and **highlight** denotes when the average value is higher. vanilla: original DREAM or MEAT approach; ORACLE: incorporation of our objective. *: We use mean pooling to compute sentence embedding. All average improvements are statistically significant with p-value ≤ 0.001.

Encoder	Objective	en-ar	en-de	en-es	en-fr	en-it	en-ja	en-nl	en-pt	en-ro	en-zh	Avg.
						Original Embedding						
MUSE ❖	-	-	-	95.40	93.50	94.30	93.80	94.00	94.90	30.00	94.30	86.90
CRISS ♥	-	-	-	96.30	92.70	92.50	84.80	93.40	-	-	85.60	90.20
DuEAM ♠	-	-	-	93.00	91.50	85.70	84.20	-	91.20	88.50	90.20	87.90
LASER	-	91.95	99.05	98.00	95.65	95.30	95.35	96.30	95.15	97.40	95.45	95.96
InfoXLM*	-	20.95	38.50	30.85	32.35	24.85	28.20	19.85	36.90	30.40	34.05	29.69
LaBSE	-	89.75	99.20	98.10	96.05	94.75	96.40	96.90	95.55	97.40	96.20	96.03
						Semantic Embedding (↑)						
LASER	DREAM	60.35	89.85	83.40	76.55	80.95	71.70	80.10	82.15	80.60	74.20	77.99
	+ORACLE	60.30	**90.00**	83.40	**76.65**	**81.00**	**72.05**	**80.35**	**82.30**	80.60	**74.60**	**78.13**
	MEAT	86.95	96.55	96.00	91.35	91.80	90.65	91.75	93.45	94.80	92.95	92.63
	+ORACLE	**87.30**	**98.05**	**96.65**	**92.75**	**92.55**	87.95	**93.70**	**94.25**	**95.40**	**93.80**	**93.24**
InfoXLM	DREAM	44.05	57.65	68.65	62.80	54.80	56.45	62.70	66.50	58.15	67.10	59.89
	+ORACLE	**44.80**	**58.00**	**68.85**	62.65	54.80	**57.05**	62.30	**66.65**	57.95	**67.20**	**60.03**
	MEAT	31.60	67.25	70.75	67.30	63.70	42.05	68.95	74.05	59.05	57.70	60.24
	+ORACLE	**31.80**	**69.00**	**71.60**	**68.35**	**64.15**	**43.10**	**70.85**	**75.25**	**60.45**	**60.30**	**61.49**
LaBSE	DREAM	89.90	99.10	98.50	95.80	95.05	95.75	97.35	95.45	97.50	95.35	95.98
	+ORACLE	89.70	**99.15**	98.50	**95.90**	94.85	**95.90**	97.30	**95.50**	**97.70**	**95.55**	**96.01**
	MEAT	90.30	99.20	98.15	98.90	94.55	96.15	97.30	95.55	97.55	95.50	96.32
	+ORACLE	**90.95**	**99.40**	**98.50**	**96.30**	**95.20**	**96.40**	**97.40**	**95.75**	**97.85**	**95.80**	**96.36**
						Language Embedding (↓)						
LASER	DREAM	1.20	1.50	2.95	1.50	4.45	1.15	2.00	3.70	1.85	1.70	2.20
	+ORACLE	**0.25**	**0.10**	**0.30**	**0.20**	**0.25**	**0.10**	**0.35**	**0.30**	**0.20**	**0.05**	**0.21**
	MEAT	19.40	9.75	13.55	6.70	14.30	5.65	9.90	16.15	16.20	10.85	12.25
	+ORACLE	**0.60**	**0.20**	**0.45**	**0.30**	**0.55**	**0.30**	**0.65**	**0.40**	**0.75**	**0.45**	**0.47**
InfoXLM	DREAM	0.10	0.10	0.25	0.15	0.45	0.20	0.40	0.20	0.15	0.20	0.22
	+ORACLE	0.10	0.10	**0.10**	**0.10**	**0.10**	**0.10**	**0.10**	**0.10**	**0.10**	**0.10**	**0.10**
	MEAT	0.35	0.55	2.00	0.90	2.75	0.30	3.35	0.85	1.15	0.40	1.26
	+ORACLE	**0.10**	**0.15**	**0.25**	**0.15**	**0.10**	**0.10**	**0.20**	**0.20**	**0.15**	**0.15**	**0.16**
LaBSE	DREAM	24.50	11.50	18.95	17.85	24.25	11.20	14.20	9.70	12.35	24.70	16.92
	+ORACLE	**2.15**	**1.20**	**1.00**	**0.30**	**1.45**	**1.15**	**1.30**	**9.30**	**0.70**	**1.00**	**1.96**
	MEAT	64.25	55.30	64.10	64.30	64.50	65.45	60.25	58.15	57.60	60.45	61.44
	+ORACLE	**8.30**	**7.25**	**5.05**	**5.00**	**8.15**	**9.70**	**7.20**	**3.90**	**6.75**	**5.65**	**6.70**

Table 9: Cross-lingual retrieval accuracy with Tatoeba task. For each language pair, we report the average accuracy of both directions (from English and into English). **Bold** represents when our method surpass the vanilla approach and **highlight** denotes when the average value is higher. ❖: results from Lee and Chen (2017) (*supervised*) ; ♥: results from Tran et al. (2020) (*weakly supervised*); ♠: results from Goswami et al. (2021) (*self-supervised*). *: We use mean pooling to compute sentence embedding. All average improvements are statistically significant with p-value ≤ 0.001.

Encoder	Objective	ar-ar	en-en	es-es	en-ar	en-de	en-tr	en-es	en-fr	en-it	en-nl	Avg.
						Original Embedding						
LASER	-	68.85	66.55	57.93	77.62	79.68	64.20	71.98	69.05	70.83	68.68	69.54
InfoXLM*	-	19.11	50.20	36.17	12.89	16.31	24.86	9.10	25.12	28.10	30.55	25.24
mSimCSE	-	69.06	74.50	65.71	79.45	80.83	73.85	72.07	76.98	76.98	75.22	74.47
						Semantic Embedding (↑)						
LASER	DREAM	57.10	53.98	46.36	43.22	41.92	40.60	32.88	48.58	49.94	47.47	46.21
	+ORACLE	**57.16**	**54.14**	**46.64**	**43.55**	**42.11**	**40.67**	32.83	**48.70**	**49.98**	**47.80**	**46.36**
	MEAT	66.87	71.95	79.16	62.41	60.44	65.06	54.63	61.94	66.27	63.90	65.26
	+ORACLE	**67.14**	**72.69**	78.75	**63.59**	60.03	**66.19**	**55.20**	61.38	65.80	63.76	**65.45**
InfoXLM	DREAM	50.28	56.39	56.16	43.35	39.54	42.71	38.42	48.02	47.80	50.18	47.29
	+ORACLE	50.25	56.38	56.16	43.35	**49.55**	42.61	38.40	47.98	**47.82**	**50.19**	**48.27**
	MEAT	35.83	61.23	51.14	11.09	25.58	33.32	20.04	29.38	41.58	37.50	34.67
	+ORACLE	**35.87**	**61.40**	50.73	**11.26**	**28.15**	**34.83**	**21.41**	**31.55**	**42.72**	**38.77**	**35.67**
LaBSE	DREAM	69.84	74.78	79.82	70.97	70.82	71.30	64.22	75.67	76.28	75.56	72.93
	+ORACLE	**70.65**	**76.03**	**81.06**	**72.37**	**72.49**	**73.33**	**66.18**	**76.13**	**76.76**	**76.29**	**74.13**
	MEAT	72.03	80.34	83.66	74.71	75.40	73.59	70.48	77.82	78.18	77.43	76.36
	+ORACLE	**72.05**	**80.41**	**83.86**	**75.09**	**75.67**	**74.56**	**70.98**	77.75	**78.57**	**77.44**	**76.64**
						Language Embedding (↓)						
LASER	DREAM	45.12	34.87	39.95	18.94	11.89	21.50	17.64	8.29	14.91	10.81	22.39
	+ORACLE	**21.43**	**12.77**	**18.40**	20.85	**11.65**	**17.12**	**15.30**	**6.14**	16.87	11.51	**15.20**
	MEAT	52.51	40.35	55.29	35.78	22.93	27.26	27.89	22.73	30.74	25.99	34.15
	+ORACLE	**21.26**	**14.97**	**21.75**	**21.48**	**6.09**	**15.71**	**15.51**	**4.86**	**15.37**	**8.49**	**14.55**
InfoXLM	DREAM	39.62	51.03	49.74	3.87	2.66	4.53	12.95	9.94	9.37	12.21	19.59
	+ORACLE	**24.62**	**31.07**	**36.01**	**-10.84**	**-7.12**	**-9.51**	**2.85**	**-3.18**	**-2.06**	**2.67**	**6.45**
	MEAT	33.00	50.01	51.02	-6.10	8.21	-2.50	-1.97	8.44	13.58	10.87	16.46
	+ORACLE	33.13	**46.96**	51.63	**-11.63**	**0.14**	**-8.14**	**-7.91**	**1.57**	**7.25**	**3.59**	**11.66**
LaBSE	DREAM	44.32	40.35	50.81	24.12	22.56	28.29	18.76	22.86	20.38	22.02	29.45
	+ORACLE	**33.10**	**19.88**	**28.60**	**1.59**	**1.14**	**17.39**	**15.57**	**12.17**	**8.36**	**12.53**	**15.03**
	MEAT	52.11	68.57	68.18	38.57	28.94	35.87	31.27	28.66	29.40	27.21	40.88
	+ORACLE	**37.25**	**27.30**	**33.61**	**0.08**	**0.79**	**16.94**	**16.60**	**10.98**	**8.01**	**13.12**	**16.47**

Table 10: Spearman's rank correlation coefficients (ρ) of monolingual and cross-lingual STS task. **Bold** represents when our method surpass the vanilla approach and **highlight** indicates when the average value is higher. *: We use mean pooling to compute sentence embedding. All average improvements are statistically significant with p-value ≤ 0.001.

Encoder	Objective	en-ar	en-de	en-es	en-fr	en-it	en-nl	en-pt	en-ro	Avg.
					Original Embedding					
LASER	-	90.82	98.75	98.26	95.17	94.63	95.22	95.91	98.37	95.89
InfoXLM*	-	13.71	39.04	37.05	36.20	29.44	29.54	41.44	31.37	32.22
LaBSE	-	90.06	99.48	98.49	95.60	93.46	97.02	96.56	98.24	96.11
					Semantic Embedding (↑)					
LASER	DREAM	59.75	88.58	84.67	73.90	84.46	80.66	82.02	82.43	79.56
	+ORACLE	59.62	**88.79**	**85.02**	73.90	84.46	80.45	**82.24**	82.18	**79.58**
	MEAT	84.91	97.82	96.28	92.70	93.34	93.84	95.05	96.86	93.85
	+ORACLE	**86.54**	97.09	**97.79**	92.59	93.22	92.67	**95.26**	96.11	**93.91**
InfoXLM	DREAM	28.05	55.14	58.07	59.72	54.09	53.99	54.90	56.46	52.55
	+ORACLE	27.80	**56.39**	**58.19**	**60.15**	**54.67**	**54.84**	**56.62**	56.34	**53.13**
	MEAT	15.35	42.26	60.51	58.22	56.43	56.43	57.70	50.69	49.70
	+ORACLE	**16.35**	42.26	**61.32**	**59.94**	**58.06**	**57.17**	**59.31**	**52.07**	**50.81**
LaBSE	DREAM	87.78	99.27	97.33	95.38	92.87	96.60	96.45	97.99	95.46
	+ORACLE	**88.30**	99.27	**98.14**	95.38	**93.22**	**96.81**	**96.66**	**98.11**	**95.74**
	MEAT	88.43	99.38	98.03	94.95	92.87	96.49	96.12	97.74	95.50
	+ORACLE	**89.56**	**99.69**	**98.37**	**96.60**	**93.34**	**97.13**	**96.34**	**98.24**	**96.16**
					Language Embedding (↓)					
LASER	DREAM	2.01	4.15	7.08	3.01	7.36	6.06	9.36	3.76	5.35
	+ORACLE	**0.25**	**0.83**	**1.39**	**0.43**	**0.93**	**0.85**	**2.48**	**0.75**	**0.99**
	MEAT	35.72	23.88	35.31	17.72	27.57	31.77	49.62	22.84	30.55
	+ORACLE	**1.51**	**1.66**	**3.02**	**1.07**	**2.45**	**2.34**	**5.06**	**1.25**	**2.30**
InfoXLM	DREAM	0.13	0.52	0.93	0.64	0.93	2.34	0.54	0.53	0.82
	+ORACLE	0.13	**0.10**	**0.46**	**0.11**	**0.23**	**0.85**	**0.11**	**0.13**	**0.27**
	MEAT	1.89	10.38	20.44	13.64	20.56	36.03	23.90	15.93	17.85
	+ORACLE	**0.38**	**1.04**	**3.37**	**1.40**	**3.15**	**8.93**	**3.12**	**1.76**	**2.89**
LaBSE	DREAM	11.57	14.54	21.24	23.52	27.69	27.21	19.38	17.44	20.32
	+ORACLE	**1.26**	**1.25**	**1.39**	**2.69**	**1.99**	**2.98**	**0.75**	**0.88**	**1.65**
	MEAT	48.81	37.80	53.31	51.34	56.54	53.35	43.27	34.00	47.30
	+ORACLE	**6.42**	**7.06**	**6.04**	**7.63**	**9.11**	**10.52**	**6.14**	**6.40**	**7.42**

Table 11: Retrieval accuracy with our code-switching dataset. **Bold** represents when our method surpasses the vanilla approach and **highlight** denotes when the average value is higher. vanilla: original DREAM or MEAT approach; ORACLE: incorporation of our objective. *: We use mean pooling to compute sentence embedding. All average improvements are statistically significant with p-value ≤ 0.001.

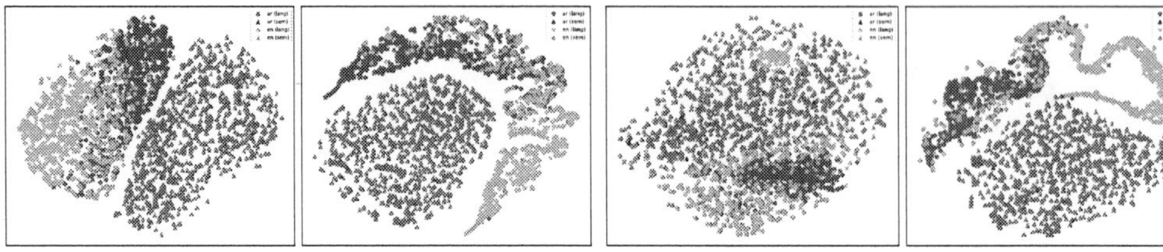

(a) DREAM (b) DREAM + ORACLE (c) MEAT (d) MEAT + ORACLE

Figure 7: LaBSE sentence embeddings for English-Arabic sentence pair.

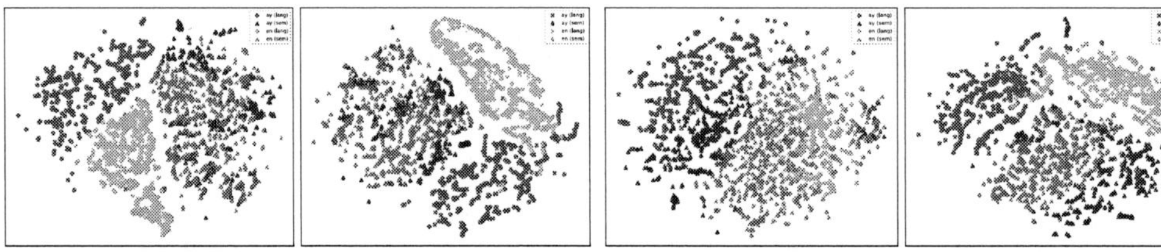

(a) DREAM (b) DREAM + ORACLE (c) MEAT (d) MEAT + ORACLE

Figure 8: LaBSE sentence embeddings for English-Aymara sentence pair.

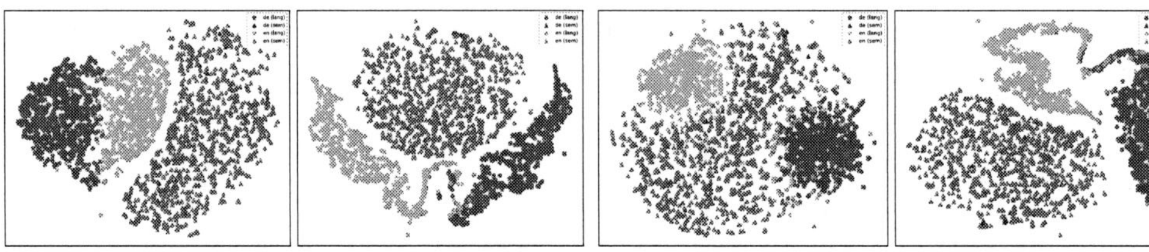

(a) DREAM (b) DREAM + ORACLE (c) MEAT (d) MEAT + ORACLE

Figure 9: LaBSE sentence embeddings for English-German sentence pair.

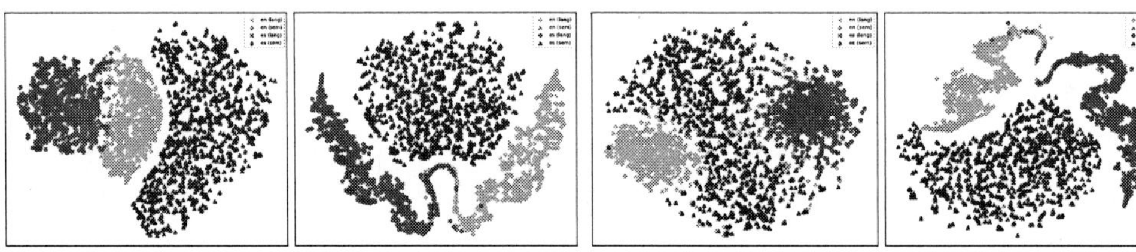

(a) DREAM (b) DREAM + ORACLE (c) MEAT (d) MEAT + ORACLE

Figure 10: LaBSE sentence embeddings for English-Spanish sentence pair.

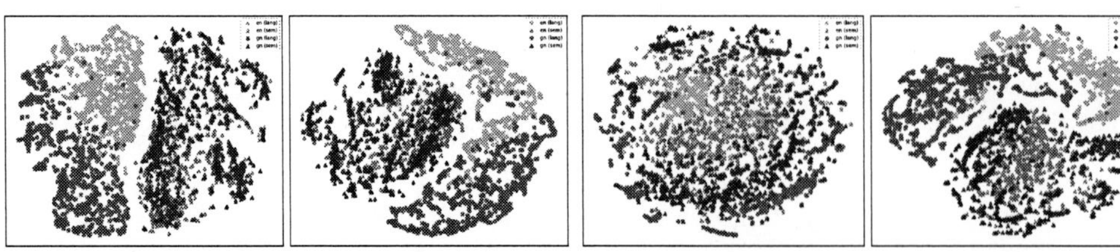

(a) DREAM (b) DREAM + ORACLE (c) MEAT (d) MEAT + ORACLE

Figure 11: LaBSE sentence embeddings for English-Guaraní sentence pair.

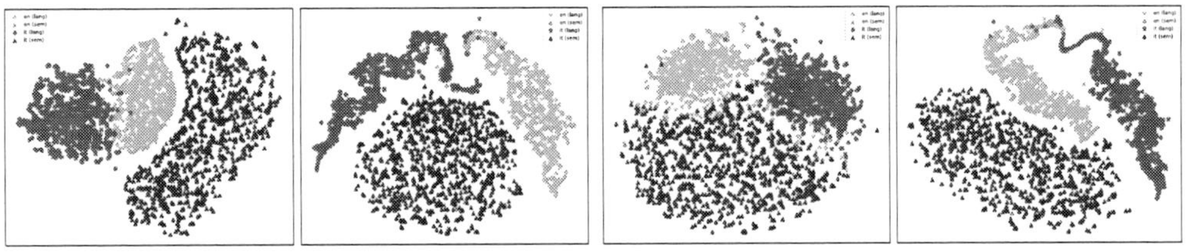

(a) DREAM (b) DREAM + ORACLE (c) MEAT (d) MEAT + ORACLE

Figure 12: LaBSE sentence embeddings for English-Italian sentence pair.

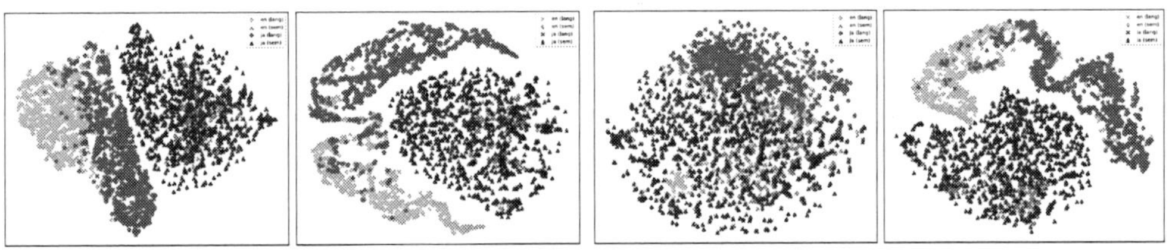

(a) DREAM (b) DREAM + ORACLE (c) MEAT (d) MEAT + ORACLE

Figure 13: LaBSE sentence embeddings for English-Japanese sentence pair.

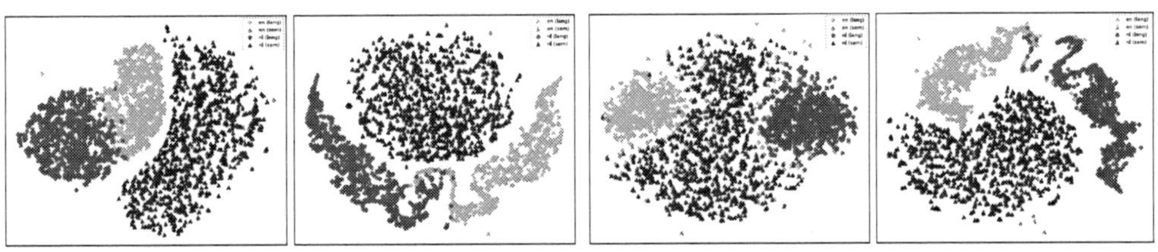

(a) DREAM (b) DREAM + ORACLE (c) MEAT (d) MEAT + ORACLE

Figure 14: LaBSE sentence embeddings for English-Dutch sentence pair.

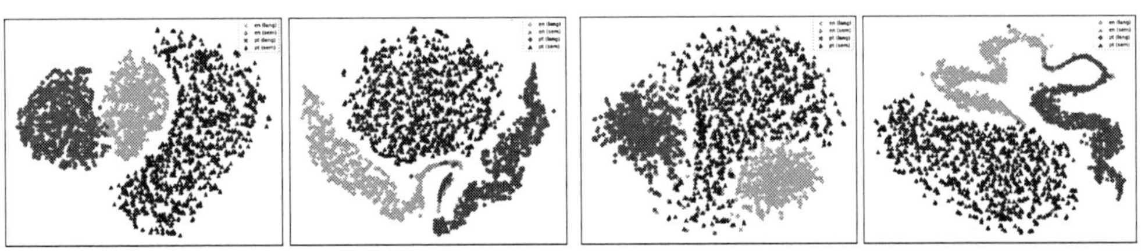

(a) DREAM (b) DREAM + ORACLE (c) MEAT (d) MEAT + ORACLE

Figure 15: LaBSE sentence embeddings for English-Portuguese sentence pair.

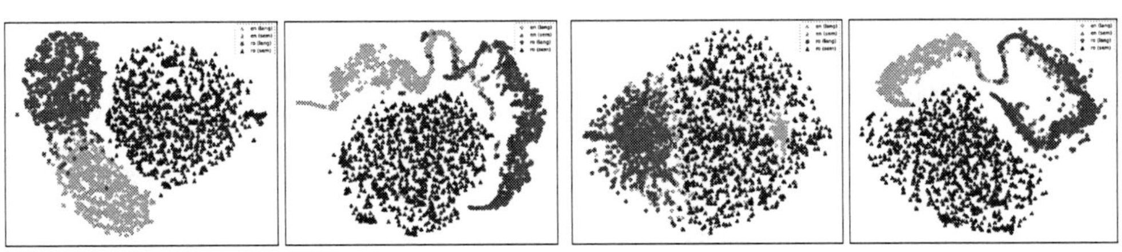

(a) DREAM (b) DREAM + ORACLE (c) MEAT (d) MEAT + ORACLE

Figure 16: LaBSE sentence embeddings for English-Romanian sentence pair.

On the Pathological Path-star Task for Language Models

Arvid Frydenlund
University of Toronto, Computer Science
Vector Institute
arvie@cs.toronto.edu

Abstract

The recently introduced path-star task is a minimal toy task designed to exemplify limitations to the abilities of language models (Bachmann and Nagarajan, 2024). It involves a *path-star* graph where multiple arms radiate from a single starting node and each node is unique. Then, given the start node and a specified target node which ends one of the arms, the task is to generate the arm containing that target node. This is straightforward for a human but surprisingly difficult for a language model, which they found failed to predict above chance. They hypothesized this is due to a deficiency in teacher-forcing and next-token prediction paradigm.

In this extended abstract, we demonstrate that the task is learnable using teacher-forcing in alternative settings and that the issue is (partially) due to representation. We analyze situations when the models fail to solve the task which leads us to introduce a regularization technique where we pack each training batch with multiple instances of the same graph but with differing target nodes to prevent overfitting. Initial results indicate this helps in solving the task.

1 Introduction

Recently, language models (LMs) have become increasingly capable of solving a variety of complex tasks (Brown et al., 2020; Zoph et al., 2022; Bubeck et al., 2023). This has led to increased interest in determining why this is and the limits to these abilities (Chen et al., 2024). Language models can do many spectacular things, which makes it all the more shocking when they fail on simple tasks. Recently, Bachmann and Nagarajan (2024) introduced one such seemingly simple task designed to showcase pathological behaviour of causal (decoder-only) autoregressive (AR) LMs trained via teacher-forcing. The task is simple by design and thus failure of AR models is both surprising and informative. We begin by describing the task in Sec. 1.1, before analyzing why it is hard for LMs in Sec. 2.

1.1 The Path-star Task

We need to describe the path-star graph, G, i.e. the data meant to be manipulated, the problem specification or question, Q, i.e. the prompt specifying the desired manipulation, and their tokenization.

Let N be the set of unique nodes forming G. A path-star graph contains one central starting node $s \in N$ and D radial arms each of length M (inclusive of s), s.t. $|N| = D(M-1)+1$. s has degree D, all final nodes which end an arm, $F \subset N$ s.t. $|F| = D$, have a single degree, and all others have a degree of 2. See Fig. 1 for an example.

Given G, and a task specification, Q, containing s and a target node $t \in F$, the task is to generate the unique arm, R_t, as a sequence of nodes starting from s until t. i.e. $R_t = \text{sort}(\{r \in N \,|\, \forall_{f \in F} \text{dist}(r, t) \leq \text{dist}(r, f)\})$.[1] Let L be the set of possible leading nodes which are adjacent to s i.e. $L = \{l \in N \,|\, \text{dist}(l, s) = 1\}$. The challenge of the task is predicting the correct leading node $l_t \in L \cap R_t$ from all other leading nodes. By design, there is a uniform $1/D$ chance of this given only G. Prediction over chance *should* be possible by inferring the correct target arm and thus l_t given t in Q. Note, as all nodes are unique, all non-leading nodes are deterministic given their preceding neighbour (closer to s).

When generating the dataset, the nodes in a single graph are uniformly sampled from a set of possible nodes, V, without replacement. G is tokenized as a series of $D(M-1)$ edges where each edge is internally ordered by distance to s and marked by special token '|' so that a given edge, (u, v), is a three token sequence 'u v |'. Q is tokenized as a sequence of four tokens with special tokens marking the beginning and end of Q as '/ s t ='. Special beginning- and end-of-sequence tokens are also used, making the final vocabulary size $|V|+5$.

[1]'dist' is graph distance. We abuse notation by treating R_t as a set and G and Q as sequences after having been tokenized.

Proceedings of the 9th Workshop on Representation Learning for NLP (RepL4NLP-2024), pages 274–284
August 15, 2024 ©2024 Association for Computational Linguistics

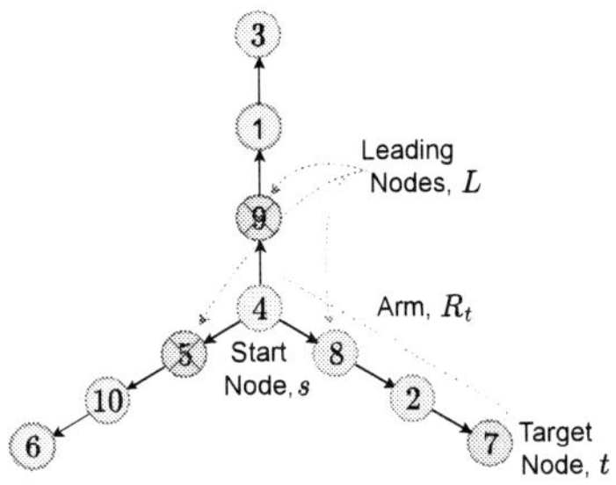

Figure 1: An example path-star graph. $D = 3$, $M = 4$, s is '4', t is '7' R_t is '4 8 2 7', and l_t is '8'. One possible tokenization of $[V, Q, R_t]$, where the arms **(and not the edges)** are permuted is: 'BOS 4 9 | 9 1 | 1 3 | 4 8 | 8 2 | 2 7 | 4 5 | 5 10 | 10 6 | / 4 7 = 4 8 2 7 EOS'.

1.2 Autoregressive models and training

A causal or decoder-only AR LM models the joint probability of a T-length sequence, y, as a factorized product of local probabilities, as in

$$p(y_1, y_2, \ldots, y_T \mid y_0,) = \prod p(y_j \mid y_{<j}). \quad (1)$$

Here, we model the path-star task as

$$p(r_1, \ldots, r_M \mid [G, Q]) = \prod_{j=1}^{M} p(r_j \mid [G, Q, r_{<j}]), \quad (2)$$

where $x = [G, Q, r_{<j}]$ is the concatenation of the tokenized graph and problem specification along with the partial ground-truth sequence, $r_{<j}$, forming the given conditioning input to the model. Such a model is trained by via maximum likelihood training, generally referred to as 'teacher-forcing' in the context of language models, as the partial ground-truth sequence is used to condition the model during training instead of the model's own predictions as done during inference (Williams and Zipser, 1989). We minimize $-\sum_{r \in R_t} \log p(\,.\mid x)$. Thus the loss is only over the target sequence R_t and not on tokens in the prefix $[G, Q]$. This is because the node ids forming G are random and Q necessarily must be provided, thus both are not predictable and can only be used to condition the model.

During inference, G and Q are provided. We consider a non-traditional 'teacher-forced' inference procedure where, instead of generating the arm autoregressively, it is conditioned on $r_{<j}$. Thus inference exactly matches the training procedure and prevents any potential training-inference bias.

We focus on transformer models (Vaswani et al., 2017), where the causal parameterization of AR models is enforced via an attention mask which prevents the token at any step j from depending on any token at step $> j$. This causal restriction applies across the entire input x. Positional embeddings make each token unique. To prevent learning a trivial answer based on position, as a data preprocessing step, **the edges in G are shuffled, which can be seen as a random permutation applied to the edge order of tokenization of G.**

1.3 Failure to learn: Clever Hans hypothesis

Bachmann and Nagarajan (2024) empirically demonstrated three different LMs – finetuned GPT2, a smaller GPT2 trained from scratch, and a state-space model, Mamaba – all fail to predict above $1/D$ chance, even in settings as small as $D = 2$ and $M = 5$ (Radford et al.; Gu and Dao, 2023). They hypothesized this was caused by teacher-forcing. The idea being that there are two possible modes of predictions which the model can learn. The first is the desired mode which learns to represent the entire path between s to t. This mode is necessary for predicting l_t. Whereas, the second mode makes trivial predictions about the next node in the arm given the previous node. This mode only needs to lean superficial information about edge structure but not graph structure and is, by design of the task, sufficient for predicting all non-leading nodes given the correct preceding node.

Bachmann and Nagarajan (2024) argued that teacher forcing will result in learning the second mode, referred to as the *Clever Hans* cheat (CHC). This is because teacher-forcing conditions on the correct ground-truth, which in this case is the correct preceding node in the arm. Also, when applied to AR models, it is restricted to making a single next-token prediction and hence precludes learning any long term planning. Then, once the CHC is learnt, it will discourage learning the desired mode necessary for predicting l_t. Their intuition, which admittedly is not proven, is that, sequence modelling relies on the intermediate training steps across the sequence to form a coherent representation of the overall sequence. In our case, that would be a representation of the entire arm structure, however, here those intermediate steps do not participate in learning such a structure but are rather absorbed into learning the trivial CHC, resulting in a loss of this intermediate training signal.

They presented empirical evidence for the CHC hypothesis by considering the overall sequence accuracy when provided with the correct preceding predictions (i.e. teacher-forced generation). Here, all non-leading tokens are learnt with 100% accuracy and the leading token is only predicted at $1/D$ chance, leading to an overall sequence accuracy of $1/D$ (See their Fig. 3 and our Fig. 3).

Interestingly, a trivial solution to the task exists if the model can look-ahead M tokens to the end of the arm as the model just needs to find and match the correct target token. Once done, it can apply the CHC in reverse order to determine the arm. This led them to provide two additional supporting empirical arguments as to why they believe the issue stems from teacher-forcing. First, they modified the task to require that the arm be generated in reverse order. This makes task trivial as the CHC can just be applied in reverse order via supervision.

Second, they introduced a 'teacher-less' model (Monea et al., 2023). This works by using M masked tokens, m, to make make all M predictions in independently of the ground-truths i.e. $x = [G, Q, m_1, \ldots, m_M]$. This completely removes teacher-forcing as it removes all dependencies between target-tokens during prediction. Of the 15 reported experiments, this method allows the model to solve the task in 5 instances: for the $D = 2$ experiment using the small GPT2, and for $D \in \{2, 3, 4\}$ (but not $D = 5$) when using large GPT2. Thus this method did not work consistently.

Importantly, they establish that, 1), the failure is not due to the amount of training data, 2), that the failure is in-distribution, and 3), that it is not due to any exposure bias or other differences between the training and inference procedures (Bengio et al., 2015; Ranzato et al., 2016; Arora et al., 2022). This allows them to disclude these alternative explanations and conclude that the CHC causes the learning problem which is itself a consequence of teacher-forcing and next-token prediction. **This leads to a discussion concerning possible fundamental limitations to the next-token prediction paradigm, with the path-star task being offered as a counter example to the paradigm being sufficient to learn any task**.

2 Methods and Results

We solely focus on the small LM setting under the belief that such models should be able to learn such a simple task and that the biases from the pretrained data and any emergent abilities of LLMs will just obfuscate the root problem. We implement our models using Fairseq (Ott et al., 2019). Our AR model have 6 layers and 200 dim. embeddings. Each layer has a feed-forward dim. of 800 and 8 heads. We use Adam (Kingma and Ba, 2014) with a learning rate of 0.0005, a dropout rate of 0.1 and a weight decay of 0.01. We train with 16-bit precision and a batch size of 1024. Each model is given a maximum of 100 epochs and stop training if the validation loss drops below 0.001 (See Fig 2). Note this is smaller than both GPT2 models used by Bachmann and Nagarajan (2024) which used 36 and 12 layers with larger embeddings.

Following Bachmann and Nagarajan (2024), $|V| = 100$ and $M = 5$. Each dataset for $D \in \{2, 3, 4, 5\}$ is made up of 2,000,000 training and 20,000 test samples of randomly generated G, Q pairs without any overlap. Unlike them, we randomly permute G at every epoch instead of just once in an attempt to prevent overfitting.

We present our work as an investigation over a series of hypotheses and corresponding experiments to get at the heart of the path-star mystery. As such, we report intermediate results and describe new methodology as it becomes motivated. We try to present results in order of our findings, however, we need to give some post-hoc explanations for our methodology in order for the reader to understand the contents of Tables (1, 2, 3, 4). First, in our initial experimentation (using $D = 2$), we found that the models would be able to solve the task seemingly at random (under modified task conditions). This motivated the use of running multiple trials for each experiment under different random seeds. For all listed experiments we consider the percent of trials that correctly succeed in learning the task across 11 trials. Second, we found it was necessary to set attention dropout to zero, which makes sense given the task requires routing node information across positions. Third, we also found that we required learned positional embeddings instead of sinusoidal embeddings. We suspect that the later results in too strong of a positional bias when randomly permuting the edges in G. As an aside, we also found that for the decoder-only model, not using any positional embeddings could also work. This is because positional information will arise out of the asymmetry induced by the causal masking.

2.1 A reproduction of empirical results

As the results of Bachmann and Nagarajan (2024) are surprising, we independently verify them as an initial step. Experiment (exp.) 1 of Table 1, confirms that the task is not learnable under the initial conditions. Exp. 2 confirms that reversing

ID	Perm.	Q	Tgt./Dir.	C.	$D=2$		$D=3$		$D=4$		$D=5$	
1	Edge	End	Fwd.	0	0%	0%	0%	0%	0%	0%	0%	0%
2	Edge	End	Rev.	0	100%		100%		100%		100%	
3	Edge	End	l_t-only	0	0%	0%	0%	0%	0%	0%	0%	0%
4	Arm	End	Fwd.	0	100%		36%	0%	9%	0%	9%	0%
5	Arm	Start	Fwd.	0	100%		100%		100%		100%	
6	Edge	Start	Fwd.	0	0%	0%	0%	0%	0%	0%	0%	0%
7	Arm	End	Fwd.	1	100%		91%	9%	91%	9%	36%	55%

Table 1: Percent of successful trials (n=11) using the AR (decoder-only) model. 'ID' is the experiment ID. 'Perm.' is the type of random permutation applied to G (Sec. 2.2.2). 'Q' is the relative position of Q to G when tokenizing (Sec. 2.2.3). 'Tgt./Dir.' is the type of target we are trying to generate (Sec. 2.2.1). And 'C.' is the number of contrastive samples used (Sec. 2.4). For each experiment in $D \in \{2, 3, 4, 5\}$, we report the percent of the 11 trials which succeeded in learning the task to at least a threshold of 95% sequence accuracy (which meant 100% for the AR models) in the first column. In the second column, we report the percent of unsuccessful trials where the valid and training loss has *not* diverged i.e. 0% means all trials have overfit

the arm results in a trivial 100% success rate.

2.2 Simplifying the task

Having confirmed the results in the original task setting, our method to investigate the issue will be to simplify the task until it becomes consistently solvable. We begin by considering the target-side.

2.2.1 Evidence against the CHC hypothesis

Under one interpretation of the CHC hypothesis, l_t is indecipherable due to the model being overwhelmed by the CHC. As such, we should be able to learn a simplified version of the task where we only predict l_t directly instead of the entire arm R_t. Exp. 3 of Table 1, shows this produces the same negative result as when predicting the entire arm.

The more charitable interpretation of the CHC hypothesis is that the core issue concerns the fact that the CHC removes necessary intermediate training signal for learning the task. Under this interpretation, we have not disproved the core hypothesis, but have shown that the entire CHC aspect is irrelevant to the underlying issue. That is, if lack of intermediate supervision is the core issue, we should just explicitly remove it from the task description and cut out the red-herring of the CHC.

However, we do not believe that lack of intermediate supervision is the real issue and take this result as a sign that something else is at play. To solve this task, all the model needs to do is 1) determine the final node, 2) trace back each arm from the final node to its leading node, and 3) predict that leading node. Importantly, this requires that we can correctly represent the arms in the graph. This motivates us to experiment with simplifying the source-side of the task instead of the target-side.

2.2.2 Alternative hypothesis: representation issues due to the permutation of G

Our first hypothesis as to what is preventing learning the solution is that it is a representation issue due to randomly permuting the edges of G. This will corrupt the arm structure with the model seemingly unable to recover the structure. In particular, when using a causal model, all information can only be routed forward in 'time' and this may induce difficulties when trying to recover and route information across the arm structure. Not only does permutation make routing information across the arms harder, or even impossible, but the difficulty in learning might also be due to the assumptions we make when we decompose the joint probability as in Eq. 1. Specifically, we are parameterizing the model to a specific decomposition (Yang et al., 2019; Liao et al., 2020). However, by permuting the arms, we are forcing the model to learn an exponential number of possible decompositions. This may be a challenge, even when using an overparameterized model like a transformer and may explain the difficulty of the task.

Thus we can simplify the task where we retain the arm structure by only permuting the order of the arms relative to each other (but not the internal order of the edges). Refer to this change as *Edge*- v.s. *Arm*-wise permutation. If this is solvable, then we know that the issue lies in the corruption of the arm information via permuting the edges. Exp. 4 of Table 1 shows this improves the results, with $D = 2$ being consistently solved, but with a diminishing success-rate as D increases. These partial improvements lead us to a related hypothesis.

2.2.3 Alternative hypothesis: representation issues due to the order of G and Q

If we can only route information into the future, maybe our representation issue stems from that fact that we have placed the problem specification after the graph during tokenanization. That is, we have placed the information needed to specify what to do with the data after the actual data. This means that the latent representation of G formed by the LM can not depend on Q. Thus instead we form our input as $x = [Q, G, r_{<j}]$. Refer to this as Q's position being either *Start* v.s *End*. Exp. 5 of Table 1 demonstrates that this consistently solves the task when combined with permuting the arms only, but goes back to being completely unsolved when combined with permuting the edges (Exp. 6). While this shows that the task is solvable, it is unsatisfying as we require stronger supervisory information in this setting. This also begs the question as to why placing Q after G is at times solvable, even if we understand why it makes the task harder.

As the causal constraint of decoder-only models potentially induces these issues, we are motivated to change the model specification to see if abandoning this constraint will solve the task.

2.3 Changing the model parameterization

2.3.1 Encoder-decoder model, or, alternative hypothesis: it's the causal constraint

Here we use encoder-decoder model with a 6-layer encoder with a 3-layer decoder with tied embeddings. Removing the causal constraint on the source-side encoding of $[G, Q]$ makes the relative position of Q to G irrelevant. If this model can consistently solve the task, it will demonstrate that the underlying issue is that the causal constraint prevents the decoder-only model from recovering the arm structure with edge-wise permutation.

Exp. 9 in Table 2 demonstrates that using a non-causal encoder representation does not solve the problem with edge-wise permutation. This motivates us to revisit the 'teacher-less' methodology as it has been shown to partially work and is an alternative non-causal methodology.

2.3.2 Non-autoregressive models

Bachmann and Nagarajan (2024) reported that 'teacher-less' models where unable to solve the task in the small LM setting. Here we attempt to improve their results. We begin by modify their their 'teacher-less' model as it was designed to modify an LM post-hoc, which is not applicable here (Monea et al., 2023). Instead, note this is actually just a kind of non-autoregressive model (NAR) (Gu et al., 2018; Wang et al., 2018; Gu and Kong, 2021).

NAR models treat all targets as independent in order to make multiple predictions in parallel instead of sequentially. This is achieved by removing the causal constraint i.e. attention mask. In the case of (fully) NAR models, full independence is assumed. However, this can lead a poor model as it limits the ability to learn from dependencies inherent in the sequence (Lee et al., 2018; Qian et al., 2021). This lead to the development of iterative autoregressive models (IAR)[2] which assume partial dependencies, both during training and inference – except in the first generation step (Lee et al., 2018; Ghazvininejad et al., 2019). Importantly, IAR models assume no order-of-generation. This allows for the model to potentially learn the reverse order solution without supervision.

To train an IAR model, an order-permutation of the sequence is sampled, along with a time-step, j such that model conditions on the permuted or 'unmasked' ground-truths prior to step j. This is equivalent to the MLM objective with a dynamically sampled masking rate, where the the uniform masking is acting as the permutation (Devlin et al., 2019; Lee et al., 2018; Ghazvininejad et al., 2019). Thus use teacher-forcing, but it is just applied to a permuted sequence order. We use CMLM (Ghazvininejad et al., 2019) for an encoder-decoder IAR model and an encoder-only model using the same hyper-parameters as the decoder-only model (i.e same model but without causal masking).

We evaluated these models both in the NAR and IAR generation setting using either 1 or M iterative steps (results not reported). Both settings produced the same results. That is, once, the model learnt the solution, it could generate the entire arm in one step just as well as over M steps. In principle, the IAR models should be able to first generate t in the last position, condition on it, and then just generate the arm in reverse order via CHC – which should be much easier than learning the true solution. This did not happen. **It should be disconcerting for practitioners of IAR models that the trivial generation order does not seem to be found.**

We demonstrate that small IAR models are capable of learning the task in Tables 3 and 4. Exp. 11 and 14 may indicate that IAR models are not as performative on the task, however, this is not true

[2] Often called iterative NAR models, which is a misnomer.

ID	Perm.	Dir.	Ctra.	$D = 2$	$D = 3$	$D = 4$	$D = 5$
8	Arm	Fwd.	0	100%	100%	100%	100%
9	Edge	Fwd.	0	0% 0%	0% 0%	0% 0%	0% 0%
10	Arm	Fwd.	1	100%	100%	100%	100%

Table 2: Results using the encoder-decoder AR model. Q pos. is 'End'.

ID	Perm.	Train	Dir.	Ctra.	$D = 2$	$D = 3$	$D = 4$	$D = 5$
11	Arm	IAR	Fwd.	0	100%	100%	82% 0%	82% 0%
12	Edge	IAR	Fwd.	0	0% 0%	0% 0%	0% 0%	0% 0%
13	Arm	IAR	Fwd.	1	100%	100%	100%	100%

Table 3: Results using the CMLM (encoder-encoder) IAR model with IAR training (teacher-forcing).

once contrastive samples are used (Sec 2.4).

2.4 Contrastive samples

Our observations of the failures of the above models lead us to conclude that, in the instances where the model failed to solve the task, the model would overfit. See the top graph of Fig 2 with $D = 2$. Here all trials end up successfully learning the task, which can be seen when the validation accuracy branches off from chance. However, the last example nearly overfits. In the third graph, we see the same experimental setting but with $D = 4$. Here only a single trial succeeded and the rest maintained a stagnant validation accuracy at chance while the training and validation losses diverge.

To prevent this, we experimented with standard methods to combat overfitting such as lowering learning rate, increasing batch size or L2 regularization, etc. without success. This lead to developing an alternative method where we supplement the training data with multiple instances of G but with different target nodes, and hence, different Q and target arms to be generated. This was achieved via expanding each batch with one or more of these *contrastive samples* per original G. These extra instances should act as interference on any spurious training signal. Note, apart from sampling, these are treated as independent and are not part of a contrastive loss. This can be viewed as extra supervisory information applied at the batch-level.

Results of exp. 7, 13, and 16 show that this prevents overfitting and leads to improved success rate across models. The arm-wise decoder-only exp. 7 shows improved rates at $D \in \{4, 5\}$. This can be seen in the first and third plots in Fig 2 in contrast to their corresponding second and forth plots where we see the validation loss tracks the training loss instead of diverging when provided with contrastive samples. This lead to learning the solutions in less epochs in the $D = 2$ case and lead to 10/11 instead of 1/11 of the trials succeeding in the $D = 4$ case.

3 Limitations and Future work

The major limitation to this extended abstract is that the experiments with contrastive samples are in progress. We included partial and preliminary results of this method in order to show the future direction of this work. Despite this, we have already demonstrated a number of interesting findings: 1) We independently reproduced the empirical results of Bachmann and Nagarajan (2024). 2) We show that the CHC is a red-herring, if the problem is due to loss of intermediate training signal. 3) We show that retaining the arm structure leads to improved results and that combining this with a better ordering of Q and G makes the task solvable. We take this as strong evidence that poor representation is a key factor in why the task is difficult. 4) We show that NAR/IAR models can successfully solve the task in limited settings, and describe a surprising failing to these models. Finally, 5), we show that overfitting is a key issue and provide initial positive results in tackling this.

We set out the hypothesis that trials where the training and validation losses do not diverge will succeed given sufficient training time. However, that has yet to be shown. It is an open question if contrastive samples will always lead to finding the solution given sufficient time or if this scales with D and M. More importantly, it is an open question as to why the models prefer to overfit instead of finding the correct solution. On lead we have is that the task hinges on a single token which determines the necessary latent representation of G, and this seems to have large consequences on the behaviour

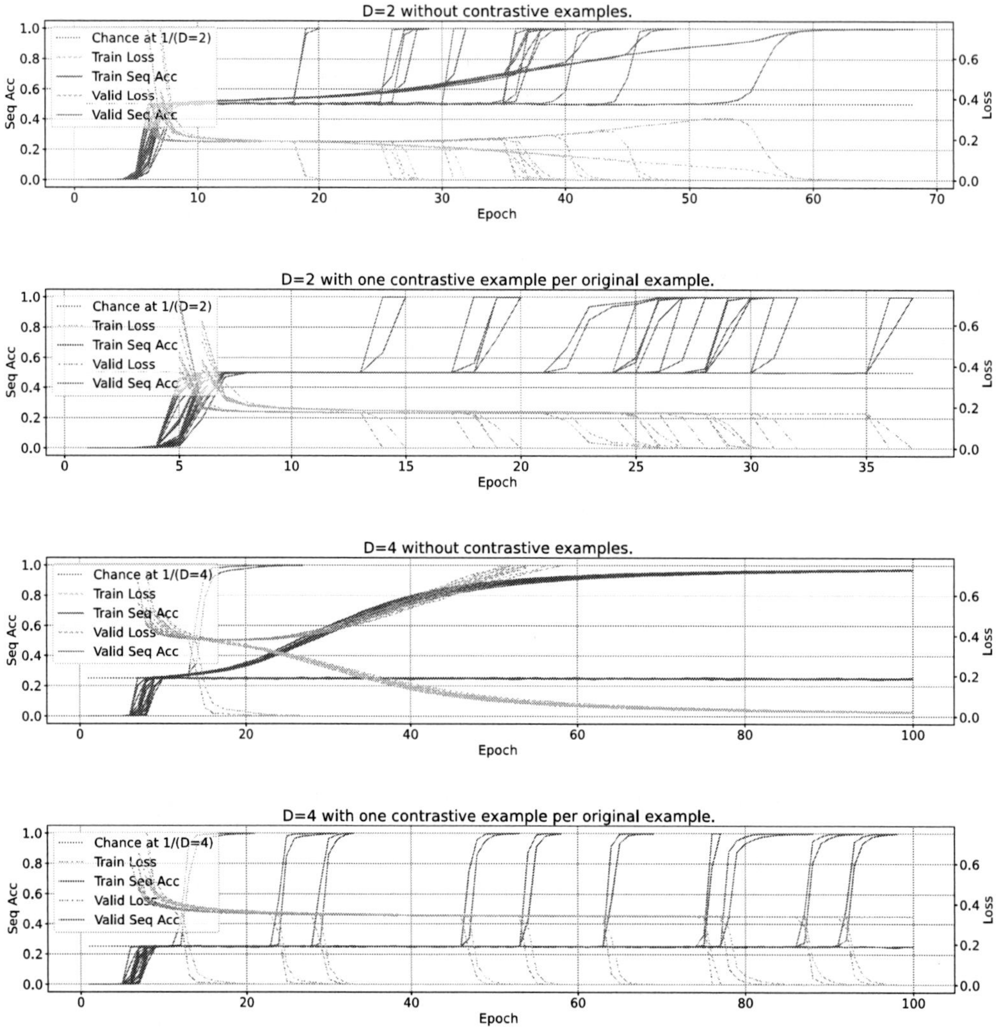

Figure 2: Plots 1 and 3 visualize the training of the experiments of row/exp. 4 in Table 1 where $D = 2$ and $D = 4$ respectively. Plots 2 and 4 visualize the corresponding experiments in row/exp. 7 when constrictive exampled are employed. Each plot shows the loss and sequence accuracy across all 11 trials of the given experiment for both the training and validation partitions. When a trial succeeds in finding the desired solution, the sequence accuracy spikes to 100% and the validation loss drops to near-zero. The loss is cutoff at 0.75 for visibility.

In plot 1, all trials succeed, however, when D is increased to 4, only 1/11 trials succeed as shown in plot 3. Here we see that the training and validation losses diverge shortly after epoch 20, resulting in overfitting. In plot 4, the use of contrastive samples prevents this divergence, leading to 10/11 trials succeeding, with the remaining trial not finding the solution within the 100 epoch limit.

ID	Perm.	Train	Dir.	Ctra.	$D=2$	$D=3$	$D=4$	$D=5$
14	Arm	IAR	Fwd.	0	100%	82% 0%	36% 0%	9% 0%
15	Edge	IAR	Fwd.	0	36% 0%	0% 0%	0% 0%	0% 0%
16	Arm	IAR	Fwd.	1	100%	100%	100%	91% 9%

Table 4: Results using the encoder-only IAR model.

of the learning algorithm and the difficulty of learning a correct solution. This indicates that the issue may stem from the sensitivity of the task to the target token (Hahn et al., 2021; Chen et al., 2023; Chakraborty et al., 2023; Bhattamishra et al., 2023; Hahn and Rofin, 2024).

A large and important part of the scientific process is testing hypotheses and putting forth counter arguments. If, as we believe, the CHC hypothesis is incorrect, then the broader discussion of Bachmann and Nagarajan (2024) concerning limitations of next-token prediction is not be supported by their findings. This is the main contribution of this work, even if, we do not have a full solution or replacement hypothesis. Even if the CHC hypothesis is wrong, the path-star task is still a seemingly trivial but deceptively difficult problem, making it worthy of study. In addition to questioning the CHC hypothesis, we make headway into the mystery of the path-start task by demonstrating multiple simplifications or alternatives of the task which make it (more) solvable. Finally, we introduce a contrastive method which has early indications of helping to solve the task, however, open questions remain as to why this method works and why it is necessary in the first place.

3.1 Post-submission findings

Between submission and acceptance, new findings have come to light, which we summarize here.

1) Constrastive samples are necessary but not sufficient to solve the task consistently. We find that, as each example is randomly sampled, there will be $|V|^{D(M-1)+1} \times D$ possible graph-target pairs to sample from. Thus it is easy to see why the models would overfit as they can learn to make many possible spurious correlations between any unique node or combination of nodes in the source-side and the targets. Contrastive samples will alleviate these spurious correlations by indicating that the targets depend on a single token only. Above, we wondered if contrastive samples will always lead to finding the solution given sufficient time. We found this is not true. However, we also conduct an analysis of the task using RASP (described below), which lead to a counter-intuitive result that, even though overfitting is an issue, we need to increase the size of the models to solve the task.

2) The RASP programming language is a formal computation model used to verify if a transformer is capable of solving a given symbolic (non-numerical) task where the existence of a valid RASP program proves there exists at least one transformer which can (Weiss et al., 2021; Zhou et al., 2024). We conduct a RASP analysis which lead us to find to many new insights to the task. We can formally prove, via the existence of RASP programs, that the task is solvable via transformers both using non-causal and causal models. Due to the graph structure, we find that the simplest RASP programs which solve the task with edge-wise permutation require $\mathcal{O}(M)$ number of layers in order to route information about leading nodes to final nodes (or vise versa). We show a $\mathcal{O}(\log M)$ algorithm exists, but conjecture than no $\mathcal{O}(1)$ exists. This would mean that the task will not be generalizable to higher values of M. However, the problem is easily solvable with a $\mathcal{O}(1)$ algorithm when using arm-wise permutation, which explains why the task is solvable under the simpler conditions demonstrated above. We also find that using a causal decoder makes the task harder as it can only route information into the future, which requires different rules depending on if the connecting edge is before or after a current edge when routing.

3) Given the RASP analysis we increased the number of layers of each model. This lead to worse in overfitting in all models, except the encoder-only model, which then is able to consistently solve the task. Both this model and the CMLM (enocder-encoder) model employ the IAR training method. The fact that it is just the encoder-only model which works indicates that the reason why it works is not due to the training method. It is an open mystery why it is only this model which can consistently solve the task.

Please look for an updated pre-print (available soon) or contact arvie@cs.toronto.edu.

Acknowledgments

We thank our reviewers as well as Siavash Kazemian, Gagandeep Singh, and Shunan Zhao for their insightful feedback.

Resources used in preparing this research were provided, in part, by the Province of Ontario, the Government of Canada through CIFAR, and companies sponsoring the Vector Institute

References

Kushal Arora, Layla El Asri, Hareesh Bahuleyan, and Jackie Cheung. 2022. Why exposure bias matters: An imitation learning perspective of error accumulation in language generation. In *Findings of the Association for Computational Linguistics: ACL 2022*, pages 700–710, Dublin, Ireland. Association for Computational Linguistics.

Gregor Bachmann and Vaishnavh Nagarajan. 2024. The pitfalls of next-token prediction. In *ICLR 2024 Workshop: How Far Are We From AGI*.

Samy Bengio, Oriol Vinyals, Navdeep Jaitly, and Noam Shazeer. 2015. Scheduled sampling for sequence prediction with recurrent neural networks. *Advances in neural information processing systems*, 28.

Satwik Bhattamishra, Arkil Patel, Varun Kanade, and Phil Blunsom. 2023. Simplicity bias in transformers and their ability to learn sparse Boolean functions. In *Proceedings of the 61st Annual Meeting of the Association for Computational Linguistics (Volume 1: Long Papers)*, pages 5767–5791, Toronto, Canada. Association for Computational Linguistics.

Tom Brown, Benjamin Mann, Nick Ryder, Melanie Subbiah, Jared D Kaplan, Prafulla Dhariwal, Arvind Neelakantan, Pranav Shyam, Girish Sastry, Amanda Askell, Sandhini Agarwal, Ariel Herbert-Voss, Gretchen Krueger, Tom Henighan, Rewon Child, Aditya Ramesh, Daniel Ziegler, Jeffrey Wu, Clemens Winter, Chris Hesse, Mark Chen, Eric Sigler, Mateusz Litwin, Scott Gray, Benjamin Chess, Jack Clark, Christopher Berner, Sam McCandlish, Alec Radford, Ilya Sutskever, and Dario Amodei. 2020. Language models are few-shot learners. In *Advances in Neural Information Processing Systems*, volume 33, pages 1877–1901. Curran Associates, Inc.

Sébastien Bubeck, Varun Chandrasekaran, Ronen Eldan, Johannes Gehrke, Eric Horvitz, Ece Kamar, Peter Lee, Yin Tat Lee, Yuanzhi Li, Scott Lundberg, et al. 2023. Sparks of artificial general intelligence: Early experiments with gpt-4. *arXiv preprint arXiv:2303.12712*.

Mohna Chakraborty, Adithya Kulkarni, and Qi Li. 2023. Zero-shot approach to overcome perturbation sensitivity of prompts. In *Proceedings of the 61st Annual Meeting of the Association for Computational Linguistics (Volume 1: Long Papers)*, pages 5698–5711, Toronto, Canada. Association for Computational Linguistics.

Xinyun Chen, Ryan A Chi, Xuezhi Wang, and Denny Zhou. 2024. Premise order matters in reasoning with large language models. *arXiv preprint arXiv:2402.08939*.

Yanda Chen, Chen Zhao, Zhou Yu, Kathleen McKeown, and He He. 2023. On the relation between sensitivity and accuracy in in-context learning. In *Findings of the Association for Computational Linguistics: EMNLP 2023*, pages 155–167, Singapore. Association for Computational Linguistics.

Jacob Devlin, Ming-Wei Chang, Kenton Lee, and Kristina Toutanova. 2019. BERT: Pre-training of deep bidirectional transformers for language understanding. In *Proceedings of the 2019 Conference of the North American Chapter of the Association for Computational Linguistics: Human Language Technologies, Volume 1 (Long and Short Papers)*, pages 4171–4186, Minneapolis, Minnesota. Association for Computational Linguistics.

Marjan Ghazvininejad, Omer Levy, Yinhan Liu, and Luke Zettlemoyer. 2019. Mask-predict: Parallel decoding of conditional masked language models. In *Proceedings of the 2019 Conference on Empirical Methods in Natural Language Processing and the 9th International Joint Conference on Natural Language Processing (EMNLP-IJCNLP)*, pages 6112–6121, Hong Kong, China. Association for Computational Linguistics.

Albert Gu and Tri Dao. 2023. Mamba: Linear-time sequence modeling with selective state spaces. *arXiv preprint arXiv:2312.00752*.

Jiatao Gu, James Bradbury, Caiming Xiong, Victor OK Li, and Richard Socher. 2018. Non-autoregressive neural machine translation. In *International Conference on Learning Representations*.

Jiatao Gu and Xiang Kong. 2021. Fully non-autoregressive neural machine translation: Tricks of the trade. In *Findings of the Association for Computational Linguistics: ACL-IJCNLP 2021*, pages 120–133, Online. Association for Computational Linguistics.

Michael Hahn, Dan Jurafsky, and Richard Futrell. 2021. Sensitivity as a complexity measure for sequence classification tasks. *Transactions of the Association for Computational Linguistics*, 9:891–908.

Michael Hahn and Mark Rofin. 2024. Why are sensitive functions hard for transformers? *ACL*.

Diederik P Kingma and Jimmy Ba. 2014. Adam: A method for stochastic optimization. *arXiv preprint arXiv:1412.6980*.

Jason Lee, Elman Mansimov, and Kyunghyun Cho. 2018. Deterministic non-autoregressive neural sequence modeling by iterative refinement. In *Proceedings of the 2018 Conference on Empirical Methods in Natural Language Processing*, pages 1173–1182, Brussels, Belgium. Association for Computational Linguistics.

Yi Liao, Xin Jiang, and Qun Liu. 2020. Probabilistically masked language model capable of autoregressive generation in arbitrary word order. In *Proceedings of the 58th Annual Meeting of the Association for Computational Linguistics*, pages 263–274, Online. Association for Computational Linguistics.

Giovanni Monea, Armand Joulin, and Edouard Grave. 2023. Pass: Parallel speculative sampling. *arXiv preprint arXiv:2311.13581*.

Myle Ott, Sergey Edunov, Alexei Baevski, Angela Fan, Sam Gross, Nathan Ng, David Grangier, and Michael Auli. 2019. fairseq: A fast, extensible toolkit for sequence modeling. *arXiv preprint arXiv:1904.01038*.

Lihua Qian, Hao Zhou, Yu Bao, Mingxuan Wang, Lin Qiu, Weinan Zhang, Yong Yu, and Lei Li. 2021. Glancing transformer for non-autoregressive neural machine translation. In *Proceedings of the 59th Annual Meeting of the Association for Computational Linguistics and the 11th International Joint Conference on Natural Language Processing (Volume 1: Long Papers)*, pages 1993–2003, Online. Association for Computational Linguistics.

Alec Radford, Jeffrey Wu, Rewon Child, David Luan, Dario Amodei, Ilya Sutskever, et al. Language models are unsupervised multitask learners.

Marc'Aurelio Ranzato, Sumit Chopra, Michael Auli, and Wojciech Zaremba. 2016. Sequence level training with recurrent neural networks. In *4th International Conference on Learning Representations, ICLR 2016*.

Ashish Vaswani, Noam Shazeer, Niki Parmar, Jakob Uszkoreit, Llion Jones, Aidan N Gomez, Łukasz Kaiser, and Illia Polosukhin. 2017. Attention is all you need. *Advances in neural information processing systems*, 30.

Chunqi Wang, Ji Zhang, and Haiqing Chen. 2018. Semi-autoregressive neural machine translation. In *Proceedings of the 2018 Conference on Empirical Methods in Natural Language Processing*, pages 479–488, Brussels, Belgium. Association for Computational Linguistics.

Gail Weiss, Yoav Goldberg, and Eran Yahav. 2021. Thinking like transformers. In *International Conference on Machine Learning*, pages 11080–11090. PMLR.

Ronald J Williams and David Zipser. 1989. A learning algorithm for continually running fully recurrent neural networks. *Neural computation*, 1(2):270–280.

Zhilin Yang, Zihang Dai, Yiming Yang, Jaime Carbonell, Russ R Salakhutdinov, and Quoc V Le. 2019. Xlnet: Generalized autoregressive pretraining for language understanding. *Advances in neural information processing systems*, 32.

Hattie Zhou, Arwen Bradley, Etai Littwin, Noam Razin, Omid Saremi, Joshua M. Susskind, Samy Bengio, and Preetum Nakkiran. 2024. What algorithms can transformers learn? a study in length generalization. In *The Twelfth International Conference on Learning Representations*.

Barret Zoph, Colin Raffel, Dale Schuurmans, Dani Yogatama, Denny Zhou, Don Metzler, Ed H. Chi, Jason Wei, Jeff Dean, Liam B. Fedus, Maarten Paul Bosma, Oriol Vinyals, Percy Liang, Sebastian Borgeaud, Tatsunori B. Hashimoto, and Yi Tay. 2022. Emergent abilities of large language models. *TMLR*.

A The Clever Hans Phenomenon

In Fig 3 we show how the CHC appears during training. Here we see that the first token to fit to 100% accuracy is the given start node, s. The next token is the given target node, t. While this might seem strange as it is generated at the end of the sequence, this token is actually easily predicable since the model can infer that the target token should always be placed in the Mth position. This is because there is no requirement that predictions be generalizable to different arm lengths and hence the target token is always in the Mth position. This is explicitly done to maintain that the test data is in-domain with the training data. Next we see that all other non-leading nodes fit via the CHC. As no trials succeeded in this experiment, the validation accuracy of the leading token becomes stagnant at chance, while the training accuracy improves.

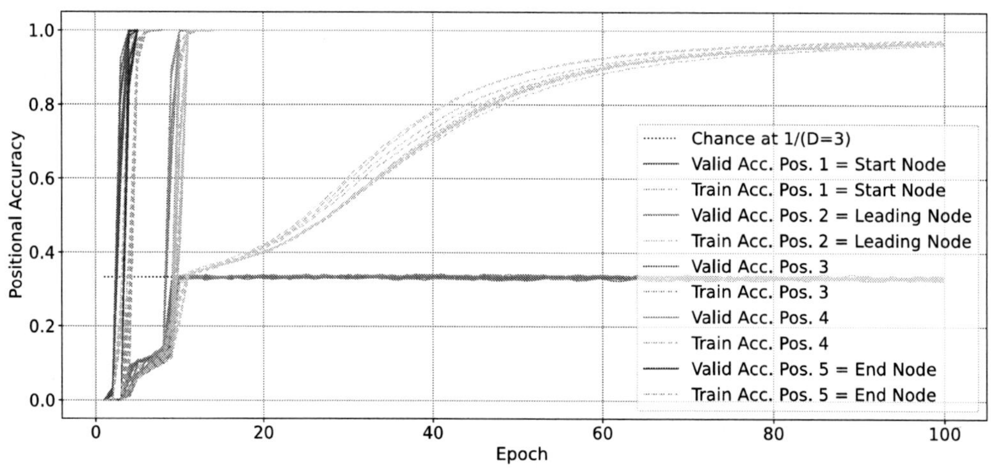

Figure 3: The appearance of the Clever Hans cheat over training. Data corresponds to row/exp. 1 of Table 1, where D=3, $M = 5$.

Whitening Not Recommended for Classification Tasks in LLMs

Ali Forooghi
School of computer science
University of Windsor
ON, Canada
foroogh@uwindsor.ca

Shaghayegh Sadeghi
School of computer science
University of Windsor
ON, Canada
sadeghi3@uwindsor.ca

Jianguo Lu
School of computer science
University of Windsor
ON, Canada
jlu@uwindsor.ca

Abstract

Sentence embedding is a cornerstone in NLP. Whitening has been claimed to be an effective operation to improve embedding quality obtained from Large Language Models (LLMs). However, we find that the efficacy of whitening is model-dependent and task-dependent. In particular, whitening degenerates embeddings for classification tasks. The conclusion is supported by extensive experiments. A by-product of our research is embedding evaluation platform for LLMs called SentEval+ [1]

1 Introduction

Sentence embedding plays a fundamental role in NLP (Le and Mikolov, 2014). Despite the widespread success of Large Language Models (LLMs) in generative tasks, embeddings obtained from pre-trained models are not impressive (Li and Li, 2023). Sometimes, they are not even competitive with traditional word2vec-based approaches on machine learning tasks such as classification and Semantic Text Similarity (STS). Consequently, there has been a flurry of research aimed at improving the quality of embeddings from pre-trained models (Gao et al., 2021; Jiang et al., 2022; Li and Li, 2023).

Among this group of work, whitening has been shown to be an effective post-processing method for improving embeddings obtained from LLMs (Zhuo et al., 2023; Su et al., 2021; Huang et al., 2021). We find that the efficacy of whitening is both model-dependent and task-dependent. Although we reproduced the result that whitening does work for some models on STS tasks, it does not work for other models. More importantly, the effectiveness of the whitening operation is restricted to STS tasks. For classification tasks, whitening degrades embedding quality consistently and sometimes with a large margin. The result is supported consistently for all the evaluated models and all the datasets in SentEval (Conneau and Kiela, 2018). To further consolidate the surprising results, we explored a variety of whitening operations, including Principal Component Analysis (PCA) (Friedman, 1987), Cholesky matrix decomposition (Siarohin et al., 2018), and Zero-Phase Component Analysis (ZCA) (Bell and Sejnowski, 1997). Although some variants of whitening induce different performances, the overall conclusion remains unchanged.

A by-product of our research is an embedding evaluation platform for LLMs, which we call SentEval$^+$, to streamline the evaluation of embedding quality. LLMs are big and costly to run. SentEval (Conneau and Kiela, 2018) provides a platform for embedding evaluation on a variety of models, tasks, and datasets. It works well on smaller models such as BERT. To facilitate the evaluation of LLMs on commodity machines, we provide the embeddings for all sentences in our evaluation datasets.

There is not much detailed comparison of the performance of embeddings from OpenAI, maybe partially due to the cost for API calls. We observe that embeddings from OpenAI are on par with LLaMA overall. Another interesting observation is that LLaMA and LLaMA2 are very close in terms of embedding performance.

Our work is important for both practitioners and researchers in LLMs. For LLM providers such as openAI, various post-processing are commonly applied to the embeddings they serve. They may want to serve different types of embeddings for different tasks, with the understanding of our result. For researchers in the area, running on a variety of LLMs is prohibitive computationally. Our SentEval$^+$ makes experiments feasible on commodity machines.

[1] Here is the link to the Github for SentEval+

Proceedings of the 9th Workshop on Representation Learning for NLP (RepL4NLP-2024), pages 285–289
August 15, 2024

2 Whitening Transformations

LLM embeddings have the isotropy problem (Timkey and van Schijndel, 2021; Kovaleva et al., 2021; Rudman et al., 2022). Whitening is a post-processing technique that converts spatially correlated, anisotropic feature representations into uncorrelated, isotropic ones (Sasaki et al., 2023; Rudman and Eickhoff, 2024). For this purpose, whitening transforms the feature representations such that the mean is centred at the origin, covariances are eliminated, and the variance is normalized to an identity matrix.

Given N number of sentence embeddings $x_1, x_2, \ldots, x_N$. Let $X = (x_1, x_2, \ldots, x_N)^T \in \mathbb{R}^{N\times d}$, where d is the dimension of the embeddings. The covariance matrix for X is $\Sigma = (X-\mu)(X-\mu)^T$, where μ is the mean of $\{x_i\}_{i=1}^N$. Whitening transformation is achieved using a matrix Wresulting in unit diagonal "white" covariance $var(Z) = I$:

$$Z = W(X - \mu) \tag{1}$$

$$W = \begin{cases} U\Lambda^{-\frac{1}{2}} & PCA \\ U\Lambda^{-\frac{1}{2}}U^T & ZCA \\ L^T & Chol \\ V\Theta^{-\frac{1}{2}}V^T & ZCA-Cor \\ V\Theta^{-\frac{1}{2}} & PCA-Cor \end{cases} \tag{2}$$

W in Equation 1 varies as in Equation 2. The most commonly used whitening operation is called PCA-whitening, which is also the one used in the first a few papers on the performance gain of whitening on LLMs. Since our initial result on PCA-whitening shows the opposite for classification tasks, and (Wang and Wu, 2023) reported different behaviour of ZCA-whitening, we exhaustively investigate all variations of whitening operations.

In Equation 2, Λ is the eigenvectors, and U is the eigenvalues of the covariance matrix, i.e., $\Sigma = U\Lambda U^T$. The matrix L corresponds to the Cholesky decomposition of the inverse of Σ, such that $LL^T = \Sigma^{-1}$. The matrices V and Θ result from the eigen decomposition of the correlation matrix P, expressed as $P = V\Theta^{-\frac{1}{2}}V^T$, where V is the eigenvector matrix and Θ contains the corresponding eigenvalues.

3 Experiments

We experimented with 8 models on classification and STS tasks. The embeddings are extracted from the last layer of the BERT and LLaMA models, following the practice described in (Reimers and Gurevych, 2019). We also explored other pooling strategies and observed similar pattern. Embeddings of SBert, AnglE, and SimCSE are generated using their provided frameworks. While AnglE and SimCSE typically use the CLS pooling method to extract embeddings, which involves using the output of the 'CLS' token from the model to represent the entire input sequence, SimCSE employs the mean pooling method instead. For all mentioned models, we used the original tokenizers. For generating ChatGPT embeddings, we choose the recent *text-small-3-embeddings*.

Algorithm 1 Whitening Operations

Input: Embeddings $\{x_i\}_{i=1}^N$
Output: Transformed embeddings $\{\tilde{x}_i\}_{i=1}^N$
Compute the mean μ of $\{x_i\}_{i=1}^N$
Compute the covariance matrix Σ of $\{x_i\}_{i=1}^N$
Compute the correlation matrix P of $\{x_i\}_{i=1}^N$
Let $U, \Lambda, U^T = \text{SVD}(\Sigma)$
Let $V, \Theta, V^T = \text{SVD}(P)$
Perform $LL^T = \text{Chol}(\Sigma^{-1})$
Transform $\tilde{x}_i = (x_i - \mu)W$ using Eq. 2

Next, we employ the *SentEval* setting to evaluate the embeddings. The classification setup involves using an MLP (Multi-Layer Perceptron) classifier with no hidden layers, utilizing the *RMSprop* optimizer. We also experimented with other classifiers including logistic regression, SVM, and Random Forests. Although the accuracy of the classification varies, the overall conclusion remains the same. Following the practice in SentEval, we report accuracy instead of F1 because the datasets are balanced.

3.1 Classification Task

Table 1 and subplot A of Figure 1 summarize our experiments on classification task. The surprising result is that whitening transformations lead to deteriorated performance on classification tasks for all models and all the datasets without exception. What is more surprising is the large gap before and after the whitening. The delta can be as large as -11 in LLaMA models on the MR dataset. The gap grows as the dimension increases–the models are sorted by their dimension in increasing order.

To understand the whitening behaviour, we visualize the embeddings before and after the whitening in Figure 2. We can observe that, indeed, whiten-

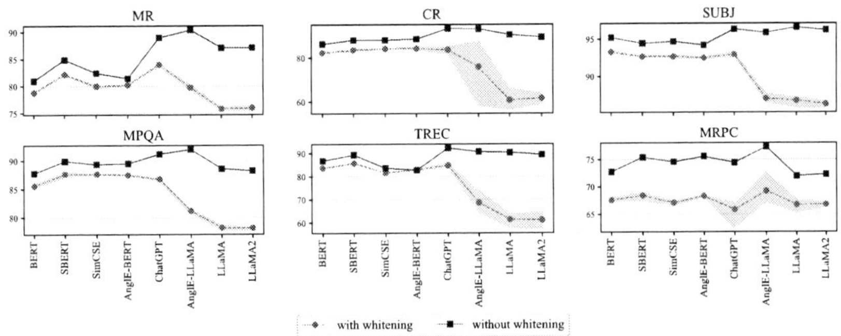

(A) Classification task. The performance is measured using accuracy per *SentEval* setting because all the data sets are balanced.

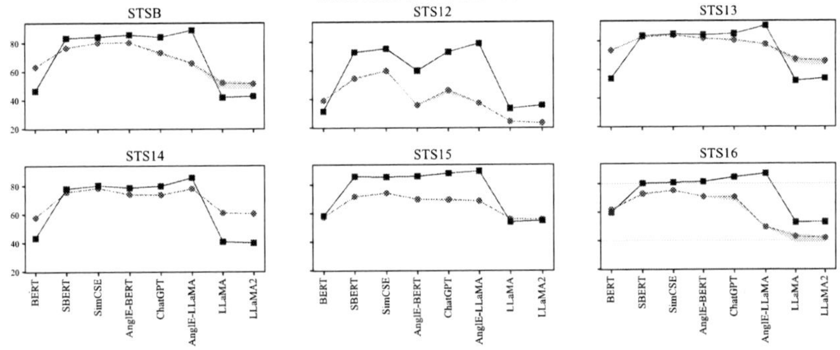

(B) STS task. The performance is measured using coefficient of Spearman's correlation, expressed as a percentage.

Figure 1: Whitening leads to a deterioration in classification tasks (subplot A), but demonstrates improvements in STS tasks on some models (subplot B). The performance is the average of five whitenings, with shaded area indicating the range.

Model	Dim.	MR	CR	SUBJ	MPQA	TREC	MRPC	SST-F	Avg
# Samples		10,664	3,777	10,002	10,608	5,956	1,513	8,544	
BERT (Devlin et al., 2019)	768	80.96	86.17	95.21	87.78	86.71	72.73	46.74	79.47
BERT$_W$		78.79	82.21	93.25	85.59	83.67	67.54	42.44	76.28
SBERT (Reimers and Gurevych, 2019)	768	84.88	87.89	94.41	89.91	89.26	75.35	50.00	81.67
SBERT$_W$		82.18	83.33	92.64	87.60	85.55	68.14	43.85	77.61
SimSCE (Gao et al., 2021)	768	82.40	87.90	94.66	89.35	83.59	74.52	48.26	80.10
SimSCE$_W$		79.96	84.04	92.66	87.63	81.44	67.16	43.67	76.65
AnglEBERT (Li and Li, 2023)	768	81.42	88.42	94.17	89.50	82.66	75.52	44.88	79.51
AnglE-BERT$_W$		80.22	84.19	92.50	87.47	82.80	68.28	43.41	76.98
ChatGPT (OpenAI, 2023)	1536	88.94	**93.14**	96.32	91.17	**92.15**	74.38	**55.02**	**84.45**
ChatGPT$_W$		83.98	83.25	92.89	86.72	84.75	65.18	44.25	77.29
AnglELLaMA (Li and Li, 2023)	4096	**90.40**	93.00	95.84	**91.97**	90.66	**77.24**	51.98	84.30
AnglE-LLaMA$_W$		79.82	72.26	86.88	81.18	67.63	68.79	37.62	70.45
LLaMA (Touvron et al., 2023a)	4096	87.08	90.36	**96.55**	88.60	90.27	71.95	46.34	81.45
LLaMA$_W$		75.90	60.80	86.67	78.15	60.82	66.81	34.73	66.24
LLaMA2(Touvron et al., 2023b)	4096	87.09	89.24	96.19	88.25	89.30	72.25	47.39	81.39
LLaMA2$_W$		76.02	61.33	86.29	78.26	60.98	66.82	35.11	66.40

Table 1: Classification task results of 8 models on 7 datasets in accuracy. Reported results derived from our classification experiments based on *SentEval* settings. All datasets are binary except SST-F, which has 5 class labels.

ing makes features more independent but, at the same time, makes the classification more difficult. An interesting pattern is that fine-tuned models, including SimCSE, SBert, AngleBERT, and AngleLLaMA, have a distinctive square shape, while vanilla LLaMA and BERT models do not have that

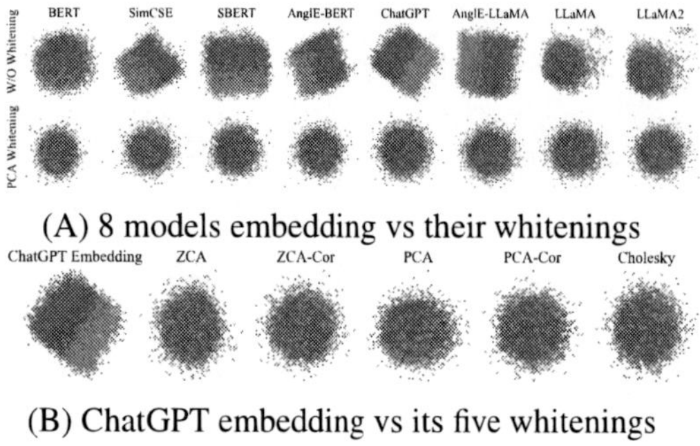

Figure 2: Visualization of embeddings before and after whitening. Dimensions are reduced using PCA.

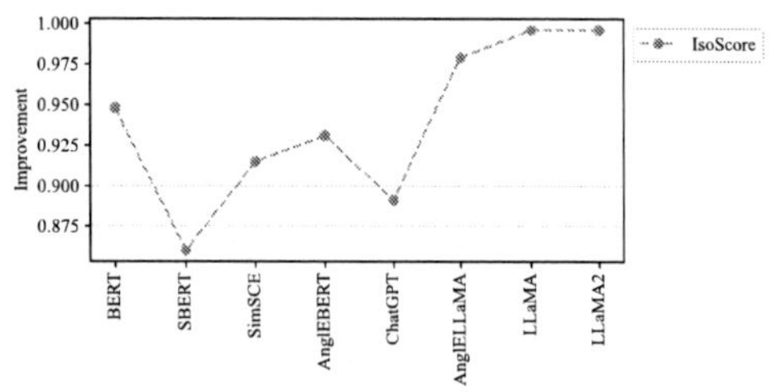

Figure 3: Improvement in Isotropy measured with IsoScore due to Whitening on MR dataset.

pattern. That prompts us that ChatGPT may have fine-tuned their embeddings, probably using the same training data, i.e. SNLI.

3.2 STS Task

Our experiments reproduced the results that are reported in (Su et al., 2021; Huang et al., 2021), i.e., the whitening improves the embedding for BERT. But that conclusion can not be extrapolated to LLMs like AngleBERT, AngleLLaMA and ChatGPT. Our experiment also echoes the results from (Zhuo et al., 2023), which shows that whitening does not work on SimCSE. Not much work has been done on the evaluation of whitening on ChatGPT and LLaMA. We find that it improves LLaMA embedding while deteriorating ChatGPT embedding. It seems that, overall, whitening does not work for fine-tuned models.

3.3 Impact of Whitening on Isotoropy

Whitening transformation ensures data isotropy by making the covariance matrix proportional to the identity matrix, thus normalizing variance across dimensions (Rudman and Eickhoff, 2024; Rudman et al., 2022; Rajaee and Pilehvar, 2021). Traditional isotropy metrics like average random cosine similarity score, partition isotropy score, intrinsic dimensionality, and variance explained ratio are often used in research to evaluate the isotropy of embeddings (Rudman et al., 2022). However, IsoScore suggests these methods do not accurately measure isotropy. IsoScore, which applies PCA to ensure dimension independence and then assesses how the normalized variance deviates from the identity matrix, ranges from 0 to 1, indicating how uniformly data occupies the vector space (Rudman et al., 2022). This makes IsoScore unique as it is mean-independent, invariant to scalar changes in the covariance matrix, and rotation-proof, offering linear scalability with dimensionality and stability across distributions with highly isotropic subspaces. Therefore, we use IsoScore to assess the isotropy of our embeddings in this study (Rudman et al., 2022).

Our results demonstrate that whitening significantly reduces isotropic bias, as evidenced by the improved IsoScore depicted in Figure 3. However, enhancing isotropy does not necessarily translate to improved performance in machine learning tasks. For instance, as shown in Figure 3, the IsoScore for the LLaMA2 embeddings increased to nearly 1 following whitening. This means that initially, the LLaMA2 embeddings exhibited a very low IsoScore, close to 0, indicating severe anisotropy. After whitening, the embeddings achieved a near-perfect isotropic distribution, reflected by an IsoScore of 1.

We also observe from Figure 3 that vanilla methods, such as LLaMA and BERT, experience a higher degree of improvement in their IsoScore compared with fine-tuned models such as SBERT and SimCSE. Suggesting that the low improvement in IsoScore of ChatGPT embeddings is a result of fine-tuning on NLI datasets.

4 Conclusion

We show that the performance of whitening is model-dependent and task-dependent. For classification tasks, we do not recommend to apply whitening. For STS tasks, the performance varies from model to model. We conjecture that it works only for LLMs before fine-tuning. Also, the technical details of ChatGPT remain to be a mystery. Based on its reaction to the whitening operation, we can infer that it may be fine-tuned, probably using NLI data. Another contribution of our work is an embedding evaluation platform for LLMs.

References

Anthony J Bell and Terrence J Sejnowski. 1997. The "independent components" of natural scenes are edge filters. *Vision research*, 37(23):3327–3338.

Alexis Conneau and Douwe Kiela. 2018. SentEval: An Evaluation Toolkit for Universal Sentence Representations. In *Proceedings of the Eleventh International Conference on Language Resources and Evaluation (LREC 2018)*. European Language Resources Association (ELRA).

Jacob Devlin, Ming-Wei Chang, Kenton Lee, and Kristina Toutanova. 2019. BERT: Pre-training of Deep Bidirectional Transformers for Language Understanding. In *Proceedings of the 2019 Conference of the North American Chapter of the Association for Computational Linguistics: Human Language Technologies, Volume 1 (Long and Short Papers)*, pages 4171–4186.

Jerome H Friedman. 1987. Exploratory projection pursuit. *Journal of the American statistical association*, 82(397):249–266.

Tianyu Gao, Xingcheng Yao, and Danqi Chen. 2021. SimCSE: Simple Contrastive Learning of Sentence Embeddings. In *Proceedings of the 2021 Conference on Empirical Methods in Natural Language Processing*, pages 6894–6910. Association for Computational Linguistics.

Junjie Huang, Duyu Tang, and Wanjun Zhong. 2021. WhiteningBERT: An Easy Unsupervised Sentence Embedding Approach. In *Findings of the Association for Computational Linguistics: EMNLP 2021*, pages 238–244.

Ting Jiang, Jian Jiao, Shaohan Huang, and Zihan Zhang. 2022. PromptBERT: Improving BERT Sentence Embeddings with Prompts. In *Proceedings of the 2022 Conference on Empirical Methods in Natural Language Processing*, pages 8826–8837. Association for Computational Linguistics.

Olga Kovaleva, Saurabh Kulshreshtha, Anna Rogers, and Anna Rumshisky. 2021. BERT Busters: Outlier Dimensions that Disrupt Transformers. In *Findings*.

Quoc Le and Tomas Mikolov. 2014. Distributed representations of sentences and documents. In *International conference on machine learning*, pages 1188–1196. PMLR.

Xianming Li and Jing Li. 2023. Angle-optimized text embeddings. *arXiv preprint arXiv:2309.12871*.

OpenAI. 2023. ChatGPT [Large language model]. `https://platform.openai.com/docs`.

Sara Rajaee and Mohammad Taher Pilehvar. 2021. How does fine-tuning affect the geometry of embedding space: A case study on isotropy. *arXiv preprint arXiv:2109.04740*.

Nils Reimers and Iryna Gurevych. 2019. Sentence-BERT: Sentence Embeddings using Siamese BERT-Networks. In *Conference on Empirical Methods in Natural Language Processing*.

William Rudman and Carsten Eickhoff. 2024. Stable Anisotropic Regularization. In *The Twelfth International Conference on Learning Representations*.

William Rudman, Nate Gillman, Taylor Rayne, and Carsten Eickhoff. 2022. IsoScore: Measuring the Uniformity of Embedding Space Utilization. In *Findings of the Association for Computational Linguistics: ACL 2022*, pages 3325–3339.

Shota Sasaki, Benjamin Heinzerling, Jun Suzuki, and Kentaro Inui. 2023. Examining the effect of whitening on static and contextualized word embeddings. *Information Processing & Management*, 60(3):103272.

Aliaksandr Siarohin, E. Sangineto, and N. Sebe. 2018. Whitening and Coloring Batch Transform for GANs. In *International Conference on Learning Representations*.

Jianlin Su, Jiarun Cao, Weijie Liu, and Yangyiwen Ou. 2021. Whitening sentence representations for better semantics and faster retrieval. *arXiv preprint arXiv:2103.15316*.

William Timkey and Marten van Schijndel. 2021. All Bark and No Bite: Rogue Dimensions in Transformer Language Models Obscure Representational Quality. In *Proceedings of the 2021 Conference on Empirical Methods in Natural Language Processing*, pages 4527–4546. Association for Computational Linguistics.

Hugo Touvron, Thibaut Lavril, Gautier Izacard, Xavier Martinet, Marie-Anne Lachaux, Timothée Lacroix, Baptiste Rozière, Naman Goyal, Eric Hambro, Faisal Azhar, et al. 2023a. Llama: Open and efficient foundation language models. *arXiv preprint arXiv:2302.13971*.

Hugo Touvron, Louis Martin, and Kevin Stone. 2023b. Llama 2: Open Foundation and Fine-Tuned Chat Models. *Preprint*, arXiv:2307.09288.

Ziyuan Wang and You Wu. 2023. Investigating the Effectiveness of Whitening Post-processing Methods on Modifying LLMs Representations. In *2023 IEEE 35th International Conference on Tools with Artificial Intelligence (ICTAI)*, pages 813–820. IEEE.

Wenjie Zhuo, Yifan Sun, Xiaohan Wang, Linchao Zhu, and Yi Yang. 2023. WhitenedCSE: Whitening-based Contrastive Learning of Sentence Embeddings. In *Proceedings of the 61st Annual Meeting of the Association for Computational Linguistics (Volume 1: Long Papers)*, pages 12135–12148.

LLM Circuit Analyses Are Consistent Across Training and Scale

Curt Tigges[1], Michael Hanna[2], Qinan Yu[3], Stella Biderman[1]
[1]EleutherAI [2]ILLC, University of Amsterdam [3]Brown University
{curt,stella}@eleuther.ai m.w.hanna@uva.nl qinan_yu@brown.edu

Abstract

Most currently deployed large language models (LLMs) undergo continuous training or additional finetuning. By contrast, most research into LLMs' internal mechanisms focuses on models at one snapshot in time (the end of pre-training), raising the question of whether their results generalize to real-world settings. Existing studies of mechanisms over time focus on encoder-only or toy models, which differ significantly from most deployed models. In this study, we track how model mechanisms, operationalized as circuits, emerge and evolve across 300 billion tokens of training in decoder-only LLMs, in models ranging from 70 million to 2.8 billion parameters. We find that task abilities and the functional components that support them emerge consistently at similar token counts across scale. Moreover, although such components may be implemented by different attention heads over time, the overarching algorithm that they implement remains. Surprisingly, both these algorithms and the types of components involved therein tend to replicate across model scale. Finally, we find that circuit size correlates with model size and can fluctuate considerably over time even when the same algorithm is implemented. These results suggest that circuit analyses conducted on small models at the end of pre-training can provide insights that still apply after additional training and over model scale.

1 Introduction

As LLMs' capabilities have grown, so has interest in characterizing their mechanisms. Recent work in mechanistic interpretability often seeks to do so via circuits: computational subgraphs that explain task-solving mechanisms (Wang et al., 2023; Hanna et al., 2023; Conmy et al., 2023). Circuits can be found and verified using a variety of methods, (Conmy et al., 2023; Syed et al., 2023; Hanna et al., 2024; Kramár et al., 2024; Ferrando and Voita, 2024) with the aim of reverse-engineering models' task-solving algorithms.

Though much circuits research is motivated by LLMs' capabilities, the setting in which such research is performed often differs from that of currently deployed models. Crucially, while most LLM circuits work (Wang et al., 2023; Hanna et al., 2023) studies models at the end of pre-training, currently deployed models often undergo continuous training or are fine-tuned for specific tasks (Hu et al., 2021). Other subfields of interpretability have studied model development during training (Hu et al., 2023; Chang et al., 2023; Warstadt et al., 2020; Chang and Bergen, 2022), but similar work on LLM mechanisms is scarce. Existing mechanistic work over training has studied syntactic attention structures and induction heads (Olsson et al., 2022; Chen et al., 2024; Singh et al., 2024), but has focused on small encoder or toy models. Prakash et al. (2024) examines circuits in 7-billion-parameter models post-finetuning, but the evolution of circuits during pre-training remains unexplored. This raises questions about whether circuit analyses will generalize if the model in question is further trained or fine-tuned.

We address this issue by exploring when and how circuits and their components emerge during training, and their consistency across training and different model scales. We study circuits in models from the Pythia suite (Biderman et al., 2023b) across 300 billion tokens, at scales from 70 million to 2.8 billion parameters. We supplement this with additional data from models ranging up to 12 billion parameters. Our results suggest remarkable consistency in circuits and their attributes across scale and training. Our contributions are as follows:

Performance acquisition and functional component emergence are similar across scale: Task ability acquisition rates tend to reach a maximum at similar token counts across different model sizes. Functional components like name mover heads,

Proceedings of the 9th Workshop on Representation Learning for NLP (RepL4NLP-2024), pages 290–303
August 15, 2024 ©2024 Association for Computational Linguistics

copy suppression heads, and successor heads also emerge consistently at similar points across scales, paralleling previous findings that induction heads emerge at roughly 2B-5B tokens across models of all scales (Olsson et al., 2022).

Circuit algorithms often remain stable despite component-level fluctuations: Analysis of the circuit for indirect object indenetification (IOI; Wang et al., 2023) across training and scale reveals that even when individual components change, the overall algorithm remains consistent, indicating a level of algorithmic stability. We also find that the algorithm also tends to be similar for dramatically different model scales, suggesting that some currently-identified circuits may generalize.

Taken as a whole, our results suggest that circuit analysis generalizes well over both pre-training and scale even in the face of component and circuit size changes. Thus, circuits studied at the end of training in smaller models can be informative for larger models, as well as models with longer training runs. We hope to see this validated for other circuits, especially more complex ones, confirming our initial findings.

2 Methods

2.1 Circuits

A **circuit** (Olah et al., 2020; Elhage et al., 2021; Wang et al., 2023) is the minimal computational subgraph of a model that is faithful to its behavior on a given task. At a high level, this means that circuits describe the components of a model—e.g., attention heads or multi-layer perceptrons (MLPs)—that the model uses to perform the task. A task, within the circuits framework, is defined by inputs, expected outputs, and a (continuous) metric that measures model performance on the task. For example, in the indirect object identification (IOI, (Wang et al., 2023)) task, the LM receives inputs like "When John and Mary went to the store, John gave a drink to", and is expected to output *Mary*, rather than *John*. We measure the extent to which the LM fulfills our expectations by measuring the difference in logits assigned to *Mary* and *John*.

Circuits are useful objects of study because we can verify that are *faithful* to LM behavior on the given task. We say that a circuit is faithful if we can corrupt all nodes and edges outside the circuit without changing model behavior on the task. Concretely, we test faithfulness by running the model on normal input, while replacing the activations corresponding to edges outside our circuit, with activations from a corrupted input, which elicits very different model behavior. In the above case, our corrupted input could instead be "When John and Mary went to the store, Mary gave a drink to", eliciting *John* over *Mary*. If the circuit still predicts *Mary*, rather than *John*, it is faithful. As circuits are often small, including less than 5% of model edges, this faithfulness test corrupts most of the model, thus guaranteeing that circuits capture a small set of task-relevant model mechanisms. For more details on the circuits framework, see prior work and surveys (Conmy et al., 2023; Hanna et al., 2024; Ferrando et al., 2024).

Circuits have a number of advantages over other interpretability frameworks. As computational subgraphs of the model that flow from its inputs to its outputs, they provide complete explanations for a model's mechanisms. Moreover, their faithfulness, verified using a causal test, makes them more reliable explanations. This is in contrast to probing, which only offers layer-level explanations, and can be unfaithful, capturing features unused by the model (Belinkov, 2022). Similarly, input attributions (Shrikumar et al., 2017) only address which input tokens are used.

2.2 Circuit Finding

In order to find faithful circuits at scale over many checkpoints, we use efficient, attribution-based circuit finding methods. Such methods score the importance of all edges in a model's graph in a fixed number of forward and backward passes, independent of model size; though other patching-based circuit-finding methods (Conmy et al., 2023) are more accurate, they are too slow, requiring a number of forward passes that grows with model size. From the many existing attribution methods (Nanda, 2023; Kramár et al., 2024), we select edge attribution patching with integrated gradients (EAP-IG; Hanna et al., 2024) due to its faithful circuit-finding ability. Like its predecessor, edge attribution patching (Nanda, 2023), EAP-IG assigns each edge an importance score using a gradient-based approximation of the change in loss that would occur if that edge were corrupted, but EAP-IG yields more faithful circuits with fewer edges.

After running EAP-IG to score each edge, we define our circuit by greedily searching for the edges with the highest absolute score. We search for the minimal circuit that achieves at least 80% of the whole model's performance on the task. We do this using binary search over circuit sizes; the initial search space ranges from 1 edge to 5% of the model's edges. The high faithfulness threshold we set gives us confidence that our circuits capture most model mechanisms used on the given task. However, ensuring that a circuit is entirely complete, containing all relevant model nodes and edges, is challenging, and no definitive method of verifying this has emerged.

2.3 Models

We study Biderman et al.'s (2023b) Pythia model suite, a collection of open-source autoregressive language models that includes intermediate training checkpoints. Though we could train our own language models or use another model suite with intermediate checkpoints (Sellam et al., 2022; Liu et al., 2023; Groeneveld et al., 2024), Pythia is unique in providing checkpoints for models at a variety of scales and training configurations.[1] Each model in the Pythia suite has 154 checkpoints: 11 of these correspond to the model after 0, 1, 2, 4, ..., and 512 steps of training; the remaining 143 correspond to 1000, 2000, ..., and 143,000 steps. We find circuits at each of these checkpoints. As Pythia uses a uniform batch size of 2.1 million tokens, these models are trained on far more tokens (300 billion) than those in existing studies of model internals over time. We study models of varying sizes, from 70 million to 12 billion parameters.

2.4 Tasks

We analyze the mechanisms behind four different tasks taken from the (mechanistic) interpretability literature. We choose these tasks because they are simple and feasible for even the smaller models we study. Moreover, as existing work has already studied them in other models, we have clues as to how our models likely perform these tasks; to verify that our models use similar circuits we briefly analyze our models' indirect object identification and greater-than circuits in Appendix A. The other task are MLP-dominant and do not involve much attention head activity; for these circuits, we verify that this is still the case in Pythia models.

Indirect Object Identification The indirect object identification (IOI; Wang et al., 2023) task feeds models inputs such as "When John and Mary went to the store, John gave a drink to"; models should prefer *Mary* over *John*. Corrupted inputs, like "When John and Mary went to the store, Mary gave a drink to", reverse model preferences. We measure model behavior via the difference in logits assigned to the two names (*Mary* and *John*). We use a small dataset of 70 IOI examples created with Wang et al.'s (2023) generator; larger datasets did not provide significantly better results, and this size fit into GPU memory more easily.

Gendered-Pronoun The Gendered-Pronoun task (Vig et al., 2020; Mathwin et al., 2023) measures the gender of the pronouns that models produce to refer to a previously mentioned entity. Prior work has shown "So Paul is such a good cook, isn't", models prefer the continuation "he" to "she"; we measure the degree to which this occurs via the difference in the pronouns' logits. In the corrupted case, we replace the "Paul" with "Mary". We craft 70 examples as in (Mathwin et al., 2023).

Greater-Than The Greater-Than task (Hanna et al., 2023) measures a model's ability to complete inputs such as $s =$"The war lasted from the year 1732 to the year 17" with a valid year (i.e. a year > 32). Task performance is measured via probability difference (prob diff); in this example, the prob diff is $\sum_{y=33}^{99} p(y|s) - \sum_{y=00}^{32} p(y|s)$. In corrupted inputs, the last two digits of the start year are replaced by "01", pushing the model to output early (invalid) years that decrease the prob diff. We create 200 Greater-Than examples with Hanna et al.'s (2023) generator.

Subject-Verb Agreement Subject-verb agreement (SVA), widely studied within the NLP interpretability literature (Linzen et al., 2016; Newman et al., 2021; Lasri et al., 2022), tasks models with predicting verb forms that match a sentence's subject. Given input such as "The keys on the cabinet", models must predict "are" over "is"; a corrupted input, "The key on the cabinet" pushes models toward the opposite response. We measure model performance using prob diff, taking the difference of probability assigned to verbs that agree with the subject, and those that do not. We use 200 synthetic SVA example sentences from (Newman et al., 2021).

3 Circuit Formation

3.1 Behavioral Evaluation

We begin our analysis of LLMs' task mechanisms over time by analyzing LLM behavior on these

[1]We exclude OLMo from our analysis due to missing checkpoints at the time of writing.

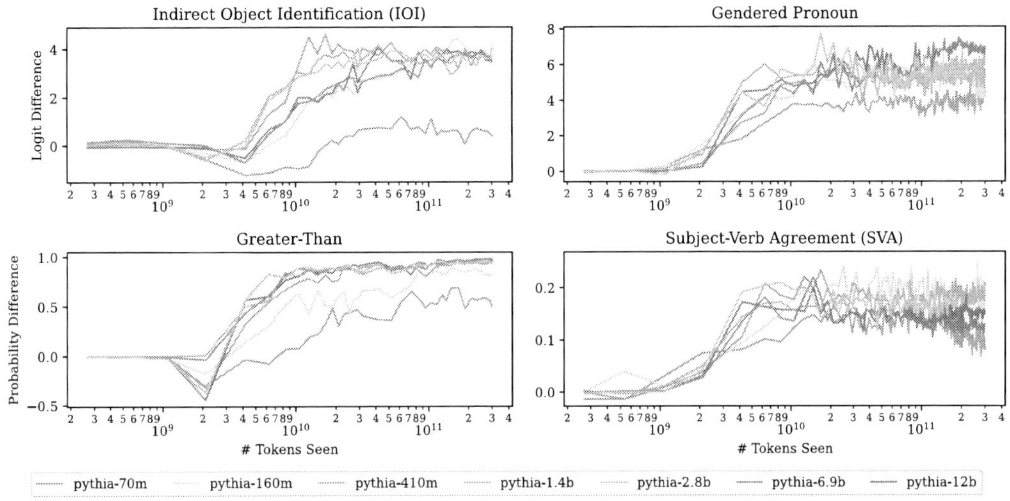

Figure 1: Task behavior across models and time (higher indicates a better match with expected behavior). Across tasks and scales, model abilities tend to develop at the same number of tokens.

tasks; without understanding their task behaviors, we cannot understand their task mechanisms. We test these by running each model (Section 2.3) on each task (Section 2.4). Our results (Figure 1) display three trends across all tasks. First, all models but the weakest (Pythia-70m) tend to arrive at the same task performance at the end of training. This is consistent with our choice of tasks: they are simple, learnable even by small models, and scaling does not significantly improve performance. Second, once models begin learning a task, their overall performance is generally non-decreasing, though there are minor fluctuations; Pythia-2.8b's logit difference on Gendered Pronouns dips slightly after it learns the task. In general, though, models tend not to undergo significant unlearning. The only marked downward trend (Pythia-70m at the end of SVA) comes from a weak model.

Finally, for each task we examined, we observed that there was a model size beyond which additional scale did not improve the rate of learning, and sometimes even decreased it; task acquisition appeared to approach an asymptote. We found this surprising due to the existence of findings showing the opposite trend for some tasks: (Kaplan et al., 2020). On some tasks (Gendered Pronouns and Greater-Than), all models above a certain size (70M parameters for Gendered Pronouns and 160M for Greater-Than) learn tasks at roughly the same rate. On IOI, models from 410M to 2.8B parameters learn the task the fastest, but larger models (6.9B and 12B) have learning curves more like Pythia-160m. We obtain similar results on more difficult tasks like SciQ (Welbl et al., 2017); for these results, see Appendix D.

What drives this last trend, limiting how fast even large models learn tasks? To understand this, we must delve into the internal model components that support these behaviors and trends.

3.2 Component Emergence

Prior work (Olsson et al., 2022; Chen et al., 2024; Singh et al., 2024) has shown how a model's ability to perform a specific task can hinge on the development of certain components, i.e. the emergence of attention heads or MLPs with specific, task-beneficial behaviors. Prior work has also thoroughly characterized the components underlying model abilities in two of our tasks, IOI and Greater-Than, at the end of training. We thus ask: is it the development of these components that causes the task learning trends we saw before? We focus on four main components, all of which are attention heads, which we briefly describe here:

Induction Heads (Olsson et al., 2022) activate on sequences of the form `[A][B]. . . [A]`, attending to and upweighting `[B]`. This allow models to recreate patterns in their input, and supports IOI and Greater-Than.

Successor Heads (Gould et al., 2023) identify sequential values in the input (e.g. "11" or "Thursday") and upweight their successor (e.g. "12" or

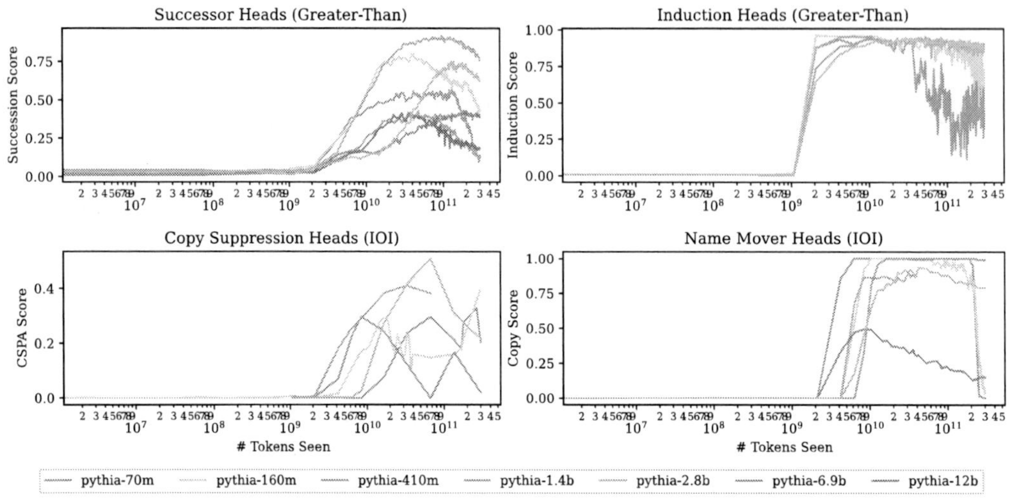

Figure 2: The development of components relevant to IOI and Greater-Than, across models and time. Each line indicates the strength of component behavior of the selected attention head from that model; higher values imply stronger component behavior. For each model and component, we plot the head in the relevant circuit (either IOI or Greater Than) that displays the component behavior the earliest.

"Friday"); this supports Greater-Than behavior.

Copy Suppression Heads (McDougall et al., 2023) attend to previous words in the input, lowering the output probability of repeated tokens that are highly predicted in the residual stream input to the head. In the original IOI circuit, copy suppression heads hurt performance, downweighting the correct name. In contrast, we find (Appendix C) that they contribute positively to the Pythia IOI circuit by downweighting the incorrect name; this is possible because both names are already highly predicted in the input to these heads, and they respond by downweighting the most repeated one.

Name-Mover Heads (Wang et al., 2023) perform the last step of the IOI task, by attending to and copying the correct name. Unlike the other heads described so far, this behavior is specific to IOI-type tasks; their behavior across the entire data distribution has not yet been characterized.

Because the importance of these components to IOI and Greater-Than has been established in other models, but not necessarily in those of the Pythia suite, we must first confirm their importance in these models. We do so by finding circuits for each model at each checkpoint using EAP-IG, as described in Section 2.2; we omit Pythia-6.9b and 12b from circuit finding for reasons of computational cost. We find that these component types indeed appear within the circuits of Pythia models' tasks circuits; see Appendix A and Appendix B for details on our methods and findings.

For each component, prior work has developed a metric to determine whether a model's attention head is acting like that component type; see Appendix C for details on these. Using these metrics, we score each of our models' heads at each checkpoint, evaluating the degree to which it acts like one of the four aforementioned heads. We then plot the earliest arising heads of each type, per model.

Our results (Figure 2) indicate that many of the hypothesized responsible components do emerge the same time as model performance increases. Most models' induction heads emerge soon after they have seen 2×10^9 tokens, replicating the findings in (Olsson et al., 2022); immediately after this, Greater-Than behavior emerges. The successor heads, also involved in Greater-Than, emerge in a similar timeframe.

For IOI, the name-mover heads emerge at similar timesteps (2 - 8×10^9 tokens) across models, with a very high strength, during or just before IOI behavior appears. Copy suppression heads emerge at the same timescale, but at varying speeds, and with varying strengths. Given that these heads are the main contributors to model performance in each task's circuit, and they emerge as or just before models' task performance increases, we can be reasonably sure that they are responsible for the emergence of performance. This said, we note an unusual trend: though model performance (Fig-

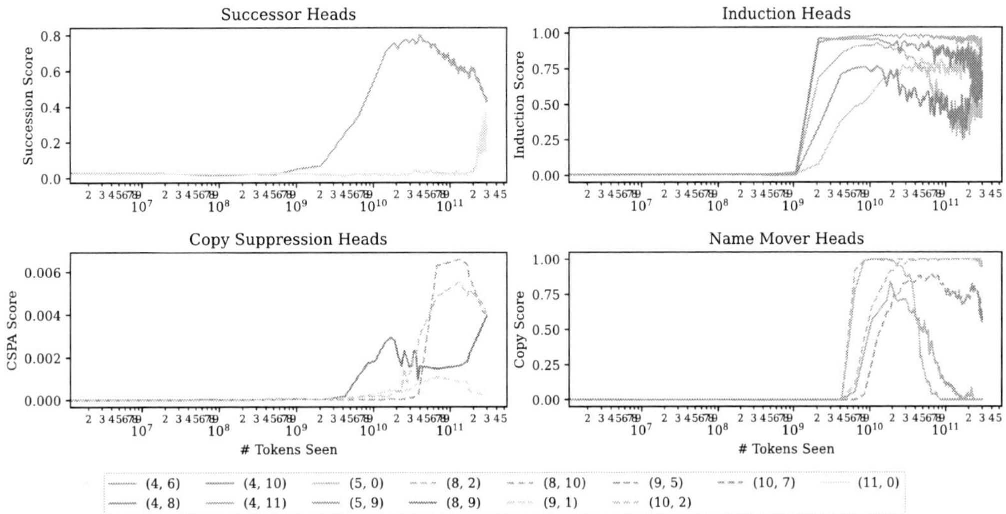

Figure 3: The development over time of components relevant to IOI and Greater-Than in Pythia-160m. Each line indicates the degree to which an attention head, denoted as (layer, head), exhibits a given function; higher values imply stronger functional behavior. Heads often lose their current function; other heads then take their place.

ure 1) does not decrease over time, the functional behavior of certain attention heads does. In the following section, we explain how this occurs.

4 Algorithms in Post-Formation Circuits

We demonstrated in Section 3 that across a variety of tasks, models with differing sizes learn to perform the given task after the same amount of training; this appears to happen because each task relies on a set of components which develop after a similar count of training tokens across models. However, in Figure 2, we observed that attention heads that had a given function earlier in behavior can lose their function later in training. This raises questions: when the heads being used to solve a task change, does the algorithm implemented by the model change too? And how do these algorithms generalize across model scale?

4.1 Model Behavior and Circuit Components Post-Formation

To understand how model component behaviors change over time, we now zoom in on the components in one model, Pythia-160m, and study them over the course of training; where we earlier plotted only the top component (e.g. the top successor head), of each model, we now plot the top 5 of Pythia-160m's heads that exhibit a given functional behavior (or fewer, if fewer than 5 exist). By evaluating components and algorithms over Pythia-160m's 300B token training span, we extend beyond previous work, which studies models trained on relatively few ($\leq$ 50M) tokens (Chen et al., 2024; Singh et al., 2024); in such work, components and task behaviors appear constant after component formation.

By contrast, our results (Figure 3) show that over the longer training period of Pythia models, the identity of components in each circuit is not constant. For example, the name-mover head (4,6) suddenly stops exhibiting this behavior at 3×10^{10} tokens, having acquired it after 4×10^9 tokens. Similarly, Pythia-160m's main successor head (5,9) loses its successor behavior towards the end of training; however, (11,0) exhibits more successor behavior at precisely that time. Such balancing may lead to the model's task performance remaining stable, as we observed in the prior section (Figure 1).

4.2 Circuit Algorithm Stability Over Training

This instability of functional components raises an important question—when attention heads begin or cease to participate in a circuit, does the underlying algorithm change? To answer this, we examined the IOI circuit, as it is the most thoroughly characterized (Wang et al., 2023) circuit algorithm of our set of tasks. Our investigation follows a three-stage approach: first, we analyzed the IOI circuit at the end of training, reverse-engineering its algorithm; next, we developed a set of metrics to

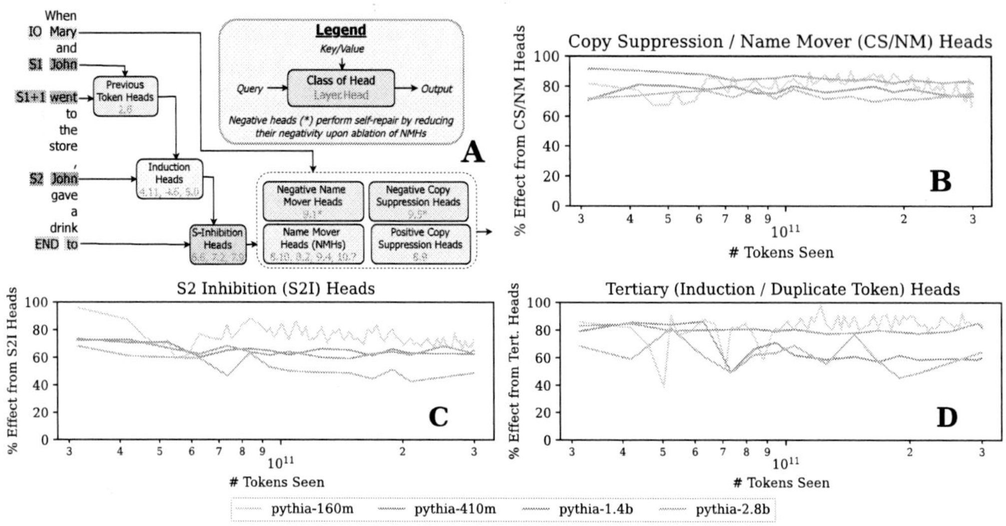

Figure 4: **A**: Pythia-160m's IOI circuit at the end of training (300B tokens). The remaining plots show the percent of model IOI performance that is explained by the Copy Suppression and Name-Mover Heads (**B**), the S-Inhibition Heads' edges to those heads (**C**), and the Induction / Duplicate Token Heads' connections to the S-Inhibition heads (**D**); higher percentages indicate that the corresponding edge is indeed important. Each of plots **B**-**D** verifies the importance of an edge from diagram **A**.

quantify whether the model was still performing that algorithm; finally, we applied these metrics across checkpoints, to determine if the algorithm was stable over training.

The first stage of our analysis is to analyze the IOI circuit at the end of training. Here, we present only the results of our analysis, but see Appendix B for details of this process, which follows the original analysis (Wang et al., 2023). Figure 4**A** shows the circuit that results from our analysis; it involves three logical "steps," each of which involves a different set of attention head types. Working backwards from the logit predictions, the direct contributors towards the logit difference are name-mover heads and copy suppression heads. The former attend to the indirect object in the prompt and copy it to the last position; the latter attend to and down-weight tokens that appear earlier in the input. In the next step, the name-mover heads (but not the copy-suppression heads) use on token and positional information output by the S-inhibition heads to attend to the correct token. Finally, S-inhibition heads rely on information from induction heads and duplicate-token heads.

Next, we quantify the extent to which the circuit depends on each of these three steps, via path patching (Goldowsky-Dill et al., 2023), a form of ablation where activations are swapped with those from counterfactual prompts (see Appendix B for details). If a step is important, ablating the connection between the components involved in that step (e.g. in step 2, between induction / duplicate-token heads and S-inhibition heads) should have a large *direct effect*, and cause a large drop in model performance. For each step, our metric measures this direct effect, divided by the sum of the direct effects of ablating each edge with the same endpoint. Our metrics range from 0-100%; higher is better.

Finally, we compute each of these metrics for each model from 160M to 2.8B parameters in size.[2] We run them on each checkpoint post-circuit emergence (that is, when all component types appear in the circuit); for Pythia-160m, we test every checkpoint, and for the larger models we space out checkpoints to save compute, using approximately 1/3rd of the available checkpoints). We find (Figure 4**B**-**D**) that the behavior measured by these metrics is stable once the initial circuit has formed. Notably, in no model or metric are there dramatic shifts in algorithm corresponding to functional component shifts within the circuit. Moreover, all scores are relatively high, generally above 50%; the core solvers of the algorithm, copy suppression and name-mover heads, have scores above

[2]We omit Pythia-70m, as it does not learn the task; due to computational constraints, we omit Pythia-6.9b/12b.

70%. This suggests that analyses of circuits in fully pre-trained models may generalize well to other model states, rather than being contingent on the particular checkpoint selected.

Generalization across model scales also seems promising, as IOI circuit metrics from Pythia-160m are also high in larger Pythia variants. However, there is variation: while the name-mover, copy-suppression, and S-inhibition heads are at work in all models' circuits, the Pythia-160m circuit does not involve duplicate-token heads, while others do. So small differences exist amid big-picture similarity. Moreover, we stress that these algorithmic similarities might not hold for more complex tasks, for which a variety of algorithms could exist.

5 Discussion

Implications for Interpretability Research While our findings are based on a limited set of circuits, they hold significant implications for mechanistic interpretability research. Our study was motivated by the fact that most such research does not study models that vary over time, like currently deployed models. However, the stability of circuit algorithms over the course of pre-training suggests that analyses performed on models at a given point during training may provide valuable insights into earlier and later phases of pre-training as well. Moreover, the consistency in the emergence of critical components and the algorithmic structure of these circuits across different model scales suggests that studying smaller models can sometimes provide insights applicable to larger models. This dual stability across pre-training and scale could reduce the computational cost of interpretability research and allow for more efficient study of model mechanisms. However, further research is needed to confirm these trends across a broader range of tasks and architectures.

Limitations and Future Work Our analysis was limited to a narrow range of tasks feasible for small models. This limits in turn the scope of the claims that we can make. We believe it to be very possible that more complex tasks, not solvable by small models, which permit a larger range of algorithmic solutions, may show different trends from those that we discuss here. Such work would be valuable, though computationally expensive due to the model sizes required. Our analysis also studied models only from one model family, Pythia. It is thus not possible to tell if our results are limited to the specific model family we have chosen, which shares both architecture and training setup across model scale. Such work is in part hampered by the lack of large-scale model suites such as Pythia; future work could provide these suites to enable this sort of analysis. Our work additionally only studies circuits over the course of training; in contrast, open-source models are more often fine-tuned, which could lead to different changes in mechanisms, though previous small-scale studies suggest this is not the case (Prakash et al., 2024). Finally, future work would do well to explore more complex phenomena, such as the self-repair and load-balancing mechanisms of LLMs, which ensure consistent task performance despite component fluctuations.

6 Related Work

Behavioral Interpretability Over Time LLMs' development over the course of pre-training has been studied via behavioral interpretability, which characterizes model behavior without making claims about its implementation. Such analyses have studied LLM learning curves and shown that models of different sizes acquire capabilities in the same sequence (Chang et al., 2023), examined how LLMs learn linguistic information (Warstadt et al., 2020; Chang and Bergen, 2022) and even predicted LLM behavior later in training (Hu et al., 2023; Biderman et al., 2023a).

Mechanistic Interpretability We build on previous work in mechanistic interpretability, which aims to reverse engineer neural networks. *Circuits* are a paradigm of model analysis that has emerged from this field, originating with vision models (Olah et al., 2020) and continuing to transformer LMs (Meng et al., 2023; Wang et al., 2023; Hanna et al., 2023). Increasingly, research has tried to characterize the individual components at work within circuits, especially attention heads (Olsson et al., 2022; Chen et al., 2024; Singh et al., 2024; Gould et al., 2023; McDougall et al., 2023) and sparse features (Marks et al., 2024). Though mechanistic interpretability is a diverse field, it is tied together by causal methods (Vig et al., 2020; Geiger et al., 2021), which yield more faithful mechanistic explanations.

References

Yonatan Belinkov. 2022. Probing classifiers: Promises, shortcomings, and advances. *Computational Linguistics*, 48(1):207–219.

Stella Biderman, USVSN Sai Prashanth, Lintang Sutawika, Hailey Schoelkopf, Quentin Gregory Anthony, Shivanshu Purohit, and Edward Raff. 2023a. Emergent and predictable memorization in large language models. In *Thirty-seventh Conference on Neural Information Processing Systems*.

Stella Biderman, Hailey Schoelkopf, Quentin Anthony, Herbie Bradley, Kyle O'Brien, Eric Hallahan, Mohammad Aflah Khan, Shivanshu Purohit, USVSN Sai Prashanth, Edward Raff, Aviya Skowron, Lintang Sutawika, and Oskar Van Der Wal. 2023b. Pythia: a suite for analyzing large language models across training and scaling. In *Proceedings of the 40th International Conference on Machine Learning*, ICML'23. JMLR.org.

Yonatan Bisk, Rowan Zellers, Ronan Le Bras, Jianfeng Gao, and Yejin Choi. 2019. Piqa: Reasoning about physical commonsense in natural language. *Preprint*, arXiv:1911.11641.

Tyler A. Chang and Benjamin K. Bergen. 2022. Word acquisition in neural language models. *Transactions of the Association for Computational Linguistics*, 10:1–16.

Tyler A. Chang, Zhuowen Tu, and Benjamin K. Bergen. 2023. Characterizing learning curves during language model pre-training: Learning, forgetting, and stability. *Preprint*, arXiv:2308.15419.

Angelica Chen, Ravid Shwartz-Ziv, Kyunghyun Cho, Matthew L Leavitt, and Naomi Saphra. 2024. Sudden drops in the loss: Syntax acquisition, phase transitions, and simplicity bias in MLMs. In *The Twelfth International Conference on Learning Representations*.

Peter Clark, Isaac Cowhey, Oren Etzioni, Tushar Khot, Ashish Sabharwal, Carissa Schoenick, and Oyvind Tafjord. 2018. Think you have solved question answering? try arc, the ai2 reasoning challenge. *Preprint*, arXiv:1803.05457.

Arthur Conmy, Augustine N. Mavor-Parker, Aengus Lynch, Stefan Heimersheim, and Adrià Garriga-Alonso. 2023. Towards automated circuit discovery for mechanistic interpretability. In *Thirty-seventh Conference on Neural Information Processing Systems*.

Nelson Elhage, Neel Nanda, Catherine Olsson, Tom Henighan, Nicholas Joseph, Ben Mann, Amanda Askell, Yuntao Bai, Anna Chen, Tom Conerly, Nova DasSarma, Dawn Drain, Deep Ganguli, Zac Hatfield-Dodds, Danny Hernandez, Andy Jones, Jackson Kernion, Liane Lovitt, Kamal Ndousse, Dario Amodei, Tom Brown, Jack Clark, Jared Kaplan, Sam McCandlish, and Chris Olah. 2021. A mathematical framework for transformer circuits. *Transformer Circuits Thread*. Https://transformer-circuits.pub/2021/framework/index.html.

Javier Ferrando, Gabriele Sarti, Arianna Bisazza, and Marta R. Costa-jussà. 2024. A primer on the inner workings of transformer-based language models. *Preprint*, arXiv:2405.00208.

Javier Ferrando and Elena Voita. 2024. Information flow routes: Automatically interpreting language models at scale. *Preprint*, arXiv:2403.00824.

Atticus Geiger, Hanson Lu, Thomas Icard, and Christopher Potts. 2021. Causal abstractions of neural networks. In *Advances in Neural Information Processing Systems*, volume 34, pages 9574–9586.

Nicholas Goldowsky-Dill, Chris MacLeod, Lucas Sato, and Aryaman Arora. 2023. Localizing model behavior with path patching. *Preprint*, arXiv:2304.05969.

Rhys Gould, Euan Ong, George Ogden, and Arthur Conmy. 2023. Successor heads: Recurring, interpretable attention heads in the wild. *Preprint*, arXiv:2312.09230.

Dirk Groeneveld, Iz Beltagy, Pete Walsh, Akshita Bhagia, Rodney Kinney, Oyvind Tafjord, Ananya Harsh Jha, Hamish Ivison, Ian Magnusson, Yizhong Wang, Shane Arora, David Atkinson, Russell Authur, Khyathi Raghavi Chandu, Arman Cohan, Jennifer Dumas, Yanai Elazar, Yuling Gu, Jack Hessel, Tushar Khot, William Merrill, Jacob Morrison, Niklas Muennighoff, Aakanksha Naik, Crystal Nam, Matthew E. Peters, Valentina Pyatkin, Abhilasha Ravichander, Dustin Schwenk, Saurabh Shah, Will Smith, Emma Strubell, Nishant Subramani, Mitchell Wortsman, Pradeep Dasigi, Nathan Lambert, Kyle Richardson, Luke Zettlemoyer, Jesse Dodge, Kyle Lo, Luca Soldaini, Noah A. Smith, and Hannaneh Hajishirzi. 2024. Olmo: Accelerating the science of language models. *Preprint*, arXiv:2402.00838.

Michael Hanna, Ollie Liu, and Alexandre Variengien. 2023. How does GPT-2 compute greater-than?: Interpreting mathematical abilities in a pre-trained language model. In *Thirty-seventh Conference on Neural Information Processing Systems*.

Michael Hanna, Sandro Pezzelle, and Yonatan Belinkov. 2024. Have faith in faithfulness: Going beyond circuit overlap when finding model mechanisms. *Preprint*, arXiv:2403.17806.

Edward J. Hu, Yelong Shen, Phillip Wallis, Zeyuan Allen-Zhu, Yuanzhi Li, Shean Wang, Lu Wang, and Weizhu Chen. 2021. Lora: Low-rank adaptation of large language models. *Preprint*, arXiv:2106.09685.

Michael Y. Hu, Angelica Chen, Naomi Saphra, and Kyunghyun Cho. 2023. Latent state models of training dynamics. *Transactions on Machine Learning Research*.

Jared Kaplan, Sam McCandlish, Tom Henighan, Tom B. Brown, Benjamin Chess, Rewon Child, Scott Gray, Alec Radford, Jeffrey Wu, and Dario Amodei. 2020. Scaling laws for neural language models. *Preprint*, arXiv:2001.08361.

János Kramár, Tom Lieberum, Rohin Shah, and Neel Nanda. 2024. Atp*: An efficient and scalable method for localizing llm behaviour to components. *Preprint*, arXiv:2403.00745.

Karim Lasri, Tiago Pimentel, Alessandro Lenci, Thierry Poibeau, and Ryan Cotterell. 2022. Probing for the usage of grammatical number. In *Proceedings of the 60th Annual Meeting of the Association for Computational Linguistics (Volume 1: Long Papers)*, pages 8818–8831, Dublin, Ireland. Association for Computational Linguistics.

Tal Linzen, Emmanuel Dupoux, and Yoav Goldberg. 2016. Assessing the ability of LSTMs to learn syntax-sensitive dependencies. *Transactions of the Association for Computational Linguistics*, 4:521–535.

Zhengzhong Liu, Aurick Qiao, Willie Neiswanger, Hongyi Wang, Bowen Tan, Tianhua Tao, Junbo Li, Yuqi Wang, Suqi Sun, Omkar Pangarkar, Richard Fan, Yi Gu, Victor Miller, Yonghao Zhuang, Guowei He, Haonan Li, Fajri Koto, Liping Tang, Nikhil Ranjan, Zhiqiang Shen, Xuguang Ren, Roberto Iriondo, Cun Mu, Zhiting Hu, Mark Schulze, Preslav Nakov, Tim Baldwin, and Eric P. Xing. 2023. Llm360: Towards fully transparent open-source llms. *Preprint*, arXiv:2312.06550.

Samuel Marks, Can Rager, Eric J. Michaud, Yonatan Belinkov, David Bau, and Aaron Mueller. 2024. Sparse feature circuits: Discovering and editing interpretable causal graphs in language models. *Preprint*, arXiv:2403.19647.

Chris Mathwin, Guillaume Corlouer, Esben Kran, Fazl Barez, and Neel Nanda. 2023. Identifying a preliminary circuit for predicting gendered pronouns in gpt-2 small.

Callum McDougall, Arthur Conmy, Cody Rushing, Thomas McGrath, and Neel Nanda. 2023. Copy suppression: Comprehensively understanding an attention head. *Preprint*, arXiv:2310.04625.

Kevin Meng, David Bau, Alex Andonian, and Yonatan Belinkov. 2023. Locating and editing factual associations in gpt. *Preprint*, arXiv:2202.05262.

Neel Nanda. 2023. Attribution Patching: Activation Patching At Industrial Scale.

Benjamin Newman, Kai-Siang Ang, Julia Gong, and John Hewitt. 2021. Refining targeted syntactic evaluation of language models. In *Proceedings of the 2021 Conference of the North American Chapter of the Association for Computational Linguistics: Human Language Technologies*, pages 3710–3723, Online. Association for Computational Linguistics.

Chris Olah, Nick Cammarata, Ludwig Schubert, Gabriel Goh, Michael Petrov, and Shan Carter. 2020. Zoom in: An introduction to circuits. *Distill*. Https://distill.pub/2020/circuits/zoom-in.

Catherine Olsson, Nelson Elhage, Neel Nanda, Nicholas Joseph, Nova DasSarma, Tom Henighan, Ben Mann, Amanda Askell, Yuntao Bai, Anna Chen, Tom Conerly, Dawn Drain, Deep Ganguli, Zac Hatfield-Dodds, Danny Hernandez, Scott Johnston, Andy Jones, Jackson Kernion, Liane Lovitt, Kamal Ndousse, Dario Amodei, Tom Brown, Jack Clark, Jared Kaplan, Sam McCandlish, and Chris Olah. 2022. In-context learning and induction heads. *Transformer Circuits Thread*. Https://transformer-circuits.pub/2022/in-context-learning-and-induction-heads/index.html.

Nikhil Prakash, Tamar Rott Shaham, Tal Haklay, Yonatan Belinkov, and David Bau. 2024. Fine-tuning enhances existing mechanisms: A case study on entity tracking. In *The Twelfth International Conference on Learning Representations*.

Keisuke Sakaguchi, Ronan Le Bras, Chandra Bhagavatula, and Yejin Choi. 2019. Winogrande: An adversarial winograd schema challenge at scale. *Preprint*, arXiv:1907.10641.

Thibault Sellam, Steve Yadlowsky, Ian Tenney, Jason Wei, Naomi Saphra, Alexander D'Amour, Tal Linzen, Jasmijn Bastings, Iulia Raluca Turc, Jacob Eisenstein, Dipanjan Das, and Ellie Pavlick. 2022. The multiBERTs: BERT reproductions for robustness analysis. In *International Conference on Learning Representations*.

Avanti Shrikumar, Peyton Greenside, and Anshul Kundaje. 2017. Learning important features through propagating activation differences. In *Proceedings of the 34th International Conference on Machine Learning*, volume 70 of *Proceedings of Machine Learning Research*, pages 3145–3153. PMLR.

Aaditya K. Singh, Ted Moskovitz, Felix Hill, Stephanie C. Y. Chan, and Andrew M. Saxe. 2024. What needs to go right for an induction head? a mechanistic study of in-context learning circuits and their formation. *Preprint*, arXiv:2404.07129.

Aaquib Syed, Can Rager, and Arthur Conmy. 2023. Attribution patching outperforms automated circuit discovery. *Preprint*, arXiv:2310.10348.

Jesse Vig, Sebastian Gehrmann, Yonatan Belinkov, Sharon Qian, Daniel Nevo, Simas Sakenis, Jason Huang, Yaron Singer, and Stuart Shieber. 2020. Causal mediation analysis for interpreting neural nlp: The case of gender bias. *Preprint*, arXiv:2004.12265.

Kevin Ro Wang, Alexandre Variengien, Arthur Conmy, Buck Shlegeris, and Jacob Steinhardt. 2023. Interpretability in the wild: a circuit for indirect object identification in GPT-2 small. In *The Eleventh International Conference on Learning Representations*.

Alex Warstadt, Yian Zhang, Xiaocheng Li, Haokun Liu, and Samuel R. Bowman. 2020. Learning which features matter: RoBERTa acquires a preference for linguistic generalizations (eventually). In *Proceedings of the 2020 Conference on Empirical Methods in Natural Language Processing (EMNLP)*, pages 217–235, Online. Association for Computational Linguistics.

Johannes Welbl, Nelson F. Liu, and Matt Gardner. 2017. Crowdsourcing multiple choice science questions. In *Proceedings of the 3rd Workshop on Noisy User-generated Text*, pages 94–106, Copenhagen, Denmark. Association for Computational Linguistics.

A Analysis of Task Circuits

A.1 IOI Circuit & Algorithmic Criteria

To determine algorithmic consistency for the IOI circuit, we apply path patching as described in Appendix B in addition to using the component scores described in Appendix C. These are used to set thresholds for classifying attention heads. Though component score thresholds can be arbitrary, applying them consistently across all model checkpoints allows us to see the degree of similarity involved with model behavior.

Concretely, we use the following metrics and thresholds:

Direct-effect heads We initially perform path-patching on all model attention heads, measuring their impact on the logit different after the final layer of the model. We then classify attention heads as name-mover heads (NMHs), negative name-mover heads, and copy suppression heads (CSHs) based on copy score (for NMHs) or CPSA (for CSHs) of $> 10\%$, which yielded a small set of heads responsible for most of the direct effect. We measure the ratio of the absolute direct effect on logit difference for these heads vs. the total direct effect of all heads (including several unclassified heads) to obtain our first value.

Next, we conduct path-patching with NMHs as the receivers. This yields a set of heads that we then test for S2-inhibition (S2I) behavior, using Wang et al.'s (2023) test for the effect of token signal vs. positional signal: does the ablation of these positional signal heads A). reduce the logit difference through the NMHs, B). reduce NMH attention (which determines what they copy) to the indirect object token, and C). increase attention to the subject tokens? If a head meets all of these conditions, we classify it as an S2I head, as it emits a signal used by the NMHs to decide what to copy. The total absolute effect of these heads on the NMHs is then divided by the total absolute effect of all heads on the NMHs, producing our second measurement.

Finally, we conduct path-patching with S2I heads as receivers. Here, we apply a simpler test since these heads can be quite diffuse throughout the model: Do the heads involved have above-average induction or duplicate-token scores? If so, we classify them as induction heads or duplicate token heads (confirming via manual examination of attention patterns and behavior), and divide the total absolute effect of these heads by the total absolute effect of all heads on the S2I heads, producing our third measurement.

These three metrics capture the extent to which known and classifiable model components contribute at each of the three primary levels of the IOI circuit. If the degree to which unknown or unclassified components contribute to any part of the circuit, we will see the corresponding score drop. As we see that in practice they tend to stay level, we conclude that there is a high degree of stability for this circuit.

B Other Circuit-Analysis Methods

Circuit analysis can be conducted via a number of different methods; the method used to find the original IOI circuit (and that we use to verify algorithmic consistency in this task) is Wang et al.'s (2023) **path-patching**. Path patching is a specialized form of activation patching, used to isolate and analyze the influence of individual model components on a given task. Starting with two datasets (identical except for the key detail we want to base our circuit on, such as the correct and incorrect names in the IOI task), x_{orig} and x_{altered}, where x_{altered} is a counterfactual version of x_{orig}, the technique involves a sender attention head h and a set of receiver nodes $R \subseteq M$ within the model's computational graph M. Initially, activations are recorded from both datasets. Subsequently, all attention heads except h are locked to their activations from x_{orig}, while h is updated with its activation from x_{altered}. This configuration allows for a forward pass on x_{orig}, capturing intermediate activations for nodes $r \in R$. A final forward pass on x_{orig} then patches R to these stored values, facilitating the assessment of h's impact on the model's output.

Path patching aims to gauge the significance of the path $h \rightarrow r$ by comparing the model's logit differences across multiple pairs $(x_{\text{orig}}, x_{\text{new}})$. By averaging these differences over many pairs, the method effectively measures the impact of specific paths on model performance, providing insights into the contributions of individual components to the overall task. The process is iterative, such that a practitioner would start by observing which nodes impact the logits directly, and then proceeding backwards to see what nodes affect those first direct-effect nodes, and so on.

C Component Metrics

In this paper, we follow the metrics from previous literature in Wang et al. (2023) for name-mover heads, McDougall et al. (2023) for copy suppression heads, (Olsson et al., 2022) for induction heads, and (Gould et al., 2023) for successor heads.

Copy Score Following Wang et al. (2023), we check if the Name Mover Heads copy over the names across training time by using the same metrics- **copy score**. To validate the Name Mover Heads, we studied what values are written via the head's OV matrix. We take the state of the residual stream after the first layer of MLP on the specific name tokens. Then we multiply it with the OV matrix of the given heads, multiplied with the unembedding matrix and also the final layer norm. This simulates what will happen if the head attended perfectly to that token. We define copy score as the proportion of samples that contain the input name token in the top 5 logits.

CSPA Score McDougall et al. (2023) introduced a novel approach named copy suppression-preserving ablation (CSPA), designed to ablate all behaviors of a specified attention head except for those related to copy suppression. This method involves two distinct types of ablation: OV ablation and QK ablation. In the OV ablation process, the output of an attention head at a destination token D is represented as a weighted sum of result vectors from source tokens S, with the weights corresponding to the attention probabilities from D to S (Elhage et al., 2021). These vectors are then projected onto the unembedding vectors of their respective source tokens S, retaining only their negative components. Meanwhile, QK ablation involves mean-ablating the result vectors from each source token S, except for the top 5% of source tokens that are most likely to be predicted at the destination token D based on the logit lens. For instance, in the phrase "All's fair in love and war," if the destination token D is "and" and the token "love" is a highly predicted follower of D and appears as a source token S, the result vector from S is projected onto the unembedding vector for "love," and everything else is mean-ablated. This demonstrates how the attention head in question suppresses the prediction of "love." To evaluate the impact of the ablation, the token distribution output by the model for a given prompt (π) is compared with the distribution following an ablation (π_{Abl}) using KL divergence $D_{KL}(\pi||\pi_{Abl})$. By averaging these values over the OpenWebText dataset, D_{CSPA} for CSPA and D_{MA} for a mean ablation baseline are obtained. The proportion of the effect explained is then calculated as $1 - \frac{D_{CSPA}}{D_{MA}}$, with KL divergence chosen because a value of 0 indicates that the ablated and clean distributions are identical, implying that 100% of the head's effect is explained by the preserved components.

Previous Token Score The Previous Token Score measures how effectively each attention head attends to the immediately preceding token. To compute this, we use a diagonal extraction on the attention pattern matrices, offset by one position. This captures the attention weights directed to the token that precedes each token in the sequence. The scores are averaged over all batches and tokens, providing a mean score for each attention head across all layers.

Duplicate Token Score The Duplicate Token Score evaluates the propensity of each attention head to focus on duplicate tokens within a sequence. We achieve this by creating input sequences where the original tokens are repeated consecutively. The attention pattern matrices are then examined for their focus on tokens that are exactly a sequence length apart, indicating duplicate attention. The scores are calculated by averaging the attention weights along the specified diagonal, representing the attention paid to duplicate tokens.

Induction Head Score Based on the prefix matching score described by Olsson et al. (2022), the Induction Head Score is designed to assess the ability of attention heads to engage in induction, where they predict the next token in a repeated sequence based on previously encountered patterns. To measure this, we generate sequences where a segment is repeated and compute the attention pattern matrices. We extract the diagonals offset by one less than the sequence length, capturing the attention from the end of the first segment to the start of the repeated segment. The mean attention scores along this diagonal provide the Induction Head Scores, averaged over all batches and tokens.

Succession Score The succession score (Gould et al., 2023) measures the degree to which an attention head performs succession, upweighting "2" in response to "1", or "May" given the input "April". As Gould et al.'s (2023) code is not publicly available, we re-implement their successor score as follows. We create a dataset of successor, consisting of numbers (in digit and written form), days of the week, and months. Then, we perform the following procedure from (Gould et al., 2023). Letting W_E and W_U denote the embedding and unembedding matrices of the model under study, MLP_0 denote the first (zero-indexed) MLP layer, and W_{OV} be the OV matrix of the head under study. Then $M = W_U W_{OV} MLP_0(W_E)$ is a square matrix whose size is that of the model vocabulary; each row thereof indicates, for the corresponding word x in the vocabulary, the degree to which an output word y is upweighted by the head under study, when x is in the input. For each (x, y) pair in our dataset (e.g. (3,4) or (Tuesday, Wednesday)) we verify that $M[x][y] > M[x][y']$ for all $y' \neq y$ in our dataset; that is, we ensure that the correct answer is more highly upweighted than any of the other possible answers in our dataset. The succession score is the proportion of examples in which that is the case.

D Additional Evidence for Task-Dependent Learning Ceilings

In addition to evaluations we performed ourselves, we also re-examined data collected during the Pythia training runs (Biderman et al., 2023b) on the SciQ (Welbl et al., 2017), PIQA (Bisk et al., 2019), WinoGrande (Sakaguchi et al., 2019), and ARC Easy (Clark et al., 2018) datasets. Each of these consist of a wide range of questions with multiple-choice answers, and accuracy was evaluated on the basis of the top choice logit produced by the model. We find that performance acquisition rates on these tasks followed the same pattern we detected with our simpler task datasets–that is, task learning rate seemed to approach an asymptote as the models increased in size. We describe the datasets below and present the results in Figure 5.

SciQ The Science Questions (SciQ) dataset (Welbl et al., 2017) consists of 13,679 crowd-

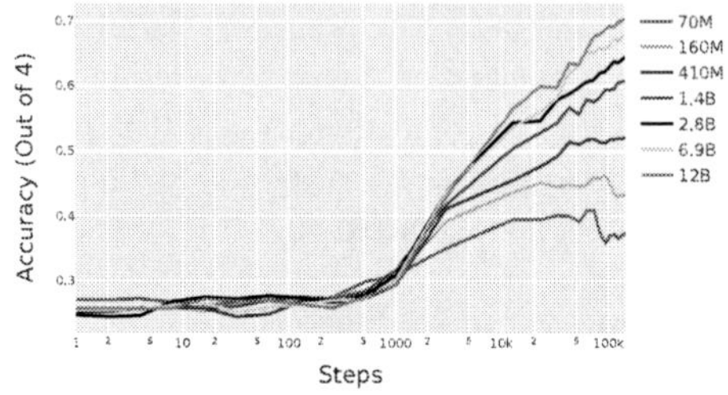

(a) ARC Easy Accuracy

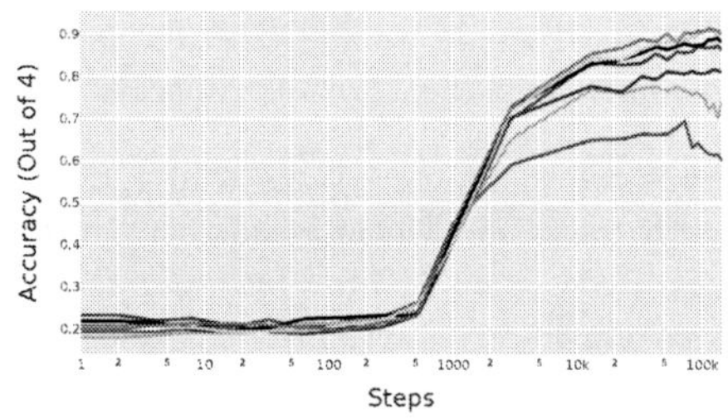

(b) SciQ Accuracy

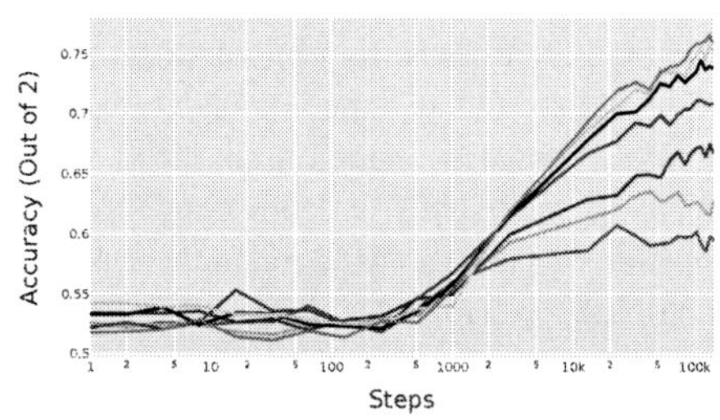

(c) PIQA Accuracy

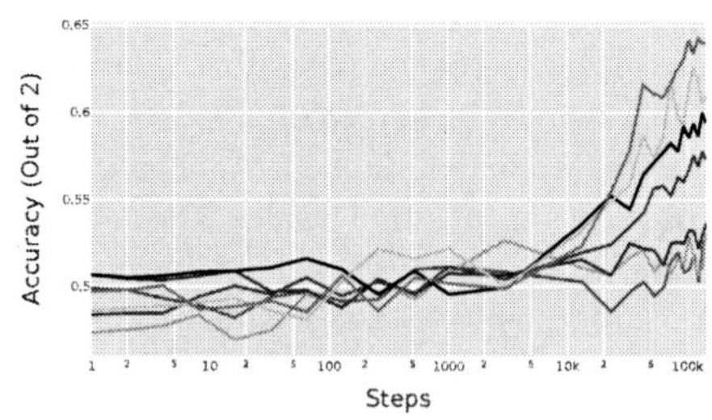

(d) Winogrande Accuracy

Figure 5: Accuracy over training for four different datasets. Step numbers each represent approximately 2M tokens, so Step 1000 would be 2B tokens. We see that the rate of capability acquisition tends to approach an asymptote as models become larger.

sourced multiple choice science exam questions ranging across physics, chemistry, biology, earth science, astronomy, and computer science. The questions cover a variety of complex reasoning skills such as causal reasoning, multi-hop inference, and understanding paragraph descriptions.

PIQA The Physical Interaction Question Answering (PIQA) dataset (Bisk et al., 2019) contains a total of 21k (across different subsets) multiple choice questions probing reasoning about basic physical commonsense knowledge. The questions test intuitive understanding of concepts like mass, volume, rigid objects, containment, stability, orientation, and more through grounded scenarios. Answering correctly requires applying physical reasoning.

ARC Easy The AI2 Reasoning Challenge (ARC) dataset (Clark et al., 2018) is a collection of 7,787 multiple choice science exam questions compiled from various grade-level sources, including a research partner of AI2. The questions cover diverse science topics and are structured as text-only prompts with 4 answer options. The ARC Easy subset consists of 5,197 of the relatively easier reasoning questions.

Winogrande The WinoGrande dataset (Sakaguchi et al., 2019) was inspired by the original Winograd Schema Challenge (WSC) and consists of 44k problems generated through crowdsourcing and systematic bias reduction algorithms. Most of these are relatively easy for humans, but often difficult for LLMs.

E Compute

Experiments were conducted over two months a pod of 8 A40 GPUs, each with 50 GB of GPU RAM. As an upper bound, our experiments would require all of these GPUs to operate for a month to run all of our experiments, but in practice we did not require all GPUs running simultaneously. We estimate that 0.25 utilization of this pod would be required in practice to run these experiments.

F Licenses of Artifacts Used

The Pythia model suite is made available with an Apache 2.0 license. Wang et al.'s (2023) IOI dataset and Newman et al.'s (2021) SVA dataset are released under an MIT license. The remaining datasets (Greater-Than and Gendered-Pronouns) are released without any license specified.

Author Index